LEATHER TANNING

The Fur and Leather Workers Union

The FUR
and LEATHER

A story of dramatic

NORDAN PRESS • *Newark*

WORKERS UNION

struggles and achievements

by PHILIP S. FONER

AUTHOR OF: History of the Labor Movement in the
United States, Business and Slavery, Jews in American
History, Jack London: American Rebel, The Life and
Writings of Frederick Douglass, Morale Education in
the American Army   EDITOR OF: The Complete
Writings of Thomas Paine, Basic Writings of Thomas
Jefferson, and the selected writings of George Washing-
ton, Abraham Lincoln and Franklin Delano Roosevelt.

MANUFACTURED IN THE UNITED STATES OF AMERICA

BY KNICKERBOCKER PRINTING CORPORATION

199

TO THE MILITANT RANK-AND-FILE

FUR AND LEATHER WORKERS

TO THE MANY

WHO MADE SUCH GREAT SACRIFICES

TO BUILD THIS DEMOCRATIC

AND PROGRESSIVE UNION

TO MORRIS LANGER AND THE OTHERS

WHO LOST THEIR LIVES

IN THIS HEROIC STRUGGLE

Preface

Between Twenty-fourth and Thirty-first Streets and Sixth and Eighth Avenues in New York City is situated the fur district, the center of America's industry that produces warm and beautiful fur garments. The visitor who passes through this area at noon will see "the fur market" filled with thousands of jostling fur workers. These are the men and women who make the sleek, elegant winter wraps displayed in shop windows on fashionable avenues in every city. And these are the men and women whose inspiring struggles and magnificent achievements are known the world over.

Known the world over, but not recorded in the histories of the American labor movement! Left out entirely in these histories is the story of the powerful rank-and-file revolt of the fur workers in the 1920's and early 1930's.

Until 1914, Socialist Party leaders like Eugene V. Debs led the resistance to the stagnating policies of the AFL bureaucrats. The IWW was a product of militant revolts of the workers against these AFL leaders. With the decay of the Socialist Party, the AFL had an open road for its bankrupt theories and practices which turned unions into the private businesses of a handful of misleaders. Workers in many industries revolted against the enslavement brought about by these policies.

The battle of the fur workers for a free union, told in this book, was a revolt against the shackles of control by terrorism. It was an eruption against the misery imposed by employers—against unscrupulous misleaders of labor—against sordid betrayals by AFL and Socialist Party officials.

In heroic battles that resounded throughout the nation, the fur workers gave expression to the struggles and hopes of all workers for a clean, democratic and progressive labor movement. Their struggle aroused a storm in the AFL and its allied Socialist Party. It opened the floodgates for revolts by workers in other trades and pointed the way for the great mass movement out of which was born the CIO. The militant progressive policies of the left wing exposed the complete bankruptcy of the AFL bureaucrats and subsequently were adopted as the policies of the CIO. It is the purpose of this book to fill this important gap in the literature of labor history.

But this is also the story of America's leather workers, their long and bitter struggles to organize, the repeated defeats, failures and betrayals they suffered, and the victories that followed after the fur workers added their experience and organizing genius to the courage and militancy of the leather workers.

For the most part the history of the Fur and Leather Workers Union is buried in the archives of the International office and the American Federation of Labor, in records turned yellowish with the dust of the years. To assemble the history of the union I had to examine hundreds of thousands of letters, leaflets and bulletins, and thousands of pages of the minutes of local meetings, executive board meetings and convention proceedings. I examined carefully the pages of the union's official journal, the files of the *Jewish Daily Forward,* the *Freiheit,* and scores of other newspapers and magazines in English, German and Yiddish. I interviewed many members of the union who personally participated in many of its long struggles. In addition, I interviewed former leaders of the union who are today members of the fur manufacturers' association, such as Mr. Abe Chalkin. In the interests of readability, I have not followed the procedure of indicating specific references to the sources. A list of all manuscript and printed sources, arranged by chapter, will be found towards the end of the book.

The months of research that went into this work have brought to light hundreds of hitherto unpublished documents that reveal in all its nakedness the unsavory role of the leaders of the American Federation of Labor and of the Socialist Party in the American labor movement. Here is the irrefutable evidence which shows how these labor leaders conspired with every enemy of the fur and leather workers, with employers, police, underworld gangs and other anti-labor agencies, to maintain their dominance over the workers in the interests of the employers. Here in their own words, in reproduction of their own writing, is proof of some of the most abominable treachery in the history of the American labor movement.

The views expressed in this book are the author's and not necessarily those of the Fur and Leather Workers Union or its officials. However, the entire organization made freely available all of its records, and afforded me full opportunity to interview members of the union, for which I wish to express my gratitude.

I am extremely grateful particularly to Mr. George Kleinman, editor of the *Fur & Leather Worker,* and to his competent assistant, Mr. Irving Stern, for their unending assistance at every stage of the work and for their many valuable suggestions and unstinting cooperation.

Space has not permitted mentioning the names of all the leaders and rank-and-file members of the Fur and Leather Workers Union who have sacrificed so much to make the union the outstanding organization it is today. Studying their history, observing them personally in action at union meetings, executive board sessions, International Conventions, at negotiations and on the picket lines, enabled me to become acquainted with the life of this organization. It has been a most exciting and rewarding experience. In the slightly more than two years I have been engaged in this work, I have received a great education. Despite all my efforts to retain complete objectivity in learning and telling this history, I must confess that my sympathies are with this inspiring body of laboring men and women who express the finest ideals of true Americanism—the fighting fur and leather workers.

PHILIP S. FONER

Croton-on-Hudson
April 1950

Contents

THE BEGINNINGS OF UNIONISM
IN FUR AND LEATHER

THE INTERNATIONAL
FUR WORKERS UNION IS BORN

THE STRUGGLE FOR
TRADE-UNION DEMOCRACY

1926—THE GENERAL STRIKE
THAT MADE UNION HISTORY

A DECADE OF HEROIC BATTLES
AGAINST GANGSTERISM, TERRORISM
AND EXPULSIONS

THE ACHIEVEMENT OF UNITY

THE FUR AND LEATHER WORKERS
JOIN HANDS

The Beginnings of Unionism
in Fur and Leather

CHAPTER 1

The Early Years

The year was 1835. American industry had grown rapidly after the Revolutionary years. A whole continent, rich in nature's bounty, was at hand for expansion and development. Land-starved, oppression-fleeing immigrants flocked from the shores of Europe to the new, free Republic. A working class that toiled for a livelihood from early dawn until dark stood ready to deliver its first powerful blows for the shorter working day.

In early June of that year, the leather workers of Philadelphia joined the Irish coal heavers and other craftsmen and laborers in a city-wide general strike that rocked the nation. They demanded the ten-hour work day. Led by a fife-and-drum corps, the strikers marched through the streets with banners reading: "FROM SIX TO SIX, TEN HOURS WORK AND TWO HOURS FOR MEALS." The city government soon yielded, granting city employees the "six to six" work day during the summer season, and the two hours for meals as demanded. Many private employers followed suit; but the leather manufacturers held out.

Faced with the bosses' strong resistance, the striking leather workers declared firmly that they would continue their fight because their claim was just and their cause righteous. "We, the working-men, the admitted bone and sinew of our country, who are looked to and determined to defend the rights and liberties of our country from foreigners in time of war, deserve and demand our right from our countrymen in time of peace . . ."

Finally, on June 20, the leather manufacturers gave in, agreeing to the ten-hour day. Two days later, the general strike was over, and the ten-hour day established throughout Philadelphia.

From earliest colonial days, fur and leather were important essentials for warm winter clothing, and for footwear, saddles and other horse-gear. Records from as far back as the Revolutionary War years give some idea of the conditions under which fur and leather workers labored. Tanners and curriers (leather dressers) of Philadelphia protested in July 1779 that they were not "able to lay up anything out of their scanty wages." Fur workers of New York joined with six hundred workers of other trades in 1797 to appeal for public relief because they were "in want of sufficient *fire* and *food*" to maintain themselves and their families.

These conditions were typical for many workers. However, while unions of various trades were formed as early as the 1790's, the trade union movement did not develop on a large scale until after 1833. The need was great. Wages were extremely low. Only the skilled craftsman could earn as much as $4 to $5 a week in 1833. Factory workers received only $2.19 to $2.53 a week. Thousands of women workers—and children, too—got as little as twenty-five cents a day. The standard work day was from sunrise to sunset. In summer, men, women and children toiled from fourteen to sixteen hours a day.

Out of these conditions sprang the American labor movement. In five years, union membership rose from 26,500 to 300,000. Between 1833 and 1837, there were 188 strikes. By 1837, city central labor bodies, known as Trades' Unions, were established in thirteen cities in the United States.

A leather workers' union appeared on the New York scene in May 1833. Other unions of leather workers came into existence at about the same time in Philadelphia and Boston: Journeymen Saddlers, Harness Makers, Leather Dressers and Curriers.

On April 20, 1836, the Philadelphia Trades' Union held its regular weekly meeting. Among the letters read by the secretary was one from the Furriers Association (Union) of Philadelphia. With it was a $50 contribution to the central labor body. This was the first union of fur workers organized in the United States.

Having won the shorter work day in 1835, the leather dressers of Philadelphia struck in the following year for a wage increase. They demanded another dollar a week, to bring their wage up to $5. Among the contributors to their strike relief fund was the fur workers' union. After a three-week struggle, the leather workers returned to work victorious.

Three months later, the fur workers of Philadelphia struck for higher wages. The leather dressers remembered the solidarity of the unions that had assisted them, and in turn contributed to the fur strikers' relief fund. Within two weeks, the fur workers' union was able to report that it had won an increase from $4.50 to $5.50 in its weekly wage.

Not every struggle was won so quickly. Employers' associations were formed to crush unions and keep wages down. The courts rushed to the aid of the employers and prosecuted unions for "conspiracy." The press, too, denounced trade unionists as "foreign agitators" who should be "deported instantly."

In the spring of 1836, when the leather workers of New York and Newark demanded higher wages, they encountered furious opposition. In April, the leather bosses in both cities locked out their workers. They declared they would not employ any man who was known to belong to an organization which attempted to "dictate" wages or conditions for employment. Union members, cried the employers, were infected with the "moral gangrene" of trade union principles.

Conducting a joint strike, the New York and Newark leather unions appealed to all workers for support. They pointed out that their employers were dictating the terms of employment, namely, the surrender of their right to belong to the Trades' Union. If they complied, it would stamp them "eternally as COWARDS AND SLAVES, unworthy to breathe in a land where all men have been declared as born free and equal."

The entire labor movement leaped to the support of the strikers. All over the country, unions adopted resolutions encouraging the leather workers "to stand fast and tremble not" in the face of the outpourings of fury of their "lordly dictators." They urged the strikers firmly to resist any attempted attacks on their rights as did the "patriots of olden times, even unto death." The strikers stood fast. On July 8, the lockout was called off. The strikers returned to their jobs with their union intact and their wages increased.

The advance of the labor movement of the 1830's, however, was short-lived. An economic crisis broke out in 1837. It lasted for several years and dealt a shattering blow to the trade unions.

For more than a decade, the fur and leather workers remained without organization until, in 1849, a group of fur workers in New York again began the struggle to build a union, the *Kurschners Verein* (Furriers Union). As the name indicated, its members were German immigrants.

Known as 48'ers, they had taken part in the Revolution of 1848 in Germany which sought to establish a democratic government. However, when the Revolution was crushed, many Germans fled to the United States to escape the terror that followed. They brought with them a strong desire for freedom and social reform, which soon found expression in the labor movement.

German-American fur workers who formed the union in 1849 were under the influence of William Weitling. Weitling preached that the fight for higher wages was unimportant compared to setting up cooperatives and a labor exchange bank which would free the workers from the cruel exploitation of the employers. Under his leadership, unions became debating societies rather than weapons of struggle to improve working conditions.

The fur workers soon became dissatisfied with Weitling's impractical schemes and looked for better leadership. They found it in Joseph Weydemeyer,* who arrived in the United States in 1851. Weydemeyer was a Communist, and a close associate of Karl Marx and Frederick Engels, the founders of scientific socialism. Weydemeyer quickly saw that Weitling's theories were of little real value to the workers. He plunged into the task of organizing the German-American workers into militant trade unions.

Inspired by Weydemeyer's leadership, the German-American workers prepared for struggles with their employers. When the fur bosses rejected the union's demands for a wage increase in March 1853, the fur workers declared a strike. After three weeks of battle against vicious police brutality, the strike was won. The fur manufacturers agreed to the union's wage demand.

Not many details are known about the fur workers' history in the next few years. However, references in various newspapers give us an occasional glimpse of their activities. Members of the union were reported taking part in a great demonstration of unemployed New York workers at Tompkins Square in 1857. The banner of the fur workers' union was prominent in the pre-election demonstration in October 1860, calling for "Lincoln and freedom." And in April 1864, when fifteen thousand trade

---

* During the Civil War, Weydemeyer was commissioned as an officer in the Union Army by President Lincoln. Acquitting himself with distinction, he rose to the rank of Brigadier General. In the summer of 1944, when asked by the United States Government to sponsor a Liberty Ship because of its magnificent record in World War II, the International Fur and Leather Workers Union chose the name "Joseph Weydemeyer" for the ship it launched.

The National Laborer.

Philadelphia, Saturday, April 23, 1836.

Printed and Published by the National Society for the Diffusion of Useful Knowledge.

EDITED BY THOMAS HOGAN.

Reported for the National Laborer.

TRADES' UNION.

A meeting of the Union was held, pursuant to adjournment, April 20th, the President in the chair.

Communicaions were received from several Societies, accompanying donations to the Union, as follow:—

From the Biscit-Bakers,	812 00
—— Furriers,	50 60
—— Hatters' ociety of Germantown,	8 00
—— Cordwaiers of Germantown,	5 25
—— Associatin of Journeymen Cabinet Makers of hiladelphia,	42 00
—— Taylors,	200 00
—— Cordvaiers (Men's Branch),	100 00

The Hatters Association communicated sundry resolutionsone of which was, that each and every menberhad agreed to pay weekly into

---

THE NEW YORK HERALD

NEW YORK, FRIDAY, APRIL 8, 1864.

THE STRIKE QUESTION.

Mass Meeting of the Trades Unions Protesting Against Legislative Usurpation.

Fifteen Thousand Citizens in Tompkins Square.

Protective Union, Iron Moulders No. 11, of Spuyten Duyvil; Laborers Union No. 2, of Spuyten Duyvil; Blacksmiths' Union of Brooklyn, New York Society of Operative Masons, Gilders' Protective Union, Pianoforte Makers, Wheelwrights and Blacksmiths No 3, Twine Spinners, Morocco Dressers, Sugar Makers, Carpenters' Union No. 5, United Cabinet Makers, Coach Painters, Ship Joiners, Operative Plasterers, Furriers, Cordwainers, Sugar Packers, Tailors, Varnishers and Polishers, Wheelwrights and Blacksmiths Union No. 2, Carpenters' Union No. 4, Upholsterers, Sash and Blind Makers, United Coopers No. 3, Blank Book Binders, Team Shoemakers, Clothing Cutters, Machinists' Association No. 1, Journeymen Plumbers, United Coopers No. 1 (Williamsburg), Car Drivers, United Journeymen Sparmakers' Society, and Machinists' Pro

---

Furriers' unions were among the earliest to make their appearance in the American labor movement. The Furriers Union in Philadelphia (1836) was the first of such unions in the U. S.

unionists gathered in Tompkins Square to protest an anti-strike bill pending in the New York State Legislature, two hundred demonstrators wore badges of the "Furriers Union of New York."

The leather workers also recovered very slowly from the blows of the crisis of 1837. Not until 1853 were they able to rebuild unions in New York, Philadelphia, Baltimore and far-off San Francisco. The following year, a leather dressers' union was also organized in Pittsburgh.

Strikes were conducted in New England in 1860 and 1861 by morocco finishers, tanners, saddlers and harness makers for higher wages, shorter hours and adjustment of grievances. But only the morocco finishers were organized strongly enough to win most of their demands. Unions of leather dressers grew rapidly and expanded to dozens of new localities including Albany, Buffalo, Louisville, Chicago and St. Louis.

In June 1864, delegates from the various leather dressers' unions met in Philadelphia and organized the National Union of Journeymen Curriers. Although it participated in founding the National Labor Union headed by the progressive labor leader, William Sylvis, the National Union of Journeymen Curriers had only a brief existence, folding up in 1868.

The crisis of 1873 and six years of economic depression that followed again wiped out fur and leather local unions, along with most of the labor movement. Wages dropped sharply. Between two and three million workers were completely out of work, a staggering figure for those years.

As economic conditions improved, the New York fur workers re-formed their ranks. The *Kurschners Verein* had a membership of fifty-three cutters and nailers in the spring of 1880. Despite its small numbers, the union put forward demands which were very advanced for the times: $20 a week for cutters, $16 for nailers, and the closed shop. During the summer and fall of 1880, the union felt strong enough to call and win a number of shop strikes. The following spring, more strikes were won against the firms of Harris, Russek, and Weinberg & Co. By July 1882, the union had over 250 members. Annual dues ranged from $5.87 to $7.50 per member.

When the union put forward a new scale of $25 for cutters and $18 for nailers, the fur bosses hit back by importing workers from Germany. To the bewilderment of the employers, these workers turned out to be Socialists and promptly reported to the union. Reluctantly, the employers granted the new wage scale.

But a new economic crisis, starting in the fall of 1882, again changed the picture completely. With widespread unemployment for the next three years, the fur manufacturers slashed wages again and again. Many fur workers were handed envelopes on pay-day with $5 and $3. A good many were forced to take home bundles of work and often worked until eleven, twelve or even one o'clock at night, so that their working day amounted to sixteen or seventeen hours.

The union did not fight back, intolerable as conditions became. Like many other unions at the time, it had lost its spirit. New members were kept out by large initiation fees and high dues. The union concerned itself mainly with setting up sick and death benefit systems and running social gatherings. Meanwhile the bosses were destroying the living standard of the workers.

With the Furriers Union doing nothing to mobilize the workers to defend their conditions, a group of militant workers set up a new organization in January 1885, called the Fur Workers Society. The new union established a twenty-five cents initiation fee and monthly dues of fifteen cents.

The guiding lights of the Fur Workers Society were members of the Socialist Labor Party. Among them was the former president of the Berlin Furriers Union. In its early years, the Socialist Labor Party followed a strong, militant policy of struggle to improve the workers' conditions. Explaining the need for organizing the Fur Workers Society, Max Bohm, one of the leaders, told a meeting of workers: "The chief aim is to protect the members from attacks and oppressive measures on the part of the bosses, and to achieve higher wages and better working conditions. In this respect, sick and death benefits alone cannot help the workers and should be considered only secondarily."

The Fur Workers Society stressed the need for solidarity with workers in other trades and for unity of all workers regardless of race, sex, color, religion or nationality. Attracted by the fighting spirit of the new organization, the overworked and underpaid fur workers flocked into it. At every meeting, new workers joined. In the short space of three months, it reached a membership of over five hundred cutters and nailers.

The activity and growth of the new organization spurred the old Furriers Union to action. After much debate, it proposed a merger of the two unions because "only a strong organization can today oppose the bosses and put demands before them." The Fur Workers Society readily agreed. When the Furriers Union lowered its initiation fee to $1, the members of the Fur Workers Society voted to join the Furriers Union in a body. Once unity was achieved, the organization grew rapidly.

An organizing committee was set up, with good results. Five new locals were organized before the end of 1885: the Fur Dressers Union; the Fur Skin Fleshers and Shavers Union; the Fur Operators and Fancy Fur Finishers Union; and the Fur Capmakers Union. By January 1886, the Dressers Union price lists had been accepted by the employers. Three months later, the Operators and Finishers Union was able to report that "most of the shops are already union shops."

Set up on a craft basis, the separate locals nevertheless saw the need for cooperation and mutual support. Delegates of each local attended meetings of the others. Complaints against employers were taken up jointly. The practical benefits of such united action soon led the five

CONSTITUTION

der

Fur Skin · Fleischer

und

Shavers' Union

VON NEW YORK.

Organisirt am Danksagungstag, den 26. Nov. 1885.

Einleitung.

Es ist die Pflicht eines jeden Arbeiters, sich mit seinen Nebenarbeitern zu verbinden, um einen genügenden Lohn für seine Arbeit zu erhalten und seine Lage in jeder Beziehung zu verbessern. Zur Erreichung dieses Zweckes wollen wir, die Mitglieder dieser Organisation, Einer für Alle und Alle für Einen einstehen.

Artikel 1. Name.

§ 1. Der Name dieser Organisation ist: "Fur Skin Fleischer und Shavers' Union von New York."

Artikel 2. Zweck.

§ 2. Der Zweck dieser Union ist, die Interessen ihrer Mitglieder gegen jede Beeinträchtigung seitens der Arbeitgeber, sowie Arbeitnehmer und Nicht-Union-Mitglieder zu wahren und zu schützen, sowie das Wohl der Mitglieder in jeder möglichen Weise zu fördern.

Artikel 3. Mitgliedschaft.

§ 3. Mitglied kann jeder werden, der das Dresserfach als Fleischer erlernt hat und erklärt, mit der Constitution einverstanden zu sein und willens ist, die darin ausgesprochenen Grundsätze und Zwecke auszuführen. Ein Kandidat soll als Mitglied aufgenommen werden, nachdem er durch Prüfung zeigte, daß er fähig ist, allerhand Waaren zu hantiren.

§ 4. Sollten Mitglieder der Union eine Stelle als Vormann annehmen, so können dieselben während der Dauer dieses Postens der Union nicht mehr angehören.

Preamble to Constitution of Fleshers Union formed Thanksgiving Day, 1885, gave its motto: "One for all and all for one."

locals to set up a Central Executive Council. By the spring of 1886, the Central Executive Council represented 1,660 members, more than half the total number of fur workers in New York.

Before long, the bosses were taking the union seriously. Thinly disguising their purpose with vague talk of "greater efficiency in the trade," 60 of the 72 fur bosses in New York proceeded to form the Manufacturing Furriers Association. But their real objective, which the workers understood, was a united front of the bosses to smash the union.

Thus was the stage set for the most dramatic episode in the early history of the fur workers—a struggle that merged with the heroic battle of the whole labor movement for the eight-hour day.

The leather workers' history during these years was closely bound to the organization known as the Noble Order of the Knights of Labor, founded in 1869. The Knights of Labor started out as a fighting union, taking in all workers in all trades, skilled and unskilled, regardless of race, color or creed. Its local assemblies conducted militant and effective strikes in many cities. Its vigorous leadership in the workers' struggles attracted strong support. By 1886, it had 700,000 members.

The Knights of Labor carried its slogan, "An injury to one is the concern of all," into the tanneries and factories of glove, harness, saddle and horse collar makers. Leather workers' unions were set up in Salem, Peabody, Stoneham, Lowell, Newark, Chicago, Milwaukee, Philadelphia, Boston, St. Louis, Baltimore and other important tannery and leather manufacturing centers. For the first time in their history, through the Knights of Labor, the New England tanneries were strongly organized and were able to carry on a series of strikes for higher wages and shorter hours.

In the same period another national labor organization came into existence, which in a few years replaced the Knights as the leading body of American labor. Started in 1881, the Federation of Organized Trades and Labor Unions of the United States and Canada later took the name of the American Federation of Labor.

In October 1884, during the fourth convention of the Federation, a resolution was passed setting May 1, 1886, as the day for a nation-wide struggle to establish the eight-hour day. This historic resolution gave birth to May Day—a day dedicated to working-class solidarity, which was soon adopted by the workers of the entire world. Reaffirmed at the 1885 Convention, the resolution stirred the imagination of the entire working class. It became the key issue of the day. Other unions took it up enthusiastically. The demand for the eight-hour day became the rallying cry of the entire labor movement. All over the United States workers sang the "Eight-Hour Song":

> "We're summoning our forces from the shipyard, shop and mill:
> Eight hours for work, eight hours for rest, eight hours for
>   what we will.
> Let the shout ring down the valleys, and echo from every hill,
> Eight hours for work, eight hours for rest, eight hours for
>   what we will."

In New England and elsewhere, local assemblies of leather workers took up the struggle for the eight-hour day and voted to join the demonstration. Simultaneously, the Furriers Union, although not affiliated to either the Knights or the Federation,* put the eight-hour day at the top

* In July 1886, the Furriers Union of New York received a communication from the Chicago Furriers Union urging it to join the Knights of Labor. The letter was tabled. There does not seem to be any further information about the Chicago Furriers Union.

of the list of demands they presented to their employers.* Thus joining hands, the fur workers and the leather workers took their place in the ranks of American labor for the historic battle that became an inspiration to labor the world over.

* The other demands called for a wage rate of not less than $12 a week for cutters; not less than $10 for nailers; and not less than $9 for ironers and finishers; overtime to be permitted only when all workmen were employed; double time for overtime and Sunday work; only one apprentice to be allowed to ten or less workers; no piece-work in the shop; no deduction of wages on legal holidays, and, if work should be required on legal holidays, the rate of wages should be the same as for Sundays. "Instead of discharging large numbers of workmen at the end of the season," the Union declared, "we recommend employment on half time."

The wage rates set in the demands were only for the lower class of workmen, "so that the more skillful may be at liberty to arrange with their employers in regard to the compensation they should receive."

CHAPTER 2

Battle for
the Eight-Hour Day

On May 1, 1886, hundreds of thousands of workers in Chicago, New York and other cities, large and small, went out on strike for the eight-hour day. It was the most powerful demonstration of labor ever witnessed in America. The movement had reached such proportions that it added a new, political significance to this economic demand of the workers.

About 185,000 workers gained their objective. Even before the fateful First of May, thousands won a nine-hour or eight-hour day by the mere threat of the walkout. In Chicago, fifteen hundred leather workers were granted the nine-hour day on April 30, the day before their strike was scheduled to start. In Milwaukee, a strike of leather tanners was averted when all but three establishments in the city agreed to allow the men ten hours' pay for eight hours' work.

Fifteen hundred fur workers, men and women, took part in the New York May Day demonstration. They met at eight in the morning and paraded through the Bowery holding aloft their union banners. That afternoon, they held a party in Beethoven Hall. In the evening, they marched to Union Square to join the large outdoor meeting. The great day over, the Furriers Union dug in for the coming struggle.

The fur manufacturers had arbitrarily rejected the union's demands. Shedding crocodile tears, the bosses wept over the "likelihood of trouble and distress falling upon the poor laborers." Using a formula that was to become very familiar to the fur workers, the Association declared: "Very many of the heads of our largest manufacturing establishments commenced at the bottom of the ladders. Some of them, who have obtained good old age, not only worked ten hours a day for thirty or forty years, but have worked twelve and fourteen hours a day; thus proving that regular hours of labor and regular hours of rest are conducive of longevity."

The fur workers, however, were unmoved by these expressions of concern for their long life. The morning of May 3 saw 875 strikers gathered at Germania Hall. Arrangements were made to pay $5 weekly relief to each striker, but most of the men refused to accept any relief.

The other unions in the trade pledged their support to the strikers. The fur capmakers promised 20 percent of their wages. The fur dressers pledged 25 percent of their earnings. A delegate from the Fur Operators and Fancy Fur Finishers announced that his local had decided to stop work in any shop where scabs were brought in. Even as he spoke, news came that the operators and fancy finishers had voted to join the strike. With cheers ringing through the hall, the strikers left to picket the shops.

On the third day of the strike, twelve independent shops settled with the union. But the Association refused to budge. It released a statement, signed by the largest employers, denouncing the union for issuing "arbitrary and bigoted mandates" and calling it "a constant source of trouble and annoyance to the employers." It refused to meet or negotiate with the Furriers Union.

At the same time the Association appealed directly to the strikers to leave the union. The Association closed its appeal with the statement that was to appear many times thereafter in strikes of fur workers: "We therefore propose to deal with our men direct, without any outside interference, and independent of the dictates of the union, we shall, henceforth, open our doors and employ all who are willing to work on these conditions."

The arrogance of the fur manufacturers was in keeping with the time. During a meeting of workers in Chicago's Haymarket Square on May 4 to protest violence against strikers, a bomb was thrown, resulting in the death of several persons. Although this was undoubtedly the criminal act of a planted employer agent, the police at once arrested and blamed the workers' leaders.* Employers all over the country

* Eight militant labor leaders were arrested on the framed-up charge, placed on trial and found guilty of a crime they had not committed. Of the eight, four were hanged, one "committed suicide," and three were later pardoned by Gov-

seized upon the incident to launch their counter-attack against labor. A "red scare" swept the country. The press, the police and the courts whipped up the hysteria to help the employers smash the trade unions. Lockouts, blacklists and legal prosecution of labor leaders became the common occurrence.

The fur manufacturers were quick to take advantage of the frenzied nation-wide "red scare." Although an arbitration committee had already been agreed upon to negotiate a settlement, the Association dismissed the committee and announced that there was "nothing to negotiate." It offered police protection to any worker who returned to work. The remainder, it threatened to blacklist.

With labor under terrific attack all over the country, the Furriers Union found it impossible to continue the battle. On May 12, the workers voted to call off the strike. Each worker was to return under the best terms he could get. The operators and fancy finishers held out a few days longer, determined that "they would never return to work until the furriers were all employed."

In spite of the defeat of the strike, some gains were scored. A few independent shops introduced the eight-hour day. Other fur workers secured a nine-hour day, some nine-and-a-half, still others a Saturday half-holiday three months in the year. Most workers received a 10 percent wage increase and some as much as 25 percent. But it was to take many years before they would obtain the eight-hour day throughout the trade.

The fur workers were by no means the only victims of the wave of repression in the months that followed. All New England leather

---

ernor John Peter Altgeld of Illinois, who was convinced of the innocence of all eight.

The fur workers were horrified by the arrest and conviction of the Haymarket martyrs, and rallied to their support. At a mass meeting of furriers on November 8, 1887, a resolution was unanimously adopted condemning the conviction of the eight men "as a criminal and shameful thing for the American Republic and the American people," and pledging "to do everything in our power to save the condemned men."

One effect of the Haymarket affair and the travesty of justice which followed was to deepen the political consciousness of the fur workers. The Furriers Union participated actively in the campaign to elect Henry George, candidate of the United Labor Party for Mayor of New York City. "About two hundred members of the Furriers Union," reported the *New Yorker Volkszeitung* on November 15, 1886, "marched in the pre-election parade, and all expenses for the latter were cheerfully paid by the union."

The Salem Gazette.

SALEM, TUESDAY, JULY 13, 1886.

A LABOR CRISIS.

A very serious labor crisis for Salem is threat-ening at the present time. Last week each leather manufacturer received the following letter in an envelope superscribed " Executive Board, Knights of Labor, D. A. 77, P. O. Box 287, Lynn, Mass."

LYNN, July, 1886.

The men employed at the tanning and currying in-dustries in Salem and the town of Peabody respect-fully ask the same privileges as the men in Boston, Woburn and vicinity are enjoying at the present time, namely: That on and after July 13, 1886, the hours of labor will be so regulated as to commence work at 7 o'clock A. M. to 12 M., and from 1 P. M. to 6 o'clock P. M., except on Saturday, when it will be from 1 to 5 o'clock P. M. Trusting their request will be granted, we are, respectfully, the executive board, K. of L., D. A. 77.

LOUIS C. T. SCHLEIBER, Sec.

This letter was looked upon as mandatory.

THE HAT, CAP AND FUR TRADE REVIEW.

TO ALL FURRIERS' BOSSES OF NEW YORK AND VICINITY.

Whereas, The working time in the furrier business be-comes more and more contracted to a shorter season every year, and that during the busy season the extra hard work is undermining the health of the workmen, while the time in which the workman is unemployed compels him and his family to undergo suffering and want, and induces him to offer his services at reduced pay; and,

Whereas, Furthermore, this system creates a competition, which is of loss both to the employers and workmen, and must eventually bring about the ruin of the business; and as this state of things can only be remedied by a uniform system of working time and wages.

Resolved, That

1. Eight hours shall constitute a day's work.

2. That the rate shall be : For cutters, not less than $12; for nailers, n t less than $10; for ironers and finishers, not less than $9. We have only fixed the pay for the lower class of workmen, so that the more skillful may be at liberty to arrange with their employers in regard to the compensa-tion they should receive.

3. Overwork will only be permitted when all workmen

Both fur and leather workers joined in struggles for a shorter working day marked by the first May Day demonstration in 1886.

manufacturers, organized in an association, locked out their workers in July and told them to sign "iron-clad oaths" agreeing to leave the union and stay out of the Knights of Labor or consider themselves fired. "Here-after," the leather manufacturers announced, "we will employ only such men as will bargain individually with us, and agree to take no part in any strike whatever." The tannery workers of Salem, Peabody and Stoneham—twenty-eight hundred strong—answered by declaring a strike on July 12, 1886. It became one of the most bitterly fought struggles of the decade.

The Boot and Shoe Manufacturers Association and other employer groups came to the assistance of the leather bosses. The police and the press gave the employers the utmost cooperation. Police escorted scabs into the tanneries and clubbed and arrested any striker who interfered.

The newspapers denounced the strikers as "vicious men led by Com-munists and Anarchists from abroad who are seeking to disturb the peace, destroy the industrial prosperity of the community and establish a Com-munist regime in New England." Any public official who expressed the slightest sympathy with the strikers was instantly threatened with im-peachment. Even the anti-labor newspapers, however, were forced to admit that the strikers had the support of the entire working class in the area, and that "almost the whole working population with their wives and children turned out every day to picket the tanneries."

The tannery strikers held out for over four months, holding mass demonstrations at the plant gates every day. But in the end, their resources exhausted, they were forced to give in. The Knights of Labor officially called off the strike on November 29. The workers returned to the tanneries with their unions smashed. Before they could get work, they were compelled to sign the "iron-clad oaths." This was the end of the Knights of Labor in New England tanneries. A Leather Workers Protective Union, not affiliated with the Knights, still remained in Lowell; but weakened by a lockout, it, too, soon passed out of existence.

Encouraged by the events in New England, the leather bosses of Newark opened the attack on their workers in the following year, 1887. After a nine-week lockout and strike, the strikers were starved and clubbed into submission. As in New England, the workers were compelled to sign the "iron-clad oaths."

The fur and leather workers were among the first groups of organized labor to feel the full effects of the employers' brutal counterattack. The Furriers Union of New York had been seriously weakened. The unions of leather workers had been driven out of the tanneries. Yet within a few years, fur and leather workers were re-forming their lines and renewing their struggles.

CHAPTER 3

Struggles and Setbacks

The German Furriers Union of New York, beaten in the strike, its militants blacklisted by the fur bosses, lost half its membership. It continued to hold picnics and social gatherings, but other activities practically ceased for the time being. Nevertheless, its remaining members were courageous enough to stop work and demonstrate on May First of the next year.

By the fall of 1888, a new campaign to organize the fur workers was undertaken. "The time for retreat in our union is passed," read one moving appeal. "The workers feel that they must belong to a labor union, that their living conditions are constantly being lowered more and more . . . There should not be a single furrier who thinks by bending his back low enough and keeping silent he can better his conditions. A man's back should never bend before another man; he should demand his rights . . ."

Gradually the union recovered its losses. At every union meeting, four, six, eight, twelve and sometimes twenty workers were admitted to membership. By the summer of 1890, a mass meeting of four hundred furriers voted to demand the nine-hour day. Within a few weeks, the employers granted their demand. The members of the Furriers Union were able to join the Labor Day parade that year with banners proclaiming that the nine-hour day prevailed throughout the trade.

Winning the nine-hour day hastened the revival and growth of the union. In January 1891 a branch was established in Montreal. The union expanded its name to Furriers Union of the United States and Canada. That summer its membership rose to twelve hundred cutters and nailers.

Influenced by the activity of the cutters and nailers, the Fur Dressers and Fur Operators and Fancy Finishers revived their unions. The Furriers Union then announced that none of its members would work with non-union operators.

The *Kurschner Zeitung* (*Furriers' Journal*) made its official appearance that year. As the months passed the *Zeitung* carried glowing accounts of victories scored by the New York fur workers. During that season, employers gave in to the union's demand to hire only union men, to pay time-and-a-half for overtime, and to place the union label on their garments. Most important, the majority of the employers agreed to the eight-hour day. In August, the union informed the employers that since the fur workers were "never able to earn enough to help them over the bad season . . . in the few weeks they are working," members of the union would "not be allowed to work on Saturday afternoon throughout the year." Once again the employers gave in.

Early in 1892 about sixty of the leading fur bosses organized the Manufacturing Furriers Exchange, Incorporated. The Exchange quickly raised a fund of over $100,000 to open a counterattack on the union, and in February it swung into action. With the familiar announcement of the "unjust demands and exactions made upon us" and "to harmonize the relations between the individual employer and workman," the Exchange declared the eight-hour day would have to go.

The employers were willing to concede a Saturday half-holiday during June, July and August. But they demanded the open shop and adjustment of grievances only with a shop committee excluding the union. If a grievance could not be settled in this manner, the dispute was to be submitted to an *arbitration committee of employers*.

Having thus at one stroke barred the union, the Exchange hypocritically concluded: "We wish to live in peace and harmony with our workmen." At the same time, the manufacturers informed the workers that if they refused to abide by these terms, they would be replaced by workers from other cities. The union promptly rejected these surrender terms. On March 1, 1892, the manufacturers locked out twelve hundred cutters, nailers and operators. To the press, the president of the Exchange, Hugo Jaeckel, cynically declared that the purpose of the manufacturers was "to rescue good workmen from the tyranny of demagogues."

The union offered to arbitrate the dispute. But the employers refused even to meet with the union, whereupon the union declared a general strike in the industry. The union held fast for thirteen weeks. On May

30, its finances nearing exhaustion and many strikers facing starvation, the union called off the strike. The employers had given the Furriers Union a tremendous blow from which that union of German fur workers never fully recovered.

During the strike, it became apparent to the Furriers Union that one important source of their weakness was the fact that the fur workers of other cities were unorganized. Before the 1880's there were no fur workers to speak of outside New York. But since the 'eighties, fur manufacturing had sprung up in other cities all over the country. Unorganized, these new workers had done little to assist the New York strikers. On the contrary, it was these very workers whom the employers threatened to bring into the New York shops.

In April, the Furriers Union applied to the American Federation of Labor for a charter. It was granted on May 3, 1892. Even after the failure of the strike, the union still made an effort to organize the other cities. By February of the following year, locals were organized in Detroit, Boston, Philadelphia, Cincinnati, St. Paul, Milwaukee and St. Louis.

A convention of all the locals was finally held in New York in May 1893. After three days of sessions, the International Union of Fur Workers of the United States and Canada was officially launched. But the organization proved to be stillborn. Before it had a chance to get started, it was caught in the most acute economic crisis the country had yet undergone. With millions of unemployed workers tramping the pavements in vain search for work, organized labor waged a hopeless struggle. Strikes were broken. Many unions were smashed completely. Those that remained alive were seriously weakened.

The fur workers' union suffered the fate of the rest of labor. Only the Furriers Union of New York survived at all. The Chicago Furriers Union held on grimly until 1895. Its end came after a bitter strike against Marshall Field & Company, the biggest fur employer in the city. Their union smashed, the workers were driven back to the shops where they faced brutal discrimination from the boss.

During the 1880's and 1890's, a large influx of Jewish immigrants came to the United States from Roumania, Bessarabia, Hungary, Austria, Poland and Russia. A number of them entered the fur trade, some having been members of fur workers unions in their native land. During the lockout and strike of the German Furriers Union of New York in 1892, the Jewish fur workers participated actively.

After 1892, the number of Jewish workers in the trade increased rapidly. Most of them were "green hands" taken in as learners in small shops clustered around Houston, Wooster, Spring and Greene Streets, in the lower East Side of Manhattan. Many of these small shops were contractors for the bigger manufacturers like Gunther's and Russek's. Wages, hours and other working conditions were, of course, worst in the contracting shops. Unable to earn enough to keep their families alive, the Jewish fur workers were forced to take "bundles" of work home.

Although alarmed by the growth of the contracting shops which threatened their own existence, the German Furriers Union looked down upon the "greenhorns" and refused to organize them. The Jewish fur workers turned to the United Hebrew Trades, which had helped organize the Jewish workers in printing, shirt, dress, millinery, and men's clothing trades.* Some small groups of Jewish fur workers were organized in 1895. But failing to achieve unity with the German Furriers Union, they made little headway and soon dropped out.

While unionism was declining among the fur workers in New York, it had a rebirth in other cities. The industrial depression, which had begun four years before, was over by the summer of 1897. With the resumption of long, busy seasons, a series of shop strikes to wipe out wage cuts swept the fur districts in St. Paul, Chicago, Detroit, Minneapolis, Toronto and Montreal. Realizing that "seasonal" strikes by themselves were no adequate solution to their problems, the fur workers in those cities began to rebuild their unions.

The most active of the new locals was the Northwestern Furriers Union No. 1 of St. Paul which, when chartered by the AFL in 1898, had a membership of 104. The local grew steadily and in 1903 helped organize the Minneapolis Furriers Union and the Ladies Furriers Union of St. Paul, the first union of women furriers in America.

The German Furriers Union of New York then had 170 members, mostly cutters, but was little more than a social organization. Chicago

---

* The United Hebrew Trades was founded in October 1888 by a committee made up of delegates from Branch 8 (Yiddish-speaking Jews), Branch 17 (Russian-speaking Jews chiefly) of the Socialist Labor Party, the Socialist-led United German Trades, and the Jewish typographical, choral singers' and actors' unions.

had about 100 cutters in the union. But in both major cities, the nailers, operators and finishers were unorganized. Everywhere, apprentices were flooding the trade. When the men threatened to strike for better conditions, these apprentices, having gained some knowledge of cutting, were put to the bench. Everywhere, too, piecework had been widely introduced, resulting "in the division of the work in separate lines . . . and a cut in the wage of the furriers."

Within a year, in response to appeals by the St. Paul local, several local unions affiliated to the AFL. In April 1904, five delegates representing eight local unions in six cities met in Detroit and formed the International Association of Fur Workers of the United States and Canada. With 590 members in St. Paul, Minneapolis, Chicago, Toronto and New York, the national union set up headquarters in St. Paul.

While seeking to "organize and elevate the fur craft," to establish the eight-hour day, win uniform wages for the same work, abolish sweatshop and child labor and promote the use of the union label, the new organization stressed that strikes were dangerous and costly. Members were urged to refrain from striking except as a last resort. Before a strike could be called by a local, its members had to approve it in a secret ballot. And even after such approval, the General Executive Board could call it off, if petitioned by ten members.

On the fourth day of the convention, Hugo V. Koch of St. Paul was elected president; C. Bruegger of New York and A. V. McCormack of Toronto, vice-presidents; C. E. Carlson of St. Paul, secretary-treasurer; and J. C. Smolensky of Chicago, chairman of the Board. The following month, the new International Union received a charter from the AFL.

The officers of the International appeared to be honest, sincere and hard-working. None except Carlson received any compensation for their union work, which was done after a full day's work in the shops. They believed in labor solidarity and equal rights for women workers in the trade, taking pride in the election of Hattie Tschida of St. Paul as a member of the General Executive Board. But these men were totally unprepared for the difficult task of building an International. They had little or no experience. Koch, 27 years old, had been in the trade only two years. He was "conservative" in his outlook and was constantly agitating justice to all—employer, employees, corporations, etc. Carlson was only 24 years old. He had been in the trade several years, but he worked in Spokane, Washington, far removed from the real center of the industry.

In keeping with the views held by many trade unionists of the period, the leaders of the International naively pinned all their hopes on the crea-

FURRIERS' JOURNAL

UNION INTERNATIONAL OF FUR OF U.S. AND REGISTERED

ORGANIZED APRIL 14, 04

LABEL ASSOCIATION WORKERS CANADA GEN SEC'Y C.E.CARLSON

♯ ♯ ♯ *Devoted to the Interests of all Fur Workers* ♯ ♯ ♯

Vol. 1   AUGUST. 1905   No. 2

ADDRESS OF PRESIDENT GOMPERS

At Civic Federation Banquet in New York City.

It is a deep cause for regret that I have not had time and opportunity to write carefully what I would like to say to you tonight. With a large number of others, I am engaged in the fight and it has not often that one who is

that the machines could be operated by night as well as by day. The conditions of the working people during the periods when they were in a state of feudalism, and when the competitive system of industry first emerged cannot be read by investigators, by sympathetic men and women, without touching them to the very core of their being. Yet we had then the highest conception of the liberty

tion of a strong demand for the union label. The International offered to give the label free of charge to the employers and to work to create a demand for the union-labeled products. In return, the employers were asked to agree to the union shop! Strikes with their "attendant bitterness" would antagonize the employers and would "not enlist public opinion." The second issue of the union's official journal, August 1905, featured AFL President Samuel Gompers' speech before the manufacturer-dominated National Civic Federation.

Experience, however, soon taught the leaders of the new International some basic lessons. The union was born at a time of furious onslaughts against the whole labor movement by various employers' organizations such as the National Association of Manufacturers, the American Anti-Boycott Association, and numerous Citizens' Alliances. During 1905, the AFL lost 200,000 members. Lockouts and court injunctions were used against unions on a wide scale. A nation-wide open-shop drive was under way. Collective agreements with unions were scrapped. And the union label, wherever it existed, was contemptuously discarded.

From the beginning, the International was caught in the tide of reaction. No sooner were locals of fur workers set up in Detroit, Boston, Cleveland and St. Louis than employers in those cities posted notices that "any man joining the Furriers Local will be discharged." In city after city, the leaders of the International were dismayed to find that appeals to the reason and good will of the bosses were fruitless. Nevertheless, in

spite of disillusionment and hardship, the International struggled to hold
on to life in the hope of organizing New York. Here, Carlson wrote to
Samuel Gompers, "the membership should reach thousands."

With $300 borrowed from the AFL, Koch and Carlson
visited New York, where they were met by a committee of Jewish
fur workers. Meetings were held in the fur market. Before Koch
and Carlson left, three hundred Jewish fur workers had been organized in a Jewish Furriers Union.

A new difficulty arose very shortly. At a meeting of the Jewish
union in May 1906, two resolutions were debated. One called for
affiliation to the International Association of Fur Workers; the second, for affiliation to the Industrial Workers of the World (IWW).

The IWW had been organized in 1905 by a small but militant
body of class-conscious workers who were disgusted with the narrow craft-unionism of the AFL, its failure to organize the mass of
workers, unskilled as well as skilled, and the bureaucratic policies
of the AFL officials. They were most bitter against the Federation's
cooperation with the employers at the expense of the workers' conditions, a policy they regarded as outright betrayal. Urging industrial unionism and the organization of the unorganized, the IWW
declared: "The working class and the employing class have nothing
in common. There can be no peace, so long as hunger and want are
found among millions of working people and the few, who make up the
employing class, have the good things of life." The IWW dubbed the
AFL the "American Fakeration of Labor."

The debate in the Jewish Furriers Union was ended by a vote to remain independent of both the International and the IWW. Nevertheless,
the character of the debate itself indicated the militancy of many of the
Jewish fur workers. They were not willing to endure the miserable conditions in the shop without a struggle. They compelled the union to act.

By 1907, locals of operators, finishers, nailers and cutters were organized, united by a Joint Executive Council. The union boasted a membership of three thousand. It was ready for battle. The determination of
the fur workers was further strengthened by a powerful strike of twelve
hundred reefer-makers (children's cloaks) that spring. Mass picketing
on a scale scarcely seen before in New York featured the strike. Despite
the brutality of police and thugs hired by the employers, the reefer-
makers held out until they won all their demands.

Inspired by the victory of the reefer-makers, the Jewish Furriers

Union drew up demands and presented them to the employers. They demanded the closed shop, hiring through the union; nine-hour day Monday through Friday, eight hours on Saturday and a half-holiday on Saturday during June, July and August; pay for all legal holidays including two Jewish holidays of Rosh Hashonah and Yom Kippur; no discharge without good and sufficient cause; top seniority for shop chairmen to be elected by each shop.

The employers, ever since their victory over the German Furriers Union in 1892, had remained unchallenged. The German fur workers did not bother them. The Jewish Furriers Union, they had laughed off with contempt. Their unconcern quickly changed when the union called a series of shop strikes in August and won settlements from a number of employers. One hundred and fifty members of the Manufacturers Association, including those employers who had signed agreements, hit back by locking out their workers. On September 16, the union answered by calling a general strike. According to the *New York Times,* three thousand workers were locked out of Association shops and an additional two thousand in independent shops were ordered on strike. The actual figures were probably somewhat higher.

A. Heilbroner, of Kaye & Edelstein, chairman of the Association, confidently told the press: "We do not anticipate much trouble as a result of this lockout. Most of our employees will return to work Monday and sign the new shop regulations . . ." The "new shop regulations" were to be a contract drawn up by the Association barring shop stewards, barring visits to shops by union representatives, and providing that "any attempt to interfere with the employer in the conduct of the shops will result in the immediate discharge of all employees connected with such action."

As picket lines appeared in front of their shops, the employers called the police. "Riot calls were sent out," the *New York Tribune* reported, "and nineteen strikers were arrested for disorderly conduct. Louis Siegel of 30 Rivington Street was arrested at 12th Street and University Place while making a speech." The *New York Herald* carried the typical headline: "FURRIERS RIOT, ARE ARRESTED."

At the end of the first week of strike, the German Furriers Union voted to call out on strike every one of its members employed at any shop where the Jewish Union was locked out. Only one member refused to abide by this decision, and he was immediately expelled.

To aid the fur manufacturers in their battle with the union, the fur skin dealers announced they were extending credit for sixty days. But no one extended credit to the strikers or to the union. Within two or three weeks, they were keenly feeling the need for funds. A back-to-work movement began after the third week and by October 9, the majority of strikers were forced back on the Association's terms. Two days later, the strike was called off. The Association gloated that it had "effectually checked the tide of Unionism as far as this trade is concerned." For years, no one dared mention the word "union" in a New York fur shop.

Failure to organize the Jewish fur workers of New York sealed the doom of the International Association of Fur Workers. The German Furriers Union withdrew from the International altogether in 1908, charging that "the American Federation of Labor is crooked, that the leaders are crooked and sell out the workingmen who compose the rank and file." Their disaffiliation represented a general trend. Matters went from bad to worse. "Inasmuch as nothing can be accomplished with such a miserable membership as ours," wrote A. V. McCormack in 1909, "there has been some talk of the International disbanding." The final dissolution came in March 1911, when the charter was surrendered.

The outlook for the fur workers was dark indeed. In the quarter of a century since 1886, all attempts to organize and win better working conditions had been smashed by the employers. With all their efforts and sacrifices, the fur workers had not succeeded in holding on to temporary gains or forging ahead to new ones. Union after union had lost ground and gone out of existence. Employers all over the country confidently predicted that the fur workers would never be organized.

But it was the darkness before dawn. Only one year after the International Association of Fur Workers folded up, a mighty general strike was to convulse the fur industry of New York. Overnight, "the miserable membership" so despaired of by previous leaders, aroused the admiration and respect of the entire labor movement.

CHAPTER 4

How to Mislead
a Union

Local unions of tannery workers, glove workers, harness makers, saddlers and horse collar makers had sprung up in the early 1880's under the banner of the Knights of Labor. But it was not until this once powerful labor body began to lose ground that the idea took hold in many trades of national unions set up on a craft basis.

Among the leather workers, the movement toward such national unions first developed among the workers on horse goods, then an important and flourishing trade. The United Brotherhood of Leather Workers on Horse Goods was launched at a meeting of several local unions in St. Louis in 1896. The new organization, which came to be known as the Brotherhood, was chartered by the AFL before the year's end. Starting out with only three locals, the Brotherhood grew steadily, reaching a membership of 8,000 in 127 local unions by 1904. Local 17 of Chicago was the largest, with 575 members. Davenport, Iowa, and New York City came next with 300 each. The rest of the locals were small, with some 60 to 100 members, and a few had only 25 members. By 1904, the locals were spread from coast to coast and from North to South, covering 119 cities and towns in thirty-five states and Canada.

Many locals of the Brotherhood chalked up important gains for their members. Chicago reported in July 1902 that it had "been successful in getting our union recognized by all the manufacturers in Chicago, and . . . in getting the prices of work raised all the way from 10 to 50 cents on the dollar." Washington, D.C., related: "This time last year we worked ten hours a day and nine hours on Saturday. At present we have a nine-hour

day, with eight hours on Saturday, and several bosses advanced wages 10
to 15 percent." Randolph, Massachusetts, reported in 1904: "Before the
local was formed, some men used to work in this city as late as nine and
ten o'clock at night. On April 20th, we received a nine-hour work day,
with an increase of 7 percent for piece hands."

Not all locals could point to such gains. In many cities, leather workers
still worked ten hours a day for "about the poorest pay of any trade in
the country." Employers often arbitrarily broke their agreements and
posted notices in the shops: "This is an open shop." One St. Louis boss
cried: "What in the h—— have saddle hands and harness makers got
to do with collarmakers ... We won't be dictated by anybody; take 'em
all out; we stand pat." He "stood pat" for three months, until forced to
change his mind and recognize the union.

With the backing of a "Citizens' Alliance," L. D. Stone of San Francisco repudiated his agreement with the Brotherhood's Local 57. The
membership responded that they were "unalterably opposed to going back
to anything that would tend to bring about the starvation wages of $7
per week on an average which we had before we organized." The strike
was "as solid as a rock" for seven weeks, the union winning complete
victory.

The fighting spirit and strong union-consciousness of the
rank and file of the Brotherhood were not isolated phenomena. Millions of
American workers, who had gone through the terrible crisis of 1893 and
suffered untold hunger and misery, were debating many fundamental
questions.

American industry had greatly expanded. Giant corporations and
trusts controlling almost all basic industries came into being, gobbling
up smaller companies. Industrial and financial power was being concentrated into the hands of a few rich families who ruthlessly crushed out
all opposition. The resentment of the people against the wealth-grabbing
trusts expressed itself in a powerful movement—known as the Populists
—that had millions of followers all over the country. At the same time
a militant Socialist Party was beginning to make its influence felt.

The rank-and-file workers were further embittered by the policies of
the top leadership of the American Federation of Labor and of many
national unions, including the Brotherhood, who shunned the struggle
against the big corporations. On the contrary, top AFL leaders developed the theory and practice of cooperating with the employers at the
expense of the workers. They confined themselves more and more to

maintaining craft unions of the highly skilled and well paid mechanics and abandoned altogether the growing mass of semi-skilled and un-skilled workers who were the poorest paid and most in need of organi-zation. Many of these unions even set up racial barriers to exclude Negroes both from membership and from their trades.

It was not surprising, therefore, that the local membership of the Brotherhood of Leather Workers engaged in lively discussions on the policies of union members. When AFL President Gompers asserted that "the interests of capital and labor are identical," Cincinnati Local 49 of the Brotherhood retorted from experience: "If such is the case, why do they antagonize one another?"

And when Gompers became a vice-president of the National Civic Federation where, with eleven other union leaders, he fraternized with August Belmont, the banker, Andrew Carnegie, retired steel mill owner, and Mark Hanna, the millionaire national boss of the Republican Party —the leather workers were furious. They were convinced that the Na-tional Civic Federation was a cunning device of the big corporation heads to check the rising discontent of the workers by winning over trade union leaders to serve as "lieutenants" to the captains of industry. Brotherhood Local 11 of Davenport, Iowa, adopted a resolution in 1902, taking Gompers to task for his connection with the National Civic Federation. The resolution, soon seconded by every local in the Brother-hood, declared that "there is no lasting benefit to be derived from the Civic Federation."

The leather locals also criticized the AFL Executive Council for making deals with the political machines in both old parties under the soothing slogan, "Reward your friends and punish your enemies." Writing directly to the leaders of the AFL, Local 49 of Cincinnati demanded: "Must we not elect men from our own class to represent our class, in the same way the Capitalist does?"

But the national officials of the Brotherhood did not reflect the strong class-conscious views of the rank and file. In fact, the national officials adhered to the AFL Executive Council's policies and repeatedly clashed with the militant membership. To perpetuate their control, the national officers of the Brotherhood decided to hold conventions every five years instead of every two years. This was typical of the methods of AFL leaders. There was a terrific outcry of protest from the mem-bership. Several locals openly accused the officers of postponing conven-tions in order to hold down the rank and file.

The outspoken sentiments of the locals must have infuriated Gompers, for in September 1901 Charles L. Conine, the Brotherhood's secretary-treasurer, found it necessary to urge Gompers to meet with the Brotherhood's national officers in order to assure himself that they did not subscribe to the views of the membership. He was confident that "we

Cincinnati Local 49 denounces the AFL policy of relying on "representatives of the capitalist class" and demands that labor work to elect "men from our own class to represent our class."

will be able to dispel some of the wrong ideas and fears as to the real intentions of our Brotherhood." Conine, however, was unable to make good on his offer to Gompers. The following year he was found guilty of embezzling $6,000 from the Brotherhood's treasury. The criminal court in Kansas City convicted him and sentenced him to jail!

The "real intentions" of the Brotherhood had already been revealed by its president, four vice-presidents, and Secretary-Treasurer Conine in a letter to the AFL in December 1900. The national officers urged the Federation to throw all its strength into a campaign for a federal law providing compulsory arbitration of all labor disputes. This proposal ranked first on the list of demands of every big open-shop employer in the country.

No single question of union policy so clearly summed up the sharp differences between the honest militancy of the membership and the double-dealing treachery of the national officers as this issue of compulsory arbitration. The rank and file saw in compulsory arbitration a straitjacket that would render them helpless and at the mercy of the bosses. But since no conventions were held between 1900 and 1904, the membership was unable to oust the top leadership and return the union to a healthy course.

In January 1904, the Executive Council of the Brotherhood and its president, Eugene J. Balsiger, signed what came to be known as the "Chicago Agreement." It provided for compulsory arbitration *for five years* of all disputes arising between members of the National Saddlery Manufacturers' Association and their employees. *For five years, the Brotherhood would give up the right to strike.* In case of an unauthorized strike or lockout, both the union and the employers' association *would have to pay damages of $2 for each worker for each day of work missed.* Nothing was said in the agreement about the union shop, or about wages or hours or other working conditions! For five years, all this would be left to arbitration. And in all negotiations with the employers, the workers were to be represented by the national officers and president of the Brotherhood—by the men who were constantly proclaiming the "partnership" and "harmony" between capital and labor.

When the text of the "Chicago Agreement" became known, a storm of indignation swept through the ranks of the Brotherhood's membership. Local 128 bluntly reminded the national officers "that slavery was abolished in the days of Lincoln." Local 136 of Waco, Texas, protested: "We do not approve of strikes until the very last resort, but if we find it necessary to strike, we don't wish to be deprived of that power." The local warned that "if this agreement should go into effect, all we have accomplished for ten years would be virtually lost; therefore, we can't stand for such an agreement." Local 108 of Shreveport, Louisiana, summed up the outraged feeling of the membership generally when it complained angrily: "A greater piece of monstrosity was never committed."

Frightened by the storm of protests, the national leaders agreed to submit the "Chicago Agreement" to a vote of the membership. The agreement was immediately voted down overwhelmingly, 1,848 to 105. President Balsiger was furious. He accused "radical elements" in the Brotherhood of having aroused "passion and prejudice" against the agreement and of having confused the membership into voting against its own interests. He was pained that the employers who had treated the union leaders "in a spirit of courtesy and fairness," should have been forced to waste their valuable time. And he insisted that he would renew the battle until the "Chicago Agreement" became an established fact.

After the rejection of the "Chicago Agreement," the national officers cracked down on the membership. To choke off all criticism, they ordered the expulsion of any member who dared oppose the policies of the leadership. Any member up for expulsion could remain in the organization only if he signed a pledge to cease speaking "disrespectfully" of the officers of the AFL and the Brotherhood.

The expulsions and betrayals disgusted the membership. Many deserted the Brotherhood altogether and joined the militant Industrial Workers of the World. The unfortunate result was that the treacherous clique remained in uncontested control of the Brotherhood. Any progressive who remained in the organization was charged by the national officers with being a "secret" member of the IWW. If he voiced any criticism of the leadership's policies, he was expelled as a "secret agent" of a dual organization. As a result of these developments, the spirit and enthusiasm was knocked out of the organization. The Brotherhood's membership rapidly declined to only four thousand in 1907.

While the invention of the automobile meant the eventual undermining of the entire horse goods industry in the years to come, the complete absence of union democracy in the Brotherhood resulted in immediate worsening of working conditions. The leadership did not fight *for* the workers. It fought only to keep control *over* them.

One last struggle was to be attempted by the fading Brotherhood—the fight for the eight-hour day. But with a cowardly, self-seeking leadership to sabotage the struggle, the Brotherhood was doomed.

A committee set up by Local 95 of New York in April 1907, to investigate conditions in the industry, reported two months later that "the eight-hour work day is the only thing that will put us any way near being on a level with other trade unions." Although the national officers found all kinds of excuses and remained cold to it, the suggestion caught fire among many locals.

Sparked by the militants, many of whom had rejoined the Brotherhood, the demand for the eight-hour day increased in intensity. The pressure on the national officers reached the point where the Executive Council was finally forced to sanction a demand for the eight-hour day in the trade. But President Baker, having in mind the "Chicago Agreement" fiasco, placed a condition to the locals that they first grant him and the Executive Council full power to settle the shorter work day proposition and any other question that came up.

On February 14, 1910, President Baker and the Executive Council finally notified all employers manufacturing harnesses, saddles and horse collars that "beginning Monday, March 31, 1910, eight hours shall constitute a day's work, with no reduction in wages for week hands, and an increase of 15 percent on all prices for piece hands."

However, instead of preparing for a strike, the national officers relied upon their "harmonious" relations with the employers. The conference took place, but the employers refused to grant the slightest concession. Knowing that the union had made no strike preparations, they remained cold to all entreaties of the Brotherhood's officers. Baker begged for some concession, and even offered to accept a nine-hour day. He guaranteed that it would be accepted by the Brotherhood's membership "if I have to take the Charter away from the Local and disrupt them and place them at your power to do as you please with them." But the employers told the Brotherhood's officers, "We really expected a strike, and we prepared for it." The employers welcomed a strike, confident that they could smash the union altogether.

Desperate, the Brotherhood's leaders called a strike on March 21. Three thousand leather workers in sixty cities walked out. The national officers insisted from the outset that the strike should be "conducted in a gentlemanly manner." Picket lines were dispensed with. Little effort was made to involve the strikers in a real mass struggle. The employers, however, had no such ideas of a "gentlemanly" strike. Scabs were brought in to replace the strikers. Workers in shops with unexpired agreements were fired and informed they could return only if they withdrew from the Brotherhood.

The strikers knew that the life of the union was at stake. They were determined to fight it out no matter how long it would take. But the national officers were jittery from the start. "We did not expect a strike," wailed the secretary-treasurer to Gompers, "but believed we could adjust the matter by meeting with the manufacturers' committee."

In the fifth week of the strike, President Baker wired Gompers pleading for him to address a meeting in St. Louis and pledge financial support. Even then, Baker told him, "if we could get assurance of support no matter how small, manufacturers will give in." Gompers came to St. Louis, but brought no financial help. On the contrary, he advised Baker to call off the strike. Baker needed little convincing. Without the slightest warning to the locals, and without even consulting the Executive Council, Baker issued an order on May 5, calling off the strike.

The protest from the membership was so strong that Baker was forced to withdraw his order and take a vote of the locals. All but one of the locals voted "to stand fast, money or no money," and the strike continued. But the damage was done. Baker's cowardice, incompetence and treachery convinced the bosses that all they had to do was hold out. The strikers started the trek back to the shops three weeks later. On June 12, the Brotherhood officially called off the strike.

In spite of the sabotage by the leadership, the workers established an eight-hour day in four cities and a nine-hour day in sixty-five cities. But some locals were completely destroyed. On returning to the shops, the strikers found printed contracts awaiting them with a pledge that they were no longer members of the Brotherhood and that they would never join any union. Almost a thousand leather workers refused to sign these "yellow-dog" contracts. They left the industry altogether rather than submit to such humiliation.

The official leadership was completely discredited. A conference of locals held at St. Joseph, Missouri, that same month removed Baker for conduct unbecoming an officer. In his place they elected William E. Bryan of Wichita, Kansas. Bryan had posed as a crusader for honest and progressive trade unionism, desiring "to give the membership a chance to express their wishes." But once in office, Bryan proceeded to establish a complete dictatorship. He raised the salaries of the officers, threw out the Constitutional provision for referendum on all important decisions, and expelled the militants from the locals.

Like his predecessors, Bryan emphasized the need for "conserving the interests of the employers," and urged the arbitration policies repudiated by the membership in the notorious "Chicago Agreement." With such continued leadership, the Brotherhood was doomed. Organizing work was neglected. The membership declined even more. The union ceased to be a factor in the industry.

The tannery workers, who had waged such militant battles against the repression of the employers in 1886, recovered very slowly from the crushing blows inflicted on the Knights of Labor assemblies. It required years for them to re-form their ranks. Not until 1900 were a number of tannery locals, now members of the AFL, able to move toward amalgamation into one national union. After a preliminary conference in Lynn, Massachusetts, delegates from several locals finally met in Philadelphia on July 4, 1901, to form the Amalgamated Leather Workers Union of America, AFL.

The union grew rapidly. Eighty-six charters were issued in the first two years. By 1903, it had gained three thousand new members and had locals in sixty-five cities and towns in thirteen states and Canada. Leather Trades Councils were set up in four regions: Philadelphia, with six locals; Newark, with eight locals; Chelsea, Massachusetts, with locals in Peabody, Worcester, Haverhill, Chelsea, Lowell, Norwood, Woburn and Danvers; and Fulton County, New York, with locals in Johnstown, Olean, Gloversville and Ballston Spa.

During the first four years of its existence, the Amalgamated adhered to a fighting policy of struggle to improve wages, hours and shop conditions. With the aid of the national union, locals in Milwaukee, Chicago, San Francisco, Newark and other cities conducted hard-fought strikes to establish the nine-hour day and abolish the vicious system of sub-contracting. Although not all strikes were successful, the union did win out in many tanneries. The California strike in 1903 for the nine-hour day involved the tannery workers of San Francisco and four other cities, and lasted seven months. The union did not win a complete victory, but the strike stimulated the growth of the organization all over the country.

The Amalgamated flourished until 1905, when the leadership made an abrupt turn in its policies. After losing four out of five strikes in 1904, President Dennis Healey and the Executive Council decided to call a halt to the program of fighting for better conditions. They took the disastrous course of the Brotherhood and other AFL unions of relying primarily on compulsory arbitration and peaceful settlement of disputes.

As in the case of the Brotherhood, the militant views and fighting spirit of the membership were completely destroyed by the surrender of the national officers to the idea of "cooperation with the employers." Unable to win concessions from the bosses with such a program, the Amalgamated made little headway in organizing the tannery centers. Moreover, the employers were quick to interpret the new policies of the national leaders as a signal to open their offensive against the existing locals. Slowly, but inevitably, the membership began to dwindle. By 1907, the Amalgamated was reduced to nine hundred members. Three years later, only half of these remained.

The end came in 1913. With only five locals left and a handful of members, the Amalgamated was nothing but a paper organization. It returned its charter to the AFL and officially disbanded.

The very same year that the Amalgamated died, however, a new international union had been born—the International Fur Workers Union of United States & Canada. A quarter of a century later, when the fur workers had succeeded in fighting through brilliant battles to build a united, democratic and progressive union, the International Fur Workers Union turned its attention to the workers of the leather industry. In a few years, as part of a new International Fur and Leather Workers Union, the leather workers accomplished what decades of previous efforts had failed to achieve—the successful organization of the leather industry.

Before tracing the history and struggles of the leather workers after 1913, it will be necessary to turn our attention to the story of the rise of the new, militant union of fur workers.

Founders of the International Association of Fur Workers of United States and Canada, organized in 1904. Seated, left to right: C. Brueger, President H. V. Koch, A. V. McCormack. Standing: Secretary-Treasurer C. E. Carlson and J. C. Smolensky.

A group of fur workers active in the 1912 strike. Fourteen-year-old Ben Gold is second from the left in the front row.

NIGHT COURT JUSTICE FOR SIX FUR STRIKERS

Five Fined $3 Each—Five Days in Workhouse for Mother of Child.

The cases of six girl strikers were disposed of in the Women's Night Court before Magistrate Herbert last night. Five of them, who were arrested in the neighborhood of the fur firm of H. Jackel & Sons, 16 West ... street, were charged with having shouted scab at strikebreakers as they were leaving the Jackel shop and with having attempted, and in some cases succeeded, in "placing their hands" on the strikebreakers. In spite of the fact that the only evidence which was adduced against them came from a policeman and Nathan Axed, a "private detective," who lives at 133 West 116th street, Magistrate Herbert fined them $... each for "disorderly conduct" ... nding to a breach of the peace.

The girls stoutly maintained that they were doing picket duty, and that they did not molest anybody. But on the contradictory and palpably vague testimony of the policeman and the private detective, who was identified ... a lawyer in the courtroom as a ...

Contrary to the expectations of the fur manufacturers that the beginning of the week would mark a break in the ranks of the strikers, not a single worker returned yesterday morning and all the shops remained shut down. Yesterday was the beginning of the sixth week of the strike and the bosses reopened their shops and

reported last night that not a single scab went to work in any of the struck shops. Special guards were placed near all the shops yesterday in addition to the uniformed cops which the city has been furnishing to the bosses since the strike started, but there were no scabs to be guarded, it was said at the strike headquarters, 210 East 5th street.

yesterday with a view of bringing about a settlement, and the workers are confident that they will come to terms within a few days.

About 150 German fur workers, it was reported at the strike headquarters, have deserted their jobs and joined the ranks of the strikers, and some of the swellest fur establishments in the city have had

Women played a leading role in the 1912 fur strike. The news item above indicates the type of justice meted out to the militant women strikers, a group of whom are pictured at the right with their signs. These news items are from the New York Call.

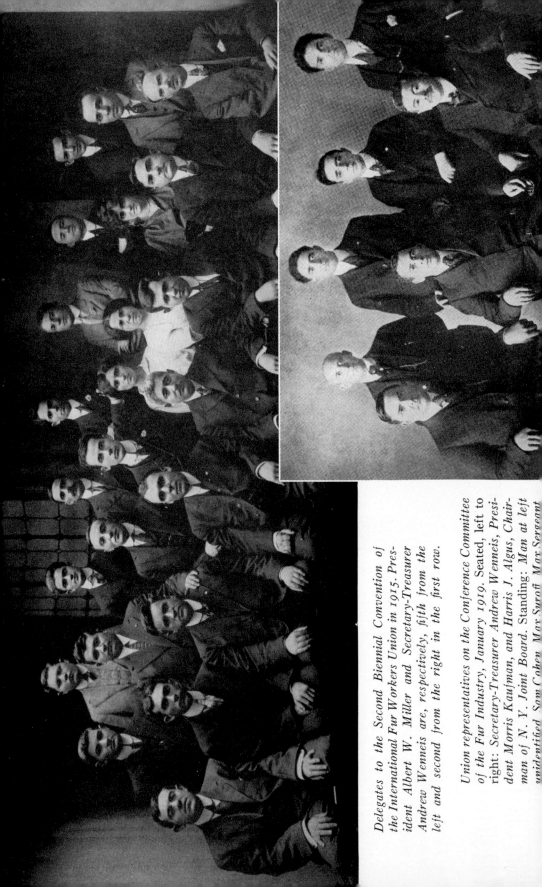

Delegates to the Second Biennial Convention of the International Fur Workers Union in 1915. President Albert W. Miller and Secretary-Treasurer Andrew Wenneis are, respectively, fifth from the left and second from the right in the first row.

Union representatives on the Conference Committee of the Fur Industry, January 1919. Seated, left to right: Secretary-Treasurer Andrew Wenneis, President Morris Kaufman, and Harris J. Algus, Chairman of N. Y. Joint Board. Standing: Man at left unidentified, Sam Cohen, Max Suroff, Max Sergeant.

The International
Fur Workers Union Is Born

CHAPTER 5

The Revolt of 1912

A powerful movement for organization swept the needle trades industries in the years of 1909-1912. It was literally a revolt against the unbearable sweatshop conditions and the long hours of toil for which the workers got a miserable wage. The workers organized and fought to smash the sweatshop system.

The waist and dressmakers, most of them Jewish and Italian immigrant girls, launched the offensive with a general strike in November 1909 known as the "uprising of the twenty thousand." It was a dramatic and bitter battle. These young girls fought employers' association, police and court magistrates who openly aided the bosses. The strike was won in February 1910.

Five months later came the "Great Revolt" of sixty thousand cloakmakers. From July 7 to September 1, 1910, the New York Jewish garment workers struck and fought militantly—and won a collective agreement. The next great blow for organization was struck by the fur workers.

The fur trade had expanded rapidly after 1907, more than doubling in five years. By 1912, there were ten thousand workers in fur manufacturing shops. About seven thousand were Jewish, practically all recent immigrants from Eastern Europe. The remainder included Germans, Greeks, Italians, French-Canadians, English, Bohemians, Slovaks and other nationalities. About three thousand were women, mainly finishers.

39

Profits of the employers were enormous. In two years, the capital in the industry increased from seven million to nineteen million dollars. It was profit extracted through the cruelest exploitation of the unorganized workers.

The poverty-ridden life of immigrant workers in New York City, the low wages, the horrible working conditions, the long months of unemployment, the constant struggle to make a living, is nowhere better illustrated than in the case of the fur workers. The majority of cutters earned about $12 a week. Operators averaged only about $6 and finishers, only $5. Most fur workers worked fifty-six to sixty hours a week, some even longer.

Morris Rosenfeld, Yiddish poet who was himself a sweatshop worker, expressed the horrors of that life in many a poem, of which the following excerpt is characteristic:

"I have a little boy at home,
A pretty little son;
I think sometimes the world is mine
In him, my only one.

"But seldom, seldom do I see
My child in heaven's light;
I find him always fast asleep . . .
I see him but at night.

"Ere dawn my labor drives me forth;
'Tis night when I am free;
A stranger am I to my child;
And strange my child to me."

In larger shops, only the merest semblance of sanitary regulations prevailed. But the majority of fur shops were filthy, disease-breeding sweatshops, usually located in ancient, broken-down wooden tenements or in basements. In one or two small rooms, without even a pretense of ventilation, about twenty fur workers would labor. Stairs, hallways, rooms and closets were packed with dust-saturated fur pieces and cuttings. Stench and dust blanketed everything. Hair, dust and poisonous dyes ate at the workers' eyes, noses, skin and lungs as they toiled at the bench or machine.

So scandalous was the disregard for sanitary conditions in fur shops that in 1911 a New York State Commission conducted an investigation. A special panel of doctors that examined many workers found conditions shocking. Out of every ten fur workers, two had tuberculosis and two had asthma. Most of the remainder suffered from bronchitis, eye sores and skin disease. The fingers of many workers were rotted by dyes. The skin on their hands turned black. The commission reported that eight out of every ten fur workers were suffering from occupational diseases.

Life insurance companies refused to issue policies to fur workers. A common saying among the workers was: "Furriers must pay with their health for the 'privilege' of working."

Heartened by the successful struggles in other needle trade industries, eighty fur operators met in the fall of 1909, and took the first steps to build the union. A few shop strikes took place in 1910. Organization spread to the other crafts. But progress was slow. The defeat suffered in 1907 was still strong in the workers' memories.

In the spring of 1911, groups of fur workers appealed in vain to the International Ladies Garment Workers Union to organize the trade. The United Hebrew Trades, however, lent a helping hand and called a mass meeting to spur the organizing drive. The speakers urged the fur workers to put an end to their miserable working conditions. A large number of fur workers present signed up with the union. Isidore Cohen, a representative of the United Hebrew Trades, was named organizer.

The cutters local was formed in June 1911. By the end of the year, locals of finishers, operators and nailers were in existence. A charter was obtained from the AFL as federal local 14263. The Fur Dressers Union was federal local 13185 and the Floor Workers Union became federal local 13196.

By the spring of 1912, having built up a membership of three thousand and accumulated some $3,000 in the treasury, the union felt itself ready for the inevitable major struggle with the employers. The workers had reached the limit of their endurance. All that was needed was a signal. As soon as the season opened in the spring of 1912, talk of a general strike spread throughout the fur market.

The union began its strike preparations, setting up a General Strike Committee of eighteen, representing cutters, nailers, finishers, pressers and examiners. Besides Isidore Cohen, the organizer, the General Strike Committee included H. Shlissel, chairman; Izzy Chalkin, hall chairman; Abe Chalkin, chairman of the picketing committee; Morris Shamroth, Barish Gerber, Max Cohen, Joseph Goldfluss, Esther Polansky, Max Suroff, and Max Metz. All members were assigned to committees on picketing, halls, speakers, relief, entertainment, law, etc. Halls were rented. Meyer London, the prominent Socialist lawyer, and other attorneys were engaged for the anticipated court cases. Other unions were contacted for organizational and financial help. Samuel Gompers assigned Hugh Frayne, New York organizer of the AFL, to advise the strike committee.

The demands of the union were: recognition of the union, closed shop, a nine-hour day (fifty-four hours a week), paid legal holidays, no homework, no contracting, sanitary conditions, union scales of wages, overtime to be permitted only during the three months of the busy season at time-and-a-half.

The decision to take a strike vote was made on June 12 by enthusiastic packed meetings at the People's Theater and Beethoven Hall. A secret ballot held by members of the union on June 14 and 15 resulted in a vote of 2,135 for a general strike, with only 364 against. Two days later, the union sent its demands to the manufacturers. Meanwhile, the workers were told to remain at their benches until final orders from the strike committee. Each shop was instructed to elect a shop chairman who would be in constant touch with the strike committee. Hundreds of workers joined the union daily and hourly. The cry was: "We have nothing to lose; we must strike this year." The new members besieged the union for the signal to start the strike. The *New York Call*, a socialist weekly, confidently reported that "soon not a worker will be outside the union."

The answer of the bosses was quick and challenging. On June 19, the two employers' associations—Associated Fur Manufacturers and Mutual Protective Fur Manufacturers—rejected the union's demands.* As usual, the employers posed as defenders of the rights of the "independent workman" and labeled the pending strike as the work of a group of outside agitators from the East Side. It was the same argument they had used in every strike as far back as 1886.

That same night, six thousand fur workers met in Beethoven Hall, Manhattan Lyceum, Astoria Hall and Casino Hall to lay final plans for the strike. Every worker present took a solemn oath to strike faithfully and devotedly until victory. Hundreds remained all night at the union office, awaiting the strike call set for the next morning, June 20. At 5 A.M., they were already in the fur district, distributing the Strike

* The Mutual Protective Fur Manufacturers Association was formed in July 1908 by the manufacturers of low and medium grade furs. By 1912 the Association had 312 members.

Call. As was the custom, the Strike Bulletin was printed in red, and was known among the workers as the *Red Special*. Calling on the fur workers to "ARISE TO BATTLE," the *Red Special* declared: "Victory is positive . . . The general strike starts today (June 20th) at 10 A.M. No one shall remain at work. Leave your shops as one man." The *Red Special* also instructed the workers to guard against provocations by the bosses or the police and to maintain strict order and discipline.

Exactly at the appointed hour, seven thousand fur workers, tools and work clothes in hand, appeared on the streets. They left not one worker in their shops to complete an order. Manufacturers who offered bribes of better conditions and bonuses were told to deal with the union. Each day more shops joined the strike. On the second day, eighty-five hundred workers were out from five hundred shops, among them fifteen hundred women. By the end of the first week, the strike was general in fact as in name. Only members of the German Furriers Union remained at work until the fifth week, when they, too, joined the strike. With nine thousand workers out, the trade was completely paralyzed. The shops were empty. The strike leaders confidently predicted that the struggle would be of short duration.

Isidore Cohen was certain that the bosses would soon yield to the demands of the workers, since the season was just beginning. Meyer London also declared on the fourth day of the strike that since the industry was a highly skilled one, the employers could not pick up professional scabs to do the work of the strikers.

Despite the optimism of these leaders, it soon became evident that the fur workers were in for a long and bitter struggle. Some small bosses settled with the union in the first three weeks of the strike. The two employers' associations, however, were determined to fight it out to the end even if it took the whole season of 1912. They were prepared to give up a profitable season and take serious losses, in order to maintain the open sweatshop system.

The associations assured the bosses with certainty that the strikers would return to work in a short time. The manufacturers would simply close their shops for three weeks, and on July 8 the shops would open for all workers to return under the old conditions. Under no circumstances would they deal with the union. The bosses felt sure that, as in previous strikes, the enthusiasm and determination of the workers would be broken after a few weeks. They would soon starve the workers out and force them to crawl back defeated.

But the strikers understood this strategy only too well. A group of women strikers, parading along the picket lines with a banner, expressed the bitter feeling of the strikers: "Masters, starvation is your weapon. We are used to starvation. We will fight on 'til victory!"

As July 8 approached, the eyes of all New York were on the fur workers. Would their ranks break? On Sunday evening, July 7, a roll call of the assembled strikers was taken. Not one striker would go back. Several thousand pickets received the instructions of the General Strike Committee at Astoria and Casino Halls: they were to remain in the halls until 4 A.M.; at that hour, mass picketing would resume throughout the fur district.

Some strikers waited outside the strike halls; others fell asleep on benches; still others sat around in groups and talked. It was a hot, stifling night. Many of the strikers fell asleep on the pavement outside the halls, or on the steps of neighboring buildings. When morning came, seven thousand strikers marched the picket lines of the fur district, keeping a sharp lookout for scabs, but not one appeared. Every shop remained empty. The strikers had won the first serious test!

"We have had many mass strikes . . . ," observed the *Jewish Daily Forward*, "but the strike of the fur workers is a rare, golden chapter in the history of the Jewish labor movement. . . The bosses thought that the sudden opening of the shops would bring the workers back. . . But the workers remained firm and united. . . The morning sun saw the wonderful result of the common effort—one of the most memorable and heroic struggles in history."

Nine times during the next ten weeks, the employers repeated their announcement that the shops would reopen. Each time they were on hand early in the morning, ready to start the machines. Each time the strikers turned out for mass picket lines to prevent scabs from going in. Each time the shops remained empty. Rumors were circulated by the bosses to spread confusion. Reports went out that many workers had come to their employers begging for work, that they had been re-hired and the shops were running full blast. The strikers spiked the rumors by militant demonstrations. "Not since the great 'Triangle' protest march," * wrote the *New York Call* on July 17, "was there a more impressive demonstration seen than the one of 9,000 fur workers which took place yesterday noon."

Inspired by the courage and enthusiasm of the Jewish fur workers,

---

* In the tragic fire in the Triangle Waist Company shop in 1911, 146 workers had lost their lives.

one thousand German fur workers joined the strike on July 23. The workers of Revillon Frères walked out. Together with two thousand strikers they marched to the shops of Ashen-Jaeckel, H. Jaekel & Sons, and Greenfield. They were joined by the other workers. Jewish and German strikers paraded together to the strike hall. The general strike was complete.

During the first few weeks, the strike had been relatively peaceful. A few strikers had been arrested the very first day, distributing the *Red Special* strike call. One worker was shot and wounded by his employer that morning as he walked out to join the strike. But in the main, the bosses had relied on hunger rather than violence to bring the workers to submission. As one boss put it: "If you will only starve these dogs for a couple of weeks more, you will see that they will run back to work."

As the weeks passed without any sign of weakening on the part of the strikers, the employers changed their tactics. Hired gangsters and gunmen brutally attacked and slugged strikers on the picket lines, making no exception of women strikers, whom they beat cruelly. Young girls walked the picket lines and gathered in the strike halls with bandaged heads and mutilated faces. By the end of July, the fur district resembled a battlefield, and the strike headquarters a hospital. A newspaperman at the strike hall reported strikers being brought in whose "clothes were hanging in tatters on them, the skin cut and bruised horribly from the bottles and iron bars with which they were attacked."

And the police? They sided openly with the employers, escorting scabs into the fur shops. Giving the run of the district to the bosses' hired thugs, the police daily dragged dozens of strikers to the police station. Over eight hundred strikers were arrested during the strike. Fifty-four got workhouse sentences. Two hundred and fifteen workers were seriously wounded by the bosses' sluggers. Some required months of hospitalization, emerging scarred for life.

That the police authorities interfered openly on behalf of the bosses was common knowledge. On August 3, a gang of thugs broke into strike headquarters and attacked several strikers. Driven out, and chased by the strikers, they took refuge in a nearby store. When the police were summoned, they escorted the thugs safely from the store and arrested the strikers who had been standing guard. A newspaperman on the spot protested the outrageous action of the police. He, too, was arrested and charged with "interfering with an officer while making an arrest."

But hunger, beatings, or arrests could not dent the spirit and morale of the valiant strikers. Every day they demonstrated anew their courage and their readiness to endure every hardship. Four strikers who were arrested while picketing turned down the offer of J. Albern, a member of the firm of Kaye & Einstein, to furnish their bail. "We have a union," they told him proudly, "if the union can't get us out we will stay here, but we don't want you to bail us out."

Of all the newspapers in the city, only the *Jewish Daily Forward* and the Socialist *New York Call* supported the cause of the strikers. The rest of the press toadied to the manufacturers and smeared both the union and the strikers. Press reports, deliberately biased, consisted mainly of propaganda statements of the employers. The *New York Times* on August 28, in a typical story, said: "An investigation of the causes leading to the strike which was made yesterday by a *Times* reporter showed that the present trouble was the direct outcome of the activities of a number of professional east side agitators."

The vast majority of the fur workers had earned very little money during the months before the strike. Their meager resources were quickly exhausted and their families were soon experiencing serious hardships. Nevertheless, many staunchly refrained from asking strike relief from the union.

In spite of the strikers' sacrifices, the union's painfully small treasury was drained by the third week of the strike. A public appeal, by several other unions, fraternal organizations and Socialist Party clubs, for funds to aid the fur strikers, movingly declared: "There is no need to speak much of the strikers. Such people are a credit to every movement. But they are poor, these heroes, so poor that in the fourth week of the strike they require help . . . In this rich trade, where they make coats of the most precious ermine and sable and mink, the workers earned so little that, even when there was work, many furriers' families lived in want . . ."

Special relief conferences of unions and other organizations were called. Concerts were held and special performances of Jewish plays were given for the benefit of the strikers. Women with handy coin collection cans waited outside shops and factories in the evening and pinned "Help the Furriers" tags on every lapel. Most of the $60,000 spent by the union in the course of the strike came from such collections.*

* Over $20,000 was raised through the *Jewish Daily Forward*. The Cloakmakers Union contributed nearly $20,000 and the Capmakers, $1,500. Special

For ten weeks, the two employer associations maintained a solid front against the union. Early in August, the members of the associations met and declared their determination to fight indefinitely until the workers would be ready to return under the old conditions. They charged that the strikers were being terrorized by their leaders. Discreetly silent about the vicious brutality of their own hired gunmen against the strikers, they demanded that the strike leaders be imprisoned for having caused a reign of terror in the fur district! Enraged, nine thousand strikers at two packed mass meetings unanimously protested against the slander of the bosses that they were forced to strike. "We will remain out on strike together until our bosses will agree to all our demands," was their ringing reply.

The first move toward a settlement of the strike came on August 20, at a secret meeting that took place between union and association committees, each accompanied by their attorneys. Two days later, the strikers packed Arlington Hall and Manhattan Lyceum to hear Meyer London's report on the conferences, which the union had told the employers would be submitted to the membership. But even before London spoke, the news had already leaked out that the employers would agree to a half-day on Saturday only during the first eight months of the year. When London was introduced, the strikers shouted, "We want a half holiday on Saturdays."

London reported that after seven hours of conference, the employers had offered: the work week to include a half-day on Saturday the first eight months of the year, but a whole day on Saturday the remaining four months; ten paid legal holidays; abolition of sub-contracting; fixing of wage rates twice a year; a joint committee to establish sanitary rules for the shops; a joint arbitration board to arbitrate disputes; and a committee of ten to decide on all other unsettled strike issues.

London was cheered as he urged the strikers to stick to their demands.

_____

strike issues of the *Forward* and the *New York Call*, tag day collections, house-to-house canvass, picnics and theater benefits netted $10,000. Lodges of fraternal organizations contributed $1,000. Other AFL unions raised another $1,000. From the Fur Dressers Union and Fur Floor Workers Union came $500, and another $200 came from fur workers in Chicago. An interesting and highly-prized contribution was received by the strikers on August 27. It was 2,000 marks ($500) from the Central Labor Union of Berlin. Some 120 small shops had settled independently with the union. On August 29, the workers in these shops voted unanimously to contribute one day's pay each week to the strike fund.

A rousing reception was also accorded to Samuel Gompers, president of the AFL, who was the next speaker. Although the AFL had given the strikers no financial aid,* Gompers struck a militant note in his speech which evoked tremendous enthusiasm. He concluded: "Since you have rebelled, which is a sign that you no longer want to stand for it, stay out and keep up your fight until your employers yield to your demands."

The strikers did not, however, get the chance to reject these proposals of the employers. Realizing that it would be overwhelmingly voted down, the employers' associations suddenly denied there had been any tentative settlement. Nevertheless, the strikers made it known emphatically that they would not accept any agreement that included more than a half-day's work on any Saturday throughout the year. "We will make no concessions on this point, even if we have to continue the strike another ten weeks," they shouted at their meetings. Their demonstration in the Labor Day Parade, when the fur strikers' division stretched over twenty blocks, was added proof that their ranks were solid.

Conferences for a settlement continued. Meanwhile, some of the most bitter battles were being fought against scabs going in to the shops. When several scabs tried to enter the shop of A. Jaeckel & Co., a group of strikers stopped them. Two private company guards attacked with drawn revolvers and threatened to shoot. The strikers, led by a woman, fought so vigorously that police reserves were called. The police clubbed and mauled the strikers mercilessly. Seven strikers, including the woman, were arrested.

The ranks and fighting spirit of the strikers remained unbroken. The employers, however, were beginning to bicker among themselves, several making overtures to the union for settlements. Others publicly blamed the association leaders for prolonging the strike, complaining that if a settlement were not reached soon, they would be bankrupt. Even the advice of the National Association of Manufacturers to the fur bosses to hold out could no longer solidify the cracking ranks of the associations.

Conferences were resumed. All day and all night on September 7, the union and association committees negotiated. The employers displayed

---

* When Morris Shamroth, a member of the Strike Committee, had gone to the AFL Executive Council in Washington for financial help, Gompers sent him back with a message: "Tell the strikers to let the world know they are hungry and keep up the fight." Unfortunately, neither the strikers nor their families could eat this message.

their full arrogance and contempt for the union by refusing to meet in the same room with the union representatives. Each committee sat in separate quarters, one at the Imperial Hotel and the other at the nearby Hotel Latham. Messengers went back and forth, carrying proposals and counter-proposals. Rabbi Judah L. Magnes, a leader of the liberal section of the New York Jewish community, acted as intermediary and conciliator.

Agreement was finally reached at 5 A.M., September 8. Its provisions included a forty-nine-hour week, 8 A.M. to 6 P.M. Monday through Friday with an hour for lunch, and a half day on Saturday (until 12 noon) *all year around;* overtime work only during the busy season, at time-and-a-half; ten paid holidays; banning of homework; wages to be paid weekly and in cash; two prices (wage rates) each year and no more; a joint committee to control sanitary conditions in the shops; a standing conference committee, five from each side, to settle all disputes with an eleventh and deciding member to be named by both sides jointly. The agreement was for two years, starting with the day of the settlement.

It was a tremendous, historic victory for the workers, this first collective agreement in the industry. After twelve weeks of general strike, overcoming all hardships, the workers had defeated the employers and had won many basic and important gains in wages, hours and other working conditions. A number of gains were even in advance of conditions in other organized industries.

Several of the original demands, however, were not won by the strikers. The most important of these were the closed shop and abolition of contracting. Despite these major shortcomings in the agreement, the union had achieved its main objectives, including the shorter work week.

News of the settlement spread like wildfire through the strike zone, where thousands of strikers had waited up all night to learn the results of the conference. Almost immediately, the halls and streets in the neighborhood of East 4th and East 5th Streets were jammed with rejoicing strikers. Men and women, old and young, embraced and kissed each other, delirious with joy. Strikers marched from hall to hall, tooting horns and rattling noisemakers.

In the evening came the victory meetings. Bedlam broke loose as fifteen members of the conference committee entered Manhattan Lyceum. As they mounted the platform, girls placed garlands of flowers around their necks. Members of the committee and rank-and-file strikers alike wept unashamedly, so great was their happiness. After the speeches,

officials and conference committee members were carried from hall to
hall on the shoulders of the rejoicing strikers. It was early morning, September 9, before the streets were again clear.

The fur workers' general strike of 1912 was hailed by organized
labor as a shining example to workers in all trades. For twelve weeks,
nine thousand fur workers, men and women, had endured hunger and
want, suffered savage beatings by hired gangsters and by the police—
but they had never for a moment flinched or wavered.

Rarely had the labor movement seen such a display of heroism and
magnificent solidarity. Many strikers' families had actually been
brought face to face with starvation. Yet a roll call by chairmen at shop
meetings just before the settlement showed that not a single striker was
missing. Even the employer-biased *Fur Trade Review* was forced to
admit that "the organization of the union ranks was remarkable."

The 1912 strike was only the first of many remarkable
struggles by the fur workers. No one then could have foreseen that
within a few years they would be locked in battle not only against a
powerful employers' association, but also against gangsters in and out
of the union and against corrupt and discredited union officials. Nor could
anyone have foreseen that within their ranks would mature forces and
leadership that would lead them to new and greater victories over all
their foes and that the fur workers were destined to demonstrate even
greater courage, morale, militancy and solidarity than in the great revolt
of 1912.

CHAPTER 6

The International Union

The successful strike of the New York fur workers laid the foundation for an international union. New York was the heart of the industry. Organization of the workers in the other cities became a necessity, not only to bring up their wages and working conditions but also to reinforce the gains won in New York.

On July 1, 1913, the International Fur Workers Union of United States & Canada received its official charter from the AFL. The founding convention, which had taken place in Washington, D.C., on June 16, 1913, was attended by twenty delegates from eight AFL federal locals in New York, Philadelphia, Washington, Boston and Toronto. (St. Paul was unable to send a delegate.) They represented some fourteen thousand organized fur workers, of whom eight thousand were members of the Furriers Union of New York, which had initiated the convention.

Copying from the Constitution adopted by the AFL itself in 1881, the new organization declared: "A struggle is going on in all the nations of the civilized world between the oppressors and the oppressed of all countries, a struggle between the capitalist and laborer, which grows in intensity from year to year."

The new organization established local unions primarily on a craft basis, all workers in every branch of the fur industry in the United States and Canada being eligible for membership. Provision was made for joint boards for two or more locals in one branch of the industry. A per capita tax of twenty-five cents a month for each member was to be paid by the locals to the International. Of this amount, ten cents went into a general strike fund. Strike benefits of $4 to $6 a week would be paid after the third week of strike, but a strike had to be properly voted by the members and authorized by the G.E.B. Initiation fees for new members were set at $5 to $25, as each local would decide. A $2 initiation fee was allowed during the first three months after a local was chartered. New York was selected for the headquarters of the International Union.

After adopting the constitution, the delegates elected officers. Albert W. Miller, formerly active in the German union, became president and general organizer, and Samuel Korman, financial secretary of the Furriers Union of New York, was elected general secretary-treasurer. Vice-presidents were: A. V. McCormack of Toronto; Philip Silberstein of Brooklyn; Julius Margolis and Andrew Wenneis of New York; and Max Shock of Washington. An additional vice-president, from either Chicago or St. Paul, was to be appointed by President Miller.

A severe economic depression set in during the winter of 1913-14. Armies of unemployed were marching the streets. The future of the new organization looked dark. The International was unable to buy stationery, much less pay salaries. "We have not two cents in our Treasury to begin with," moaned President Miller.

Hampered by lack of funds, the new organization was slow in getting started. The two locals of fur dressers in Brooklyn, the German Furriers Union, and locals in St. Paul and Philadelphia showed little enthusiasm and at first refused to apply for charters. Aside from the fact that President Miller did not enjoy their confidence, the locals objected to the amount of per capita.

After many appeals, the AFL lent a hand by placing President Miller on its payroll as an organizer at $30 a week. A turn in the affairs of the International eventually came with the strike of fur dressers and floor workers early in 1914. The fur dressers and floor workers had won an agreement with the Fur Dressers Association after an eight-week strike in 1912. In that agreement the fleshers and shavers obtained the nine-hour day Monday through Friday and half-day until noon on Saturday. The floor workers received a ten-hour day during the week and a half-day until one o'clock on Saturday. Wages had been raised only slightly, averaging between $12 and $15 a week for fleshers and shavers, and $8 a week for floor workers.

The locals now asked a 20 percent raise for the dressers and 10 percent for floor workers. Negotiations for the new agreement failing to produce a settlement, seven hundred dressers and floor workers went out on strike on February 13, 1914.

For thirteen weeks, the Fur Dressers Association refused to negotiate. Finally, shaken by the firmness of the strikers, the employers accepted the proposal of E. S. Ulmann, one of the biggest fur dressers, to act as mediator. When the conference between the union and the employers was held on May 4, President Miller was invited to participate, even though the two locals had not yet affiliated to the International.

The agreement resulting from the conference was an important victory for the union. All members of the Fur Floor Workers Union, including drivers, watchmen and all other employees doing floor work received a $1 a week raise. Overtime was limited; and when permitted, was to be paid at time-and-a-half. The fur dressers, piece workers, received a 5 percent increase for 1914, 7½ percent for 1915, and 10 percent for 1916. Both locals were recognized by the employers in a closed shop agreement. The International agreed to be guarantor for the two locals for the carrying out of the three-year contract. Several weeks later, both locals affiliated to the International. The Fur Dressers became Local 2, and the Floor Workers, Local 3.

The next big test of the International's strength was the renewal of agreements of the New York Joint Board with the fur manufacturers. The Joint Board's main demands were minimum wage scales, closed shop, abolition of sub-contracting and apprenticeship systems, and the setting up of a permanent Grievance Board to adjust complaints.

Two associations of employers existed in the industry at this time: the Associated Fur Manufacturers, known as the "big association"; and the Mutual Protective Fur Manufacturers, known as the "little association." Conferences were begun by the union jointly with the two associations. However, a split developed between the two. The Associated appeared to be ready to accept all the union's demands except the closed shop. The Mutual Protective, however, not only rejected the union's demands but even insisted that the fur workers should work on Saturday afternoons during three months of the year and that five of the ten paid holidays be dropped. When the union rejected these counter-demands, the "little association" withdrew from the conferences.

The conference committee of the union and the "big association" reached agreement as early as July 13, 1914. The new contract was to last until January 1, 1917. Working hours remained the same, forty-nine hours a week. The union had the right to designate shop chairmen. Minimum wage scales, beginning January 1915, were to be worked out by a joint committee of the union and association, with Dr. Magnes acting as chairman. The same committee was also to work out a reasonable system of apprenticeship. A Committee of Immediate Action, similarly composed, was set up to adjust all disputes during the life of the agreement. The contract also barred piece work and home work, and outlawed inside contracting beginning January 1915. But outside contracting was permitted provided that the contractors maintained the same union conditions as the manufacturers. Wages were to be paid weekly and in cash. Overtime was permitted only between September and March, but for not more than thirteen weeks. Women workers were not to work more than fifty-four hours a week at any time, nor more than ten hours a day.

The employers retained the right to hire and fire at will, promising only not to discriminate against union members. While ten legal holidays were retained, the employers were given the right to exchange them for Jewish holidays. Also, firms that were closed on Saturdays to observe the Jewish Sabbath could work a half day on Sunday in exchange.

Within ten days after the agreement was concluded, however, the members of the Associated rejected the contract. Their committee came back with a new proposal which President Miller termed "not worth the paper it was written on." It threw out the union shop, cut three paid holidays, and lengthened the work week to fifty-three hours during the three busy months. The union rejected these counter-proposals.

An independent agreement was signed by Jaeckel & Sons, the largest fur manufacturer in New York, on the same terms as originally agreed by the Associated, but the union was pledged not to reveal this at the time. Conferences continued with the "big association." Meanwhile, the union prepared for a strike. Faced with a general strike at the height of the season and informed, moreover, that the AFL Executive Council had approved it, the employers reconsidered. On August 13, the "big association" settled with the union on the identical terms reached one month before.

Refusing to deal further with the "little association," the union notified the rest of the bosses that they would have to sign independent agreements. The union also demanded $200 bond from each independent boss as "security for the faithful performance of the agreement." Many signed up quickly. The remainder of the independents were struck. Eighty-six independents joined the "big association" and over two hundred were signed up directly by the union. By September 8, all shops were settled.

The new agreement, which covered about nine thousand workers in the industry, had gained a number of important improvements. However, the contract also contained many serious weaknesses. The right of the employer to discharge "in accordance with the necessities of his business" was an axe over the head of every active union member including the shop chairman. It was a loophole for all kinds of violations, for speedup and wage-cutting, that were to plague the union for another thirty years. The "outside" contracting system was legalized, which in practice made it almost impossible to enforce union conditions anywhere. And the expiration date of the agreement had been shifted from September to December 31, the beginning of the slack season, which was highly unfavorable to the workers.

Despite these shortcomings, and the delays in establishing minimum scales and abolishing "inside" contracting (not until January 1915), the Joint Board ratified the agreement. It became the pattern for all locals of the International, with minor modification in various cities.

Following quickly on the heels of the successful shop strikes in the independent fur factories, the muff bed workers, organized as Local 51, went out on strike. Most of these workers were young girls, poorly paid, employed in typical sweatshops located in attics, cellars and basements. Of seventy such shops, forty signed a collective agreement after ten days of strike. The remainder were rooted out, organized and signed, one by one. By the end of October, practically all were unionized. Their agreement corresponded largely to the Joint Board contract, with a forty-nine hour week, ten paid holidays, union shop, and a wage increase of $2 a week.

In the same month, October, Miller visited Boston. Eighty-five women fur workers and several men joined the union within one week. Fully aware of the gains and strength of the union in New York, twenty Boston fur shops, organized into an association, quickly signed an agreement with Local 30. The International acted as guarantor for the local. All points of the New York agreement were included in the Boston contract, except that only nine legal holidays with pay were recognized. In another two weeks, the smaller independent shops were all signed up.

The next task tackled by the International was the organization of the biggest fur dressing and dyeing plant in the industry—A.

Hollander & Sons in Newark, New Jersey. Over seven hundred workers were employed in this shop, two hundred of them women. Established in 1890, the firm had always been an open shop. Every device had been employed to prevent its organization. Men who joined a union—or were even thought to be interested in union—were immediately discharged. Any worker who dared to protest was kicked out. Wages were low, and women workers, frequently hired to replace the men, worked for even lower wages.

The average weekly earnings of the Hollander workers were $6 to $10. In the unionized dressing shops of Locals 2 and 3, the unskilled laborer began at $12 and in the third year received $15 a week. The low wages in Hollander's open-shop plant threatened the wage scales in the organized shops. Moreover, every time Local 2 and 3 members struck for higher pay, the Hollander plant continued to work in full force, enabling the manufacturers to get their skins dressed and thus weakening and prolonging the strike.

So strong was the atmosphere of fear in the Hollander plant that Miller declared that to reach the workers was "just like fighting your way through a stone wall." After a number of workers were contacted, a mass meeting was called. Despite warnings from the employer to each worker before he left the factory "that any worker that dared to go to this mass meeting or attempted to join the union would be immediately discharged," practically the whole crew marched to Semmels Hall. When they arrived, they found the members of the firm and their private detectives standing at the doorway, taking note of all who entered. Some seventy-five workers defied the Hollanders and the detectives and went into the meeting. Nevertheless, they were still too fearful to join up.

A secret meeting of workers from Hollander's shop was called the following month at Windsor Hall. This meeting was more successful and Local 54 was chartered. A committee was elected to present the union's demands: a wage increase and union recognition.

When Miller and the committee called on Hollander to present the demands, they were turned down cold. Resolutely, the committee prepared to fight it out. Backed by promises of support from the Essex County Trade Council, the Socialist Party of Newark and local branches of the Workmen's Circle, the strike date was set for April 1, 1915. Only a few workers responded to the union call during the first few days, but on April 6, the entire plant walked out.

From the beginning, it was a bitter struggle. Hollander refused even to discuss recognition of the union. And on that issue the workers were adamant. Violence marked the picket lines right at the outset. The firm imported scabs and hired gangsters to smash the picket lines, and as usual, while the pickets were being attacked and brutally beaten, the Newark police stood by and even encouraged the thugs. In the third week of the strike, the attacks reached a fatal climax. On April 16, Morris Rubin and Abraham Novick, two of the most militant strikers, were shot and killed in cold blood by the gunmen. The day before, Rubin and Novick had told the rest of the strikers, "We must have a Union. Conditions in the shop are unbearable." Singled out as determined fighters, they paid with their lives.

The mourning strikers buried their dead and vowed at the funeral not to return to the plant until the strike was won. They kept their oath. They remained out until an agreement was finally won, to last until December 1, 1917. It provided a $3 weekly increase for skilled workers, $2 for unskilled, and $1.50 for apprentices. The work week was cut to fifty hours a week, with a half-day on Saturday. Overtime was paid at time-and-a-half. The union was recognized. Preferential union shop was written into the contract. New workers hired had to join the union after two weeks. A shop chairman would be elected by the workers in the plant.

The end of the strike was celebrated by a parade through the streets of Newark. Behind brass bands and flags marched the victorious strikers. Proudly they carried aloft a huge banner: "THROUGH STRUGGLE TO VICTORY. WE RETURN TO WORK AS UNION MEN."

The Second Biennial Convention, marking the first two years of the International Union, took place in Philadelphia on June 7, 1915. Sixteen locals had been chartered: seven in New York, two in Brooklyn, two in Toronto, and one each in Boston, Chicago, St. Paul, Philadelphia and Newark. All strikes had been won. Important concessions had been gained in agreements. These were by no means small achievements, especially since the union had started out at a time of economic depression and widespread unemployment.

But many of the locals still had no real foundation. Philadelphia, with twenty members, appeared lifeless; Boston had 163 members on the books, but only ten were in good standing; Toronto reported a "baker's dozen" present at meetings of Local 40, composed of Jewish operators; and Local 35, consisting of non-Jewish workers, was hardly any better off. Many locals were sadly in arrears on their per capita payments, Chicago and Baltimore being unable to afford even sending delegates.

The main base of the International was New York, which supplied the bulk of its income.

The delegates stressed the need to organize the fur dyers and urged the organization of new trade centers. The G.E.B. was instructed to start a campaign to establish minimum wage scales throughout the industry. Miller and Korman were unanimously re-elected to their posts as president and secretary-treasurer.

Meeting less than one year after the outbreak of the war in Europe, the convention delegates strongly denounced the war "as caused by the capitalistic system and decaying monarchy." The delegates unanimously went on record "that this Convention protest against this wholesale slaughter of the workers, and we hope that this terrible cataclysm will soon end, and the workers of the whole world will come to their senses and put an end to the damnable capitalistic system which makes possible such terrible calamities."

The outlook for the future of the union was bright. The fur trade had already recovered from the first effects of the war. New York was well on its way to becoming the main fur market of the world, a title formerly claimed by London and Leipzig. In addition, American dressers and dyers, cut off from European dyestuffs, developed their own dyes and processes, no longer shipping skins to London for this purpose. But most important, the war in Europe created a tremendous boom in American industry as a whole, which was shared by the fur trade.

The fur workers were now fully employed. There was even a shortage of labor. In a strong bargaining position, the workers felt more independent. Manufacturers, reaping huge profits, were not inclined to invite strikes by battling the union. The International was able to march from city to city, establish locals and win agreements after brief strikes, and in most cases at the mere threat of strike.

In Philadelphia, most of the fur employers signed agreements in October 1915, upon receiving the union's demands. Three shops that resisted were struck, the employers giving in after a few days. The workers received the New York agreement, increases of 25 to 30 percent, and the two-price system of wages (slack season and busy season).

The same result was achieved in Chicago within the space of a few days. Presented with the union's demands, many employers promptly signed agreements. A few bigger manufacturers were determined to resist. But the workers were "steamed up to a pitch," wrote Miller, "and they are willing to fight to the limit." The mass meetings "looked like New York in 1912 on a smaller scale."

A strike was called in all unsigned shops. The response of the workers "was wonderful and a pleasure to see." While the strikers marched up and down on the picket lines, Miller busied himself signing agreements and ardently urging certain big manufacturers to form an association. With the aid of Mike Hollander, who happened to be in Chicago, Miller convinced the employers that an association should be formed. On October 30, 1915, the newly-formed manufacturers' association signed an agreement with Local 45. It followed generally on the order of the New York agreement, except that it provided a fifty-hour week, only six paid legal holidays, and a three-price wage system (January 1 to April 30; May 1 to August 31; and September 1 to December 31).

Day by day, the Chicago fur workers won agreements from more independent employers. Strikers were arrested as they pulled scabs out of the shops, but this did not stop the drive. By November 12, every shop had been "pulled" and agreements had been signed with all employers. The union had won recognition from all employers, association and independent, had reduced working hours, and had won increases of about 30 percent.

The union's next achievement in Chicago was the organization of the dressers and floor workers into Local 56. The employers promptly agreed to the union's demands and signed an agreement similar to the contract of Locals 2 and 3 in Brooklyn.

Next stop, St. Paul. News of the Chicago victory had already reached there and upon Miller's arrival, the enthusiastic workers gave him "a royal reception." Agreements were soon reached with practically all the employers without a strike. Piece work was abolished and week work instituted with minimum wage scales. Local 52 was recognized, establishing the union shop, a one-price system throughout the year, seven paid legal holidays, a fifty-hour week with a half-holiday on Saturday, time-and-a-half for overtime, and an apprenticeship system.

Until now the women operators and finishers had been completely unorganized. They were now chartered as a separate union, Local 57. Their agreement with the employers was identical with that of Local 52, except that the wage scale was lower.

Toronto, too, gave Miller "a grand reception" when he arrived there in June 1916. As in the other cities, the spirit of the fur workers was high. Miller found them determined to win an agreement and ready to strike "for the 44-hour week, nothing more or less." There was no difficulty in mobilizing the workers at mass meetings. Even the women workers, who had never belonged to a union, now joined up. In a few days, a committee of the three locals (35, 40 and 65, the new local of women workers) drew up demands and sent letters to the manufacturers, demanding an agreement under the threat of strike.

The Toronto employers answered by demanding that the immigration authorities deport Miller, who had been born in Germany, with whom Canada was then at war. The Canadian authorities readily complied. They seized Miller and began deportation proceedings. The Canadian Trade and Labor Congress leaped to Miller's defense and protested vigorously to the government. This enabled Miller to secure a temporary stay. The manufacturers retreated. They hastily formed an association and settled, granting full recognition of the union, a forty-four-hour week, time-and-a-half for overtime, two-and-a-half times the regular rate for holiday work and a wage increase amounting to 25 percent. "Toronto is practically a 100 per cent organization," reported Miller.

Inspired by the events in Toronto, a group of Montreal fur workers organized a union in July 1916. When Miller arrived later that same month, he chartered the union as Local 66. With twelve hundred fur manufacturing workers in the city, more than half of them women, and with an additional three hundred dressing and dyeing workers, Montreal was an important center of the fur trade. At a union mass meeting attended by Miller, more than six hundred fur workers showed up, strong for the union.

The Montreal employers formed an association and cold-bloodedly discharged every worker who refused to leave the union. The workers clamored for action. The showdown was not long in coming. Declaring that "the standard of working conditions of the Employees of Montreal is much lower than cities like Toronto, New York, Philadelphia, etc.," the union demanded the equivalent of the Toronto agreement. The employers were given until September 12 to reply to these demands. At the same time, an urgent wire was dispatched to Miller in New York by Sol Schacher, secretary of Local 66: "People demanding action—something must be done—impossible to hold them back—decided to make demands on the manufacturers—situation very serious—must have you here at once—impossible for me to further control them—sure of walkout if you don't come."

At Miller's request, the expiration date of the ultimatum was delayed. He arrived a few days later. While the manfacturers were discussing the union's demands, Local 67 was set up, composed of one hundred women workers who, as in Toronto, insisted on a separate local. Fur dressers, dyers and floor workers were also organized into Local 68, the three locals together forming a Joint Board.

No collective contract was concluded with the Association, but individual agreements were signed with nearly all the manufacturers. These agreements fell far short of the original demands. Nonetheless, they reduced the work week from sixty to forty-nine hours, increased wages about 15 percent, established time-and-a-half for overtime, seven paid legal holidays, cash weekly wages and a preferential union shop.

Before the close of 1916, the first issue of the union's journal, *The Fur Worker,* appeared. Consisting of eight pages in all, it was published semi-monthly in English and Yiddish, with occasional columns in Italian, German and French. Aided by prosperity in the trade, the International had by the end of 1916 made considerable progress. Twenty-seven locals had been chartered, with a greatly increased membership. Agreements with significant gains had been signed in almost every organized fur center. These achievements bespoke a sound and vigorous organization. However, this was only on the surface. Already alarming signs of incompetence, corruption, and bureaucracy were evident in the conduct and dealing of leading officers of the union. Within a year, both Isidore Cohen, manager of the New York Joint Board, and Albert W. Miller, general president of the International, were ousted from their posts. Behind their forced resignations lay the story of a tragic state of affairs within the union.

CHAPTER 7

Union or

Private Business?

When the union was organized in 1912, its leaders were mainly from the Socialist movement. Like many of the immigrant fur workers, they had participated in Socialist movements in Germany, Russia, Poland, Italy, Roumania, Hungary, etc. These were people who had fought against all kinds of oppression, exploitation and discrimination. But before long, many of these leaders forgot their ideals. They abandoned militant policies. Yielding to the pressure and bribery of employers, to their greed for money and to other temptations, they became corrupted.

In the American Federation of Labor as a whole, many union leaders developed a system of regarding unions as a sort of business. The bigger the income from dues, initiations and assessments, the bigger their "business." Salaries and expense accounts were heavily padded. Leaders pilfered the union treasury and accumulated private fortunes. Financial reports were doctored and, in many cases, not given to the membership at all. Many such union leaders lived in fine homes and mingled freely with the rich, looking down upon the workers with contempt. They became "respectable" in the eyes of the employers and betrayed the interests of the workers to maintain that position. The employers actually used such union leaders to keep the workers down.

Many leaders in the fur workers union, particularly among the paid officials, were affected by these ideas. Although agreements with improved conditions had been won through the militant struggles of the workers, these union leaders were soon cooperating with the bosses instead of enforcing the agreement. The rude awakening among the fur workers in many cities was marked by bitter but unheeded complaints about the abuses of the employers. "The owners and foremen . . . do anything they please with us and our leaders only laugh when we complain to them," was a typical charge.

The Chicago workers openly accused their officials of conspiring with the bosses to violate the agreement. When they produced evidence of rank discrimination against union members and stacking of shops with non-union workers, the bosses laughed in their faces. The officers of the local assured the bosses that the complaining members did not have the support of the union.

In St. Paul, the workers accused their business agent, Charles Gmeiner, of advising the bosses not to pay older workers the union scale on the excuse that they were nowhere near the "efficiency scale." Newark workers accused their business agent, Nick Roman, of drawing up a new agreement with Hollander without their knowledge. Boston workers informed their president, Benny Lederman, that they were getting less than the union scale. They were told they could "go to a lawyer." Montreal workers complained of discrimination against active union members and that non-union workers were being given preference, but "our leaders say nothing." Philadelphia workers charged that their leaders agreed with the bosses that "hot-headed" union workers should be kept out of the shops. The union leaders themselves helped to blacklist the militants by calling bosses and warning them against "troublemakers."

And so it went, local by local. These union leaders talked about fine agreements, but the workers complained "the bosses will sign mostly anything, but it is a hard thing to make them live up to the same."

In the hands of Isidore Cohen, the leader of the New York Joint Board, the agreements won in 1912 and 1914 became worthless scraps of paper. The bosses simply ignored the agreement and fired any worker who dared to complain. Shop chairmen who took up grievances were told to look for jobs elsewhere. Business agents meanwhile pocketed both the bosses' bribes and the workers' money.

At first, the workers had rushed to the union office with their complaints. They were treated with the utmost cynicism. When a worker persisted despite all rebuffs, the business agent sarcastically told him: "I get thirty dollars a week. Your share is a penny. Here is your penny and go home." Other workers were told to keep their mouths shut or they would get into trouble. The next day, the boss would fire them as "agitators." The bosses didn't even hide the fact that the union officials advised them to get rid of these "troublesome" workers.

Although the 1914 agreement provided that minimum wage scales should go into effect on January 1, 1915, Isidore Cohen did nothing to enforce this provision. As a result, an operator might get $30 a week in July and August, but only $15 the rest of the year. Some workers got as little as $10 or $12. Having done nothing to enforce minimum scales, while permitting the bosses to cut wages, Cohen at the same time rejected all arguments that the union should demand wage increases. Without a minimum scale, he declared, the union "has no right" to ask for increases. Even more, without such minimums, "the union cannot hold the manufacturers responsible for reducing the wages of their employees and taking up others who are willing to work for a lower price."

"How long can this go on?" complained the workers of Jake Hollander's shop. "We work for twelve and thirteen dollars per week. These are bitter times; we have barely enough for our daily bread. If there is the faintest suspicion that a worker takes things a little easier, he is watched like a hawk, lest he lead too 'luxurious' a life. We cannot so much as turn our heads. To put it briefly, things are very bad. We want a strictly union shop. But we are being misled."

The 1914 agreement also required the bosses to improve sanitary conditions in the shops. Under Cohen's leadership, this provision was ignored. In 1915, the New York Department of Health conducted an investigation of the industry. It found so many violations of sanitary laws that it considered the life of every fur worker was in grave danger.*

---

* The Department of Health investigated working conditions in 113 fur factories and arranged for the medical examination of 542 furriers. Only 77 of these workers, a little over 14 percent, had no physical defects. The striking fact is that 72 percent of these 542 furriers examined were under 40 years of age and only 10 percent were over 50 years of age. From this the report drew the conclusion that "the working people engaged in the fur trade are surely not in such financial circumstances as to be able to retire voluntarily from business before the age of 50; therefore it would seem to conclude that physical disability compels their early retirement from vocational activity." In other words, the fur workers were compelled to leave the industry because their health and strength had been shattered.

The report showed that 251 workers of those examined, over 46 percent, were suffering from disturbances of the nose, throat and air passages. In addition, there were 12 cases of furriers' asthma, 11 cases of tuberculosis, 7 of emphysema (a disturbance of the lung tissue), and 32 of sub-acute and chronic bronchitis. Regarding bronchitis, the report stated: "Although only thirty-two (slightly less than 6 percent of those examined) were found to have definite signs of

The Department of Industrial Hygiene recommended sweeping changes in shop conditions, and called upon the union to cooperate in forcing the employers to carry out these proposals. But Cohen, considerate as ever of the employers, refused to cooperate. Dr. Louis L. Harris, chief of the Department, protested in vain that "we pointed out dangers that severely and gravely menaced the health of the workers in your trade. Up to the present time there has been no active cooperation between your organization and the Department of Health."

It was inevitable that the fur workers, who had proved their militancy in the 1912 strike, should turn against the corrupted, graft-ridden administration headed by Isidore Cohen. The workers soon regarded the union as "a suite of offices and paid officials." With such policies, Cohen carried his "business unionism" a step further.

At one time Isidore Cohen had been a "revolutionary," a member of the Jewish "Bund" in Russia. After the failure of the Russian revolution of 1905, he had fled from Vilno to the United States. In this country, he was a speaker for the Socialist Party, and continued to orate for socialism "in words." In deeds, however, Cohen bowed to the will of the employers in all basic issues facing the fur workers.

Following the practice of many anti-union employers, the fur bosses had brought notorious gangsters into the fur market during the 1912 strike. After the 1912 strike, Isidore Cohen used the same strong-arm tactics to protect his "vested interests" in the union "business" against the resistance of the membership. Moreover, Cohen made no bones about it. As early as 1913, he publicly admitted using such methods. He wrote in the *Jewish Daily Forward* that "one must use the whip" against the workers.

To justify such actions, the administration callously coined the slogan that a union must have gangsters to survive. To explain away the militant struggles of the Jewish workers to build the union, Cohen argued, "Jews are good strikers but poor union men. They are always complain-

---

bronchitis, it is our feeling that a much greater number of cases exist than could possibly be discovered at a single examination." Similar comment was made on the tuberculosis cases and attention drawn to the fact that if the workers in the trade "had more freely shared their confidence as to their personal history, instead of a scant 12 percent of respiratory ailments and a still smaller number of skin diseases which were discovered, the number would undoubtedly have been more than doubled." There were actually 163 cases of skin disease due to the poisons used in the trade.

ing. . . But do they so much as lift a finger to help the union? No. They are satisfied with merely tearing down and discrediting the union leaders." They would never pay dues. They would not attend union meetings. Hence the need for "the whip."

The tragic truth was that the outrageous conduct of the business agents and the strong-arm men was calculated to terrorize the workers and drive them away from the union. It required the utmost courage for a worker to stand up at a meeting and criticize the actions of the leadership. Sluggers and a machine clique were spread out in the hall, stationed like watchdogs at posts assigned in advance. A worker applauding any speaker who criticized Cohen was openly threatened. Workers who escaped unharmed from the meeting hall itself found a strong-arm gang outside.

Many workers refused to attend meetings. Often, the business agents, accompanied by sluggers, would round up reluctant workers and drive them to a scheduled meeting. The clique of administration speakers would seize the floor and insult and threaten any critic. Proposals favored by the administration were inevitably carried by counting the "aye" votes and completely ignoring the "nays." When a worker protested the count, he would promptly be hit on the head with a club or a chair.

Instead of relying upon the workers for support, the administration had to depend upon the sluggers. Elections became a formality honored only in the breach. Unable to get the workers' votes, the administration openly stole the elections. A committee of workers investigating the Joint Board election held in 1914 reported "that the election held by this union on September 24, 25, 26, 1914, was fraudulent through the fact that . . . the Ballot Box used in the East 10th Street voting place was exchanged for another box previously prepared and into which fifty or more ballots were cast with the intention of swinging the election. . ."

Cohen and the Joint Board paid no attention to such findings. As a result, the workers were far from enthusiastic about paying dues. Cohen met this problem in the same manner. As workers left their shops, strong-arm men would be waiting for them outside. "Hey, you," a slugger would shout at a worker, "Cohen wants you to come down to the union." The workers would be forced down to the union office to pay their dues.

The scandalous conditions in the fur workers union were a reflection of what was taking place in many unions at the time. In the needle trades unions, both the membership and the leadership stemmed largely from the Socialist movement. One group, which eventually be-

I. COHEN. Organizer   Tel., Madison Sq. 10244   A. ROSENTHAL. Sec'y-Treas.

JOINT BOARD
Furriers' Union, of Greater New York
Locals 1, 5, 10 and 15
INTERNATIONAL FUR WORKERS UNION OF UNITED STATES AND CANADA

We, M. Zuckerman, J.B. Salutsky and A. Held compose the committee appointed by the Furriers' Union to investigate supposed frauds in the conduct of election for "Business Agents" and "Manager", held September 24,25,26 1914, and taking cognizance of the fact that this committee was selected with the consent of the men accused of the fraud, namely:

            Messrs. Ackerman, Moses, Chalkin and Margolis, find,

(1)   That the election held by this Union on September, 24,25,26,1914, was fraudulant through the fact that it was proved beyond a shadow of doubt that the Ballot Box used in the East 10th Street voting place was exchanged for another box previously prepared and into which fifty or more ballots were cast with the intention of swinging the election for either Margolis or Moses or both as Business Agent of the Furriers' Union.

(2)   We find that all the four accused Messrs. Ackerman, Moses, Chalkin and Margolis had knowledge of the fraud before it was perpetrated and we therefore find them guilty of the offense as charged by the Joint Board of the Furriers' Union.

(3)   We find that Ackerman actually perpetrated the fraud and actually substituted for the legal ballot box another box.

(4)   The Committee finds however, that although it is convinced that Margolis had guilty knowledge of the fraud before it was committed, it is not convinced that he actually took part in either the planning or bringing about the fraud:

                           J.B. Salutsky
                           A. Held
                           M. Zuckerman   *SECRETARY:*

The stealing of elections during Isidore Cohen's administration is revealed in this report by a workers' investigating committee.

came known as the "left wing," believed in a militant, fighting policy of struggle by the workers for better conditions, greater democracy, and the whole philosophy of a socialist system to do away with all forms of exploitation and oppression. The other, the "right wing," gradually grew cynical and corrupt. Its leaders adopted the bureaucratic and self-seeking practices current in many AFL unions. Right-wing Socialist union leaders like Isidore Cohen—who had completely abandoned all Socialist principles and ideals, and established corrupt administrations—nevertheless still found it expedient to continue to masquerade as Socialists.

Under cover of this once-militant label, they unashamedly practiced the concept of "business unionism." In contrast to former Socialist beliefs, they now argued that the bosses and the workers had the same basic interests. They were striving for the same things. What helped one helped the other. Therefore, they said, the workers should cooperate with the bosses, and the union with the bosses' association.

The developing progressive "left wing" among the Socialists hotly disputed these policies and tactics. They denounced the "right wing" leaders for their "class collaboration." To the progressive workers, the union was not a private business belonging to a few leaders. The union belonged to the workers and should be run in their interests. They maintained that the interests of the workers were just the opposite from those of the bosses. The boss ran his business for profit; the less wages he paid, the more profit he squeezed out of the labor of the workers; the longer the hours of work, the more profit the boss made; if the boss speeded up the workers and made them produce more within the same number of hours, his profit grew.

The progressives, expressing the program of the workers, demanded a constant struggle for higher wages, for shorter hours and for improved conditions of work. They demanded that every gain won in the agreement should be vigorously enforced; that instead of ignoring or overlooking the bosses' violations of the agreement, the union should be trying to win improvements in wages and working conditions even during the life of the agreement.

The progressives called for a democratic administration. Only a union that was democratic, that was checked and controlled at every step by the workers themselves, that gave every member the right to speak, to vote, to run for office and to participate in all the affairs of the union from top to bottom—only such a union would carry on a militant, progressive struggle at all times for the workers. Strong-arm methods, the lack of democracy in the union, the deals with bosses, the bribery and graft of union leaders, the failure to enforce union conditions and to adjust complaints of the workers properly, were the inevitable accompaniment of Isidore Cohen's "class collaboration" policies.

The protests of the rank and file and of some honest local union leaders against the undemocratic methods of Cohen and his henchmen, mounted from month to month. In the shops, at meetings and in the fur market, the workers voiced their dissatisfaction.

One of the earliest spokesmen to express the indignation of the workers at the time was Samuel Leibowitz. A founder of the union and active striker in 1912, thoroughly honest and devoted to the workers and the union, Leibowitz had risen to the position of president of the operators' local. This was not a salaried office. Disregarding the threats of physical violence, Leibowitz strenuously assailed the bureaucracy and its neglect of conditions in the shop. He was particularly bitter in denouncing the failure of Cohen to establish the minimum scales as provided in the agreement. Leibowitz and his group complained repeatedly that many workers got only "two-thirds and many a time less" than the wages due them.

Indignation over Cohen's sell-out policies swelled to the point where, in July 1915, a committee of militant rank-and-file fur workers went from shop to shop gathering signatures on a petition demanding an end to the reign of terror. Several thousand workers signed the petitions, which was presented to the Joint Board. For a few months, Cohen was compelled to comply with this demand and the fur market was free of the strong-arm gang. But it was only a temporary respite. In the absence of an organized opposition, Cohen was able to bring his sluggers back in full force the following year.

The dissatisfaction of the workers with Cohen's gangster administration finally came to a head at the time the agreement was renewed in the spring of 1917. The workers demanded an eight-hour day, minimum wage scales, a one-price system of wage payments instead of three all year 'round, equal division of work, a definite apprenticeship system, full recognition of the union and provisions for better enforcement of the agreement. A mass membership meeting of all the locals voted that any proposition of the manufacturers must be submitted to the membership for approval before acceptance by the Joint Board.

A new agreement was quickly concluded by the union's conference committee. Cohen hastened to hail it in the press as a great victory. But when its provisions were made public, the workers were dismayed. The contract did provide a forty-eight hour week, wage increases, minimum wage scales, closed shop, and other improvements. But there were so many loopholes in the agreement that the workers smelled a rat.

The employers retained the right to hire and fire any worker "in accordance with the necessities of his business." Bitter experience had taught the workers that under the excuse of "necessities" of business, the bosses always fired the militant union workers. The forty-eight hour provision gave them the right to vary the working hours at will each day. Another provision permitted overtime work between September and March. Such a long period of overtime would keep the unemployed out of the shops.

The classification of second-class work (and lower pay) included such a wide variety of furs that only a few workers would get the first-class rates. Women operators were rated as second-class workers, enabling the boss to replace men with women doing the same work for less money. Finally, the equal-division-of-work clause also permitted the boss to "reorganize" his shop at the beginning of each season. This made the "equal division" benefit practically valueless. The boss could get rid of any worker he did not like. The door was open for wholesale discharges.

The workers stormed with protests. They accused Cohen of selling out to the employers. With a show of indignation, and hoping to sow confusion in the ranks of the workers, Cohen pretentiously resigned as Joint Board manager. No doubt he expected the bewildered workers to plead with him to remain at this critical hour of negotiations for the new agreement. However, his plans sadly miscarried. The local meetings of operators, nailers and finishers joyfully accepted his resignation, which they hailed as the beginning of a new era in the union. The locals then went on to reject the six clauses of the agreement dealing with discharges, distribution of the forty-eight hour week, overtime, exchange of holidays, second-class work, and reorganization of shops.

When his union business was abruptly ended, Isidore Cohen went into the fur business and operated an open shop. During the strike of 1920, Cohen refused to settle with the union, running his factory as a scab shop. It was a logical continuation of the cynical, self-seeking, corrupt policies he had followed as manager of the union.

CHAPTER 8

Exit Albert Miller

The ill-fated agreement that precipitated Cohen's ouster was signed by Albert W. Miller, the International president. In his own way Miller, too, had been building up an unsavory record that was to result in his forced resignation.

From the start, Miller rode the crest of the strength and influence gained by the union as a result of the great strike of 1912 and the militancy of the fur workers themselves. Lacking real ability as a leader, Miller alternated between over-confidence and easy discouragement. The mere threat of strike with hardly any actual organizational preparations often proved sufficient for him to win an agreement. And when the workers were inadequately mobilized to carry on a strike, as in Philadelphia in 1915, Miller blamed the workers, declaring: "The Philadelphia furriers are rotten. They want something for nothing and don't even want to assist in getting it."

In St. Paul, Toronto and Montreal, he agreed to setting up separate locals of women workers, yielding to the pressure of divisive prejudices that weakened the structure of the union. In Toronto, he went even further, agreeing to separate locals based on religion: one local for Jewish workers, another for Gentile workers.

The conscientious International secretary-treasurer, Andrew Wenneis, was compelled to caution Miller that his excessive expenditures had been "commented upon by members of the General Executive Committee." The warnings were useless. While on "organizing tours," Miller even used the opportunity to make his own business deals. Coming into a

71

city, he would immediately contact some fur dealer for a "good buy" in
fur skins. "Don Ome expects some skunks soon," he wrote on one occasion. "Walter Mahon has some beauties already dressed and has offered them to me to pick at cost price."

Of course, the rank and file knew nothing of this racket. Miller's affairs with women, however, were notorious. To these faults, Miller added
a consuming thirst for liquor. Although few of his misdeeds were openly
known to the membership generally, Miller was sharply criticized by
the union's Third Biennial Convention in Boston, June 1917, for having
squandered the union's funds. Especially bitter condemnation was voiced
at the convention for Miller's vote at a special AFL meeting in favor of
American entry into World War I, after the fur workers' convention had
characterized that war as an "imperialist conflict."

Miller was re-elected president, but one third of the delegates voted
against him. The time was not far off when he was to find himself in the
company of Isidore Cohen—out of the union.

Agreements of the locals were renewed easily enough, especially under war-time conditions. Industry had billions of dollars of
war orders. There was a growing shortage of labor. Wages were going
up even in unorganized shops. The fur business, too, was booming and
the manufacturers were anxious to avoid interruptions of work. They
readily made small concessions in wages and working conditions modeled
after the New York agreement. Only in Montreal and Newark was any
difficulty encountered by the union.

On July 28, 1917, the Montreal employers abrogated their agreement
and locked out their shops. J. O. Benoit, business agent of Local 66, felt
that a strike would be a "big mistake." He appealed to President Miller
to come in, and meanwhile restrained the workers from making any decision to meet the lockout. But Miller was having too good a time with
Business Agent Charles Gmeiner in St. Paul to worry about Montreal.
He was busily engaged in long sessions with Gmeiner in the Twin Cities'
leading saloons.

While the Montreal workers fretted, uncertain as to what action to
take, a young fur worker who had recently arrived from New York for
a visit to Montreal, demanded action. Why wait for Miller, he said. The
only way to meet the lockout and save the union was to answer with a
strike. The French-Canadian fur workers eagerly seized upon this proposal. They demanded that a strike be called. That young New York fur
worker was Ben Gold.

Ben Gold was born in Bessarabia, then part of Czarist Russia, in 1898. He was the son of Jewish parents, Israel Gold, a watchmaker and jeweler, and Sarah Gold. The boy's family background was steeped in Socialist struggle against oppression. His sisters took part in the student revolutionary movement, and one was severely beaten and crippled in a demonstration against Czarist tyranny. The young boy soon learned the meaning of the dreaded knock on the door by Czarist police in the deep of night, and the horrors of pogroms against the Jewish people.

Israel Gold came to the United States in 1908. He saved enough to bring his wife and children here in 1910. His son, Ben, began to work at all kinds of trades—a few weeks on pocketbooks, then on dresses and paper boxes. Finally, a friend of the family took him up to the fur shop of Agines & Son in Bleecker Street. Israel Gold paid the boss ten dollars to teach his son the trade.

Ben Gold was thirteen years old when he took his first job in a fur shop. He was supposed to learn cutting, but since he was still too small to reach the table, it was decided that he should become an operator. In 1911, when he worked for the season as an operator at Board & Hauptman, he earned $9 a week. The money was welcome, for he was the only member of the family then employed.

The Furriers Union was just about being organized at this time. In May 1912, Israel Gold gave Ben $1.25 to pay for a union book, and the young boy joined the union. When the 1912 strike started, Gold was assistant chairman of the shop of Pike & Rabinowitz. He became an active striker, constantly on the picket line, in the strike hall, patrolling struck shops. Throughout the strike, together with other strikers, he slept near the shop to prevent scabs from being brought in or out during the night.

During the strike, Gold became acquainted with men and women who were active in the Socialist Party. Though much older, they took the young boy into their confidence and taught him many things about the struggles of the workers. The progressive atmosphere at his home also contributed to his education in the labor movement. Several of his sisters were active in the cloak and dressmakers' union, and their friends would frequently gather at his home on East 13th Street to discuss union problems. The boy would listen with rapt attention to the conversation as it roamed over the fields of literature, trade unionism and politics. He read Dostoevsky, Gorky, Zola, Tolstoy, De Maupassant, and drank deeply of the socialist writings of Jack London, Eugene V. Debs, Upton

Sinclair and others. While working in the fur shop of Kaufman & Ober-
lander during the day, Gold was rounding out his education by attending
the Manhattan Preparatory School at night. He was determined to study
law, but this ambition was never realized.

During the early years of the Furriers Union, Gold participated in
many rank-and-file actions to halt the corruption and bureaucracy in the
union. In 1916, he joined the Socialist Party. In 1917, Gold went to
Montreal to visit several friends of his family. Some of them worked in
the fur trade, and they took Gold to meetings of the Montreal Fur
Workers Union. Although he was not yet working in the trade in Montreal, Gold became interested in the problems of the fur workers there.
When the strike started, he was already looked to by the workers for
leadership.

This then was the background of the young man around whose dynamic leadership the whole progressive opposition was to be crystallized
in the Furriers Union. Destined to lead the fight against gangsterism
and to clean the union of its bureaucratic, corrupt officials, Ben Gold
gave his first example of militant leadership of the fur workers in the
twelve-week Montreal lockout and strike.

President Miller arrived in Montreal eight days late with
the excuse that the train had been delayed. He was told about the young
fur worker from New York and sent for Gold. Impressed by the widespread support among the Montreal workers for Gold's strike proposal,
Miller agreed to call a strike if the employers did not immediately recall
the lockout.

Miller's pleas to the employers were of no avail. They refused even
to meet with him. Since the employers had tried to bribe the workers
with an offer of a forty-four-hour week and a 25 percent wage increase
if they would only quit the union, a general strike was called by the
union, setting these conditions plus a closed shop and minimum wage
scales as the union's demands. Heading the strike were Gold, Maurice
H. Cohen, Sol Schacher, Albert Roy and Ben Sheraga.

As the Toronto employers had done the year before, the Montreal manufacturers asked the Canadian immigration authorities to deport Miller.
But a mounting protest by the labor movement quickly forced them to
withdraw their request.

As in almost every other strike, the Montreal bosses hired thugs to
beat up and intimidate the strikers. And as in strikes in the States, it was
the strikers, not the gangsters, who were arrested and jailed. Dragged

into court, the handcuffed, bruised and beaten strikers were heavily fined.

Having tried in vain to break the strike by gangster violence, slanders in the press, provoking religious prejudices of Catholic French-Canadians against Jewish workers, and outright starvation—the association now tried to put over a double-cross. On October 12, they proposed a one-week truce. The workers should return to work while the conference committee of the union and the association negotiated a settlement. If no agreement should be reached in one week, each party could then do as it saw fit.

The strike committee accepted the truce proposal, but suspecting a trap, alerted the workers for instant action. Confident that once the workers were back in the shop they would not go out again, the association refused to make the slightest concession during the week that work resumed. They were certain that the strike was done for. But to their amazement and consternation, on October 20 the workers voted to stop work again.

Their trick having failed, the manufacturers reached an agreement with the union two days later. Although the open shop was retained, the employers recognized the union and agreed to the forty-four-hour week with only a half-day on Saturday; time-and-a-half for overtime, which was permitted only between September and March; six paid legal holidays; no contracting or sub-contracting; and a 20 percent increase in wages.

On October 23, the twelve-week strike ended. The victorious workers returned to their shops, hailed far and wide as heroes of the Canadian labor movement. Ben Gold, the young New York fur worker, was singled out for distinction as a leader of the picket lines. *The Fur Worker* was lavish in its praise. "Gold was a hard worker during the strike in Montreal. Never lost a chance to show that he was a striker and a good captain in picketing."

Miller returned to New York in time to enter the negotiations for renewal of the agreement with A. Hollander & Sons in Newark. This was to be the final episode in Miller's career as president of the union.

The Newark local submitted its demands for a shorter work week, a $5 increase for unskilled workers and a two-cent piece rate for fleshers, but Hollander refused to discuss wages or hours. Instead he proposed that the firm have the right to shift workers from one department to another, but retain the lower wage rates even when a worker was going into a higher-paying department. The union rejected this proposal. On the date of the expiration of the old agreement, Hollander locked out his six hundred workers.

All signs pointed to a long and difficult struggle for the union. The firm was rich, the largest in the industry. Even before the lockout, Hollander had established factories in two other cities—Middletown, New York, and Long Branch, New Jersey. The Middletown plant paid men $12 a week and women $8 a week, far below the Newark scale.

The Newark workers were woefully inexperienced and the International did nothing to help them. Instructed by the G.E.B. to devote his time to Newark, Miller casually departed for a two-week vacation. He finally returned, and intervened in the Newark situation, but the locked-out workers soon were complaining that they would have been better off had he extended his vacation indefinitely.

Accompanied by the AFL general organizer of Newark, Henry F. Hilfers, Miller went to Middletown to discuss a settlement with the firm. Hollander then revealed his alleged reason for the lockout. The union in Newark, he complained, was controlled by a "radical element, 'Bolsheviki' . . . who had no respect for the American Federation of Labor." Hollander wanted to drive out the "radical element" and have a free hand in the shop. Miller and Hilfers expressed deep sympathy for this aim, agreeing that the "radical element" was a thorn in their side as well.

Returning to Newark, Miller set out to convince the workers that the only way to end the lockout was to get rid of the "radical element" and thus prove to the firm that they would be "good boys." But when he made this proposal, Miller was howled down by the strikers. They said plainly that he was the "paid agent of Hollander," and that he had sold out the workers. Unable to carry out his betrayal, Miller left the meeting in a huff, announcing that he would do nothing to help the strikers.

A few days later, Miller's conduct was discussed at a meeting of the G.E.B. The Board instructed him to attend a mass meeting of the Newark workers on January 20. Miller refused, but the Board voted that it was his duty as president to attend. Miller knew better than to face the Hollander workers. On January 18, he handed in his resignation.

Miller's subsequent career paralleled that of Isidore Cohen, the ousted manager of the Joint Board. Starting up an open-shop fur factory in Chicago, he soon achieved a reputation as a bitter opponent of the union. When a union delegation asked Miller to sign an agreement, he refused.

His excuse was that since neither the local nor the International would be able to enforce it, he saw no necessity for a union contract.

Although he had failed to put across his sell-out, Miller's sabotage of the Hollander workers' struggle proved quite effective in undermining the strike. In the nineteenth week of the strike, the strikers finally accepted a proposal tendered by Hollander through Mayor Gillen of Newark. Hollander promised a wage increase, shorter hours, no discrimination against any union man, preference for strikers in employment, and settlement of grievances with department committees elected by the workers. Hollander refused to recognize the union. However, in view of these pledges delivered through the Mayor, the strikers ratified the settlement and returned to work on April 2.

As soon as the strikers were back in the factory, Hollander repudiated his promise to recognize department committees. Enraged by this treachery, the workers walked right out again. Despite the severe hardships that the workers and their families had already endured, the strikers valiantly held out another three weeks. At the end of the twenty-second week, they ended the strike on virtually the same terms as three weeks earlier.

Hollander pledged that if 51 percent of the workers wanted a union agreement at the end of the year, he would negotiate a preferential union shop. But these pledges and promises soon proved to be as worthless as Hollander's earlier ones. Strikebreakers from the Long Branch plant were brought back to Newark and placed in the shop before the strikers. Union members were discriminated against and assigned to the most difficult and disagreeable work. Workers who had proved themselves militant strikers were deliberately excluded from the plant altogether.

The defeat of the Hollander strike hung like a dark cloud over the union for many years. Hollander plants remained open shops for almost twenty years, until a powerful International Union, united and organized under the leadership of Ben Gold, compelled the Hollander open-shop fortress to come to terms and conclude a union agreement.

CHAPTER 9

Emergence of the
Kaufman Machine

Isidore Cohen was replaced as manager of the New York Joint Board by Morris Kaufman. And when Miller some months later resigned as International president, Kaufman was named acting president, holding both positions at the same time.

Morris Kaufman was an immigrant from Minsk who claimed to have participated in the revolutionary struggles of the Russian workers. He had been one of the principal leaders of the ill-fated 1907 strike. Associated with the defeat of 1907, he had been completely eliminated from leadership in the great strike of 1912.

The opposition to Isidore Cohen's corrupt administration had been led by a group of young militants, mainly from the operators' local. Samuel Leibowitz, Louis Weiser, the Sargent brothers and Alter Newman were the leaders of this group. Kaufman's appointment to office stemmed in large part from the fact that he was associated with neither Isidore Cohen nor with the opposition to Cohen's administration.

The United States had entered World War I in April 1917. The labor movement was sharply divided in its attitude toward the war. The fur workers' convention had taken a strong stand against America's participation. Practically all the delegates felt that it was a war of power politics and economic rivalry.

Their refusal to view the war as a battle "to preserve democracy" was sharpened by the brutal wave of repression carried out by government agencies against progressive sections of the labor movement. Under cover of war hysteria, perjured testimony was used to frame Tom Mooney, militant labor leader of San Francisco. Law enforcement officers turned their backs while squads of soldiers and sailors terrorized the Wobblies, wrecked their halls, stoned the homes of some IWW members and murdered others in cold blood. "Radical" publications were barred from the mail. Federal agents raided the offices of the Socialist Party and the IWW.

The Socialist Party, which had many followers among the fur workers, held a national convention in St. Louis in April 1917. In a resolution approved by referendum vote, it branded the declaration of war by our government as a "crime against the people of the United States and against the nations of the world." Many Socialist leaders and members took this declaration seriously. They forthrightly expressed their anti-war views and suffered great hardships as a result. Eugene V. Debs, Charles E. Ruthenberg, Kate O'Hare and hundreds of others were arrested and imprisoned. But others in the Socialist Party abandoned the principles avowed by the convention and joined with top leaders of the AFL to sell the workers the idea that it was a war for democracy.

The differences within the Socialist Party ranks were further deepened by the October Revolution (1917) in Russia. The end of the brutal, repressive Czarist regime had been acclaimed almost universally by the most diverse groups, including Catholics, Jews, liberals, democrats, trade unionists and militant Socialists. The militants in the Socialist Party hailed the new Soviet government as one in which the workers and poor farmers had achieved power for the first time in all history. However, others in the Socialist Party, known as the right wing, bitterly condemned the Soviet government. In the fur workers' union, and in the labor movement as a whole, the war and the Russian Revolution naturally became an additional dividing wedge between the militants and those who practiced cooperation with the employers at the expense of the workers.

The newly-elected Kaufman denounced Gompers and other leaders of the AFL, and even went so far as to urge the fur workers to leave the "reactionary and conservative" Federation. But at the same time he imitated Gompers and other high AFL officials by appealing to the fur workers to give their all in the war which the Socialist Party had condemned.

Kaufman's political hypocrisy was matched by his double-dealing in internal union affairs. When he visited St. Paul, a group of fur workers presented him with a long list of appalling charges against Charles

Gmeiner, their business agent. They accused Gmeiner, among other things, of aiding the employers "in *not* carrying out the agreement." When the workers got up at union meetings to criticize Gmeiner's autocratic rule, they were shouted down as "Bolsheviks and Socialists." Kaufman listened to the charges of the St. Paul workers with a show of sympathy. But on returning to New York, he coldly informed the St. Paul workers that he could do nothing against Gmeiner because of "the principle of local autonomy." The St. Paul workers bombarded the G.E.B. with charges against Gmeiner, a member of the Board. But even after an investigation committee of the G.E.B. found Gmeiner guilty of every charge, Kaufman voted to whitewash "Charlie" and upheld his right to remain as business agent and International vice-president.

Nor were the workers of Toronto any more successful in their pleas for action against J. McEwan, their business agent and likewise an International vice-president. A petition, signed by thirty Toronto workers, accused McEwan of having "continually neglected the interests of the workers." The petition was ignored by Kaufman.

By July 1918 a spontaneous demand for wage increases had spread throughout the New York fur market. Although they were coining enormous profits, the fur manufacturers refused to bargain with the shop committees. Moreover, they conspired not to engage any new workers that month who had left another job. Refusing to be intimidated, one shop after another stopped work and marched in a body to the union office demanding action. By the end of the first week in July, thirty shops were down, including some of the largest.

Frightened by the outpouring of the workers, and afraid it might develop into a general strike, Kaufman persuaded the workers to end their stoppages and to allow him to take up the issue with the Conference Committee and the impartial chairman. But the workers first exacted Kaufman's pledge that the union would not accept less than a sliding scale of 40, 45 and 50 percent raises. The decision finally handed down by the impartial chairman granted increases ranging from 40 percent for the lower-paid workers down to 30 percent for the higher-paid mechanics— about a third less than the minimum demanded by the workers. Kaufman accepted the decision enthusiastically, but the workers were furious and accused him of betraying his word. The increases, though substantial, were still inadequate compared to the enormous rise in the cost of living. And the workers knew that had the union supported their stoppages, the employers would have been compelled to grant the original demands.

Notwithstanding Kaufman's assurances that the agreement would be renewed without trouble at the end of the year, the workers insisted on preparing a strike fund that fall. Within a few weeks they collected $100,000. When negotiations for the new agreement started in December, the principal demands of the union were a forty-four-hour week, one-price minimum scale throughout the year, equal division of work, registration of contractors, and higher minimum scales. Weeks of conferences yielded no results. On January 20, 1919, when a strike referendum was taken, the vote was almost unanimous. Of 4,723 votes cast, only 39 were opposed to strike. A general strike was set for February 4.

It was an exceptionally favorable moment for the workers. The war-born prosperity was at its peak. When the war stopped the importation of furs from Paris and London, the demand for domestic furs increased enormously. The employers were making tremendous profits. There was a shortage of labor. Had the union been under proper leadership, a golden opportunity would have been at hand for the workers to win not only shorter hours and higher wages, but real job security in the form of equal division of work throughout the season and no discharge without just cause.

During that same week, an eleven-week strike in the men's clothing industry had ended with the establishment of the forty-four-hour week. Alarmed by the overwhelming strike vote of the workers, and confident that the existing union leadership would not enforce the agreement anyhow, the fur manufacturers hastily settled with the union on the eve of the strike date. The forty-four-hour week was established with one minimum wage scale for each class of work throughout the year and a 40 percent increase in the minimum.* However, even with this increase, the minimums remained extremely low. In addition, equal division of work was granted only during the months of June, November and December. The Conference Committee was to certify outside contractors. Only a slight limitation was placed on the right of the manufacturer to "reorganize" his shop, firing workers, at the beginning of each year.

At his local meeting, Ben Gold opposed acceptance of this agreement because of its many weaknesses and because much more could have been gained under the prevailing economic prosperity. The failure to achieve

---

* The following schedule of wages was established: *Cutters:* first class, $42; second class, $36. *Operators:* first class, $34; second class, $28; female, $28. *Nailers:* first class, $32; second class, $26. *Finishers:* first class, $31; second class, $25.

equal division of work and no discharge, at a time when the industry was busy and suffering from a labor shortage, was Kaufman's most damaging concession to the employers. All the needle trades, except the fur workers, had obtained job security. But Kaufman did not press for this demand.

There were other weaknesses in the agreement. The new minimum scales were still too low in view of the inflated cost of living. Women operators justifiably felt discriminated against by being classified as "second-grade" workers at "second-rate" pay. The certification of contracting by the Conference Committee in effect legalized and perpetuated this evil. And the agreement failed to provide a more effective system of enforcement, a key problem in the light of the sad experiences of the fur workers in the preceding years. With all its shortcomings, the New York agreement became the pattern for Boston, Chicago, Montreal and other cities.

Although there was no organized opposition to the settlement, there was a strong division of opinion among the workers. They were far from enthusiastic about the agreement. Kaufman was rapidly losing their support. Having put across this kind of agreement, he embarked upon the path of cooperation with the employers, although still trying to play the role of a militant. Before long, the workers saw that Kaufman had, in the words of one member, "little by little absorbed the philosophy of the boss."

It was in accordance with "the philosophy of the boss" that Kaufman administered the agreement. New workers were hired without union cards. Overtime was worked in violation of the contract. A deaf ear was turned to the complaints of the workers. "For the twenty-one cents weekly dues," Kaufman sneered, "they would have the union not only increase their pay-envelopes and reduce the working hours, but do their bidding whether reasonable or unreasonable; get even with the employers whenever they feel aggrieved in a few cents, and call the shop on strike upon every hasty word or action on the part of the foreman. And they are unable or unwilling to consider possibilities and impossibilities."

The language was familiar. The fur workers had heard it for years from Isidore Cohen. And like Cohen, Kaufman surrounded himself with a group that looked upon the union as their personal property. In Cohen's time, the Joint Board did not have a very big income. But after 1917 conditions changed. Due to wartime prosperity, the membership of the Joint Board grew rapidly and the income almost doubled. In January

1918, the receipts increased to $76,122.25 as against $43,826.39 the year before. The union offered a rich field for exploitation.

Whenever a young, strong and pliable fur worker who looked like a suitable candidate for the "Educational Committee" was discovered, he was put on the union's payroll. The new recruit's duties consisted of disciplining workers, keeping order at shop meetings, openly terrorizing workers who spoke up at these meetings, and intimidating workers at local meetings. In critical periods, gangsters from New York's East Side came in to aid the strong-arm squad. At election time, the strong-arm men made sure that the "right" candidates were voted in.

"The Derbies are coming!" Week in and week out this cry rang through the fur market as the furriers saw the East Side gangsters, velvet collars on their coats and derbies on their heads, walk into the union headquarters ready to do the latest dirty work for the administration.

In due time, whole gangs, including the notorious Chrystie Street gang

An example of Kaufman's attitude: Baltimore furriers "have water in their veins" and are "ignorant as you can make them."

led by "Little Augie," entrenched themselves as the real rulers of the union. The gangsters did very well for themselves. They collected huge sums from the union for keeping workers in check. And they exacted tribute from the employers for protecting their shops against militant workers. In the "protected" shops the workers did not dare to dream about a raise, a strike, or even complaining to the union. Another source of income for the strong-arm men was the money they extracted from the non-union workers who paid weekly for permission to work in the shops. When these workers wanted to become members of the union they were forced to pay graft in order to obtain a book.

The mobsters did so well, in fact, that they established themselves as dictators in the industry. "Big Jake," "Little Louie," "Cut-'em-up Charlie" and other criminals used union officials as front men to cover up their racket. The union officials, on the other hand, needed the under-world to suppress the workers and perpetuate themselves in power. And the bosses found it cheaper to pay tribute to the racketeers than to pay union wages and observe conditions provided in the agreement. The mass of workers, of course, were the victims.

The struggle that was opening for trade union democracy and against bureaucracy in the trade unions was also sharpening within the Socialist Party. Those Socialists, known as the "left wing," who were followers of Eugene V. Debs, fought for industrial unionism, organization of unorganized workers, and a policy of struggle for better conditions.* The right-wing followers of the Hillquits and Bergers copied the AFL's policies of craft unionism and cooperation with the employers at the expense of the workers.

Kaufman and his cohorts in the top leadership of the Furriers' Union were allied to the right wing in the Socialist Party. On the other side were the rank-and-file progressives like Ben Gold, Samuel Leibowitz and Aaron Gross, identified with the left-wing Socialists as members of the left wing of the Jewish Socialist Federation. In the spring and summer of 1919, this group launched a rank-and-file movement to clean the gangsters out of the union and to replace the bureaucratic machine with an honest leadership devoted to democratic unionism.

* A majority of the Socialist Party membership supported the left-wing militants. In 1919, the left wing won twelve of the fifteen seats in the National Executive Committee. But the right-wing executive autocratically declared the election void and expelled sixty thousand left-wing supporters. From the ranks of these expelled left-wing Socialists grew the Communist Party.

Under the leadership of Samuel Leibowitz, the membership of the fur cap, head and tail makers, muff bed and trimming locals developed into union-conscious militants. These locals were known as the "small joint board." Earning even lower wages than the workers in the fur coat manufacturing shops, the workers of these locals were not impressed by Kaufman's double-talk. When Kaufman visited these locals and urged the workers to make the "greatest sacrifices" for the war, he was shouted down by the workers and denounced as an agent of the bosses.

In February 1919, the small joint board struck the notorious open-shop Star Fur Manufacturing Company, known in the trade as Kassel Cohen. Without consulting the local or the strike leaders—Leibowitz and Simon Schachter—Kaufman entered into secret negotiations with the firm. The strikers, however, refused to allow Kaufman to sell them out by a private deal with the firm. They suffered hunger and hardship and endured beatings by thugs.* And they held on grimly for seventeen weeks, until they forced the firm to surrender. They won a wage increase, the forty-four-hour week and the union label.

Although not representing a large or decisive section of the workers, the leadership of the small joint board spearheaded the fight against the Kaufman machine at the 1919 International Convention. A majority of the delegates at the 1919 Convention were hand-picked by the machine. Kaufman engaged in red-baiting tirades against the progressive delegates, especially those of the small joint board. But the progressives nevertheless succeeded in getting a number of important resolutions adopted, including a drive for the forty-hour, five-day week, the union label, elimination of contracting and equal pay for men and women. Also adopted was a demand for a referendum of the membership on the proposal for a general strike of fur workers, a demand for the release of Tom Mooney, and another for the recall of American troops that had invaded the new Soviet Republic.

Although Kaufman was again named president, the progressives succeeded in electing one of their leading spokesmen, Samuel Leibowitz, as third vice-president.

A few weeks after the convention, a "Furriers Agitation Committee"

---

* Many of the strikers were past fifty, and even the court officials were moved when they saw these gray-haired workers with their faces bloody and swollen from repeated beatings. Magistrate Nolan publicly criticized the terroristic tactics of the firm, sent one gangster to the workhouse for sixty days, and put another under bail of $1,000, until trial in General Sessions.

put out a circular attacking Kaufman for his conduct in the Kassel Cohen strike. That same month, July 1919, two progressive leaders, Ben Gold and Aaron Gross, were elected to the New York Joint Board.

The youthful Ben Gold became the leader of the left-wing Socialist and progressive forces in the union. Personally, Gold was faring well, earning $100 a week as a fur cutter. He was enraged, however, by the gangsterism and bureaucracy in the union, and moved by the struggle of the small group of progressives to restore the control of the union to the workers. Together with the other progressives, Gold dedicated himself to breaking the right-wing machine. With his election to the Board, the rank-and-file opposition movement began to crystallize. The battle for democratic unionism now got under way in earnest.

At every meeting of the Joint Board, Gold lashed out at the gangster system and methods. He demanded that the rank and file be organized to carry on the work of the union. Gold would introduce a motion, Gross would second it. At each meeting workers would appear to present their complaints. Arguments on these complaints lasted for hours, with Gold championing the workers' rights. Battling Kaufman every inch of the way, Gold and Gross soon made their influence felt, even though all their proposals were voted down by Kaufman's majority.

The machine finally decided that this situation could not be allowed to continue. Somehow, they had to get rid of Gold. When Gold exposed the improper conduct of the business agent in the Helfenbaum case, the machine brought charges against him and decided on a special membership meeting that was to vote Gold's impeachment as a Board member. Over a thousand fur workers poured into Beethoven Hall on July 31. The meeting opened amid terrific tension. One after another, the business agents and other Kaufman supporters took the floor. They denounced Gold as a "troublemaker," said he was stirring up complaints, and demanded his expulsion.

When Gold arrived at Beethoven Hall, the meeting had been going on for some time, with Kaufman trying to whip up an expulsion sentiment. In fact, Kaufman was just about ready to call for the vote when Gold walked in. A clamor arose that he be given the floor. After a hurried consultation with his henchmen, Kaufman decided it would be dangerous to defy the workers' insistent demand. As soon as Gold walked up to the platform and began to speak, Kaufman knew he had made a serious mistake.

Gold talked for a solid hour. Burning with indignation, he exposed the trumped-up charges against him. His words exploded like a bombshell among the assembled workers. Dealing with the Helfenbaum case, Gold revealed the facts of the complaint this worker had brought to the Joint Board. Helfenbaum, an operator, had worked half a day without receiving pay. After repeated complaints, Hyman Sorkin, the business agent of Local 5, agreed to look into the matter. Together with the Association representative, Pike, he visited the firm to examine the books. But it was Pike who actually examined the records while Sorkin, the union business agent, spent his time having a friendly chat with the boss. Pike reported that there was nothing to the worker's complaint. Sorkin took his word for it, and didn't even look at the books himself. Gold proposed a motion at the Joint Board that the books of the firm be brought before the Joint Board for examination. Even after four solid hours of debate, the Kaufman machine refused to take action. Nor was this an isolated case. Hundreds of complaints were handled in a similar way.

Gold did not merely defend himself against the charges. Going far beyond the Helfenbaum case itself, he proceeded to draw up a factual indictment of Kaufman and the Joint Board leadership. He attacked the use of gangsters to rule over the workers. He condemned the denial of the most elementary democracy to the membership. He gave example after example of how Kaufman's policies of cooperation with the employers resulted in wholesale violations of the agreement. The workers were being underpaid, overworked and discriminated against, he charged.

Kaufman and his henchmen were paralyzed by Gold's indictment and the indignation openly displayed by the audience. They did not even try to answer. To escape the wrath of the workers, they rushed out of the hall without even waiting for Gold to finish speaking. Instead of impeaching Gold, the meeting encouraged him to go on with the fight for a clean union. At the next meeting of the Joint Board, Kaufman's henchmen set up an "impartial committee" to try Gold! A hearing was held, but the committee never dared reveal the results.

Stymied for the moment in his plot against the progressives in the Joint Board, Kaufman had the Sub-Committee of the G.E.B. expel Simon Schachter, militant business agent of Local 74, which was part of the small joint board. The charge was that Schachter was a "troublemaker," that he had abused the union leadership and that he had anonymously written the leaflet of the "Furriers Agitation Committee." Local 74, however, refused to accept the Sub-Committee's action. Instead, it adopted a vote of confidence in Schachter and re-elected him business agent. Kaufman answered by revoking the local's charter.

The same meeting of the Sub-Committee that revoked Local 74's charter had before it an appeal by Joe Cohen, a Newark fur worker. Joe Cohen had been fined $25 by his local because he had publicly protested against the exclusion of Negro members from a ball given by the Newark Union. "These men carry cards in our Union," argued Joe Cohen in his appeal, "work alongside us in the shops, bear the burden of the union's expense. . . . I, as a good-standing and active member, could not see these men humiliated in this fashion." The Sub-Committee was not interested in Joe Cohen's appeal. The Newark leadership was part of Kaufman's machine. Men like Joe Cohen were probably progressives anyway. The appeal was rejected.

Although the progressive forces in the Joint Board did not represent a fully crystallized opposition movement in 1919, their campaign against gangsterism and corruption in the union won support from the rank-and-file fur workers. By the end of 1919, the original progressive group consisting of Gold, Gross, Leibowitz, the Malamud brothers and Max Cooperman, now included Max Suroff, Esther Polansky, Fanny Warshafsky and Lena Rabinowitz. At the same time, Harris J. Algus joined the progressives. Chairman of the cutters' local and of the Joint Board, the venerable and highly-respected Algus was also a vice-president of the International. With his tremendous standing and popularity, particularly among the cutters, Algus now joined the struggle of the progressives against the Kaufman machine for trade union democracy.

A bloc of progressives was elected to the Joint Board in January 1920.* With that development the picture changed. No longer was it possible for Kaufman to present a proposal to the Board and have it ratified without question. The progressives demanded the reason behind the proposal. They wanted to know where the union's money was going. How much was being used to pay off the gangsters? Why was so little used for organizing purposes and for enforcing the agreement?

Accusing the progressives of advancing a "theory of ultra-democracy," Kaufman insisted that the Joint Board had no right to inquire into "the manager's acts and motives." But the progressives were not put off by high-sounding phrases. The first encounter came at a meeting of the Joint

---

* Gold and Gross were not delegates to the Joint Board in 1920. Having become a cutter and working at the bench as such, Gold had to transfer from the operators' Local 5 to the cutters' Local 1. According to the union's constitution, he could not, therefore, run for office in the Joint Board for one year. Gross did not run for office in 1920 because of ill health.

Board on January 22, 1920. Chairman Algus accused Kaufman and A. Rosenthal, secretary-treasurer of the Board, of planning to lend B. C. Vladeck of the *Jewish Daily Forward* $25,000 of the union's money without the knowledge or consent of the Board. Vladeck, manager of the *Forward*, said this loan was to be used for a building to house the paper in Chicago. Kaufman argued in self-defense that if he had turned Vladeck down, the union would be attacked in the press.

The Joint Board rejected the argument and passed a resolution condemning Kaufman for dealing with the *Forward* behind the union's back. If the *Forward* wanted a loan from the union, the Board declared, it should send a formal request to the union asking for it, and the matter would be decided by the fur workers themselves.

Kaufman did not take this setback lightly. Accustomed to doing as he pleased, he was unwilling to accept the fact that the fur workers were demanding a voice in the operation of their union. A break was inevitable.

It came over an important issue. For several years funds collected from the employers for violation of the agreement had been placed in Kaufman's hands for use by the Organization Department. How much money there was in the fund was known only by Kaufman and a few of his cronies, as the manager kept the books and never reported to the Joint Board on the matter. As soon as the progressive delegates were elected to the Board, they insisted that a committee, made up of one member from each local, be authorized to investigate the books of the Organization Department and that the money be turned over to the Board. As was to be expected, Kaufman fought this proposal, and even after the committee had been set up, he refused to turn over the books for inspection. The Joint Board, he declared angrily, had no right to interfere with the affairs of the Organization Department. The money would remain in his own name, and regardless of what the Board said or did, would be administered only by himself.

For weeks, a battle raged over this question. Finally the progressive delegates succeeded in persuading the Joint Board to present Kaufman with an ultimatum, warning him that if he did not turn over the books to the committee, the issue would be taken to the local meetings.

Refusing to turn over the books for inspection, and in order to becloud the issue, Kaufman resigned both as manager of the Joint Board and as International president. At the same time, he worked out a deal with his lieutenants to bring him back as soon as things were straightened out.

As soon as Kaufman stepped out, however, while still officially agitating for his return, the strong-arm group secretly made plans to take full control of the union without him. Learning of this, Kaufman prepared to go into the manufacturing business and even concluded a partnership for this purpose with Chernyak, a member of the Joint Board.

As more and more evidence came to the surface showing that Sam Cohen and the strong-arm groups were plotting to seize complete control, the progressives realized that to press for Kaufman's ouster would in effect mean that the underworld would take over. They therefore decided to offer Kaufman a united front if he would change his previous policies and agree to eliminate the strong-arm men and practice trade union democracy. The progressives in turn would mobilize all their forces to assist Kaufman in rank-and-file organizational work.

Leibowitz, Gold and Gross visited Kaufman at his home. After hours of discussion, Kaufman agreed to the terms set down by the progressives. But he laid down conditions for his return as manager: the entire Joint Board must resign, and a new Joint Board with whom he could work must be elected. Partly because of their immaturity and partly because they were prepared to make every sacrifice necessary to save the union from complete domination by the underworld, the progressives reluctantly accepted Kaufman's conditions. At a general membership meeting in Webster Hall on March 30, 1920, Chairman Algus declared that the Joint Board delegates had decided to resign since they could not work in harmony with Kaufman and the office staff. They asked the workers to accept their resignations, but they wanted it understood that they did not intend to give up their work for a clean, democratic union.

Kaufman took the floor after Algus. He immediately turned his back on the united-front program and launched an attack on the progressives. He assured the workers he was now returning as manager for keeps. Anyone who dared to criticize him would not stay in the union. Before any member could rise to answer him, Kaufman closed the meeting.

It was in this sorry way that Kaufman returned as manager of the New York Joint Board and president of the International. Having demobilized the progressive group and lulled it into the illusion that he had accepted their terms, Kaufman began the drive to eliminate the progressives from the union. The gangsters were now able to take over in full force.

The Struggle for
Trade Union Democracy

CHAPTER 10

The Disastrous Strike of 1920

The wave of wild speculation in the fur trade which had started during the war years reached its height during the opening months of 1920. The fur skin market became a vast gamble. Men became rich overnight, and anyone who bought raw skins made huge profits. Skins were sold and resold several times without the goods being seen or examined. Prices for garments shot up beyond all reason. A Hudson Seal coat of good quality had sold for $200 before the war. In September 1919, the same garment brought $700, and in January 1920 it brought $800.

In the early part of April 1920, a break occurred in the fur market. Overnight the price of skins fell 50 percent below their former value. Orders were cancelled, buyers stopped placing new orders. The banks shut off credit, and bankruptcies of smaller manufacturers mounted daily. By April 25, more than half of the ten thousand fur workers in New York were out of jobs.

Pressed by the unemployed, Kaufman called together the executives of the locals and the delegates to the Joint Board. He proposed that all members be taxed $10 to enable the union to build a great treasury with which to face the employers. He also proposed that the union call the leaders of the Association to a conference and demand a shortening of the working week from forty-four to forty hours and an extension of the principle of equal division of work throughout the year.

The progressive delegates at the conference agreed with Kaufman's proposal but opposed the tax. The membership endorsed the stand of the progressive delegates. The workers were opposed to entrusting their money to the machine and did not take seriously the talk of using the money for the unemployed.

At a meeting of the Conference Committee, Kaufman proposed that a forty-hour working week for the entire trade should begin on the fifteenth of May. Kaufman was confident that he would have no trouble convincing both the employers' representatives on the Conference Committee and the impartial chairman of the justice of the union's proposals.

However, Dr. Magnes, the impartial chairman, ruled that the issue was outside his province. The employers' representatives on the Conference Committee denied that there was a serious unemployment problem in the trade and flatly rejected the union's proposals. Kaufman pleaded with the Association to remember all that the union had done for the employers during the war, and how he personally had "stretched many points in the agreement in order to satisfy your members."

Fully aware that the practices of the Kaufman machine had weakened the union and robbed it of the strength to fight, the employers adopted an arrogant attitude at the conferences. The president of the Association, Samuel N. Samuels, declared, "If you people have unemployed workers and don't know what to do with them, why don't you drown them."

Thus, the bankruptcy of Kaufman's policy of cooperation with the bosses was revealed at one stroke. Faced with the collapse of the theories they had pursued for years, Kaufman and his associates sought to rebuild their prestige among the workers by posing as militant fighters against the employers. With their eyes glued on the union's big treasury, Sam Cohen and the strong-arm men suddenly began to agitate for a general strike.

The progressive forces viewed this campaign for a general strike with alarm. It was dangerous at this unfavorable time to involve the union in such action. The labor movement was on the defensive all over the country. Everywhere the employers were instituting the "American Plan," a sugar-coated title for the open shop. Workers in many industries were being forced to sign "yellow-dog" contracts binding them not to join a union. In many cases they were required to pledge themselves not to strike.

Reactionary forces in the government gave the employers valuable support in this anti-labor offensive. Injunctions based on wartime legislation poured out of the Attorney-General's office. Employers had only to petition for injunctions against strikes and the courts hastened to comply.

The government had also begun an unprecedented witch-hunt attack on militant union men. Building up a fake "red scare," and violating every principle of the Bill of Rights, the Department of Justice under Attorney-General A. Mitchell Palmer launched an onslaught against radicals. On January 2, 1920, in the most widespread of the notorious Palmer raids, agents of the Department of Justice arrested 2,758 men and women, and held 556 for deportation. Foreign-born workers were illegally jailed for months without charges being placed against them. They were deported without proper hearings, and many were convicted on the flimsiest evidence of violating criminal syndicalism or criminal anarchy laws. Nicola Sacco and Bartolomeo Vanzetti, a shoemaker and a fish-peddler, both anarchists, were pronounced guilty of murder on utterly insufficient proof and condemned to die for a crime they had never committed.

Gold and other progressives pointed out that such a political situation was highly unfavorable to the workers in a strike. Moreover, the manufacturers did not care if the workers went out. Business was bad anyway and there was little the employers would lose by a strike. The progressives were convinced that the strike was being promoted for sinister purposes. The majority of the workers also did not want the strike. To Kaufman, however, a strike was an opportunity to prove he was a truly militant leader. To the strong-arm group, of course, a strike would provide an opportunity to get their hands on the union's funds.

Although the progressives opposed a general strike and sought to persuade Kaufman not to call one, they did not agitate publicly against it. To do so, they knew, would weaken the union in its negotiations with the employers, and destroy all possibility of a peaceful settlement.

Ignoring the warnings of the progressives, Kaufman proceeded with his program. At a meeting of the fur workers in Cooper Union on May 17, he argued that there was no alternative but a strike and warned that it was useless to criticize the plan.

The progressive workers were faced with a difficult question. Should they participate actively in the strike when it was called? Some of them advocated remaining on the sidelines during the strike. Gold disagreed, arguing that the progressive workers could not stand at a distance and look on while their union was involved in a struggle with the employers. They must participate in the struggle if only to lessen the suffering of the workers. They would be close to the workers and in a better position to help them solve their problems.

Convinced by Gold's arguments, the progressive group demanded of

Kaufman that before he called the strike a committee of one hundred workers should be elected from the four locals. Kaufman acceded to this demand, and a committee of one hundred was set up. On the eve of the calling of the strike, Kaufman met with the committee and presented the names of the twenty persons who would serve on the General Strike Committee. Over their protest, he appointed Sam Cohen and Hyman Sorkin as leaders of the strategic Picketing Committee.

The strike started on May 27. Kaufman assured the workers that it could not last long since "the manufacturers will not dare to prolong the strike, and very soon will concede to the union on its demands." It did not take long for the workers to realize how completely they had been misled by their manager and International president.

The employers immediately took steps to break the strike. They set up shops outside of New York. They brought scabs into their shops and farmed out work to the Greek open shops, which had never been organized because of the leadership's policy of keeping the Greek workers out of the union. The Greek shops worked day and night. In fact, many new ones were opened just before and during the strike.

Some settlements were made with small and independent manufacturers, but most of these settled shops were doing scab work for the big Association firms. Still Kaufman continued to predict an early end to the strike. On August 7, he practically guaranteed the "near future collapse" of the manufacturers. Ten days later, he boldly announced that the strike "will be over the end of this month or the very beginning of September, because the employers are on the verge of bankruptcy." September went by, but the Association showed no sign of settling with the union. On October 10, Kaufman ventured his last prediction. "I think the strike will be over this week," he told the press.

The strike ended on December 20, 1920. It had lasted for thirty weeks. It was the longest strike that any union of the needle trades had ever gone through. And it had come to a heartbreaking conclusion, with the union itself practically destroyed. The membership, weakened by the loss of the strike and thoroughly disgusted with the leaders of their union, dropped from 10,000 to 650.

The 1920 strike exposed the union leadership, as well as the harmful theories of the AFL and Socialist Party officials. For the first time, the workers were able to convince themselves of the tragic state of affairs in the union.

The strikers themselves had nothing to do with the work of the all-important Picketing Committee. This committee was made up of about sixty sluggers, some of them members of the union, the majority brought in from the outside. The right-wing theory was that a little intimidation by gunmen would persuade a manufacturer to settle; a visit to a shop by the gangsters would teach the scabs a lesson they would never forget; a beating by sluggers would convince workers in the settled shops that they had better pay their strike assessments. Each slugger was placed on the union's payroll at a rate of from $20 to $25 a day. Thus, from the very beginning, the strike was stripped of any possible semblance of a workers' struggle. The longer the strike, the more gravy for the goons!

The utter futility of conducting a strike according to this formula was never better demonstrated than during the 1920 furriers' strike. The gangsters made deals with both the union and the bosses, and they double-crossed both. Instead of forcing the scabs down from the shops, the sluggers supplied the bosses with scabs. When an occasional picketing committee of workers set out to visit a shop, the mobsters went ahead to warn the bosses of their approach. When rank-and-file workers on the picket lines outside the shops tried to stop the union's strong-arm men from bringing scabs into the building, they were slugged. Yet if these same workers refused in disgust to report for picket duty, the mob would visit them in their homes and again give them a thorough beating. Most shameful of all, as they left the strikers' homes, the strong-arm squad would make off with money, clothing and even household furniture!

In addition to robbing the workers, the sluggers stole vast quantities of furs from the bosses. They would go into a shop, ostensibly to check up on scabs. Even when they were paid off by the boss, the hoodlums would beat him up, grab his skins and throw them out of the windows. Other gangsters in the street would be waiting to pick up the skins and load them in trucks. Most of the skins were sold back to the manufacturers. And to top it off, the union was forced to provide these thieves with bail and legal defense!

At the beginning of the strike, the employers had also hired an army of gangsters. But as the strike progressed, the gangsters of the bosses and the gangsters of the union joined forces. The headquarters of the combined strong-arm committee was in Astoria Hall, on Fourth Street. Whenever the pickets succeeded in persuading a strikebreaker to stop work and register for strike duty, he was taken into the strike hall for "questioning." On many occasions the strong-arm committee would relieve him of his watch and wallet and tell him to go back to work.

The strikers learned very quickly of what was happening in Astoria Hall. When a committee of rank-and-file workers protested to Sam Cohen, he told them bluntly, "If you don't shut up, you'll get your heads split." At a mass meeting of the strikers in Manhattan Lyceum, a worker arose and asked Kaufman why he let the gangsters run the strike. As he was talking Alex Fried, one of the chiefs of the strong-arm squad, walked over to the worker and hit him over the head with a chair. When Kaufman, fearing the reaction of the workers, ordered Fried to leave the hall, he was told to shut up and continue with the meeting. Kaufman shut up.

As early as the second week of the strike, the progressives asked their three delegates on the General Strike Committee to demand an immediate investigation of the shameful role of the gangsters. When Algus and Suroff raised this question, Kaufman shouted that anyone who dared to criticize the Picketing Committee would pay dearly. "I am responsible and I alone am responsible for the management of the strike," he cried.

As the days passed, the morale of the strikers collapsed. Even the pro-Kaufman *Forward* had to admit that there was no enthusiasm among the furriers for the strike. Gone was the militant spirit that had marked the 1912 strike. In its place was sullen resentment so great that when a mass meeting was called in one of the strike halls, the strong-arm squads had to threaten the workers to get them to applaud Kaufman. Most of the hall committees found it impossible to get the workers to report for picket duty. The workers would reply, "Let those go picketing who get $20 a day."

In this bleak and sordid picture there were a few bright spots. The furriers pointed with pride to the activities in Casino Hall, the strike hall under Ben Gold's leadership. In the district covered by Casino Hall, stretching from 25th Street down to East Broadway and over to Brooklyn and including some shops on 38th Street, the workers themselves carried on the strike, did the picketing and stopped the scabs from working. As soon as Gold was appointed chairman of Casino Hall by the General Strike Committee, he set up a rank-and-file picketing committee. The gangsters were afraid to enter the district, let alone Casino Hall itself.

The results achieved under Gold's leadership aroused such attention that reporters were sent to investigate the situation. They found that the workers were involved in every aspect of the struggle. Even the right wing had to admit this.

"In the [Casino] Hall circles here and there," wrote a reporter in the

Kaufman-controlled *Fur Worker,* "they would see the workers all absorbed in listening to some one of our active committees talking to them in a spirit of comradeship. For instance, the Hall Chairman, B. Gold, with his keen logic and irrefutable arguments explaining to the workers the situation of the trade, and compelling the weakest man of the circle to pay full attention to his remarks. At another circle, we would find his righthand man Gross, or Shapiro, or Rackow, or any of those who are working under his guidance and inspiration, or his Secretary Maurice Cohen, paying minute attention to the various details of the clerical work necessary in the conduct of the strike, keeping records of each and every man in the hall, knowing his whereabouts, his faithfulness to the strike and everything to be known of every man and woman registered therein. They would find them all deeply engrossed in their work, the atmosphere leavened with activity; every striker, man or woman, fully appreciating the seriousness of the situation and ready to do his or her utmost to assist in whatever work is necessary to carry on this great struggle."

The majority of the shops and strikers, however, were in halls under the control of men who leaned on gangsters in the operation of the union and the conduct of the strike.

In an effort to save the strike and rekindle the enthusiasm of the workers for the struggle, Gold appealed to Kaufman to get rid of the professional hoodlums on the union payroll. "The Picketing Committee," he told Kaufman, "must be organized and composed of the best devoted and loyal class-conscious men that are able to fight for the interests of the union, not to protect the scabs. No strike can be won when you kill the morale and spirit of the workers. You engage the workers in their own fight and they will do it."

The progressives assured Kaufman that they could guarantee to furnish a picketing committee of more than a hundred workers who would work without pay. Gold was willing to accept the post of chairman of such a committee, provided that he was not required to handle any money and provided that Kaufman got rid of Sam Cohen, Hyman Sorkin and all of the gangsters. But Kaufman and his henchmen rejected the plan. "The answer was fists and blackjacks," Gold pointed out later.

In the fifth week of the strike, when it was clear that Kaufman would do nothing to improve the conduct of the strike, a committee of progressives visited Congressman Meyer London and urged him to use his influence in saving the situation. The committee was composed of Ben Gold, Aaron Gross, Esther Polansky, Harris Algus and Max Suroff. London informed them that in his opinion Kaufman would rather lose the strike than allow anyone else to intervene. At the same time, London refused to get the leaders of the Socialist Party to repudiate Kaufman.

In mid-July, the International called general strikes in Philadelphia and Boston to stop scab work being done in these cities. Unfortunately, the conduct of these out-of-town strikes duplicated the situation in New York. Kaufman gave the management of the Philadelphia strike to H. F. Somins, one of his henchmen who also happened to be a contractor! Every week Somins received $2,000 from the International and he was answerable for this money only to Kaufman.

Some of the workers actually came to New York to complain personally to Kaufman, but he refused to hear a word of criticism about the Philadelphia strike. The progressive delegates on the General Strike Committee warned Kaufman that if he did not order the withdrawal of the gangsters from Philadelphia, they would inform the New York workers about it. Kaufman finally agreed to the appointment of a committee to investigate the situation in Philadelphia. This committee, composed of three Kaufman men and two progressives, reported that a group of sluggers, paid large sums of money from the union treasury, had fastened themselves on the two hundred Philadelphia workers and were constantly terrorizing them.

The same situation prevailed in Boston, and in both cities there was only disgust among the workers. David Mikol, who was supervising the strike in Boston, admitted that the members of Local 30 "were never warm about the strike," and that only the terror instituted by the strong-arm squads kept the workers from returning en masse to the shops. "I had to assume complete dictatorship of the strike," he wrote to International Secretary-Treasurer Wenneis on August 15.

Towards the end of July and early in August, a real possibility existed of settling the New York strike on the basis of a forty-two-hour week and the arbitration of other points raised in the union's demands. The manufacturers had to make their fur skins into coats or go bankrupt. They were willing to negotiate. But, infuriated by the continuous robbing of their shops by gangsters, they stipulated that Kaufman should not participate in the negotiations.

With Kaufman's consent, a committee composed of Gold, Algus, Goldenberg, Brownstein (chairman of the hall committee) and Suroff went to see the impartial chairman. They informed Dr. Magnes that the union would accept a forty-hour, five-day week, and equal division of work. Dr. Magnes felt that the union could get forty-two hours, but that while the other demands were justified, he believed the manufacturers would put up a stiff fight against them.

When the committee reported back to Kaufman, he rejected negotiations by anyone other than himself and shouted, "We started the strike and we will finish it." Ironically enough, when the strike was finally settled in December, in the thirtieth week of the battle, Kaufman did not participate in the negotiations. And the settlement was much worse than what the union could have secured in July, when the employers were anxious to end the battle. But in July the gangsters were still having a good income from the strike and did not want it to end.

On July 27 Max Yurman, a militant young striker, was shot by a policeman. The policeman refused to allow the other strikers on the spot to call a physician to attend to the fatally wounded Yurman. He died within a few minutes.

A veteran who had volunteered and served in the expeditionary forces in France, Yurman had joined the union after the war. He was twenty-three years old and only recently married. The wanton and deliberate murder of this young fur worker aroused the fury of the strikers. Thousands of fur workers paid their respects when Yurman's body lay in state at the funeral parlor. The workers in the settled shops stopped work on the day of the funeral in tribute to the memory of the labor martyr. Over fifty thousand workers of all needle trades attended the funeral.

Even the killing of Yurman did not change the conduct of the strike. Every day the *Forward* carried reports of individual settlements with the union. It did not report the fact that if one day a shop of five workers would settle, the next day there would be fifty workers in the shop, all of whom would be doing scab work for the bigger manufacturers still on strike.

Kaufman actually welcomed this development. The more workers who were hired in these shops, the more money the union would take in, since they had to contribute 40 percent of their earnings to the union as strike assessments. The fact that they were doing scab work, he insisted, was not important. "The scab work does not amount to enough to make much difference in the final result," Kaufman declared on September 18.

One incident in connection with the individual settlements illustrates clearly the way in which the strike was conducted. Without the knowledge of the General Strike Committee, a firm was lent $3,000 in cash and $2,000 in notes to induce it to sign a settlement. The firm, Hoffman and Rubin, employed about thirty workers. After the settlement, the firm went into bankruptcy. The union lost the $3,000 cash and had to make good on the notes as well.

The *Forward* kept reporting that the Association was on the brink of settling on the union's terms. Later Kaufman admitted that he had found it necessary to "color" the news. By the middle of October, it was no longer possible to conceal the fact that the strike was lost and the only thing that remained was to end it as quickly as possible.

On October 13, Mikol confessed that his "complete dictatorship" in Boston had failed. "The workers are tired of the strike and they want the end of it one way or the other," he informed Wenneis. Twelve days later the strike in Boston was officially called off, and the workers went back to the shops, in most cases under open-shop conditions.

In New York, the strike was entering its sixth month. Several members of the Association had settled, but the majority were still holding out, either operating with scabs or getting their work done in the settled shops. The union's treasury was exhausted and even substantial loans from the Joint Board of the Cloakmakers, which contributed $50,000, and from the Amalgamated Clothing Workers did not help the situation.

The strike began petering out and some shops returned to work without a settlement. When the whole sorry mess caved in, and the gangsters realized that the goose was no longer laying golden eggs, they began gradually to withdraw from the strike, leaving only a few strong-arm men in charge. Sam Cohen and Hyman Sorkin also retired. Cohen went away for a rest. Sorkin bought a bakery and went into business. The news that Sorkin, the head of the Picketing Committee, had gone into business, spread like wildfire through the fur market and added to the disgust and demoralization of the strikers.

In mid-October, Motty Eitingon, one of the biggest fur dealers in the trade, appealed to the Association to renew the old agreement with the union for another year and settle the strike on this basis. Following Eitingon's proposals, the manufacturers agreed to settle the strike on the basis of the 1919 agreement. Kaufman, however, rejected this proposal. He urged the strikers to sit tight, assuring them that "the union is ready to continue the strike through the next spring season if necessary." But no one took him seriously. Fed up with the whole business, the majority of the workers threatened to return to the shops on whatever terms the employers offered.

A committee of the General Strike Committee went to see Sidney Hillman of the Amalgamated Clothing Workers, Benjamin Schlessinger of the ILGWU and other union leaders. At a meeting with these trade union leaders in Meyer London's office, Ben Gold, who had been invited by Kaufman to join the Strike Committee, and Esther Polansky, argued that it was utterly impossible to go on with the strike without funds. The conference recommended that the strike should be ended and the Association's terms accepted.

On December 17, the General Strike Committee voted to accept the terms of settlement proposed by the Association. Kaufman still demanded that the strike be continued. Not only was he voted down, but the Association again refused to negotiate if he were a member of the union settlement committee.

At a meeting in Manhattan Lyceum on December 18, attended by a total of 324 fur workers, the terms of settlement were ratified. Thus, the thirty week strike came to a tragic end.

The union's treasury was exhausted. A large part of the $897,000 spent by the union had ended up in the hands of gangsters. The union was heavily in debt. Its prestige was shattered. Its membership was but a shell of what it had been before the strike. The 1919 agreement on which the settlement was based was a dead letter. Those fur workers who were fortunate enough to find jobs were forced to work fifty hours a week, to accept wage cuts ranging from 25 to 50 percent, and to do unlimited overtime work at the regular hourly rate. In all of the shops union control was a thing of the past, and in most of them the open shop was in effect.

On January 11, 1921, Locals 1, 10 and 15 adopted resolutions by overwhelming majorities which demanded the resignation of the entire office staff of the Joint Board. "With other officers such a strike in the industry would have been avoided," they declared. With new officers, said all three locals, the fur workers could begin "to do some really worthwhile and energetic work to continue the building of our union."

Convinced that the jig was up, Kaufman resigned as manager of the Joint Board late in February. With the resignations of the business agents and other officers, the workers made a clean sweep of the Joint Board. On February 26, 1921, an entirely new administration was elected. Abraham Brownstein, who had been chairman of the General Hall Committee during the strike and had moved close to the left wing as a result of his experience with Kaufman's tactics, was elected manager. Maurice Cohen, S. Felder and Esther Polansky were elected business agents. Among the progressive men and women elected as unpaid officers of the Joint Board were Algus, N. Rosenberg, Fanny Warshafsky, I. Shapiro, S. Falperin, Aaron Gross, Max Suroff and Sam Mencher.*

Though the new administration was influenced by the left wing, it was largely composed of middle-of-the-road progressives. Maurice Cohen was the only left-winger to accept a paid office and he did so reluctantly after considerable persuasion. It was considered unbecoming for a progressive to hold a paid office in a union since it meant that he would be living at the expense of the workers. It was to take some time before this idea—which grew out of the contempt of the workers for their right-wing officers—disappeared among progressives.

The vote cast in the election for the new administration of the Joint Board held out hope for the future of the union. Sixteen hundred fur workers had cast their ballots, the greatest outpouring of voters in the history of the union up to this time.

The fur workers were not yet rid of Kaufman. After resigning as manager of the Joint Board, Kaufman went to Long Island City, the headquarters of the International, and continued to operate as International president. This was an unpaid position, but Kaufman's group on the G.E.B. apointed him general organizer of the International and editor of *The Fur Worker* at a salary of $90 per week.

Under the International constitution, less than 20 percent of the membership spread across the country had greater weight in the union than New York's 80 percent. By controlling the small out-of-town locals, many of which were only paper organizations created to provide convention delegates who would be cogs in Kaufman's machine, the president could dominate the International and use it as a weapon against the New York members.

As we shall see, the small, reactionary clique which controlled the International did not hesitate to use its power to gain its ends. An appeal to the members of the New York Joint Board issued by the Press Committee of Locals 1, 5, 10 and 15, early in 1921, was prophetic. It declared: "A new chapter is opening in the history of the Furriers Union. This chapter may be written in blood and tears, but it will be remembered by the American working class."

* Ben Gold, who was not in New York during the time of the elections, did not assume any office in the new administration until several months later.

CHAPTER 11

Battle in the
New York Joint Board

The end of the 1920 strike found the International Fur Workers Union in a deplorable condition. Only a few hundred members were left in New York. Union control in the shops had vanished. Not a single shop chairman was functioning throughout the industry. Unemployment was widespread. The union was over $136,000 in debt, and had no means to help workers who were facing prison terms as a result of arrests during the strike.

Outside of New York conditions were no better. In several cities the union practically ceased to exist. In Boston and Philadelphia, the open shop prevailed. Chicago fur workers were demoralized. Pittsburgh was "half dead"; Milwaukee was "sound asleep"; Detroit was "shot"; Atlantic City's condition was "very poor"; San Francisco and Los Angeles had "just a handful of paid-up members"; and Montreal and Toronto were facing wage cuts of 20 percent. Everywhere there was despair and disintegration. Everywhere the workers were embittered against the union.

It was generally recognized that the future of the International revolved around New York. If New York remained lifeless, the entire union would go to pieces.

As soon as the new administration in the New York Joint Board was installed in February 1921, it tackled the job of rebuilding the union through the zealous energy of the few remaining active members. New shop chairmen, selected for their honesty and devotion to the union, were placed in every shop. They assured the workers that their union was no longer a haven for gangsters and racketeers. Leaflets emphasizing this theme were distributed every day in the fur market. At first skeptical, the workers gradually began to visit the union headquarters to see for themselves. Every day a few more shops would meet. By the second week in March, 107 shop meetings had been held in the union headquarters. Members coming in with complaints were met sympathetically by the union officers. They found that their grievances were recorded and attended to promptly. Money due the workers from the employers was collected.

Week after week the number of members in good standing grew. After a visit to the Joint Board late in March, International Secretary-Treasurer Wenneis informed the out-of-town locals that "the situation in New York City is slowly but surely improving. The members are showing a livelier interest than they did immediately after the strike, and it will only be a question of time when New York will be back where it was before the strike."

Although pretending at first to be in full sympathy with the efforts of the progressives to rebuild the union, Kaufman exposed himself rapidly. In order to induce the workers to come back into the union after the disastrous strike, the Joint Board issued a manifesto informing the furriers that they were released from the payment of dues for the time of the strike if they had not worked during this period. Kaufman immediately informed the Joint Board that the manifesto was illegal and would not be recognized by the International. The Joint Board ignored Kaufman's protests and proceeded with its plans.

This was just the beginning. At the same time that he was assuring the fur workers of his cooperation, Kaufman was cooking up a new plan for a comeback. Cooperating with Kaufman in this plan were Max Sergeant, Charles Stetsky, Sam Cohen, Harry Yurman, Alex Fried, Isaac Wohl, Max Ash and others who had been repudiated by the fur workers after the 1920 strike. With the cooperation of the *Forward*, Kaufman's henchmen organized a society which bore the benevolent-sounding name, "Welfare Club." The Club was founded in April 1921 at a banquet attended by Kaufman and leaders of the International Executive Board, together with leaders of the Socialist Party, including Meyer London.

Directed by Sam Cohen and Charles Stetsky, its contact men with the strong-arm gang, the Welfare Club swung into action shortly after it was organized. The sluggers began to break up local meetings. Workers were threatened, and those who refused to heed the warnings of the Welfare Club soon had bandaged heads to show for it.

Sam Mencher, left-wing member of the Joint Board, was one of the first victims. On several occasions Mencher had been warned by Sam Cohen that he would be "fixed." The threat was carried out brazenly in the office of the Joint Board. Mencher was attacked by several members of Cohen's squad. Cohen stood by, watching, as the hoodlums beat Mencher mercilessly. Hurried to a hospital after he was found lying unconscious in a pool of blood, Mencher hovered between life and death for several weeks. He finally recovered after months in the hospital.

The brutal attack on Mencher was followed by assaults on scores of rank-and-file workers. By the second week in May, the reign of terror instituted by the Welfare Club had become a scandal. Andrew Wenneis was so shocked by the events in New York that he complained to Kaufman on May 10, 1921: "Conditions in New York City have taken on quite a serious aspect. The rough element of the union is on the rampage. Brother Mencher, one of the active members, has been beaten up and is in the hospital. No doubt the result of a conspiracy as far as I can see. Local meetings are not attended because this element terrorizes the members. They even go so far as to terrorize the members of the Joint Board demanding money. So far as I can learn they are purposely doing these things so as to hinder the present administration in the conduct of the necessary business of the union. They have even threatened to get the rest, even going so far as naming the officers. It is needless to say that some action will have to be taken by us in this situation if it continues. Such actions are outrageous and should not be tolerated."

Wenneis' proposal that the International do something in the "situation" was promptly vetoed by Kaufman. The violence continued. When Brownstein, manager of the Joint Board, went to the International to urge the removal of the strong-arm men, he was told by Kaufman: "We can't sit in your office and take care of you."

Had the International Convention been held in June 1921, as scheduled, the progressives would have had the majority. The crimes of the 1920 strike were fresh in the minds of the workers, and progressive delegates would have been elected in overwhelming numbers to the Convention.

But Kaufman moved quickly to prevent this development. With the help of his lieutenants on the G.E.B., he submitted to the locals a proposal for postponing the convention one year. The New York Joint Board rejected the proposal and sent a call to all locals urging them "to join in the demand that the convention should take place this year." Chicago and San Francisco responded favorably to the Joint Board's appeal, but the other locals, most of which were merely paper organizations, voted for postponement. In May, the International announced that the convention was postponed until June 5, 1922.

Kaufman now proceeded to use every device to entrench himself in his position as International president. The first step was to rescue his friends who had been arrested for attacking Mencher. After spending union funds to get the sluggers out on bail, Kaufman pressured Mencher into withdrawing the charges against his associates with the argument, "We must not bring union affairs to a capitalist court." Mencher yielded to Kaufman's pleas when the latter promised that the charges would be presented to an impartial labor body to be chosen by both parties.

No sooner were the charges withdrawn, than Kaufman repudiated his pledge. A special committee to investigate the incident was set up, but only right-wingers were appointed to the body. The committee, consisting of S. E. Beardsley, Max Zaritsky and Alexander Kahn of the *Forward*, met for three days and heard witnesses. Mencher himself was not called to testify. Only members of the Welfare Club were given a hearing. The committee cleared Sam Cohen of any connection with the attack.

Amazingly enough, in spite of the disruptive tactics of the Welfare Club, the union continued to make progress. The facts spoke for themselves. In nine months the Joint Board had cleared up $40,000 in debts. It had returned $10,500 to the Amalgamated Clothing Workers, $2,300 to the Cap Makers and $10,000 to the International. Other debts for trials and counsel had also been paid.

Proud of these achievements, which were recorded despite the Welfare Club's reign of terror, the new administration prepared for negotiations for a new agreement. Representing the union on the Conference Committee were Ben Gold, Samuel Leibowitz, H. Algus, Max Suroff, A. Halpern, A. Shapiro, Jack Schneider, Spivak, Miss Horowitz, Miss Dora Fialo and L. Tellis—men and women who had proved their devotion to the union.

On the eve of the negotiations, Harry Lang, labor editor of the *Forward* and a close friend of Kaufman, assured the manufacturers in a lengthy article that the union was in no position to put up a fight, that it was weak, disorganized and hated by the workers. Indignant at this stab-in-the-back from a so-called workers' newspaper, the fur workers demanded an immediate retraction. After a visit to the *Forward* by a committee of Joint Board delegates with an ultimatum for a public correction, Lang was compelled to publish an apology.

The manufacturers entered into negotiations in an arrogant mood. They demanded the lengthening of the hours of work from forty-four to forty-nine per week, abolition of pay for legal holidays, provision for changing the minimum wage scale during the life of the agreement in accordance with changed conditions, and the regular rate for overtime. The union's answer was short and swift—"No!" A petition signed by several thousand fur workers declared "that under no circumstances should the union enter into an agreement with the manufacturers reducing any of the standards." This position was reaffirmed at a mass meeting of four thousand fur workers at Cooper Union on January 21. A week later, the Association withdrew all of its demands, and renewed the existing agreement for two years ending January 31, 1924.

While many independent manufacturers quickly accepted the Association agreement for their own shops, a large number refused to sign up with the union. These shops were declared on strike. By the third week in March, the union had forced all but a small number of the independent manufacturers to sign the agreement.

While negotiating the new agreement, the Joint Board took steps to organize the retail fur workers, about twelve hundred of whom worked in the expensive shops in the uptown district. The Joint Board succeeded in organizing a good number of retail shops and was planning to step up the drive once the new agreement was concluded. At this juncture Kaufman, as International president, moved in, and, over the protest of the Joint Board, proposed setting up a separate "Gentile local" among the retail fur workers. By splitting the union and by pitting Gentile workers against Jewish workers, Kaufman evidently hoped to create chaos in New York. Experience in Toronto had proved that division of the fur workers into separate Gentile and Jewish locals was a powerful weapon in the hands of a bureaucratic leadership.

Completely ignoring the protests of the Joint Board, Kaufman issued a circular calling on all fur workers of the retail shops to meet on January 18 "to organize an English-speaking local." The Joint Board was furious. It denounced Kaufman for betraying his previous promise that the retail workers would be "part and parcel" of the Joint Board, and for trying to set up a separate "Gentile local."

Locals 1, 5, 10 and 15 shared the Joint Board's indignation. In a letter

found that although as an International Union, it is your
duty to organize non-organized workers of the fur industry,,
at the same time you have no constitutional or moral right
to dissect our organization into a racial congregation. We
are all toilers regardless of our religious
Furthermore, our Joint Board in permitting y
the retail workers has never given you the p
organize them into a separate local. On the

Local 15, among others, protests against the setting-up of a separate local for Gentile workers in the retail shops of New York City.

to the International, signed by Joseph Winogradsky, Goldie Horowitz, Lina Bramen and others, the Executive Committee of Fur Finishers Local 15 wrote: ". . . Although as an International Union it is your duty to organize non-organized workers of the fur industry, at the same time you have no constitutional or moral right to dissect our organization into a racial congregation. We are all toilers regardless of our religious beliefs." The Executive Board of the Fur Cutters Local 1 protested "against the creation of racial and religious barriers against our working masses." And the Executive Committees of the Fur Operators Local 5 and Fur Nailers Local 10 were convinced that Kaufman's action would "divide the workers, create discord, and prove detrimental to our fur workers' union."

As a result of the vehement protests, the Sub-Committee of the G.E.B., consisting of those board members residing in New York, was finally compelled to return the jurisdiction to the Joint Board.

Defeated temporarily in this maneuver, the Welfare Club stepped up its terroristic activities, preparing for the March elections for paid officers of the Joint Board.

Alex Fried, the Club's candidate for Local 10's business agent, was a past master at the art of terrorizing workers. It was common knowledge that Fried had participated with a gang in burglaries and served a term in jail. His job in a fur shop was only a front for his main occupation as a representative of the outside gang in the Furriers Union. During the 1920 strike, "Big Alex" had furnished scabs to the employers. At the same time he was receiving $20 a day from the union for supposed work on the Picketing Committee.

A few days before the election, the fur market was flooded with gangsters. Fried and his friends went about the market threatening the workers that if they did not vote for the Welfare Club's slate they would be attacked in their homes. As the election approached, the rank-and-file fur workers became more and more nervous. After contacting influential figures in the political world for assistance in preventing attacks on the workers when they came to the polls, the Joint Board notified the furriers that they would be protected in their right to vote and urged them to turn out in record numbers. On the day of the election, three men in civilian clothes appeared at the union office and announced that they had been sent to see that things passed quietly. They were told not to make themselves conspicuous and to interfere only if anyone tried to start a battle.

The election took place on a Saturday. At twelve o'clock there were huge crowds of fur workers outside the union office waiting to vote—the greatest turnout in the history of the union. Suddenly there was a commo-

A leaflet issued before the March 18th election challenged the "Welfare Club" and endorsed a slate of progressive candidates.

FURRIERS, UNMASK THEM!

Furriers! Who is the "Furriers Welfare Club"? Who are the directing spirits, and for what purpose was this "Club" organized? Why are they afraid that their names become known? Is it true that this Club was organized from the well known General Picketing Committee? Members of this so-called Club, show your faces!

Why don't you tell the truth about the aims of your Club? Why

of your own interests, that you should be careful for whom you are voting at this election.

FURRIERS' AGITATION COMMITTEE
FOR RESPONSIBLE REPRESENTATIVES.

J. Algus,	G. Horowitz,	Kaplan,
B. Gold,	D. Greenberg,	Ferfer,
A. Schapiro,	S. Malamud,	S. Mencher,
S. Leibowitz,	Shechter,	J. Skolnik,
A. Gross,	Meltzer,	H. Schneider,
M. Suroff,	L. Breiman,	S. Malamud,
D. Fialer,	Poland,	D. Jakobowsky,
L. Rabinowitz,	Nestel.	

tion. Alex Fried, who had been going about with his gangsters threatening workers in the line, was heard shouting that the union had brought in detectives who were employed by an anti-labor detective agency.

Chairman Algus of the Joint Board immediately ordered the three men out of the office, and the election continued. The Welfare Club's threats had proven futile. Over seventeen hundred workers voted, and they overwhelmingly re-elected the officers of the Joint Board, Manager Brownstein and the business agents.

The next day, the *Forward* carried an editorial accusing the left wing of having brought in gangsters to terrorize the workers! A few days later, Sam Cohen and the leaders of the Welfare Club called a rump meeting of the right-wing members in Local 5 and adopted a resolution demanding the withdrawal of the local's delegates from the Joint Board. However, Local 5's delegates refused to recognize the illegal procedure of the Welfare Club clique and continued to serve on the Joint Board. Furthermore, at local meetings, the membership endorsed the action taken to guarantee a peaceful election.

Repudiated at the local meetings, the Welfare Club ran to the International for help. Kaufman suggested calling a local meeting to vote on the question of withdrawing Local 5's delegates. This was all the Welfare Club needed. They called a meeting of Local 5 but were careful not to notify the workers that the withdrawal of the Joint Board delegates would be discussed. Then, taking no chances, they packed the small meeting with gangsters, and forcibly drove away any worker who they suspected might vote against them. With the meeting thus completely under their control, they approved a resolution to withdraw the local's delegates from the Joint Board. The moment the coup in Local 5 was completed, the Welfare Club used the same methods to put across a similar resolution in Local 10.

Once again the Joint Board refused to surrender to terrorist tactics. It challenged the legality of the rump meetings run by the Welfare Club, and the elected delegates of Locals 5 and 10 refused to resign from the Board.

But the Welfare Club had not yet played its trump card. It appealed to the United Hebrew Trades for assistance. On Tuesday, March 28, the Joint Board received a letter from the United Hebrew Trades requesting that all union officials appear before a trial committee the following Saturday to answer questions concerning the hiring of detectives at the elections. The Joint Board was given just four days to prepare its defense.

In deciding to appear before this committee, the young left-wing leadership showed its inexperience. They naively believed that by revealing the truth even to a right-wing committee, they would gain support. Only later did they realize the serious mistake they had made.

The committee was composed of Max Pine, Max Zuckerman, Isidore Korn and Isidore Feinberg. Feinberg made it clear in his opening remarks that the committee was already convinced that the Joint Board was guilty. He also made it plain that the committee would not hear any evidence dealing with the role of the Welfare Club.

The Joint Board delegates and many of the fur workers went to the *Forward* building on April 2, 1922, to present the union's case. Brownstein, the Joint Board manager, who was even then preparing to make a deal with Kaufman, had promised to present the union's case in a militant manner. But when he appeared before the committee he seemed to have lost his powers of speech. Not wishing to antagonize the right wing, he said little and retired.

Disgusted with Brownstein's timidity, Gold took over the presentation of the union's case. For two hours he lashed out at the conspiracy against the union. Gold charged that the trial committee was fully aware of the terrible state of the union when Kaufman resigned as manager and fled to Long Island City. They knew that the 1920 strike was not called for the benefit of the workers. They also knew, he said, that gangsters had terrorized the workers.

"We came to you as younger brothers to older ones, and told you that the underworld was trying to break our union, and you were silent. Now when we have rebuilt our union in a short time, when we have taken a union which had only 650 members after the 1920 strike and restored it to a membership of 10,000 and brought back all the workers into their union, you start to do something. Yes, we are guilty; we are guilty of having taught the lesson that you can build a union of workers without the help of strong-arm men and gangsters. We are proud to be guilty of this."

Thunderous applause greeted Gold's speech. As far as the fur workers were concerned, the trial was over. The entire delegation of the Furriers Union left the building. The trial committee hastily adjourned, and announced that it would reveal its decision at the convention of the International Fur Workers Union. Meanwhile, Kaufman ruled that the delegates of Locals 5 and 10 should be suspended from the Joint Board until the decision of the United Hebrew Trades was announced.

The time was fast approaching for the International Convention. All signs pointed to a victory for Kaufman's machine. The postponement of the convention for a year had enabled Kaufman to line up a corps of lieutenants in the out-of-town locals, ready to do his bidding: Gmeiner of St. Paul, Millstein of Chicago, Roy of Montreal, Currie of Toronto, Lederman of Boston and others. Although the Joint Board had contributed the bulk of the International's treasury. Kaufman was using the money to build a machine for use against the Joint Board. Many of the out-of-town locals were paper locals set up solely to enable Kaufman to control the convention.

Through the strong-arm men of the Welfare Club, the right-wing machine had gained control of the delegates from Locals 5 and 10, the operators and nailers, in the New York Joint Board. But Locals 1 and 15, the cutters and finishers, elected a slate of progressives delegates. On the last day of voting, however, the progressives sustained a tragic setback. Harris J. Algus, chairman of the Joint Board, died suddenly.

A bitter foe of the right-wing machine and friend of the progressive forces in the union, Algus had come to be regarded by many furriers as the father of the Joint Board. His death took place under very mysterious circumstances. After the voting had been completed and tallied, a number of leaders had a round of drinks in the union office. A stiff drink was handed to Algus by one of the right-wing group. Algus drank only half, which was still a sizeable quantity. He poured out the remainder with the remark that it was the worst whiskey he had ever tasted. He died suddenly that same evening. No investigation or careful examination was ever made. The doctor's report read "attack of indigestion."

So highly was Algus revered by the fur workers that when Kaufman ordered that his seat at the convention be filled by another delegate, the Joint Board voted that his place should remain empty.

On June 5, 1922, the Fifth Biennial Convention opened in Philadelphia. In his report to the delegates, Kaufman spoke of the importance of achieving unity and harmony in New York, called for an end to "internal strife and factional fights," and pledged himself to cooperate with all groups prepared to achieve this goal.

The progressive delegates from New York, led by Ben Gold, Samuel Leibowitz, Joseph Winogradsky and Max Suroff, were prepared to make important contributions toward achieving unity and harmony. But they soon discovered that Kaufman's emphasis on unity was simply for the record. Making ruthless use of his machine, Kaufman saw to it that not one of the progressives was appointed to the all-important Credentials Committee or any other important committees.

Over the opposition of the progressive delegates, Kaufman's machine adopted red-baiting resolutions labeled by the progressive delegates as "open provocation to bar unity from entering the ranks of the union." Kaufman also jammed through a resolution granting a charter to the retail fur workers over the opposition of the Joint Board. The machine approved a resolution, proposed by Charles Stetsky and Sam Cohen, endorsing the Socialist Party.

Designated by Kaufman for the purpose, Max Pine of the United Hebrew Trades approached the progressive delegates and told them that Kaufman was ready to cooperate with them. However, they had to denounce the publications of the Workers' (Communist) Party and agree to fight the Amalgamated Clothing Workers, which had undertaken a project to assist the Soviet workers in reconstructing their war-devastated industry. The progressives, however, once again proposed as conditions for unity: elimination of the strong-arm men from the union and dissolution of the Welfare Club; organization of the unorganized fur workers; and real democracy in the union, including election of the International president by a referendum vote of the entire membership. Their proposals were quickly dismissed by Kaufman.

On the fifth day of the convention, the trial committee of the United Hebrew Trades announced its decision on the election charges against the New York Joint Board. Before the report was read, Kaufman's machine put through a motion that "no discussion be permitted on the matter." "The Committee," this truly amazing report concluded, "is of the opinion that the action of the Joint Board in hiring protectors was against the ethics of the labor movement, and in this particular case there was no justification nor necessity to hire protectors."

The depths to which Kaufman and his associates descended at the convention disgusted even some of the right-wing spokesmen. "You have no right to gamble with the fates of the men and women whose future and happiness depend upon the life and growth of the movement," warned Congressman Meyer London, turning to Kaufman. "I would recommend that those who happen to be in the majority should not attempt to force things outside of the union upon the minority. I would cooperate with any man, no matter what his political belief, so long as he has at heart the interest of the organization. I never inquire about his political opinions."

London's words were wasted on Kaufman. The machine went ahead with its policies. Kaufman's election was a foregone conclusion. Control of the out-of-town delegates gave Kaufman the votes, and he was re-elected by a vote of 37 to 8. The same control gave Kaufman a General Executive Board composed almost entirely of his henchmen, men like Sam Cohen, Jack Millstein, Charles Gmeiner, Philip Silberstein, Albert Roy.*

Barely had the convention adjourned, when the Welfare Club swung into action again, determined to recapture control of the Joint Board. In the election for delegates to the Board in June and July, the Club employed all their weapons. They broke up meetings and slugged workers unmercifully.

The employers made their own contributions to the disruption of the union, firing progressive workers, freely violating agreements, refusing to pay for overtime, discharging workers at will and replacing them with others at lower wage scales. The purpose, *Women's Wear* frankly admitted, was to convince the workers that their conditions could not be improved until the left-wingers were ousted from control.

The Welfare Club's new reign of terror produced results. The progressives had neither the strength nor the experience to defend themselves and the workers against the constant waves of terrorism. Forced to battle the gangsters as well as to carry the weight of all the union work, many progressives became demoralized. Weak and incompetent at his best, the manager of the Joint Board, Brownstein, had tried to ride two horses at the same time, working with both the progressives and the right wing. As he became terrified by the power of the gangster elements in the Welfare Club, Brownstein looked about for ways of uniting with the right-wing machine. By the time of the June and July elections, the surrender was complete. Brownstein was using his influence in behalf of the right-wing candidates.

With many of the fur workers absenting themselves from the polls out of fear of being attacked by gangsters, the right-wing clique carried the election. Only in Local 1 was the left wing successful, re-electing the same delegates who had represented the Local on the Joint Board since early in 1921. In Locals 5, 10 and 15, however, most of the left-wing candidates were defeated. One of the few to be re-elected was Joseph Winogradsky of Local 15, the Finishers Union.

* Abraham Brownstein and Max Suroff were also elected vice-presidents. They were in a completely minority position on the G.E.B.

Joseph Winogradsky, was born in Bessarabia, the son of a poor tailor. Winogradsky passed the examination for high school, but he was not allowed to enter. The one place set aside for Jewish students was given to the son of a wealthy merchant who had failed the examination. Winogradsky went to work as a tailor, and in 1917 obtained a job in a sugar factory in Odessa. Here he participated in his first strike. Later he returned to his home town and joined a committee to organize the tailors.

Winogradsky came to the United States in 1920. He left behind a wife and daughter who waited until he found his place in the new world. Soon after he arrived, Winogradsky found work as a finisher in a fur shop (his brother was already a fur worker), and joined Local 15. He joined immediately with Gold in the rank-and-file fight against the corruption of the right-wing machine and gangster rule. Winogradsky quickly won the confidence and respect of his union brothers and sisters. They elected him an Executive Board member a few months after he had joined the local. In 1922 he was elected a delegate to the International Convention.

The members of Finishers Local 15 were among the first to feel the effects of the right-wing victory. The finishers had long been plagued by the contracting evil. Non-union contractors would take the garments out of the shops for the finishing work. The wages and working conditions of the finishers in the manufacturing shops were constantly threatened by the substandard conditions of the contractors' shops.

The finishers demanded action to eliminate the contracting plague and called on the Board to appoint an additional business agent for this purpose. After some discussion, the Board agreed to undertake the campaign, but for four weeks it did nothing. All of its time was taken up deciding who should get the job of business agent. The Welfare Club had many rivals for the job. No one was more deserving of a reward than Alex Fried, for no one had been more energetic in attacking the furriers. But Fried was so thoroughly hated by the fur workers that the right-wing leaders of the Joint Board hesitated to appoint him.

In a letter to Kaufman, Charles Stetsky, newly-elected chairman of the Joint Board, unwittingly revealed the rivalry in the Welfare Club for union jobs: "The Joint Board has decided to engage another Business Agent and from all appearances Alex Fried will be the one. The Bunch here is very much opposed, yet, there seems to be no other alternative. I personally am not very much in favor of him, but if we do not elect him it may mean the breaking up of the activity of the group—and the question remains—does it pay?" But the gang leaders had given the command, and Fried was soon to be appointed.

While the right-wingers debated for weeks the wisdom of giving Fried the job, the members of Local 15 took matters into their own hands. Max Suroff, chairman of the local, and Joseph Winogradsky, Executive Board member, called together the active workers and plans were laid to call a strike in the contracting shops under the leadership of Fanny Warshafsky. The workers threw themselves energetically into the campaign.

Suddenly the right-wing Joint Board awoke. Warshafsky was a progressive business agent. If the campaign against the contractors was successful, the prestige of the progressives would rise. Moreover, a strike against contractors would be an opportunity for the members of the Welfare Club to make all kinds of deals. The right wing leaped into activity. Sam Cohen and a squad of his strong-arm boys moved in on Local 15 and laid plans for taking over the strike. Winogradsky and Suroff insisted that Local 15 would not tolerate a repetition of what happened in 1920. By their vehement stand they forced Kaufman to order Cohen to call off the strong-arm squad for the moment.

On the first day of the strike, more than fifty contracting shops were stopped. The shop chairmen bluntly told the manufacturers on behalf of the other three crafts that they must not give out the finishing work but have it done in the shop. "Where the cutters, operators and nailers work," they insisted, "there also the finishers must work. We won't allow you to send out the work to be finished in the cellars of the contractors." It was the first time these bosses had heard such talk from their workers.

Suroff was severely beaten when he went into a contracting shop to persuade the workers to walk out, and he was forced to remain in bed for several days. When he returned to the union, he discovered that the gangsters, equipped with union books, had been working day and night to take over control of the strike. They would barge into meetings of the strikers, terrorize them, and hurl vile epithets at Fanny Warshafsky. Since the contracting shop workers had just been brought into the union, they were soon bewildered and alarmed by the gangsters.

There came a time when Fanny Warshafsky had been goaded beyond endurance. Subjected to the foul obscenity of one of the gangsters, she answered him with a resounding slap in the face. This was exactly what Kaufman's henchmen had been waiting for. They ran straight to the International and preferred charges against Miss Warshafsky. At a special meeting of the Joint Board, Kaufman rammed through the suspension of Warshafsky, right in the midst of the strike.

At first Brownstein feigned indignation, even threatening to resign as manager in protest. His devotion to "principle," however, was fully revealed in Stetsky's letter to Kaufman dated September 1: "Knowing as we do that Mr B. does not care to part with One Hundred and Ten Dollars per week we played for that weak spot, and the result is that he is not resigning."

In protest against Warshafsky's suspension, Maurice Cohen, a progressive, resigned as business agent. Immediately, the Joint Board appointed four new business agents, all of them members of the Welfare Club. The dispute over Alex Fried was settled. He was one of the four. With Suroff sick, and new (Welfare Club) business agents appointed, the strike against the contractors became demoralized. As soon as the gangsters got what they wanted out of it, it was abandoned. And to stop the protests of the finishers on the sabotage and destruction of their strike, the Welfare Club terrorized the workers and broke up the meetings of the local.

As early as December 1922, in the election for local officers and delegates to the Joint Board, the tactics of the right-wing machine were revealed in all their sordidness. Without bothering to notify the members, the machine called together its followers in Locals 1 and 15 and set up election and objections committees to arrange and conduct

Stetsky: "... Mr. B. does not care to part with $110 per week ..."

The Joint Board suspended Mrs Warshawsky for four weeks and as soon as that was done the political machine began to work The Manager and the office staff were almost Bull Dosed in to tender their resignations. but knowing as we do that Mr B. does not care to part with One Hundred and Ten Dollars per week we played for that weak spot, and the result is that he is not resighning

I still am at the Joint Board and probably will be there as its Chairman untill things quieten down

Yours

[signature]

Regards to you from the Bunch

the election. The committees proceeded to remove from the ballot the names of all candidates opposed to the right-wing machine.

To give a more respectable air to the conspiracy, a committee from the International was sent in to aid in supervising the election. Since both election committees consisted of machine men, there was no limit to the number of repeaters. No matter how many workers voted legitimately, the right-wing machine naturally won the election. The final irony was that any appeal would have to be ruled on by Kaufman as International president.

Denouncing the fraudulent character of the elections, the Executive Boards of the two locals declared them illegal and null and void,* and resolved "to carry on a fight against the unjust and unlawful methods which were rampant in the Union." The fight opened at a meeting of Local 15 in February 1923 when Kaufman attempted to install the newly-elected local officials and Joint Board delegates. The workers were told that first the officers would be installed and only afterward would the report of a committee that had investigated the elections be made. Led by Joseph Winogradsky, the workers demanded that the order be reversed, and they refused to allow the meeting to continue unless the investigating committee first made its report. The machine had to give way when the motion was overwhelmingly adopted.

Once the reading of the report started, it became clear why Kaufman had insisted on first installing the officers. The whole story was revealed —the elimination of opposition candidates from the ballot for spurious reasons, the use of repeaters, and the stealing of the election. As the names

---

* In a statement to the press, the Executive Board of Local 15 listed the following reasons for having recalled the elections:

"1. The machine took away the constitutional rights from the members to elect their officers at the regular local meetings as provided by the constitution of the International Fur Workers Union.

"2. The machine of the 'Rights' took off the ballot active members without any reasons and they added on the ballot their own people among whom we find a Store Keeper, a Foreman, and one of their own boys who stands under fine for betraying and spying against the workers in the shop.

"3. The machine wilfully falsified an important paragraph of a letter written by the Executive Board to the members concerning the elections and in such a way manipulated the elections to suit themselves. Thanks to these shameful and illegal methods used by the machine, they succeeded in smuggling through the elections against the will of the Executive Board.

"It is important to remark that scores of members refused to participate in the election and only 45 members of the whole local, consisting of 2,500 members, took part in voting."

of the elected local officials and Joint Board delegates were read aloud, cries of indignation arose from the workers: "That man on the Executive Board is a spy of the boss," "That fellow is a foreman," "That member of the Joint Board isn't a worker, he owns his own store and is an employer." Soon the entire meeting-room reverberated with the cry: "New elections! We want new elections!"

A motion calling for new elections was proposed. But before it could be seconded, Kaufman stepped to the front of the platform, and shouted: "I am the president of the International, and I will not allow any such thing. Installations, and that's all. Mr. Chairman, I order you to proceed with installations. If you do not obey the order, I shall take over the chair." When the chairman protested, Kaufman ordered him to leave the platform. As he started to descend, Kaufman was heard shouting above the din of the clamoring workers: "I declare the newly-elected officers legal representatives of the masses, and they are hereby installed. The meeting is closed." As he finished, the lights were turned off. The meeting was over.

By such tactics, Kaufman and his machine appeared to be victorious. But in a broader sense, they had really lost. In the heat of the battle, the spirit and morale of the progressives revived, never again to decline.

CHAPTER 12

The Trade Union
Educational League

In the course of their struggle against the Kaufman regime for clean, honest and democratic trade unionism, the progressive forces in the Furriers Union soon learned that they were battling a disease which had infected the entire American labor movement. They discovered that Kaufmanism was based upon the theory and program of the leadership of the American Federation of Labor and of the Socialist Party, and was practiced in almost every union.

In earlier times, the Socialist leaders of the needle trades unions had opposed Gompers' machine. They had exposed the AFL bureaucracy's class collaboration policies and protested the participation of Samuel Gompers and other labor leaders in the National Civic Federation together with representatives of big business. But by the 1920's, the Socialist leadership of the needle trades unions had repudiated every semblance of militancy in their attitude towards the employers. They became just as ardent advocates of cooperation with the employers as were the most conservative AFL leaders.

When Morris Sigman, President of the International Ladies' Garment Workers' Union, presented Samuel Gompers with a bronze bust at a convention of the AFL in the 1920's, his act was symbolic of the complete surrender of the Socialist trade union bureaucrats to the policies and leadership of the Gompers machine.

The complete degeneration of the Socialist leaders of the needle trades unions paralleled the decay of the Socialist Party after it expelled its left-wing militants in 1919. Even the superficial pretense of honesty and of desire to protect the workers' interests were for the most part openly abandoned as they sought to curry favor with the employers and to hang on to their fat sinecures in the unions.

The fight against the reactionary bureaucracy of the AFL and the Socialist Party took on an organized form with the emergence of the Trade Union Educational League.

The Trade Union Educational League is associated inseparably with the name of one man—William Z. Foster. Born in Massachusetts, the son of political refugees from Ireland, Foster was forced by poverty to seek a job at the age of ten. He took part in his first strike when he was fourteen years old and joined the Socialist Party as a youth. Like Eugene V. Debs, he opposed the Party's reformist right-wing leadership, and because of it was expelled from the Party. An ardent believer in industrial unionism, he joined the IWW. He soon saw the necessity of battling for progressive trade unionism in the existing trade unions, and he tried in vain to convince the IWW leaders that their practice of isolation from the conservative trade unions was wrong.

Foster returned to the AFL. In 1917, as a delegate to the Chicago Federation of Labor from a local of the Brotherhood of Railway Carmen, he initiated a drive to organize the mass production industries. His role in the packinghouse strike of 1918 and as leader of the great steel strike of 1919 established him as the ablest organizer in the American labor movement.

Following the steel strike, Foster again undertook to rally the militants to the program of building a progressive rank and file in the existing unions. For this purpose, he organized the Trade Union Educational League in November 1920. A month later, in an article written especially for the fur workers, Foster pointed out that the failure of the steel strike had convinced many American workers of the need for a new program for the labor movement. The purpose of the League was "to unite the progressive forces in conservative unions and to pull the unions away from the conservative methods which for too long a time hampered the growth of the American labor movement."

The League was not a union. It issued no charters and collected no dues or taxes. Financially the organization depended on voluntary contributions of individuals and local unions, and the sale of its organ, *The Labor Herald*. In the words of the League itself, it was simply "a virile educational league, operating within and in support of the trade unions, and by no means in opposition or in competition with them."

T̲H̲E̲ LABOR HERALD

Published monthly at 118 N. La Salle St.   Subscription price $1.50 per year.   The Trade Union Educational League, Publishers.
"Entered as second class matter March 28, 1922, at the postoffice at Chicago, Illinois, under the Act of March 3, 1879."

Vol. II.   APRIL, 1923   No. 2

Getting Together
By Eugene V. Debs

THE urgent. imperative need of thorough-going working-class unity was never so glaringly manifested as it is today. Recent lessons growing out of the defeated steel strike, the defeated mine strike, and the defeated railroad strike, are tragically in evidence in the appeal they make to the workers of the nation. Each of these strikes that resulted in such disastrous failure could and should have achieved a clear cut victory. The grievances in each instance ... ters and misleaders, and to their own detriment and undoing. There can be no possible excuse for it, in the light of its recent tragic failure to achieve anything for the members save only the

> The Trade Union Educational League, under the direction and inspiration of Wm. Z. Foster, is in my opinion the one rightly directed movement for the industrial unification of the American workers. I thoroughly believe in its plan and its methods and I feel very confident of its steady progress and the ultimate achievement of its ends.

Eugene V. Debs wholeheartedly endorses the TUEL's militant trade-union program.

The League subscribed to the program of amalgamation of the existing craft unions, industrial unionism, organization of the unorganized, independent political action by labor and international labor unity. In the League were gathered the workers who refused to follow blindly the dictates of trade union bureaucrats; who struggled for the right to discuss union policies at meetings; who maintained that the rank and file could and must develop a militant and honest trade union movement.

Eugene V. Debs, the militant Socialist leader, expressed the opinion that the League was "the one rightly directed movement for the industrial unification of the American workers." David J. Saposs, then one of America's leading labor historians, wrote of the TUEL: "There is a vital need for an organization that will at least develop an intelligent opposition to the reactionary, routinized and visionless leaders controlling the labor movement."

Hundreds of locals in the Miners Union, the Carpenters Union, the Railroad Unions, the Machinists Union, textile, printing, shoe and leather, and building trades unions endorsed the League's program, and had begun a campaign against the autocratic machines of the reactionary bureaucracy. In the needle trades, a splendid opportunity presented itself to realize many features of the League's program. The workers in the needle trades were the most politically advanced in the whole labor movement, and their long socialist tradition had already created a mass sentiment for many of the progressive policies advocated by the TUEL.

Before long, there were many League branches in the needle trades, but they were mostly local and of a craft character. The obvious need was to unite these local bodies, known as Shop Delegates Leagues, into one sweeping, active movement. On November 22, 1922, forty rank-and-file delegates from shops of the Amalgamated Clothing Workers, the International Ladies Garment Workers Union, Millinery, Capmakers, Journeymen Tailors and Furriers Unions met in New York City and formed the Needle Trades Section of the Trade Union Educational League. Ten days later, the Furriers Section of the TUEL was born.

The struggle of the progressive forces for democratic trade unionism in the needle trades was at the same time a struggle to break the influence of the *Jewish Daily Forward*. In the opening years of the twentieth century, the *Forward* had helped the Jewish workers in their struggles to organize unions and conduct strikes for better conditions. As a result, the majority of Jewish immigrants read the paper.

Before many years had passed, however, the character of the *Forward* changed sharply. As its circulation soared and its revenue from advertisements increased, the *Forward* became a wealthy and powerful organization. The interests of the *Forward* were paramount to any other consideration. Those trade unionists who "played ball" with the paper were assured of its powerful support. Those who dared to take issue with Abraham Cahan, head of the Forward Association and editor of the paper, would be attacked as enemies of the labor movement.

When the Socialist Party split into right and left wings in 1917, Cahan and his associates became the most embittered enemies of the Soviet Union. Jewish trade unionists who did not immediately join the "Soviet-haters," were accused of having been bought by "Moscow gold." Not even Attorney-General Palmer, J. Edgar Hoover or Hearst outdid the *Forward* in red-baiting.

Right-wing union leaders, facing revolts of the rank and file, rushed to the Forward Association for loans to enable them to remain in power. Soon many of the needle trades unions were actually in receivership, with the *Forward* holding the reins as creditors. The *Forward* also dominated the United Hebrew Trades, the Workmen's Circle and the Socialist *Call*.

A Yiddish paper was needed which would expose the role of the *Forward* and its right-wing allies in the union leadership. It was needed to clarify the issues and problems of the workers, and to present the rank-and-file program without distortion. To meet this need, the *Freiheit* appeared on April 22, 1922.

Organized by progressive left-wing Socialists and Communists, including former members of the *Forward* staff who had resigned in disgust over its policies, the *Freiheit* expressed the militant aspirations of many Jewish workers. Under the leadership of Dr. Moissaye J. Olgin, the *Freiheit* faithfully mirrored the life and struggles of the Jewish workers and gave them a sense of their own dignity and strength.

Dr. Olgin had been a shining light in the Socialist Party, and became a prominent leader of the newly-organized Communist Party. A brilliant writer, lecturer and critic, and author of *The Soul of the Russian Revolution,* he was an outstanding figure beloved by thousands of Jewish workers, especially in the needle trades. He was largely responsible for the *Freiheit's* growing influence, and for its high literary quality.

In the battle against corruption in the Furriers Union, the *Freiheit* became an indispensable weapon. It was a means of mobilizing the furriers in the struggle to uproot the system represented by the coalition of Kaufman, the bosses, the Welfare Club, the Socialist Party leadership and the *Forward*. It was in the *Freiheit* of January 11, 1923, that the Furriers Section of the Trade Union Educational League issued its first call to the fur workers. Written by Ben Gold, the call read in part:

"Brothers and Sisters! We know from experience that when control of the union is put into the hands of a small group of individuals, no matter how fine their intentions, the union cannot remain the instrument which successfully protects the workers from the abuses of the bosses. And, needless to say, the intentions of the present leaders of the Furriers Union are not the best.

"The Furriers Section of the Trade Union Educational League desires to draw the workers into union activity in order to assure that no clique shall be able to retain control of the union and deal with it as they see fit in their own interest.

"The League strives to guarantee that the leadership of the union shall come from the rank and file. The League believes that the shop chairman system should become the established system for running the union."

Within two years, the Furriers Section of the Trade Union Educational League grew into a mass movement representing the vast majority of the fur workers and serving as their spokesman in the battle for progressive, militant trade unionism.

CHAPTER 13

Sit Down or I'll
Knock You Down!

A newspaper reporter who made a careful study of the trade union movement wrote in the early 1920's: "In no union in the American labor movement is gangsterism such a big factor as in the Furriers Union. The officialdom of the furriers outbid every other officialdom in the extent of using violence to gain and hold control of the organization."

In February 1923, a delegation of young fur workers headed by Ben Gold asked the *Forward* to take a vigorous editorial stand against the sinister practices in their union. The workers produced eye-witnesses and other evidence to prove that the beating and slugging of union members were daily practices of the administration.

"Nothing doing," the workers were informed.

After their fruitless visit to the *Forward,* the committee wrote a letter to the *Freiheit*. It appeared on February 28, 1923, under the headline, "THEY BEAT YOU IN THE FURRIERS UNION." The introduction read: "A group of furriers comprising several active members of the union have sent us the following letter. We do not disclose their names at this time, for their protection."

The letter read in part: "Do you know that the situation in the Furriers Union is such that no member dares criticize the administration lest he be beaten mercilessly? Are you aware that almost every week a worker is beaten, and the attacker goes unpunished by the union officials? . . . We ask that our *Freiheit* tell the world about our plague, and place the guilt where it belongs. . . ."

In a brief editorial postscript, Moissaye J. Olgin, editor of the *Freiheit,* assured the furriers that "all facts pertaining to conditions in their union, if supported by reliable evidence, will be published in our newspaper."

The next day the Joint Board put through a motion to present libel charges to the district attorney against the editor of the *Freiheit.* In a letter to Kaufman, Dr. Olgin demanded that the charges against the *Freiheit* be brought "to a court of labor representatives which will be chosen by impartial methods." He promised to abide by any decision handed down by this court and urged Kaufman to agree to do likewise.

Kaufman succeeded in dragging the editor of the *Freiheit* before the district attorney, but Dr. Olgin stood his ground and refused to divulge any information concerning affairs in the union. He insisted that he was prepared to turn over evidence to an impartial labor court, but not to any agency outside of the labor movement. He maintained that neither the *Freiheit* nor the Furriers Section of the TUEL would come to the aid of employers by giving the courts a chance to probe into the union's records and books.

District Attorney Lehman fumed, raged and finally threatened to prosecute the *Freiheit* for libel. But it was all in vain. Dr. Olgin again challenged Kaufman to bring the case to a labor tribunal. But Kaufman claimed that he had been vindicated by Olgin's refusal to furnish evidence to the district attorney. As far as he was concerned, the incident was closed.

The fur workers had a different viewpoint. After the final hearings in the district attorney's office, the Furriers Section of the TUEL issued a call for a mass protest meeting. As soon as the leaflets announcing the meeting at Webster Hall were distributed, Kaufman arranged to call a mass meeting on the same day in Manhattan Lyceum. The Joint Board dispatched telegrams to all shop chairmen urging them to "advise" the workers to go to Manhattan Lyceum and not to Webster Hall. Over ten thousand letters were mailed to individual members of the union, and the fur market was showered with leaflets.

At twelve o'clock on Saturday, March 17, hundreds of fur workers left their shops and formed a procession toward Webster Hall. As they approached the hall, they were met by an army of sluggers stationed near the entrance who tried to block the way. But the throng of workers moving toward the hall grew greater and greater. The strong-arm squad could do nothing to stop this tidal wave. Over fourteen hundred workers, union books in hand, crowded into the auditorium.

Isidore Shapiro, staunch rank-and-file member of the union, opened the meeting and acted as chairman. The speakers included Ben Gold, Louis Weiser, formerly an administration supporter but now an active left-winger, Max Suroff and Fanny Warshafsky. Dr. Olgin and Alexander Bittelman spoke for the *Freiheit,* and J. Manley brought greetings from the TUEL.

After several speakers had exposed the corruption of the union leadership and the widespread terror in the fur market, Gold introduced a resolution thanking the *Freiheit* for the assistance it had rendered the Furriers Union and demanding an investigation by an impartial workers' tribunal of the charges against Kaufman and his henchmen. The resolution was unanimously adopted.

"The entire labor movement must get into this battle," Gold concluded. "We furriers are the vanguard of the labor movement. Let us lead the work. Let us from this day on lead a new way in the Furriers Union. We have the forces to win, and we can win."

Gold's words were to be borne out. The letter from the fur workers and the *Freiheit's* editorial comment started a chain of events of the utmost significance to the entire labor movement. During the next few years, the attention of progressive workers all over the country was riveted on the battle against the machine in the Furriers Union.

The *New York Times* reported that only two hundred people were present at the Manhattan Lyceum meeting called by the officers of the union. All the speakers expressed the attitude that the union belonged to the present leadership and that those opposed to their policies were seeking to rob them of their property. "Let them go to Moscow," declared Meyer London in winding up a long tirade against the *Freiheit* and the left wing.

The small Manhattan Lyceum meeting then adopted a resolution that authorized the Board to "take suitable action against those that seek to discredit or destroy the union." In fact, the strong-arm men did not even wait for the meeting to end before they began interpreting the words "suitable action."

David Kass of Local 1, who was a member of the Workmen's Circle and had never been associated with the left wing, described his experience at Manhattan Lyceum: "I asked for the floor, and then stated that I did not think that we had the right to bring workers to court. This would make a bad impression and our bosses would utilize this far more than the court. I think it would be better for us to solve our problems by ourselves. Later, as I was leaving the hall, I was attacked and beaten, because of what I said."

Sam Lipton, also a member of Local 1, dared to ask why the union did not enforce the part of the agreement dealing with equal division of work. "For this question," he complained to Kaufman, "I was attacked by your 'disciples' and beaten. As if this alone were not enough, I was attacked again after the meeting on Monday at noon, at 29th Street in the fur market. I ask you: what will be the outcome of such activities?"

Elections for local officers and delegates to the Joint Board were scheduled to take place in June 1923. Realizing that the revolt of the rank and file was growing every day, the "election" committees decided to remove all opposition candidates, but some "legal" pretext was still necessary. Local meetings, screened by gangsters, approved the resolution voted at Manhattan Lyceum. With this authorization, the "election" committees were ready to proceed.

On June 16, 1923, candidates Fanny Warshafsky, Lena Greenberg, Joseph Winogradsky, Ray Katz and Lina Bramen were called before the "election" committee of Local 15. They were asked a single question: "Did you attend the Webster Hall meeting on March 17, 1923?" When they answered in the affirmative, their names were removed from the ballot.

When Esther Polansky was asked if she had attended the meeting, she replied that she had been in Europe at that time and therefore could not have attended. Still not satisfied, Kaufman's henchmen asked her whether she would have attended the meeting if she had been in New York on March 17. When Miss Polansky replied that she might have attended, her name too was removed from the ballot.

Following the pattern set in Local 15, the "election" committees in the other locals removed all candidates from the ballot who admitted having attended the Webster Hall meeting. The Sub-Committee of the General Executive Board quickly approved these actions. Stealing of elections, terroristic acts against opposition candidates, even the elimination of candidates from the ballot on the ground that they were not members in good standing, were common practices of trade union bureaucrats. But now the leaders of the Furriers Union had added the new device of simply refusing to recognize candidates who were open opponents of the machine.

On December 12, 1923, the union representatives conferred with the manufacturers' association for renewal of the agreement. But the workers did not know what demands the union had presented. How did the union propose to solve the serious problem of contractors, the influx of learners, the widespread unemployment and the power of the manufacturer to fire a worker any time it suited his interests? Kaufman and Brownstein assured the workers that they were aware of these problems, but they were very vague when it came to revealing the demands. In answer to all questions from the workers, Kaufman replied: "It is my heartfelt wish that both parties [the manufacturers and the union] shall further continue their contractual relations in the spirit of unified understanding and hearty cooperation."

From personal experience the fur workers had plenty of reason to be suspicious of Kaufman's "hearty cooperation" with the employers. In the past it had always resulted in an agreement which was useless in the shops. "Hearty cooperation" had meant that the worker was completely dependent upon the good will of the boss. With the boss having unlimited power of discharge, the worker could not afford to complain when the manufacturer violated the agreement. He knew that to complain to the union was to put his job in jeopardy.

To insure that the betrayals of the past would not be repeated, the Furriers Section of the TUEL called a mass meeting at Webster Hall on December 15. Close to one thousand furriers, unable to express themselves through regular organizational channels, answered the call and heard Ben Gold, Fanny Warshafsky, Max Suroff and A. Shapiro outline demands which should be incorporated into the new agreement. These demands boiled down to three main points: (1) equal distribution of work throughout the year, (2) no discharge, and (3) guarantee of fulfillment of union conditions in the contractors' shops.

Frightened by the success of the Webster Hall meeting, Kaufman called together the shop chairmen to inform them of the union's proposals to the Association. The left wing distributed leaflets urging the chairmen to attend the meeting, and advised them to ask questions and speak up on the demands for the agreement.

In addition to the shop chairmen, many active workers attended the meeting. When Kaufman saw the great number of workers responding, he ordered that no left-wingers should be permitted to enter the hall. A sharp outcry of protest from the workers forced him to let everyone in. But from the beginning of the meeting Kaufman made it clear that he would not permit any discussion. He would simply outline the proposed terms of the new agreement. Local meetings were to be held in the next few days, and here the workers would have an opportunity to discuss the terms. After this announcement, Kaufman quickly read the proposed terms of the agreement and adjourned the meeting.

The first of the local meetings was that of Local 15, the finishers. The left wing distributed leaflets in the market calling on all finishers to attend the meeting. The response was an indication of the workers' concern over the agreement. The meeting-hall was crowded to the doors. As was the custom in the Furriers Union when important issues were to be taken up at any local meeting, workers from the other Joint Board locals attended to hear the discussion. Ben Gold and Max Suroff came, and took seats in the rear of the hall.

Although the workers demanded discussion of the agreement immediately, Kaufman dragged out the proceedings so that it was late in the evening before he came to the main purpose of the meeting. Obviously disappointed because none of the workers had left on account of the delay, Kaufman began to read the agreement, following each point with a bitter blast against the left wing. Meanwhile, he gave the workers no opportunity for discussion.

Finally, Max Suroff arose and asked Kaufman a question. Kaufman ignored the interruption, but Suroff persisted. "Brother President," he asked, "if you do not answer questions and do not allow discussion of the agreement with the employers which all of us will have to abide by for two years, then in whose name will you sign the agreement?"

Kaufman's reply was another tirade against the left wing. He ended his attack with the threat: "Whoever asks such questions tonight, will pay for it with his blood."

Protests arose on all sides: "If you try to put over an agreement without discussion, we will not recognize it! This is no longer 1920!"

Meanwhile, Suroff was still standing and waiting for an answer to his question. Kaufman had an answer: "Drag him out of the hall."

Strong-arm men surrounded Suroff and Gold, who had leaped to his defense. Sam Cohen, Charles Stetsky and about ten others closed in on Gold and began to beat him brutally with chairs and clubs and slash him with knives. Bedlam broke loose. The gangsters did not spare the women. Chairs aimed at heads flew in every direction. Suroff, Fanny Warshafsky and Lena Greenberg were beaten.

Gold's head required eleven stitches. While Dr. Marie Lerner was working on him, a policeman entered the office and asked for Ben Gold. Even the officer was stunned by Gold's ghastly appearance when he was pointed out. He told the doctor that he had been sent to bring Gold to the police station, but he obviously could not take him in this condition. Later a hundred workers followed Gold and Dr. Lerner to the police station where they encountered Stetsky and several of the strong-arm men. When the police captain heard the workers describe the attack on Gold, he arrested Stetsky and Kramer, a Kaufman lieutenant, and ordered Gold to return the next morning for a hearing.

Although the doctor had forbidden Gold to appear in court the next morning, he left his bed and showed up on time. He knew that if he failed to appear, the blame for the battle would be placed on the shoulders of the left wing. As soon as Gold arrived in court, he was arrested on the charge of assault and battery. When the furriers heard that Gold had been arrested, hundreds of them left their shops and marched to the Essex Market Court, where they packed the largest room.

In spite of this demonstration by the furriers, the judge released Stetsky and Kramer immediately and ordered Gold to be placed in custody. District Attorney Markewich demanded prompt action, crying that were it not for men like Kaufman and his allies, the left-wingers would set up a "Communist" administration.

While efforts were being made to raise the $1,000 required for bail, Gold was thrown in the Tombs. He remained for only two hours. Workers threw dollar bills into the hats that were passed around to collect the bail money, and Gold was quickly released from jail.

While Gold was in jail and the bail fund was being collected, hundreds of fur workers left the court and marched spontaneously to a demonstration of protest at the *Forward* building on East Broadway. They were especially enraged by the report in the *Forward* that the left-wingers themselves had beaten Gold in order to have a martyr!

The furriers marched two abreast around the *Forward* building, carrying placards which read: "WE PROTEST AGAINST GANGSTER ATTACKS IN OUR UNION!" "KNIVES AND CHAIRS ARE THE WEAPONS THAT THE RIGHT-WING MACHINE USES AGAINST THE MEMBERS OF THE UNION!"

The workers' protests were largely responsible for the fact that the charges against Gold were dropped. His wounds kept him in bed for two weeks, however. "Is there anything we can do?" hundreds of fur workers asked. They offered to donate blood. They collected funds to pay the doctors' bills. Even the anti-labor newspapers were impressed by this unusual devotion of the fur workers for the left-wing leader.

"You have become a symbol," Dr. Olgin wrote to Gold in a public letter. "To me, you symbolize the new spirit which has imbued a section of the working class on this side of the Atlantic. You are an example of the new youth which by means of heavy sacrifice and long struggle, will revitalize the entire American labor movement, and with it, the rusted, stagnant, muck-laden political life of America."

Gold's courageous stand gave the fur workers the will to fight back. A few days after the attack on Gold, hundreds of fur workers of all political views organized themselves into a defense committee to prevent attacks upon members, and, in case of assaults by gangsters, to aid the victims. As its first act, the defense committee issued a call for a mass meeting at Webster Hall on January 5, 1924.

Despite warnings by Kaufman, Webster Hall was filled when Harry Kravitz opened the meeting. He unwrapped a package and showed the audience its contents. "You see here the blood-stained clothes of Ben Gold," Kravitz cried, "the man who was murderously attacked because he fought for you and me, and for all the fur workers." A tremendous demonstration greeted this statement. One after another, workers stood up and asked, "How long will we stand for it?"

Over his doctor's objections, Gold addressed the meeting. With ringing defiance of the strong-arm squad, he declared: " . . . Our workers were frightened, they were afraid of everyone. They were afraid of the bosses. They were afraid of the foreman, of the union, and especially of the people whom they themselves had elected as leaders. The union officials know this and that is why they are so brazen. They have kept the workers in check through their gangster tactics. They are determined to hold on in the same way."

But the events of the past few weeks, Gold pointed out, marked the beginning of their end. "We have decided that no more blood shall be spilled. We will not go to the courts, for we know the nature of the courts under our present system. Instead we will build a strong defense organization of the workers themselves. If it was possible to end the Czar's regime in Russia, should we be afraid of Kaufman's regime? . . . We will not stop with protest meetings. With an organized defense committee, we will take practical steps to free the workers from terror."

The reaction to the attack on Gold marked a turning-point in the struggle within the Furriers Union. With the formation of the defense committee, the fear that had paralyzed so many fur workers gradually disappeared. The machine's chief weapon—violence—was soon to be destroyed by the courage and spirit of the workers themselves.

On February 2, 1924, Kaufman announced that "a satisfactory settlement" had been reached with the New York Fur Manufacturers Association. "Settlement," he wired to the leaders of the AFL, "is a splendid victory for the union and membership is overjoyed."

The "overjoyed" membership chose a most peculiar way of showing it. Only twelve hundred out of nine thousand members voted in the referendum on the settlement, and even this figure undoubtedly included numerous machine repeaters. Having lost all confidence in voting controlled by the right wing, the workers voted with their feet by staying away from the polls.

Kaufman boasted that the new agreement vindicated his program of "hearty cooperation" with the employers. But no guarantee existed that the manufacturers would adhere to the terms even of this settlement. Moreover, the employers retained the full power to discharge workers whenever they pleased, the contracting menace still continued to plague the fur workers, and the problem of learners became even more serious as a result of concessions to the employers. The important demand that all the work, including finishing, be done in one shop, had been abandoned. In short, the new agreement gave the bosses what they wanted. The workers were helpless so long as the union remained under control of the machine.

CHAPTER 14

Expulsions

To squelch all opposition to his "hearty cooperation" with the employers, Kaufman now embarked on a program of expulsions. On January 10, 1924, M. Markoff of Local 15 filed charges against Ben Gold before the Grievance Committee of the Joint Board. He charged the left-wing leader with "maliciously slandering members and officers of the union," and with "disturbing the last meeting of Local 15 held on December 19th and causing there a disturbance and physical fight." Thus, the victim of the attack was now to be tried by the very people responsible for it. Kaufman himself was, of course, behind these charges. Markoff later admitted that he had no idea of what he was doing and was merely following Kaufman's bidding. "I never preferred charges against Gold, never," he confessed. "I can't read English. He told me to sign."

Similar charges were preferred against Max Suroff, Esther Polansky and Fanny Warshafsky of Local 15, Isidore Shapiro of Local 1 and Harry Kravitz of Local 5. Gold and the other left-wingers were ordered to appear on January 31 to answer the charges.

According to the International constitution, the Grievance Committee of the Joint Board had no authority to try any members on charges. The constitution specifically stated that "all charges shall be referred to a committee of investigation to be selected by the local union. The accused shall have the privilege of challenging any three members of said committee." The right-wing machine knew only too well that the charges would be dismissed by committees elected by the local unions.

136

The Grievance Committee of the Joint Board, on the other hand, was completely dominated by the machine.

Acting on the advice of their counsel, Joseph R. Brodsky, the brilliant labor lawyer, the left-wingers refused to appear before the Joint Board Grievance Committee. They demanded that the charges be sent to a committee of investigation to be selected by the local unions of which they were members, and insisted on their constitutional right to challenge any three members of the committee. At the same time, they expressed their readiness to submit all of the charges to an impartial committee of seven, three to be selected by the Joint Board, three to be selected by the accused, and the six together to select an impartial chairman.

The Joint Board Grievance Committee slapped a fine of $10 on each of the accused for refusing to appear and recommended that Ben Gold, Fanny Warshafsky, Esther Polansky, Max Suroff, Isidore Shapiro and Harry Kravitz be suspended from the union for two years. During this period they were to be deprived of the right to run for office or to participate in local meetings. Two weeks later, the recommendation was unanimously adopted by the Joint Board.

The haste with which the right-wing machine had acted in unconstitutionally suspending the left-wing leaders stemmed from a fear of the forthcoming elections for paid officers and convention delegates. Despite the suspensions, the machine men were still nervous about their ability to carry the elections. So they proceeded to multiply the seven hundred votes actually cast into sixteen hundred ballots. Putting into practice Kaufman's "hearty cooperation," the bosses and the foremen campaigned for the right-wing ticket. In many shops, the bosses distributed printed cards which instructed the workers to vote for right-wing candidates. Scoring a "smashing victory" in the election, Kaufman turned confidently to the International Convention to be held in Chicago.

Every local in the United States and Canada was weak and disorganized. The condition of the New York fur workers was truly tragic. The small New York Joint Board was broken and ruined. Out-of-town open shops had moved to Connecticut, New Jersey and Springfield. New York retail shops were unorganized. Seventy-five per cent of the fur workers in Montreal were not organized. In Detroit and other cities, there was no union at all, even though the workers had appealed frequently to the International to help them organize. In Boston the local had practically ceased to exist. Thousands of others employed in the fur industry were not organized.

But none of these things seemed to disturb Kaufman, whose main concern was to retain control of the International. The locals outside of New York were dependent upon the International for financial support and would have to vote as Kaufman ordered at the convention. Although the money to finance these locals came from the New York Joint Board, which had 80 percent of the International's membership, the locals outside of New York had the majority of delegates at the convention. Moreover, the New York fur workers had no opportunity to express their real opinions, since the elections were stacked.

"We cannot expect that the Convention will do anything of value for the fur workers," wrote Ben Gold on the eve of the gathering. "The delegates simply do not have the will nor the power to do this. They will follow Kaufman's bidding and punish the left-wingers. Then they will attend banquets, take pictures, and, after hectic enjoyment, go home."

Gold's prediction was borne out. The Sixth Biennial Convention held in Chicago from May 12 to 17, 1924, and attended by fifty delegates from eighteen local unions and five Joint Boards was the most reactionary convention in the union's history. Of the fifty delegates, eighteen were paid officers of the union, men like Cohen, Stetsky, Rosenthal, Brownstein and other members of the right-wing machine. Most of the other delegates had only one function at the convention—to approve every proposal submitted by the machine.

By holding the convention in Chicago, the Kaufman machine had hoped to make it impossible for large groups of New York furriers to attend as visitors. In the main, the plan worked. But at a great open forum in the fur market sponsored by the left wing, the workers voted to send Ben Gold to Chicago to prefer charges of corruption, graft and gangsterism against Kaufman and his henchmen.

At the convention, the machine quickly tabled all issues which Kaufman did not want to have discussed. It shelved Max Suroff's appeal against his impeachment by the G.E.B. as an International vice-president because he had written an article in the *Freiheit* criticizing the policies of the Kaufman administration. Ben Gold's charges against Sam Cohen and A. Soifer for the assault upon him at Local 15's meeting in December 1923 were also tabled. Through some slip, Gold's charges were allowed to be read in part. But before the reading was completed, Meyer London interrupted the proceedings and advised Kaufman to stop the speaker. Not only were the charges tabled, but Gold was even forbidden to attend the remaining sessions as a visitor. And, after taking

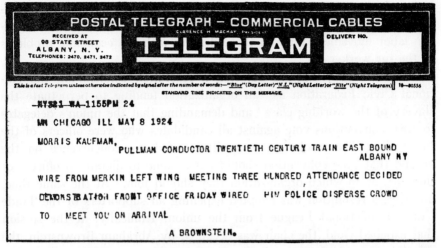

POSTAL TELEGRAPH – COMMERCIAL CABLES

CLARENCE H MACKAY, PRESIDENT

TELEGRAM

RECEIVED AT
98 STATE STREET
ALBANY, N. Y.
TELEPHONES: 2470, 2471, 2472

DELIVERY NO.

This is a fast Telegram unless otherwise indicated by signal after the number of words:—"*Blue*"(Day Letter)"*N.L.*"(Night Letter)or"*Nite*"(Night Telegram) 10—80556
STANDARD TIME INDICATED ON THIS MESSAGE.

-NY521 WA-1155PM 24

MN CHICAGO ILL MAY 8 1924

MORRIS KAUFMAN,
          PULLMAN CONDUCTOR TWENTIETH CENTURY TRAIN EAST BOUND
                                                    ALBANY NY

WIRE FROM MERKIN LEFT WING MEETING THREE HUNDRED ATTENDANCE DECIDED
DEMONSTRATION FRONT OFFICE FRIDAY WIRED HIM POLICE DISPERSE CROWD
TO MEET YOU ON ARRIVAL
                        A BROWNSTEIN.

*Brownstein, attending the Chicago convention, calls in police
to stop a rank-and-file demonstration against the machine.*

such actions, the convention blandly adopted a resolution condemning
"all forms of dictatorship."

The report of the General Executive Board, a fat document of seventy-
nine pages, was hurriedly read to the delegates, and speedily adopted.
When some of the delegates criticized the officials for failing to provide
copies of the report in advance, and complained that they did not understand most of the contents, they were told that they "should have listened
to the reading of the report and they would then be acquainted with the
contents." Delegate Steinberg of Local 40 in Toronto asked about the
elections in New York, where it was reported left-wing candidates had
been removed from the ballot. He also inquired why the report had made
no mention of the fact that a great number of fur workers had been
beaten by gangsters in New York. Steinberg was promptly labeled
a tool of "the agents of Moscow." Later, the right-wing machine explained that "due to his poverty of outlook on life and his general inexperience, Steinberg fell an easy victim to the wily agents of the foreign
group."

The International had spent over $313,000 in the two years since the
last convention. But when a delegate asked for a detailed examination
of the financial report, the machine answered by calling for a "vote of
confidence" in Kaufman and his administration. The vote was quickly
secured.

Over a hundred resolutions were jammed through in less than five hours. As was to be expected, much more time was devoted to resolutions denouncing the Soviet Union and the left-wing forces in the American labor movement than on those dealing with the economic problems of the fur workers.

The right-wing machine rejected a resolution condemning the National Civic Federation as "an organization tending to perpetuate the slavery of the working class" and demanding that the union's delegates to AFL conventions vote against all candidates who were officers of the Federation. The resolutions committee voted non-concurrence on the ground that "the convention should not assume to dictate to officers of the AFL as to which organization they should join." At the same time, however, a resolution was adopted expelling all supporters of the Trade Union Educational League from the union. Ironically, at the session that expelled Gold, the chair was occupied by Abraham Brownstein, the third vice-president.

The right-wing machine appropriated $100 for the "political prisoners" of Soviet Russia; at the very same time an appeal for aid to Sacco and Vanzetti was not acted upon, but referred to the G.E.B.

Without consulting the members of the union and without the slightest discussion at the convention, the machine drastically amended the constitution. Having already outlawed membership in the TUEL, the machine put through a constitutional amendment calculated to suppress all opposition. It empowered the G.E.B. to suspend or expel any member "who attempts or takes part in a protest meeting or unauthorized meeting against the union, or anyone who will slander or libel the union or the officialdom."

A significant section was added to the constitutional provision dealing with charges and trials. The new section permitted charges to be tried by the Joint Board or a committee of the Joint Board instead of a committee selected by the local. By hastily amending the constitution *after* the left-wingers had been suspended, the right-wing machine confirmed the left-wing charge that the New York Joint Board had acted unconstitutionally in suspending Gold and other left-wingers for their refusal to appear before its Grievance Committee to answer charges against them.

The convention continued the existing Board in office, adding Sam Gurwitz, a Kaufman supporter, to take the place made vacant by the impeachment of Vice-President Suroff. Kaufman closed the convention accepting his re-election as president "as an endorsement of my policies as president of the International Union."

So outraged were the workers by the actions of this convention that the officers did not dare to submit a report to the local unions for approval.

The New York fur workers quickly demonstrated what they thought of Kaufman's policies. Defying the constitutional amendment of expulsion for attending meetings where the leadership's policies were criticized, over one thousand fur workers were present at a meeting in Webster Hall on May 25, called by the Furriers Section of the TUEL.

Gold described how the right-wing machine at the convention had cut off discussion on real problems facing the fur workers, how constitutional amendments and resolutions had been jammed through without discussion, how the convention ignored unemployment and other pressing issues in the trade. Gold closed his report with a challenge: "We want Kaufman to know that neither he nor the *Forward*, nor the entire bureaucracy, will crush our belief in our cause."

Resolutions adopted by acclamation at the meeting declared the fur workers' protest "against the despotic laws and regulations created at the convention; against the neglect of their tasks and duties to the workers by the union officials, particularly at this critical time; against the dictatorship which our officers have set up in our union; against the fact that certain individuals use the union for their own personal ends."

In the next few months, the supporters of the left wing grew into thousands. The fur workers were fed up with the complete failure and bankruptcy of the right-wing machine.

"Inside of one year," Gold predicted on his return from the Chicago convention, "this International will collapse and the left wing will take over." An outburst of merriment from the right wing greeted this prediction. The *Forward* pointed to Gold's remark as proof of the arrogance and stupidity of the left wing. "Here is a strong International union with twelve thousand members, a treasury, and agreements with employers, and this young, arrogant leftist is stupid enough to predict that within a year it will collapse and its leadership be replaced. It is pointless to argue with such stupidity."

Exactly one year later, in May 1925, the right-wing machine was to be kicked out of the New York Joint Board and Ben Gold elected manager. Six months after that, at a special convention in Boston, Kaufman was to be removed as International president.

CHAPTER 15

The Revolt
of the Workers

The fur market seethed with rising indignation in the spring of 1924. The long-repressed wrath and bitterness of the fur workers swelled higher with every new outrage of the strong-arm regime in control of the union. Rallying around the left wing, the workers' resistance stiffened and sharpened daily. The sluggers attacked, the workers fought back. Even when they were mauled and bruised, and their heads bandaged, the workers walked about the market boldly, ready to hit back against their attackers. They took plenty of punishment, but they learned how to dish it out too. Before long, the sluggers even began to be careful about appearing alone in the market.

The district began to hum and sizzle with new life. There was a new confidence, enthusiasm and determination. An exhilarating fighting spirit —planted and carefully cultivated by the militant left-wing leaders— swept through the ranks of the workers. Kaufman, secluded in the International office in Long Island City, trembled at the growing resistance of the furriers. "At present we have our hands full of various difficulties and troubles," he complained in a letter on May 29, 1924.

Kaufman's "hearty cooperation" with the employers was bearing bitter fruit. The number of unemployed union members increased. Contractors were busy, working until late in the night with non-union help, while thousands of union workers remained without jobs for seven and eight months at a time. Those in the shops, straining to keep up with the speedup, were uncertain of their jobs. The worker unwilling to take a wage cut would be replaced by a new worker from the army of unemployed. It was a miracle to find a shop where the minimum wage scale was being enforced.

To stop the influx of new workers used by the employers to break down the existing wage scales, the local unions had voted to limit the number of learners. But the Kaufman administration was more interested in a big income from selling learners' permits and union books than in maintaining wage standards. At every session of the Joint Board's executive committee a long line of new workers would form outside of the meeting room, waiting for their chance to obtain a union book. Agents of the strong-arm squad went down the line. Those workers who were ready to pay $100 would be brought before the executive committee for a favorable decision. When the meeting was over, the "boys" would retire to the washroom and divide the take. A certain percentage was usually set aside for the "outside" underworld leaders.

With the union officials doing nothing to help the unemployed, the workers under left-wing leadership began to take matters into their own hands. On June 2, 1924, a great mass demonstration of unemployed workers was called by the Furriers Section of the TUEL. With Ben Gold and other left-wingers leading the way, the unemployed furriers marched to the union headquarters. Manager Brownstein, caught by surprise, was forced to permit them to meet in the union office. The building was packed with workers. Hundreds who could not get in waited in the street for a report.

Gold spoke for the unemployed, putting forward demands for action that had been set forth in numerous leaflets issued by the left wing. He proposed that the union set aside $50,000 from its treasury for loans to unemployed furriers, to be paid back as soon as they began to work. A second proposal called for the immediate election of a rank-and-file committee of one hundred who, working without pay, would visit all shops under the union's direction, and see to it that only union workers were employed. This action would result in obtaining jobs for hundreds of union members.

Brownstein hedged on the question of loans, arguing that the Joint Board would have to discuss the matter. But he was unable to get around the second demand, and a committee of one hundred was elected on the spot. Brownstein promised that he would have credentials, and the names of the shops to be inspected, ready for the committee the next morning.

When the volunteers came to the union headquarters the following morning, a squad of strong-arm men stood at the door and blocked the entrance. Anxious to avert a bloody battle, the committee elected two delegates to speak to the manager. Brownstein told the delegates that President Kaufman had forbidden him to deal with the committee of one hundred on the ground that it was unconstitutional.

The rank-and-file furriers began to shout their defiance at local meetings. When the strong-arm gang would snarl, "Sit down or we'll knock you down," workers would stand up and shout in a chorus, "O.K., let's see you try it." Sluggers approached Jack Schneider (one of the leading rank-and-filers) at a meeting of Local 1. In an instant, a group of cutters leaped to their feet and cried, "We dare you to lay a hand on Schneider." The gang beat a hasty retreat.

Jack Schneider was born in Bessarabia in 1897. He migrated to Palestine where, as a construction worker, he became a union member. He aroused the opposition of the union leadership when he came out in favor of unity between the Jewish and Arabian workers. Schneider emigrated to the United States, arriving in New York in 1921. He went to work in the fur industry as an operator and joined the union. In 1922 he had the first of hundreds of encounters with the strong-arm men of the Welfare Club who had the workers terrorized. He soon allied himself with the left-wing forces.

In 1924, Schneider became a cutter and joined Local 1. He quickly won the admiration of the workers, who looked to him for leadership in the struggle against the machine. Never having been suspended, he was able to fight at union meetings for the left-wing program. And day in and day out, he kept talking to the workers in the market, urging them to resist the machine and to unite, regardless of political belief, for a clean, democratic union.

A strong bond of solidarity, friendship, loyalty for one another and readiness to sacrifice in the common struggle was emerging among the rank-and-file fur workers. The machine was tottering. At a meeting of Local 5, on June 5, an election was held for temporary secretary of the local. An opposition candidate was elected by the vote of the majority of the members. Nevertheless, in typical fashion, the officers declared that he had been defeated, and announced the election of the machine's candidate. One worker, unable to restrain himself, shouted that the officers had no right to rob the members of their vote. Several of the sluggers immediately rushed to attack him. Instantly, the rest of the workers arose to his defense, and a terrific battle broke out. Many workers came to the market the next day with bandages on their heads, but the mood was, "We shall fight it out, even if it costs us our lives."

Local 1's meeting on June 11 was the scene of another battle between the workers and the "organization" committee. As soon as the chairman opened the meeting, the workers shouted: "Admit Gold and Shapiro." A motion to admit them was immediately carried. Thereupon Manager Brownstein declared that the vote was unconstitutional since the officers had suspended Gold and Shapiro for two years. The workers insisted on again putting the motion to a vote—the result was 146 for and 26 against admitting Gold and Shapiro to the meeting. Brownstein ordered the meeting closed and the lights turned out immediately. Instead of disbanding, however, the furriers moved to another hall, and unanimously adopted a resolution protesting the decision of the officers to bar Gold and Shapiro from meetings "simply because they have the courage to criticize the actions of the officers." Thus the pattern was set and it continued from week to week. Soon Kaufman and his henchmen simply gave up the idea of holding union meetings altogether.

Prevented from holding forums in the union office and from attending local meetings, the workers came in increasing numbers to the open forums sponsored by the Furriers Section of the TUEL. They knew that here they could express themselves freely without reprisals. These forums imbued the workers with greater courage to fight back against the reign of terror. The workers themselves contributed nickels and dimes to pay for the leaflets and for the rent of the halls. They were both amused and indignant to read in the *Forward* that the money was coming "from Moscow." Strong-arm squads had to go into the shops to force the furriers to pay their union dues, but the same furriers willingly contributed the cost of meetings and circulars sponsored by the left wing. They even paid the fines imposed on left-wingers by the right-wing machine.

The entire picture in the New York Joint Board began to change during the summer and fall of 1924. Even Socialist supporters of Kaufman were beginning to criticize the scandalous situation in the Furriers Union. Late in October, William Karlin, a leader of the Party who had helped the fur workers repeatedly in the 1912 strike, was speaking at an open-air election rally in an area where many fur workers lived. A well-known labor lawyer and brilliant speaker, Karlin attacked the "crooked officers" of the Furriers Union, and charged that Kaufman and his machine had "succeeded in depleting the treasury to such an extent that this Union is now on the verge of insolvency." Karlin's remark was wildly applauded by many Socialist fur workers who had formerly supported the right-wing machine.

Under the terrific pressure of the rising resistance of the workers, which was now spreading even into the ranks of former Kaufman supporters, the machine began to crack. "Things are not running smooth in New York," Kaufman wrote to Philip Silberstein late in May 1924, "and there is a great deal of patching up work that has to be done now amongst our own people. . . ." A short while later, Stetsky urged Kaufman to return immediately from Portland, where he was attending the AFL convention, in order to put down a minor revolt in the machine. "The situation in New York (I mean the political)," Stetsky wrote, "is

Socialist leaders repudiate Karlin's attack on "crooked officers" and reassure "Comrade Kaufman" of continued "pleasant relations."

Phone Stuyvesant 4620   Socialist Party Local New York

7 East 15th Street

For Governor
Norman Thomas

October 25, 1924

Morris Kaufman, Gen. Pres.,
Fur Workers' Union,
9 Jackson Avenue,
Long Island City, N.Y.

Dear Comrade Kaufman:

Replying to your letter of the 23rd inst., permit me to say that I am calling personally on Comrade Karlin and the other candidates and speakers in that section. I will take up with them the complaint in your letter and I want to assure you and the entire Fur Workers' Union and other unions that we will not permit the Socialist platform to be used to make attacks upon organizations of this kind. I sincerely regret that anything has happened to mar the pleasant relations that have so long existed between the Fur Workers and the Party, and I shall do everything in my power to prevent these relations becoming strained, and I want to assure you not only the position of the Party is against such attacks, but I personally feel that we must not have a repitation of them, and that the Party must work to get the good will not only of our progressive unions but eventually of the union movement, in that I feel we will have the fullest cooperation of the Fur Workers Union, and surely we will endeavor to merit it.

Thanking you for the very pleasant way you have taken this matter up and also for the many considerations you have given the Party in the past, I am

Fraternally yours,

SOCIALIST PARTY, LOCAL NEW YORK,

ACTING SECRETARY

not very encouraging. . . . Last Tuesday Sam [Cohen] and Alex [Fried] had a scrap and it raised quite a rumpus. . . . The Bunch here is very anxious to have you come back. They imagine that you can whip things into shape."

In this situation, a new group, seeking to utilize the discontent of the workers for their own advantage, began to play an independent role in the union. Hyman Sorkin, the leader of this group, had been head of the Picketing Committee during the 1920 strike. For several years after the strike, Sorkin had been away from the industry, busy with the bakery that he bought. In the late spring of 1924, he returned to the fur trade. But Sam Cohen, Abraham Brownstein, Charles Stetsky, Harry Begoon, Alex Fried and others had taken over and did not want Sorkin as a partner. Sorkin, Oizer Shachtman, Isidor Winnick, Jacob Strauss and others of the cracking right-wing machine, who saw in the rising wrath of the workers an opportunity to take over for themselves, organized a so-called "Progressive" group.

The "Progressives" realized that their only chance of gaining control of the union was by working with the left wing, which had the support of the workers. Together with the left wing they could revive the confidence of the workers in the union and carry an election against Kaufman. Without the cooperation of the left-wing, they would get only contempt from the workers.

In July 1924 the "Progressives," therefore, took the first step by asking the leaders of the left wing for their support in the forthcoming elections for local officers and delegates to the Joint Board. They promised that they would not deal with the strong-arm committee, and they agreed to allow the left wing to draw up the program of a united front, provided they were assured of a number of important paid positions.

Some among the left-wingers opposed a united front with the Sorkin group. These said it would violate the principles of the left wing to make a "partnership" with Sorkin. They preferred to remain "Simon-pure" even at the risk of permitting a new corrupt strong-arm group to form.

Gold led the move in the left-wing camp for the united front. He agreed with everything that was said about the past role of Sorkin, Shachtman, Wohl, Winnick and the other "Progressive" leaders. Nevertheless, he argued, the united front was essential to save the union from the clutches of the right-wing Socialists of the Kaufman machine, the *Forward* crowd and the underworld. The united-front program would embody the policies for which the left wing had been fighting. It would be up to the workers to compel adherence to the program, Gold insisted.

"We will tell the workers precisely on what conditions we are having unity and indicate clearly that while we are uniting on a minimum program, the left wing will not abandon its broader and more comprehensive program for the workers," declared Gold. "As we fight for the workers' interests, we will make our position clear at all times. Understanding this, the workers themselves will help us thwart any attempts of the Sorkins and Shachtmans to go back on their pledges."

After much discussion, Gold's position was upheld, and the left wing agreed to join the united front. The decision showed that the left-wingers had matured politically in the course of the past few years' struggle. In 1921, the left-wingers had refused to take union positions as paid officers. They had left these posts in the hands of Brownstein and other middle-of-the-roaders. In 1925, having learned from experience that the Brownstein group could not be depended upon to carry on a consistent struggle for clean and progressive trade unionism, the left-wingers understood the necessity of taking a direct part in the union leadership. They now realized that it would require a constant struggle to clean up the union. The only assurance that this struggle would ultimately be successful was if the mass of workers themselves were drawn into it.

The left wing supported the "Progressive" candidates. As a result, a large bloc was elected and the Sorkin-Winnick-Shachtman group gained a majority in the Joint Board. As one of the first moves to prove their sincerity, this "Progressive" majority reinstated Ben Gold in November 1924, with full rights of membership. The action was almost unanimously approved by three of the four locals in the Joint Board. Immediately afterwards, Gold was elected to the executive board of Local 1. He was now again able to function in an official capacity.

The right-wing machine in the International moved swiftly to nullify the decision of the Joint Board locals. At its meeting in Montreal in January 1925, the G.E.B. ruled that "Brother Gold stands suspended, but he may appeal to the General Executive Board if he so desires." As far as the workers and the "Progressive" leaders of the Joint Board were concerned, however, the suspension was a thing of the past. Gradually, other ousted left-wingers were reinstated over the International's opposition.

The "Progressives" also agreed to fulfill the demand of the left-wingers for a thorough investigation of the widespread corruption in the Joint Board. In November 1924, the Joint Board appointed a committee to investigate irregularities in the issuance of membership books. The committee, composed of a majority of "Progressives," obtained affidavits from several workers and employers which proved all that the left-wingers had been charging for years. The strong-arm men had taken union books and dues stamps from the finance office and sold them like so much merchandise outside the union. They got money for beating up workers. They collected money from non-union workers in the shops. One worker testified that he had paid $99 to his boss for a book.

An employer told the committee how he had obtained a union book for a worker in his shop:

"I met the man on Sixth Avenue, and I asked him if he could do anything for this fellow, if he could get him a union book."

"Q. What made you ask that man that question?"

"A. I know he hangs out in the union and that he could probably do something. He told me that he will let me know. He later called me on the phone and told me that he got a book and asked me the man's name."

"Q. When he called you up to find out the name of the man for whom you wanted the book it was only natural for you to know what the price of the book would be."

"A. He asked $65. He brought up the book to the office and gave it to the girl."

There had never before been an investigation. The deeper the committee probed, the more it became obvious that they were dealing with an organized system of corruption. To get to the root of the evil, the committee resolved to investigate the entire financial structure of the Joint Board, the operation of the manager's office and all other cogs in the machine.

At this point, Kaufman decided to put himself at the head of the investigation, in order to control and divert it. He was afraid that the investigation might develop into a probe of Kaufman's own finances within the G.E.B. He, therefore, became the "investigator."

After consulting Meyer London, Kaufman issued a statement which for sheer double-talk has seldom been equalled. He had been concerned for years over the "irregularities and dishonest practices of certain individuals," who "committed improper, dishonest and wrongful acts against the organization and individual applicants for membership." He welcomed the investigation. He and other International officers had waited patiently for the Joint Board to "prosecute those guilty of the crime of stealing and selling union books and taking commission or graft from applicants." But since no action had been taken, the International felt that "it was its painful duty to step into this situation, to make an end to a condition of terror, to rid the union of such elements, to go through with a thorough investigation of all wrong and ill practices, to try to prosecute those who are guilty and to safeguard the interests and well-being of the members as individuals and the organization as a whole."

With Kaufman conducting his own "investigation" the Joint Board Committee continued its work. Two weeks after the investigators began delving into the operations of the manager's office, Abraham Brownstein submitted his resignation.

Before accepting the resignation, the investigators continued their probing. On April 15, Brownstein testified before a joint committee of the International and the Joint Board. The testimony, corroborated by documentary evidence, proved conclusively that for several years Brownstein had taken sums of money from workers who wanted to join the union. He had issued signed receipts without the authority of the Joint Board or the local executive boards, but the money went into his own pocket. It was proved that this stealing had been going on since October 1922, a few months after Brownstein had broken openly with the left-wing forces and allied himself with the right-wing machine.

Brownstein himself confessed these facts. He pleaded, however, that he had fallen a victim to the machine. He insisted that everything he had done had been with the knowledge of Abe Rosenthal, secretary-treasurer of the Joint Board and one of Kaufman's strongest supporters. He admitted that the money should have gone into the union's treasury. Rosenthal told the committee he had not considered it his duty to report such matters to the Joint Board.

The next morning the Joint Board accepted Brownstein's resignation. The "Progressives" were none too anxious to proceed further against Brownstein for fear of what he might reveal about their own connections with the machine.

On the day that Brownstein left the union, the Joint Board appointed a management committee of five consisting of Harry Begoon, chairman of the Board, Jacob Strauss, Philip Stefanesco, Oizer Shachtman and Ben Wexler. With Shachtman as acting manager, the committee would run the union until elections were held.

Kaufman and his associates had felt no hesitation in throwing Brownstein overboard. They hoped that with this action the investigation would be stopped from going into Kaufman's activities. As Jack Millstein, Kaufman's lieutenant in Chicago, put it in sustaining Brownstein's removal as International vice-president: "Let us hope that this incident will soon be forgotten by our membership."

But the "incident" was not forgotten by the furriers. A jammed membership meeting of Locals 1, 5, 10 and 15, the first mass meeting in five years, was held in Cooper Union on April 25. The object of the meeting was to report to the membership on Brownstein's resignation and the appointment of the management committee.

Harry Begoon was chairman, and Kaufman was sitting on the platform. Oizer Shachtman, of the Sorkin group, opened with a lukewarm talk. As soon as he finished, Gold asked for the floor. Since Gold had again been declared "suspended" by Kaufman, Begoon refused to recognize him. Immediately, the meeting was afire. Bedlam broke loose. The workers jumped to their feet angrily and began to shout: "Give him the floor." "Let him talk." "To hell with them." For half an hour the meeting was in a turmoil, the shouting continuing. Begoon couldn't stop it. At previous local meetings, the right-wing leaders had adjourned in the face of such a storm. But here they were afraid that the left wing and the "Progressives" would take over and continue the meeting.

It was a contest between the infuriated mass of workers and the machine—and the rage of the workers broke the backbone of the machine, which had been dictating to them for years. Gold spoke for about fifteen minutes. His every word was an indictment of the whole system of corruption in the union. He gave expression to the bitterness of the workers for their years of suffering at the hands of the strong-arm sluggers, how they had been betrayed in the shops, how they had been beaten on the streets and in the union. He unmasked the grafters and their system of terror in the union. And he concluded with a fervent call to the workers to unite their ranks to clean up the union. Before he was through, he had sealed the doom of the right-wing machine.

Kaufman got up to speak. The workers would not let him. "Get out of this union," they shouted angrily. Again and again Kaufman attempted to speak. Each time the workers drowned him out. He stood on the platform five minutes, ten minutes, fifteen minutes. His face turned purple, then pale. Still the workers would not let him talk.

Finally, Gold mounted the platform again. There was an outburst of cheering. Gold began to plead with the workers, in the name of democracy, to let Kaufman speak. Hundreds of workers shouted back: "Don't do it, Gold." "Are you getting soft?" But Gold repeated: "Give him a chance. Maybe it's his last speech. Maybe he just wants to say good-bye."

The meeting finally quieted down. Kaufman rose to speak. He began with his usual tirade about "agents of Moscow," "Foster's agents" and so on. But no sooner had his first red-baiting words been spoken, than the workers again stopped him cold. Red-baiting was more than they could take. Kaufman had to give it up. He was finished.

The meeting went on to adopt a number of resolutions by unanimous vote. One resolution, into which was poured the accumulated hatred of the workers, condemned "the system of dictatorship" which had existed for years, "which distinguished itself with a policy of unwarranted persecutions and expulsions." Another resolution demanded immediate reinstatement of all suspended workers.

Immediately after the Cooper Union meeting, the management commitee of the Joint Board proceeded to take further steps to clean up the union. A trial found Abe Rosenthal guilty of neglect of duty in having failed to report Brownstein's stealing. Over Kaufman's objections, Rosenthal was suspended as secretary-treasurer of the Joint Board, the office he had held for over twelve years.

Stuart Chase, certified public accountant for the Labor Bureau and noted economist, was engaged to make an examination of the books and records of the Joint Board since 1922. After only a brief investigation, Chase reported many discrepancies in the union's finances: "Large donations and appropriations are being made without proper record in the minutes of the Joint Board. . . . There has been a very serious increase in expenses during the past three years without a corresponding increase in income. . . . There is a strange difference in the balance between stamps and dues—amounting to over 26,000 stamps."

One of the items in Stuart Chase's report aroused especial indignation. Money contributed by the fur workers to assist strikes of other unions had never been contributed to the strikers. A special assessment had raised a fund to help the steel strike of 1919, but "nothing was paid to the steel workers." Thus, it appeared that not only had Gompers and the AFL sabotaged the great steel strike led by William Z. Foster in 1919, but the corrupt leaders of the Furriers Union had actually stolen the money collected for the strikers' relief!

Seven thousand dollars had been collected to aid the 1922 miners' strike, but only $2,000 went to the miners. "Thus, the Joint Board seems to have a habit of collecting special assessments for beneficiaries," Chase concluded, "from which the beneficiaries receive no benefit!"

Since the management committee was only intended to be a temporary body, the Joint Board now decided to hold elections towards the end of May. Kaufman insisted on postponing the election until July and threatened that it was "illegal." The Joint Board nevertheless went ahead with its plans.

This was no ordinary election. The united front between the left wing and the "Progressives" in the Furriers Union was an historic event in the American labor movement. It was the first achieved since the formation of the TUEL.

In conferences between the "Progressives" and the left wing, it was decided that Gold should draw up the program of the united front. Of the eight business agents to be elected, five would be from the "Progressives" and three from the left wing. Gold agreed to become manager of the Joint Board. Sorkin was to be the assistant manager, and Shachtman the secretary-treasurer. Of the other officials, seven would be "Progressives" and three, left-wingers.

The united-front program, released to the fur workers by a united-front committee,* was based on five points:

"1) The united front pledges to do everything possible to do away with the terroristic methods which have ruled the union in the hands of the former administration.

"2) To establish a completely democratic system of elections and action of officers, assuring the complete right of the members to differences of opinion and complete freedom to express these opinions as well as complete responsibility for organizational activities on the part of the administration to the membership.

"3) To remove from power every person found guilty of breaking of union principles, in order to do away with corruption in the union.

"4) The recognition of the right of every member to belong to whichever political party he chooses.

"5) The united front pledges to mobilize every capable union member to assure and improve the economic conditions of the fur workers."

The Furriers Section of the TUEL endorsed the united-front program and spelled it out even further. The left wing proposed to eliminate "grafters and shady persons from union activities"; dismiss shop chairmen who betrayed the workers; elect "shop committees who will protect the workers' union conditions in the shop"; dissolve local executive boards "who are under charges of graft"; organize "the devoted union members into a permanent organization committee"; remove "the gangsters from the local meetings and union committees"; enforce the agreement and force the bosses to register their contractors; launch a campaign

* The united-front committee consisted of Max Schlossberg, Louis Weiser, Alter Newman and Max Goldfield. All had formerly supported Kaufman.

"to defeat the contractors and do away with the contracting evil"; call regular local and membership meetings; clean out "the filthy and unsanitary sweatshops and firetraps"; reinstate the honest and able active union workers who were "illegally expelled from the union."

The left wing declared: "The united front will do its utmost to do away with the tactics and systems of graft, betrayal and lack of union discipline. The united front will do its utmost to protect the workers from unnecessary and wrong oppression, punishment, insult and terror. The right of free speech and criticism, the rights of the members to belong to whichever political group they desire is the fundamental principle and guarantee of the united front. These principles the united front pledges to uphold. The united front pledges to do everything within their power to improve the economic conditions of the workers."

At the same time, the left wing also pointed out that it still maintained its own far-reaching principles that went beyond the points agreed upon in the united-front program. These included amalgamation of all needle trades unions and political organization of the workers in a great farmer-labor party.

The following candidates for business agents were endorsed by the united front: Local 1—Ben Gold and I. Winnick; Local 5—Aaron Gross and M. Goldfield; Local 10—B. Wexler and I. Wohl; Local 15—Fanny Warshafsky and J. Strauss.

On May 23, 1925, the most important election in the history of the Furriers Union up to this date took place. Held under the supervision of representatives of the American Civil Liberties Union, it was the first honest and orderly election in the Joint Board in many years. Four thousand workers poured out to vote. After casting their ballots, hundreds of furriers remained near the union headquarters for hours to hear the results. A tremendous shout of joy greeted the announcement that every candidate endorsed by the united-front committee had been elected by an overwhelming majority.

A few days later came the announcement that the Joint Board had elected Ben Gold as manager. On the day of installation of officers, the platform at Webster Hall was a veritable garden. It was completely banked with flowers, the joyful greetings of the triumphant workers. After years of intense struggle, the New York fur workers had taken the first great step toward freeing their union from the Kaufman machine.

CHAPTER 16

United-Front Administration

Incredible difficulties confronted the new united-front administration of the New York Joint Board. Almost all of the shops were disorganized. Wages were at the lowest level in years. A large number of contracting shops and all the Greek shops were filled with non-union workers. Many manufacturers in Association shops were contemptuously ignoring the agreement, while paying tribute to hoodlums for "protection" against the union.

The Joint Board and the local executives were still infested with strong-arm men, who were not going to give up their graft without a terrific battle. Admitting that the problem was serious, the "Progressive" leaders urged Gold to wait until the July elections before taking any step to clean out the gangsters. But at a meeting of the Joint Board, Gold recommended that he, as manager, be authorized to take immediate action. Every member of the Joint Board voted for the proposal, the strong-arm men laughing and enjoying the prospect of an early defeat for this young left-wing upstart who dared to challenge their power.

But the very next day the laughter died on their lips. All the local executive boards met that day. Over three hundred furriers were milling around the union headquarters waiting for union books. Suddenly the line parted outside the room where Local 5's Executive Board was meeting, and Ben Gold entered the room. He picked up the union records lying on the table and told the stunned members of the Executive Board: "You are not going to meet any more. I place all of you under charges of graft." As he left the room, the union books in hand, Gold informed the waiting workers that they should return next week to apply for membership in the union. Gold went from one executive-board meeting to another, repeating this procedure. Inside of twenty minutes, all the union records were deposited in Gold's desk.

It took but a few moments for the strong-arm men to recover from the shock of this bold action. Suddenly, with "Big Alex" in the lead, they rushed into Gold's office and demanded the union books. Gold answered that he had been given full power to handle the matter. At the same time he handed them written charges of corruption calling upon them to answer before the proper union body. He also informed them that they had a right to appeal to the Joint Board. The Joint Board could, if it wished, decide to give them the union books.

"Big Alex" threatened, "If you don't put the books in our hands, we'll put you in the hospital and bust up this office."

Taking his watch out of his pocket, Gold calmly replied: "If you don't clear out of this office in three minutes, we'll see who'll land in the hospital." He opened the door to the foyer and raised his voice: "What do you say, are you leaving?"

When the workers in the foyer heard Gold raise his voice, they rushed toward his door. The gangsters in Gold's office cowered with fear. They were ready to forget their own threats. All they wanted now was to get out safely. And looking at the crowd of workers, they knew they couldn't. Desperate, they turned to Gold and begged him to get them through safely.

And so, to prevent the bloodshed which he knew was inevitable, Gold escorted the gang through a narrow lane formed by the workers. Only his strict order held the workers back. Within ten minutes, the whole incident was over.

There were other showdowns with the gangsters before they learned that the union office had become an unhealthy spot for them. On one occasion, as Gold returned from settling an important complaint with an employer, he found several hundred workers congregated outside the union building. Stetsky and a strong-arm squad had occupied the office! Police in front of the building had refused to do anything about it.

Gold went in and told the gang: "I give you five minutes to get out. If not, the workers will put you out." He counted off the minutes. One minute. Two, three. Four! Five! The workers moved into the room, grabbed one gangster and threw him out bodily on the sidewalk. The rest of the gang didn't wait longer. They ran.

Every day, promptly at twelve noon, hundreds of workers came to the union office to protect their organization from the gangsters. At night, after work, they would be back again, prepared to fight off any attack. The executive boards remained dissolved. At local meetings, each attended by over fifteen hundred workers, Gold's action was approved. The beginning of the end of the reign of terror was at hand.

Some two weeks later, several gangsters swaggered into Gold's office. Pulling a gun from his pocket, the leader of the gang demanded "back pay" due them from the union. He insisted that the union owed thousands of dollars to the strong-arm men for past "services" rendered. Gold coldly informed the gangsters that he had not hired them, and that if they wanted payment they should go to the men who had used their services. "Give us the money or we shoot," the gangster snarled.

While this drama was unfolding in the union office, a signal had been flashed to the market and shops. Hundreds of workers dropped their tools and rushed to the union office. They seized the gangsters, disarmed them, and drove them toward the stairway. On the stairs, scores of other workers gave the gangsters a taste of their wrath. Their clothes torn to shreds, their faces and bodies mauled and bleeding, the gangsters finally staggered out of the building and collapsed in the street.

Defeated, the strong-arm men still tried to make a deal with Gold. If they were paid off, they would remain neutral. Nothing doing, was the reply! If they were put back on the payroll, they would help the left wing against the right wing. Again: Nothing doing! Gold had only one answer to all their propositions—get out and stay out, and if you don't, the workers will make you regret it. And the workers' guard outside the union office, day in and day out, made the Furriers Union out-of-bounds for any strong-arm squads.

Having thrown the strong-arm men out of the union the new leadership decided to push the drive for July increases, to organize the Greek workers, and to begin a campaign against contractors. To do this required an extraordinary mobilization of the workers. For this reason, a mass demonstration was called for June 23, at four o'clock, two hours before the usual quitting time.

The trade was busy on the day of the stoppage and the vast majority of the workers were employed. But when the clock struck four, the workers dropped their tools, left the shops, and marched as one man to Cooper Union. Within fifteen minutes, the workers jammed Cooper Union, Webster Hall and Astoria Hall. Unable to get in, crowds of furriers waited outside the halls for reports of the meetings.

The workers were in full swing at these meetings. With an ovation for the leadership, they roared unanimous approval of the program outlined by the union. At the same time they served notice "that the furriers are united, ready to meet all attacks from every source." The meetings adopted a resolution demanding a special convention in order to restore democracy throughout the union.

As the fur workers left the three meeting halls, many were attacked by squads of strong-arm men. Several "near-riots" took place, but the workers stood their ground and beat back their assailants. Before long, the gangsters were fleeing in wild panic, pleading for mercy.

The June 23rd stoppage proved to the employers once again that the fur workers solidly supported the united-front administration. The new administration eliminated shop chairmen who had been the tools of the bosses and replaced them with chairmen loyal to the union. Previously, no honest worker would want to be a shop chairman and associate with the right-wing machine. Now it became an honor and a real responsibility to be a shop chairman. Workers were now called to shop meetings, and they responded enthusiastically. Every night, twenty to thirty shops would meet at one time—in the brief period of four months, a total of 1,143 shop meetings took place.

Even more important than the number was the nature of the shop meetings. Previously, such meetings had been called merely to collect dues and taxes. Trade and shop questions were never taken up. The workers were afraid to raise complaints lest the strong-arm men be called in or the employers learn of it and fire them. Now it was different. The workers talked freely and brought forward their grievances. Brushing aside the strong-arm men, the union's complaint department, headed by Irving Potash, went directly to the employers and insisted upon settling every complaint.

Irving Potash was born in Russia in 1902, the son of working-class parents. He was only ten years old when his parents brought him to the United States. He attended public and high school in New York City and became active in the progressive student movement. In 1916 Potash joined the Socialist Party. Allying himself with the left wing, he became a charter member of the Communist Party after the split in the Socialist Party.

In 1919 when the notorious Palmer raids against the progressive and labor movement swept over America, Potash was arrested. He was charged with having attended a dance given by a progressive students' organization. The law upon which he was jailed was later repealed because of public protest. When he was released, Potash sought citizenship, but his efforts were rebuffed.

Potash obtained work in a fur shop, but, in 1923, anxious to complete his education, he left to enter the College of the City of New York. When his second college year ended, Potash, like many City College students, looked for work to earn money for his fall tuition. He turned first to the fur industry where he had worked years before. He went to Ben Gold and asked for a job. But there were no jobs available. Potash called at the office several times. Gold put him to work, helping out, until a shop job would come along.

Potash never returned to City College. His work as Complaint Clerk convinced Gold that he had outstanding contributions to make to the labor movement. Association with Gold, Schneider, Winogradsky and other progressives in the Furriers Union convinced Potash that he should devote himself completely to the labor movement.

For years, the manufacturers had ignored the provision in the agreement calling for July increases. Now, as July approached, the new administration started a wage drive. Shop after shop demanded collective increases ranging in many cases up to $20 a week. When the employer refused to meet the collective demands of the workers, the shop struck.

On July 9, three hundred employers of the Association met and denounced the union for encouraging the workers to demand collective wage increases. Association President Samuels called a conference and attempted to lay down the law. The shop strikes, he fumed, violated the collective agreements, and they would not be tolerated. Undisturbed, Gold replied that if the employers would abide by the agreement and grant the July raises, the union would call off the stoppages. Until then, the stoppages would continue.

Deprived of the assistance of the right-wing machine and of the strong-arm squads, there was nothing the employers could do but comply. The new administration obtained July increases totaling many thousands of dollars a week for the workers.

The month of July also saw a successful strike against more than two hundred finishing contractors employing approximately one thousand workers. The majority of these workers were not union members, yet they responded eagerly to the union's call. All efforts of the sluggers to interfere with the strike were in vain. In the course of the three-week strike, many contractors went out of business. Settlements were made with about forty, permitting them to do business until January 1, after which they would have to shut down. Manufacturers who did not have the space to do their own finishing would be allowed to send work to these shops only until January, on condition that they would be responsible for union standards within these recognized finishing shops. During the strike, moreover, wage rates were raised and back pay was collected for the workers for long-neglected complaints. Each boss had to put up a minimum of $250 in security against any future violations.

In the four-month period ending October, the united-front administration collected $23,297 in back pay for the workers for overtime, differences for working below the minimum, various wage claims and loss of time while striking. While the union collected close to $30,000 as security from employers against violations of the agreement, the united-front administration did not depend upon security money as the real guarantee of maintaining union conditions in the shops.

The rank-and-file workers became the mainstay of the organization. About three hundred volunteers, women as well as men, served without pay on the organization committee. This committee watched the shops day and night, Saturdays, Sundays and legal holidays against unauthorized overtime. They stopped over two hundred shops for working overtime and another two hundred for organizing purposes. The remarkable activity of this devoted rank-and-file organization committee was one of the proudest achievements of the new administration.

The united-front administration next undertook the organization of the Greek fur workers. For a number of years, about fifteen hundred Greek fur workers, employed in about three hundred shops, had been virtually enslaved. With many brought to this country by the Greek manufacturers under a system approaching forced labor, they were compelled to work under miserable conditions. As one Greek worker described it: "We have been living in darkness for years. We never have happiness in our lives, working from six o'clock in the morning to seven o'clock in the evening every day. . . . We never saw a holiday like other humans, we never had enough to support ourselves. . . . Family men working for $18 a week. . . ."

During the 1920 strike, a large part of the scab work was done in the Greek shops. Following that disastrous strike, many Greek shops did finishing contracting for the big manufacturers. Time and again during the Kaufman administration, resolutions were passed urging the G.E.B. to organize the Greek workers. The resolutions were simply filed and forgotten. The Greek workers were forced to endure the cruelest exploitation for years.

The united-front administration now set up a special committee to organize the Greek workers. Gold was a regular speaker at their weekly meetings, his speeches in English translated into Greek by members of the organizing committee. By August, five hundred Greek furriers were attending meetings. The Joint Board reduced the initiation fee to one-third of the regular amount. Greek workers began to fill out membership cards and assist in the organizing campaign.

On Tuesday, October 27, the call was issued for a general strike in the Greek shops. The demands of the union were a forty-four-hour week, pay for ten legal holidays, time-and-a-half for overtime, a minimum scale of wages, and all other union conditions prevailing in the industry.

The next morning, fifteen hundred Greek fur workers conducted a magnificent demonstration on the picket line. They proved themselves militant strikers, and put everything they had into the strike. Many pickets were clubbed by the police and several were arrested. But their enthusiasm for the strike swept over all obstacles. The shops continued to be picketed day and night.*

The Greek employers formed an Association to break the strike. Spreading false rumors combined with threats, the Association told the Greek strikers they had been duped by "Jewish propaganda." Gold exposed this trickery with a pledge that the Joint Board would "carry on the struggle as long as necessary and money will be no object in making the Greek fur workers an organized power in the industry along with their Jewish fellow workers who are standing shoulder to shoulder with them."

The ten-day general strike of the Greek workers ended in complete victory. On November 4, the union signed closed shop agreements with the majority of the Greek manufacturers. The workers won all their demands, including substantial wage increases. The agreements would expire on January 31, 1926, together with the contract of the Associated Fur Manufacturers. Negotiations with the Greek manufacturers would

---

* Among the most active leaders of the Greek strikers were John Papagianos, Tom Pappas, Vasiliki Maliaron, George Arvanitis, Steve Leondopoulos, James Stephenson, John Demelis, Louis Hatchios, Gus Rossios, Anthony Julios, Harry Parrisis, Aristides Sotiropoulos and A. Payvouris.

then be conducted simultaneously with the Associated Fur Manufacturers.

The news that the agreements had been concluded was flashed to the fifteen hundred Greek workers waiting anxiously outside the conference hall. Instantly, a joyous victory parade began. Many of them dressed in native costume, they marched through the market with banners and placards proclaiming their victory. As they paraded through the streets, they received a stirring ovation from the Jewish workers.

The victory was a triumph for the united-front administration, for it had clearly demonstrated that it could carry through the left-wing program of organizing the unorganized. Moreover, the organization of the Greek shops placed the union in a stronger position in the impending big battle with the employers. As *Women's Wear* observed:

"In the trade it is declared that the successful culmination of the Union's drive on the Greek shops will make its position much stronger when it meets the employers across the conference table in December to work out a new agreement.

"During the strike of 1920, it is pointed out, by far the greater part of the production that helped break the strike came from the Greek shops. Should there be a strike because of the failure to reach an agreement to replace the one expiring by limitation on December 31, the union will be in a much stronger position with the Greek workers organized than it has been in strikes heretofore."

At the same time that it wrought all these remarkable changes in the conduct of the union, the united-front administration was forced to wage a ceaseless struggle against the slanders and attacks of the manufacturers, the *Forward* and the right-wing machine in the International. The right-wing machine tried to obstruct the Joint Board's organization work by calling separate meetings under the protection of the strong-arm men, breaking into the union offices, and attempting to disrupt shop meetings. Top officials of the International openly proclaimed in the *Forward* that any means were justified to discredit the united-front administration because it "is dominated by the Communists."

By decision of the locals, elections of local officers and Joint Board delegates were scheduled to take place on July 21. A group of Kaufman's henchmen, without consulting the membership, immediately announced that the election of Local 5 was to be held on July 9. The International designated Philip Silberstein, Kaufman's lieutenant, to supervise the "election." But heeding the Joint Board's call, all but eighty-two operators out of a membership of thirty-five hundred in the local boycotted Kaufman's "election."

The Joint Board then went ahead with the election of local officers and Joint Board delegates on July 20-21. There was nothing the machine could do. International Secretary-Treasurer Wenneis warned Kaufman that it would be futile at this point to interfere. "Should the general officers take any action in disciplining the Joint Board," he wrote, "I believe it would be a very costly matter and leave the result very much in doubt."

Every candidate elected in Locals 1, 5, 10 and 15 was pledged to support the united-front administration. Every candidate associated with the right-wing machine was overwhelmingly defeated. It was a clean sweep. The local executive boards and the Joint Board were rid of the corrupt elements who had heretofore dominated the union. Their places were taken by men like Jack Schneider, Sam Resnick, Isidore Shapiro and others who had distinguished themselves in the struggle for clean, honest and progressive unionism.

Kaufman then publicly appealed to "those supporters of the 'United Front' who claim not to be Communists, to refuse to take part in the installation of the new Joint Board." He also proposed an "investigation" of the New York situation by a committee of "impartial" labor men acting in conjunction with representatives of the International. Kaufman even named the people who should constitute the "impartial" committee —Meyer London, his legal adviser, B. Vladeck and N. Rogoff of the *Forward* staff, and Max Pine, Isidore Cohen and M. Feinstone of the United Hebrew Trades. These gentlemen, Kaufman assured the "Progressives," would help them "to re-establish a strong, healthy, constructive union, headed by a truly responsible administration, which shall respect the laws of the union and protect the interests of the workers."

Kaufman had no illusions that Gold would go before this committee. Gold had learned a lesson from the mistake of submitting to the rigged "impartial investigation" by the United Hebrew Trades in 1921. He understood now that it was the same outfit, preparing to do the same hatchet job. But Kaufman thought he would be able to persuade the so-called "Progressives" to agree. Instead, the management committee of the Joint Board turned down the "impartial committee."

Unknown to Gold and the left wing, and certainly to the membership as a whole, a new attack against the union was even then being prepared. Every politician in the Socialist Party was being brought into the picture to create a split in the united front in the Furriers Union.

Joseph Bearak, a member of the Boston law firm of Roewer and Bearak and an associate of the *Forward* group, approached Shachtman with the proposal that the "Progressives" and Kaufman unite against the left wing. Bearak was joined in this attempt by Louis Waldman and Joseph Liederman, right-wing Socialists. On July 25 he wired Kaufman: "Yesterday conferred with Waldman and Liederman. When I told them what I want they said it would do no good, it's gone too far. But to please me they would talk to Shachtman who was in the waiting room. I asked Louis [Waldman] to call him in, but he went out and spent a few minutes with him outside and returned saying 'nothing doing!' Shachtman then came in and said he appreciates what I am trying to do, but it is too late to confer now. 'You had all the chances before but now you are licked and conferences would do no good.' Later Liederman told me they are afraid they would be double crossed. . . ."

Events were to prove that the "Progressives" were merely biding their time for a more opportune moment to betray the united front and come to terms with the Kaufman machine.

Meanwhile, at the installation of the newly-elected Joint Board on July 28, the fur workers condemned Kaufman and the *Forward* and reaffirmed their faith in the united-front administration. After reporting on the achievements of the new administration, Gold concluded: "There is a great deal to be done. . . . We took over a union which was completely demoralized. We will not rest until we have succeeded in accomplishing everything, until every pledge we have made to the workers is fully redeemed."

CHAPTER 17

The Ousting of Kaufman

Like a spreading circle in a great pool, the revolt of the fur workers broadened out until it reached great masses of workers in the other needle trades. A few weeks after the united-front administration took office in the Furriers Union, a revolt broke out against the bureaucratic machine in the International Ladies Garment Workers Union, of which Morris Sigman, right-wing Socialist, was president.

Aware that both struggles against corruption were linked together, the Joint Board of the Furriers Union proposed a loan of several thousand dollars to the rank-and-file Joint Action Committee which was leading the revolt in the ILGWU. The fur workers approved the loan at a mass meeting. Kaufman, convinced that his own fortunes were linked with the right-wing bureaucrats in the ILGWU, viciously attacked the Joint Board and questioned its right to make such a loan. But he refused to accept the Board's challenge that he present his case to another mass meeting of the fur workers.

Two weeks later, the Joint Board hurled a second challenge at Kaufman. Six hundred fur workers in Montreal had gone out on strike, under the direction of Charles Stetsky. The conditions of the Montreal fur workers had completely deteriorated under Kaufman's administration. Local 68 had vanished completely. The two remaining locals, 66 and 67, had lost two thirds of their membership. The gains secured in the 1917 strike had been taken back by the employers. The wages of the

Montreal workers were the lowest in the entire industry, operators getting as little as $10 a week.

Shortly after the strike began, the New York Joint Board, with the approval of its members, sent a contribution of $4,000 to help the strikers, and offered to lend $10,000 to the Montreal union. No one from Montreal came to claim the loan. The $4,000 was immediately wasted by Kaufman's "strike committee." While the strikers and their families were desperately in need of assistance, very little went to them.

A committee of the New York Joint Board, headed by Shachtman, went to Montreal and informed the strike committee that it would turn over an additional $3,000 on condition that the money be given directly to the men and women on strike. The Montreal strike committee demanded that the money be turned over unconditionally.

Knowing from experience how Stetsky managed strikes, the Joint Board representatives asked for a meeting of the strikers so that the question could be put before them. They also suggested that a committee from Montreal visit the New York Joint Board membership meeting. When the Montreal strike committee rejected both proposals, the representatives of the Joint Board refused to hand over the money to the machine men and returned to New York.

Kaufman attacked the New York Joint Board, accusing the "Communist united-front administration" of refusing to aid the Montreal strikers. He charged that "the Communist Joint Board of New York" were "guilty of treason" to Montreal fur workers because they had refused to give the money "to be used at the discretion of the strike committee."

The Joint Board replied by challenging Kaufman. If he was really interested in the success of the Montreal strike, he would agree to let the Joint Board lead the strike to victory. This challenge too went unanswered.

The strike dragged along, hopelessly mismanaged, until the strikers became completely demoralized. Even under these circumstances, the New York Joint Board continued to aid the strike. By March 1, 1926, three months before the strike drew to a disastrous conclusion without any gains for the workers, it had contributed $20,000. As Gold had predicted, however, very little of this money was used to aid the strikers. After the strike ended, Emile Perrault, a member of the Montreal Joint Board, blamed the International, writing that "the members are disgusted. A good many are talking of a National Union and it is very hard to get them to our meetings."

The Joint Board initiated a movement for a special International convention. Kaufman tried desperately to block the movement, but the pressure among the rank and file was too strong for the machine to resist. On August 4, the General Executive Board reluctantly approved a resolution providing for a referendum to hold a special convention in November. The resolution was, nevertheless, worded to suit Kaufman's purposes. It charged that the convention was needed "to rescue the organization from the control of Communists and irresponsible elements."

To restore Kaufman's sinking prestige, Local 45 of Chicago, where Kaufman's lieutenant, Millstein, was strongly entrenched, was selected for a debate between Kaufman and a representative of the Joint Board. After the debate, the local was slated to adopt a resolution condemning the "Communist Joint Board" and hailing Kaufman as the saviour of the Furriers Union. It was to be a dress rehearsal for the special convention.

The New York Joint Board chose Gold to present its case against the International. Sorkin was designated to accompany Gold.

The debate took place on August 28 in the Capitol Building in Chicago. Kaufman exuded confidence. He assured the press that the Chicago local would stand with the International "in its fight against the Communistic element in the local New York Joint Board." As he entered the auditorium, accompanied by Millstein and Siskind, editor of the Chicago *Daily Forward*, he was greeted with a storm of applause. The machine boys greeted Gold and Sorkin with booing and shouting, "Who wants you here? Go back to New York."

Kaufman opened the debate. He spoke for over an hour. Beginning with a description of his recent operation, he continued with a tearful recital of how he had risen from a sick-bed to prevent the union from being seized by "Communist agents of Moscow." The rest of his speech was devoted to red-baiting. The Communist International, he charged, was "paying Ben Gold" and all the rest of the left-wingers in the New York Joint Board to force him, Morris Kaufman, out of the presidency. Only his staunch resistance was saving the union from being taken over, lock, stock and barrel, by the "Communists."

Yes, there had been some evidence of corruption in the New York Joint Board, but he, Kaufman, claimed credit for removing Brownstein from his post. The talk of slugging tactics, graft and corruption in the union, he declared, was nothing but typical "Communist propaganda." Kaufman concluded his red-baiting with an appeal to rout the "Communists" and restore the union to "sensible, reasonable" men.

Millstein's introduction of Gold was coldness personified. The audience was hostile. "If you want to debate Communism," Gold began, turning to Kaufman, "I am ready at any time or place, but at this membership meeting of the Chicago union, I want to acquaint the membership with the facts of the present controversy between you and the New York Joint Board."

Then Gold described in detail the system of graft, corruption and slugging that had prevailed under the right-wing administrations. To this he contrasted all the positive achievements of the united-front administration. Gold did not speak in generalities. He produced pictures of workers beaten up by sluggers, receipts showing union money had been paid to underworld elements, quotations from the press acknowledging the accomplishments of the united-front administration. As these undeniable facts piled up, Kaufman's henchmen began to squirm and turn pale. By the time Gold was midway through his speech, they were looking towards the exits. When he concluded, they rushed out of the hall, Siskind of the *Forward* leading the way.

The place was in an uproar. Worker after worker leaped up and shouted to Kaufman: "Why didn't you tell us these things instead of yelling about Communism? Why, we have the same terrorism in Chicago!" Some workers even threatened to attack Kaufman, and Gold found it necessary to plead with the audience to allow the International president to answer the facts. The audience finally quieted down sufficiently to enable Kaufman to speak. But he was a changed man. Mumbling a few more charges against the "Communist Joint Board," Kaufman ran from the hall, not even waiting to hear Gold's summation.

Gold's final remark was brief. He assured the Chicago fur workers that the special convention would see the ousting of Kaufman and the beginning of new opportunities for the fur workers all over the country. On this note, the debate ended. Thereafter, there were no more debates scheduled by Kaufman in local unions.

Approved by overwhelming vote of the locals, the Seventh Biennial Convention opened at the American House in Boston on November 9, 1925. The machine controlled 34 votes, chiefly from small out-of-town locals; the opposition numbered 41 delegates from the New York Joint Board with its twelve thousand workers. Among these were 26 left-wingers under the leadership of Ben Gold and 15 "Progressives" controlled by Hyman Sorkin.

The forty-one delegates representing the united front in the New York

POSTAL TELEGRAPH – COMMERCIAL CABLES

CLARENCE H. MACKAY, PRESIDENT

TELEGRAM

CLASS OF SERVICE DESIRED

FAST TELEGRAM

DAY LETTER

NIGHT TELEGRAM

NIGHT LETTER

The sender must mark an X opposite the class of service desired, otherwise the telegram will be transmitted as a fast telegram.

RECEIVER'S NUMBER

CHECK

TIME FILED

TELEGRAMS TO ALL AMERICA   CABLEGRAMS TO ALL THE WORLD

STANDARD TIME

Send the following Telegram, subject to the terms on back hereof, which are hereby agreed to.   Form 2

NIGHT LETTER

Oct. 8th, 1925.

Mr. J. Millstein,
Fur Workers Union,
8 So. Dearborn St.,
Chicago, Ill.

Letters received this morning upon my return from Montreal.
No change in that situation. Am advised by our office
that you paid per capita for the year ending September thirteeth
for less than two hundred. and that including your payment of
October second your paid up membership xit is xm brought up
to two hundred fifty two. This will enable your local to have.
three delegates. Would suggest that you accept as delegate to
convention also have one of the girls and a third one either
the old man or Goldberg. So far the subcommittee did not
act upon your expenditure and that is the reason whey that
amount could not be sent to you. Will write you in detail
next week.

MORRIS KAUFMAN.

How conventions were packed by the right-wing machine is told
by Kaufman's frank "suggestions" in this telegram to Millstein.

Joint Board came with specific instructions adopted at local meetings just
two weeks prior to the convention. They were instructed to present a
solid front against the machine on all issues. They were to fight for a
militant program to help solve problems in the fur trade and to ally the
fur workers with the most progressive sections of the labor movement.

The first real battle arose over the machine's attempt to bar Ben Gold
and Sam Mencher from the convention. The majority report of the credentials committee (appointed by Kaufman) recommended that Gold be
barred immediately from the convention because he had been expelled
and because charges were being brought against the Joint Board. The
machine then attempted to postpone the debate on seating Gold until
after the whole case against the Joint Board was presented by the G.E.B.

The majority of delegates were determined to seat Ben Gold before
taking up any charges against the New York Joint Board. The battle
raged throughout the morning and afternoon sessions and late into the
evening of Tuesday, November 10. But despite all the maneuvering and
stalling tactics engaged in by the machine delegates, the motion to seat
Gold immediately was finally passed.

This was merely the opening skirmish. The next three days were taken up with the battle over the report of the General Executive Board on the controversy between the International and the New York Joint Board. The officers' report was divided in two parts. One was devoted to activities outside of New York. The other, a 32-page document, known as the "Supplementary Report," dealt with the New York situation. Kaufman's aim was to separate the fight of the left wing from the general issues of the union.

In the first few paragraphs, the Supplementary Report hastily glossed over the ill-fated 1920 strike and the four years of corruption that followed under the right-wing leadership. Then the Report went into thirty pages of red-baiting against the left-wing militants, the TUEL, "Moscow agents," and "Communists." It accused the left wing of "sabotaging" the 1920 strike, of arousing "passion and discontent," of "slander and undermining the organization," of "provoking fist fights" at meetings, and many other fantastic charges.

The Supplementary Report generously gave Kaufman the credit for ousting Abraham Brownstein. At the same time it exonerated Abe Rosenthal, who had been kicked out by the Joint Board for concealing Brownstein's stealing. It ended by "sounding the alarm" against "the lawless actions of the Communist group." The officers demanded "the necessary steps to re-establish law and union discipline."

As soon as the reading of the Supplementary Report was finished, one of Kaufman's lieutenants leaped up and moved that it be referred to the committee on officers' reports. No time was specified for this committee to report. And until the committee reported, all discussion could be stifled by Kaufman.

Gold immediately moved to instruct the committee to bring in its report the very next morning. Over the objection of the machine men, Gold's motion was carried. Despite the crucial nature of the issue, the machine men proposed a five-minute time limit for any delegate discussing the report. But Gold's motion for unlimited discussion was also carried.

The next morning, the committee on officers' reports submitted its report. As was to be expected, Kaufman's handpicked majority on the committee recommended finding the New York Joint Board guilty.*

---

* The report was signed by H. Foucher, I. B. Hertzberg, Ed Freedman, Frank Barossi, Milton Corbett, and Wm. Ritchie. Hyman Sorkin was a member of the committee. He did not sign the report. Neither did he join with Jack Schneider in presenting the minority report.

Although thirty delegates had asked to be allowed to present their version of the veracity of the Supplementary Report before the committee, they had been given no opportunity to speak. A minority report was then presented by the left-wing delegate, Jack Schneider, moving to reject the Supplementary Report and to condemn the International Officers.

At this point, Kaufman was riding high. Everything seemed to be going according to schedule. Then suddenly the storm broke loose. When it was over, the Kaufman machine was a total wreck. Ben Gold, symbol of the battle between the right and left forces, took the floor for two hours to defend the Joint Board against the accusations set forth in the Supplementary Report. Step by step, he covered the history of the union since 1919, related the story of assaults upon members—the corruption and graft—the maintenance of a spy system—the protection of favored shops—the dictatorship of fear—and the alliance with the underworld to wipe out opposition in the union at whatever cost. As he proceeded, the right-wing machine was stripped naked of every vestige of decency and of any pretense of its rights to leadership in the union.

Gold asked why less than one page of the Report was devoted to the years 1920-1924. "These four years," he emphasized, "are the most important years of the happenings in the Joint Board and it was then that the question came up which made necessary the calling of a special convention to discipline the Joint Board."

Gold pointed out that even in 1919 when there were no Communists in the union and certainly "no crystallized left wing," there was already "strong opposition to the leaders" because of their dictatorial tactics and the "strong-arm methods against those who had other opinions." In fact, Kaufman had been forced to resign as manager of the Joint Board before the 1920 strike.

Taking time for only a brief analysis of the disastrous 1920 strike, Gold completely disposed of the false charges that the opposition elements had sabotaged the strike. He described the deplorable state of the union after the strike, and the organization of the "Welfare Club" to sabotage the constructive work of the left-wing elements in restoring life to the organization. Gold told of his frequent visits to Kaufman to urge him to stop the beating and terrorizing of the membership. On every visit he had received the same answer: "Nothing doing!"

Not for a moment did Gold disavow his membership in the TUEL, without which, he said, "the union would have been ruined today." "The TUEL left-wingers," he said proudly, "are a factor in the labor movement, standing for the interests of the rank and file in the building up of a powerful union to fight the bosses."

Gold told how the right-wing machine had paralyzed the union, destroyed the self-confidence of the workers, placed the union under the control of the manufacturers and the underworld, and intensified the persecution of all opposition elements. Gold related how Kaufman had gone to the district attorney—a union-hater—to destroy the left-wing movement. And how, failing in all measures to overcome the left-wing's growing influence among the fur workers, the red-baiting right-wing machine resorted to suspensions and expulsions of the left-wingers.

Then Gold showed how the fur workers learned to fight back and finally swept the united front of left-wingers and "Progressives" into office. Within a few weeks, the manufacturers knew "that the union was no longer broken down and decayed," and the gangsters knew that their hold over the union had been smashed. The membership backed the new administration in the Joint Board to the hilt.

Gold was ready to conclude. In a moving statement, he appealed to the delegates: "If you think this Joint Board is guilty because we got rid of the graft system—if you think we are guilty because we enforced union conditions—if you think we are guilty of organizing the unorganized—if you think we are guilty because we have a union that has never been organized before—if you think we are guilty because we delivered the union to the members with free speech, with free determination of policies—if you think we are guilty of this crime, if this is a crime—you can convict us. I don't think any delegate who claims he is interested in or works in the interests of the workers, will be against the other workers of the International Furriers Union. I hope on examining the facts and the evidence, you will say, 'Joint Board, greetings! We are going to help you fight your internal and external enemies for a better union.' "

As Gold closed, the majority of delegates rose amid prolonged cheering for his magnificent speech. Many delegates outside of New York were horrified by Gold's disclosure of the years of corruption and misconduct resulting from Kaufman's policies. They were anxious to disassociate themselves from responsibility for these events. Had the vote on the Supplementary Report been held then and there, the outcome would have been a foregone conclusion. But Kaufman hurriedly recessed.

As the afternoon session opened, the anti-Kaufman forces again took up the cudgels. One after another, the delegates from New

York cited their own experiences to corroborate the charges Gold had hurled at the right-wing machine. Mencher described how he had been attacked and sent to the hospital in a critical condition. Skolnick told how he used to come home from local meetings "beaten up, my garments torn into shreds," ashamed to tell his wife and children that he was a member of a trade union. Elster, one of Kaufman's own supporters, speaking in Yiddish, described the unjustified and brutal attack on Gold by gangsters at Local 15's meeting in December 1923. The simple words of this aged delegate made a profound impression on everyone.

These revelations were too much for many of the out-of-town delegates. Albert Roy of Montreal arose and announced in a choking voice that he wished no longer to be considered "a lieutenant of Kaufman." He declared that many delegates were wondering "whether they are a part of a real International Fur Workers Union or if they are not a part of an International Gangsters Union."

With their machine crumbling, Kaufman's henchmen could only resort to red-baiting in their support of the Supplementary Report. Gmeiner, Stetsky and Kaufman himself cried that the issue was only one of "outside interference" by the Communist Party.

Red-baiting alone, however, could not overcome the terrible indictment that had been presented by the New York delegates. Something extraordinary was needed if the machine was to save the Supplementary Report.

Two years previously, when the Conservatives in England were faced with the danger of a Labor Party victory in the elections, they had brought forward the infamous "Zinoviev forgery" at the eleventh hour. The forged letter purported to be a communication from the Soviet foreign minister to Ramsay MacDonald, then British premier and viciously anti-Communist. The letter suggested how MacDonald could aid in spreading Communist propaganda in Great Britain. The Soviet Union immediately branded the letter a forgery. But it had already served its purpose. It was the decisive factor in turning the tide in favor of the Conservatives, and causing the defeat of the MacDonald cabinet.

Taking a leaf from the English Conservatives, Kaufman and his henchmen sprang their own "Zinoviev forgery" on the convention. As Kaufman closed the debate on the Supplementary Report, he announced dramatically that he held in his hand a telegram which contained orders from the Central Executive Committee of the Workers' (Communist) Party to William Weinstone, organizer for the TUEL and *Daily Worker* correspondent at the convention. The telegram, said to be signed by Charles Ruthenberg, the general secretary of the Workers' Party, contained instructions to the left-wing delegates as to how the various offices in the International should be distributed at the elections. Significantly, it dealt mainly with the necessity of breaking the power of Hyman Sorkin and his "Progressive" followers. Here was proof, Kaufman cried, that "an invisible power" was seeking to control the union.

Ruthenberg immediately denied the authenticity of the telegram, and publicly declared that its use "shows up the machine as the unscrupulous clique resorting to every device to maintain power." Nevertheless, like the "Zinoviev letter," the machine's desperate strategy paid off. Out-of-town delegates who had been wavering in their support of the machine, were brought back into line by the hysteria created by the alleged telegram. And most important, the forged message from the Workers' Party gave Sorkin and his followers an excuse to break the united front.

Sorkin had been looking for an opportunity to make his own deal with the right-wing machine. Fearing that Kaufman would expose his unsavory role during the 1920 strike, he had remained silent during the entire discussion on the Supplementary Report. Now the forged telegram lent an air of righteous indignation to his double-cross of the left wing.

To hasten the split in the united front and to make the treachery of the "Progressives" more palatable, the right-wingers withdrew the committee's report and substituted a compromise. The compromise justified the International and "forgave" the Joint Board. In return the International was to be recognized as supreme. Refusing to allow any further debate, Kaufman rushed the matter to a vote. A group of the "Progressives" voted with Kaufman. The result was 37 to 28 in favor of the compromise. Eleven "Progressives" abstained. Thus was the united front split. The schemes of the right-wing Socialist leaders had borne fruit.

The betrayal of the united front took place at Friday night's session. Rallying their forces, the left wing reopened the fight the next morning to get a clear-cut condemnation of the machine. Alarmed that their action would be repudiated by the membership in New York, those "Progressives" who had split with the left wing on the compromise proposal, now joined with them in seeking a reversal of Friday night's vote.

As soon as Saturday's session opened, Gold introduced a resolution declaring that the New York Joint Board had cleaned out corruption, and fought against suspensions and the reign of terror that had been built up by the machine. The resolution instructed the incoming General

Executive Board "to work in closest harmony with the New York Joint Board for the purpose of maintaining a strong and unified International."

Kaufman refused to take up Gold's resolution unless the convention would give its unanimous consent. Gold fought back doggedly, demanding the right to appeal to the convention against the President's ruling.

Finally, sensing the growing resentment of the delegates at his bureaucratic methods, Kaufman allowed the appeal to the convention. By a vote of 40 to 30, with some of Kaufman's own delegates voting against him, Gold won the appeal. Again Kaufman attempted to prevent a vote on Gold's resolution. Six o'clock was approaching, the time for the final adjournment of the convention. Kaufman tried to stampede an adjournment, but his move was blocked by the left wing and the "Progressives." When this maneuver failed, Kaufman introduced a new "compromise" proposal in the form of an interpretation of the substitute resolution adopted on Friday night. The new resolution declared that the disputes between the New York Joint Board and the International were "liquidated and that the incoming G.E.B. shall not revive them or take any action upon matters that occurred between the two bodies prior to the convention."

The machine was beginning to crawl. Still the left wing did not yield. Kaufman finally had to agree that both resolutions—Gold's and Kaufman's—be handed to a committee of five which should begin immediately to work out a new resolution acceptable to both sides.

This committee brought in a unanimous declaration that the Joint Board had fought against violation of democratic principles, and membership suspensions, and that under the chaotic conditions created in the organization by the internal struggle, not all constitutional interpretations had been lived up to by the Joint Board. Nevertheless, under these special circumstances, the actions of the Joint Board against the International were justified. The resolution pledged support to the Joint Board and declared that the dispute between the Board and the International had been liquidated. It urged the incoming General Executive Board not to revive it or take any action upon matters that had occurred between the two bodies prior to the convention. The entire Supplementary Report was thrown overboard.

In the last two days of the convention, the alliance between the machine and Sorkin's group in the "Progressive" bloc had made itself fully evident. The "Progressives" voted with the left wing on a large number of resolutions, in order to give the appearance of conforming to the membership's instructions, but on the decisive issue such as the Supplementary Report they either abstained or voted with the right-wingers.

The ultimate betrayal of the united front came at the final session during the election of officers. Before the convention, Shachtman had agreed with Gold that it would be tragic for the union to elect Sorkin president. Shachtman indicated his own willingness to accept the presidency, if elected. During the convention, the united-front delegation agreed to support Shachtman for president, Skolnick, a left-winger, for secretary-treasurer and Gold for first vice-president. Several of the Sorkin group and several left-wingers would receive the remaining posts.

At a conference with the Sorkinites the machine agreed to throw its support to the "Progressive" candidates but not to the left-wingers. The Sorkin group made the deal and split the united front. Shachtman was elected president by a vote of 42 to 31, the left-wing delegates keeping their pledge to support him for office. But in the nominations for first vice-president, the so-called Progressive, Winnick, was named to oppose Gold. On the first ballot, Gold received 29 votes and Winnick 17, with 26 delegates not voting. On the second ballot, the 26 blank votes which had been cast by machine supporters were thrown to Winnick. He was elected, 41 to 29.

The remaining votes followed closely along these lines. In the end, the General Executive Board was composed of four members of the Sorkin group, two members of the machine, two wavering between Sorkin and Kaufman, and two left-wingers (Aaron Gross and Harry Englander). Two other Board members from St. Paul and Montreal were slated to fall to the machine, which controlled the elections in these locals.

In spite of the betrayals by the so-called "Progressives" under Sorkin's leadership, the convention marked an important advance for the fur workers. Kaufman had been forced out of leadership. His policies had been repudiated. The strength of the left wing had made its imprint on every resolution. The effort of the right-wing machine to destroy the Joint Board had failed. That the machine was not cleaned out altogether was due to the treachery of the "Progressive" group. But, as Gold declared:

"Only for a short time has the machine saved itself from complete annihilation. . . It is not as in the days gone by. The force of the organized membership has shown how it may combat its enemy. . . Furriers know no half-way battles. The fight against Kaufmanism will be brought to its completion."

1926—The General Strike
that Made Labor History

CHAPTER 18

The Battle Line Forms

Never had the American labor movement been in a more discouraging position than it was when the year 1926 opened. Organization was at a low ebb. Undermined and demoralized by a reactionary AFL leadership, union after union lost ground under the employers' open-shop offensive. The AFL declined from over four million members in 1920 to less than three million in 1926. Even the powerful United Mine Workers was defeated in a series of strikes in 1926 and weakened by the growth of non-union coalfields in West Virginia and Kentucky.

Company unions abounded throughout the country. "Baltimore and Ohio" speedup plans were being forced on the workers. William Green, Matthew Woll and other top leaders of the AFL kept announcing that the old days of struggle between capital and labor were past, and that the strike as a weapon against employers was no longer necessary. "Co-operation with the employers" became the theme of labor leaders all over the country.

In February 1926, a general strike broke out in the New York fur industry which was destined to influence the course of the American labor movement for years to come. For seventeen weeks, the fur workers demonstrated a fighting spirit seldom equalled in the annals of labor struggle. The forces of "law and order" were vainly invoked by the employers to break the strike. Right-wing Socialists and top leaders of the AFL lent their assistance to the employers. The press leaped in to smash the strike. Lurid headlines and inflammatory newspaper reports daily screamed out the fearful news that a "revolution" was taking place in New York. But the fur workers withstood every attack with heroic solidarity and tireless endurance. By the time the strike had run its course, it had taught American workers invaluable lessons.

The agreement was due to expire January 31, 1926. Directly after the Boston Convention, the New York Joint Board adopted demands to be presented to the manufacturers' association. First drawn up by a special committee that included Manager Gold, the business agents and the shop chairmen, the demands were discussed at numerous meetings of the workers. Explanatory pamphlets and bulletins were published. Suggestions from rank-and-file workers were eagerly accepted and embodied in the final demands approved at membership and local meetings.

These demands were not advanced frivolously. They grew out of long and bitter experience, out of wasted and broken lives of fur workers, out of exhaustive knowledge of trade evils. They included:

1. Forty-hour, five-day week.
2. Thirty-two-hour week during the slack periods.
3. Equal division of work during the entire year, instead of only during three months of the year.
4. An unemployment insurance fund to which every manufacturer was to contribute 3 percent of the amount he paid out in wages.
5. Punishment of manufacturers who broke the agreement.
6. A 25 percent increase in wages over the old minimum, and one minimum scale.
7. No section contracting.
8. Corporation shops and retailers not to be given any contracting work.
9. Any manufacturer who employed less than ten workers not to be admitted into the Association.
10. Foremen must not be permitted to work in any branch of the fur trade.
11. Manufacturers to use only those skins which were prepared in a union shop and bore the union label.
12. May First to be observed as a holiday with full pay.
13. Shops to be inspected by representatives of the union.
14. Agreement to last for two years.

A number of these important demands had been advanced during the Kaufman regime, too, during negotiations for agreements. But in those days they had been presented for window-dressing purposes exclusively.

As soon as negotiations began, the employers were privately informed not to take the demands seriously. This time, the employers knew that the union meant business. They saw how the fur workers, under left-wing leadership, had revived the union and placed it on a solid footing. They had witnessed the shop strikes for July increases, the organization of the Greek workers, and the union's drive against the open shops. They were therefore under no illusion that they would be able to put across their previous deals in these negotiations.

The first conference with the Associated Fur Manufacturers was held on December 8, 1925.* The union presented its demands. The Association's answer came at the second conference a week later: "We absolutely refuse to discuss any of your demands if you do not first remove the equal division of work clause." The union's reply was a brief: "Nothing doing!" At the suggestion of Dr. Abelson, the impartial chairman, the Association and the union agreed to set aside the equal division of work clause for the moment. But as soon as the conferees turned to the other demands, the Association stated firmly that it would only renew the old agreement without any change. Once again, the union's answer was: "Nothing doing!"

A joint conference of the officers and executive committees of the four locals met with the entire Joint Board on December 30 at Manhattan Lyceum to hear a report of the negotiations. Upon learning of the manufacturers' extreme hostility, the meeting unanimously voted to mobilize the entire membership and to alert them to meet any emergency that might develop during the negotiations. The meeting also expressed full confidence in the Conference Committee and warned the manufacturers: "The fur workers are resolved to gain their demands under all circumstances."

The union leadership genuinely desired a peaceful settlement. New conferences with the Association, however, revealed that the manufacturers did not share this desire. The spokesmen for the employers insisted on the withdrawal not only of the equal division of work demand

---

* The union was represented by a Conference Committee consisting of representatives of each local—Shapiro, Local 1; Baraz, Local 5; Ozeroff, Local 10; Elster, Local 15—the chairman of the Joint Board, Zeitlin; the manager, Gold; the president of the International, Shachtman; and the two business agents who attended to the Association shops, Gross and Winnick. The employers had the same number of representatives on their delegation which was headed by Samuel N. Samuels, president of the Association. Dr. Paul Abelson, the impartial chairman, also attended the conference.

but of the demands for the forty-hour week and the fund for the unemployed.

When the conferences had ended in a deadlock, the Joint Board called
a mass meeting for January 23 in Cooper Union and Webster Hall. The
slogan was, "Prepare for struggle!" By one o'clock the two large halls,
with a normal capacity of about forty-five hundred seats, were packed
to the rafters with some six thousand workers. Hundreds more had to be
turned away.

After the chairmen, I. Shapiro at Cooper Union and M. Polinsky at
Webster Hall, had briefly explained the importance of the gatherings
and the issues confronting the fur workers, Fanny Warshafsky addressed the meetings. Arvanitis addressed the workers in Greek and his
speech was then translated. He hailed the achievements of the union in
organizing the Greek furriers and improving their miserable conditions.
Declaring that in past strikes the Greek workers had been misled by
their employers into acting as scabs, he pointed out that if a strike became necessary now, the Greek workers would fight shoulder-to-shoulder
with the other furriers on the picket lines.

Gold gave a detailed report of the conferences. "The manufacturers,"
he said, "revealed themselves in their true colors as greedy employers,
who care for nothing but their profits." He analyzed the conditions in
the trade that made it necessary to insist on the union's demands. While
the bosses were getting richer every year, the workers were becoming
poorer, physically exhausted, and more and more often exposed to actual
starvation. "No one in the union wants a strike," he emphasized, "but
we will not forfeit our human rights." He appealed especially to the
young workers to take their places in the front lines of the pending
battle and help lead the union to victory.

The International president, Shachtman, pledged all the resources of
the International Union to support the Joint Board, should a strike become necessary. The fur workers were to remember these words when,
only a few weeks later, they saw the leaders of the International unite
with the manufacturers in an effort to smash their strike.

The membership at both meetings endorsed the stand taken by the
union's Conference Committee. The meeting instructed the union leadership "to mobilize all forces of the fur workers and prepare the whole
union machinery for a struggle with the manufacturers until the demands
submitted by our union are granted." Two other resolutions were
adopted: full support to the striking Montreal fur workers, and solidarity
with the striking mine workers, then in a bitter five-month struggle.

The powerful demonstrations in Cooper Union and Webster Hall left no doubt about the spirit of the fur workers. They were determined to win their justified demands. If no other course were left, they were ready to enter into a prolonged battle. One after another Locals 1, 5, 10 and 15 membership meetings voted to empower the Joint Board to call a strike if the employers continued to reject the union's demands.

On January 25, six days before the existing agreement expired, Dr. Abelson called another conference in a last attempt to settle the dispute. That same day, the *Jewish Morning Journal* published a statement by Samuel N. Samuels, president of the Association, which made it clear that the employers were determined to fight it out with the union. As his predecessors had done as far back as 1886, he declared that the manufacturers were faced with a conspiracy to "bolshevize" the fur industry. The manufacturers, he continued, would never "allow a political group who knows how to trick the membership into electing them as union officials to ruin the industry." He said nothing about the demands or the vote of almost the entire membership of the union at mass meetings and local meetings.

The conference went on until midnight. In the end, the representatives of the Association merely repeated the ultimatum they had made two weeks before. If the union was willing to withdraw its three main demands—equal division of work, the forty-hour week, and the 3 percent unemployment fund—the Association would make an effort to come to an understanding about the other points. But if the union refused to withdraw these three demands, the Association no longer wished to conduct any conferences.

"Fur workers!" Gold appealed, in calling all active workers to a meeting in Manhattan Lyceum on January 30. "It is now clear that the manufacturers are determined to enter into a struggle with the union. A fight is unavoidable. Our rightful demands must be won. All the forces of the union must be concentrated for this effort. Everyone must be ready for the fight."

It was at this historic meeting in Manhattan Lyceum that a new technique in strike strategy was introduced into the American labor movement. The famous General Picketing Committee of one thousand fur workers was set up. And when Gold cried out in appealing for volunteers for the committee: "Don't volunteer if you are afraid of a bitter struggle! No one will hold it against you. Whoever does not feel able to take police clubs on his head and body, whoever fears to go to prison for his ideals, should not volunteer for the general picketing committee. What is your answer?"—a forest of hands went up with demands of "Sign me up in the union's army."

Within half an hour the General Picketing Committee was organized. Gold announced that a women's battalion would be needed in the strike. Nearly two hundred women rushed to sign up.

These volunteers represented a merging of the best fighting elements in the union. Men and women, white and Negro, Jewish and Greek, people of all shades of political belief formed this solid phalanx for the battle that lay ahead.

The last conference with the Association started in the Hotel Pennsylvania shortly after the meeting in Manhattan Lyceum. Spokesmen for the Association resumed exactly where they had left off five days before. They again insisted that the union withdraw its three principal demands. The union, of course, refused. Dr. Abelson intervened and asked the union's representatives to state the minimum terms upon which they would consent to sign a new agreement. The union's Conference Committee then retired to one room, and the Association representatives to another directly adjoining it.

At the caucus of the union's Conference Committee, Gold suggested that a final effort be made to break the deadlock and avoid a strike. He proposed that the manufacturers be told that if they agreed on all other demands, the union would be ready to discuss how far the present three-month period of equal division of work should be extended.

Gold then asked each member of the Conference Committee for his opinion. Every member voted in favor of the proposal. When it came to Shachtman's turn, he threw a bombshell into the proceedings with a vicious attack on the Joint Board leadership. He suddenly accused Gold and his associates of being "agents of Moscow" and charged that the negotiations were being conducted at the command of the "Communist Party." The Conference Committee turned on Shachtman and blasted him for using language that was identical with that of the employers.

Gold conveyed to Dr. Abelson the union Conference Committee's compromise offer on the demand for equal division of work. He assured the impartial chairman that it was "a bona fide offer to reopen the discussions so that an agreement might be reached without a strike."

The leaders of the Association had made their decision even before Dr. Abelson informed them of the union's compromise proposal. They rejected the offer coldly. To absolve themselves from responsibility in the eyes of the public, they subsequently denied that the union had made any concession which would have provided a basis for continued discussions.

The union promptly submitted the issue to a referendum vote of the entire membership of the four locals: "Shall the old agreement as offered by the manufacturers be accepted, or shall the Joint Board be authorized to call a general strike for the enforcement of the new demands presented to the Fur Manufacturers' Association."

On February 3 and 4, the fur workers cast their ballots. President Samuels of the Association published an "Open Letter to the members of the Furriers Union." He publicly urged the workers to repudiate their leadership in the strike referendum. He was confident that the workers could still defeat the "Communist conspiracy" by voting "against a strike." But if they allowed themselves to continue to be misled by their revolutionary leaders, he warned, the manufacturers would "fight the union to the bitter end."

The fur workers' answer came swiftly. By a vote of 6,702 in favor and only 629 against, the secret ballot referendum authorized the general strike.

The *Forward* came out with a bitter blast against the union. It praised the employers for refusing to sign an agreement with the Furriers Union, and stated that it was impossible to negotiate with "Communists." The identical language of the employers, Shachtman and the *Forward* was no mere coincidence. Had the facts then been known to the union, the fur workers might have been spared many weeks of suffering.

Even after the overwhelming strike referendum, and even as strike preparations went on, the union leaders still explored all possibilities of a peaceful settlement.

The Association brought matters to a head. Meeting behind closed doors on February 11, they decided to lock out the workers. As of that date, the members of the Association were to cease all production. Every Association member would pay a sum equal to one-half of the yearly dues for a "special emergency fund . . . for whatever purpose may be deemed necessary and proper." The Association leaders cracked the whip and forced every manufacturer to join the lockout.

Reports began to appear in the press indicating that "already the gangsters of the city were getting ready for action." As in all previous strikes, the "necessary and proper" purposes evidently included "hiring plug-uglies to beat up strikers and protect scabs."

The only reason it resorted to a lockout, the Association declared, was to "protect the workers, the bosses and the shops from these Communist terrorists. . . . Under no circumstances will we deal with the Furriers Union as long as its leaders insist upon becoming dictators in the fur industry, in order to force upon it new and radical changes in working conditions, which are not economical, are impossible, impractical and which only oppress and destroy the individuality of the workers." The Association made no attempt to explain why the workers' demands were "impossible and impractical."

The workers in the fur market answered to the point: "The bosses said the same thing in 1912 and 1920 when there was no left-wing leadership. Why didn't they grant the workers' demands then, and why was the union compelled to conduct a thirteen-week strike in 1912 and a thirty-week strike in 1920?"

On January 27, President Samuels of the Association significantly declared in a public statement: "If a group should arise in the union which has a sound organization, and wishes to submit other demands to the manufacturers, it will find the Association reasonable." In reply, a leaflet signed by former members of the right-wing machine appeared in the fur market on February 8. It denounced the union leadership. It further charged that the demands presented to the employers were utopian and had as their sole purpose forcing a strike from which only the "Communists" would benefit.

The talk from both sides about a "Communist conspiracy" had a definite purpose. It was intended to hide the fact that a real conspiracy was in full swing—the conspiracy between the leaders of the Association and the men who had formerly terrorized the union and collected a good income while in control of the organization. The goal of both parties was to unseat the militant, progressive union leadership. By forcing this battle upon the union, the employers hoped that, with the aid of the underworld, the right-wingers and the *Forward,* the discredited former leaders would come back into power. Once back, they would restore the policy of "hearty cooperation" which had proved so profitable to the manufacturers and so disastrous to the fur workers.

Bolstered by this heart-warming prospect, the fur bosses practically oozed confidence as they locked out the workers. The *Fur Age Weekly,* an employers' organ, put it frankly on February 1, 1926: "The strike cannot endure. The leaders cannot offer the workers anything but hopes. They cannot support their members during a strike. They cannot expect help from other unions because other unions are not in sympathy with the left-wing movement. . . . *If the leaders of the union do not make swift progress toward the promised goal it will not be long before they are cast aside.*"

Gold was authorized by the Joint Board to prepare all the arduous details involved in the forthcoming battle. The plan he evolved was unanimously adopted by the General Strike Committee. It was described by those familiar with strike strategy as the most careful and thorough organization of a strike machinery they had ever witnessed.

There was a committee for every phase of the strike: a picketing committee, a law committee, a publicity committee, a control committee, a relief committee, a women's committee, a committee for the Greek strikers,* a grievance committee, a settlement committee and an out-of-town committee. Even the old workers were organized into a special committee. These committees were staffed entirely by rank-and-file workers.

The separate committees were part of the General Strike Committee which was given full power to answer the lockout with a strike and carry it through to victory. Ben Gold was the chairman and Jack Skolnick the secretary. Among the other members of the General Strike Committee were Aaron Gross, Maurice H. Cohen, Samuel Leibowitz, Jack Schneider, Joseph Winogradsky, Max Suroff, Esther Polansky, Louis Elster, Simon Malamuth, Sam Mencher, Sam Resnick, Harry Farber and Isidore Shapiro. International President Shachtman was also a member. In addition to the committees, there was the powerful body of fifteen hundred shop chairmen who joined with the strike committee in formulating the strike policies.

Several halls were engaged where the workers were to register and hold their mass meetings. A list of all shops and buildings was drawn up. Legal defense was arranged. Finances were organized. Literature was prepared. Contacts were made with speakers and entertainers for lectures, forums and concerts. The union was organized in such a manner that nothing could happen in any shop, building or hall without the General Strike Committee being immediately informed. In this magnificently-organized strike apparatus every fur worker had his place and his role to play.

---

* At this time 90 percent of the Greek fur workers did not understand English. It was necessary to have groups of Greek fur workers who understood English to talk to the Greek strikers. The Greek strikers met in a special hall, and had their own hall chairman, hall committee, finance committee, picket committee, etc.

Meanwhile Gold received visits from "Little Augie," Lepke, Gurrah, and other underworld characters who were looking for an opportunity to cash in as they had done in previous strikes. "Why, we built this union," they informed him. But Gold's curt answer to all of them was: "Nothing doing! There'll be no gangsters and no hired men in this strike!"

As soon as the strike machinery was organized, Gold announced the Joint Board's decision that no one would be paid for his work in the strike. Another decision was that for the entire duration of the battle, the officials of the union would not receive their salaries. And if relief would be distributed to the workers to enable them to live, it would be allotted on the basis of need rather than on personal connections with the top leaders. The leaders themselves would have to set the example and be the first to make the necessary sacrifices.

The organization of the strike was in itself an education to the workers. One fur worker later described it:

"The union headquarters was like a school. Day and night every room was filled with workers who were discussing the operations of the particular committee to which they belonged. The business agents and the other union leaders participated in the discussions, but the workers themselves were often the teachers. Many of the workers who had gone through past struggles could tell the newcomers into the union how a strike should not be conducted.

"The leaders of the union were determined that the workers should know everything. They told the workers that not every strike ended in victory, but that one that was fought by the power of the rank and file could not be a complete loss, as had been the disastrous strike of 1920. They prepared the workers for the brutality of the police, and warned them that every power at the bosses' command would be used against the union."

Many unions, before entering a strike struggle, add up their assets on the basis of dollars and cents in their treasuries. On the eve of the 1926 furriers' strike—a strike which was to go down in American labor history as one of its most heroic and brilliant chapters—the union measured its assets in much more vital terms:

1. *Democratic control of the whole strike machinery by the rank and file.* From the very start, the workers were made to feel that it was their own fight. They would have to rely on their own powers. The leaders had to submit every policy and program to the rank and file for approval.

Nothing was concealed from the rank and file. And every motion or proposal from the ranks was given the most careful consideration.

2. *The strike apparatus, consisting of the General Strike Committee, the shop chairmen's meetings, and the well-organized "strike halls."* The General Strike Committee was the executive organ—planning, supervising and executing the major steps of the strike. The shop chairmen meetings, an institution hitherto unknown in the union, was the legislative body deciding on the most important issues. Every shop chairman was in close contact with the members of his shop. The "strike hall" was the meeting-ground of the strikers. Each shop and each cluster of shops housed in the same building was assigned its space in the "strike hall." Each shop chairman kept a check on the workers of his own shop. Should anyone be missing, the union would immediately send a committee to investigate his whereabouts and make certain that there was no scabbing. There was strict discipline from top to bottom. In all, a splendid manifestation of trade union democracy in action.

3. *A general picketing committee from among the most devoted union members.* Wherever a check had to be put to strikebreaking activities, it was to be done by the members themselves and not by professional outside strong-arm men.

4. *An ideological foundation.* The intensive educational campaign among the workers made it clear that their strike for these important economic improvements was also part of the historic struggles of the American workers.

5. *The leadership of the strike was a united front.* It was a real grass roots united front of the mass of workers. No political passport was asked of anyone. Communist workers, Socialist workers, progressives, active rank-and-file workers of every description. All that was demanded was that they prove in action their honest devotion and loyalty to the union.

Confident that the union was thoroughly prepared, the workers waited impatiently for the union's answer to the lockout. It came on Thursday, February 16, 1926. Early that morning the streets in the fur market were flooded with the "red circular" issued by the General Strike Committee. It called on all twelve thousand members of the Furriers Union to leave the shops at 10 A.M. and begin the historic battle for "bread, freedom and human living standards."

The great battle was on!

CHAPTER 19

The First Seven Weeks

At ten o'clock in the morning of February 16, 1926, the fur workers streamed toward the strike halls. Within an hour, Manhattan Lyceum, Beethoven Hall, Astoria Hall, and Webster Hall were filled. The workers turned in their union cards and were handed strike cards.

The manufacturers continued their attack with the cry of "Bolshevism." They charged that the leaders of the strike had "their feet in America and their heads in Russia"; that they represented not the workers but the interests of "Moscow" and the "Communist International." The strike, the manufacturers shrieked, was a plot "to bring about the overthrow of the government of the United States." The furriers answered these red-baiting slanders with a series of great demonstrations.

On Monday, February 22 (Washington's Birthday), after picketing three hours, seven thousand strikers marched in line through the fur district. At their head were Gold, Gross, Leibowitz, Maurice Cohen, Schneider, Winogradsky, Suroff, Potash, Mencher, Warshafsky, Polansky, Resnick, Shapiro, other members of the strike committee, hall chairmen, important shop chairmen, picketing and law committees and others. They marched up Seventh Avenue to West 30th Street, past the Association's offices. The procession moved through street after street in the fur district, picking up more and more strikers as it went along. By nine o'clock, there were close to ten thousand—Jews, Greeks, Negroes, men and women—marching six abreast in tightly-packed rows.

As the strikers marched with picket signs, shouting slogans and singing spirited songs, the police charged the demonstration. Despite the force and violence hurled against them, the workers maintained solid ranks and continued down to the strike halls. The demonstration swept clean everyone who stood in the way—police, "industrial squad," scabs in the buildings, and the thugs hired by the employers to terrorize the pickets.

Rain or shine, this mass demonstration was repeated every Monday, and it seemed as if the entire New York police force was patrolling the fur market. Scores of police and detectives would be on duty long before a demonstration started, and the moment Gold, Schneider, Gross and the other strike committee members appeared, mounted police would dash into the district. The clubs would begin to swing. Strikers would be arrested and piled into waiting police wagons. But nothing could break the spirit of the strikers. Even under harsh court sentences, this determination proved unbreakable. Striker Charles Melvin, for example, was fined $25 for disorderly conduct. He told the magistrate: "I am an American citizen. I have the right to defend my job so that nobody else should take it." The magistrate sentenced him to ten days' hard labor.

"THIRTEEN STRIKERS ARRESTED ON THE PICKET LINES!" was a typical headline in the press. Before two weeks had passed, more than two hundred strikers had been arrested while picketing. Many were arrested several times over. Barely were they released from jail than they would be back on the picket line. Respect for the Negro and Greek workers grew rapidly among the Jewish furriers as they saw their extraordinary loyalty and militancy on the picket line. In 1912 and in 1920, the Greek workers had been tricked into scabbing. In 1926, they became one of the staunchest pillars of the strike. Esteem for the women strikers, including Greek women, mounted by leaps and bounds as the fur workers saw them arrested, thrown in prison, and, when released, back on the picket lines. Every few days, Gold himself was arrested, released and back on strike duty.

The Bill of Rights flew out of the window as New York's police Industrial Squad joined the employers' thugs in attacking the pickets. On one occasion, the Industrial Squad raided the strike headquarters at Beethoven Hall and beat up active strikers mercilessly. They packed the entire strike committee into a patrol wagon and took them to the police station. On another occasion, the police invaded the office of the union's physician, Dr. Marie Lerner, while the doctor was treating badly bruised pickets, and arrested all but four patients.

Rev. Harry F. Ward, chairman of the American Civil Liberties Union, denounced the conduct of the police in the furriers' strike as a "reflection of the Department's record in industrial disputes." Magistrate Louis

D. Brodsky censured the police for "undue coercion" of the fur strikers.

"I know," Ben Gold declared at a mass meeting, "that the terror campaign the bosses are carrying on through the police and hired gangsters will not in any way lessen the determination and militancy of the fur strikers to fight for their just demands in order that they may live like human beings and not like slaves. Neither the police force, nor all the gangsters of the United States can break the solid ranks of the fur workers. The instructions for Monday morning are: all workers out for the mass picketing demonstration."

Ten thousand strikers responded to Gold's call on Monday, March 8. The police lunged into the mass of workers and beat down hundreds of strikers, men and women. The workers fought back. Frail girls leaped up fearlessly and returned blows squarely in the policemen's faces. As the line of strikers continued to forge ahead, police in patrol cars drove with breakneck speed into large numbers of workers on the sidewalks. Still the mass of strikers did not budge. In spite of every new assault by mounted police and motorized squads, the line grew. In the face of this immovable force, the police were powerless. Finally the great mass of pickets broke through completely and marched triumphantly to the strike halls. Besides the hundreds of strikers beaten up in that single demonstration, one hundred men and twenty-five women were arrested.

Such heroism compelled even the big-business-controlled newspapers to admit that the furriers "are running their own general strike." It completely refuted the employers' false charges that the workers did not support the strike leaders. A great force had emerged in the labor movement—rank-and-file mass picketing. It drove out the underworld elements, beat back policemen's clubs and nullified the dreaded raids of the Industrial Squad. This power was also capable of protecting the strike leadership from attacks by the employers' hired thugs. Strong-arm characters, lurking in nearby buildings waiting for a chance to attack Gold, thought better of it when they saw thousands of workers escorting him on his rounds of the strike halls.

Patrolling the fur district seven days and seven nights a week, the strikers wiped out the scab work in New York City. The bosses began to rely more and more on getting work done in out-of-town shops. In overcoming this new problem, the strike committee faced a serious obstacle—the open cooperation between the right-wing leaders of the International and the out-of-town employers who were doing scab work.

In the midst of these developments, Shachtman disappeared. Reporters looked for him high and low. When Gold visited his home, Shachtman's wife said she didn't know where he was. When Gold sent an inquiry to the International office in Long Island City, Secretary-Treasurer Wohl curtly informed him that President Shachtman was "now on tour throughout the country in behalf of the strike." Meanwhile Winnick kept issuing statements as "Acting President."

Reports poured in to the strike committee from workers outside New York that scab work was being done in their shops. The representatives of the International were doing nothing to stop it. Members of Local 53 in Philadelphia, led by Sam Burt, protested to J. Bowman, their business agent, that scab work was being done for New York manufacturers. They were bluntly told that it did not matter because the strike in New York was being led by Communists. When these workers complained to the International, Acting President Winnick advised Bowman to inform the protesting workers that the strike in New York was "nothing but a political maneuver." The scab work in many Philadelphia shops continued.

In Boston, too, enraged members of Local 30 informed their business agent, Beckman, that their shops were doing scab work for New York. Beckman asked the International to authorize him to call out the workers. His letters and telegrams went ignored. On March 10, he wrote to Acting President Winnick: "We wrote several letters to the International in reference to the New York situation and informed them that some of our shops are doing work for New York. . . . We also have information that quite a few shops around Boston, in the little towns, have opened up and are also doing work for New York. We were ready to make an investigation and to help the New York workers, but as we did not hear from you, we did not know what action to take. Kindly give this your immediate attention."

In reply, Winnick repeated that the strike in New York was a "political maneuver" by the Communists. He added quite frankly: "Therefore we shirk responsibility of any scab work that is being done outside of New York."

The International also sent letters of instruction to the out-of-town locals that they were to keep out representatives of the striking Joint Board locals who sought to stop scab work being done for the New York fur manufacturers.

The fact that the International permitted scab work in the out-of-town shops was not the only injury the right-wing officials of the International did to the strikers. On March 4, Winnick wrote confidently to Shachtman in Cleveland that everything was "pretty safe" in New York, and that by the time he returned, the International would have control of the strike. He wrote: "Happens the party I look at, meaning no 'lefts,' have the better of the situation for they are better schemers and you know it."

The "better schemers" included International officials, right-wing Socialist leaders, and the *Forward*. Winnick's letter to Shachtman was written two days after a meeting had been held in the office of the International in Long Island City, with Winnick, Sorkin, Wohl and a representative of the *Forward* present. The plan adopted for defeating the strike included:

1. That the *Forward* should play up news that the workers were dissatisfied with the strike leadership and the manner in which the "Communist leaders" were conducting the strike.

2. That the use of the strike funds should be criticized to make it more difficult for the strike leaders to carry on the struggle.

3. That contacts would be established with underworld leaders to supply sluggers to beat up strikers.

4. That when these attacks had demoralized the strikers, the right-wing officials of the International should step in and take over the leadership of the strike.

It was this plan that enabled Winnick to assure Shachtman so confidently that things were "pretty safe" in New York and that everything would soon be in the hands of the International.

The *Forward* wholeheartedly fulfilled its "holy mission." Daily it delivered a barrage of red-baiting against the strike. "This is not a strike. This is a revolution," blared the *Forward*. The very organization of the strike was patterned on the system in Russia. The shop chairmen's committee was based on local Soviets. The aim of the Communist leadership of the strike, the *Forward* cried, was to show Stalin "that his American followers have begun to make the revolution." Since the fur workers were not interested in this "revolution," they were being terrorized by the Communists to continue striking. The *Forward* even "discovered" a mysterious "Room C" in the strike headquarters. There, it narrated, hundreds of fur workers who refused to support the strike were taken and beaten into submission by the "Communist terrorists."

The *Forward* carried advertisements which urged all furriers who wished "to become financially independent" to apply at certain strikebreaking employment bureaus. The workers angrily ripped into shreds copies of the paper handed to them outside of the strike halls. Many burned their copies publicly.

When the manufacturers locked out the workers, the majority of the furriers had already been out of work for many weeks. Many strikers applied for strike relief during the first week of the strike. The relief committee investigated all who turned to them for support. A resolution had been adopted not to pay general strike benefit before the sixth week of the strike. The bosses had made the lockout during the slack period deliberately in the hope of starving out the strikers. The union's strategy was to preserve its funds until the critical period of the strike. Nevertheless, in view of the extreme difficulties of certain strikers who had been unemployed for a long time, the shop chairmen voted to begin paying benefits in these exceptional cases only.

The right-wingers, seeking to exhaust the union's funds as quickly as possible, seized upon this action of the shop chairmen. Their followers began to agitate the strikers to storm the offices of the union for strike benefits. When shop after shop endorsed the shop chairmen's decision, the right-wing clique demanded benefits for themselves and their families. "Give us benefits or we won't picket," they cried.

At the same time, the *Forward* charged that Communist strike leaders were giving benefits only to their comrades and discriminating against all others. The *Forward* also claimed that while the Jewish strikers were starving, the Greek strikers were receiving huge benefits.

On the other hand, Morris Zeitlin, chairman of the Joint Board and a right-wing supporter, refused to sign checks needed to carry on the strike and to pay benefits to those strikers who had been found to be desperately in need of financial aid. Echoing the *Forward* in long statements to the press, Zeitlin charged that the strike leadership intended to use the strike funds for Communist purposes. "I will not sign any checks as long as the Communists are the leaders of the strike," he threatened. Simultaneously, Winnick, Sorkin and Wohl announced that the International had notified all banks not to honor Joint Board checks which did not bear Zeitlin's signature.

The shop chairmen, fifteen hundred strong, answered the "better schemers" by notifying Zeitlin that if he did not stop interfering with the strike and sign the checks, he would be impeached. The locals were ready to follow up this warning. Zeitlin was compelled to yield. Thereafter he signed checks.

On March 8, the strike leaders heard that Abe Beckerman, later expelled by the Amalgamated Clothing Workers for corruption, was meeting with Winnick, Sorkin and Wohl. They suspected a serious provocation was afoot. Two days later, Gold received a call in the union office that a riot was going on at Webster Hall. When he reached the strike hall, he found the battle raging along the entire block between the strikers and Beckerman's gunmen. The gangs had tried to push their way into the hall. The strikers blocked them. Hundreds of the strikers from within Webster Hall and from the nearby strike halls rushed out to drive off the gangsters. Although some strikers were clubbed and beaten, hundreds more boldly joined the fight and overpowered the thugs. Pursuing the gangsters as they fled, the workers stripped them of guns, blackjacks, knives and clubs, and all but trampled them to death. When the battle was over, it was certain that these gunmen would never go near the strike halls again.

The bosses, meanwhile, were doing their share. They hired nearly every gangster in New York City, from the East Side and the West Side. They imported gunmen from Philadelphia and Chicago. They engaged private detective agencies.

Groups of gangsters paid visits to the picketing committee on 4th Street and to the strike halls. But after the first few visits, they steered clear of these places. One day, Gurrah and two of his gang were caught by the strikers on the street near one hall. After a battle, the workers chased them out of the area.

Jack Schneider, one of the most effective strike leaders, was a favorite target of the gangsters. On one occasion, Schneider was slashed up in the fur market by a group of gangsters and bosses. On many other occasions, he narrowly escaped from assaults carefully planned by hired thugs.

Gold, of course, was the prize target of the mobsters. Once a gangster walked into his office and demanded that certain shops be returned to work. When Gold refused and ordered him out, the gangster told him: "I'm coming back in ten minutes and I'll tear this office apart. You can order your ambulance now!"

"I'll wait for you," replied Gold. He walked over to the door, opened it, and told the gangster, "Get out!"

The thug looked at Gold and at the crowd of workers in the foyer. He dashed down the stairs and out of the building. Gold called out to him, "Don't come back or you'll regret it." With that, things quieted down. Gold resumed his work and dismissed the incident from his mind.

At seven that evening, Gold was in Child's Restaurant on Broadway with S. J. Zuckerman, labor editor of *The Day*. As they emerged from the restaurant, they saw the entrance surrounded by a group of mobsters, among them the thug Gold had thrown out of his office earlier in the day. Zuckerman removed his spectacles and said, "Gold, do you see?" "We're in a bad spot," Gold answered. Both remained standing tensely with their backs to the restaurant door.

At that very instant, as if by a miracle, several hundred people filtered into the block, from both ends and on both sides of the street. Before the mobsters could make their move, the block was filled with more than five hundred strikers. Hopelessly outnumbered, the mob fled. The workers would have slaughtered them and they knew it.

When Gold had left the union office with Zuckerman, some strikers had followed watchfully. As soon as the gang appeared, a striker dashed back to the union office and sounded the alarm. The general picketing committee, always alert for emergencies, arrived at the restaurant in the nick of time!

The fur workers did such a thorough job on the gangsters that they demanded ever greater sums of money from the employers. Towards the end of the strike, no gang was willing to risk the job, no matter how much the bosses offered.

The amazing solidarity of the strikers in the face of police brutality, arrests, gangsters and sluggers, won the admiration and support of broad sections of the American labor movement. On March 23, the Central Trades and Labor Council of New York City, composed of delegates from all AFL unions in the city, heartily endorsed "the management and conduct of the Joint Board Furriers' Union . . . in their strike," and pledged its full support to the Joint Board.

Many manufacturers were by this time privately conceding that they could not defeat the union. Their samples were not made. Even the scab work they were having done in out-of-town shops with the connivance of leaders of the International did not solve their problem, since the scabs could not produce one-tenth of the work that was needed. Many manufacturers knew that they would be forced into bankruptcy if a settlement did not come soon. As the weeks passed, more and more members of the Association pressured their leaders to end the strike and settle with the union.

There were two distinct groups on the Association's Board of Directors.

One group, headed by President Samuels, represented the most vicious anti-union elements. Aggressive and arrogant, they were determined to smash the union as in 1920. The second group represented the richer, more influential, comparatively "liberal" manufacturers. Their financial losses during the strike were much greater than those of the group headed by Samuels. They were anxious for a settlement. But they were neither organized nor aggressive. They did not dare challenge Samuels because of the hysteria he had whipped up to terrorize the workers and keep the shaky employers in line. They were also reluctant to be labeled disloyal if they called for a settlement.

This more influential group of employers turned to the fur skin dealers and importers for assistance to end the strike. The dealers and importers had huge investments in fur skins which were seriously jeopardized by the paralysis in the trade. The manufacturers owed them considerable sums. They were alarmed at the prospect of numerous bankruptcies among the manufacturers. They, too, were therefore desirous of ending the strike.

Outstanding among the dealers and importers was Motty Eitingon of the Eitingon-Schild Company, the wealthiest fur importer in the trade. Eitingon, it will be recalled, had been instrumental in ending the 1920 strike when the right-wingers had been in control of the union. His influence in the trade had increased enormously since 1920; in fact, many manufacturers were dependent on the credit extended them by Eitingon. It was a foregone conclusion that with the votes of the group that wanted a settlement, and with the influence he exercised in the industry generally, Eitingon's pressure on the Samuels group in the Association's leadership would result in an agreement within a short time.

Eitingon stepped into the picture on March 25, in the seventh week of the strike. The strike was actually settled that week with an outstanding victory for the union. The amazing reasons for its continuation beyond the seventh week have never before been told in full.

The story begins long before the seventh week of the strike. Among the reporters assigned to cover the strike was S. J. Zuckerman of the Jewish paper, *The Day*. Although he was labor editor, Zuckerman knew little about the furriers' dispute when he was assigned to cover the strike. He obtained numerous interviews with Samuels and other leaders of the Association. He then interviewed a number of leaders of the Joint Board and spent several hours discussing the strike with Gold.

Impressed by Gold's earnestness, his concern for the needs of the workers, and his unwavering faith in the rank and file, Zuckerman devoted every moment of his time to the fur workers. He went from one strike hall to another. He talked to strikers on the picket lines. He listened to conversations among rank-and-file groups. He was with the strikers so much that many came to regard him as a true friend. Through his detailed reports of the strike in *The Day*, Zuckerman's writings, together with the factual reports that appeared in the *Freiheit*, did much to counteract the enmity of the *Forward*.*

Through Zuckerman, Gold met Joseph Mayer, labor reporter for *Women's Wear*. Mayer was a highly talented writer, with prestige in the fur industry. He had the utmost contempt for the type of labor leaders he frequently met in the course of his work. At first, he had taken it for granted that Gold, too, was corrupt and bureaucratic and that he would sell out to the bosses for a price. But at his very first meeting with Gold, Mayer developed a wholesome respect for the young left-wing leader of the Furriers Union. The occasion was a press conference held by the union. James O'Leary, reporter for the *New York World*, asked Gold whether the reports that he was a Communist were true. "Sure, since 1919," came Gold's proud reply. That was "sensational" news for most of the reporters. Mayer and Zuckerman, however, were greatly impressed by Gold's frankness and fearlessness.

* Zuckerman was bitterly attacked by the *Forward* and Morris Sigman, right-wing Socialist President of the ILGWU, and accused of violating the ethics of his profession and of being in the pay of the Communists of the Furriers Union. Towards the end of the strike, Sigman influenced Joseph Barondess, the early leader of the New York Cloak Makers and a power in Jewish progressive circles, to investigate the charges against Zuckerman for his coverage of the strike. While the investigation was taking place, Zuckerman waited outside all afternoon and was not even called in to defend himself. However, he needed no defense, for the publisher, Shapiro, informed him that he and Barondess had agreed that the charges were unfounded and false. However, to appease the right-wing Socialists, Shapiro informed Zuckerman that if he wished to continue as labor editor of *The Day*, he would have to submit his articles in advance of publication for editorial review. Zuckerman refused to submit to this obvious attempt at censorship and gave up the post of Labor Editor for *The Day*. He continued to work for the paper in other capacities, but refused to allow any article he wrote to appear in the paper under his signature. In 1943, Zuckerman asked to be re-assigned to cover labor news, and his request was granted unconditionally.

It is important, in connection with Zuckerman's accounts of the 1926 strike, to bear in mind that at no time was he a left-winger either before, during or after the strike. He was simply an objective journalist who developed the utmost respect for the honesty and sincerity of the fur workers and their leaders, and who felt that the attacks against the strike leadership were outrageous.

Informed by the dealers and many leading manufacturers that the continuation of the strike would be ruinous for them, Mayer talked to Motty Eitingon. He convinced him that it would be suicidal for the manufacturers to prolong the strike in the vain hope that the union would weaken.

Zuckerman then arranged for Gold to meet Eitingon to discuss the terms of a settlement. Knowing Eitingon's role in settling the 1920 strike, and aware of the great influence he exerted in the industry, Gold accepted the invitation. He received permission from the General Strike Committee for a confidential committee, consisting of himself, Gross and Leibowitz, to conduct negotiations toward settling the strike. The terms of any settlement, when and if reached, would then be submitted to the General Strike Committee and to the strikers themselves for approval.

Gold's first conference with Eitingon took place on March 25. Eitingon made it clear that his main purpose at the first conference was to find out all he could about the union, its leadership, and the demands of the strikers. Gold made it equally clear that the demands for equal division of work, the forty-hour week and no section contracting were very important to the fur workers. He presented a detailed analysis of the significance of these demands. He informed Eitingon that the wages of most fur workers averaged between $28 and $30 a week. Since they worked only seven or eight months in the year, it was impossible to earn a living. Eitingon expressed amazement at these facts. From what the manufacturers had told him, he was under the impression that the fur workers earned as high as $125 a week. Gold explained what equal division of work meant to the workers. They were threatened with unemployment every Saturday. Active union men were in danger of being discharged at a moment's notice. Eitingon agreed that this was a bad situation. He declared that a reasonable plan of equal division of work would be good for the industry. However, Eitingon refused to commit himself further. He insisted that he wanted to hear the manufacturers' side of the question.

That same evening, Eitingon called Gold and asked him to keep the news of the first conference in strict confidence. The manufacturers, Eitingon continued, had informed him that Gold was a "bolshevik" and would "make capital" of everything he was told. With the approval of Leibowitz and Gross, Gold agreed that the news of the conference would be kept secret.

At a second conference on March 27, Eitingon questioned Gold minutely about the facts Gold had given him concerning the conditions of the fur workers and the importance of equal division of work. Eitingon revealed that he had spoken with School, former manager of the Association's labor department, and had obtained an entirely different version of the issues in the strike. For over two hours, Gold patiently went over the major demands of the union. After listening attentively, Eitingon's conclusion was: "Between you and School I cannot come to a decision. You say one thing and he says another."

Eitingon met with Gold and School two days later. School led off with the argument for the manufacturers. If they granted the union's chief demands, he insisted, they would be placed in a vulnerable position. He was brutally frank. With equal division of work and a forty-hour week, he declared, unemployment would be reduced and wages could no longer be arbitrarily cut. If, in addition, section contracting was abolished, the manufacturers would be completely powerless to reduce wages. If wage rates were raised and overtime eliminated, the workers would have to be kept working steadily at good wages. The only way the manufacturers could then exist would be by raising their prices. Since this would be difficult, the union's demands, if adopted, would force many manufacturers out of business, concluded School.

Gold hammered School's arguments to bits. He showed that conditions in the fur industry were chaotic. Adoption of the union's chief demands would actually solve many of the existing problems. Equal division of work would mean more stability in the industry and end most of the moving about of workers from shop to shop. If there was security on the job and more steady employment, there would be less pressure on wage rates. The employers would have to recognize that they could not discharge their workers at will. If they spent less time concocting schemes to get rid of "troublemakers," they would devote themselves more to operating on a stable basis.

Gold made it clear that the fur workers were ready to fight to the limit to secure the forty-hour, five-day week. He described the terrible working conditions in the fur shops and their destructive effect on the workers' health; the determination of the religious Jews in the union who refused to work on Saturdays; and the unemployed who saw in the shorter work-week a chance to get work.

Eitingon announced that he would reach a decision within a day or two. The next day, March 30, Gold received a message through Zuckerman that Eitingon wished to see him. With Eitingon at the conference was R. L. Lindheim, the vice-president of the Eitingon-Schild Company.

Eitingon revealed that he had been convinced by many of Gold's arguments, and that he had already discussed with Samuels the need to settle the strike. He was now ready to negotiate. He assured Gold that whatever he would agree upon would be approved by the employers as the terms on which the strike would be settled.

Eitingon proposed settling on a 50-50 basis. This meant a forty-two-hour week; equal division of work six months during the year; no section contracting; no overtime, except two hours on Saturday during September to December at the option of the workers; and a 10 percent wage increase. Gold refused to commit himself before consulting Leibowitz and Gross.

At the next conference, Gold declared that the strike committee might compromise on equal division of work, but would not give up the forty-hour, five-day week. Eitingon argued that the union would get an extension of equal division of work, an increase in the minimum scale and other points, hence it should be willing to agree on the forty-two-hour week.

After much bargaining, the next day, at the final conference, Eitingon agreed to the following terms as the basis for the settlement:

1. Forty-hour, five-day week.
2. Equal division of work during four months of the year.
3. No contracting.
4. 10 percent wage increase.
5. No overtime except during the period from September to December when workers could work two hours on Saturday at regular rates if they wished to do so.
6. Abolition of the second-class minimum wage scale.
7. Other points to be negotiated.

The forty-hour week was won! Eitingon and Gold shook hands on this settlement. The wealthy importer promised to call the strike leader within two days to arrange for the signing of the agreement.

Two days went by. No call from Eitingon. Two more days passed—still no call.

On Friday, April 7, the call came. Eitingon asked Gold to meet him at his suite at the Ansonia Hotel. When Gold entered, Eitingon had his hat and coat on. A porter was carrying out his suitcases. Eitingon was curt. "I am leaving for England within half an hour," he told Gold. "But before I leave, I wanted to wish you luck with the settlement. My sole reason for calling you is to tell you that if you negotiated a settlement

with Samuels and William Green in Washington, you should at least have
had the courtesy to inform me of it."

Gold was speechless! When he recovered his bearings, he assured
Eitingon that he did not know what he referred to. It was Eitingon's turn
to be startled. He asked Gold if he had not signed a settlement in Washington. When Gold again denied any knowledge of such a settlement,
Eitingon said he had failed to call him during the past week because he
was under the impression that the strike had already been settled at a
conference in Washington.

It was in this manner that Gold learned for the first time
that a secret agreement had been signed in Washington behind the backs
of the strikers and their democratically-elected leaders—one of the most
disgraceful chapters in the history of the American labor movement.

Shachtman, Sorkin and Winnick had learned that Eitingon was discussing a settlement of the strike with the manufacturers. When they heard
from the employers that Eitingon was about to settle the terms of the
agreement with Gold, they became frantic. A successful outcome of the
strike under left-wing leadership, especially after the right-wing's open
sabotage, would doom their control of the International. They determined
that at all costs, the negotiations by Eitingon must not be permitted to
result in a settlement.

The leaders of the Fur Manufacturers Association and the right-wing
officials of the International turned in desperation to the top officials of
the AFL. Both knew that the AFL officials would be alarmed at the prospect of a left-wing victory in the fur workers' strike. It would jeopardize
the hold of the conservative labor leaders over other trade unions too.

As early as the summer of 1925, the top officials of the Federation had
started to maneuver secretly to aid the right-wing clique in the needle
trades unions against the rising rank-and-file revolt led by the left wing.
In June 1925, two representatives of the right-wing machine met secretly
with William Green at Unity House, the ILGWU's summer resort, and
discussed plans to halt the growth of the left-wing movement in the New
York Joint Board. That same month, directly after Locals 2, 9 and 22
of New York were expelled by the Sigman machine in the ILGWU, Hugh
Frayne, New York representative of the AFL, joined the leaders of the
Sigman machine in secret conferences with the police officials of New
York. A plan was devised to use the police power against the members
of the three expelled locals.

"I have just returned from police headquarters," Frayne wrote to

NEW YORK OFFICE

AMERICAN FEDERATION OF LABOR

Executive Council.
President, SAMUEL GOMPERS,
Secretary, FRANK MORRISON,
Treasurer, DANIEL J. TOBIN,
801 E. Michigan St., Indianapolis, Ind.

First Vice-President: JAMES DUNCAN,
M. Gilmore Street, Washington Mass.
Second Vice-President, JAS. P. VALENTINE,
A Sixteenth Building, Cincinnati, Ohio.
Third Vice-President, FRANK DUFFY,
Carpenters' Bldg., Indianapolis, Ind.
Fourth Vice-President, WILLIAM GREEN,
Merchants Bank Bldg., Indianapolis, Ind.

Fifth Vice-President, T. A. RICKERT,
Room 505, 116 W. Washington St., Chicago, Ill.
Sixth Vice-President, JACOB FISCHER,
325 East Michigan Street, Indianapolis, Ind.
Seventh Vice-President, MATTHEW WOLL,
Room 901, 166 W. Washington St., Chicago, Ill.
Eighth Vice-President, MARTIN F. RYAN,
Aet Rail building, Kansas City, Mo.

HUGH FRAYNE
REPRESENTATIVE
1416 BROADWAY CORNER 39TH ST.
ROOMS 606-606
TELEPHONE, PENNSYLVANIA 5666

A. F. OF L. BUILDING
WASHINGTON, D. C.

LONG DISTANCE TELEPHONE, MAIN 3671-2-3
CABLE ADDRESS, 'AFEL'

New York, June 17, 1925.

RECEIVED
JUN 18 1925.

Mr. William Green, President,
American Federation of Labor,
A. F of L. Bldg., Washington, D. C.

Dear Sir and Brother:.

I am enclosing clippings from the New York World and
Times, as the subject may not have been brought to your attention.

In connection with this matter I desire to say that I
had a conference at the Aberdeen Hotel on Tuesday night with
President Sigman and Vice-President Perlstein of the International
Ladies Garment Workers Union. It was decided to take this question
up with the police authorities.

I have just returned from police headquarters where I
spent several hours with President Sigman, Vice-Presidents Halpern
and Sideman of the International, and Chief Inspector Lahey.
The whole subject was laid before him, with the additional understanding that President Sigman would furnish a written memorandum
giving names and locations where the members of the ousted unions
are active and where they have succeeded in getting police protection under false pretenses.

This matter was brought to a head by the International
officers ousting the three executive boards of these unions and
while it is a serious situation, I feel sure that the Communistic
activities of this group will be very much weakened by removing
them from official positions in the unions, where they have been
able by authority of their offices to practically dominate the
organizations through a minority group of Communists.

With the true facts placed in the hands of the police
through Chief Inspector Lahey, and the determination of President
Sigman and the Executive Board to clean house, it is only a short
time when what might be considered a death blow will be given
to this insidious movement which is a menace not only to the labor
movement but to the safety of the nation as a whole.

I have been cooperating with and rendering every
possible assistance to President Sigman and his associates in
this work, which I know will meet with your full approval.

With best wishes, I am,

Fraternally yours,

General Organizer
American Federation of Labor

*AFL and right-wing ILGWU leaders rush to the police for help
in crushing the revolt of the militant cloak and dressmakers.*

William Green on June 17, 1925, "where I spent several hours with President Sigman, Vice-Presidents Halpern and Sideman of the International, and Chief Inspector Lahey. The whole subject was laid before him, with the additional understanding that President Sigman would furnish a written memorandum giving names and locations where the members of the ousted unions are active. . . With the true facts placed in the hands of the police through Chief Inspector Lahey, and the determination of President Sigman and the Executive Board to clean house, it is only a short time when what might be considered a death blow will be given to this insidious movement which is a menace not only to the labor movement but to the safety of the nation as a whole."

The plan met with Green's approval. "I recommend most heartily the brave, courageous and aggressive stand which you and your associates have taken," he wrote to Sigman on June 24, 1925.

Sorkin and Shachtman went to Washington to discuss their plans with Socialist Congressman Meyer London. He readily agreed to collaborate with them. Together with Feinstone, a leading figure in the Forward Association, the United Hebrew Trades and the right-wing machine in the ILGWU, Winnick conferred with Hugh Frayne, New York representative of the AFL. They arranged to have Frayne inform William Green personally of the importance of intervening in the furriers' strike on behalf of the leaders of the International.

After conferring with Frayne, Green met with Shachtman, Sorkin and Congressman London in Washington. The latter group insisted that the fur workers had been "jockeyed into the strike by leaders who are tools of the Soviets." They assured Green that as soon as the strikers saw that the AFL had come to their rescue, they would throw out the "Communist" strike leaders who had been terrorizing them. The strikers would ratify any agreement with the manufacturers concluded by the International officers and endorsed by the Federation.

When it appeared certain that the Eitingon-Gold conferences were bringing the strike to an end, the plotters rushed ahead. On April 1, the day after Gold and Eitingon began their actual negotiations, Green met in Washington with Samuels, Shachtman and Meyer London. A tentative settlement was reached, the final details to be worked out in New York City by Frayne, Shachtman and Samuels. This agreement, drawn up behind the workers' backs, surrendered some of their most important demands. It provided:

POSTAL TELEGRAPH - COMMERCIAL CABLES

TELEGRAM

CLASS OF SERVICE DESIRED

FAST TELEGRAM
DAY LETTER
NIGHT TELEGRAM
NIGHT LETTER

TELEGRAMS TO ALL AMERICA   CABLEGRAMS TO ALL THE WORLD

Send the following Telegram, subject to the terms on back hereof, which are hereby agreed to.

To   Mr. H. Sorkin, Hotel Washington,   March 19, 1926
Washington, D.C. c/o O.Shachtman.

President Green will be in New York Saturday ten o'clock. He will
not be back in Washington before some day next week. Feinstone
arranged with Frayne to have appointment in New York on Saturday.
Think it advisable that you make first train back to New York. If you
think that everything is arranged with Shachtman to meet Green. Wire
immediately if appointment will be kept. Wire answer to my home, thirteen
thirty seven Grant Avenue, Bronx.

I. Winnick.

WESTERN UNION TELEGRAM

NEWCOMB CARLTON, PRESIDENT   GEORGE W. E. ATKINS, FIRST VICE-PRESIDENT

CLASS OF SERVICE
TELEGRAM
DAY LETTER   BLUE
NIGHT MESSAGE   NITE
NIGHT LETTER   N L

If none of these three symbols appears after the check (number of words) this is a telegram. Otherwise its character is indicated by the symbol appearing after the check.

The filing time as shown in the date line on full rate telegrams and day letters, and the time of receipt at destination as shown on all messages, is STANDARD TIME.

Received at

WB481 91 NL

WASHINGTON DC 30

OZIER SCHACTMAN

9 JACKSON AVE LONGISLANDCITY NY

I AM DEEPLY INTERESTED IN THE STRIKE OF THE MEMBERS OF THE
INTERNATIONAL FUR WORKERS UNION AND AM DESIROUS OF BEING
HELPFUL IN BRINGING ABOUT SUCCESS TO THE MEMBERS OF THE
INTERNATIONAL FUR WORKERS UNION ON STRIKE AND SATISFACTORY
SETTLEMENT TO ALL CONCERNED STOP BECAUSE OF THIS FACT I AM
ASKING YOU TO COME TO WASHINGTON FOR A CONFERENCE ON THURSDAY.
APRIL FIRST STOP IF YOU DEEM IT ADVISABLE I SUGGEST YOU
INVITE MR SAMUEL N SAMUELS PRESIDENT OF THE ASSOCIATED
FUR MANUFACTURERS INCORPORATED TO ACCOMPANY YOU STOP
PLEASE WIRE REPLY

WILLIAM GREEN.

Winnick and Green set the stage for the betrayal in Washington.

1. The old agreement shall form the basis for a settlement.
2. Elimination of overtime as far as possible.
3. A three-year agreement.
4. No apprenticeship from February 1, 1926, to February 19, 1928.
5. No sub-contracting.
6. A 10 percent increase over the present minimum wage scales.
7. At the end of two years the second-class minimum to be abolished.
8. A forty-two-hour week.

At one stroke, the character of the 1926 strike was altered. It was no longer simply a battle for economic improvements. Now it took on the broader significance of a fundamental struggle for trade union democracy, for the right of workers to determine their own destiny, and for freedom from the days of terror and betrayal that had marked the Furriers Union before the spring of 1925. If the manufacturers could get away with this, then everything the fur workers had fought for since 1920, everything they had gained since the spring of 1925, would be lost.

"The end of the left-wing rule is in sight," the *Fur Age Weekly* gloated when the news of the Washington agreement was made public. All the right-wingers needed now was to force the agreement down the strikers' throats.

Could they do it?

CHAPTER 20

Carnegie Hall
to 69th Armory

On April 13, 1926, the fur workers received letters from the International signed by President Shachtman and Secretary-Treasurer Wohl. Intimating that a satisfactory settlement of the strike was in sight, the letters announced that the terms would be made public at a meeting in Carnegie Hall on Thursday, April 15. The letters enclosed a ballot, to be returned unsigned to the International officers. If the workers wanted to return to their shops, they had only to mark "Yes" next to the question: "Shall the International Fur Workers Union forthwith go into conference with the Associated Fur Manufacturers for a settlement of the strike?"

Although their plans had been worked out in careful detail, the right-wingers were still jittery over the temper of the strikers. "Would be of great help to us if you would address our meeting," Shachtman wired William Green. "We feel that your presence would save the situation."

Perhaps President Green had a premonition. At any rate, he decided that it would be unwise for him to appear at the meeting. The right-wing leaders of the International had to content themselves with a message in which Green pledged the Federation's support to the International "in such action as may be taken in negotiating a settlement with the fur manufacturers upon a fair, just and satisfactory basis."

The shop chairmen were called to a meeting at Manhattan Lyceum on April 14, the day before the Carnegie Hall meeting. Gold opened the meeting with the declaration that the General Strike Commit-

208

tee did not care "who brings a settlement, so long as the workers' demands are satisfied." The one vital point, Gold insisted, was that the workers themselves must be the ones to decide on the terms of the agreement. "What difference does a 'signed contract' make, if the workers won't work under it?" he asked. "No matter who signs the 'contract,' the workers are the final judge."

Gold offered to withdraw from the General Strike Committee if that was the wish of the workers. The shop chairmen emphatically refused to consider his proposal. One after another, the chairmen declared that the workers of their shops were indignant at the letter sent out by the International. They reported that the workers were turning in their ballots to the shop chairmen, who in turn handed them over to the Joint Board for use as a check on the results of the balloting that might be announced by the International.

When the discussion ended, Gold advised the shop chairmen: "First, don't lose your heads. Retain contact with the workers. Second, be at Carnegie Hall tomorrow morning at eleven o'clock. Line up around the hall. Carry your striking cards. Get in. We have been invited, and we will go."

"Boycott the meeting!" shouted the shop chairmen.

Instantly Gold was on his feet. "No! Be there. Your place tomorrow is in Carnegie Hall. The International would like you to boycott the meet-

Shachtman begs Green to "save" the right wing at Carnegie Hall.

POSTAL TELEGRAPH - COMMERCIAL CABLES

TELEGRAM

Send the following Telegram, subject to the terms on back hereof, which are hereby agreed to.

To   Mr. William Green, President,   April 13   193 6

American Federation of Labor,

Barcli Theatre,

Barrett St., Schenectady, N.Y.

Mass meeting called for Thursday April fifteenth, our situation favorable. Would be of great help to us if you would address our meeting. We feel that your presence would save the situation.

O. Shachtman.

ing. Then a small group of right-wing scabs and strong-arm men will vote to end the strike. The next day, the newspaper headlines will shriek: 'FUR WORKERS VOTE TO ACCEPT SETTLEMENT AND END STRIKE.' This will cause confusion and division among the workers. We can prevent this by being at Carnegie Hall. Every furrier, including those who work in the settled shops, must be at Carnegie Hall tomorrow morning. There we will show where the furriers stand."

Gold went on to point out that it was necessary at this stage for the workers to differentiate between the right-wing leaders of the International and leaders of the AFL. It should be assumed for the present that President Green had been "indirectly misinformed as to the true facts in the furriers' strike." An open conflict with the Federation must be avoided if possible. If the manufacturers saw that the strikers were in a fight with the American Federation of Labor, that would "create even more difficulties."

After exhaustive discussion, the shop chairmen agreed with the logic of Gold's reasoning. They voted unanimously to instruct the workers to attend the Carnegie Hall meeting in full force.

A resolution from the floor reaffirmed complete confidence in the strike leadership and asserted that the fur workers would return to work only under an agreement signed by their elected leadership. *Women's Wear* reported that "the reading of the resolution brought loud cheers from the meeting." However on Gold's insistence that the issue was not *who* signed the agreement, the resolution was not put to a vote.

At nine o'clock the next morning, all the strikers gathered in the fur market, received a bulletin prepared overnight by the General Strike Committee. It described the heroic battle waged by the fur workers for almost nine weeks and the continuous maneuvers of the leaders of the International to break the strike.

The strike, the statement continued, was not being conducted in order to decide who would confer with the manufacturers for a settlement. It was for better conditions that the fur workers were battling so valiantly. The General Strike Committee did not claim that it alone possessed the power to settle the strike. But it insisted:

"No one will be allowed to confer or to make a settlement with the bosses without the consent of the striking furriers. The furriers, who are carrying the yoke of battle on their shoulders, must and will be the ones to decide for themselves who shall represent them, and what conditions they wish to accept.

"This question will not be settled by any fake ballots which bear no signatures and which can be counted in any number desired, but by an honest vote of the membership. No earnest discussion on the points of settlement can be conducted today at Carnegie Hall. This can be done only in a gathering at which all strikers may participate."

The statement urged the strikers to go to Carnegie Hall and tell the betrayers: "Hands off our strike! Get out of our way! We alone have borne the brunt of the battle up to now, and we will lead it to a victorious end!"

The right-wing leaders were thrown into a panic by the efforts of the General Strike Committee to impress the workers with the necessity of attending the Carnegie Hall meeting. "That the right wing had apparently expected the left to take steps to keep the workers from participating in today's mass meeting," *Women's Wear* reported on April 15, "was indicated by measures resorted to by right-wing leaders. Reports have even gained currency in the market yesterday that such steps had been taken. It was heard that there had been rioting in Webster Hall where workers were alleged to have been intimidated. The same sources which transmitted this information to WOMEN'S WEAR later retracted the story."

Thrown off balance by the General Strike Committee's instructions to the strikers to attend the Carnegie Hall meeting in full force, the right-wing leaders resorted to the most despicable trickery to save the day. Their conduct at Carnegie Hall marked a new low for treachery, deceit and arrogant contempt for the rank-and-file workers.

At ten o'clock Thursday morning, the fur workers began to assemble outside of Carnegie Hall. By 11:15, about four thousand were lined up; a half-hour later, there were about six thousand. By one o'clock, when the doors were scheduled to open, the line which started at the entrances, four or five abreast, circled around the entire block between Sixth and Seventh Avenues.

Large numbers of police were on the scene. Mounted officers were posted every ten feet along the line. Plainclothesmen and uniformed guards were at the doors. Stationed near the entrances were so-called "private detectives," none other than the gangsters who had been serving the bosses since the outbreak of the strike.

At ten minutes after one, the phones in the union office began to ring. Excited workers informed the General Strike Committee that hundreds of strikers were being refused admittance even after they showed their strike cards. A committee of the International and the gangster elements

—"Bullet-proof Ashie," Yurman, "Big Alex" Fried and a whole crowd of strong-arm men—inspected everyone who approached the entrance. They instructed the police and detectives that those strikers whose cards showed a large number of strike-hall punches should be refused admittance to the hall. Those who were allowed to enter were first "frisked" for hidden weapons. Those rejected as active strikers were hustled away from the door. They remained in the vicinity, however, and assembled in the streets outside of Carnegie Hall. Each moment they were joined by other "suspects" who were taken out of the line.

The entire General Strike Committee left immediately for Carnegie Hall. Meanwhile, Gold instructed the strikers who phoned that all were to conduct themselves peacefully and not to give any grounds for disturbance.

"When we came to 57th Street near Fifth Avenue," Suroff wrote later, "it became difficult for us to get near the hall. The streets were black with people. The traffic was halted for blocks around. Police mounted on horses were in the hundreds.

"When the strikers saw their leaders, a great cry arose, 'We want Gold! We want the General Strike Committee!' Those strikers who were near us told us that they had been shamefully mistreated at the entrance to the hall. The police and detectives searched their pockets as if they were common thieves. Any striker who managed to get inside the hall was forced to walk through cordons of police, and if someone regarded suspiciously by the leaders of the International was allowed to enter by mistake, he was thrown out bodily by the gangsters stationed around the auditorium.

"I wanted to convince myself of the truth of this incredible story, so I walked over to the entrance on Seventh Avenue. The workers who saw me made way for me. Near the door I saw first the strong-arm boys from the underworld whom we had driven out of the union. Here they were a real power. They wore red bands on their arms, and strutted about shouting insults at the workers. I recognized them. They were the same gangsters who now worked for the bosses, beating up the workers who picketed the shops.

"As they saw me, one of them cried out to a policeman, who stood near the door, 'Throw him out!' I took out my credentials as a member of the General Strike Committee, thinking that this would get me into the hall immediately. The policeman was confused. He did not know what to do, and answered me that he could not help it.

"Then I saw Isaac Wohl, secretary-treasurer of the International. I asked him, 'Why don't you let the strikers inside the hall?' His gruff answer was, 'Get away from here! We don't recognize you Communists!' "

When Gold and the other members of the General Strike Committee came to Carnegie Hall, they were surrounded by detectives outside the hall. "This time you will not get in," the strong-arm men sneered at Gold.

Meanwhile, the police received orders to disperse the workers who had been refused admittance. By this time they had filled the streets in a densely-packed mass for five or six blocks around Carnegie Hall. A squadron of police on horseback dashed headlong into the crowd. But every group that was splintered off came right back and reassembled. Several times the swarming rows of strikers were broken. Each time they regrouped and resumed their places. The police eventually abandoned their efforts.

Suddenly an uproar from inside Carnegie Hall rang through the streets. It drowned out the shouts of the police. "We want Gold! WE WANT GOLD! WE WANT GOLD!" The thousands of workers in the streets took up the cry. "WE WANT GOLD!"

A shower of paper cups, cigarette wrappers and other paper objects streamed out of the upper windows of Carnegie Hall. The workers in the street snatched up the papers as they fell. On each scrap was a message from a group inside. "Brothers, stand fast and solid," the notes read. "We won't let them open their dirty mouths until they let our leaders in."

Tears flowed from the eyes of workers in the streets as they read these words. The curious policemen too began snatching the falling pieces of paper. When they came upon Yiddish writing, they asked the workers to translate the messages for them. Many policemen frankly confessed that they had never seen anything like this in their lives. Even the most cynical newspaper reporters were moved by this extraordinary demonstration of working class solidarity.

Meanwhile, what had been happening inside Carnegie Hall? Word that Gold had been barred soon reached the auditorium, crowded from orchestra pit to the highest galleries with restless strikers. Jeers and hisses immediately broke out, directed at the four men on the stage: Hugh Frayne, John Coughlin, Secretary of the New York State Federation of Labor, Oizer Shachtman and Morris Zeitlin, chairman of the Joint Board.

Frayne arose to call the meeting to order and to read William Green's telegram of greetings. He was met with an avalanche of boos. The workers shouted that they wanted Gold. For more than a half-hour Frayne stood there, unable to make himself heard. The workers outside picked up the cry until it reverberated through the packed streets: "Gold! Gold! We want Gold!"

Every time one of the four men on the stage stood up, the outcry rose higher and higher. It was impossible for any of the four "speakers" to utter a word. Time and again, the strong-arm men sought to still the crowd. They pulled many of the shouting workers out of their seats. But the strikers refused to budge. Other workers stood up and dared the bruisers to start any trouble. "Bring Gold in and we'll keep quiet," the workers shouted.

Frustrated, the four officials on the platform decided to give up the meeting. But the workers did not even allow them to announce that the meeting was called off. Finally, at 3:20 P.M. a tall man in a light overcoat strode onto the stage and held up his hand for silence. The shouts and cries showed no sign of abating until he pointed to a gold shield on his lapel. When the tumult subsided, the speaker said:

"If you will be quiet, I have an announcement to make. I am Inspector Lyons of the Police Department and I am in charge of the policemen who are here today. This committee has decided not to hold this meeting. In the name of the Police Department I ask you to leave quietly and peacefully. The police will assist the crowd in leaving the hall."

The fur workers applauded this announcement. Like disciplined soldiers they filed into the aisles and marched out to the street, where, together with those already outside, they lined up two by two and marched thirty-five blocks to the headquarters of the Joint Board.

To save face, the right-wing leaders of the International charged that the demonstration inside Carnegie Hall had been "engineered by communist agitators under Gold's direct supervision." *Women's Wear* promptly labeled this "ridiculous." "If the demonstration was engineered by the left wing," the trade journal declared, "it was executed by a leaderless left wing. Those in charge of arrangements had taken steps to keep out every person whose presence was not welcome to them."

Carnegie Hall became a symbol of what workers could accomplish when inspired by the ideals of a great struggle. Years of theoretical discussion could not have taught the American workers what they learned from the fur workers that day. Ultra-conservative leaders of labor and their right-wing Socialist allies would have to yield before the power of an aroused, united and union-conscious working class.

On the following day, Hugh Frayne released to the press the terms of the eight-point settlement made behind the backs of the fur workers. At the same time, he induced the Central Trades and Labor Council of New York to withdraw their endorsement of the strike. Asked by reporters what the Federation would do if the strikers refused to recognize the settlement and continued the strike, Frayne replied bluntly: "Then the strike will be outlawed."

The leadership of the Furriers Union was not to be caught napping. At a mass meeting of the strikers, Gold declared that the eight-point offer was "a betrayal of the workers' cause." The Joint Board, Gold pointed out, could have secured the terms embodied in the eight-point pact without having to go through a strike. More important, the union was on the verge of securing the workers' major demands when the International stepped in and sabotaged a settlement by the duly elected strike leaders.

Gold warned the strikers not to be provoked into any action that would play into the hands of the bosses and their agents. Amid the cheers of the strikers, he vowed that the strike would go on until they obtained a "satisfactory settlement."

Once again, Gold refrained from attacking the AFL and its leaders. In part, his attitude was based on the belief that William Green had been misled by the right-wing leaders of the International and the manufacturers. But primarily, Gold's approach was an attempt to frustrate the efforts of the right-wingers to isolate the strikers from the mainstream of the labor movement, the American Federation of Labor.

William Green now had to choose between arbitrarily settling the strike without the consent of the workers or dealing with the recognized representatives of the strikers. After Carnegie Hall, Green could no longer claim that he was saving the strikers from "Communist terrorists" who kept the furriers on strike against their will. By refraining from identifying the Federation with the attempted sell-out, Gold deliberately gave Green a means of retreating from his untenable position.

Learning that Green was at the Hotel Cadillac in New York, Gold secured an appointment with the President of the Federation. Together with Leibowitz and Gross, he spent two hours in conference with Green on Saturday, April 17. He went over the union's demands, and proved that there was a real possibility of winning the forty-hour week and equal division of work. He pointed out, moreover, that in 1912 Samuel Gompers had spoken for the fur strikers and the Federation had assisted them in winning their strike. But now the fur workers were beginning to believe that they were being betrayed by the Federation and its leaders.

The telling arguments made Green wince. He began to retreat. Green confessed that he knew very little about the problems of the fur workers or the basic conflict between the Joint Board and the International. He had become involved in the strike because he had been told by Shachtman and Meyer London that a small body of Communists held the fur workers in their grip and were forcing them to strike against their will. Now, he admitted, he saw that he had been operating under a misconception. He was still anxious to bring about peace between the International and the Joint Board and to help the fur workers win their strike. He therefore proposed that a joint Conference Committee consisting of representatives of the AFL, the International Union and the Joint Board be set up to negotiate a settlement with the manufacturers.

The following day, Green and Frayne, representing the Federation; Shachtman, Winnick and Sorkin, representing the International; and Gold, Gross, Shapiro, Leibowitz and Polansky, representing the General Strike Committee, met at the Hotel Cadillac. After a good deal of polite discussion, the conferees agreed * that a committee composed of repre-

---

* The text of the agreement is presented below in full not only for its importance in the strike itself, but also because after the strike was over, Green, Frayne and Shachtman claimed that the agreement included a provision calling for an investigation of the strike by the AFL. Gold denied this contention, and it is clear from the text of the agreement that the truth was on Gold's side.

"First, it is agreed that a committee composed of a representative of the American Federation of Labor, the President of the International Fur Workers Union and his colleagues, and a committee representing the general strike committee of locals 1, 5, 10 and 15, shall meet with the representatives of the fur manufacturers for the purpose of negotiating an agreement.

"Second, it is further agreed that any terms of settlement which may be considered acceptable to the Conference Committee shall be immediately submitted to a referendum vote of the membership of locals 1, 5, 10 and 15 of the Fur Workers on strike in New York City, for their acceptance or rejection in accordance with the Constitution of the International Fur Workers Union.

"Third, For the purpose of promoting the economic and social interests of the Fur Workers, and for the further purpose of creating solidarity and understanding, a mass meeting shall be held on Wednesday, April 21st, which will be addressed by the President of the American Federation of Labor who will set forth the position of that body in connection with the present strike of locals 1, 5, 10 and 15 of the Fur Workers in New York City.

"By unanimous consent it was agreed that the General Organizer, Frayne, would preside at the mass meeting; would arrange with the fur manufacturers for a time and place of conference; and also to arrange for counting the ballots cast in the referendum vote, when taken, in connection with the strike.

"This agreement and understanding was unanimously agreed to and accepted by all those participating in the conference."

sentatives of the AFL, the International and the General Strike Committee should negotiate an agreement; that the terms of the settlement should be immediately submitted to a referendum vote of the membership of Locals 1, 5, 10 and 15; and that a mass meeting should be held on April 21st which would be addressed by the President of the AFL.

This arrangement was a tremendous victory for the strikers. It proved the correctness of Gold's strategy in defeating the attempted sell-out, in not boycotting the Carnegie Hall meeting, and not permitting the strikers to be isolated from the official body of the AFL. The back-door settlement was rejected. Equally important, no agreement could be concluded without the consent of the General Strike Committee elected by the workers and any settlement would have to be ratified by the strikers.

Gold related the details of the Hotel Cadillac conference to fifteen hundred shop chairmen who packed Manhattan Lyceum to capacity. He pointed out that the events of the past few days were a tactical victory for the Joint Board. The employers now knew that the International represented nobody but themselves. The very language of the agreement with Green was the best proof that the strikers were represented not by the International or the Federation, but only by their own strike committee.

Naturally the chairmen bitterly attacked the right-wingers. But Gold insisted that "the International is ours, even if the officers are not." The shop chairmen voted unanimously to approve the agreement of April 18 with William Green.

April 21, 1926, was a clear, sunny day. As early as 6 A.M., the subways and elevated lines adjoining the fur district disgorged masses of fur workers. Men and women, dressed in their best clothes and carrying American flags, paraded for several hours in the fur market. At 10 A.M., they proceeded to the 69th Regiment Armory on Lexington Avenue at 26th Street. The police were out in full force. But for a change they were not brandishing clubs in the faces of the fur workers. Carnegie Hall had instilled a healthy respect among the police. Moreover, this was a "respectable" meeting. None other than William Green was to bestow his blessing on the striking fur workers.

The doors of the Armory opened at noon. Within half an hour, the huge auditorium was packed. A large overflow of strikers remained outside, quietly awaiting the report of the proceedings. The crowd outside was almost as numerous as the audience inside the Armory.

William Green and Hugh Frayne were the first to appear on the platform. Trailing after them came Shachtman and a few vice-presidents of the International. Green was politely applauded as he took his seat.

A few minutes later, Gold arrived at the Armory. As soon as he entered the door, a tremendous shout arose from the workers: "Gold is here!" Every worker in the Armory leaped to his feet, and began cheering, applauding and waving his flag. Green himself was so stirred by the spirit of the greeting that he too stood up and applauded. "I am sure," wrote a fur worker who attended the meeting, "that for the first time in his life, President Green saw what it meant when workers love their leader. Certainly he had never before seen such a heart-warming and sincere greeting extended to a leader of the working class."

When the applause finally subsided, Green arose to speak. He recalled the chartering of the International Fur Workers Union a bare thirteen years before by the AFL and called the Furriers Union the child of the Federation. Cheers greeted his statement that the Federation was solidly behind the fur workers and would do everything in its power to help them win their demands. These demands, he continued, were fully justified. Few workers had thus far gained a forty-hour, five-day week. It was more than proper that the fur workers should lead the labor movement in securing this demand. Not only were they entitled to the forty-hour week because of the menace to their health arising from the special nature of their work, but they deserved it because of the brave battle they had been waging for almost ten weeks.

The manufacturers had been asked for conferences, Green declared. The answer would be known in a few days. "If they refuse to meet us, we will fight them to the end, with all the forces of the American Federation of Labor," he thundered amid great applause.

When Shachtman arose to speak, outcries of "Shame! Shame!" arose from every side, even though the workers had been asked by Gold to give Shachtman a respectful hearing. The outburst was finally quieted. Shachtman was allowed to finish his speech without interruption. The patience of many workers was sorely tried when Shachtman asserted that it was "dangerous" to give the manufacturers "the chance to sabotage the strike by placing a Communist label upon it." Sensing the deep resentment of his audience, Shachtman hypocritically bemoaned the fact that the "bosses have used the charge of political affiliation against the strike as a smokescreen." But when he claimed that he had done all in his power to help the strike, he was answered with stony silence.

The moment Gold was introduced, the entire audience leaped to its feet. Again, the cheers and applause rang out.

"This meeting," Gold began, "will demonstrate to the fur bosses that the claim of certain elements that there is dissension in the ranks of the union is false. What is more, this meeting proves that the fur strikers are not fighting for themselves alone but for the cause of organized labor in America."

With a passionate denunciation of the callousness and arrogance of the manufacturers, Gold fired the great audience to new heights of enthusiasm. He contrasted the wealth of the employers to the conditions of the fur workers, and concluded amidst tremendous applause: "All this wealth we, the workers, created. We are not going to be cheated out of it. We are going to ask for all we can get, so that our lives may be more human and decent."

Many in the audience regretted that Gold had delivered this speech in Yiddish. Had he spoken in English even William Green might have learned something. The furriers were deeply moved by Gold's inspired speech. At the end of the meeting, they carried the 27-year-old leader of the strike out of the Armory on their shoulders.

What a remarkable contrast in a single week! April 15, Carnegie Hall. April 21, 69th Regiment Armory! At Carnegie Hall, the strikers and their leaders had been shamefully and brutally treated like criminals. At the 69th Regiment Armory, the President of the American Federation of Labor spoke from the same platform as the left-wing leader of the strikers, and listened to thunderous applause for Gold and the left-wing, militant movement he symbolized.

It was an amazing chain of events within a single week that has no equal in the history of the American labor movement. It will always rank as a triumph of left-wing leadership and strategy, based on an educated, militant rank and file.

The ranks of the strikers were more closely united than ever. They had learned invaluable lessons. They held their leaders in even higher esteem. They were determined to fight on until victory. And they were convinced that however long they would still have to battle—the strike would be won!

CHAPTER 21

'Til the End of 1926—
if Necessary

William Green told the strikers at the Armory that the manufacturers had been invited to new conferences. He pledged the full support of the Federation for the strikers' demands. However, even then he was secretly making an important concession to the employers that nullified much of his pledge to the workers. On April 20, a day before the Armory meeting, Hugh Frayne sent a letter to Association President Samuels in behalf of the new union Conference Committee requesting a conference for the purpose of negotiating a wage agreement. Samuels answered the same day, reminding him that an eight-point agreement had already been concluded with Green in Washington. Before the Association would agree to a new conference, Samuels wished to know what the Federation's attitude was "with reference to the agreement made and entered into between Mr. Green and myself and subsequently confirmed by you and which you saw fit to make public."

The Association chose to ignore the understanding reached at the Hotel Cadillac by representatives of the Federation, the International and the General Strike Committee in which the eight-point pact had been dropped. Gold promptly informed the press that the understanding to abandon the pact "does exist, did exist and will continue to exist."

Green, however, refused to endorse Gold's statement. In a letter to Samuels, he protested that he had only acted in the capacity of "mediator" when he had conferred with Samuels at his office in Washington. A new situation had arisen since that time which required the reopening of conferences. However, Green assured Samuels, "You would have a perfect right, at such conference, to present for consideration the basis for settlement which you outlined to me at Washington and which, at a later date, you submitted to Mr. Frayne."

Still the Association was not satisfied. Samuels answered that both Green and his New York representative had been acting "as the direct and authorized representatives of the workers" when they had conferred in Washington and New York. He repeated that even if they had served as "mediators," nevertheless they had reached an understanding on the terms and conditions that should be the basis for settling the strike. If Frayne would agree to present the eight-point pact at the new conference, the Association would attend.

Green replied he was "pleased" with the tone of Samuels' communication. There would be no difficulty, he assured him, in meeting the Association's conditions. The eight-point pact "could be submitted to the conference for its consideration and action."

On April 29, Samuels informed Frayne that the Association was ready to accept the invitation to a joint conference and that its representative would "insist upon the eight points."

Gold quickly disillusioned the leaders of the Association. As far as the strikers were concerned, they had given their answer to the eight-point pact at three mass meetings. The union, Gold informed the shop chairmen at another mass meeting on April 26, was prepared to continue the struggle for its demands until the end of 1926, if necessary.

Negotiations with the Association were set to reopen May 1 at the Hotel Cadillac. On the very eve of the new conference, *The Fur Worker*, speaking for the leaders of the International, praised the eight-point pact as the most reasonable basis for the settlement of the strike. The *Fur Age Weekly* reprinted the article under the headline: "INTERNATIONAL SAYS EIGHT POINTS ARE GOOD." Small wonder that the shop chairmen unanimously denounced the latest maneuver of the International officials as clear proof that "the whole clique is working hand-in-glove with the manufacturers." The manufacturers, however, felt that all they had to do was stick to their guns, and everything would turn out well.

The week before the new conference, Morris Polinsky, chairman of the out-of-town committee, went to Philadelphia to investigate reports that shops in that city were continuing to do scab work for New York manufacturers. Accompanied by Sam Burt, militant leader of the left-wing forces in Local 53, Polinsky investigated two of the largest shops in Philadelphia, Kushner & Weiss and Walloch & Walloch. The

Below are excerpts from the correspondence of William Green, Hugh Frayne and Samuel N. Samuels which reveal how the

Frayne to Samuels: ". . . I request that you meet us . . ." Samuels to Frayne: ". . . before we can act upon your kind invitation . . ."

> In behalf of the American Federation of Labor, the Officers of the International Fur Workers' Union and the local strike committee I request that you and your associates, representing the Fur Manufacturers' Association, meet us in joint conference for the purpose of negotiating a wage agreement, to be followed by the termination of the strike now existing in the fur manufacturing industry.

> My conferees are astonished at the fact that you failed to give these points recognition in your communication of the 20th inst. inviting us to a conference, and they are now seeking to learn from me where the American Federation of Labor stands on the tentative agreement they entered into with the President of the Associated Fur Manufacturers, Inc.
>
> Therefore, before we can act upon your kind invitation, we desire to know what is the attitude of the American Federation of Labor with reference to the agreement made and entered into between Mr. Green and myself and subsequently confirmed by you and which you saw fit to make public.

Green to Samuels: ". . . you would have a perfect right . . ."
Samuels to Green: ". . . if Frayne will agree to present . . ."

> It was with this object in view that Mr. Frayne addressed a communication to you requesting a conference. It was intended that at this conference the points of difference existing between the striking fur workers and their employers would be discussed and settled. You would have a perfect right, at such conference, to present for consideration the basis of settlement which you outlined to me at Washington and which, at a later date, you submitted to Mr. Frayne. I firmly believe that at such a conference where these matters could be fully discussed an honorable and satisfactory settlement could be brought about.

> You are now extending us an invitation to attend a joint formal conference at which proposed conference, you state, that I have the right to present the basis of the settlement of the strike which you, Mr. Frayne and myself worked out after many lengthy discussions. We, however, feel that as mediators the presentation of the basis of settlement worked out by us, is solely your right as well as your duty.
>
> Therefore, if Mr. Frayne, who is to preside at the proposed conference, will agree and is ready to present to the conferees the basis of settlement jointly worked out by us we are willing and ready to attend a joint conference at any time and place you may designate.

CORRESPONDENCE—APRIL 20-29, 1926

AFL President agreed to revive the eight-point pact at the same time that he was telling the fur workers he fully supported their demand for the forty-hour, five-day week. This exchange of letters has never before been published.

Green to Samuels: ". . . I am very much pleased with the tone . . ."
Samuels to Frayne: ". . . we assume this condition is accepted . . ."

I read with very great interest your letter of April 22nd which reached me this morning. I understand you forwarded a copy of this communication to the New York representative of the American Federation of Labor, Mr. Hugh Frayne. I am very much pleased with the tone of your communication. I cannot help believing, based on what you say therein, that a conference will ultimately be held between the representatives of the Associated Fur Manufacturers, Inc., and the Committee representing the striking fur workers -- of which Mr. Frayne is the Chairman -- for the purpose of reaching an agreement and a settlement of the strike.

Acting on Mr. Green's request, I am writing you with reference to the proposed conference, and in this connection I desire to quote a part of my letter to Mr. Green of the 22nd inst., which is as follows:

"Therefore, if Mr. Frayne, who is to preside at the proposed conference will agree and is ready to present to the conferees the basis of settlement, jointly worked out by us, we are willing to attend a Joint Conference at any time and place you may designate."

This paragraph is quoted to you because we assume from Mr. Green's letter that this condition is accepted.

Frayne to Samuels: ". . . the eight points may be discussed . . ."
Samuels to Frayne: ". . . we will insist upon the eight points . . ."

Your request that I pledge the committee to certain conditions before going into conference is one I regret it is not possible for me to comply with for the reason that I have not the authority to do so. That does not mean, however, that if the Associated Fur Manufacturers, Inc., through you, agree to go into conference, that the eight points tentatively accepted, or any other phase of the old or new contract, may not be discussed to the end that an agreement acceptable to all concerned would be reached.

Therefore, in view of the contents of your last letter, we feel that the situation is sufficiently clarified to warrant our acceptance of your invitation for a Joint Conference. We, however, desire you to know that in accepting your invitation for a Joint Conference, we will insist upon the eight points, tentatively accepted.

investigation left no doubt that the shops were doing scab work; the charge books of these manufacturers revealed that they made coats for New York firms whose workers were on strike.

Work was stopped in the shops, but the moment Polinsky returned to New York, Secretary-Treasurer Wohl ordered the workers to return to work, asserting that "the Philadelphia manufacturers have a right to sell their garments to New York firms affected by the strike."

The General Strike Committee appealed to President Shachtman on April 30 to suspend Wohl and take immediate steps to stop the scab work in Philadelphia. Shachtman did not even bother to answer the letter.

Jack Millstein, right-wing manager of the Chicago local, gave Shacht-man some advice on the forthcoming conference with the manufacturers. He urged Shachtman to repudiate his agreement to work with the General Strike Committee and renew the battle against the "communistic elements" leading the strike. "In such a fight with such a crowd," Millstein wrote on April 26, "we cannot act impartial. The sooner we kill them off and don't let them grow, the better it is. . . . I feel that the time has come for the International to fight this battle to the end, regardless of the outcome—we have nothing to lose, and a lot to gain."

The right-wing leaders of the International planned to arrange matters at the new conferences in such a way that the representatives of the Joint Board would be forced "to withdraw or try to break up the conference." Then, Shachtman assured Joseph Bearak, the Boston Socialist lawyer, "we, together with Mr. Hugh Frayne, representative of the American Federation of Labor, will aim to continue the same. If such developments should take place as above mentioned, that will be the time when your services will be sought and we hope that you will not refuse to render."

At conferences with the employers on May 1 and 2, negotiations went on for fifteen hours without any agreement being reached. Samuels repeatedly brought forward the pact which he insisted Green, Frayne and Shachtman had agreed to. Gold was equally emphatic in maintaining that it was a thing of the past and had no place in the negotiations.

Putting aside the discussions on the pact for the time being, Gold proposed that both sides accept the plan of equal division of work in principle and elect a committee of union and Association representatives to work out a detailed plan to introduce the system in the industry. The manufacturers flatly turned this down. During a recess, the spokesmen for the union agreed to postpone the discussion of equal division of work, in order to get on to the forty-hour demand. With the resumption of conferences, Shachtman introduced a motion which stated that the union "was ready to waive the demand for equal division of work." Gold immediately interrupted Shachtman and amended the motion to read very clearly that the union was not waiving the demand, but was simply willing to postpone further discussion of it for the present.

But the damage was done. Samuels insisted that unless Shachtman's original motion was adopted, negotiations would cease. Gold refused. The conference remained deadlocked. However, contrary to Shachtman's plan, Gold refused to bolt the conference. Finally, at 1:30 P.M. the next day, Frayne closed the meeting without arranging for future negotiations.

The General Strike Committee immediately made clear its position that further conferences with the manufacturers would serve no purpose unless the employers agreed in advance to the forty-hour week. While there was room for compromise on other issues, they would listen to no more double-talk from the Association on this point. Fifteen hundred shop chairmen enthusiastically approved this decision.

Time and again during the strike, fur workers from other cities sent contributions to the strikers through the International. They soon discovered that the money was not being turned over to the strikers. By May, the scandal became so great that many fur workers of other

International leaders "neglect" to forward money to the strikers.

Mr. I. Wohl, General Sec'y-Treasurer,
International Fur Workers Union,
9 Jackson Avenue,
Long Island City, N.Y.

Dear Sir and Brother:-

           I have been instructed by the Joint Board to communicate with you as to the reason why, you did not forward all the contributions received during the strike from all locals for us.

           Please send us a list of the donations of all the locals received, and also forward a check for the amount to us, by return mail.

           Fraternally yours,

           JOINT BOARD FURRIERS UNION,

SEC'Y-TREAS. *Maurice Moker.*

Millstein is alarmed by rank-and-file protest against withholding of their strike relief contributions from N. Y. Joint Board.

cities were planning to send committees to the International to demand that their contributions be turned over to the strike committee. When the Chicago fur workers threatened to send a delegation to the International, Millstein hurriedly wrote to Shachtman on May 5: "We would like to have a letter from you stating explicitly that the money will go direct to the strikers for strike benefits only."

Arrangements were made with the bank of the International Ladies Garment Workers Union for a loan of $200,000 to carry on the strike. The General Strike Committee requested that the International endorse the notes for the loan. The Sub-Committee of the General Executive Board answered with a resolution refusing to endorse the notes unless the General Strike Committee turned over complete control of all funds to a committee appointed by the G.E.B.

Gold put the question to the shop chairmen. "If your decision is that we should give over the management of the strike funds to the International," he told the chairmen at a mass meeting, "we will follow your decision."

The shop chairmen answered indignantly: "We are willing to die of hunger rather than turn over the management of the strike funds to those people." They criticized Gold for even posing such a question. As one chairman expressed it: "If we have to battle without money to avoid getting it from them, then we will fight without money as strongly as with money. We will battle as long as is necessary to win." The assembled chairmen unanimously rejected the International's conditions.

Without the International's endorsement, the ILGWU bank refused to go through with the loan. The General Strike Committee, however, obtained endorsement of part of the loan from Locals 2, 9 and 12 of the cloak and dressmakers' locals of the ILGWU so that some money did come in. In addition, the workers in the settled shops voted unanimously at a mass meeting that beginning May 7 each worker would pay 25 percent (it was 15 percent before) of his weekly salary to the strike benefit fund. Many workers insisted on a higher percentage, but Gold refused to entertain these motions. "Twenty-five percent is high enough," he said, "and we will not have even that change unless you want it." There was loud applause when one worker compared this statement with the practice followed in the 1920 strike, when a 40 percent payment was levied upon the workers in the settled shops without their being consulted.

Assured of funds sufficient to carry on the strike and pay benefits for the next three weeks, the union intensified its mass picketing. The day and night picketing of buildings increased. No task was too difficult for the pickets. The heroism of the women strikers exceeded even the spirit displayed in previous weeks. What a contrast between this rank-and-file picketing committee and the 1920 gangster-and-thief committee!

The attacks on the pickets by the police and the gangsters continued without let-up. Every few hours, the patrol wagons would roll up to the fur district and haul away loads of strikers. But as they sped away, the stirring strike songs of the arrested workers rose higher than the clanging bells of the patrols.

The spirit of the strikers who were sent to jail on charges of disorderly conduct was amazing. From the Tombs came a message from Mencher, Bauer, Felsher and Isersky addressed to the General Strike Committee.

The first three had received prison sentences of three months each, and the last, thirty days.

"Dear friends! Don't worry about us. We are well. Continue to fight until victory is attained. Go forward, forward, friends, without stopping. Victory will surely be ours. Greet the twelve thousand strikers in our name, and tell them that we are waiting impatiently for the time when we shall join their ranks and be able to help our strike with even greater courage."

From David Wexler, an imprisoned striker in the New York penitentiary, the strike committee received an extraordinary letter: "I request that you do not spend any money in trying to obtain my release. I know that the money is necessary for more important matters. Let me serve my sentence. I hope that when I come back, I will find that you have had a great victory."

More and more members of the Association were convinced that they could not break the strike. On May 7, a group of the most influential manufacturers, employing from three to four thousand workers, threatened Samuels that either he settle with the union or they would make a settlement of their own. That very day, an important fur importer contacted Gold and assured him that he could arrange a meeting with Samuels and reach a settlement with a forty-hour, five-day week.

After the Hotel Cadillac conferences with the manufacturers on May 1 and 2 had ended in a deadlock, Frayne sent Green a detailed account of the proceedings. He admitted that if the eight-point pact were submitted to a referendum vote of the strikers, "there would be no question but that it would be rejected." He admitted further that "each day I come in contact with these phases I realize that any attempt to settle, leaving Gold and his associates out, is impossible as they have sufficient influence over the strikers to prevent any terms of settlement being accepted either in a mass meeting or by referendum vote."

In the same confidential report to Green, Frayne made another observation which fully exposes the true colors of the leaders of the AFL. *"While we must support the International officers,"* Frayne wrote, *"they are no asset but rather a liability in this case. If President Shachtman had told us in the very beginning the real situation, we would have planned differently. . . ."*

On May 7, Frayne informed Gold that President Green was in New York City and had requested a meeting with the representatives of the General Strike Committee at the Hotel Cadillac the following morning. Green had already arranged a conference with the Association on the afternoon of May 8 and wanted to discuss the strike situation with the strike leaders first. The General Strike Committee was bitter against Green's new move, in view of the fact that he knew of their decision not to confer with the manufacturers unless they agreed in advance to the forty-hour week.

Still determined to avoid an open break with the AFL, Gold persuaded the General Strike Committee to authorize its representatives to meet Green and confer with the manufacturers. The next morning, Gold assured Green that a real possibility of securing a forty-hour, five-day week existed if the strikers remained firm in their demands.

That afternoon, the representatives of the Association again attempted to revive the eight-point pact and insisted that the General Strike Committee should present this proposal to a referendum vote of the strikers. To Gold's amazement, neither Green nor Frayne raised any objection.

"How can you even speak of it?" Gold asked Green at a caucus of the union's Conference Committee. "You know as well as I the answer the workers gave to the eight-point pact at Carnegie Hall. If not for your interference, the manufacturers would have given us the forty-hour, five-day week."

Green's reply was that Shachtman and the other right-wing officials of the International had told him that the strike was lost, and that most of the shops were already operating. Shachtman, Winnick and Wohl also spoke at length for the eight-point pact. Again and again they repeated that the only way to retrieve anything out of the strike was to accept a forty-two-hour week.

Enraged, Gold pointed out that the right-wing leaders knew nothing about the actual condition of the strike, never came to the strike halls, and spent all of their time plotting against the strike leadership. The strike, he assured Green, was in a splendid condition. The closer the battle approached to the August sales, the more certain was a complete victory. He insisted that the forty-hour week could be won.

Green concluded the heated meeting with an ultimatum to the strike committee's representatives. If he did not have evidence before the week-end was over that the strikers could secure a forty-hour week, he would declare the strike ended on Monday morning. He would settle with the Association himself on the basis of the eight-point pact. The representatives of the strike committee were so shocked by Green's conduct that for a moment they were speechless. Then Gold cried out: "We detest the thought, President Green, of falling at your feet and begging you to let us settle our own bitter battle with the bosses. But in the interests of the strikers, I must plead for a chance to prove my point. I promise you that tomorrow, I will give you all the evidence you need to prove that we can get the forty-hour week."

Late that same evening, May 8, the representatives of the Association and the union reconvened. There were two adjoining rooms for each group to meet in separately. These rooms were connected by sliding doors. During one caucus of the Association group, the connecting doors were slightly open. The union representatives in the adjoining room heard several of the most influential manufacturers angrily say: "Let's give them the forty-hour week and settle the strike." Turning to Green, Gold said: "Did you hear what they said?" Green refused to comment. But even Wohl had to admit: "Yes, I heard it."

While the conferences were going on in the Hotel Cadillac, thousands of fur workers waited in the lobby and in the streets for a report. It was already one o'clock in the morning, but no worker thought of leaving and going home to sleep.

When the representatives of the General Strike Committee came down at 1:30, the workers surrounded them and asked what had happened. "The news is not joyful," Gold replied. "Come to the union office and we will tell you everything."

"The forty-hour week or we continue to strike," was their unanimous opinion, when Gold reported on the latest developments. Then Gold told the workers of Green's ultimatum. "We must bring such a demonstration to the hotel that Green will see where the workers stand," he concluded.

It is doubtful if any workers at that meeting slept the rest of that night. Somehow, even though it was Sunday, they managed to get the news to thousands of strikers. Early next morning, a great mass of fur workers was mobilized around the hotel. With each passing hour, their numbers increased. By noon, the streets around the hotel were jammed.

That morning at the conference with the manufacturers, Green called Gold out of the room and gave him until seven o'clock that same evening to bring forward his proof that the strikers could get the forty-hour week. If Gold did not produce the evidence by that hour, he would announce to the press that the strike was over.

What followed would make a Hollywood thriller, if Hollywood scenarios had a working-class setting. The script begins with a flash-back. On Thursday, May 6th, one day before Green arrived in New York,

Gold had a conference with R. L. Lindheim, vice-president of the Eitin-gon-Schild Company. A clever and highly capable lawyer, Lindheim was one of the most respected figures in the fur industry. Lindheim told Gold that he had been authorized by a majority of the Board of Directors of the manufacturers' association to settle the strike on the basis of the forty-hour week. While he made it absolutely clear that this was a real and definite settlement, the matter was to remain confidential until the official conference on Monday. Until then, he asked Gold not to divulge the information to anyone.

Determined not to break his word, Gold had neither revealed these facts nor mentioned Lindheim's name to William Green at the Cadillac Hotel on Sunday, May 9. Now it was necessary for the president of the Federation to hear the truth from the lips of Lindheim himself.

Lindheim was spending the week-end in a suburb out on Long Island. Whatever was to be done, it had to be done posthaste. In an automobile driven by a striker, Gold and Zuckerman of *The Day* drove out to Lind-heim's home, where Gold explained the critical situation to the wealthy fur importer. "I am expecting guests," Lindheim replied, "but if Mrs. Lindheim releases me, I will go with you and speak to Green." He returned in ten minutes, his hat and coat on, and said, "Let's go." In the car, he told the driver that every minute counted. The race against the deadline was on!

Back in New York City, the crowd of workers outside of the Hotel Cadillac was growing more and more nervous. It was already five o'clock in the afternoon, two hours before the deadline. No one seemed to know where Gold was. Workers stood at the corners, worry written on their faces, and peered anxiously into every automobile that approached.

5:30 P.M.! 6:00 P.M.! 6:30 P.M.! Still no sign of Gold. A shudder ran through the crowd. The whole strike, the union itself, was at a turning point. Suppose Gold could not furnish the evidence in time? Green would announce that the strike was over. Would it be possible to stop workers from going back to the shops? Would the pangs of hunger break their endurance? With so many leading officials of the labor movement lined up against the strike, would it be possible to maintain the morale and fighting spirit of the strikers?

Suddenly, a few minutes before seven, an automobile drew up before the hotel entrance. Gold was the first to leap out. "Gold is here!" the workers near the entrance shouted out. Hundreds of workers ran eagerly towards the hotel. Gold's eyes were misty as he saw the huge crowd of fur workers that had assembled at such short notice.

Gold, Zuckerman and Lindheim went in for the meeting with Green. The evidence was at hand—just in time. Green asked Gold to step out of the room for a few minutes. "No," Gold replied, "I want to be here when Lindheim tells you the story." It was only when Lindheim too asked Gold to let him speak with Green alone for five minutes that Gold agreed.

Once alone, Lindheim assured Green that notwithstanding all that Samuels had said, the fur manufacturers had agreed to grant the forty-hour week. Furthermore, he told Green that the majority of the manufacturers were faced with bankruptcy and most of the fur dealers were not far behind. Millions of dollars of merchandise would become worthless unless the strike was settled quickly. "You will carry the responsibility for interfering in the strike," he assured Green.

When Green asked how this could be squared with what he had heard from Samuels, Lindheim told him that the majority of the manufacturers were disgusted with the arrogant stand and maneuvering of the leaders of the Association, which spelled ruin for the entire industry.

A few minutes later, Gold rejoined them. A deflated Green said somewhat wearily: "You win, Ben!"

Outside the hotel, many hundreds of workers were still waiting. As Gold stepped out of the elevator, scores of workers rushed up to him. Gold was beaming. "We have proved our point!" he cried out. A cheer rose from the workers who had maintained their vigil at the hotel the entire day.

His interview with Lindheim concluded, Green told Shachtman and the other right-wing leaders of the International that he now had the true facts. Samuels had misinformed him. He no longer trusted him. He was convinced that the forty-hour week could be obtained. The AFL would support the strikers in winning this important demand.

The next day William Green issued a statement to the press. It was not the statement the leaders of the Association, the right-wing leaders of the International, the *Forward* and its allies had been eagerly awaiting. Instead, Green declared: "Because of the seasonal character of the fur manufacturing industry, I am of the opinion that the forty-hour week should be granted. For that reason, the American Federation of Labor joins with the officers and members of the Fur Workers organization in insisting upon a forty-hour week."

CHAPTER 22

Victory

The fur workers' battle for the forty-hour, five-day week attracted nation-wide attention. Workers all over the country began to realize that if the fur workers won this demand, it would pave the way for them too. The fur workers themselves saw the national significance of their struggle. The demand for the forty-hour week became the focal issue in the strike.

Nine thousand and eighty-three fur workers signed a pledge endorsing the stand of the General Strike Committee on the forty-hour, five-day week. Taking into account the one thousand strikers who had been released for work in other trades, and the workers in the settled shops who already worked forty hours and did not have to sign, it is clear that almost 100 percent of the strikers signed the pledge.

"At any future conferences on the settlement of the strike," said Gold, "if there is any question as to how the fur workers feel about the forty-hour week, we will present these ballots."

On May 17, the General Strike Committee issued an appeal to all labor organizations in New York City to join the drive for a forty-hour, five-day week. Already, the New York section of the International Ladies Garment Workers Union had adopted the demand in principle. The Cap Makers endorsed it. The Amalgamated Clothing Workers had accepted it at their convention in Montreal. President Green of the AFL had given the forty-hour week his endorsement. Now, therefore, was the time for the workers of New York to come to the aid of the striking fur

A Call by the Striking Furriers
FOR A FORTY - HOUR WEEK

FELLOW WORKERS:

We, the Fur Workers of New York, have been on strike for 13 weeks. We have shown our employers a solid wall of working class unity. We have repelled all the open and secret attacks upon our ranks. Our demands for the improvement of our working and living conditions have all concentrated around this, the most vital and far-reaching demand: the FORTY-HOUR WEEK.

We are fighting for five eight-hour days and two full free days a week.

This demand has become the storm centre of our strike. The employers are determined to fight it with all means at their command. The Fur Workers will utilise all their energy, solidarity and endurance to see that the forty-hour week becomes a fact.

In this way, Fellow Workers, the Fur Workers of New York are blazing a new path for the labor movement.

The Furriers launched the nation-wide drive for forty-hour week.

workers and make the demand for the forty-hour week the demand of New York's organized labor.

The call closed with a stirring appeal:

"A new era is dawning upon the working class. New vistas open before the laboring masses. Let us all unite in raising the banner of the FORTY-HOUR WEEK. Let us become the battle-cry of labor all over New York, all over the country.

"LONG LIVE THE 40-HOUR WEEK!

"LONG LIVE THE SOLIDARITY OF THE WORKING CLASS!

"LONG LIVE THE WORKERS' STRUGGLE FOR FREEDOM!

"ONWARD TO NEW STRUGGLES AND NEW ACHIEVEMENTS!"

Along with the call went invitations to all branches of organized labor in New York City urging them to participate in a giant rally at Madison Square Garden on May 22. President Green, Shachtman, John Coughlin of the State Federation of Labor, representatives of the Amalgamated Clothing Workers, ILGWU, Hat and Cap Makers, Teachers Union and other labor organizations were invited to address the meeting.

Madison Square Garden was jammed on the afternoon of May 22, 1926. It was the greatest indoor labor mass meeting ever held in New York City up to this time. "Not Barnum's elephants nor Tex Rickard's leather pushers were the attraction that filled the monster new Madison Square Garden this time," wrote one reporter. "The forty-hour week fight of the striking furriers did it." Cloak and dress makers, shoe workers, food workers, bookkeepers, printers, teachers, building trades workers, waiters and others, joined the striking fur workers in demanding a forty-hour week for all organized labor.

Telegrams of support came from all over the nation: the Pennsylvania, Minnesota and California State Federations, Minneapolis, St.

Paul, Milwaukee, and St. Louis central labor organizations, Pittsburgh, Philadelphia, Boston and New York needle trades unions. "The mound of AFL telegrams," commented a reporter, "was spectacular proof that the furriers' strike was not the outlaw movement that certain groups have tried to represent it, but a bona fide trade union struggle that has inspired New York labor and the labor movement outside as have few strikes."

The packed Garden and the pile of telegrams more than offset the failure of William Green, Oizer Shachtman, Sidney Hillman, and Morris Sigman to come to the rally. Hillman and Sigman sent telegrams declining to attend on the ground that one union alone should not have taken the initiative to call a mass meeting of this character. Neither one, however, offered any explanation as to why no other labor organization had the courage to launch the nation-wide demand for the forty-hour week.

John Coughlin brought the official endorsement of the forty-hour campaign from the AFL unions in New York. He congratulated the furriers on standing firm for this demand. John Sullivan, president of the New York State Federation of Labor, also heartily endorsed the demand of the fur workers. The manager of the Cloak and Dress Makers Unions and the president of the Teachers Union were among other AFL leaders in New York who endorsed the demand and brought greetings.

But it was Ben Gold who brought the meeting to the highest pitch of enthusiasm. He pledged that the strike would go on with renewed vigor and determination. Highly indignant at Hillman's refusal to attend,* after having helped plan the meeting and after giving his promise, Gold was sharp in his criticism of Hillman as well as Sigman. With scorn, he told the vast assembly: "They declared themselves in favor of the forty-hour week. But when it comes to the test of appearing on the public platform to favor it, they fail to appear." The importance of the meeting, he assured the cheering audience, was not diminished in the slightest by the absence of timid labor leaders. This rally would help the fur workers win their strike. And this, in turn, would spur other workers in the United States to gain the forty-hour week.

"The bosses now acknowledge," Gold said in conclusion, "that if it had not been for the intervention of our International officials, the strike

* The Madison Square Garden meeting was planned by Gold in consultation with Sidney Hillman, president of the Amalgamated Clothing Workers Union. Hillman had given $25,000 to the fur strikers and had promised another $25,000. He had agreed to be one of the speakers at the Garden mass meeting.

would have been settled by this time. They are still not convinced that the fur strikers are firm in their determination not to compromise. Some manufacturers realize this; the others need further proof. Today's meeting, with its endorsement by labor unionists all over the country, will be the last great blow. Victory is ours if we fight on in the same splendid fashion we have carried on our struggle for the past fourteen weeks. The strike was never in better shape. We are sure to win—and very soon."

Even as the Madison Square Garden meeting was being arranged, the fur manufacturers sent messengers to the Joint Board with compromise proposals. They offered a forty-hour week four months during the year, and a forty-two-hour week during the remaining eight months. The strike leaders refused to bite at this bait. The manufacturers raised their bid to five months. This proposal, too, was rejected. Then came another offer: the forty-hour week, but withdraw the three months' equal division of work period, decrease the number of paid legal holidays, abandon the demands for the abolition of contracting, and retain the second-class minimum wage scale. This was also refused.

The union's treasury, meanwhile, was being depleted. Contributions sent through the International were not forwarded to the Joint Board. Locals that sought to send funds directly to the strike committee were threatened with disciplinary action by the right-wing leaders of the International. And the bank refused a loan, because the International would not endorse the Joint Board's notes.

Appeals had been sent by the General Strike Committee to all labor organizations in the country. Some financial assistance came in, but scarcely enough to meet the dire needs of the strikers.*

Unknown to the strike committee, the appeal for funds was being sabotaged. Winnick secretly dispatched letters to Green enclosing newspaper clippings and translations from the *Freiheit*. He claimed that they proved the strike leaders were making "slanderous remarks" against the AFL and its President. He urged that they were not entitled to financial aid from AFL affiliates. Publicly, the right-wing leaders of the International proclaimed their 100 percent support of the strikers.

---

* Local 9, Cloak and Suit Tailors Union, sent $5,000; Local 100, Barbers Union, $500; Bessarabian Podolier Cultural Society, $200; Radical Branch 436 of the Workmen's Circle, $50; Kodzer Branch of the Workmen's Circle, No. 324, $100; Branch No. 89, $25; Branch No. 122, $25; Branch No. 69, $5; Ridomer Branch, $10; collection from members of Local 91 of the ILGWU working in the shop of Klein and Kravitz, $15.

Working hand-in-glove with the right-wing leaders of the International, Hugh Frayne was playing an equally two-faced role. He wrote privately to Frank Morrison, secretary-treasurer of the AFL: "Personally, I feel that no encouragement should be given to the appeal for funds for these people as their tactics and methods in handling the strike are anything but praiseworthy. See President Green by all means as you may be called upon by organizations who receive the circulars for advice as to whether they should make contributions or not." It is clear from his letter that William Green fully shared his attitude.

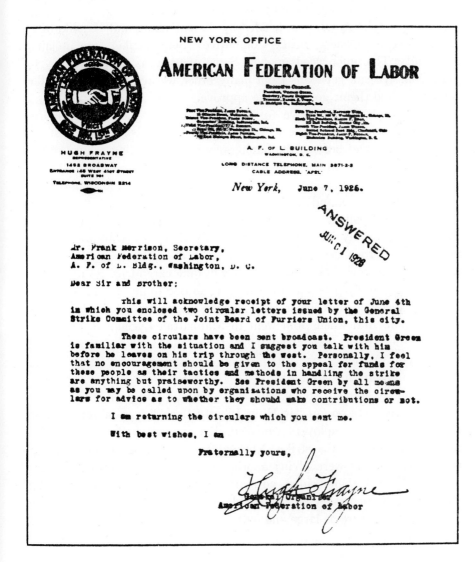

The leaders of the Association may or may not have known of this behind-the-scenes sabotage of the union's appeals for contributions, but they continued to exhort the manufacturers that the strikers were on their last legs. All they had to do was wait another week or two. The strikers would be starved into submission.

On Thursday, May 27, mass meetings were held in the bigger strike halls. The members of the General Strike Committee were worried. There was exactly $70 in the treasury. At least $50,000 was needed on the following Monday for strike relief.

A group of shop chairmen, headed by Trachtenberg and Hershkowitz, came to see the General Strike Committee. "Some strikers are in jail," they said. "The union needs money. Some of us want to lend money to the union. We can get loans from many other workers too." The strike committee told them: go ahead, we approve.

Thus a rank-and-file drive for "40-Hour Liberty Loans" was born. When Gold announced at the strike halls that from this day on the strikers themselves had become the bankers and were building a huge strike fund through loans to the union, there were shouts from every side of the hall: "I will bring $500 tomorrow!" "I will bring $300 tomorrow!" Many pledged $100, and still larger numbers pledged $50.

One striker walked to the platform, and announced: "I have paid fifteen years on my insurance policy. Many times my wife and I have not eaten in order to have the money to meet the next payment. But now I know that we have a union that will take care of us. So tomorrow I am cashing in my policy and I will bring $1,000 to my union."

At the meeting in Webster Hall alone, $19,000 was pledged as loans to the union. And when Gold went to Manhattan Lyceum to bring the news to the strikers assembled there, the same kind of demonstration took place. Another $9,000 was pledged. The union issued bonds to the donors, to mature in six months.

On Monday, June 1, strike relief was paid out as usual!

When over $100,000 of "40-Hour Liberty Loans" was subscribed, the final hope of the employers vanished. Every maneuver, every attack, had failed to break the strike. Now, at the beginning of the fifteenth week, the workers were giving another remarkable demonstration that they would back their leaders no matter how many months of suffering would still be necessary to win. And to top it all the mass picketing demonstrations were as large and enthusiastic as during the first week of the strike.

While Samuels was still proclaiming to the press that the Association would never sign an agreement with "the Communist leaders of the strikers," many manufacturers were cabling Motty Eitingon in Europe. They beseeched him to return and force the leaders of the Association to settle the strike. The cables told him that they were "ruined if he did not come back."

Gold received word that Samuels wished to have a private discussion with him. They met near the New York Public Library, and then went to Central Park and talked over issues for several hours. Samuels fairly wept as he implored Gold to be reasonable and to help "save face" among the members of the Association. He asked for some concessions to enable him to persuade his associates to grant the forty-hour week. Gold refused. Nothing came of the conference.

At this point, Eitingon returned from Europe and he invited Gold, Gross and Leibowitz to his home at the Hotel Ansonia on the evening of June 8. After discussing the strike with the union's representatives for several hours, he called Samuels at his home and asked him to come to the meeting immediately.

The conferees argued until six o'clock in the morning. Samuels finally agreed to the forty-hour week, but demanded that the union give up equal division of work and six legal paid holidays. The union representatives refused. As a compromise, Eitingon suggested that they give up the legal holidays in January and February when the furriers usually didn't work anyway.

The General Strike Committee was hastily called together. Gold reported on the meeting that had taken place in Eitingon's home. The committee approved Gold's suggestions for a compromise in return for the forty-hour week and authorized the union representatives to negotiate for a settlement on that basis. Gold, Eitingon and Samuels spent the night of June 9 together, hammering out the general terms of the settlement. After several hours of negotiations, they reached agreement.

Early in the morning of June 10, Dr. Paul Abelson, the impartial chairman, announced that he had invited the Association and the union to meet with him at three o'clock at the Hotel Pennsylvania.

Long before 3 P.M., the streets in the vicinity of the Hotel Pennsylvania were jammed. Side by side with the thousands of fur workers stood many manufacturers. They could be overheard saying hopefully to each other that the strike would be settled today.

Shortly before three o'clock, a shout rose from the crowd. Gold, Leibowitz, Gross, Shapiro, Cohen and Warshafsky stepped out of a car and entered the hotel. The cheers died down suddenly as the workers saw Shachtman, Wohl and Winnick follow the strike leaders. Even at the last minute, the strikers suspected the right-wingers of some new maneuver.

Every few minutes, one of the strike leaders left the conference room and released details of the proceedings. The workers soon learned that a battle was taking place over the question of the scabs who had worked in the Association shops during the strike. The strike leaders demanded that the scabs be discharged and their cases be left to a special committee of the union. The bosses insisted that the scabs remain in the shops, and they were supported in this stand by the leaders of the International.

The conference was stuck on this point for several hours. If the union representatives obtained this point, it would be the first time in American labor history that such a provision was won by a union. To leave the scabs in the shops without punishment for their treason, the strike leadership knew, would give the bosses a nucleus for new conspiracies against the union. To every appeal from the employers for a fair deal for the scabs, Gold replied: "Fire them first. Turn them over to the union for discipline. Then we will consider each case on its merits." The manufacturers had no choice but to yield.

The conference lasted twelve hours, until 3 A.M. Friday, June 11. At that hour, the tentative agreement, subject to ratification by both the fur workers and the manufacturers, was signed by Gold, Samuels and Abelson. Shachtman and the other right-wing officers of the International refused to affix their signatures to the agreement and left the conference room in a huff. The strike was settled upon the following terms:

1. A forty-hour week, five eight-hour days.

2. A 10 percent wage increase over the existing minimum wage scale and a reclassification of minimum standards which, in the words of the *New York Times*, "will mean a considerable wage increase for many workers."

3. Ten legal holidays, all paid except three—New Year's Day, Lincoln's Birthday, and Washington's Birthday—which came in the dull months when most of the fur workers were not employed.

4. No overtime work to be allowed except during the four months from September through December, when shops might work for four hours extra on Saturday—at extra pay.

5. No workers to be discharged the week before a holiday, thus ending the employers' old trick of avoiding payment for the workers' day off.

6. No apprentices to be taken on for two years.

7. No section contracting—every garment had to be made entirely in one shop and no individual part of the garment could be given out to contractors.

8. The Conference Committee was to decide whether any manufacturer was abusing the privilege of the number of foremen in his employ.

9. All scabs were to be discharged. They were to be penalized by a special committee of the Joint Board acting together with Dr. Abelson.

10. The collective agreement was to run for three years, retroactive to February 1, 1926, when the old agreement expired. The agreement applied also to the United Fur Manufacturers Association and the Fur Trimming Manufacturers Association.

Twelve thousand strikers thronged to meeting halls that day to celebrate. Workers openly kissed and embraced each other for joy. Many wept publicly as they expressed their happiness over the union's triumph.

The platform was gaily bedecked with a multitude of flowers as the shop chairmen gathered at Manhattan Lyceum that afternoon to listen to Gold's report. Thousands of workers crowded in. They jammed the hall to the rafters. Thousands more outside joined in the general jubilation.

Exhausted though they were by the long vigil of the last few days, the workers all but tore the roof off the building when Gold entered the hall. "We did not win a one hundred percent victory," he said after the demonstration had died down, "but we won a victory against the most difficult obstacles ever placed in the path of the fur workers. And it was a clean-cut victory." Then Gold read the terms of the settlement. The workers listened quietly and broke into loud cheers when Gold said: "We have the forty-hour week. We have abolished section contracting once and for all."

On Monday morning, June 14, the strikers ratified the agreement by an almost unanimous vote. Only forty workers, out of all the thousands of strikers, were against the settlement. When the vote was announced, the workers decided to hold their last demonstration on the following day. They assembled in the strike halls in their best clothes. Many brought their wives and children with them. Banners and signs decorated the walls. With several bands on hand to furnish the music for the festivities, they paraded through the streets.

As the first column of fur workers marched out of Manhattan Lyceum, they were thunderously applauded by workers from other trades who had gathered to pay tribute to the heroic strikers. From the cloak and dress shops, the furriers were greeted joyfully by workers who were soon to occupy the very same strike halls. Thousands of cloak and dress makers hurled confetti from the windows, and shouted: "Long live the Furriers Union! Long live the forty-hour week!" The jubilant strikers cheered and waved their flags and cheered again in answer to the applause of thousands who crowded the buildings along the line of march. As they passed the *Freiheit* building, their resounding cheers voiced their appreciation for the paper that had proved an indispensable ally in their bitter battles against gangsterism, the employers and the right-wing officials.

For four hours, the twelve thousand furriers paraded the streets, demonstrating their joy over their great victory. With music, flowers and unforgettable rejoicing, the great seventeen-week strike came to a glorious end.

All over the United States, workers hailed the victory of the New York fur workers.* Progressives everywhere shared their joy.

The victory was an overwhelming one. The fur workers had won more than a forty-hour, five-day week, wage increases and other important gains. The significance of this strike far exceeded the purely economic gains, important as these were. The strike had erased the blot of the 1920 disaster from the union's history. It had given the twelve thousand fur workers of New York a new confidence in themselves, a new outlook and pride in their own achievements. A true unity of the rank and file

---

* In Passaic, New Jersey, fifteen thousand textile workers were on strike for decent conditions under the leadership of the TUEL since February 1926. They eagerly seized copies of their strike bulletins, which proclaimed the wonderful news: "NEW YORK FURRIERS WIN! NOW FOR PASSAIC TEXTILE STRIKERS' VICTORY! VICTORY OF FUR WORKERS WILL CARRY PASSAIC OVER THE TOP! FURRIERS UNION CELEBRATES VICTORY IN BIG DEMONSTRATION AND PARADE. BUSINESS IN NEW YORK STOPPED ALONG STREETS OF MARCH FOR FOUR HOURS."

The Furriers Union had contributed financially to assist the Passaic strikers. One student of the strike observes: "Considering the precarious state of its treasury after the seventeen-weeks' strike, the Furriers Union contributed proportionately one hundred times as much as the Amalgamated Clothing Workers to the Passaic strikers." (Interview with Morton Siegel, New York City, March 1949.)

had been created—Jewish, Hungarian, Greek, Slavic and Negro workers had been molded into one great family. A magnificent tradition had been born among the fur workers—the tradition of 1926—that was to inspire them in later struggles and make new victories a certainty.

But in the headquarters of the right-wing Socialists and among the leaders of the American Federation of Labor, there was only gloom. Their worst fears had materialized. The fur workers, under left-wing leadership, had won their strike.

For the American working class as a whole the furriers' general strike of 1926 was an event of the utmost significance. It stood out like a beacon light in a period of labor defeats, "union-management cooperation," wage cuts, blacklistings, company unionism, open-shop drives and reactionary national, state and local politics. At a time when workers were suffering setbacks on all fronts, the fur workers proved that a militant rank and file led by an honest, progressive leadership could win their demands against the greatest opposition any strike could possibly face. They proved that conducting a labor struggle by involving the whole membership was infinitely more effective than relying on professional gangsters. These striking truths were a tremendous stimulant to the whole labor movement. They demonstrated the correctness of the policies of left-wing trade unionists. And they exposed the class collaboration theories of the right-wing Socialists and the conservative labor bureaucrats.

Out of the strike emerged a labor leader whom few in the entire trade union movement could equal for popularity among the workers and for ability to lead workers in militant struggle. This was the 27-year-old Ben Gold. The *New York Times* paid Gold its highest compliment when it said that American capitalists had begun "to fear him as among the most dangerous labor leaders," and were giving him "full credit for winning the forty-hour week and other concessions."

Gold himself constantly emphasized that the strike had been won by a united rank-and-file leadership at the bottom and a collective progressive leadership at the top. Yet if every fur worker had been asked who more than anyone else was responsible for the victory, the immediate reply would have been—Ben Gold. No historian who studies the fascinating story of this strike can come to any other conclusion.

Confronted by unprecedented attacks by the employers, the right-wing Socialist leaders of the International, the bureaucratic leaders of the American Federation of Labor, the right-wing Socialist power in the needle trades and the entire right-wing Socialist and commercial press, Gold defeated every maneuver to break the strike. One slight misstep at a critical moment might well have spelled defeat for the fur workers. Had the workers boycotted the Carnegie Hall meeting, the strike could have been lost. Had Green been allowed to continue his open cooperation with the right-wing leaders of the International instead of being forced, publicly at least, to retreat, the strike would have suffered. These as well as many other strategic decisions during the strike, were the result of Gold's astute analysis of the forces involved in the struggle.

At no point in the strike did Gold fall a victim to the isolating policies into which left-wing ultra-militants in the American labor movement so often slipped. In spite of every provocation of the right wing to cause a break between the General Strike Committee and the AFL, the union, as a result of Gold's leadership, maintained its position. It was this policy, that made it possible for the union to overcome all the propaganda of the manufacturers, the *Forward*, and the right-wing Socialists that the strike was a "Moscow-inspired revolution."

The fur workers had gone through a school of struggle during the seventeen weeks of the strike. From this struggle emerged a mighty Furriers Union composed of a militant and unified rank and file and guided by a left-wing leadership that had proved itself worthy of the trusted position it held. The fur workers were now ready to undertake new struggles against their combined enemies. The future was to bring new victories of tremendous scope and significance for the American labor movement.

One of the great mass picketing demonstrations during the 1926 strike. Irving Potash can be seen in the lower-right corner.

N. Y. Daily News Photo

A picketing parade of 1926 strikers.

N. Y. Daily News Photo

A Decade of Heroic Battles
Against Gangsterism,
Terrorism and Expulsions

CHAPTER 23

Expulsion of the
New York Joint Board

Fur workers all over the country felt the stimulating effects of the tremendous victory in New York. They were guided by the lessons of the great New York battles; in many instances they were actually assisted in their negotiations by representatives of the New York Joint Board. A number of locals struck, and won in most cases.

Furriers in Boston, Philadelphia, South Norwalk, Toronto and other cities won agreements based on the terms of the settlement in New York —a forty-hour, five-day week all year 'round and an increase in the minimum scale. These victories were achieved without any real support from the leaders of the International. Wherever leaders of the International did enter the picture the workers usually lost.

In Chicago, the workers were on the verge of winning their demand for the forty-hour week when their right-wing leader, Jack Millstein, called off the strike. He accepted the employers' offer of a forty-four-hour week for the busy season and a forty-hour week for the rest of the year. Shachtman, who was present in Chicago, later admitted to the General Executive Board that if the strike had lasted another week or two, the strikers would have won their full demands.

As a result of the victory in New York and its helpful effect on their own struggles, the fur workers outside of New York City rallied to the left wing. Sam Burt, militant left-winger, was elected manager of Local 53 in Philadelphia by an overwhelming majority. In the elections for executive board members in Local 30 of Boston, the left-wing candidates emerged victorious.

In Newark, the right-wing Corbett machine was ousted and Morris Langer, left-wing leader, was elected manager of Local 25 by a three-to-one vote. In spite of repeated demands, Corbett had refused to render a financial accounting to the local. In the summer of 1926, a committee began investigating the union's books. But on the day the committee started its work, Corbett announced that someone had "broken into" his office and stolen certain pages from his records. The missing pages covered the receipts for the months of March to July, 1926.

Corbett tried to accuse the left-wingers of the theft. But Louis Belfour, vice-president of the local and formerly one of Corbett's assistants, disclosed that at a "fishing party" a few days earlier, Corbett had outlined his plan to rip out and burn the incriminating pages. On the basis of the evidence, the local's committee found Corbett guilty of destroying financial records and misusing funds of the union. Both Shachtman and Wohl defended their colleague, but the verdict of the investigating committee was accepted by a membership vote of 138 to 7. The International leaders, however, retained him as a vice-president of the International.

A similar scandal rocked the Chicago local and led to the ousting of Jack Millstein. During their 1926 strike, the *Jewish Daily Forward* sent a loan of $5,000 to the local. Instead of turning the money over to the union, Millstein kept it for himself. Shachtman wrote Millstein about the $5,000. Through Millstein's carelessness, the letter fell into the hands of opponents of the right-wing machine, who published it in the press. The disclosure forced Millstein to resign. In the local elections in September 1926, despite Shachtman's support, his machine was swept out of office by a progressive-left-wing coalition.

The election of left-wingers to positions of leadership in many of the out-of-town locals was a definite sign that the days of the right-wing officials were numbered. The fur workers were now in a position to sweep the right-wing leaders of the International out of office at the convention scheduled for May 1927. But this could not be allowed to happen.

In a letter to Charles Stetsky, dated August 23, 1929, William Green boasted: "It is clearly evident that the American Federation of Labor saved your organization from the Communists. At the time we took charge of the situation in New York, the membership of your International Union was about to elect Communists as officers of your International organization. The influence of Communism and Communist leaders was very great. They had practically captured your International Union."

It was a foregone conclusion that the workers would elect the left wing to lead the entire union. To prevent this, it was necessary to deprive the workers of their democratic rights—to subject them to every type of force and violence—and to split the union apart, even at the sacrifice of all their gains in working conditions. The blunt denial of the democratic right of the workers to choose their own leaders, as expressed in Green's own words, is the key to the history of the Furriers Union and, for that matter, of a large part of the American labor movement in the years after 1926.

On July 19, 1926, Ben Gold, manager of the New York Joint Board, received notice from William Green that the Executive Council of the AFL had "authorized and instructed the President of the American Federation of Labor to appoint a committee representing the Executive Council for the purpose of making an investigation into the internal affairs of the International Fur Workers Union, the recent strike of the New York membership of that Union, the developments which took place in the working out of a new wage agreement and the general policy pursued by the Strike Committee which directed the strike in New York City."

"The Executive Council desires to know," the communication continued, "whether those in charge of the recent strike in New York City were conforming to the laws, usages and administrative policies of the American Federation of Labor, in their management and conduct of the strike."

The committee appointed by Green consisted of Matthew Woll, vice-president of the AFL, as chairman; Hugh Frayne and Edward F. McGrady, general organizers of the Federation; John Sullivan, president of the New York State Federation of Labor; and Joseph Ryan, president of the New York City Central Trades and Labor Council.

"Please give the committee access to all books, records and accounts of the local strike committee of which you were chairman, and the books, records and accounts of any sub-committee created by the local strike committee," Green's letter to Gold demanded.

To give the investigation an air of impartiality, Green sent a similar letter to Shachtman, asking him to give the committee access to all books, records and accounts of the International Union which the committee might consider pertinent to its investigation. But in a private letter to Shachtman on July 23, 1926, conspicuously marked "confidential," Hugh Frayne secretly reassured Shachtman and told him that the committee had already met and drawn up its plan of operation. It was essential that Shachtman be present when the committee met, he wrote, to "enlighten us with such information as will be helpful in the work."

In the weeks to come, the investigation committee issued statement after statement to the press, announcing that it was conducting an impartial inquiry and that it was neutral in the conflict between the International and the Joint Board. It was extremely unfortunate that the Joint Board did not know of the "confidential" letter. Its publication would have exposed the collusion of right-wing leaders of the International and the AFL officialdom.

After a discussion of Green's letter at a full meeting of the Joint Board, Gold sent a vigorous protest to the President of the AFL expressing amazement at "such an unexpected and extraordinary investigation."

"What are we accused of?" Gold asked. Green had neither stated the grounds upon which the investigation had been ordered, nor disclosed upon whose initiative it was being undertaken, he pointed out. "This is an unusual procedure indeed," the letter continued. "Is the AFL in the habit of ordering special investigations of strikes simply because it is generally interested in the welfare of the organizations concerned? We think not. On the contrary, the AFL policy has always been to grant the affiliated organizations great latitude in the conduct of their strikes. Such an investigation as the one proposed is almost, if not altogether, without parallel in American trade union practice. Our Joint Board requests from you a definite statement of the specific reasons for the proposed investigation."

The Joint Board also desired to know if the investigation was proposed by the Executive Council itself or by the International? If it was initiated by the Executive Council, was this not an invasion of the autonomy of the International? And if the investigation was asked for by the International, why did not Green's letter make this clear? Since this issue touched on one of the most vital features of trade union practice—the question of the rights and duties of the affiliated organizations —the Joint Board was entitled to specific information.

"We are proud of our long, hard-fought and successful strike," Gold's letter concluded. "We have no objection to its being investigated by a fair and properly authorized committee. The Joint Board is a loyal and disciplined section of the AFL. But we insist upon knowing why the investigation is being undertaken and upon whose initiative. We also propose that our Joint Board be allowed three members upon any such

NEW YORK OFFICE

AMERICAN FEDERATION OF LABOR

Executive Council.

President, William Green,
Secretary, Frank Morrison,
Treasurer, Daniel J. Tobin,
521 B. Michigan St., Indianapolis, Ind.

First Vice-President, James Duncan,
15 Hancock Street, Quincy, Mass.
Second Vice-President, Frank Duffy,
Carpenters' Building, Indianapolis, Ind.
Third Vice-President, T. A. Rickert,
Room 303, 175 W. Washington St., Chicago, Ill.
Fourth Vice-President, Jacob Fischer,
528 Reed Michigan Street, Indianapolis, Ind.

Fifth Vice-President, Matthew Woll,
Room 501, 175 W. Washington St., Chicago, Ill.
Sixth Vice-President, Martin F. Ryan,
Mill Hall Building, Kansas City, Mo.
Seventh Vice-President, James Wilson,
Second National Bank Bldg., Cincinnati, Ohio
Eighth Vice-President, James P. Noonan,
Machinists Building, Washington, D. C.

HUGH FRAYNE
REPRESENTATIVE
1482 BROADWAY
ENTRANCE 145 WEST 41st STREET
SUITE 701
TELEPHONE, WISCONSIN 2214

A. F. OF L. BUILDING
WASHINGTON, D. C.

LONG DISTANCE TELEPHONE, MAIN 3871-2-3
CABLE ADDRESS, "AFEL"

New York,   July 23, 1926.

<u>CONFIDENTIAL</u>

Mr. Oiser Shachtman, President,
Fur Workers International Union,
Hotel Morrison, Chicago, Ill.

Dear Sir and Brother:

You no doubt received a letter from President Green advising you of the appointment of the committee to investigate the internal affairs of the Fur Workers Union.

We had a meeting here today and organized and made up our plan and scope program. The first meeting to begin the hearings will be held in this office on Thursday, July 29th, at 10:30 A. M. It was suggested that I communicate with you urging you to be here at that time to appear before the committee and enlighten us with such information as will be helpful in the work. We have decided to carry on this work quietly, without any publicity whatever for the present, at least.

We are asking you to appear before the committee and if necessary you can return to Chicago again, but we want you to appear before the committee first so we can have the benefit of first-hand, valuable information which you can furnish us. No substitute will do in this case and because of the importance of the matter we urge you to come. One or two hours of your time will be sufficient; any other material may be given through such channels as you decide on.

Urging that you give this your favorable consideration and advise me whether we can expect you here in this office on Thursday morning, July 29th, at 10:30 o'clock, I remain, with best wishes,

Fraternally yours,

Hugh Frayne

General Organizer
American Federation of Labor

(BS&AU)
(12646)

While claiming to be conducting an impartial inquiry, Frayne urges Shachtman to attend a secret conference and give the committee "valuable information" to frame the Joint Board.

committee and that it conduct its hearings publicly in a hall which will permit the attendance of the largest possible number of trade unionists and the press."

In another letter—this one to President Shachtman—Gold again asked why and by whom the investigation was ordered. Since Shachtman was fully aware that the strike had enormously strengthened the union in New York and inspired victories for fur workers all over the country, he should be the first to point out that no investigation was necessary. But if the International still insisted that it was needed, why not have the investigation conducted by the union itself? "The Joint Board has no objection to such an investigation by our International," Gold affirmed.

Green and Shachtman groped for some plausible explanation which would not reveal the conspiracy against the Joint Board. Both claimed that an understanding had been reached on April 18, 1926, at the Cadillac Hotel conference, to the effect that "after the strike an investigation into the internal affairs of the International Fur Workers Union would be made by a committee representing the American Federation of Labor." Since the document released to the public after this conference [reprinted in full on page 216] contained no reference whatever to any investigation, Shachtman came up with the excuse that "it was not advisable at that time that this part of the agreement be made public."

For almost a year, the question of who initiated the investigation went unanswered. But on March 14, 1927, when the real purposes of the investigation had been achieved, Green wrote: "The International Fur Workers Union appealed to the American Federation of Labor to make an investigation of the 1926 strike of the Fur Workers of New York City which was originated, directed and administered by the Joint Board of the International Union."

How the membership felt about the impending investigation was expressed on August 12, 1926, when thousands of fur workers packed Cooper Union to hear a report from the leadership of the Joint Board. Inside the auditorium, a huge banner carried the slogan: "WE ARE PREPARED TO MEET THE NEW ATTACKS OF OUR ENEMIES."

Gold accused the AFL officialdom of seeking to throw the union into receivership. The leaders of the Federation, he declared, had never bothered to investigate the betrayal of the 1920 strike by the right-wing clique; nor had they ever looked into the terroristic activities of the Welfare Club or the links between the right-wing machine and the underworld. For that matter, they had never questioned the conduct of strikes in which the workers of various unions had been sold out by their leaders.

"They seek to investigate us, however," he went on, "because we got rid of the grafters and the thieves and the underworld, because we organized the unorganized workers and conducted a strike in a responsible fashion, faithful to the interests of the workers."

"If they mean to destroy our union, if they mean to uproot the new spirit of the furriers, they are making a grave mistake. The furriers," Gold warned, "are prepared to meet all their enemies on the field of battle."

With one enormous shout, the thousands of fur workers present answered "aye" to a resolution which expressed their "complete trust in those who served us on the General Strike Committee and in our present progressive leadership of the Joint Board, against whom the present investigation is aimed. We pledge them our full support against these latest attacks on our union."

The workers also demanded that the hearings of the investigation committee "be public and aboveboard, and that they be open to the press representatives and to the workers."

Ignoring the protests of the workers, the investigation committee went ahead with its prearranged plans, drawn up in consultation with President Shachtman. All requests for a specific statement of charges and for open hearings were denied. The committee also brusquely rejected the Joint Board's protest against the men appointed to investigate it—particularly against Hugh Frayne, who had worked so hard to sabotage the 1926 strike. Protesting that the investigation was in violation of the International Constitution and the laws of the AFL, the Joint Board nevertheless finally agreed to make its books and records available to the committee, so that "the American labor movement might learn how to conduct a strike."

The committee assigned Walter M. Cook as the accountant to investigate the books and records. The Joint Board immediately lodged a furious protest with Matthew Woll that Cook was closely linked with the leaders of the International and had been on the International payroll for several years. Again the Joint Board's protest was ignored.

Throughout August and September, 1926, the committee met in secret session. It inspected the books of the Joint Board and took personal testimony. The testimony of the witnesses was kept secret. Had it been made public, the record would have revealed very plainly the difference in treatment accorded to the spokesmen of the Joint Board and those of the

International. The former were repeatedly asked if they were members of the Communist Party, if they supported and endorsed the *Freiheit*, and other questions intended to give the impression that the leaders of the strike were "Moscow agents" and that the strike itself was a "Communist plot." On the other hand, spokesmen for the International were not asked if they were members of the Socialist Party, if they endorsed the *Forward*, or if they had held any meetings with other right-wing trade union leaders during the strike to betray the strikers.

Shachtman, Sorkin and other right-wing leaders of the International accused the strike leaders of squandering the union's money, of bribing the police, of forcing strikers to join the Communist Party, of terrorizing workers who refused to continue on strike, of prolonging the strike at the order of the Communist Party, and even of placing "Communist agents" in the offices of New York newspapers—including the *New York Times*—to report the strike in a manner favorable to the Communists.

These accusations, unsupported by the slightest shred of evidence, were readily accepted without question by the investigation committee. All requests by representatives of the Joint Board for the right to cross-examine witnesses were rejected. At one point, Gold burst out angrily: "If any of the furriers can prove satisfactorily that they were frightened or forced to join the Communist Party, I state on behalf of the Joint Board that we will be willing to cooperate with the AFL committee, to go to any extended discipline in accordance with the methods of the AFL constitution against those who are guilty." His protest was ignored.

Likewise rejected was the Joint Board's request for an opportunity to cross-examine some fifty-eight signers of affidavits who claimed that they had been victims of beatings during the strike. When the Board offered to prove that the majority of the affidavits were submitted by thugs and strikebreakers, like "Cut-'em-up Charlie" Psomberg, Woll at first agreed to permit their cross-examination. But as soon as he was informed by the International leaders who these characters were, he changed his mind.

It was upon such "evidence" that the investigation committee submitted its report to the Executive Council of the AFL. Taking their "facts" from "Cut-'em-up Charlie" and other gangster and right-wing elements, the committee claimed that the Communist Party had dictated appointments to the strike committee; that right-wing officials had been eliminated from the strike leadership; that furriers had been beaten for criticizing Communist control of the strike; that union funds had been misused; and that police and court officials in New York City had been

bribed in order to secure protection for the strikers. Even Motty Eitingon, who was instrumental in settling the strike, was charged with
being an "agent of Moscow" and was reported to have an $8,000,000-a-
year fur importing concession from the Soviet Government.

Aside from the charge of police bribery, everything in the committee's
report had been said time and again during the strike by the employers
and the *Forward,* and refuted by the mass picket lines of the fur workers.
As to the bribery charge, even the commercial newspapers were forced to
comment that the police and the Industrial Squad had acted very
strangely for men who were supposed to have been bribed by the union.

At a meeting of the Executive Council of the AFL in St. Petersburg,
Florida, on January 13, 1927, the committee solemnly announced that
"a most serious state of affairs" existed in the International Fur Workers Union "due to the fact that a communistic leadership had gained the
ascendancy in the New York locals. Unless drastic measures of defense
are resorted to at once," this same leadership would gain control of "the
whole of the International Fur Workers Union."

"This must not come to pass!" the committee proclaimed. They therefore recommended that the Executive Council of the AFL urge the International Fur Workers Union "to expel from its membership all who
admitted affiliations to the Communist or Workers' Party, or the Trade
Union Educational League, or those who may be found to have such
affiliation." Should this prove to be insufficient to meet the crisis, the
International was asked to revoke the charter of the New York Joint
Board and of all local unions which refused to comply with this directive.

On January 8, 1927, a week before the report was made
public, Shachtman had already assured Green of the International's decision "to reorganize the Joint Board." He appealed to the AFL's Executive Council to appoint a committee "to give the International Union
assistance and advice as well as active support" in carrying through the
expulsion of the Joint Board. The Executive Council approved the report
of the investigation committee and authorized Green to appoint a special
committee to cooperate with the International Fur Workers Union "to
rid this organization of its communistic leadership."

"AFL TO RESCUE THE FUR WORKERS!" ran the headline of the International newspaper.

It was to take a few weeks to carry out the plot to expel the Joint
Board and "rescue the fur workers." Meanwhile, bankrupt financially,
the right-wing leaders of the International wanted to grab as much as

they could from the Joint Board before announcing the expulsion. Although strike debts of $400,000 placed the Joint Board in extreme financial difficulties, it had already paid the International $30,000 in per capita during the brief period between August and December, 1926. In addition, the Joint Board had helped the International with enormous sums of money; it had sent $3,000 weekly to the Montreal strikers, and $5,000 to the Chicago strikers. (It had to borrow money to make this contribution.) It contributed to the Winnipeg fur strikers. The Joint Board also gave financial assistance to the forty thousand cloakmakers in their bitter strike, to the Passaic strikers and the paper box strikers. This was of little concern to the right-wing leaders of the International. Late in January 1927, at the very time that they were outlining the plan to expel the Joint Board, they demanded $15,000 from the Board.

When the Board rejected the demand, the conspirators moved ahead swiftly. "Will meet you Cadillac Hotel Saturday," Green wired Shachtman on February 1. "Suggest you arrange affairs so we can carry out recommendations of Investigation Committee immediately." At this conference, Green appointed a committee composed of Matthew Woll, Edward F. McGrady and Hugh Frayne to work with the leaders of the International in expelling the Joint Board and reorganizing the New York union.

Cooperating with the AFL committee was a so-called Committee for Preservation of the Trade Unions. This ironically misnamed committee had been organized in December 1926 by right-wing Socialist union officials, including Morris Sigman and Julius Hochman of the ILGWU, Abraham Beckerman of the Amalgamated Clothing Workers, Morris Feinstone of the United Hebrew Trades, Abraham I. Shiplacoff of the International Pocket Book Workers, and Alex Rose of the Millinery Workers. This committee declared war on the left-wing forces in the needle trades unions, and called for the expulsion of all Communists from the labor movement. The National Executive Committee of the Socialist Party hailed the organization of this committee and enthusiastically endorsed its program.

In the years when Socialist trade union leaders had waged militant battles against the employers and sweatshops, they had clashed with the reactionary policies and tactics of the AFL. They had denounced the participation of Samuel Gompers and other labor leaders in the National Civic Federation together with open-shop employers and other enemies of labor. Now, however, they cooperated enthusiastically with Matthew Woll, acting president of the same National Civic Federation.

The "Committee for Preservation of the Trade Unions" had helped Morris Sigman expel the militant New York Joint Board of the ILGWU without trial or hearing, on 24-hour notice.

On February 8, 1927, the "Committee for Preservation of the Trade Unions" met with the AFL special committee to discuss plans for expelling the New York Joint Board of the Furriers Union.

"It was pointed out by everybody at this meeting," Woll, Frayne and McGrady wrote to Green, "that the communists in the fur industry were much better entrenched than they were in all of the other needle trades and that consequently the fight would be more bitter and costly. . ."

"The International Fur Workers Union," Woll, McGrady and Frayne also sadly informed Green, "was not only bankrupt, but owed considerable money and could give no financial assistance." The money, then, would have to come from outside sources. This from men who were charging that the leaders of the Joint Board were directed by "outside" forces!

The "Committee for Preservation of the Trade Unions" pledged "to devote their time to raise money among the Hebrew trades" and appointed the Socialist Party leader, Abraham Shiplacoff, treasurer of the fund to keep the bankrupt International alive. The AFL leaders agreed to get the Central Trades and Labor Council of New York to issue a letter asking for funds. (During the 1926 strike, they had sabotaged the collection of relief for the strikers!)

Thus, in February 1927, the International Fur Workers Union went into receivership. The International office became nothing more than a front for the right-wing Socialists and reactionary AFL officials in the attacks upon the fur workers of New York.

No act was too contemptible for these trade union leaders. On February 23, 1927, Edward McGrady wrote to Edgar Wallace, chairman of the AFL Legislative Committee, informing him that he had received "confidential information" that Aaron Gross, one of the left-wing leaders of the New York Joint Board, had sailed for Europe. He added: "Would you go to the State Department and find out whether or not any passports have been issued in the name of Aaron Gross recently and if so, what his destination is. If no passports have been issued to this man, find out what the penalty is for sailing on false passports. I would like to get this information as soon as possible."

Shachtman was only too happy to cooperate in this degrading plot. When the State Department asked for a picture of Gross in order that it

AMERICAN FEDERATION OF LABOR

A. F. OF L. BUILDING

Washington, D.C.

February 25, 1927.

Mr. Edward F. McGrady, Organizer,
American Federation of Labor,
1452 Broadway, New York City.

Dear Sir and Brother:

Your letter of February 33 in relation to
Mr. Aaron Gross received.

This matter was taken up with the state
department and it was learned that three men by the name
of Gross had sailed from New York during the last two
weeks. Two, named Arthur B. Gross (probably father and
son), were oil operators and sailed for South America.
The third, Alexis Gross, was also an oil operator and he
sailed for Mesopotamia.

All passports applied for in New York are sent
to the state department here for approval. Each passport
contains the picture of the person for whom it is issued.
It was suggested that if anyone knew Aaron Gross by sight
or you could obtain a picture of him, comparisons could
be made at the state department to learn if he was
traveling under a forged passport or one issued to someone
else.

I was requ[...]
regarding Aaron Gros[...]
take it up with the[...]
could send a photo[...]
his passport if he[...]
passport of some on[...]

With best[...]

Feb 26 · 1927

Mr Ed. Wallace

Dear Sir and Brother

Enclosed you will find
the picture of Mr A. Gross
as per Communication sent
to you by Bro McGrady.

With best regards I am
fraternally yours

C Shachtman

---

*Shachtman and AFL officials forward Aaron Gross's photograph
to State Department. Obvious purpose: to railroad him to jail.*

could check up on his passport, Shachtman hurriedly forwarded a photograph through Edgar Wallace in Washington.

On February 17, in answer to a request from William Green,* the New York Central Trades and Labor Council expelled the Fur Workers Local Unions, Nos. 1, 5, 10 and 15, and the International Ladies Garment Workers Local Unions, Nos. 2, 9, 22 and 35. Against this united attack, the workers in the needle trades began to consolidate their forces. A week later, thousands of fur workers jammed into Cooper Union, denounced the attempt "to undermine both unions" and called for the formation of a joint committee "for the purpose of defending our unions and maintaining the labor standards in the shops."

"This struggle is a historic one for the entire labor movement," Ben Gold declared, "and we are going to mobilize the workers in defense of their unions as we did in the last general strike of twelve thousand furriers."

Late in February 1927, the General Executive Board of the International Fur Workers Union received an urgent appeal from the Toronto Joint Board. The Toronto fur workers called upon the G.E.B. to cease its destructive campaign against the New York Joint Board and "issue immediately a call for a convention to be held in May 1927."

This plea for sanity was ignored. Instead, on March 2, 1927, the G.E.B., acting through Shachtman, Wohl, and its Sub-Committee, expelled thirty-seven officials of the New York Joint Board and of Locals 1, 5, 10 and 15 from membership in the union.** It ordered the immediate dissolution of the Joint Board and the local unions, and demanded the immediate delivery of all funds and properties of the Board and these unions to the special committee of the AFL.

---

* Green's letter to the New York Central Trades and Labor Council came in response to telegrams from Sigman and Shachtman requesting this action. "You will observe in reading this enclosure," Green wrote to Shachtman on February 17, 1927, "that I have thoroughly and fully complied with your request and recommendation as submitted in your telegram." The "enclosure" was a copy of Green's letter to the New York Central Trades and Labor Council.

** Those expelled were Ben Gold, I. Shapiro, J. Schneider, M. Pinchefsky, B. Baraz, W. Woliner, H. Kravitz, L. Schiller, S. Mencher, L. Cohen, S. Resnick, Lena Greenberg, J. Winogradsky, A. Cohen, S. Leibowitz, M. Polinsky, Fannie Warshafsky, S. Malamud, M. Suroff, A. Gross, J. Skolnick, E. Polansky, F. Farber, M. Cohen, Julius Fleiss, Frank Brownstone, B. Frieman, M. Intrator, H. Cohen, J. Hershkowitz, Esther Gumberg, S. Kass, M. Gursky, Lena Rabinowitz, I. Horn, M. Spivack and B. Garff.

That same day, March 2, a leaflet distributed in the fur market, signed by Shachtman and Wohl, declared the Joint Board and the four local unions to be "illegal" bodies. Members of the suspended locals were instructed not to take any orders from the expelled unions or pay any dues or assessments at the office of the Joint Board. Instead, they should bring their dues to the office of the new union, called the Joint Council, opened by the special committee of the AFL at 31-33 East 27th Street.

Shachtman and Wohl did not state who was supplying the funds for the new union office. But in a private letter to William Green, Woll, McGrady and Frayne disclosed that the money had been raised from "the Hebrew trades" by the "Committee for Preservation of the Trade Unions."

"The Joint Board brands your action as utterly illegal and in defiance of the Constitution of the International Fur Workers Union," Gold wrote the G.E.B. in the name of the Board. "Your attention is called to the fact that our Constitution prescribes that anyone charged

No charges—no hearing—no trial. You're expelled—period.

OIZER SHACHTMAN
General President

TELEPHONE, HUNTERS POINT 0068
9119

ISAAC WOHL
General Secretary-Treasurer

ISIDOR WINNICK
First Vice-President
HYMAN SORKIN
Second Vice-President
LUIGI DELSIGNORE
Third Vice-President
HYMAN KALMIKOFF
Fourth Vice-President
AARON GROSS
Fifth Vice-President
MILTON CORBETT
Sixth Vice-President

INTERNATIONAL

FUR WORKERS' UNION

OF UNITED STATES AND CANADA

AFFILIATED WITH A. F. OF L.

9 JACKSON AVENUE

SAMUEL BUDKOWITZ
Seventh Vice-President
IDA WEINSTEIN
Eighth Vice-President
JACOB DISSIN
Ninth Vice-President
MOE HARRIS
Tenth Vice-President
HARRY ENGLANDER
Eleventh Vice-President

LONG ISLAND CITY, N.Y., March 4, 1927.

Mr. H. Cohen,
Joint Board Furriers Union.
22 E. 22nd St.,
New York City.

Dear Sir & Brother:

Enclosed herewith find copy of charges and findings of the Sub-Committee of the General Executive Board of the International Fur Workers Union.

Fraternally yours,

Isaac Wohl

General Secretary-Treasurer.

with an offense is entitled to have written charges preferred against him in a prescribed manner, and to be given an impartial trial and an opportunity to be heard. Nevertheless, no attempt has been made to serve the so-called charges upon anybody, and, as you know, the first intimation of any charges pending against the Joint Board, its locals and the persons expelled, was given in the letter of expulsion itself.* First, you expelled us, and then you generously informed us of the charges. Such action not only violates the letter and spirit of our Constitution, but it also outrages the most elementary rules of conduct of the organized American labor movement which you profess to uphold. . . .

"As to the attempted expulsions and re-organizations, we shall leave the answer to the membership, which will give it in due time and in no uncertain terms. As to the charges, we unhesitatingly brand them as a tissue of falsehoods and flagrant inventions, evidently not made in the expectation that they would be believed, but in an attempt to find some excuse for their actions, which are not only utterly illegal, but, if successful, would result in utter ruin of the union itself.

"We, therefore, challenge our accusers to present these charges to a convention of duly and honestly elected representatives of the rank and file of our International membership, as we stand ready to answer all charges before our own membership, who are very well familiar with the principles, tactics, traditions and usages of the labor movement and ready to uphold the same."

The unconstitutional and undemocratic expulsions, dissolution of the Joint Board and the four locals, and setting up a new union under the AFL—all clearly revealed the new conspiracy of leaders of the International and of the AFL who had failed only a few months before in the efforts to break the general strike of 1926. As Gold declared in his letter to the G.E.B.: "Your final act offers to the Joint Board an opportunity to unmask before all workers your type of labor misleaders who shamelessly serve the interests of the employers against the workers. Your actions will go down in labor history as the most shameful and cowardly attempt to betray the labor movement."

* In all, thirty charges were listed in the expulsion order, although not all of those expelled were included in each one of the charges. Most of them were based upon the report of the AFL's investigation committee, and one, the seventh charge, directed only against Gold, charged a conspiracy "to permit the Communist Party to shape the policies and the conduct of the strike." Several charges referred to the fostering of dissension among the fur workers, attending protest meetings against the union, and joining an organization (the name of which was not mentioned) said to be "hostile to the union."

CHAPTER 24

The Plot Thickens

Thousands of fur workers, filled with indignation over the attempt to destroy their union, assembled in Cooper Union and Webster Hall on March 10, 1927. Pledging their loyalty to the Joint Board, they swore to defend their union, their rights, and their working conditions. They instructed the Joint Board to mobilize its entire strength to defend the union.

"The union is ours," the fur workers cried, "and the officers whom we elect are our leaders and our servants. We will not be ruled by force. We will not be ruled by dictators. We demand the right to elect our own officers. We demand the right to make our own decisions."

A rank-and-file defense committee of five hundred was organized. They patrolled the fur district and routed the sluggers who had been hired to force the workers to register with the new Joint Council. McGrady himself ventured into the fur market with a strong-arm gang. He was greeted by shouts of: "Get out of the market!" "Go back to Washington!" "Take your dirty hands off our union!" McGrady ordered his lieutenants to call the police. He was soon "saved" by a squad of policemen who escorted him back to his office amid the jeers of the workers.

Two weeks after the Joint Board had been officially "dissolved," the *Forward* announced that thousands of furriers were waiting in line to take out books in the Joint Council and blessed the AFL for rescuing them "from the grip of Communist tyrants." In truth, however, only a few dozen had signed up, mostly men who had scabbed during the 1926 strike.

The International office and the Joint Council, dismayed by the resistance of the workers, stepped up the attack on the Joint Board. Within the next few weeks, every union-busting force was again brought into action against the fur workers. Woll, Frayne and McGrady informed Police Commissioner McLaughlin it was absolutely essential that they receive the "full cooperation of the police department." McLaughlin instructed Deputy Inspector McGrath and Captain Hanley of the 30th Street Police Station to devote their full time to assisting the AFL leaders. "At the request of these two police officers," Woll, Frayne and McGrady reported to Green, "it was agreed to pull off all the pickets from the streets and let the police handle the situation. This procedure has ever since been followed."

The fur market became an actual battlefield as police on motorcycles and on horseback and detectives of the Industrial Squad moved in and attacked the workers without any reason. "Arrests are being made everywhere," Woll, Frayne and McGrady wrote to Green.

Still the workers stood fast. The AFL "reorganizers" did not succeed in registering more than a handful of workers. "Time is a very important element in this question," declared the "Committee for Preservation of the Trade Unions," as it summoned all "moral and material resources in the Labor Movement" to the attack on the Furriers Union.

The union-busters then enlisted the aid of the district attorney and the courts. On March 16, 1927, Jack Schneider was arrested and third-degreed. The detectives demanded that he sign a statement that Ben Gold had sent a committee to break up a scab shop in Mineola during the 1926 strike. His body was black and blue. His head and face were swollen unrecognizably. The detectives would let him recover for a few minutes and then they would start in all over again. It went on for six solid hours. But Schneider refused to be bludgeoned into such a statement even if it meant his life. It almost did.

The next day, eleven active workers and leaders of the Joint Board, including Gold, were arrested. They were charged with felonious assault in connection with the picketing of a small scab shop in Rockville Center, Long Island, near Mineola, during the 1926 strike.* For several days,

* In addition to Gold, the men arrested were: Jack Schneider, Isidore Shapiro, Samuel Mencher, Otto Leonard, Oscar Maileff, J. Katz, Martin Rosenberg, N. Malkin, Leo Frankel and George Weiss. Malkin and Frankel had been arrested several months before in connection with the Mineola affair and were

Barney Bassoff, a stool-pigeon informer, had scoured the fur market with detectives, pointing out active members of the union. He charged them with having been implicated in the Mineola affair. Upon the unsupported word of this stool-pigeon, the leaders of the union were imprisoned in the Nassau County jail.

Judge Lewis J. Smith of the Nassau County Court at first refused bail, on the grounds that he had received "information" that Gold and the others were such "criminals" that they should not be permitted to go free. Finally, weakening under the pressure of protests from thousands of fur workers, the judge released the union leaders on bail of $10,000 each. Gold publicly accused the officials of the AFL and the right-wing leaders of the International of direct responsibility for the arrests and of having supplied Judge Smith with the "information" on which bail was first denied.

The next phase in the attack on the union was planned at a conference on January 21, between William Green, Matthew Woll and Mayor James J. Walker of New York. On March 23, 1927, Mayor Walker announced an investigation of the AFL charge of police bribery during the 1926 strike. He had become "convinced that the allegations were sufficient to warrant a thorough inquiry." Magistrate Joseph Corrigan was named to conduct the official court investigation.

To insure their success, the AFL "reorganizers" secretly took steps to deprive the accused of adequate legal defense. Woll, Frayne and McGrady wrote to Green: "About April 1 your committee was informed that Clarence Darrow was coming to New York to confer with the communist leaders who desired to engage his services at a trial which was to be held at Mineola, New York where they were the defendants on a felonious assault charge and also to represent them at the investigation of the alleged police graft in New York City. Your committee met with Mr. Darrow and as a result he promised not to handle their case."

Fortunately, there were other prominent lawyers willing to defend militant union leaders. George Z. Medalie, a member of the National Committee of the Republican Party, and former State Attorney-General, agreed to serve as counsel for the union. Medalie headed the group of lawyers for the defense. The Joint Board also appealed to Frank P. Walsh, a distinguished member of the bar, to undertake the defense of

---

awaiting retrial. Bassoff was arrested along with them and was used by the district attorney in the effort to frame and imprison the leaders of the union. Bassoff was a scab, who had joined the union professing a change of heart.

Committee for Preservation of the Trade Unions

7 EAST 15th STREET, NEW YORK CITY

Telephone, Stuyvesant 7082-3

Provisional Executive Committee

ABRAHAM BECKERMAN
LOUIS D. BERGER
SAMUEL A. BEARDSLEY
MORRIS FEINSTONE
SAMUEL HERSHKOWITZ
ROSE SCHNEIDERMAN
A. I. SHIPLACOFF

March 18th, 1927

Dear Friend:-

A conference of a small number of representative men in the Labor Movement will be held on WEDNESDAY,
March 23rd, 1927 in the Forward Building, #175 E. Broadway. We are calling this conference for the purpose of
getting the advice and cooperation of the best minds in
the Movement in connection with the work of the Committee
for the Preservation of the Trade Unions.

As a result of a large conference that was
held in the latter part of December at Beethoven Hall,
considerable work has been accomplished in a number of
unions, particularly in the International Ladies' Garment
Workers' Union. The back-bone of the Communist conspiracy
against labor unions has practically been broken. Their
only real stronghold today is the Furriers Union. Time
is a very important element in this question. There are
enough of moral and material resources in the Labor Movement to put an end to the work of the wreckers if we will
pull all our forces together at this time.

You are urgently requested to attend this conference which will begin at 3:00 P.M. sharp. All of the
people that are being invited are busy folks. You are
therefore requested to be on time so that we can accomplish
our aim.

Fraternally yours,

A. I. Shiplacoff,
Chairman

BS&AU
12646
AFoL

M. Feinstone,
Secretary

*A meeting of right-wing leaders is called in the Forward Building
to step up the all-out attack on the fur workers. Note: These
are the same people who always shouted "outside interference."*

its leaders.* Walsh refused to accept the cases until he had an opportunity to make an exhaustive investigation of the charges and counter-
charges. For several weeks, Walsh and his entire staff of attorneys investigated the Mineola affair and the police-bribery charges. They
reached the inevitable conclusion that the charges against the leaders of
the fur workers were "of the flimsiest nature," most of them being "based
upon false accusations," and inspired by right-wing leaders of the International and the AFL "to eliminate the present Joint Board and their
officers."

Convinced that a vast frame-up was in the making, Walsh agreed to
take the cases and threw himself energetically into the preparation of the
defense of the furriers' leaders. In addition, he helped to organize a Committee of One Hundred to defend needle trades' workers who were either
in prison or were facing imprisonment as a result of their activities in the
furriers' and cloakmakers' strikes of 1926. The committee included leading writers, artists, playwrights, editors, ministers and men and women
prominent in humanitarian movements.**

The formation of the Committee of One Hundred threw the leaders of
the AFL and their right-wing Socialist allies into a frenzy. The liberals
who were serving on the committee, McGrady declared, were being used
as "window dressing" by the "Communist Joint Board of the Furriers
Union." There was "no issue of civil or industrial rights" involved, he
cried, since they were all "Communists."

Emissaries from Woll, McGrady and Sigman of the ILGWU warned
Forrest Bailey, director of the American Civil Liberties Union, against

---

* In addition to a long and distinguished legal career, Walsh had held, among
others, the positions of President of the Kansas City Board of Civil Service;
Chairman of the Federal Commission on Industrial Relations; Joint Chairman
with ex-President William H. Taft of the War Labor Conference Board; and
representative of the people on the National War Labor Board. He was also
Chairman of the American Commission on Irish Independence and in that capacity argued the case of Ireland at the Versailles peace conference.

** Among them were Forrest Bailey, director of the American Civil Liberties
Union and President of the Civic Club of New York; Susan Brandeis, lawyer
and daughter of United States Supreme Court Justice Brandeis; Professor
Henry W. L. Dana; W. E. B. DuBois, outstanding Negro leader and editor of
Crisis; James Weldon Johnson, leader of the National Association for the
Advancement of Colored People; Arthur Garfield Hays, prominent lawyer active
in the American Civil Liberties Union; Rev. John Haynes Holmes; Upton Sin-
clair, famous novelist; John Howard Lawson, noted playwright; Hugo Gellert,
artist; Rev. Eliot White of Grace Church; and Rev. Harry F. Ward of the
Union Theological Seminary.

serving on the committee. When Bailey refused to be intimidated, Sigman wrote personally to the directors of the ACLU, advising "the individual Civil Liberties members participating in this so-called 'defense committee' to keep their hands off."

"Your letters indicate that your emotions have destroyed your sense of humor as well as your sense of fairness," Arthur Garfield Hays replied to Sigman. ". . . You write letters to the effect that this will cause me the loss of your respect and that of others in the labor movement, something I would wish to avoid. You even state that we who serve on the Committee must be 'inextricably bound up with the gangsterism, fraud and corruption employed by those former leaders.' You must know that this sort of thing is preposterous and that statements of that kind merely reflect on your judgment and good faith."

Woll, Frayne and McGrady were also busily engaged in conferences with the leaders of the Associated Fur Manufacturers. Originally it had been planned that the employers should remain in the background while the leaders of the International and the AFL carried the ball in smashing the Joint Board. In this way, it was hoped, the fur workers would not see how deeply their employers were involved in the scheme to smash their union. But the continued resistance of the workers forced the conspirators to drop the mask. The employers came openly into the campaign of terror to force the fur workers to register in the dual union.

"As a result of these conferences," the AFL trio wrote to William Green, "the Associated Fur Manufacturers agreed to recognize the contract of the International organization and the American Federation of Labor. It further agreed that it would instruct all members of the Association to employ none but workers in good standing in the International organization affiliated with the American Federation of Labor."

On April 1 there was a public announcement of the terms of the agreement. When the furriers entered the shops the next day, Friday, they were informed by signs posted on the walls that anyone who did not bring a book from the Joint Council on Monday morning would not be allowed to work. As they left the shops that afternoon, they were again warned by the bosses that they must register with the Joint Council.

So enraged were the fur workers that in the vast majority of the shops they ripped the signs off the walls. That evening, workers from over 120 shops came to the Joint Board office and demanded immediate strike action against their employers.

"The period of slavery in the United States is past," the Joint Board

warned the manufacturers. Should they continue their attempts to dictate
to the fur workers what union they should belong to, the Joint Board
would take steps to defend the workers' rights.

It is important here to note a most grievous mistake committed by Ben Gold at the conclusion of the great strike of 1926. It was a
mistake that cost the fur workers dearly in 1927 and the years that followed. It is dealt with here for the valuable lesson to be learned from it.

At the end of the strike, the actual wage rates of the fur workers went
up as much as 40 percent. The union was heavily in debt. Many workers
urged Gold to recommend an assessment which would provide enough
money for the union to liquidate all debts and still remain with an adequate union treasury. The fur workers would have joyfully given a
week's pay for that purpose, and over a million dollars could have been
raised within a few weeks. With this financial reserve, the Joint Board
would have had the resources needed to defeat the new conspiracy against
the union in 1927.

But in 1926, Gold still seriously underestimated the desperation and
viciousness of the enemies of the union and the union-busting methods
they would pursue even after the strike. He failed, therefore, to place the
question of finances as a matter of utmost organizational importance to
the union; a necessary resource to defend it against the attacks to come.
In a reaction to the policies of the discredited Kaufman administration
which had levied tax after tax upon the workers, Gold took the position
in 1926 that he wanted to give the workers a breathing spell. They had
suffered and starved during the strike. Many were in debt. Hence Gold
wanted them to be able to pay off their debts and save up a few dollars.
Therefore, no assessment.

It should be added that this was also a serious underestimation of the
readiness of the workers—when they were in a position to do so—to put
the union on a solid financial basis. It was no favor to them not to pay
an assessment. They would have saved a hundred times that much afterward by being able to smash the union-busting attacks at the start.

Having made this mistake, Gold then compounded it by permitting
the union to use its income after the 1926 strike to pay off the accumulated debts immediately at the expense of the union's financial strength.
The union made it a point of honor to pay off the debts—even to the bank
of the ILGWU, whose officials were now assisting in the attack upon the
Joint Board. The treasury was depleted to the point that not enough was
left for organizers' payroll.

Rarely, if ever, had a union faced attacks on so many fronts at one time. Every day more and more shops reported to the Joint Board that they had not been allowed to go to work because they had refused to register with the scab "union." Meanwhile, with the aid of the police and gangsters, the Joint Council was trying desperately to fill the shops with scabs to replace workers who had refused to register.

Under the threat of terror and starvation, some workers did capitulate. The vast majority held fast, however, even though they were thrown out of their shops and deprived of their livelihood. Because the fur garments were not being produced, many employers frantically offered to pay the registration fee for the workers in the dual union. Invariably, the answer was: "We won't register with the scab 'union.'"

Under pressure from the manufacturers, the leaders of the Association demanded action from the AFL. "The Associated Fur Manufacturers called in your committee," Woll, Frayne and McGrady wrote to William Green, "and said they were willing to go through with this fight provided your committee would pledge that the American Federation of Labor would stay until conditions were stabilized. This we promised to do."

Suddenly, on April 11, bail for Gold and his ten associates was lifted and they were again arrested, handcuffed and locked up in the Nassau County jail to await trial in the Mineola affair. Realizing that it was impossible for the furriers' leaders to obtain a fair trial in Mineola —a well-known center of the Ku-Klux-Klan, where hatred for Jews and trade unionists was rampant—the union's lawyers asked that the trial be transferred to the Supreme Court of Brooklyn.

On the same day that the union's request was argued before Judge Gallagher of the Brooklyn Supreme Court, the newspapers featured a story in which Matthew Woll accused the leaders of the Furriers Union of preparing for "a revolutionary industrial war which is to end in Communist dictatorship directed from Moscow." District Attorney Elvin N. Edwards of Mineola made effective use of Woll's red-baiting article in his argument opposing the transfer of the trial. Not only did Judge Gallagher refuse to grant a transfer of the trial, but he even refused to discuss the question of releasing the prisoners on bail.

While handcuffed in jail awaiting trial together with the other union leaders, Gold dictated a message to the fur workers in the name of all the imprisoned leaders: "They may chain our bodies, but not our spirit. Prisons and chains have no rule over our ideals and opinions. On the contrary, our courage and spirit for justice for the oppressed working class is strengthened. Hold high the banner of our holy struggle. Close your ranks for defense against the enemy. We hope to see you soon. Long live the struggle for justice."

Events fully justified the union's request for a transfer. The defendants were supposedly on trial for having broken into a scab shop and attacked the owner. But a good deal of the trial was conducted as if the defendants were guilty of political crimes. They were asked if they read the *Freiheit* and endorsed its principles. Did they know Charles E. Ruthenberg, general secretary of the American Communist Party? Did they oppose the capitalist form of government? Were they in favor of war? Frank P. Walsh protested bitterly that these questions had nothing whatsoever to do with the charge against the defendants and were asked only to prejudice the jury. Judge Smith overruled his objections and encouraged the district attorney to probe further into the defendants' political beliefs.

So obvious was the prejudice of the judge and the district attorney throughout the trial in Mineola, that Supreme Court Justice Mitchel May in Brooklyn was later forced to grant a certificate of reasonable doubt in the case on the grounds that even "a superficial examination of the records of this trial" revealed "an atmosphere around the Mineola trial which would influence the jury against the accused." Justice May bluntly accused the presiding judge and the district attorney of going far out of their way in order to assure an "unfavorable verdict against the accused." "It is seriously questionable whether the defendants were able to secure the fair and impartial trial which the law insures," he concluded.

Two defendants—Gold and Shapiro—were acquitted. Nine others were found guilty. They were sentenced to two-and-a-half to five years in prison.*

The reactionary anti-labor forces were not yet satisfied. As soon as the

---

* George Z. Medalie, one of the most brilliant lawyers in the country, was heartbroken over the Mineola trial. Enraged at the treachery of the AFL and the attempts to frame the union militants, Medalie told Gold: "I have defended all kinds of criminals, even murderers. Whenever their cases were lost, they were ripping mad. Here, for the first time in my life, I defended labor men, men who were not guilty of any crime, but were declared guilty. Yet they come over and shake hands with me and express their thanks for my efforts. . . . I never knew there were such people in existence."

Henry A. Uterhart, another of the defense attorneys, declared movingly: "To me Gold, Shapiro, Mencher and the others are apostles in the struggle for justice."

jury had brought in its verdict, the district attorney demanded that Gold and Shapiro be held in the Mineola prison until they could be brought to trial for the second time. The first trial, just concluded, was based upon charges brought in by Michael Barnett, boss of the Mineola shop; the second would be based upon charges presented by his brother, Jack Barnett. As a result of vigorous protests by the defense, Judge Smith magnanimously permitted Gold and Shapiro to go free on parole until the district attorney demanded a new trial on the second indictment.*

In the midst of all of the bitterness of the year 1927, there was a moment of joy for the fur workers when Gold returned from the Mineola jail, a free man. Their happiness was mingled with grief over the fate of the men who were still imprisoned. Thousands of furriers packed Cooper Union, Webster Hall and Manhattan Lyceum to welcome Gold home. When he entered Cooper Union, an indescribable demonstration broke loose. Tears of joy flowed freely down the cheeks of young and old alike.

The mass protests of the fur workers and other needle trades workers forced the district attorney of Mineola to drop the second indictment against Gold and Shapiro. But the attempt to frame the furriers' leaders on the police-bribery charges continued. Hearings were resumed by Magistrate Corrigan.** Woll, Frayne, McGrady, Shachtman and Winnick literally stumbled over themselves in their eagerness to imprison the entire leadership of the Joint Board on the ground that they had bribed the police during the 1926 strike. But the elaborate structure built up by the AFL and International leaders to railroad the furriers was completely demolished by the defendants. By proving the actual conduct of the police during the strike, they exposed the ridiculous accusation. Never before in the history of the labor movement in New York City had there been so many arrests and prosecutions of workers during one strike. Police records put into evidence showed 874 arrests in three precincts alone and 477 convictions. In all, about fifteen hundred strikers had been arrested. Hundreds had been brutally beaten by the police. The right to picket had been denied. Hostile judges had imposed harsh sentences. Some workers had been jailed for two to three years. Throughout

* After two years of legal appeals in the courts and continuous mass pressure, seven of the nine were finally acquitted, and the other two were imprisoned for two and one-half years. Medalie submitted the brief for the appeal.

** The hearings actually started on April 6, 1927, but after a few days an adjournment was taken because Gold, Mencher, Shapiro and others were called to trial in Mineola.

the strike vigorous protests had been lodged against the brutal police attacks on the strikers. The terror unleashed against the fur workers had even compelled the Central Trades and Labor Council of New York to investigate the police outrages.

Despite the overwhelming evidence of police brutality against the strikers, the leaders of the AFL still charged that Mencher, Resnick, Shapiro, Gold and other left-wingers had confessed during the AFL investigation that they had paid graft to the police.

But the accused leaders of the Joint Board firmly denied any such statements. They insisted that the testimony in the AFL investigation had been deliberately falsified to railroad them to jail. They presented the stenographic notes taken by the secretary of the Joint Board during the investigation to prove that none of the admissions attributed to them had ever been made.

"What we say is true," Gold declared. "If they can prove what they say is true, they can prove the earth is flat."

"Do you think that these things were put there to injure you?" Gold was asked.

"I have no doubt of it," he replied.

"They would send a man to the electric chair so that they might take the leadership of the union from us," Shapiro added.

The investigation lasted for about two weeks. Judge Corrigan finally ruled that there was "no evidence obtainable to sustain the charges" of the AFL officials. "Nothing has been brought out during this examination which in any way reflects upon the honesty of the Police Department or any members of the force." He dismissed the whole charge. The police had rendered valuable service to the employers by arresting and terrorizing the fur workers. Any charge that they had been bribed to be partial towards the strikers was simply too preposterous to hold water.

The defense against the Mineola trial and police-bribery investigation frame-ups absorbed much of the union's time, energy and finances. Meanwhile, the so-called "reorganization committee" continued to terrorize the fur workers in order to force them into the Joint Council. At least five policemen stood near each building in the fur market, prepared to arrest any furrier who tried to stop scabs from taking the places of loyal union members. Underworld characters cruised the fur district in automobiles, ready to attack militant workers with blackjacks and iron bars. Accompanied by members of the Industrial Squad and professional sluggers, a representative of the Joint Council (usually a strong-arm man) made the rounds of the shops. Workers found without Joint Council books were slugged and thrown out into the street.

As the reign of terror mounted, the workers resisted desperately. Workers in shop after shop, locked out because they refused to register, went on strike. Every morning the newspapers carried photographs of policemen dragging fur workers off in patrol wagons.

A fur worker at Geller Brothers described how he and others in his shop were forced to register:

"4 P.M. The boss goes up to the workers.

" 'Now, people, you will have to go and register with the new union.'

"The workers: 'Nothing doing. Nobody is going to decide for us which union we'll belong to.'

" 'Very well then if you want your Communist union you can't work here.'

"And he turns off the power. The machines stop. The workers file down stairs. At the entrance a reception committee awaits them. A strong delegation of cops and plainclothesmen of the Industrial Squad. . . The workers sense trouble. They try to walk past.

"The police and the squadmen let them pass. Then suddenly a group of furriers is sectioned off. A cordon is made around them. Another group and another group is surrounded. And quickly the order is given: 'Walk along!' There are tussles. Some of the workers break through the cordons. Cries of 'Let me go!' 'They want to take us to the scab union!' Shrieking girls struggle with the squadmen. Police shove and drag workers to keep them within the ring. 'Move along, you damned bolshevik!' 'I'll stretch you out if you don't move on!'

"Crowds of workers gathering on the pavements shout: 'Don't let them take you!' 'Don't let them take you to the scab union!' The police get rougher. 'Move along damn you!' they growl and dig their clubs into the ribs of the ringed-in workers. 'Move along, move along!' And the ambuscade marches on."

The following day the *Forward* and several English papers reported with bold captions the news that a hundred workers in the shop of Geller Brothers had "deserted the ranks of the Communist Joint Board and marched in a demonstration to join the bona fide union."

This went on for days, weeks and months.

The leaders of the Joint Board were deeply moved by the plight of these workers. They saw furriers who courageously defended their union being beaten and arrested. They saw and felt the hunger of these workers and their families. Their problems had to be faced. After full and free discussion with the shop chairmen, the leaders of the Joint Board decided early in May to instruct the workers to register in the scab "union" as "a beginning in the important, necessary work to defend the lives of the workers and the unity of our union."

When the furriers were informed of the decision at their shop meetings, tears streamed unchecked down their faces. They realized that there was no alternative in view of the hunger and terror facing them, but the thought of having to humble themselves before their bosses by joining the scab "union" less than a year after their tremendous victory, was unbearable. "We refuse to degrade ourselves," many workers cried out in anger. To this Gold replied: "Go to work, brothers and sisters, and catch your breath; the battle is by no means over. We are merely retreating in order to be in a better position to make further advances. When your union will be prepared, it will call you and you will come back to your union."

Thus it was that fur workers, with tears in their eyes and their heads low, returned to the shops. By May 10, about sixty-five hundred names, carefully screened to keep out the known militants, were registered with the AFL Joint Council. But the headquarters of the Joint Council remained empty. For the vast majority of the furriers did not go to register and obtain books in person. Their employers registered for them, paid their initiation fees and obtained their union books. The bosses paid their dues to the Joint Council. But the workers still continued to pay dues to the Joint Board and to attend shop meetings in the Joint Board office. When the bosses distributed the books to the workers, some furriers, unable to control their rage, would tear them up.

Thousands who refused to register with the Joint Council wandered from shop to shop, worked a day or two in each place, until the boss ordered them to register or get out. Most of them were unemployed for months on end. Some were reduced to sleeping on park benches and lived on handouts.

In the Association shops, the employers lost no time in claiming the full benefits of the chaos created by the expulsion of the Joint Board and the AFL "reorganization." Working hours were increased to forty-four and forty-six a week, and many furriers were forced to work fifty, sixty and seventy hours a week without overtime pay. Wages were cut sharply, in many shops about 50 percent. The sweatshop system now returned in full force. Contracting and subcontracting again infested the industry. The contractors did not even have to hide their violations of union standards. They went so far as to advertise their businesses in the New York telephone directory. Once again, contractors were seen freely taking bundles out of the shops.

Once again, too, it was useless for the workers in the Association shops to complain. "Go complain to your new union," the bosses would answer, laughing. At the union headquarters, the complaining worker would get his answer from a gang of strong-arm men. If he did not heed this warning, he would find himself out in the street, his job in the shop taken by a "more reliable" worker.

This was the price the fur workers had to pay for the privilege of being "liberated."

The "reorganizers" became confident that they were accomplishing their mission. In May 1927, Harry Begoon, acting secretary-treasurer of the International, wrote jubilantly:

"Our work is going on exceptionally well and there is no doubt in the minds of the people in the labor movement in the city of New York that this clique of communists are out. With the assistance of the American Federation of Labor we have them licked and it is only a question of a few weeks that we hope to have them entirely wiped off the map as labor leaders of a labor organization."

Begoon's rejoicing was premature. The Joint Board was mobilizing the workers to resist the breakdown of working conditions in the shops. They had told the workers to register with the Joint Council and stay in the shops until the signal was given. The time had now arrived for the Joint Board to take the offensive.

CHAPTER 25

The 1927 Strike

The Joint Board took the offensive on June 3, 1927, by calling the fur workers out on strike. The demands of the union were: reinstatement of the 1926 agreement, enforcement of the agreement in the shops, and recognition of the Joint Board.

Besides these specific demands, the strike had a carefully calculated purpose. The employers were set up as two associations, coat manufacturers and trimming manufacturers. In addition, a large number of shops were independents, belonging to neither association. Many of the most militant and loyal union members worked in the trimming and independent shops which, together, employed about six thousand workers.

The trimming association dealings with the union, however, were through the Labor Department of the coat manufacturers' association. Although the trimming association had signed an agreement with the Joint Board on May 3, they repudiated this pact a week later as a result of the combined pressure of the manufacturing association and their allies. They then laid plans to join the Associated and deal exclusively with the Joint Council.*

---

* On May 11, 1927, Woll, Frayne, and McGrady wrote to William Green: "The Fur Trimmers Association which recently had recognized the deposed New York Joint Board of Furriers Union, yesterday May 10th repudiated that arrangement and voted to join with the Associated Fur Manufacturers Association in dealing with the New York Furriers organized under the direction of the Special AFL Committee and under the jurisdiction of the International Fur Workers Union."

Two demonstrations during *1927* strike. Above, *Irving Potash reads resolutions denouncing the AFL strikebreaking trio, Woll, Frayne and McGrady. Below, wives and children of fur strikers protest at City Hall against suppression of mass picketing.*

The big parade to the police stations during the 1927 strike. These scenes are typical of the daily mass arrests of fur strikers.

The objective of the Joint Board leadership in calling the 1927 strike was threefold. First, to block the "reorganization" in the trimming shops and split away the trimming association from the coat manufacturers. Second, to consolidate the union's position in the independent shops. The trimming and independent shops together would give the Joint Board control in a majority of shops in the industry. Third, to blunt and, if possible, destroy completely the company union conspiracy of the AFL "reorganizers" in the shops of their strongest ally, the Associated Fur Coat Manufacturers.

The decision to strike was not reached lightly. Not a single fur worker underestimated the magnitude of the difficulties that faced the union. The mighty army of strikers who had fought victoriously a year before was now no longer united. Their ranks had been weakened by the relentless attacks of the employers, the AFL and the International leaders and the courts. These same forces would resort to every underhanded tactic to break the strike. But the workers knew that no other decision was possible. The union could not stand by helplessly and watch the destruction of the conditions they had won at such sacrifices.

Dozens of Association shops held meetings in the Joint Board. Most of these workers had registered with the dual Joint Council because of the unbridled reign of terror. Nevertheless, they assured the union leadership that they would be on the picket line when the strike officially started. If the union had no money, they would battle without funds.

"Only through a struggle can we force the bosses to return our last year's wages," declared the call of the Joint Board. "There is nothing left for the fur workers to do but to fight against piece work, against speed-up systems, against slavery and for the recognition of the Joint Board, which is the Fur Workers Union."

Frantic conferences took place at the headquarters of the Joint Council. The mobilization call of the Joint Board and the response of the fur workers at their shop meetings threw the "reorganizers" and the International leaders into a panic. A telegram brought Matthew Woll flying to New York. After a hurried consultation, Woll, Frayne and McGrady turned for assistance to Joseph A. Warren, New York Commissioner of Police. The strike must not take place! "To this end," the triumvirate wrote to Commissioner Warren, "we venture to suggest, if it is within the propriety of your Department, that you call to your office the communistic leaders of the Joint Board."

At the same time, the trio spread red-baiting leaflets in the fur market threatening the furriers. Any worker who joined the strike, whose sole aim was "to Sovietize the fur industry," or even went to the office of the "Communist Joint Board" would be "severely dealt with." "They will lose their right to work in any Union shop in New York or any other city in the United States." The threat to blacklist striking fur workers all over the country was even a step ahead of the manufacturers!

The fur workers did not retreat. The arrest of workers distributing Joint Board mobilization leaflets only intensified their determination to be there in full force. They packed Cooper Union and Manhattan Lyceum to the rafters, and they unanimously passed a resolution pledging full support to the Joint Board when it issued the strike call.

Joining the New York fur workers at these rallies was a large delegation from Newark, Local 25. This local was already on strike against both the bosses and the right-wing leaders in the International. Since the ousting of Corbett and the election of left-wing officers, the International officials had been busy trying to break the unity of the membership. They had even secured an injunction against the local and its officials and compelled the local to appear in court. When this scheme fell through, the International Executive Board suspended Local 25 on the ground that the union's leadership "consists of the same crowd that the special committee of the American Federation of Labor helped the International Union purge from our ranks in New York."

As in New York, the International opened a dual union office in Newark and tried to force the members of Local 25 to register. The Newark bosses proceeded at once to lock out all workers who refused to register with the dual union. Outraged, the membership of Local 25, four hundred strong, answered with a general strike. The members of Local 25 came from Newark in busloads to mobilization meetings. With their manager, Morris Langer, at their head they marched into the halls singing "Solidarity Forever." The placards they carried said: "THROUGH SOLIDARITY WE WILL WIN." "DOWN WITH THE TRAITORS!"

On the first morning of the strike, the fur market was crowded with thousands of men and women peacefully picketing. At 10 A.M. the striking fur workers marched in an impromptu procession from the fur market to four East Side halls where they were addressed by members of the General Strike Committee. After receiving working cards from the Joint Board, members of the independent and fur trimming shops voted to give 10 percent of their wages as a strike assessment.

These workers, who had come out for a one-day stoppage, were instructed to return to their shops on Monday, June 6, but not until they had participated in the mass demonstration in the fur market.

Thus the workers who had been forced, under the threat of blackjack, knife, police club and discharge, to register with the Joint Council were showing where they really belonged. While this demonstration of thousands of workers was at its height, the right-wing leaders were denying there was any strike at all. H. Schlissel, member of the "reorganization committee" of the International, declared that only fifty workers had walked out of Associated shops.

The manufacturers knew better. Their shops were empty. Panic-stricken, they rushed to Woll, Frayne and McGrady. When they had locked out their workers and forced them to register with the Joint Council, they had been assured that the "Communist Joint Board" was already dead and buried. The manufacturers had gained immense benefits through the AFL "reorganization" in the form of lower wages, longer hours and worsened conditions in the shops. But now the strike showed that the Joint Board was very much alive.

The AFL triumvirate reassured the manufacturers. They had no reason to be worried. There would be no difficulty in getting scabs to do the work in the shops. But the AFL representatives were themselves thoroughly frightened. The strike had to be smashed.

Once again the trio rushed to the police for assistance. In a letter to Police Commissioner Warren, McGrady predicted that the mass demonstration set for June 6 would be completely successful "unless these groups are awed by the presence and activity of the police assigned to this district. . . . We are confident that your Department will adequately handle the situation."

The police leaped to do their bidding. From the first day of the strike, numerous squads of police and Industrial Squad detectives patrolled the fur market and assaulted the pickets. Arrests of strikers increased daily.

On the morning of the first great mass demonstration, the entire fur district was flooded with policemen and detectives. No sooner had the thousands of strikers started their march, than the police and detectives launched their attack. Within a few minutes, the fur district was turned into "a war zone." An army of police and detectives, swinging clubs and blackjacks, tried desperately to break up the demonstration. "At times the press of strikers was halted only when detectives drew revolvers," wrote one reporter. But it was only a temporary halt, for the strikers moved along relentlessly and swept all scabs out of the market.

Unable to break up the mass demonstration, the Industrial Squad men took bloody revenge on individual strikers, singling them out and beating them mercilessly. The police, however, were forced to permit the strikers to proceed on their one-way parade. They circled completely around each block and marched past the shops a second time. Gold announced that the union would have seven thousand pickets on duty every day until the strike was ended. The shops of the Associated would be picketed three times a day—in the morning, at noon, and in the evening.

Not even the most reactionary labor leaders could have dreamed of the depths to which Woll, McGrady and Frayne now descended in their last-ditch efforts to crush the fur strike. In letters to Police Commissioner Warren and Mayor Walker, they openly demanded that the police absolutely forbid mass picketing in the fur market. In justifying their demand, they pointed with approval to the fact that the police had stopped mass picketing in other strikes in New York.

"Surely then," they pleaded, "if the action of the police is justified in these latter instances there can be no justifiable reason for such discrimination in favor of the Communists who are parading the streets of New York in one of its busy centers, not in twos and threes but in hundreds and thousands."

The AFL leaders had deliberately lied in telling the press that only a handful of men and women were picketing. And in demanding police interference, they were ready to surrender the right of all workers to conduct peaceful picketing. So shameful was this betrayal that the New York City Central Trades and Labor Council could not stomach it. When this AFL body received a circular from the AFL special committee asking it to protest the "leniency" of the Mayor and Police Commissioner in dealing with the strike situation in the fur market and demand that mass picketing be prohibited, the delegates to the Council, most of them strongly anti-Communist, denounced the request.

"They are trying to tell us in fact," said J. Prechtl of the Brewery Workers Union, "that we should go to the police and ask them to let loose with the greatest possible brutality against striking workers. It does not make any difference who these workers are. . . . We have here a case in which the police are being incited by an AFL committee against strikers."

"If we now demand imprisonment for Communists," asked the rabid anti-Communist Joseph Ryan, "what shall we do when we ourselves are in the same predicament. Shall we expect consideration from the police?"

After other delegates had bitterly denounced the AFL "reorganizers," the Council voted that all local unions in New York should ignore the circular and under no circumstances protest to the city administration.

Under the protection of the police, gangsters overran the fur market, spreading terror on every block. They rode through the district in big cars filled with weapons. At intervals they would leap out, slash the pickets with knives or beat them with iron bars and other weapons. Then they pushed back into the waiting cars and sped away to escape the wrath of the other pickets.

Even the metropolitan press, totally out of sympathy with the struggle of the furriers, could no longer conceal the fact that organized crime was rampant in the fur market in the very sight of the police.

"In a free-for-all-fight yesterday afternoon at Sixth Avenue and Twenty-Seventh Street," the *New York Sun* reported on June 25, 1927, "four left-wing pickets were beaten with iron bars and stabbed within sight of police on strike duty." The strikers themselves literally had to force the police to arrest these gangsters. "The seven men tried to escape after the attack on the pickets," the *New York Times* reported, "but their car was surrounded and stopped by an angry crowd of furriers." "Eight iron bars, about a foot and a half long and an inch in diameter, were found in the car," the *New York Evening Post* added, "and police declared that two of the men arrested had previous prison records."

Who imported these gangsters into the fur district to terrorize the pickets? "The prisoners," the *New York Sun* reported, "told Inspector Coughlin that a man named Mandell had hired them to 'work' for the International Fur Workers Union, the right-wing group under the domination of the AFL at a salary of $50 each per week." "Schwartz [one of the gangsters]," the *New York Sun* further reported, "has served four years in Sing Sing for participation in a hold-up, and Eagen [another gangster] has served one year in the New Jersey State Prison at Trenton for robbery."

On the seventh day of the strike, Aaron Gross was suddenly attacked by gangsters, members of the notorious "French gang." Isaac Walter, an executive board member of the Joint Council, accompanied the gangsters. "There he is," shouted Walter, pointing to Gross. Then the brutal slugging began. Fur workers in the immediate vicinity came to Gross's assistance, but too late to save him. Gross was stabbed twice, almost fatally. At Bellevue Hospital, doctors worked over him for more than three hours before they were able to stop the flow of blood.

Fur workers seized two of the gangsters who had attacked Gross. The police rushed over and arrested the attackers. In the court, they were revealed to be Ben Cohen and Meyer Friedman. Cohen had been arrested four times for robbery and had served terms in Elmira and Sing Sing prisons. Meyer Friedman, also with a long prison record, told Judge Collins that they had been hired to beat up Communists as a "patriotic duty." As in the cases of other gangsters arrested on complaint of the strikers, the cases of Ben Cohen and Meyer Friedman were dismissed. The International Union's attorney, Samuel Markewich, was on hand to bail out the gangsters. The bail records tell the story: "That the said surety has been promised from the International Fur Workers Union of New York residing at 31 E. 27 St. the sum of $300.00 as consideration for becoming such surety on said bond."

International furnishes bail for Ben Cohen, Gross's assailant. Prison record: Burglary—1915, burglary—1917, burglary—1919.

PEOPLE OF THE STATE OF NEW YORK

-against-

Ben Cohen

STATE OF NEW YORK
CITY AND COUNTY OF NEW YORK } ss:

Samuel Rothberg being duly sworn,
deposes and says, that he resides at _75 St. Nicholas Pl_
and is the attorney-in-fact of the EQUITABLE SURETY COMPANY, the
surety on the bail bond of the defendant in the above entitled
action.

That the said surety has been promised from _International
Fur Workers Union of N.Y_ residing at _31 E. 27 St_
the sum of $300 dollars as consideration for becoming such
surety on said bond.

That the said surety has received from _International
Fur Workers Union N.Y._ residing at _31 E. 27 St_
as security in the event of the forfeiture of said bail bond the
following described property: _Confession of
Judgement_

That the said surety has received from _____
_____ residing at _____
In business as _____ at _____
an agreement in writing, duly executed, whereby the said _____
_____ has contracted and agreed with the said
surety to indemnify the said surety against any loss under said
bail bond.

That the said surety, or any one on his behalf has not
received, nor has been promised, any consideration, security or
indemnity, except as herein set forth.

That this affidavit is made pursuant to the provision
of Section 554A of the Code of Criminal Procedure as added by
Chapter 415 of the Laws of 1926.

Samuel Rothberg

Sworn to before me this
10 day of _June_ 1927.

In the midst of the sorrow over the brutal assault against one of the leaders of the Joint Board came a joyful announcement. The general strike of the Newark furriers had ended in a complete victory. The Consolidated Furriers Association had agreed to keep their hands off Local 25, and to stop interfering in the union's internal affairs. They also agreed to recognize the local's duly elected representatives, employ only members of Local 25 and discharge scabs who had worked during the strike. The bosses' agreement to recognize the progressive administration headed by Morris Langer was a smashing defeat for the AFL-International combine.

On Tuesday, June 14, the appeals of the AFL leaders to Mayor Walker and Commissioner Warren brought new action. The police were instructed to arrest all pickets in excess of twelve on a block. By seven o'clock, when the strikers began to pour into the fur district, four hundred police, armed with nightsticks and revolvers, were stationed at fifty-foot intervals along the streets.

Within a few minutes, thousands of strikers were parading back and forth. A number wore steel helmets and carried placards reading, "OUR HEADS ARE NOT SAFE." The police swung into action. Scores of men and women were herded into hallways and beaten with nightsticks. Police wagons crashed through the crowd and backed up to the hallways. With their brothers and sisters shouting their protests, the workers were shoved and jostled into the wagons.

All through the morning the arrests continued. But the thousands of strikers continued to show their power. In the face of the police brutality and the threatening hoofs of the horses, they held the line. Several hundred strikers were arrested and hauled away in patrol wagons. On their way they sang working-class songs, and improvised new words to such tunes as "On the Picket Line."

> "On the line! On the line!
> On the picket, on the picket line.
> We'll save the 40-hour
> With our mass power
> On the picket, on the picket line."

A few hours later, in the Jefferson Market Police Court, the sounds of singing and cheering floated up from the cells into the dingy court room. The court was packed with sympathizers and fellow strikers. Cheers rang through the court room when 110 of the strikers announced

THE EVENING WORLD,
MONDAY, JUNE 20, 1927

POLICE ARREST 116 FUR STRIKERS FOR PARADING

Alleged Picketing Demonstration Was Obstructing Traffic

One hundred and sixteen striking furriers, including Ben Gold, their leader, and forty women, were arrested on a charge of obstructing traffic shortly before 9 o'cclock to-day when eevry available policeman in the neighborhood of Seventh Avenue and 28th Street surrounded a picketing parade and turned it to the West 30th Street Station.

There it required more than an hour to book the prisoners on charges of disorderly conduct. Later all available

THE NEW YORK TIMES,
SATURDAY, JUNE 25, 1927

IRON BARS CAUSE FUR STRIKE ARRESTS

Implements Found in Car of 7 "Right Wing" Men After Attack on Pickets.

GOLD SEES CHARGES PROVED

Leader of Ousted Faction Says He Will Renew Complaint of Terrorism by Opponents.

Eight iron bars were found yesterday in an automobile occupied by seven men arrested in the fur district yesterday morning after two pickets had been beaten and bruised by a heavy weapon. The seven men tried to escape after the attack on

While known gangsters run riot, hundreds of peacefully picketing fur workers are herded to the police station and courts.

that due to the excessive bail asked by the judge, they preferred to sit in jail rather than put their union to a terrific expense.

"I have been in war," wrote one New York reporter the following day, "but I have yet to see anything which will compare with the indomitable courage and guts displayed yesterday by the striking furriers—men and women—on the picket line."

The bloody events of June 14 were only the beginning. Deputy Inspector McGrath, in charge of police in the strike district, threatened to arrest "the strikers wholesale in the future." "Next time they start mass picketing we are not going to run a few batches of them in," he announced, "but we are going to run them in by the hundreds. We'll start their parade right for the West Thirtieth Street police station and keep it going until it's all inside."

Newspaper headlines told the rest. "ARREST 350 FUR STRIKERS!" "224

FUR STRIKERS ARRESTED!" "FORTY FUR PICKETS SENT TO PRISON!" "131 MORE PICKETS SENT TO PRISON!" "POLICE BREAK UP FURRIERS' PICKETING PARTY; ARREST 173 STRIKERS!" "THE BIG PARADE—TO COURT!"

One day's score: One worker sentenced to eight months in prison. Four sentenced to six months in prison.* Sixty-two sentenced to fifteen days in prison. Thirty-four sentenced to ten days in prison. Eight sentenced to five days in prison. Among those to whom this AFL-police court "justice" was meted out were fifty-four women.

In vain the Joint Board pointed out that the pickets marched two abreast and left room for passersby to go through; that even the police admitted the pickets were peaceful; that the penalizing of the workers, picketing peacefully, violated a recent decision of the New York Court of Appeals upholding "peaceful picketing." ** The police continued their mass arrests and the magistrates continued to sentence the pickets to jail.

The AFL "reorganizers" were overjoyed. McGrady hailed the mass arrests and the sentencing of the pickets to jail as a "vindication of the attitude taken by the American Federation of Labor that mass picketing is illegal." His sole complaint was that the authorities were still not dealing "severely enough" with the fur strikers. And when Magistrate Rosenbluth, who had sentenced scores of pickets to jail, ventured to suggest that the AFL leaders reach some agreement with the Joint Board "on the number of pickets to be used," McGrady immediately released a statement criticizing the judge. "There is no strike. There is no legitimate need or right to picket."

After studying the situation as an observer for the American Civil Liberties Union, Norman Thomas, leader of the Socialist Party, who could hardly be accused of being biased in favor of the left-wing leadership of the Joint Board, wrote privately to Forrest Bailey: "As far as I could judge, the present attitude of the police would make proper picketing of the most peaceful sort a practical impossibility. For instance, the attempt to hold the number of pickets down to twelve on the blocks be-

* Max Shusterman and Ethel Shusterman, Ida Ishman, Sam Broad and Frank Jeave were the famous five who were sentenced to eight and six months in prison for having "disturbed" the court, when, outraged at the vicious sentences given their fellow picketers, they expressed indignation and horror. One of the prisoners, a boy of 19, was brought up on three charges: one for smiling, one for making a face at the judge and the third for having booed.

** The case passed upon by the New York Court of Appeals was that of an injunction taken out by the Exchange Bakery and Restaurant, Inc., against officers of the Waiters' and Waitresses' Union, Local 1. The decision was handed down on June 1, 1927.

tween Sixth and Seventh Avenues means that there cannot be efficient peaceful picketing. This is especially true since the pickets aren't allowed to wear signs or carry banners."

The right of peaceful picketing and every cherished constitutional right and civil liberty of American workers vanished completely. False arrests without warrants, unjustified and malicious attacks, attempts to murder, beatings, and the most shameful oppression of peaceful men and women were daily occurrences in the assaults of the police and detectives of the Industrial Squad. A. C. Sedgwick, a *New York Times* reporter, graphically described the treatment of arrested strikers at the hands of the police and the Industrial Squad:

"One detective takes a piece of rubber hose, which is part of the equipment of the detectives' bureau and is favored because it leaves no marks. Another takes out his blackjack. Others grab for anything— blackjacks and night-sticks. The prisoners fall to the floor. The blood pours from their faces. They spit and cough blood. The detectives still in a rage, look at them. The door opens. A young policeman in a uniform pokes his head in. 'You fellers is easy with 'em,' he says. 'Is that so?' roars a detective and kicks a prisoner in the face, pulls him to his feet, props him against the desk, then with the butt end of his revolver makes a gash in his head. . . .

"If it were asked of any official source what happened to the men it would be said that they received their injuries resisting arrest, or perhaps that the 'sidewalk came up and hit 'em.' "

Such were the horrible atrocities that must be charged not only to the police and the employers, but also to the AFL leaders who inspired these acts in the name of "brotherhood," "democracy" and "free trade unionism."

Magistrate Brodsky, one of the more decent judges, could not stand these public atrocities any longer. He dismissed the case against a group of strikers, stating: "I was observing the picket line when some of these workers were arrested, and in my opinion none of them was violating the law. I am going to have it entered on the court record so other magistrates who may try similar cases can use my experience as a criterion."

More than a thousand strikers marched to City Hall to petition Mayor Walker to protect them from persecution and gangster raids. A committee of seven was admitted. They gave the Mayor's secretary a letter signed by the fur workers, protesting the "systematic persecution of the fur strikers." Outside, the assembled strikers and their families carried placards reading, "WE ARE STRIKERS AND NOT CRIMINALS."

Meanwhile, thousands of New York trade unionists in various trades and professions were eagerly signing petitions addressed to Governor Alfred E. Smith and Mayor Walker demanding that "the right of peaceful picketing—a fundamental right of all workers which recently has been upheld by the Court of Appeals in New York State—shall not be denied to the workers of New York City through the arbitrary action of the police and the courts." The appeals and the petitions were ignored. Both the AFL and the employers had built a solid front with the Tammany Hall machine.

In spite of the most ferocious attacks, the strikers remained firm. Fearlessly and bravely, they marched on, their spirit unbreakable. Among them were some of the most courageous strikers in the history of the American labor movement. The extraordinary heroism of these strikers is shown by the attitude of forty women pickets who were arrested and imprisoned on Welfare Island. They were serving sentences of five, ten and, in some cases, thirty days and even six months. They were being treated by the prison authorities as if they were common criminals. Those given five or ten days could have been freed if they were willing to pay their fines. But when a representative of the Joint Board came with funds to release every woman, they refused to allow the union's funds to be exhausted for payment of fines. "We will serve our sentences," they declared. Not even the pleas of anxious relatives could sway them.

The 1927 strike was an example to all American workers of magnificent heroism displayed by workers struggling for their conditions, their union and their democratic rights.

As a result of these heroic battles, the Joint Board succeeded in achieving its main objectives in the strike. Both independents and trimming association recognized the Joint Board and the 1926 agreement. Union control and union conditions were re-established in shops employing the majority of workers.

In the coat association, the Joint Board was unable to secure formal recognition. Many association members, however, agreed not to compel their workers to register with the Joint Council. Other association employers went through the motions of asking their workers to register, but made no reprisals when workers refused. In other association shops, where the Joint Board was weaker, loyal union members who were compelled to register nevertheless reported regularly to the Joint Board, paid dues and considered themselves in good standing.

CHAPTER 26

Betrayal in Washington

While thousands of fur workers were battling police clubs, gangsters' knives, arrests and imprisonment on the picket line in New York, the Eighth Biennial Convention of the International Fur Workers Union opened on June 13, 1927, in the AFL Building in Washington, D.C. According to the union's constitution, the convention was to have taken place in May, but a new constitution was now in effect—Woll, Frayne and McGrady. The AFL trio ordered the International officers to ignore all demands from the locals and insisted as late as April 21 "that no call be sent out at this time for the holding of a convention."

Lest the International officers forget the facts of life, the AFL "reorganizers" added the following postscript to their warning: "As you well know, your International Union is today being financed to a great part by the reorganizing activities going on here in New York City and that without this income your organization would be practically bankrupt."

In a private letter to William Green on May 7, the AFL "reorganizers" gave their reason for postponing the convention: "There is an agitation being worked up around the country for the convening of the convention of the International Fur Workers' Union. This should have taken place in the month of May. Your committee delayed calling this convention until we had assurances that the International Organization would be able to control the situation. On May 4, at a conference with the International President Shachtman, together with Vice-President Winnick, your committee was assured that if a convention was called outside of New York City, the International Union would have thirty-one favorable delegates and six unfavorable delegates. With this understanding we have tentatively agreed to call the convention June 20th. It has been suggested that the convention be called in Washington in the conference room of the American Federation of Labor." *

What a cesspool this hitherto-unpublished letter uncovers! The fur workers all over the country were demanding the convention in May. Had the union's constitution been observed, the entire conspiracy against the fur workers would have been smashed. The AFL leaders' solution was simple: throw the constitution into the wastebasket.

Shachtman and Winnick made sure that the right wing would control the convention. They refused to recognize the delegates from the New York Joint Board elected by the thousands of fur workers who constituted more than 85 percent of the total International membership. The General Executive Board had chartered a number of paper locals in New York and elsewhere in order to pack the convention.

Finally, they arbitrarily increased the number of delegates from the "reliable" locals and made certain that rubber-stamp delegations were selected. On May 24, 1927, Joseph Bearak, the lawyer connected with the *Forward* and the Socialist Party, wrote to Shachtman from Boston: "It would seem to me that somebody ought to come to Boston the end of this week to help elect our own delegates, and if possible, we ought to allow local #30 two delegates instead of one." To the AFL and to the International this, of course, was *not* outside interference.

When the convention opened, the hand-picked delegates from the paper locals set up by the G.E.B. were on hand in Washington. But present, also, were thirty-five delegates, headed by Ben Gold, elected by the fur workers to represent the New York Joint Board. Although they knew that the AFL and the International leaders had already decided to bar them from the convention, these delegates were determined to conduct a militant battle for recognition.

The thirty-three "delegates" from the New York Joint Council sat around a long, yellow table in the middle of the small hall. The Joint Board delegation, admitted as "visitors," sat in three rows on the right side of the hall. Near them was stationed a squad of strong-arm men.

Shachtman, seated between William Green and Matthew Woll, intro-

---

* Shachtman explained his proposal to use the Federation's small council chamber in Washington as the meeting place on the grounds that it would "prevent any possible demonstrations on the part of the vast majority of the Communists and their followers."

NEW YORK OFFICE

AMERICAN FEDERATION OF LABOR

A. F. of L. BUILDING
WASHINGTON D. C.

LONG DISTANCE TELEPHONE MAIN 3871-2-3
CABLE ADDRESS. AFEL

HUGH FRAYNE
REPRESENTATIVE
1493 BROADWAY
ENTRANCE 148 WEST 41ST STREET
SUITE 701
TELEPHONE WISCONSIN 2214

New York, April 21, 1927.

Mr. Oiser Shachtman, President,
International Fur Workers Union,
9 Jackson Ave., Long Island City, N. Y.

Dear Sir and Brother:

We, the undersigned members of the Special Committee of the American Federation of Labor to whom has been delegated the task of cooperating with your International Union and its executive officers in enforcing the decisions reached by your body and giving enforcement to recommendations made by the Executive Council of the American Federation of Labor which have subsequently been approved by your International Union, having full and complete knowledge of conditions prevailing in your International Union, in your local affiliated unions, as well as those prevailing in New York City, unequivocally and unhesitatingly recommend that the next convention of your International Union be postponed until the earliest possible date when it is feasible and practicable for your International Union to hold a convention.

We sincerely trust that your General Executive Board will conform in action and attitude to the foregoing recommendations urgently presented to you.

Fraternally yours,

Special Committee
American Federation of Labor.

The AFL Special Committee "recommends" postponement of the International convention until, as they later informed Green privately, they would be "able to control the situation."

duced Green to the convention. Green began calmly enough, but quickly lapsed into invectives against the left-wing leaders of the New York Joint Board. He charged them with "furthering a movement whose avowed purpose was the destruction of the American Federation of Labor" and "the organized labor movement." Admitting that the AFL was interfering in the internal affairs of the Furriers Union, he justified this unprecedented action on the ground that the Federation could not permit the Communists to "inject their strange philosophy in the trade unions."

Green bemoaned the fact that even at the moment fur workers "are marching up and down the streets of New York City in the fur manufacturing district." "It is a most distressing situation," he confessed. But, he explained to his own satisfaction, "many of them are misled. They do not understand."

Then Green announced that there was a strong movement among the fur workers for peace and unity in the union. He thundered on: "Peace can be made through the supremacy and the jurisdiction of the American Federation of Labor. No peace can be established that will give any recognition to those destructive forces that are attempting to tear down our great trade union institution. My friends, I leave the subject to you."

Was this a slip? Was this a confession that the conspiracy against the fur workers was doomed to failure?

The truth was that Green's use of the word "peace" was no accident. The night before, McGrady had sought out Gold and Leibowitz at their hotel and conferred with them at length. Green was fed up with the situation, he told them, and so was he. "I think even worse about the Socialists than you do," McGrady confided to Gold and Leibowitz much to their surprise. "I can't stand the right-wing Socialists, and the left-wing Socialists, and the Anarchists, and the rest of them. They are a bunch of crooks and I can't stand the whole bunch. Bill feels the same way. The only one pressing is Matthew Woll. Let's call it off."

Amazed, Gold demanded to know in whose name he spoke. In reply, McGrady called Green on the telephone. "He wants to know whether you are in favor of stopping the battle," McGrady asked Green on the phone. "Tell him I'm in favor of stopping it," was Green's reply.

McGrady then asked Gold to remove the picket line the Joint Board had placed in front of the AFL building. Gold refused, regarding it as a trick of some kind. McGrady told him: "What do you give a damn about the convention. The hell with it. You'll deal with Green and me." But Gold still suspected some maneuver and the pickets remained.

"Peace!" The very word spoken by Green at the first session of the convention sent a shudder through the right-wing International officials. They had ignored a unity resolution circulated by the Toronto Joint Board throughout the International even though several locals had already acted favorably on it. They were trying to keep the word "unity" buried at this convention. Now along had come William Green and uttered that horrid word, "peace!"

But the die-hard Matthew Woll, following Green, quickly calmed the fears of the right-wingers. He denounced the left-wing leaders of the New York Joint Board and reiterated the hoary tale that the 1926 strike was a "Communist plot," financed by "Moscow," to start the "revolution" in the United States. Like Judge Thayer in the Sacco-Vanzetti frame-up, he declared in a tearful voice that he had disregarded his own "personal well-being in attending to the affairs of the fur workers," had been singled out for attack by the Communists, and had even received threatening letters. As for the fur workers who were battling on the picket line in New York, Woll contemptuously called them "the scum of New York City." Repeatedly, he assured the right-wingers that there would be no peace in the union. He guaranteed that their control over the organization would be complete when the convention was over.

Immediately, Ben Gold stood up and demanded the floor in order to answer Woll's attack on the courageous fur strikers. Shachtman refused to recognize Gold, since he was not a "legitimate delegate" to the convention. Shachtman threatened that not only Gold, but all of the other left-wing delegates would be ejected from the convention hall if they persisted in "interrupting the session."

Then Shachtman sanctimoniously called upon the delegates to rise and bow in silence for one moment in memory of Eugene V. Debs and Meyer London, both of whom had passed away since the last convention.

When the delegates had resumed their seats, Shachtman announced that nominations for the Credentials Committee were in order. Vice-President Harry Englander of Toronto arose and asked by what right the International leaders had packed the convention with delegates from hastily-organized paper locals. He also demanded to know if the thirty-three "delegates" from the New York Joint Council would be allowed to vote for members of the Credentials Committee. Shachtman ordered Englander to sit down. Englander protested, "Who authorized you to suspend and expel the leaders of the New York fur workers, institute forced registrations, and split the union into pieces? We demand an answer. We demand an investigation of the facts." The right-wingers shouted, "Kick him out!"

Immediately, several of the hired thugs attacked Englander. Delegate Stein of Philadelphia rushed over to protect the Toronto delegate, but he too was soon covered with blood. Englander appealed to Green to stop the hoodlums, but the President of the AFL played deaf, dumb and blind. Delegate Garff of New York rushed up to Green, displayed a handkerchief covered with Englander's and Stein's blood, and asked whether this represented the principles of the AFL. He received no answer. Instead, a hoodlum attacked him.

Thus, in the high temple of American labor—the headquarters of the AFL—workers who dared to ask questions were attacked with blackjacks and chairs. To complete the sordid picture, Vice-President Englander was instantly suspended from the General Executive Board for "repeated attempts at obstruction!"

The Credentials Committee, composed entirely of right-wingers headed by Harry Begoon, presented its report the following morning. It recommended seating the delegates from the New York Joint Council. Together with the paper delegates they made up the convention majority. The legitimate New York delegates were not seated, nor were any anti-administration delegates from Newark, Montreal, Boston, Chicago, Winnipeg and Toronto.

Despite the sluggings, the delegates from Toronto and Philadelphia, led by Sam Burt, bitterly fought the report of the Credentials Committee. Disregarding threats and warnings from Shachtman, they denounced the "mob rule" at the convention and exposed the methods used by the right-wingers to guarantee their control of the convention. The steamroller was in full swing, however, and the report of the Credentials Committee was adopted.

That same afternoon, the Joint Board delegates were barred from the convention. They immediately called a unity conference at the nearby Harrington Hotel. Many delegates from other locals left the convention in disgust and answered the call. Together with the New Yorkers, they set up a Unity Conference Committee. A small committee was appointed to meet with President Green and urge him to use his office "to the end of terminating the internal union war."

In the AFL building, meanwhile, the remaining delegates were treated to a new orgy of red-baiting by Morris Sigman, Abraham I.

Shiplacoff, Morris Feinstone, Louis Berger and other right-wing Socialists. Sigman frankly told the delegates that they were "fortunate in
Washington in this hall . . . which affords no possibility for an audience at your open sessions." The Communists, he cried, were always denouncing cooperation with the employers. They made peaceful relations
with the employers impossible. He pointed with pride to the fact that the
ILGWU, under his leadership, was operating "on the basis of class collaboration." He considered it a "tremendous accomplishment on our
part" that his leadership had won the "sympathy" of the biggest employers. He hoped that the furriers would learn from his union and complete the expulsion of the left-wingers.

That night, Gold and Leibowitz once more met with McGrady. When
McGrady again talked about burying the hatchet, Gold insisted that the
left-wing delegates must not be barred from the convention. McGrady
told him, "Walk into Bill Green's office and tell him you want to go into
the convention. You'll get in."

The next morning, Gold went to Green's office. The entire rank-and-
file delegation was promptly assured admittance, more proof that Green
was ready to call it quits.

In the convention room, Shachtman reluctantly agreed, over the opposition of Sorkin and Winnick, that the delegates of the suspended locals
be permitted to defend themselves on the floor of the convention. Woll
supported Shachtman's move and proposed that the convention act as a
large trial committee before which the locked-out delegates might appear.
Though he secretly opposed Green's desire to end the fight, Woll pointed
out that hearing the delegates of the suspended locals would disqualify
any appeal in the courts on constitutional grounds.

In keeping with this advice, the convention decided to go into session
as a Committee of the Whole, with Matthew Woll as chairman, at the
Thursday afternoon session. The representatives of the suspended locals
and the expelled members were to be allotted two hours to refute the
charges against them. But, fearful that the left-wing delegates would ex-
plode the whole conspiracy of the AFL and the International officials at
the Thursday afternoon session, Woll and Shachtman made haste to complete the expulsions. On Thursday morning, before the Joint Board delegates were to be heard, Shachtman proposed that the convention approve
the expulsion decisions of the International leaders and consider the case
closed. Despite the appeal of the Toronto delegation to delay action at
least until the New York Joint Board representatives had presented their
side of the case, Shachtman's proposal was adopted.

The cards were stacked against the Joint Board delegates. Nevertheless, they appointed Gold, Sam Leibowitz, Esther Polansky and Maurice Cohen to represent them. They were under no illusions as to the outcome. But it was important that the true voice of the fur workers should find expression at the convention and be recorded for all to judge.

Leibowitz, Cohen and Polansky spoke briefly. Following them, Gold, in an impassioned speech which lasted over an hour, branded as false the "charges" against the Joint Board.

"We came here knowing that we could not expect justice from your convention," he began. "This convention will not settle our disputes. The New York Joint Board and its four thousand members of the settled shops and over four thousand who are on strike will not recognize this so-called convention which is filled with people who represent no one except themselves."

Then Gold summarized the events of the last year and a half in the Furriers Union and showed that none of the acts of the right-wingers had solved the problems of the fur workers; on the contrary, they had only resulted in worsening their conditions.

Turning to the organization of the convention itself, Gold observed that scabs and hoodlums had been seated as delegates, and the fate of the thousands of fur workers placed in their hands. He cited specific cases of "Joint Council delegates" from New York who were strikebreakers in both the 1920 and 1926 strikes.

"The furriers will not permit such action," Gold declared vehemently. "The activities of the men who control this convention have annihilated the working conditions for which the furriers have fought so long and so hard and for which they paid with blood, hunger and prison terms. They are responsible for the Mineola trials. They tried to kill Aaron Gross. They are determined to destroy our entire union. But they will not succeed. The fur workers will continue to fight for a united union on and off the picket lines."

Gold emphasized that neither the issue of offices nor of Communism should concern the convention. The problem was to achieve unity and a more effective union to serve the interests of the workers.

"I am ready to resign as manager of the Joint Board," he challenged. "We want only peace and unity within the International. The cry of 'Communism' is raised as a bogey to cover up the dastardly efforts of certain International officials to break the spirit of the New York fur workers."

"The real issue," Gold concluded, "is whether we shall be sold out to the bosses or whether our union shall fight to win better conditions for the workers. The real issue is majority rule versus gangster and boss control. It is democracy in the union; effective strikes and mass picketing versus surrender to the bosses; honest trade unionism versus stool-pigeonism by so-called labor leaders; the right to fight for decent wages and working conditions without being treated worse than the lowest criminals. Finally, the real issue is the creation of a strong, honest, democratic union in the industry."

The right-wingers speaking in reply produced not a single shred of evidence to prove the charges against the Joint Board. They contented themselves with red-baiting. By approving the expulsion activities of the International leaders that very morning, they cried, the convention had actually made a tremendous contribution towards saving the United States from the "revolution."

Gold asked: "Will this convention of the local delegates agree, under their supervision and their direction, to call together all the thousands of fur workers, put the charges that have been made here before them, and let them decide who is right and who is wrong? Let us have a referendum vote of the membership of the union, supervised by an impartial body, to decide this issue."

Gold's proposal immediately brought Woll to his feet. There was no need for a referendum, he shouted. Only the convention would decide "these questions."

The two-hour speech of Matthew Woll was practically a word-for-word repetition of the report of the AFL "investigation" into the 1926 strike. He recapitulated the same story of "Communist terrorism," "Moscow plot," "police bribery" that had filled many columns in the *Forward* during and after the strike. Then he urged that the "reorganization" of the union be completed. He predicted that the New York police would soon succeed in breaking the current Joint Board strike in New York. Meanwhile, the convention should reject "any plea for peace and unity" and revoke the charters of the suspended locals.

The next morning, the International officers called for reaffirmation of the convention's decision approving the expulsions and lifting the charters of the Joint Board locals. The recommendation was adopted.

As soon as the vote was announced, the Toronto delegates headed by Englander walked out, declaring they could no longer participate in a convention that was splitting the union. Other delegates followed suit. All told, forty-three bona fide delegates representing New York, Newark, Toronto, Montreal, Winnipeg, Philadelphia and Chicago left the convention and took a train to New York, where they joined the striking fur workers on the picket line.

Thus ended the International's hand-picked, machine dominated convention in the AFL's Washington building. Green's secret avowal of desire to end the fight came to nought. With Matthew Woll's irreconcilable hand at its helm, the convention had made the expulsions final.

Philip Silberstein, Kaufman's old lieutenant in the fur dyeing and dressing locals in Brooklyn, was elected "honorary president" of the bankrupt International. Harry Begoon, Woll's right-hand man in the International and the darling of the Forward Association, was elected secretary-treasurer.

For the fur workers, of course, the convention was a tragedy. However, during this same week in Washington, another conference had taken place which was to mean much more for the future of the fur workers than the proceedings at the packed convention. In the name of more than 90 percent of the International membership, a Unity Conference Committee of fur workers pledged itself to unite all forces to build a powerful furriers' union.

CHAPTER 27

The Struggle for Unity

The Socialist leaders were ready to sacrifice even the most elementary interests of the workers in their determination to prevent unity with the left wing. On July 7, 1927, twenty thousand workers gathered in New York's Union Square to protest the approaching execution of Sacco and Vanzetti. Ben Gold, who came with thousands of fur workers to join in the demonstration, was recognized in the crowd and carried bodily to the platform while the entire audience clamored that he speak. The right-wing Socialists on the platform ignored the demand of the workers. And when Gold, helpless in the surging crowd, was pushed up onto the stand, they kicked him in the face and body. Then they called on the police to disperse the crowd. "I'd rather have the meeting broken up than have Gold speak," cried Samuel Friedman, one of the Socialists in charge.

"As an eyewitness of the Sacco and Vanzetti affair at Union Square," Adolf Wolff wrote to the American Civil Liberties Union, "I wish to inform you that in all my life I have never seen such shameless display of the betrayal of the workers in the hoops and clutches of the police as that perpetrated by the cowardly traitors who call themselves socialists in charge of the platform.

"More than 20,000 workers were clamoring to hear one of their tried, true and trusted leaders. They shouted 'Gold!' 'Gold!' 'We want Gold!' until they were hoarse from shouting. Then they booed the cowards on the platform who had kicked and pushed Ben Gold off and called on the police to discipline the crowd thus breaking up the meeting.

"Twenty thousand voices against five and the five won for they had the police on their side. If this be democracy, for God's sake give us anything else."

This attitude on the part of the Socialist Party leaders doomed to failure all efforts to establish peace in the furriers' union. In the year following the Washington convention, there were many movements for unity among the fur workers. Three, in particular, stand out.

While the convention was still in session, McGrady called Gold and suggested that Magistrate Rosenbluth of New York be asked to intervene to end the split in the union. Wary of McGrady's proposal, Gold suggested that he include Magistrate Brodsky, who had proved himself liberal-minded and had expressed his outrage at the brutal, unprovoked assaults on the strikers. McGrady readily agreed.

A few weeks later, the two judges invited the leaders of the Joint Board and the representatives of the International and the AFL to attend a conference to discuss peace terms. When the AFL "reorganizers" and the International leaders finally agreed to send a representative, Rosenbluth and Brodsky asked the Joint Board to submit the terms upon which unity could be achieved. The Board sent the following proposals:

"1. The AFL officials should eliminate their hired sluggers from their dual union.

"2. Reinstatement of the expelled locals and individual members.

"3. The AFL should nullify their agreement with the bosses and should recognize the agreement which was signed by the Joint Board and the Association representatives in June 1926, after the victorious general strike, i.e., a guarantee of the forty-hour week and the other recent gains of the workers.

"4. That all the appointed dictators of the AFL be eliminated and elections be held. In order to insure an honest election, an impartial committee agreed to by both sides to be selected to supervise the elections."

At the conference, Markewich, the International's attorney, stated that the AFL would like to withdraw from the furriers' situation "with honor," but that some way had to be found to enable it to "save its face." Gold promptly suggested that in the interest of peace and unity, he and Shapiro, who were acting as spokesmen for the Joint Board, would agree not to run for any paid office at the supervised election for officers. He emphasized that they were prepared to waive their constitutional right to run for any paid office, because "the interests and welfare of the workers are more important than anything else."

When the meeting with the two magistrates was over, it seemed almost certain that the Joint Board's conditions would be accepted as a basis for peace and unity. The AFL was reluctant to continue pouring money uselessly into the paper union known as the Joint Council. Woll, Frayne and McGrady had complained to Green that "we have received almost no support either moral or financial from the unions affiliated with the Central Trades and Labor Council of New York City," and they had planned "to remain at this task" only until the International convention was over "and possibly for a week or two thereafter."

But directly after the conference with the magistrates, the Socialist Party leaders went to work on the AFL. They implored the AFL leaders to reject any proposal for peace and unity and to continue operating in the Furriers Union. To withdraw now, they pleaded, would be a tremendous setback for the right-wingers in all needle trades unions. It would even affect the hold of the AFL on unions throughout the country. Shiplacoff of the "Committee for Preservation of Trade Unions" and Feinstone of the United Hebrew Trades promised that their organizations would undertake to carry the main financial burden in the campaign against the membership of the Furriers Union.

The pressure exerted by the Socialist leaders brought results. The day after the conference with Magistrates Rosenbluth and Brodsky, the International issued a statement rejecting the Joint Board's peace terms. It charged that Gold had sinister, un-American motives in seeking unity. The left-wing leader of the Joint Board, it declared, was soon to depart "for Moscow" and he only wanted to be reinstated in the AFL in order to be able to pose there "as an influential American labor leader."

The fur bosses made no effort to conceal their satisfaction over the rejection of the Joint Board's peace terms. One manufacturer frankly told a reporter for *Women's Wear* that the thing the employers dreaded most was the success of the unity conference.

"We manufacturers can dicker with workers on wage questions much more easily than we could when they were united," he gloated. "I myself have been able to handle the wage increase question this year more to my own advantage than for some time past, chiefly because I can deal with the workers individually.

"Formerly the workers in the shop drew up a list containing each man's name, his present wage, and the increase demanded. Then the shop chairman presented it to the boss, who had to deal with the whole list at once.

"With conditions as they are now, I simply throw away the list and say that I'll deal with each worker individually on the wage question. And they are afraid to insist because they aren't unified."

The second major move for unity came late in August, the same year. This time it was initiated by the Toronto District Labor Council, an affiliate of the Labor Congress of Canada and the American Federation of Labor. The Council, composed of delegates from the Toronto trade unions, adopted a resolution "to appeal to the Executive of the AFL and the Executive of the Fur Workers Union to withdraw the special committees and bogus and artificial locals that have been set up and to restore rank-and-file control, which in our estimation is the only method of re-establishing peace and unity in the Fur Workers Union in New York City."

The AFL "reorganizers" and the International leaders were seized with consternation when they learned of the Toronto District Labor Council's action. Begoon demanded an investigation of the Council to discover why it should have the "impertinence . . . to interfere in our affairs and adopt a resolution in such insulting terms." There could be only one answer. "Has it recently turned Communist or near Communist?" he asked.

McGrady also called for an investigation. The Toronto Council, he informed AFL Secretary-Treasurer Frank Morrison, "has been hoodwinked and misled. I would suggest that they be instructed to withdraw the action they have just taken."

When the Council remained adamant, the International leaders sent it a letter telling it to mind its own business. "We consider the controversy settled, finally and forever," Begoon wrote in behalf of the G.E.B.

The conditions of the fur workers in Association shops, however, made it impossible for them to "consider the controversy settled, finally and forever." Unemployment was mounting by leaps and bounds; speedup increased; the contracting epidemic spread.

The competition for jobs drove workers to accept the ever-worse conditions. The forty-hour week became only a memory. Gone, too, was payment for legal holidays, time-and-a-half for overtime, the minimum wage scale and all the other union conditions won in 1926. The employed fur worker sapped himself of the last bit of energy to meet the mounting speedup. Hungry, discouraged, unemployed fur workers waited in the market for the boss or the foreman to give them jobs.

By the spring of 1928, with eight thousand of the twelve thousand furriers unemployed, conditions reached the point where even McGrady had to admit that the fur workers and their families "are actually starving." The employers themselves admitted as much when they offered to donate $15,000 from their "Charity Chest" for the relief of unemployed furriers.

Other than accepting the employers' handout and thanking them for their "big-heartedness," the AFL officials and the International leaders

Back pay collected for two workers by Joint Council returned to the boss in accordance with Stetsky's secret arrangement.

Babby, Kaden & Schwartzman

(Manufacturing Furriers)

150 WEST 30ᵀᴴ STREET

NEW YORK November 23rd, 1927.

Furriers Joint Council,
28 West 31st Street,
New York City.

Gentlemen: Attention Mr. Mc Grady.

We wish to call your attention to an item of $84.

which Mr. Charles Stetsky requested us to pay to two of our

workman, Max Crystal and Jack Lemberg the week of April 2nd,

1927.

It was agreed that this amount would be returned to us

in the near future but up to the present writing we have not

received same.

We trust you will find it convenient to send us your

check by return mail.

Very truly yours,

BABBY, KADEN & SCHWARTZMAN

Received to pay —

H. Schwartzman

had no solution for the unemployment problem. It was all the fault of
the Communists, they wept piously. They advised the fur workers to pray
for better times.

The solution of the workers' problems, Ben Gold declared at a meeting
of several thousand unemployed workers in March 1928, would come
from "fighting the bosses bitterly and struggling to rebuild the union into
that powerful instrument for the improvement of our conditions that it
once was."

But the right-wing leaders of the International were concerned only
with fighting the left wing. "We are only 20 percent organized," several
locals appealed to Begoon in March 1928, "and if the General Executive
Board will help us, we are sure that during the spring season we can
organize at least 35 percent more. We feel that this work has been greatly
neglected, and it is time that the open-shop movement be checked." "The
time just now is not opportune for organizing," was Begoon's answer.

"We are always advising the locals to avoid strikes as much as possible for at such times it is impossible to win them," wrote Begoon privately in the spring of 1928. When Local 25 of Newark and Local 58 of
Brooklyn refused to accept the International's advice and went on strike
in the early spring of 1928, the International leaders stepped in and
signed an agreement with the employers behind the backs of the strikers
accepting a $15-a-week wage cut.

Local 30 of Boston, in March 1928, made a new effort to
end the disastrous war being waged by the International leadership
against the thousands of New York fur workers. Local 30 proposed that
a conference of all out-of-town locals be called as soon as possible "in
order to discuss how unity and harmony can be brought about within the
International." The local sent its appeal to the G.E.B. and to all of the
out-of-town locals.

Labeling the call as "another move of Communist disruption" and
Local 30 as a "tool in Communist hands," the G.E.B.'s Sub-Committee
warned every local in the International to ignore the call. "Table this
communication with the contempt it deserves," the order stated.

At the same time, the Sub-Committee sent a strongly-worded warning
to Local 30 threatening it with "severe discipline" if it did not revoke its
call for a unity conference. The move to call a unity conference must
be stopped, Begoon wrote on March 30, 1928, even "if necessary to suspend or expel the local union." Local 30 temporarily abandoned the
effort.

The collapse of working conditions throughout the fur industry proceeded at a tremendous pace. In the rabbit dressing industry, for example, open shops, employing non-union workers, dressed about 40 percent of the rabbit and lamb skins.

"This open shop danger has already touched the bread and butter of our members," Locals 25 and 58 wrote to the Sub-Committee on May 3, 1928. "Our members are not only losing the work which is being done in these open shops, but they also had to submit to a wage cut amounting to about $15 per week.

"Now it appears that this wage cut does not satisfy the appetites of the bosses, and they are demanding a still further reduction of more than 25 percent in wages. There seems to be no doubt that if the bosses succeed in carrying through this second wage cut, they will demand a third wage cut . . .

"Where will this stop? We feel it our duty and also think it should be the duty of the International officers to defend the broad interests of our members under all circumstances."

Everywhere the fur workers saw their conditions wiped out, their organizations reduced to helplessness, and the open-shop movement spreading rapidly through the industry. Still the International officials were ready to see the union demolished rather than permit unity.

In this situation, Boston Local 30 decided that no matter what the consequences might be, it was necessary once again to issue a call for a unity conference. On May 14, 1928, Local 30 adopted a new resolution calling the G.E.B.'s attention to the spread of open shops in the fur manufacturing and fur dressing industries which was "breaking down the power of our local unions, cutting our wages to the bone and generally bringing in worse conditions in the union shops." The resolution went on to point out that because of the internal struggle in the union, the International was "spending all the money and energy on the war against the left wing instead of using them for organization purposes and for strengthening the locals." In view of these tragic developments, Local 30 again appealed to the Sub-Committee to immediately call together a conference of local representatives for the purpose of putting an end to the fight in the union. The resolution was forwarded to every local.

Within two weeks, three locals—Local 53 of Philadelphia, Local 40 of Toronto and Local 58 of Brooklyn—had endorsed Local 30's demand. In addition, several locals, despite instructions from Begoon warning them not "to take this communication up at all," were seriously debating the resolution.

The answer of the Sub-Committee to Local 30's communication came on June 5, 1928:

"I am directed by the Sub-Committee of the General Executive Board in reply to this resolution," wrote Begoon to Local 30, "that we recognize in it the same kind of song you have sung us before. This is sufficient evidence that you are acting for the Communists who have instigated the officers of your local to this in order to get some publicity.

"The International Fur Workers Union as well as the American Federation of Labor have once for all taken the stand that there can be no unity, peace or compromise with the Communists."

While answering Local 30, Begoon was also busy preparing a reply to another letter he had received on May 25, 1928. Indeed, it was a most unusual type of correspondence for an American trade-union official. At the top of the letter in bold type were inscribed the words: "IMPERIAL JAPANESE NAVY." The letter was signed by Captain T. Matsuda. The captain in the Imperial Japanese Navy wrote to Begoon:

"Yesterday when I called upon Mr. Hugh Frayne, New York Representative of the American Federation of Labor, he suggested to me to write to you, and therefore, I shall be much obliged if you will supply me with any literature or information you may have concerning the action you have taken against Bolshevism or Communism."

On May 29, 1928, Begoon proudly related to Captain Matsuda "the action we took against the Communists." He told how the Joint Board had been suspended and its leaders expelled, and how "with the aid of the American Federation of Labor" the International officials had reorganized the locals in New York. He described how the convention held in Washington in June 1927 had endorsed this action and "revoked the charters of the affected locals."

Then Begoon closed on a triumphant note, proclaiming: "Since then we have declared again and again publicly, that peace pleas and similar maneuvers of the expelled Communists are not to be trusted and we shall have no peace with them."

On the following day, Captain Matsuda thanked Begoon profusely in the name of the Imperial Japanese Government. Whether the imperialist government of Japan actually needed Begoon's advice or not, newspaper reports subsequently told of the expulsion of left-wingers from the Japanese trade unions, of the arrest and imprisonment of militant leaders of

IMPERIAL JAPANESE NAVY

INSPECTORS' OFFICE

ONE MADISON AVENUE

NEW YORK CITY

METROPOLITAN BLDG
ROOM 212-213
PHONE NO ASHLAND 2030 2031

In reply refer to
Captain T. Matsuda.

May 25, 1928.

Mr. Harry Begoon, Secretary-Treasurer,
International Fur Workers Union,
9 Jackson Ave.,
Long Island City, N. Y.

Dear Sir:-

Yesterday, when I called upon Mr. Hugh
Frayne, New York Representative of the American Federation of Labor, he suggested to me to write to you,
and therefore, I shall be much obliged if you will supply
me with any literature or information you may have concerning the action you have taken against Bolshevism or
Communism.

If you make an appointment, I should like
to send my representative to see you and discuss this
matter with you.

Thanking you for your prompt reply, I remain

Yours very truly,

T. Matsuda

ENGINE CONSTRUCTOR CAPTAIN, I.J.N.

IMPERIAL JAPANESE NAVY

INSPECTORS' OFFICE

ONE MADISON AVENUE

NEW YORK CITY

In reply refer to
Captain T. Matsuda.

June 1, 1928.

Mr. Harry Begoon,
General Secretary & Treasurer,
International Fur Workers' Union,
9 Jackson Ave.,
Long Island City, N. Y.

Dear Sir:-

Thank you for your letter of May 29th
giving me information as to the action you have taken
against Communism and Bolshevism.

Very truly yours,

T. Matsuda

ENGINE CONSTRUCTOR CAPTAIN, I.J.N.

*Captain T. Matsuda of the Imperial Japanese Navy finds no
lack of cooperation when he seeks information from Frayne
and Begoon on how to get rid of "Bolshevism or Communism."*

the Japanese working class, and even of the wholesale slaughter of workers who dared to strike against these edicts.

The cooperation of the AFL representative and International officials with Captain Matsuda of the Imperial Japanese Navy exposes the complete lack of scruples or principles of the right-wing Socialist leaders bent on preventing unity in the Furriers Union.

On the surface, the struggle to re-unite the union had appeared to produce no real results. But beneath the surface, the influence of the unity movement was making itself felt even within the ranks of right-wing supporters. The pressure of the dissatisfied workers created fertile ground for a split in the leadership of the right-wing New York Joint Council. The rival Stetsky-"Big Alex" Fried clique and the Sorkin-Winnick group fought over control of the Council. The Stetsky-Fried clique, closer to the AFL "reorganizers" and in control of the strong-arm squads, held the dominant position in the Council and most of the offices. The Sorkin-Winnick group knew perfectly well that all the boasting that thousands of workers were registering with the Joint Council and that the "Communist Joint Board" was dead—was just so much hogwash. As a matter of fact, the registered workers did not even pay dues unless they were forced to do so by the strong-arm squads. Stetsky himself admitted that only a few hundred workers were in good standing. As in 1924, the Sorkin group saw an opportunity to gain support of the workers by again posing as "Progressives," and thus win control of the Council.

The Socialist Party leaders hastily intervened to prevent an open split in the New York Joint Council. On October 21, 1927, Shiplacoff and Feinstone called a conference to discuss healing the breach in the Joint Council and thereby preventing "a serious tragedy." They conjured up threats of Communist reprisals if the left-wingers won out as a result of the internal split in the Joint Council. Still the Sorkin-Winnick group refused to be kept in line.

The Socialist Party itself stepped into the picture. A resolution adopted at the convention of the Jewish Socialist Federation on December 1, 1927, was specifically directed at the Sorkin-Winnick group. The resolution declared that "the socialists in the unions must act in all important matters as a unit in line with a fixed policy. It is not permissable for one socialist to fight another socialist on the floor of the union. All differences must be adjusted among themselves or through the intervention of the socialist organization."

This from an organization that justified expulsion of Communists on the grounds that they were under "domination of an outside organization" and could not act as "free agents" in trade unions!

Despite the pressure applied by the Socialist trade union leaders and the Socialist Party, the factional struggle inside the Joint Council grew with every passing month. William Collins, general organizer for the AFL in Yonkers, who had assisted in "reorganizing" the Furriers Union, wrote to McGrady on January 3, 1928, that he was disgusted with the "mess" in the Joint Council, and was glad to get away from "furriers who are fighting for office." In his public statements Collins, like Woll, Frayne and McGrady, stoutly insisted that the battle in the Furriers Union was between the principles of Communism represented by the Joint Board and the principles of Americanism represented by the Joint Council. But in this private letter, Collins admitted that the right-wing Socialists were really fighting for positions in the union. Significantly, when McGrady forwarded Collins' letter to Begoon, he added the note: "This letter must not be read to the Sub-Committee. It is strictly confidential."

The open split in the Joint Council convinced the AFL leaders that their entire campaign against the fur workers had disintegrated to a point where it was no longer possible to retrieve it.

On top of this, the conspirators suffered another blow. The "Committee for Preservation of Trade Unions" informed the AFL leaders that their treasury was bankrupt and they could no longer carry the burden of financing the Joint Council. The AFL itself had indicated months before that it could not keep pouring money into the Joint Council. It was clear that the jig was up. Writing from Washington on July 6, 1928, Edward McGrady informed Shiplacoff that the AFL had decided to throw in the sponge and withdraw from the fur situation in New York:

"The committee representing the American Federation of Labor feels very much discouraged over this situation and as a result of the action of your Committee I have conferred with President Green on this situation, and we feel that inasmuch as the Preservation of Trade Unions Committee is not in a position to render any further assistance, the American Federation of Labor will surrender its control of the situation just as soon as we can close the various matters up.

"If there is anything further that you think might be done in the immediate future I will be very glad to hear from you. Otherwise the American Federation of Labor will get out of the situation within the next few weeks."

McGrady's letter to Shiplacoff vindicated the firm belief of the rank and file that it was only a matter of time before the right-wing union-splitters would be crushed and the task of rebuilding the shattered Furriers Union would be accomplished by the membership.

In the right-wing camp there was consternation and despair. McGrady's letter had struck them a devastating blow. The deals with the employers, assistance from the police and the underworld—had been all for nothing. Once the AFL withdrew from the fur situation in New York, the Joint Council would be exposed for the paper organization it really was. Only the horrible memory would remain of the methods that had been used to force the workers to register and pay dues. The repercussions would be felt in other needle trades unions where the rank and file was battling corrupt, bankrupt and bureaucratic officials.

The desperate Socialist leaders, however, quickly overruled all suggestions that they retire from the scene. On July 11, 1928, five days after he had received McGrady's letter, Shiplacoff sent a hurried call for help to the right-wing leaders of the needle trades unions, inviting them to an emergency meeting in the Council Room of the ILGWU.* Calling their attention to McGrady's letter, Shiplacoff reminded the right-wing leaders "that we cannot very well afford to have the Communists re-intrench themselves in the Furriers Union." "Just what can be done I don't know," he fairly wept, "but I do know that it would weigh heavily on your conscience and on mine if we did not make a serious attempt to prevent the recapture of the Furriers Union by the Communists." At the emergency conference, desperate efforts were made to raise funds so that the AFL leaders might be persuaded not to pull out.

A copy of McGrady's letter to Shiplacoff came into possession of the Joint Board, and was published in the press on August 6. Instantly, the right-wing leaders sent frenzied telegrams to the AFL officialdom asking for an immediate statement to offset the impression that the Federation had acknowledged its failure. If a statement was not immediately released to the press, all would be lost.

Green leaped to rescue the hard-pressed Socialists. In a telegram to the *Jewish Daily Forward,* he announced that not only would the Federation

---

* The call was sent to thirty individuals including A. Cahan and B. C. Vladeck of the Forward Association, M. Feinstone of the United Hebrew Trades, M. Sigman and Luigi Antonini of the ILGWU, Joseph Schlossberg, A. Beckerman and Sidney Hillman of the Amalgamated Clothing Workers, Max Zaritsky of the Cap and Hat Makers Union, and Alex Rose of the Millinery Workers Union.

A. I. SHIPLACOFF
53-55 West 21st Street
NEW YORK. N. Y.

July 11th, 1928.

Dear Friend:-

        A moments reflection on the enclosed will
probably bring you to the conclusion it brought me that
we cannot very well afford to have the Communists re-
intrench themselves in the Furriers Union.

        Just what can be done I don't know, but I
do know that it would weigh heavily on your conscience
and on mine if we did not make a serious attempt to
prevent the recapture of the Furriers Union by the
Communist.

        Knowing that you have a sincere sense of
responsibility toward the labor movement I am calling
upon you and those listed below to meet on Tuesday, July
17th in the Council Room of the I.L.G.W.U. 3 West 16th St.
at 3 P.M.

M. Brown	A. Cahan	Luigi Antonini	A. Miller
M. Sigman	A. Beckerman	B. Schlesinger	M. Guskin
B.C. Vladck	M. Gillis	M. Feinstone	A. Held
L. Fuchs	D. Berger	Hershkowitz	Gertler
J. Roberts	Stetsky	Mr. Imhoff	A. Rose
C. Goldman	Sm. Ninfo	H. Orlofsky	S. Hillman
J. Schlessberg	M. Zaritzky	M. Spector	J. Weiss
	E. McGrady	Dogccn	

        If the destruction of the Furriers Union
is really to be consummated, let none of us feel that we
haven't made a last attempt to save it.

                    Fraternally yours,

                    A.I.Shiplacoff

Tuesday, July 17th, 3 West 16th Street.

*McGrady's letter to Shiplacoff indicating that the AFL is
ready to pull out of the furriers' situation, calls forth a
new appeal for outside interference with the fur workers union.*

not "withdraw from the furriers' situation," but it would continue "to give its service" in the "fight against Communism and Communist influence" in the International Fur Workers Union. The Executive Council again assigned Woll, Frayne and McGrady "to the fur workers for an indefinite period." At the same time, Shiplacoff disclosed that the organizations represented at the emergency conference had promised to provide the additional financial resources necessary to enable the AFL "to control the situation" in the Furriers Union.

But statements could not breathe new life into the "corpse," as the workers called it. All the money poured into the Joint Council would only pay the salaries of the right-wing clique and their strong-arm squads, and preserve the "corpse" as a useful instrument of the employers to destroy the furriers' working conditions.

On the other hand, the Joint Board was very much alive. It had just completed a highly successful drive for July raises. It had called and won several shop strikes despite the fact that the employers had new "agreements" with the Joint Council and did not recognize the Joint Board. These successful strikes enabled thousands of workers in other shops to obtain July raises from their bosses.

The Joint Board connected the battle for wage increases with the campaign for peace and unity. Why, it asked, had wages been cut more than 50 percent? Why were cutters, operators, nailers, and finishers now receiving $30 and $40 less per week than they had received in 1926 although they were now producing twice as much work?

"One strong, united union," declared the Joint Board, "under the leadership of competent, devoted and militant workers will restore the union conditions, will put an end to the merciless exploitation in the shops, increase the wages, curb the appetites of the greedy manufacturers and re-establish the furriers' self-respect and pride."

For over a year, the campaign to end the internal warfare and build a strong, united union had been centered upon attempting to reach a settlement of the struggle between the right and left wings in the International. Now it became clear that unity could not be achieved under these circumstances. The right-wing clique would make every concession to the employers rather than yield an inch to the workers' demands for unity.

The fur workers had no recourse now except to take new measures to defend their union.

CHAPTER 28

The Needle Trades Workers Industrial Union

On August 12, 1928, delegates representing nearly every furriers' local in the United States and Canada, plus the New York Joint Board and the former so-called Progressive Bloc of the right-wing Joint Council, met in New York City. The conference formed an international united-front committee for the purpose of building a new International union in the fur manufacturing and fur dressing industries upon the scattered ruins of the right-wing organization. As a first step, the united conference called a mass mobilization meeting of the fur workers. The declaration announcing this historic decision read in part:

"We repudiate the policy of expulsion of members because of their political convictions and affiliations, and we declare for a union of all workers, recognizing the right of every worker to his race, color and religious and political beliefs.

"We are fully cognizant of the probable persecution of every worker signed to this declaration, but we also recognize that the urgent task of building one united international union of all fur workers, a union demo-cratically controlled and managed by the workers only, and the task of restoring and bettering of the union conditions and union wages stand above every consideration of self-interest and safety. . . . All of those who are honestly and sincerely desirous of helping the workers to build their union are welcome to join our ranks.

"International United-Front Committee." *

* The signers were Ben Gold, representing the New York Joint Board; S. Leibowitz and Jack Schneider, Local 1; Aaron Gross and Benjamin Baraz,

The largest meeting ever to fill Cooper Union was held on August 15, 1928, when over four thousand fur workers literally jammed tight every inch of available space, including the large corridors behind the doors; even at that, many were turned away. They had come to hear reports from representatives of locals in New York, Brooklyn, Newark, Philadelphia, Boston, Toronto and Winnipeg, and the so-called Progressive Bloc. They knew that they were participating in one of the most exciting events in the history of the Furriers Union.

This meeting was to take the most important step in the two-year-old struggle against the International leadership and its allies. A living symbol of this struggle sat on the platform, his face swathed in bandages. Meyer Weinstein, fur worker, had just been slashed by a right-wing thug in the shop where he was working because he had refused to attend a Joint Council meeting.

Following a number of stirring speeches, the meeting unanimously resolved to organize a new International. It empowered the representatives of the thirteen locals and the "Progressive Bloc" to form a provisional National Executive Committee "for the purpose of uniting and mobilizing all of the locals and all of the fur workers . . . for the organization of a real union." It also empowered the Committee to call a convention of all local unions "for the purpose of forming a new International Union of fur workers of the United States and Canada." Another resolution opened a drive to raise the sum of $25,000 for an immediate campaign to organize the open shops.

Even before the furriers had taken this step to set up a new International union, the majority of the members of the International Ladies Garment Workers Union had made a similar decision. The internal struggle in the Furriers Union had been paralleled by that in the women's garment unions. There, too, the right-wing leadership had adopted wholesale expulsion policies on the pretext of meeting the threatening "Red Menace." They too had expelled the New York Joint Board,

---

Local 5; Louis Cohen and Hershkowitz, Local 10; Joseph Winogradsky, Local 15; S. Soulounios, J. Pappas, G. Perdicaria, the Greek Branch of the Joint Board; I. Winnick, Hyman Sorkin, Dave Goodman, S. Strauss, the "Progressive Bloc"; Morris Langer, B. Yudkowsky, F. Yadkofsky, Louis Jaffee and Mike Hudyma, Local 25; David Mathoff, G. Perlman, Local 30; H. Englander, Local 40; J. Newman and Sam Burt, Local 53; Philip Getz, Irving Ader and Morris Stein, Local 54; Louis Bricca, Julius Weil, Local 58; G. Satrople, Local 70; Louis Canter, Simon Lunin and Boris Prokofin, Local 88.

and "reorganized" the most powerful locals of the International Union.*

For twenty-one months, a struggle for unity took place in the ILGWU, as in the Furriers Union. Every movement in the direction of unity, however, was rebuffed by a leadership indifferent to both the needs of the membership and to their appeals. The final act in the tragedy was performed at the International convention in May 1928. Afraid to admit the representatives of the membership, the office-holding and office-seeking cliques, led by Sigman, Benjamin Schlessinger, David Dubinsky and Salvatore Ninfo, called upon the Boston police to keep out of the hall the delegates of the deposed Joint Board, who had come to make still another overture of peace. In the police-barricaded hall William Green fumed and threatened that if the militant rank and file of the union "gains control in spite of all we can do, then the last step will be taken. The charter of the Union will be revoked."

The barred delegates, together with the Committee of Fifty and delegates from various needle trade centers, met for three days in Boston and set up a National Organization Committee. This formed the cornerstone for a new organization of cloak and dressmakers. On August 8, 1928, at a monster mass meeting of fifteen thousand workers at the Bronx Stadium in New York City, the Committee presented a proposal for building a new union. Amidst great enthusiasm, a resolution was adopted that "the time has come when the workers of the ladies garment industry must begin building our new union, controlled by the rank and

---

* "It is superfluous to dwell at length upon the evils arising from such a situation," the Committee of Fifty, composed entirely of non-Communist cloak and dressmakers, had written to William Green on February 4, 1928. "It is enough to state that all the horrors and chaos which existed in this industry prior to 1910 are gradually coming back. Unscrupulous employers, glad to take advantage of the situation, are pitting one faction of the workers against the other. Union standards are disappearing. The sweatshop employer is again thriving."

The right-wing Administration, the Committee of Fifty informed Green, "exists by virtue of the fact" that the employers "are discharging all workers who refuse to join the newly organized locals. It is conceded on all hands that the present administration cannot survive one day without that support. This means that the Union has become not a labor organization, but an employers' organization. . . . *Such employers' union* can only breed corruption inside and chaos all round."

Completely ignoring the tragic picture outlined by the Committee of Fifty, Green replied: "We shall assert our authority and power to protect those who place trade union principles and trade union philosophy above Communism and the Communist philosophy."

file, which will lead us in struggle against the bosses and the company union."

Thus within a week of each other, the cloak and dressmakers and the furriers moved to finally rid themselves of the nightmare of corrupt right-ring leadership. Henceforth, for six years, these groups of needle trades workers were to combine their heroic courage and skill in the building of a real workers' union.

The announcement of the fur workers' decision to organize a new union brought forth a broadside of vituperation from the right-wing leaders and the AFL officialdom. The old cry of "Moscow domination" arose from Begoon, Woll and McGrady. Unperturbed, the provisional National Executive Committee began a campaign to mobilize the fur workers. By mid-September, 1928, Locals 1, 5, 10 and 15 of New York, Local 30 of Boston, Local 25 of Newark, Local 40 of Toronto and Local 58 of Brooklyn voted to stop paying dues to the AFL International and to join the new union.

The right-wing leadership of the International threatened all sorts of reprisals and immediately declared the locals officially dissolved. The banks were instructed that "all money and property in the name of such dissolved local must be turned over to the General Secretary-Treasurer of the International Fur Workers Union." The following blanket authorization handed out by the International leaders to an AFL official was typical:

"August 27, 1928.

"To whom it may concern:

"This is to certify that Brother Harry P. Grages, Secretary and Business Representative of the Boston Central Labor Union is fully authorized to represent the International Fur Workers Union of the United States and Canada, *in any action he may desire to take.*

H. Begoon, General Secretary-Treasurer."

In September 1928, Begoon and McGrady exerted strenuous efforts to get the Philadelphia fur bosses to break off their agreement with Local 53, which was participating in the movement for the new union. The manufacturers' association informed Sam Burt, Local 53's business agent, that they would sign a new agreement only "if underwritten and sponsored by the International Fur Workers Union . . . and the American Federation of Labor." Begoon made a hurried trip to Philadelphia, set up a paper union overnight in the office of the right-wing Cloakmakers Union, and met with the employers' association to arrange for an agreement with the new local. In return for this cooperation of the employers, the new agreement would include a wage cut and would surrender the forty-hour week.

"This morning Mr. Polin and I were up in Ritchie's office," Begoon wrote to McGrady from Philadelphia on September 12, 1928. "We explained him the situation. Ritchie and I then had a little conference with a group of manufacturers in Carl Blumer's office. The Association meets tonight to discuss the situation. Mr. Blumer and the rest impressed me that their meeting tonight will uphold the actions of their conference committee, but they persistently wanted to know how much protection we will be able to give them, and how soon will New York send enough workers to fill the places of those that will respond to Mr. Burt's call. Ritchie told them that they need not worry about protection, he will take care of it. In regard to workers, I repeated the assurance that you gave them while in conference."

When the employers were about to conclude the agreement with Begoon's paper local, Local 53 issued a call for a one-hour strike in all Philadelphia fur shops. One hundred percent of the workers answered the call. Unanimously, Local 53 voted for a general strike and began to mobilize the general strike machinery that was to go into operation the moment the employers announced signing with the AFL union.

Despite Ritchie's assurance of gangster protection and the promises of McGrady and Begoon to bring in scabs from New York, the spectre of empty shops finally forced the Association to concede defeat. On September 20, Local 53 obtained a three-year contract, retaining the forty-hour week and providing for additional improvements for the workers.* Thus even before the new union was officially launched, Local 53's victory showed the fur workers the only way in which they would be able to retrieve their devastated working conditions—the way of united, militant struggle against the employers and their allies. This victory had been achieved to a great extent through the sound leadership of Sam Burt.

Sam Burt was born in Russia in 1905. His father was a poor shoemaker, and Burt was forced to go to work at the early age of twelve to help keep the family of nine alive. He came to the United States in

---

* Instead of equal division of work "during slack seasons only" with interpretation of slackness in the hands of an impartial chairman, the new agreement provided for equal division of work from May to March, or over ten months a year.

1922, and went to Philadelphia where his mother and two younger brothers had already settled. That same year he went to work in a fur shop, earning $10 a week as an operator. For two years, Burt fought in vain to force Local 53's Executive Board to allow him to become a union member. This would enable him to earn $35 a week for the same work for which he was receiving $10. Finally, in 1924 he was admitted into the union.

While serving on a committee to check the union's finances, Burt obtained a real insight into how the local was being run by the right-wing machine. Although not a single meeting of the committee was called, the chairman reported to a local meeting that the books were in order. Burt denounced the report and demanded a real investigation. This time a committee meeting was held, but instead of studying the books, the evening was devoted to drinking and card-playing. Again the report to the local was that the books were in order. When Burt related what had happened at the committee's meeting, he was laughed at by the union leadership. But this stand won the support of the workers, and soon Burt was elected recording secretary of Local 53.

During the 1926 fur strike, Burt did a great deal to stop the scab work being done in the Philadelphia fur shops. It was during the strike that he made his first contacts with the progressive leaders of the Furriers Union in New York. He allied himself with them in their struggle against the right-wing International leadership, and when the New York Joint Board was expelled, Burt rallied the Philadelphia furriers in opposition to the ruinous policies of the International leadership. During the next few years, Local 53, with Burt as manager, was a potent force for unity in the Furriers Union. When the Industrial Union was established, Burt became one of its outstanding leaders, first in Philadelphia, and later in New York.

While the furriers' provisional National Executive Committee was engaged in sponsoring a series of mass meetings throughout the country in support of the new union movement, it was invited by the National Organization Committee of the cloak and dressmakers to join in forming a single industrial union as the first step toward complete amalgamation of the needle trades unions. The letter pointed out that the workers in these industries "have had to contend with and meet the same enemies. On the picket line we were faced with similar gangster squads. Our enemies are the same; our problems are the same."

The idea of an industrial union which would include all needle trades workers was by no means a new one. It was a burning issue especially after the war years when the employers began their open-shop drive and cloakmakers, dressmakers, furriers and other workers on strike saw the bosses importing scabs from other needle trades. Sidney Hillman, head of the men's clothing workers union had strongly advocated amalgamation of all needle trade unions. The right-wing leaders, much as they feared the eventual loss of their jobs, were forced to give lip-service support to the idea and held several conferences on the question of combining all unions in the garment industry. In typical fashion, they tried to stifle the growing demand for amalgamation, by creating a loose, meaningless federation known as the Needle Trades Workers' Alliance. Formed in December 1920, it remained only a paper organization.

The amalgamation movement took sharper form with the formation of the needle trades section of the Trade Union Educational League in 1922. The TUEL thereafter repeatedly called for amalgamation to increase the effectiveness of the unions in organizing and to intensify their striking power. To head off this demand, the right-wing leaders revived their Alliance in 1923. Again it was only a meaningless gesture. Before long the Alliance disintegrated and passed from the scene.

Hailing the amalgamation proposal, Irving Potash, secretary of the provisional National Executive Committee for a new Furriers International Union, replied to the National Organization Committee of the cloak and dressmakers: "We are convinced that the immediate amalgamation of the cloak and dressmakers and furriers unions, which have freed themselves of the grip of the bureaucrats, will place in the hands of our workers the most effective weapons in their struggle for better working and living standards and lay the basis for the all-embracing unification of all needle trade workers despite the sabotage of the labor bureaucrats."

Two conventions, one of the cloak and dressmakers and the other of the furriers, opened in New York City on December 28 and 29, 1928. Two days later, after the amalgamation proposal had been unanimously adopted by both conventions, the Needle Trades Workers Industrial Union was organized by delegates representing thousands of workers in all the important centers of the garment industry.

The joint convention settled down to the job of laying the foundation of the new union. A constitution was drawn up, resolutions were adopted, and national officers and a General Executive Board were elected.

The principles and structure of the new union marked an important advance in democratic trade unionism. It recognized the principle of proportional representation and the election of general officers by referendum, with the right of recall. It established the shop delegate system, with the shop as its basic unit, as the foundation for the union, an important step toward drawing more and more of the rank and file into the union's activities.

The economic program adopted by the Convention included: a forty-hour, five-day week; minimum wage scales; wage increases; abolition of piece work and the establishment of week work; abolition of standards of production; forty-week yearly time guarantee of employment; limitation on contractors with the aim of their eventual elimination; the right to the job with no discharge or reorganization; elimination of sweatshops, home work, section contracting and sub-contracting; unemployment insurance to be paid by the bosses and administered by the workers; protection of youth and women in industry.

The Convention adopted a series of important resolutions. It voted to send delegates to all conferences called by militant unions in the country and to conferences called by the Trade Union Educational League. It demanded immediate release of Tom Mooney and Warren K. Billings and all other class-war prisoners languishing in jails. It recognized the special need of organizing Negro workers and women workers. It recognized the international character of the trade union struggle, by sending fraternal delegates to the next congress of the new International of Labor Unions that had been organized to combat the bankrupt policies of the practically defunct Socialist-dominated Amsterdam trade union international.

At its last session, the Convention elected the new union's officers. Louis Hyman of the cloak and dressmakers was elected president, and Ben Gold of the furriers, secretary. An executive board composed of thirty-nine other well-known militant needle trades workers was chosen to lead the new union. The members of the executive board included Negro workers, Russian-Polish and Greek workers, women and a representative from the youth.*

* The following were the members of the general executive board: Sam Burt, Irving Potash, Jack Schneider, Samuel Leibowitz, M. H. Cohen, Joseph Winogradsky, Joseph Borochovich, Rose Wortis, Virginia Allen, B. Baraz, H. Berlin, L. Cohen, S. Cohen, J. H. Cohen, A. Digiralemo, Oswaldo Eusepi, Aaron Gross, M. Jensky, S. Kaplan, E. Kaplan, H. Kessler, E. Kudrenetsky, H. Koretz, J. Levine, I. Lutsky, J. Petrofsky, G. Perlman, J. Pappas, J. Portnoy, H. Rosemond, Lena Rabinowitz, J. Strauss, I. Stanger, M. Shapiro, J. Weil, A. Weiss, E. Yannunsky, Charles S. Zimmerman and A. Zierlin.

The Negro members of the Board were Virginia Allen, dressmaker, and Henry Rosemond, furrier. M. Jensky was the youth delegate.

CHAPTER 29

Retreat

At secret conferences among McGrady, Woll and top leaders of the Fur Trimming Association, a plan was conceived to wipe out the newly-born Industrial Union. The AFL "reorganizers" offered the fur trimming employers still greater concessions to withdraw recognition from the Joint Board and to unite with the Associated Fur Manufacturers in recognizing only the AFL union. "If we can put this over," McGrady wrote to William Green, "our troubles will be largely over."

The self-appointed "conference committee," Woll, McGrady and a handful of right-wing officials, signed an agreement with the Associated Fur Manufacturers and the Fur Trimming Association, and an identical agreement with the Greek Fur Manufacturers Association. All the conferences were held in secret. Only after the agreements had been signed were the workers informed of the terms.

The agreement was to run for three years, from January 30, 1929, to January 31, 1932. The minimum wage rates were frozen as they were in the old agreement. The "minimum" rates had already become the "maximum" rates in the shops controlled by the employer-Joint Council alliance. Therefore the fur workers could expect no wage increase for the next three years.

The new agreement gave the employers the unlimited right of discharge. Equal division of work, a crucial issue among the furriers, was reduced to a myth with the general remark that it "shall be carried on *wherever possible* during the months of June, November and December, for those who have worked with the firm not less than seven consecutive weeks

prior to the period when equal division of work is begun in each establishment."

The sweatshop contracting system, one of the worst evils in the trade,
was now openly legalized: "The same conditions as prevail in the shops
of the members of the Association shall be maintained in the shops of
contractors working for the members of the Association."

The *Jewish Daily Forward* announced the new agreement in big headlines. It was a "great victory" for the furriers. The fur workers were
"filled with joy" over the terms of the agreement and "gratitude" towards
the AFL leaders. A few days later, buried on an inside page, the *Forward*
reported that 615 fur workers had participated in the referendum. As
usual, the right-wingers declared that the fur workers were so "satisfied"
with the new agreement that they had "no reason to vote."

The AFL leaders were not fooling themselves, however.
They knew how bitter the fur workers were over the concessions granted
the employers in the new agreement, and that it could be put over only
through police terror and the threat of starvation. This was especially
true of the workers in the fur trimming shops who had been represented
by the left-wing Joint Board in their dealings with the employers.

"Many of the Fur Trimming shops that have just signed up with us,"
McGrady wrote to William Green on February 2, 1929, "are manned
entirely by left wing workers who are antagonistic to the American Federation of Labor. We are going to give them an opportunity to join our
union at a minimum charge of $12.50 each. . . If they fail to become
members of our organization, we will then ask for their discharge and
fill their places with workers affiliated with the American Federation of
Labor . . ."

McGrady also arranged for another appointment with Mayor Walker
on February 6 "at which time," he informed William Green, "Vice President Woll, Mr. Joseph Ryan of the Central Trades and Labor Council
and myself hope to have the Mayor instruct the police commissioner to
assist us in maintaining order in the needle trades district."

The AFL leaders were confident that they would now have easy sailing. William Green informed Begoon that "the time has now arrived
when you and your associates are in a position to take charge of and
direct the affairs of the International Fur Workers Union . . ."

McGrady turned over the manager's office in the Joint Council to
Charles Stetsky. He left New York to continue his work for the employers, this time in the Southern textile district.

Before many weeks had passed, William Green was deluged with desperate appeals from Begoon, Stetsky and other right-wingers in the Joint Council. Send McGrady back to New York! A new crisis has arisen!

The workers in the trimming shops could not be forced to register with the Joint Council. Stetsky complained to Green that the "Trimming Manufacturers Association . . . lacked the courage of rigid enforcement of the agreement calling for the employment of none but members of the International." The efforts made by the Joint Council to get control of these trimming shops, he admitted, "brought about little results because most of the workers in these shops were left wing sympathizers."

In the fur manufacturing shops, too, things were beginning to hum. Following a series of successful shop strikes, a number of manufacturers signed up with the Industrial Union. Others sent in applications for settlements. Hundreds of workers who had been forced to register with the Joint Council took out membership cards in the Industrial Union. Many held these cards secretly. They waited for the opportune time to openly proclaim themselves members of the Industrial Union.

With reports of a general strike in the air, Begoon implored Green "to lend us again the services of Brother Edward McGrady, it would help a great deal. . . . Brother McGrady is well acquainted with the situation and knows precisely what action to take in the case."

Green to Begoon, February 4: We're through. You're on your own. Begoon to Green, May 11: Help! Send McGrady back to us.

> We will be glad to help and assist you in every possible way. I feel, however, that the time has now arrived when you and your associates are in a position to take charge of and direct the affairs of the International Fur Workers' Union in accordance with the authority conferred upon you by the American Federation of Labor.
>
> With all good wishes, I beg to remain
>
> Fraternally yours,
>
> *[signature] Green*
>
> President,
> American Federation of Labor.

> I am writing to you President Green, suggesting that if it were possible to lend us again the services of Brother Edward McGrady it would help a great deal. I need not tell you that Brother McGrady is well acquainted with the situation and knows precisely what action to take in the case. As the matter stands we really have no other friends to help us in

But McGrady's talents were busily engaged elsewhere. Green was forced to reject Begoon's frantic appeal. He assigned Matthew Woll, William Collins, the AFL organizer, and Joseph Ryan of the Central Trades and Labor Council of New York to assist the right-wingers in the Joint Council "to resist the attack of the Communists."

Woll did just what McGrady would have done. On May 13, 1929, he telephoned Green and asked the AFL president "to write to the Mayor and Police Commissioner asking for adequate police protection." Green complied, and authorized Woll, Collins and Ryan to use his name in presenting the situation in person to Mayor Walker.

Ironically, on the very same day that the AFL leaders and their Socialist assistants in the Joint Council were conferring with Mayor Walker on the details of the new campaign of police terror and brutality to be launched against the fur workers, a letter from Norman Thomas to "Comrade Stetsky" arrived in the Joint Council. The Socialist leader invited the Socialist manager of the Joint Council to attend a meeting to discuss the necessity of defeating Mayor Walker and Tammany in the fall elections.

"Surely we do not have to endure the scandals of the last four years," wrote Thomas, "the shocking conditions of the Police Department and the Magistrates' Courts, the do-nothing policy of the Mayor on all large issues without protest."

It is to be wondered that Norman Thomas expected "Comrade" Stetsky to attend such a meeting. Thomas knew from his own experience in the 1927 strike just how dependent the right-wing Socialist leaders of the Joint Council were on Mayor Walker, the Police Department and the Magistrates' Courts. Indeed, when Roger Baldwin, director of the American Civil Liberties Union, dared to discuss with Police Commissioner Grover A. Whalen the right of fur workers to picket unmolested by police, "Comrade" Stetsky urged the Mayor and Police Commissioner to ignore Baldwin. Whalen assured Stetsky that he understood his objections to Baldwin's demand. He "promised the full cooperation of his department." Nor is there any record that Norman Thomas condemned "Comrade" Stetsky's intrigue with the Police Department.

Woll, Collins, Ryan, Stetsky and the other right-wing leaders made full preparations to crush the impending general strike. The police were alerted. Any fur worker who wanted to join the picket line was to be taught a lesson that would change his mind. The right-wingers were confident that they were "ready to meet the emergency."

Unfortunately, the Industrial Union was anything but ready. On the contrary, the union that entered the 1929 strike bore no resemblance to the mighty, coordinated, thoroughly-prepared organization that had made labor history in 1926. A well-organized, well-prepared strike in 1929 would have knocked the props from under the bosses, the AFL leaders and the right-wing Socialists. The sell-out in the new agreement had fanned the flames of discontent in the fur market. The right-wingers themselves admitted that conditions were ripe for a successful general strike. The "broke and discontented" workers, Stetsky frankly told William Green, were convinced "that the American Federation of Labor was responsible for the existing condition." It was only natural to expect, he added, that when the strike call would be issued the workers "would respond to that call."

It was this understanding of the critical situation they faced in the event of a general strike that had caused the right-wingers to run to William Green begging for help. "As the matter stands," Begoon wailed, "we really have no other friends to help us in this difficulty than the American Federation of Labor." The employers, too, doubted the value of an agreement with the right-wingers, with all its concessions. Unless fur coats were produced, the sell-out would turn out worthless to the bosses.

At this critical moment, the right-wingers were saved from an unexpected source. The task of mobilizing the fur workers for the struggle against the bosses and their allies was assigned to Aaron Gross, manager of the Fur Department of the Needle Trades Workers Industrial Union. No greater mistake could have been made.

Gross was Ben Gold's assistant and best friend. But Gold had opposed the selection of Gross for the post of manager. Although Gross had worked with Gold, Leibowitz and other left-wing leaders since 1919, he lacked both organizational ability and the capacity for managing the union. In addition Gross was a member of the Lovestone group in the Communist Party.

According to the theories of Jay Lovestone, American capitalism was the "exception." It had entered the "Golden Age" of eternal prosperity. Even though there already were undeniable signs of a developing crisis in a number of industries in 1928, with over two million workers unemployed, Lovestone and his followers insisted that American capitalism was exempt from the crisis that was enveloping all the capitalist countries. "American national economy as such is not declining fundamentally," Lovestone declared in May 1928. "Quite the contrary. It is on the ascent."

Although Lovestone's followers felt that American workers were not ready for a militant trade union movement, they had assumed leading positions in the new Industrial Union. Events soon demonstrated that they had done so for a devious purpose—to sabotage its work, force its liquidation and make peace with the right-wing and AFL bureaucracies. The 1929 fur strike, led by Gross, was an outstanding example of their disruptive work in the new union.

Gross failed utterly to prepare the workers for the impending strike. Few of the shops were contacted. Shop chairmen most devoted to the Industrial Union were neglected. No steps were taken to organize rank-and-file committees for conducting the strike. Only a half-hearted attempt was made to even call the workers together in mass meetings.

In addition, Gross failed even to publicize a victory won by the Industrial Union in the fur dressing and dyeing industry. Early in June, the Industrial Union signed an agreement with the Federated Rabbit Dressing Corporation which included the forty-hour, five-day week, 25 percent wage increases, and other important gains. Here was an agreement that stood in sharp contrast with the sell-out of the workers' interests negotiated by the AFL leaders and the Socialists with the three Associations. But Gross did not trouble to distribute a single leaflet in the fur market informing the workers of it or pointing up the lesson that similar victories could be won in the forthcoming general strike.

Ben Gold, unfortunately, was completely unaware of Gross' mistakes or his sabotage of the program of the Industrial Union. As secretary-treasurer of the national union, Gold was out of New York most of the time, devoting himself to organizing locals of dressmakers, cloakmakers and furriers in Philadelphia, Baltimore, Boston, Chicago and other cities. In addition, he was compelled to take on other duties. Louis Hyman, the national president—incapable, indecisive, and continually wavering between optimism and defeatism—lacked the qualities necessary to head the union. Most of his time was spent at home. The bulk of the work fell on Gold's shoulders. During the weeks when the general strike in the New York fur industry should have been prepared, he was moving about from city to city performing the combined duties of president and secretary-treasurer of the Industrial Union.

A few days before the strike was called, Gold returned to New York. He was called back by a group of active fur workers who complained vigorously against Gross' failure to prepare for the forthcoming struggle.

They informed Gold that when they had voiced similar complaints to Gross, he had assured them that conditions were so bad in the fur shops that the workers would respond spontaneously to a strike call whether adequate preparations had been made in advance or not.

Seriously disturbed, Gold called a meeting of the active Joint Board leaders. He questioned whether or not the strike should be called. Gross and his Lovestoneite followers argued vehemently in favor of calling the strike. They insisted heatedly that criticism of Gross' management was wrong.

To call the strike off at that late date would have been a terrible blow to the whole union. It would have demobilized the workers and strengthened the company-union Joint Council. Still not fully informed of the extent of Gross' neglect of the strike preparations, Gold came to the conclusion that the strike had to be called as scheduled, a few days later. Events proved this a most serious mistake on Gold's part.

The strike call, issued on June 19, 1929, appealed to the fur workers to: "Open battle against the bosses in order to wipe out the system of slavery, exploitation and oppression which exist in the shops . . . win back your 40-hour week, higher wages and all the other demands for which you bled and fought 17 weeks in the general strike of 1926 . . . force the bosses to stop the terror and the persecution which they have been carrying on with the help of the Socialists and the AFL traitors . . . fight unemployment, hunger and need which most of the furriers have suffered in the past two and a half years . . . struggle for your living needs and elementary rights as workers."

The Industrial Union also demanded work for the unemployed; a wage increase; equal division of work; a thirty-hour week during slower times; no discharges; an unemployment fund paid by the bosses and managed by the union; better conditions for younger workers in the trade; pay for legal holidays; no work on legal holidays; no piece work; no section contracting; no speedup system; no sweatshops; no discrimination or blacklist against union members.

The police went into action with a vengeance on the very first day of the strike. This time, the police and the detectives of the Industrial Squad did not merely club and arrest the workers. They blocked the exits of the buildings and did not allow anyone to join the picket line. As Stetsky boasted: "The Police Department also showed its readiness to meet the emergency."

Because of the inadequate preparations for the strike, the majority of the fur workers yielded before the police and gangster terror. Many had not even been contacted before the strike and remained at work in the shops. The tried and true militants answered the strike call and did their utmost to contact and organize others in spite of Gross.

The response to the strike call was poor. But those who did join the picket line gave battle valiantly. For over three weeks, a small group of devoted, class-conscious, militant fur workers battled unprecedented gangster and police terror. They fought back courageously, were arrested and sent to jail. The moment they were released, they would be back on the picket line.

On July 22, its forces inadequate to continue the battle, the General Strike Committee officially called off the strike. Though the strike had to be abandoned, the struggle was by no means over. Gold assured the fur workers: "This strike is one of the stages in the fight of the furriers for union conditions. It is not a fight of a day or a week, but it will continue until the Stetsky company union is wiped off the face of the earth, the sweatshop is destroyed, and every furrier works under union conditions."

The right-wingers were fulsome in their praise of Police Commissioner Grover A. Whalen. Stetsky wrote expressing "deep appreciation of your splendid work." He and his right-wing colleagues, he assured Whalen, "are eternally grateful to you."

"Permit me to mention," Stetsky continued, "the splendid work which has been performed in carrying out your program by Inspector Bolland, Deputy Inspector Walsh and Lieutenant O'Grady of the 30th Street Precinct. These police officers are, in our judgment, a credit to your department. As to yourself, Mr. Commissioner, your name will always be cherished not only by my organization, but by every member in the organization as the one who helped them rid themselves of the irresponsible Communistic elements in the fur industry."

To William Green, Stetsky reported that the determining force in breaking the strike was the fact that "Police Commissioner Whalen assigned 500 uniformed men to the fur district." Again Stetsky announced the end of the Communists in the fur industry. "The American Federation of Labor has attained a glorious triumph in removing, for all time, the communist influence in our trade unions. Our fur workers are eternally grateful to you for your splendid support and cooperation."

Begoon shared Stetsky's opinion. "I think that in New York they [the Communists] are out of the fur industry for good," he wrote on July 12.

A month later, after the strike was called off, Begoon was absolutely certain. "They are no more a factor in the industry."

In the critical period following the unsuccessful strike, the Industrial Union faced a new difficulty. The Lovestoneites centered their main disruptive activity in the new left-wing unions. Seizing upon the failure of the fur strike, for which their own sabotage was mainly responsible, they demanded the instant liquidation of the Industrial Union. In seeking to win the support of the large number of militant fur workers, the Lovestone group did not hesitate to use radical phrases like "fighting the bureaucrats" and "class-struggle unionism." But their deeds soon proved these to be empty words, employed deliberately to confuse the workers and undermine the Industrial Union. It shortly became clear, too, that the Lovestoneites had established connections with the right-wing Joint Council.

Demoralized by the failure of the general strike, weakened by the dissension sowed by the Lovestone clique, the Industrial Union appeared on the verge of collapse in the summer and fall of 1929. Only about six hundred workers paid dues to the Fur Department of the Industrial Union. There was scarcely enough money in the treasury to pay the office rent, to say nothing of officers' salaries. To many observers, it seemed as if the right-wingers were finally justified in claiming that the left wing and the Communists were dead and buried. To many it seemed, too, that the right wing was now firmly entrenched. It had contracts, recognition from the bosses, official standing with the AFL, connections with the police. It had everything—except the workers.

CHAPTER 30

Battle for Spoils

On October 24, 1929, the Wall Street stock market crashed, and with it the entire false structure of so-called prosperity. Investments and savings of thousands of people were wiped out in a single day. Industries cut down their production. With the number of unemployed mounting month by month, millions of families in the richest country of the world were reduced to actual starvation. Ragged apple vendors on every street-corner vainly sought to eke out a few pennies for bread for their families. Soup lines stretched for many blocks. Thousands of the unemployed in every state, evicted from their homes, were forced to build the crudest huts out of refuse timber on vacant city lots. Soon the entire nation was dotted with colonies of these shambles, aptly known as "Hoovervilles."

The extraordinary human misery and suffering caused by the worst economic crisis in American history did not come up for discussion at the Ninth Biennial Convention of the International Fur Workers Union which opened at Montreal on January 13, 1930. One thought alone dominated the right-wing delegates—the supposed death of the left-wing Industrial Union.

AFL and right-wing leaders, as usual, hailed the "successes" achieved during the past year. But privately they admitted that there were no successes to point to. Begoon confessed that he was having difficulty in preparing the report of the General Executive Board "because this report will have to explain why things were not done. It will be more of a negative report than a positive."

The only "success" they could point to was the breaking of the 1929 strike in New York. Priding themselves on their contributions towards this "achievement," Shiplacoff, McGrady, Woll and David Dubinsky assured the right-wingers that they were no longer in need of outside assistance. "I feel that I can safely say that you have reached an absolute state of safety in your work and in your organization," declared Shiplacoff joyfully. The left wing and the Communists were finished. "All that we have to do is to get rid of the bad odor that is left." Dubinsky told the right-wingers, "You have captured the organization for yourself."

The right-wingers now had a free hand. No more worries about exposures of graft and corruption by left-wing leaflets and bulletins, about mass resistance to the gangsters, about demonstrations for an honest, democratic union. The Industrial Union was shattered. It would soon pass out of existence.

After enacting a series of new taxes and assessments on the members, the convention began to wrangle about control of the union. There were two factions in the right-wing camp. One was the Stetsky-"Big Alex" Fried group in the New York Joint Council. The other was the group led by Harry Begoon, the representative of the Socialist Party bureaucrats and the Forward Association. The Stetsky-Fried group now tried to extend its control over the entire International. Hungry for a higher position, Stetsky felt that he was entitled to a handsome reward for his role in breaking the 1929 strike.

Everything seemed to be going smoothly for the Stetsky-Fried faction. For a while, Stetsky ran the convention just as he pleased. One delegate was prompted to propose sarcastically that the next convention "take place in Mr. Chas. Stetsky's apartment, somewhere in the Bronx."

Actually, Stetsky was riding for a fall. Despite his service to the right-wing camp, he was frowned upon by the Socialist Party bureaucracy. Stetsky's intimate connections with the underworld and his well-organized strong-arm squads under the direction of "Big Alex" had been extremely useful to the right wing in the battle to force the fur workers into the Joint Council. However, they were afraid that he would now be difficult to control. They feared Stetsky would use the same methods against any right-wingers who threatened his power. For Stetsky was just as cynical about the Socialist Party leadership as he was about the workers.

The Begoon group, who spoke for the Socialist Party and the Forward Association, therefore brought forward Morris Kaufman as their candidate for International president. Kaufman was not eligible for a union office under the International Constitution since he had not been a worker in the trade and a union member for at least two years. But constitutional provisions were blandly ignored when it came to right-wingers.

In command of the Socialist Party strategy was Joseph Bearak, the Boston lawyer who was closely linked to the Forward Association. While Bearak operated behind the scenes (several delegates signed a petition protesting "most emphatically on the prominent part played by this Boston lawyer at the furriers' Convention"), Abe Cahan himself was brought in to lay down the law to the delegates.

Abe Cahan, editor of the *Forward,* had built up a reputation as one of the most cynical leaders of the Socialist Party. Through the *Forward,* Cahan exerted a powerful influence over the Workmen's Circle, the United Hebrew Trades and the bureaucrats in the needle trades unions. Cahan made it clear to the delegates that the *Forward* and the Socialist Party leaders wanted Kaufman as president. "The *Forward* will be your organ more than ever," he declared, "will help Mr. Kaufman, will help all of you and will help every man that is connected with the organization that we can."

The very same right-wingers who had shrieked to high heaven that Communists in the union were dominated by "outside influences" now proceeded to take Cahan's orders. They elected Kaufman president of the International, constitutional or not.

In closing the convention, Kaufman praised the "wonderful spirit of unity and cooperation" in the right-wing camp and called for setting aside all personal rivalries in the future. "I hope that this is the spirit that will prevail amongst all of us in the time between this convention and the next one," he concluded.

The "unity" achieved among the right-wingers had about as much value as a Confederate dollar. Within two months, warfare broke out in the right-wing camp in every section of the International. In Toronto, a battle raged between the right-wing group led by Harry Markle (who was soon to be convicted of looting the union treasury) and another right-wing group headed by Albert Gilbert. In Chicago, there was a bitter struggle between the right-wing group led by Jack Mouchine (allied to gangsters connected with Al Capone) and the right-wing group headed by Jack Millstein. And in New York, the most important center of the International, a fierce battle was in full swing between the Kaufman-Begoon and Stetsky-Fried factions. All of these inner rivalries in the right-wing camp revolved around greed for position and power in the union.

The International presidency was important to the Kaufman group as the means of gaining control of the New York Joint Council, the major source of the union's income. Although very few workers paid dues to the Joint Council of their own free will, there was a huge potential income to be derived from New York.

No one knew better than the right-wingers themselves that a revolt against the Joint Council was in the making. For all their talk that the left-wing Industrial Union was dead and buried, they knew the furriers hoped to see the left wing back in leadership. After they had broken the 1929 strike, the Stetsky-Fried clique openly conducted the Joint Council as a company union. The agreement was completely forgotten. Wages in the shops were cut to the bone. In most shops the furriers worked sixty, seventy and even eighty hours a week. The speedup system was such that workers produced twice as many garments at half the wages they received in 1926. Overtime without pay became the established practice.

Contracting became so widespread that the Association itself admitted vast numbers of furriers "work under sweatshop conditions in unsanitary basements, behind stores and in their homes. They work nights, Sundays and holidays." Meanwhile thousands of fur workers were unemployed. Even those workers who had fallen prey to the right-wing anti-Communist propaganda were beginning to complain that they had been sold a false bill of goods. This mounting discontent and pressure of the workers was in fact sharpening the split between the Stetsky-Fried and Kaufman-Begoon groups.

To get rid of the Stetsky-Fried gang by calling in the underworld was not a simple matter for Kaufman. Both Stetsky and "Big Alex" Fried were experts in that game. They would not hesitate to use every weapon to hold on to their control.

Kaufman, therefore, chose a different course of action. He assumed the pose of a knight in shining armor who had returned to rescue the poor, exploited furriers and end the terrible conditions in the shops. Kaufman hoped by this means to build a mass following against the Stetsky-Fried gang and kick them out of the leadership, to induce the workers to pay dues (meanwhile accumulating a substantial treasury), and to take the "steam" out of the left wing by giving the workers the impression that he would wage a vigorous campaign against the bosses.

Soon after the International convention, Kaufman opened his attack upon his enemies in the Joint Council. In a surprise "manifesto" to the New York fur workers, he announced a so-called "reform" program. He admitted that the union had failed "to safeguard the interests of the workers," and that there had been a sharp increase in "the evils of corporation [shops] and sweat shops." He attributed all this to "the prolonged period of severe unemployment" and "the interference and tactics of the Communists." All that, however, belonged to the past. Now an opportunity existed "to remedy the situation." Kaufman called on all fur workers to become good-standing members again by wiping out their debts to the union. Through the payment of the sum of $17.25, of which $5 would be an assessment for use of the Joint Council, every fur worker, except those expelled and suspended since 1926, could establish himself as a good-standing member and join in the campaign "to help us build and strengthen the union." If the majority of fur workers would cooperate, Kaufman was "confident that our union will be able to overcome the present difficulties and will in the near future regain the strength and prestige it had enjoyed in former years."

Taken by surprise, the Stetsky-Fried gang at first went along with Kaufman. For a few weeks, there was a good deal of hustle and bustle in the fur market to give the impression that a real campaign was under way to end the evils in the shops. On Saturday morning, February 1, 1930, Kaufman in person led a parade through the fur market as a demonstration against overtime work. The demonstrators assembled in the headquarters of the Joint Council and heard speeches by Kaufman and Stetsky. Committees were sent to various shops to stop overtime work.

After a few such demonstrations, Kaufman announced with a great flourish that the problems of the fur workers were on the way toward solution. "The good old days" were just around the corner. The employers, he cried, were literally trembling as "they saw with their own eyes that the union was coming back and gaining strength."

The "reform" program did not yield a single concrete improvement in the conditions of the fur workers. This did not disturb Kaufman. It was part of his scheme. He blamed the failure of the "reform" program on the Stetsky-Fried gang and insisted that once the leadership of the Joint Council was cleared out, real results would follow.

On March 14, 1930, in a letter to the Joint Council, he declared: "A large number of our members are of the opinion and under the impression that his [Fried's] activities direct or indirect, and his influence in our ranks are harmful to the union. Such impressions and rumors are even widely spread outside the furriers' organization. This has become the talk amongst the ranks of many other labor organizations." In addition, Kaufman noted, Fried was reported to be a contractor for the firm of Feuer and Steinberg.

For years, the left wing had denounced Fried's terroristic activities in the union. But as long as "Big Alex" was useful to the right-wing machine, they had made no objections to his holding a leading position in the union or being a contractor.

Now Kaufman announced that a committee of outstanding Socialist leaders had volunteered to assist in ridding the Joint Council of all undesirable elements. The so-called Committee of the Labor Movement for the Fur Workers Union consisted of Shiplacoff, Feinstone, Judge Jacob Panken, N. Chanin of the Forward Association, and Dr. Louis Hendin, a dentist active in Socialist Party affairs.

While lining up the Socialist leaders against the Stetsky-Fried faction in the forthcoming Joint Council elections, Kaufman was "impatiently waiting for the favorable action of the Forward Association." On March 25, 1930, he wrote to Vladeck: "To you I may say in confidence that our treasury is practically empty and if I don't get money from the *Forward* in a few days I will be stuck. . . ." The Forward Association came through with a loan of $5,000.

Stetsky did not sit by idly. On March 7, 1930, he resigned as first vice-president of the International. "The reasons are well known to you," he wrote angrily to Kaufman. Denouncing Kaufman for "causing such factional dissensions among the members of the Furriers Union," he appealed to Matthew Woll to stop the Kaufmanites from attempting to take over the Joint Council. "The situation," he warned Woll, "is developing to a point of danger to the organization." Stetsky warned Woll that the Industrial Union was distributing leaflets urging the fur workers to "take advantage of the conflict between both treacherous cliques, to destroy the scab agency Joint Council, and build and fortify the Industrial Union!"

After a hurried consultation with Green, Woll informed Kaufman that he was authorized to arrange a conference to end the "unfortunate situation" existing in the relationship between the officers of the International Union and those of the Joint Council. Kaufman was urged to meet with Woll, McGrady and Stetsky at the earliest possible moment.

Kaufman postponed the meeting on the grounds that he had to attend to duties in locals outside of New York. Meanwhile he issued a new blast against the Stetsky-Fried gang in the *Forward*. He called upon the fur workers to elect a Joint Council that would cooperate with the International president in carrying through his "reform" program and in eliminating "those elements whose activity and impulse are harmful to the Union and are demoralizing to its leaders." Stetsky immediately accused Kaufman of deliberately splitting the union in order to gain personal control of the Joint Council.

Infuriated by this turn of events, Matthew Woll reminded both Kaufman and Stetsky that the AFL's supervision of the affairs of the Furriers Union was "still in force." Neither side was to make further statements "until the committee of the American Federation of Labor has had an opportunity of inquiring into the entire situation. . . ." Although Woll's request was sent to both Kaufman and Stetsky, his anger was mainly against Kaufman. "I have talked with Matthew Woll over the telephone," Joseph Bearak informed Kaufman. "Matt Woll is angry not only because you have disappointed him, but because the Committee which you created, known as the Panken Committee, did not have a representative of the AFL on it."

Woll would have liked the Stetsky-Fried gang to remain in power, since it was closer to the AFL bureaucrats than the Socialist Party-Kaufman group, but there was little he could do about it. The more open the battle in the right-wing camp, the greater the danger of a rank-and-file revolt. Woll and McGrady finally informed Kaufman and Stetsky that they would take no part in the Joint Council elections. At the same time, they wrote Kaufman that they "regret exceedingly that the internal misunderstandings between the international officers and the officers of the Joint Council of New York could not have been settled amicably within the organization and that you should have had to appeal to others outside the organization to settle your troubles for you." No threats of expulsion from the AFL here although the right-wingers were working with outside forces!

The propaganda issued by Kaufman's group in the June 1930 Joint Council elections claimed that "we are endeavoring to bring in a new spirit into the union. We believe that the union ought to be a fighting instrument in the hands of the workers. The union must be watchful and fight for the interests of the workers. The union must establish control in the shops in which chaos and demoralization now exist; and must see to it that the workers shall make a living." Once the Stetsky-Fried gang was ousted and a Joint Council pledged to work with Kaufman was elected, the fur workers were assured they would see "something real big . . . a general stoppage in the trade."

But militant phrases borrowed shamelessly from left-wing leaflets did not dispel the feeling of the vast majority of workers that the only issue was who would control the spoils. They refused to have anything to do with the war between the two right-wing groups. With less than a thousand workers taking part in the vote, the Kaufman slate, led by Begoon, Harold Goldstein, Sol Weiner and other right-wingers, was elected to office. "Operators vote approximately four hundred," Kaufman reported to Joseph Bearak. "Cutters three hundred twenty-five. Consider it big vote."

On June 5, 1930, Bearak further advised Kaufman: "I think that as soon as the new Joint Council is installed that you, as General President, ought to arrange a conference with Charlie, Begoon, and four or five others and reach an understanding on the workings of the organization and that it would show Charlie that this is not a question of getting 'even' with anybody or taking revenge. . . . Please let me know how Charlie has taken this."

In no mood to occupy a subordinate position in Kaufman's machine, "Charlie" Stetsky resigned as manager of the Joint Council. Kaufman was distressed. "That in my opinion was a foolish move," he reported to Bearak. "This is exactly what I was fearing all the time. I had seen this coming in the last two or three months. It is only regrettable that Charlie did not understand the situation right along. There is one thing that I told Stetsky and that is, that my intention is not to eliminate him altogether from the organization. I assured him that I will take it upon myself to have the International engage him as soon as possible as an organizer, and that in time there might be a chance for him to work himself in again in the New York situation. Meanwhile, the Joint Council gave him four weeks' salary. I suggested to him to go away for a couple of weeks, and by the time he gets back I will manage to have the Sub-Committee act on his behalf."

Poor Stetsky! He did not "understand" that if the Kaufman group was assured control of the income they had no objection to his remaining on the staff. As soon as he was ready to play ball and obey orders, he could return to the Joint Council as Kaufman's lieutenant.*

* A similar situation was developing at this time in Local 45 of Chicago. In the spring of 1930, Kaufman started a war to oust the Mouchine gang and install his own machine, headed by Shachtman, the former International President. As in New York, Kaufman advanced a "reform" program and accused the Mouchine gang of every crime in the book, from being paid off by non-union employers to stay away from their shops, to pocketing the initiation fees of the workers. With the assistance of the Chicago Federation of Labor, the United Hebrew

Kaufman was out for personal and complete control over the entire Joint Council. A slight hitch developed. A number of right-wingers wanted to elect Harold Goldstein as manager to replace Stetsky. Bearak urged Kaufman to move quickly to prevent this. "You must be particularly careful as to the ambitions of Goldstein," he warned Kaufman. "Whatever you do, watch your step that Goldstein does not become manager of the Joint Council. I am afraid that the day he steps in there will be started the beginning of a disruption of the organization."

Kaufman assured Bearak that the matter had been properly handled. "In order to offset this," he wrote, "Begoon prevailed upon the 'crowd' that they should eliminate the question of managership for at least six months by asking the president to supervise New York for that period." The fur workers themselves, it is worth noting, had no part in this decision. Kaufman assumed the "heavy burden" because the organization had appealed to him "to help them extricate themselves from the grave situation," as he put it. Actually he initiated the proposal himself and had it seconded by his own henchmen.

Kaufman's scheming was fully revealed in a letter sent him by Stetsky. Pointing out that the decision to make Kaufman supervisor of the Joint Council had been decided upon at "many secret caucuses which you held months prior to the election of local officers of the New York locals," Stetsky wrote, "I admit I was much amused with the earnestness of your tone and particularly by the heartrending appeal made to you by the New York organization to come to their rescue and save them from their miserable plight, as you state. . . . It is indeed tragic as well as comical."

Trades and the Forward Association of Chicago, Kaufman succeeded in defeating the Mouchine gang. Once Kaufman was in control of the local, the cliques got together. Kaufman assured the Mouchine gang that he was "not interested in any act of revenge," and that if they would play ball with his people, all would be forgiven.

The Mouchine gang accepted Kaufman's peace offer, agreed to serve as lieutenants in his machine, and to obey orders handed down by Shachtman. "I am satisfied to hear that Mouchine and his group are finally coming to terms," Kaufman wrote to Shachtman on July 16, 1930. ". . . I will have no objection . . . that no further claims be made on him as far as the accounting of money is concerned. Some definite understanding should be reached so that the records of the local will contain something to that effect. If the matters are straightened out, a representative of the Chicago Federation of Labor should be called in as a signatory to the agreement, so that Mouchine and his followers will respect the adjustment that will be in effect."

Once Kaufman had control of the Joint Council, the so-called reform program was scuttled. Forgotten were the highly-publicized demonstrations against overtime. On the contrary, several workers offered proof that Kaufman gave Dr. Paul Abelson, the impartial chairman, "full power to grant overtime permits to all members of the Associated and Fur Trimming Association." Forgotten were the July raises the workers were supposed to receive. Forgotten, too, were the pledges to enforce the union agreement, rid the trade of sweatshop conditions, wipe out contracting, and provide for the needs of the unemployed. Instead, the boses enjoyed a Roman holiday, slashing wages whenever they felt like it, dismissing workers in the middle of the week or in the middle of the day, handing out garments to contractors where workers toiled sixty hours a week and earned starvation wages while thousands of unemployed furriers starved. Kaufman himself privately admitted that most of the work in the industry was being done in "hundreds of small contractors, sub-manufacturers and corporation shops," and that the union had "no way to combat these small shops."

Kaufman and his henchmen now attributed their failures to lack of funds. "Without funds, organization work cannot even be begun," the Kaufmanites cried. In October 1930, over the opposition of many workers, Kaufman rammed through a proposal to raise the dues from thirty cents to forty cents a week. Kaufman railed at any opposition to the dues increases, charging that "the Communists, their souls rest in peace, had set the fashion to attack the officers for propaganda purposes." The opponents of higher dues, he complained, had "fussed and fumed about it as though it were a question of $10,000."

In November of the same year, the *American Federationist*, official organ of the AFL, published an article by A. Rosebury, Kaufman's right-hand man, entitled "Model Collective Bargaining in the Fur Industry." According to Rosebury, the fur workers were living in a blissful paradise. Relations between the employers and the workers in the fur industry had reached such a stage of "perfect equality" that the union was able to solve every problem facing the furriers "by sheer moral force." In the entire article not one word was said about unemployment, sweatshop conditions, speedup in the shops, inhumanly long hours and miserably low wages.

Describing conferences between "influential employers and leaders of labor" in the fur industry, Rosebury noted: "It would be difficult to distinguish these representatives in session, bargaining for conditions and discussing terms, from a board of directors deliberating on affairs of common interest."

Thus, proudly, Rosebury hailed the "common interests" of Kaufman, Stetsky and the other right-wingers with the employers. Certainly they acted more like members of the Board of Directors of a financial corporation than labor leaders. They called themselves "economic statesmen of the labor movement." "Militant tactics" were outdated since "the spirit of conflict prevents clear thinking and retards progress." And while they discussed "affairs of common interest" with the employers, the workers they were supposed to represent slaved under sweatshop conditions or stood gaunt-faced and hungry in the fur market praying for jobs.

It was no wonder that the fur workers were so bitter over Kaufman's action in raising the dues. They had not the slightest confidence in the right wing's sincerity.

When Kaufman first announced his "reform" program, some workers, in their desperation, believed him. Afterwards they learned from bitter experience that they had simply been used as tools in the battle between rival groups, each serving its own interests and the interests of the bosses. It was a costly experience for these fur workers, although perhaps a necessary process of education. Nothing the left wing said in leaflets and bulletins so effectively exposed the selfishness and corruption of the right-wing groups, their indifference to the plight of the workers, as did this sordid battle for spoils. The accumulating evidence reminded the furriers that they could place no faith in a union leadership which was maintained only with the connivance of the bosses.

The events of 1930 destroyed any lingering illusions about the role of the right-wing leadership. The events of the next year proved to the furriers that only the Industrial Union, with its progressive policies and leadership, could be depended upon.

Break-up of Sacco-Vanzetti protest meeting following refusal by Socialist leaders on platform to allow Ben Gold to speak.

N. Y. Daily News Photo

Pickets arrested during the 1929 fur strike being herded into court.

Ben Gold on the shoulders of workers who demanded he be allowed to address the Sacco-Vanzetti meeting. He was brutally attacked by the Socialist leaders in charge of the rally as the crowd tried to get him onto the platform.

SACCO VANZETTI MUST BE SAVED FOR THE

CHAPTER 31

The First Offensive

As the economic crisis deepened throughout the land, poverty and destitution gripped the mass of toilers everywhere. By the end of 1930 fully half of all industrial workers in the United States were out of work. The rest suffered wage cuts of 20 to 50 percent. Between January and March 1930, demonstrations involving hundreds of thousands of unemployed took place in many cities.

The AFL Executive Council was deaf and blind to the needs of the unemployed. Speaking through the die-hard red-baiter, Matthew Woll, the AFL declared: "Behind the demonstrations are paid propagandists and agitators taking their orders from Moscow and acting in accordance with a plan aiming at fanning the fires of social conflict, sowing hatred and promoting the communist will-of-the-wisp called 'world revolution.'"

It was not until May 31, 1931, that William Green even recognized that there was an unemployment problem. Only then did he come forward with vague proposals for a shorter work day and work week, higher incomes, federal employment agencies, and vocational guidance service. The AFL leaders, however, said nothing about resisting the merciless wage-cutting that was taking place all over the country. And they vehemently denounced compulsory unemployment insurance for workers. Charging that it was the forerunner of the "dole," they warned employers not to be stampeded into support of the principle. John Edgarton, president of the National Association of Manufacturers, and Ralph Easley, reactionary president of the National Civic Federation, took exactly the

341

same position on this question. Once more the AFL "leaders" of labor saw eye-to-eye with "capital."

To cover up its own indifference to the plight of the workers, and to silence all opposition, the leadership of the AFL suddenly discovered a new cause for the depression—"Soviet dumping." Uniting with Hamilton Fish, one of the most reactionary leaders of the Republican Party, Matthew Woll started a campaign to forbid imports from the Soviet Union. Although the total imports involved were so negligible as to be of no economic significance whatsoever, this was Woll's "contribution" toward solving the economic crisis. The right-wing Socialists in the Furriers Union joined eagerly in the Woll-Fish anti-Soviet campaign. At a meeting in Carnegie Hall in February 1931, Kaufman congratulated Fish and Woll for having initiated the boycott of products from the Soviet Union. The success of the campaign, declared Kaufman, would solve the unemployment problem among fur workers. Seated with Kaufman on the platform, in addition to Fish and Woll, were representatives of the American Legion, American Vigilantes Alliance, American Patriotic Society, National Patriotic Council and other organizations notorious for opposing trade unions and foreign-born workers. Only Captain Matsuda of the Imperial Japanese Navy was needed to complete the picture.

The Socialist Party leaders were not far behind the AFL. As the soup lines grew longer and millions of unemployed warmed their hands over bonfires in city dumps, the Socialists had to make some pretense of action. They called a "Socialist Emergency Conference on Unemployment" headed by Shiplacoff and Feinstone. The latter two were among the most active participants in the AFL conspiracy against the fur workers. The "Emergency Conference," as was to be expected, turned out to be a fruitless gesture.

Morris Hillquit, who was both a wealthy corporation lawyer and a leader of the Socialist Party, later confided to Kaufman that "with the tide of unemployment still rising and the misery of the workers growing daily, some concerted and effective action must be speedily organized by the Socialist and Labor movement unless we are prepared to abandon the field to the spectacular and futile Communist campaigns."

The only real resistance of the workers against destitution, starvation and wage-cutting in this period of crisis, was that organized and led by the newly-organized industrial unions and by militants in the Communist Party. The onset of the industrial crisis came as no surprise to left-wing trade unionists and Communists. As early as July 1923,

William Z. Foster wrote in the *Labor Herald,* official organ of the Trade Union Educational League: "If Labor neglects this splendid chance to organize the unorganized, it will pay dearly for it in the near future. Our prevailing prosperity is only a passing thing. It cannot last long. A year or two at the utmost is its limit. Then, as sure as fate, will come one of the worst periods of depression that this or any country has ever seen. All signs are pointing that way. And when the inevitable industrial breakdown comes, woe betide Labor if it has not had the intelligence and initiative to strengthen its lines by organizing the unorganized."

Although efforts to prepare the workers for the inevitable crisis were sabotaged by the Lovestone group with its theory of "American exceptionalism" and "unending prosperity," the Communists and the left-wingers swung into action soon after the stock market crash. United in the Trade Union Unity League, the successor to the Trade Union Educational League, the new industrial unions undertook to mobilize the workers against starvation.* They conducted strikes and mass campaigns for unemployment insurance and relief, in sharp contrast to the shameful do-nothing policies of the AFL and Socialist leadership. At the same time the fur workers in the Needle Trades Workers Industrial Union launched an offensive against the employers during the summer and fall of 1931.

The Industrial Union had suffered defeat in the 1929 strike and lost a large part of its membership. At its second convention in August 1930, the Lovestoneites proposed that the Industrial Union should be liquidated and that the workers in the needle trades should return to the right-wing unions.

Leading the struggle against the Lovestoneites, Ben Gold showed that their policy led inevitably to the abandonment of all struggle in the interests of the workers. The idea of conducting a struggle inside the right-wing unions was indeed very important to the extent that such a struggle could in fact be carried on. But simply to liquidate the Industrial Union would actually play into the hands of the bosses and their corrupt allies. Without the Industrial Union to lead the fight for better conditions in the shops, the workers would be exposed to even more merciless exploitation.

* The Trade Union Educational League was reorganized into the Trade Union Unity League at a convention held in Cleveland September 1, 1929, which was attended by 690 delegates representing seventy thousand organized workers, some of them already representing new industrial unions, and others opposition groups in the AFL and Railroad Brotherhood.

The Lovestoneites were overwhelmingly defeated. Only seven votes were cast in favor of liquidating the Industrial Union, and the Lovestone-ites were removed from important positions.

Among the fur workers, the results of the Industrial Union's convention were immediately felt. The furriers began to break through the bonds of the Joint Council. Instead of staying away when the right-wingers called meetings and forums, the workers came to demonstrate their opposition to the corrupt leadership. When strong-arm squads could not quell the outbursts of the workers, the frightened right-wingers halted the meetings. "The bad feature about the open forum," a Joint Council announcement cancelling all forums declared, "is that the majority of those who participate in the discussion do not keep to the subject. Some of those who speak make campaign speeches and attempt to discredit the work of the present administration."

Prevented from expressing their opposition at the Joint Council forums, the fur workers rallied to meetings called by the Industrial Union. Demonstrations of rank and file, climaxed by a mass meeting in Irving Plaza on March 10, 1931, were attended both by Industrial Union members and those who had been forced to register with the Joint Council.

The mass of furriers was beginning to revolt against the AFL bureau-crats. In the shops and the market, the workers kept repeating: "If only Gold were here, we would show the bosses and their stooges."

In September 1930, Gold had taken a leave of absence from the Indus-trial Union to survey labor conditions in various European countries. He particularly studied the conditions of the workers in Germany, then under a Social-Democratic government, and in the Soviet Union. Through correspondence with his close friends and associates in the Industrial Union, he remained in close touch with developments in the fur market. In April 1931, while still abroad, Gold received a letter from Jack Schneider, now manager of the Fur Department of the Industrial Union. Schneider reported a meeting he had with committees of fur workers who were members of the right-wing union. "Write to Gold," the commit-tees had implored Schneider, "urge him to return immediately. Tell him the workers are ready to start."

"Tell the workers," Gold immediately replied, "that I will return in a short time. Tell them, too, that their hardships will make all the more sweet the coming victory."

During the week of June 14, 1931, a series of unforgettable scenes took place in the fur market. Gold was back! As he walked along Seventh Avenue, spontaneous demonstrations broke loose. Even the police, sensing the power of the fur workers as they greeted their leader, abandoned their attempts to prevent the open-air meetings organized to welcome Gold home.

On June 17, 1931, thirty-five hundred workers crowded into the Central Opera House to hear Gold report on his experiences in Europe. After describing the unemployment and misery he had witnessed in Germany, he told of his visits to factories and farms in the Soviet Union.

"Today," he concluded this part of his report, "the old capitalist system is in an ever-deepening crisis, with ten million unemployed and their families in the richest country in the world, facing starvation; today, the capitalist system is helpless to solve the problem of the crisis—but there is no unemployment in the Soviet Union. Workers and peasants in that country are disproving every prediction of capitalist economists who sneered at their attempt to build Socialism."

Gold devoted the rest of his report to mobilizing the fur workers for the struggle for better conditions. He rejected the claim of the right-wing leaders that the crisis was mainly responsible for the terrible conditions in the fur shops. He insisted that these conditions would not have become so unbearable had it not been for the betrayals of these same leaders. In like manner, he denounced the argument of the AFL bureaucrats that it was impossible to obtain higher wages and better conditions in times of economic crisis. "This is a bosses' theory," he cried, "which the agents of the bosses use in order to beat the workers into submission, into forcing them to accept hunger wages and conditions of slavery."

Actually, Gold insisted, the objective conditions were ripe for a mass movement to wipe out many evils in the trade and establish union conditions. The workers now knew that the Joint Council was a company union supported by the bosses. Even staunch AFL supporters were discontent. Right-wing and left-wing workers alike suffered from horrible conditions in the shops and from unemployment.

The bosses themselves, Gold further pointed out, were weaker than before. Many were bankrupt. Others were owned outright by bankers, factors and rich building owners. The Association was weak. The large coat manufacturers and the small trimming manufacturers were again split. While they would unite against the workers in the event of a mass struggle, it was nevertheless possible to derive much advantage for the workers from the rivalry of these two employer groups.

Finally, Gold emphasized, the left-wingers had defeated the agitation of the Lovestoneites for the liquidation of the Industrial Union. This strengthened the workers and made possible a successful mass struggle for better living conditions.

Gold did not minimize the difficulties involved. The terrorization by the bosses, the AFL and right-wing leaders, with their new partners, the Lovestoneites, would be intensified the moment the furriers took the offensive. The police and the underworld would again be brought in. Workers would again be slashed and clubbed. Hundreds would be sent to jail.

In order to overcome these difficulties, Gold declared, the Industrial Union must develop a united front of the workers, regardless of political affiliations. Past differences among the workers must be dropped. All workers must be invited to participate in the struggle. They were not to be questioned whether they wanted to be in the right-wing union or in the Industrial Union. The only question was to unite the workers in the struggle to secure human conditions in the shops.

This united front mass movement, under the leadership of a large representation of the rank and file, supported by the Industrial Union, would assure victory. Mass activity, mass picketing, mass defense would overcome every obstacle the bosses and their agents would place in their path—the gangsters would be driven out of the market and police interference would prove futile.

Gold's penetrating analysis aroused the fur workers to the highest pitch of enthusiasm. The entire audience leaped to its feet and cheered him for ten solid minutes. The fur workers endorsed the united front policy. They empowered Gold and Jack Schneider to organize a conference of delegates from the shops and from the ranks of the unemployed—the rank-and-file body that would lead the struggle.

Together with this rank-and-file shop delegate committee, Gold worked out the strategy for the offensive. The dog-skin trimming shops were chosen for the first big blow. The workers in these shops were the most militant group of union members. Organized by the left-wing leadership in 1925, they had received one wage increase after another. By the end of 1926, dog-skin cutters and operators were earning from $80 to $100 a week and more. The dog-skin workers had fought bitterly against the AFL "reorganization." They were among the last to register under compulsion with the right-wing Joint Council, and never paid dues there.

With the "reorganization," their wages were cut to the bone. Speedup and contracting tore down conditions to the point where cutters earned only $50 a week and operators only $40. Nailers earned even less. Negro workers, militant union members, received much lower pay for the same work. The bosses openly discriminated against them, while the right-wing leaders remained totally indifferent.

A joint committee of the Industrial Union and the shop chairmen of the dog-skin shops prepared for the strike. At the same time, a special "July increase" committee was organized in many of the coat manufacturing shops. They began to agitate, organize and unite the workers to fight for July raises. The foundation was carefully laid; this time there would be no dependence on spontaneous outbursts of the workers to conduct the struggle.

On June 25, 1931, Samuel N. Samuels, executive director of the Associated Fur Coat and Trimming Manufacturers, announced that the employers had decided not to grant July raises. There was no point even to discussing the matter, Samuels declared brusquely. The issue was closed!

Three days later the offensive began with a call to action, signed by Gold, addressed to all fur workers, employed and unemployed: "Attack! Go forward! There is no stepping backwards! To the struggle! Hardships? Of course. But we will overcome them. Let the bosses hire the whole New York underworld. Let them hire all professional scabs who are found in the fur industry. Let them mobilize all politicians, the police department. Let them begin anew their frame-ups and their base provocation and savage persecution against the workers—their devilish plans of enslaving and starving the workers will not be realized. . . The picket line will give the bosses their proper answer."

The shop of Prince Brothers & Shapiro, 345 Seventh Avenue, started the ball rolling the very next day with a strike for a July increase. Almost overnight more than a hundred shops walked out. The headquarters of the Industrial Union became a beehive of activity. Every hour Jack Schneider and other left-wing leaders walked into the building with new groups of strikers following them. From seven in the morning until late at night, all rooms were occupied with shop meetings, chairmen's meetings, committee meetings. The Industrial Union assisted all workers whether they were members of the left-wing organization or not. They were not required to join, yet by July 14 one thousand furriers had taken out books in the Industrial Union.

After the most thorough preparations, the dog-skin workers struck on July 9. In addition to a wage increase, they demanded full responsibility of the manufacturers for their contractors; union conditions and union control in every dog-skin shop; and equal wages and union conditions for Negro and white workers.

Ninety-six dog-skin shops went out on the first day of the strike. The next day, one hundred and forty shops were out. Altogether they involved eight hundred workers. The employers themselves admitted the strike was 95 percent effective in the dog-skin trade.

The picket lines of the dog-skin strikers were an inspiring sight. "Revive the spirit of 1926," these militant workers shouted as they marched through the streets of the fur market, Negro and white, fighting side by side in complete unity. Furriers from the coat manufacturing shops came down to join the picket lines in increasing numbers. The dog-skin workers infused the struggle with so militant a spirit that in one swoop the majority of the furriers overcame all hesitation and fear. Once again they marched in mass picket demonstrations. On the second day of the dog-skin strike, four thousand fur workers jammed 29th Street between Seventh and Eighth Avenues. The police had to close the street to traffic.

The strikes crashed like thunder over the heads of the right-wing leaders of the Joint Council, heralding the revolt of the workers after four years of terror, exploitation, and hunger.

At first, Kaufman and Stetsky thought that they might stem the rising tide by "demanding" July raises themselves. They announced in the press that they were asking the bosses for a 25 percent wage increase. But early in July, *Women's Wear* reported that a conference between the right-wing leaders and the bosses had resulted in the "withdrawal of demands" for July raises and had "cleared up" the fears entertained by some employers.

The right-wingers now mobilized to meet the new crisis. Squads of goons invaded the fur market. Conferences were held with Matthew Woll and Edward F. McGrady. Letters to Police Commissioner Mulrooney again appealed for immediate aid "to please nip this Communist move in the bud." Names and addresses of the strikers were obtained from the employers. The Joint Council telegraphed these workers at home: "If you fail to return within twenty-four hours, your stoppage will then be not for an increase, but for political reasons, and the Union will be obliged to place union men in the shop that don't play Communist politics."

Matthew Woll publicly denounced the strikes as a "conspiracy on the part of Soviet Russia to destroy the fur industry in the United States." He urged the fur workers "not to be misled by any new policy or honeyed words advanced by Gold and his hirelings." Police Commissioner Mulrooney assigned one hundred extra policemen to the fur market.

POLICE DEPARTMENT
CITY OF NEW YORK

July 25, 1931.

Mr. Morris Kaufman,
General President-Secretary,
Fur Workers' Union,
9 Jackson Avenue,
Long Island City.

Dear Sir:

      The Police Commissioner directs me to acknowledge receipt of your communication of July 22nd, 1931.

      The Commissioner is glad to know of the cooperation you are receiving from Sergeant Pike and his men, and will be pleased to bring your letter to the attention of his Commanding Officer.

Very truly yours,

N. V. Neary.
Secretary
to Police Comm'r.

Mulrooney's secretary acknowledges Kaufman's letter of gratitude for police assistance in battling the striking furriers.

The old pattern of strikebreaking was all there. But this time, the furriers refused to be divided. Right-wing and left-wing workers in the shops united against the common enemy. The committees of unemployed workers worked hand in hand with the strikers. Negro and white workers were united against the enemy, with Negro workers represented on the organization, strike and shop committees.

The strikers and the unemployed picketed together. Together they chased the underworld agents from the market. As soon as the strong-arm boys were seen in the fur market, the word "gangsters" spread like fire among the strikers. In a flash, the gangsters were encircled and disarmed. Battered and bleeding, they fled from the market in wild panic.

Mass defense, which foiled the gangsters, also rendered the police powerless. Many a cop had to release his intended victim when he found himself encircled by a crowd of angry pickets. Only a large guard of policemen, including mounted police, enabled them to make any arrests.

On July 20, 1931, McGrady secretly informed William Green that despite everything done to crush it, the strike movement was developing and spreading. "This is made possible," he continued, "because the workers willingly go out with them, hoping that the Communists will get them increases in wages." (On the very same day, Kaufman claimed that the only reason so many fur workers were on strike was "because of fear of Communist methods.")

The remainder of McGrady's private letter to William Green is difficult to match. McGrady wrote:

"Vice-President Woll and I had a conference with Police Commissioner Mulrooney. He also had his official staff at the conference. We suggested:

"First. That he place more detectives in the fur market and assign extra men to watch the headquarters of the fur workers, and when the strike committee of the Communists would leave the headquarters the detectives should follow them in order that they might protect the workers when the committee entered that shop;

"Second. That they prohibit the noon-day open air meetings;

"Third. That they stop the distribution of circulars in the market. . . .

"I went into the fur market two mornings from 7 to 8:30 A.M., and again from 12 to 1:30 P.M., and in the evening. I talked with hundreds of workers and listened to their complaints. There is no question about the unrest.

"On July 14th ten of the strike committee of the Communists were arrested when they entered a shop to drive out our workers. These men were find $10.00 or three days in jail. They all accepted the imprisonment.

"On Thursday July 16th, ten more of their committee were caught. When they went before the Magistrate, the Magistrate released them all, so that it will be necessary for us to call attention of the Chief Magistrate to the situation, urging him to inform the other Magistrates as to what should be done to meet the situation. There is no use in having arrests if the courts are to free them afterward. . . ."

AMERICAN FEDERATION OF LABOR

A. F. OF L. BUILDING

Washington, D. C., July 20, 1931

Mr. William Green, President,
American Federation of Labor

Vice-President Woll and I had a conference with Police
Commissioner Mulrooney. He also had his official staff at the
conference. We suggested:

First. That he place more detectives in the fur market
and assign extra men to watch the headquarters of the fur workers,
and when the strike committee of the Communists would leave the
headquarters the detectives should follow them in order that they
might protect the workers when the committee entered that shop;

Second. That they prohibit the noon-day open air meetings;

Third. That they stop the distribution of circulars in
the market.

The Police Commissioner said he allowed the street meetings with the understanding that these meetings did not obstruct
the traffic. We pointed out to the Police Commissioner that the
policemen on duty diverted the traffic so that the Communists'
meeting should go on without disturbance. The Commissioner replied that traffic was not to be diverted, and if the meetings
did interfere with traffic the meetings were to be stopped. If
there was no interference with traffic, he thought he would allow
the meetings to go on.

On my request that the distribution of circulars be
stopped, the Police Commissioner said it was no violation of the
law to distribute circulars, but if any one receiving a circular
throws it in the street he would be subject to arrest, but the
man who gave out the circulars was immune.

On the question of assigning more detectives in the market
he agreed to do this, although at the present time he was handicapped
because many of his men were on vacations.

I went into the fur market two mornings from 7 to 8:30
a.m., and again from 12 to 1:30 p.m., and in the evening. I talked
with hundreds of workers and listened to their complaints. There is
no question about the unrest.

On July 14th ten of the strike committee of the Communists
were arrested when they entered a shop to drive out our workers.
These men were fined $10.00 or three days in jail. They all accepted
the imprisonment.

On Thursday July 16th, ten more of their committee were
caught. When they went before the Magistrate the Magistrate released them all, so that it will be necessary for us to call attention of the Chief Magistrate to the situation, urging him to inform
the other Magistrates as to what should be done to meet the situation. There is no use in having arrests if the courts are to free
them afterward.

Yours fraternally,

Edw. F. McGrady

One of the most damning documents in American labor history.

McGrady and Woll were at it again. And William Green, the President of the AFL, to whom this report was sent, was not at all shocked. Not for a moment did he falter in his eloquent speeches about "democracy" and "principles of trade unionism."

At the very time McGrady was sending his report to Green, many of the strikers had already won wage raises of from $5 to $15 a week. The dog-skin workers secured even greater increases and recognition by the employers. All told, the shop strikes won increased wages amounting to $20,000 weekly for three thousand fur workers, an average of $7 a week. The Dog Skin Workers Rank-and-File Strike Committee issued a public challenge to Woll, McGrady, Kaufman, Stetsky and other leaders of the Joint Council: "We are ready to prove publicly to all fur workers, that we won wage increases of $15, $20 and even $30 for the dog-skin workers as a result of the strike." The challenge went unanswered.

The right-wingers saw their house collapsing. Their efforts to break the strike were failing. Shop after shop went out and won increases. More and more workers were joining the Industrial Union. In desperation, the right-wingers conceived a new strategy. On July 16, even as the AFL leaders were moving heaven and earth for police and court action against the strikers, Stetsky issued a "Declaration" of "unity." The condition for unity, declared the "Declaration," was that the left-wingers must abandon the Industrial Union!

That the true purpose of this "Declaration" was to get the workers to abandon the struggle for increases and improved conditions is fully borne out in the hitherto unpublished secret minutes of the Joint Council. At the very meetings where the decision was reached to issue the "Declaration," the leading right-wingers explained that they were not in the least interested in achieving "unity with Communists." The whole idea of the "unity" proposal was "for the purpose of tearing off the mask under which the Communists are trying to mislead the fur workers." Once the left-wing offensive was halted by the discussions of the "unity" question, everything would again be under control.

An especially demagogic role in this fake unity maneuver was that of the Lovestoneites, still operating as a group within the Industrial Union. The "unity" proposal of the Joint Council was used by the Lovestoneite group to try to disrupt the continuing offensive of the Industrial Union. At a conference of shop delegates to discuss broadening the strike movement for wage raises, B. Baraz and I. Shapiro, leaders of the Lovestoneite group, insisted that it was useless to continue the struggle until everything had been done "to unify the ranks of the fur workers by establishing one union in the trade."

Gold quickly exposed this attempt to scuttle the developing offensive against the bosses. "To give up the Industrial Union," Gold emphasized, "means to give up shop strikes, the campaign for higher wages, the struggle against the speedup system, the struggle against contracting. It means giving up the struggle to defend the interests of the workers."

The idea of "one union," Gold declared, was an excellent one. The left wing had been the first to raise the slogan. But was there a single worker, Gold asked, who was naive enough to believe that the "one union" advocated by the right-wingers was the type of "one union" the workers had in mind? Gold charged that the Lovestoneites covered up their real designs with all sorts of militant phrases "so that the workers will not openly see their treachery. Their slogans sound very innocent; but when you scratch a Lovestoneite, you find an agent of Matthew Woll, Stetsky, Kaufman, the same sort of misleaders parading in a different guise."

Gold's conclusion was to prove prophetic. Defeated in their proposal to liquidate the Industrial Union, the Lovestoneites decided to work openly with the right-wingers "to build one union in the fur industry." At a secret conference at the Social-Democratic Rand School on July 30, 1931, the right-wingers and the Lovestoneites agreed that their primary concern in the "unity" move was to find "ways and means regarding the extermination of the Communists from the Furriers Union." Publicly these two groups were proclaiming their great desire for unity in the Furriers Union. But secretly, both groups admitted that their real aim was to continue the same policies that had brought so much misery to the mass of the fur workers.

At the first "unity" conference on September 8, 1931, the Industrial Union was not represented. But the views of the fur workers who were actively engaged in struggles for better conditions were put forward by the representatives of the Rank-and-File Opposition Group in the AFL Joint Council.* They demanded, first of all, that a chairman be elected instead of being appointed as the right-wingers proposed.

---

* Seven groups were present at the conference which took place at the Governor Clinton Hotel: the sub-committee of the Joint Council, the sub-committee of the International Executive Board, the so-called Committee of the Labor Movement, the "Progressive Bloc" (Sorkin-Winnick group), the "Progressive League" (Lovestoneite group), United Registered Furriers (Schlissel group), and the Rank and File Opposition in the Joint Council.

Secondly, they insisted that Socialist Party leaders Vladeck, Feinstone, Shiplacoff and other members of the so-called "Committee of the Labor Movement," a body completely outside the union, be forced to leave the conference on the ground that they spoke for no one but themselves. They were successful on both demands. Louis Cohen, a shop worker and leader of the Rank-and-File Opposition Group, was elected chairman of the conference, and the representatives of the "Committee of the Labor Movement" were forced to withdraw.

The Rank-and-File Opposition Group emphasized that the Industrial Union was the main factor in the industry. Any talk of unity without the left-wing organization was fraudulent. After a hurried discussion, the various right-wing groups and the Lovestoneites agreed to invite the Industrial Union to the next conference, confident that the left-wing union would not accept the invitation. The Rank-and-File Opposition signed the invitation which asked the Fur Department of the Needle Trades Workers Industrial Union, as "an important factor in the fur trade," to elect five delegates to the next "unity" conference.

The Industrial Union responded immediately. At a special mass meeting in Cooper Union on September 17, attended by thousands of fur workers, the Industrial Union proposed that the invitation to the "unity" conference be accepted on the following terms: (1) the conference to be an open one—all furriers to be admitted; (2) complete unity among the fur workers, left-wingers and right-wingers, employed and unemployed, on a program of struggle for union conditions to be proclaimed immediately; (3) all discrimination against workers for their political beliefs to cease immediately; (4) every fur worker, left-winger or right-winger, registered or non-registered, should have the right to work in every shop where he could secure employment, regardless of whether it was a Joint Council or Industrial Union shop.

As soon as unity was proclaimed, shop struggles should be launched to secure the following conditions: (1) the 40-hour week; (2) wage increases, time-and-a-half for overtime, pay for legal holidays; (3) abolition of piece work, sub-contracting, and speedup; (4) limitation of overtime during periods of unemployment and jobs for the unemployed; (5) no discrimination against Negro workers; (6) no discrimination against active members; (7) no interference by the bosses in union affairs; (8) no dues to be collected by the bosses; (9) no committees to stop workers from shops so as to force them to pay dues or taxes; (10) abolition of all hired professional gangsters who are used to terrorize the fur workers; (11) no police or detectives to be used against the workers; (12) no workers to be thrown out of the shops, and (13) strict enforcement of all other union conditions won by the furriers in 1926.

The Industrial Union further proposed that a committee of fifty active shop workers be elected, twenty-five by the membership of the Joint Council and twenty-five by the membership of the Industrial Union. This committee would immediately initiate the shop strikes for better conditions. The workers in every shop were to elect unity committees who, together with the rank-and-file committee of fifty, would carry on the struggles. Finally, a broad conference of elected unity shop committees would be called to discuss the question of one union led, administered and controlled by the workers in the shops. This would be unity achieved "from below," by the workers themselves and not just a paper unity proclaimed by a few top leaders.

The program of the Industrial Union was unanimously adopted by the Cooper Union mass meeting. A committee of fifty was elected to attend the "unity" conference. Gold cautioned the workers, however, not to place too much hope in the conference. The Joint Council leaders, he predicted, would fight tooth and nail against the Industrial Union's proposal simply because it was based on a rank-and-file struggle for better conditions in the shops. Their aim was to divert the workers from the struggle, not to further it.

Gold's prediction was all too rapidly fulfilled. The right-wingers engaged a small room in the Imperial Hotel for the "unity" conference. When the fifty delegates of the Industrial Union arrived, the room was so crowded that it was impossible to open the meeting. The hotel management called the police to maintain order. The workers insisted so strongly that the Industrial Union's proposal for an open conference be accepted that the right-wing leaders of the Joint Council were forced to agree. It was overwhelmingly voted that the next conference should be held in a large hall and all furriers should be allowed to attend.

The right-wingers promptly ignored this vote and called another conference in a small room in Irving Plaza, a room which could hold about thirty people. The leaders of the Joint Council also had police on hand to bar the workers from attending the conference. Gold pointed out to Stetsky that five hundred furriers had come to the conference and were waiting in the street to be allowed to enter. The right-wing leader cynically replied, "Let them remain outside." Gold proposed that the conference be transferred to the large auditorium in Webster Hall. This was flatly rejected. There was no need for discussion, he was told. Everything was already decided.

The following morning, the fur workers in the market were informed by leaflets of what had transpired at Irving Plaza. "The Sub-Committee of the Joint Council does not dare to continue its maneuvers when the fur workers are present," the Industrial Union declared. "Their plan is to make deals behind closed doors." The "deals" of right-wingers and the Lovestoneites, however, would have no meaning. The fur workers would pay no attention to them.

Reluctantly, the leaders of the Joint Council announced that the first open mass "unity" conference would be held on October 1 at Webster Hall. At the same time, they issued a leaflet outlining their program. It did not contain a single word about struggles against the bosses. It emphasized that the Industrial Union must be liquidated and that the "one union" must be organized under the banner of the AFL.

Two thousand furriers assembled at the Webster Hall conference and roared their approval of the Industrial Union's unity program. Stetsky and the right-wing groups, supported by the Lovestoneites, remained adamantly opposed. For hours the discussion continued on the Industrial Union's program as adopted at the Cooper Union mass meeting. To all proposals, the Stetsky group and the Lovestoneites had only one answer. They insisted on an immediate referendum among the fur workers to determine what sort of union they wanted—the AFL Joint Council or the Industrial Union. Stetsky demanded that Gold agree in writing that the furriers' section of the Industrial Union would be liquidated in the event the vote went in favor of the AFL Joint Council.

Aside from seriously interfering with dozens of shops strikes being conducted at that time by the Industrial Union, which was the right-wing's primary aim, the right-wing leaders and the Lovestoneites believed that the "referendum" proposal would enable them to label Gold a "tool" of the Communist Party. Without even permitting him an opportunity to place the question before the membership of the Industrial Union, they demanded that Gold agree to give up the Industrial Union if the vote was in favor of the AFL Joint Council.

Gold's reply completely exposed the trickery of the right-wing leaders and their Lovestoneite allies. He turned the tables. In the presence of the two thousand furriers and the representatives of the press, he declared that the Industrial Union would accept and carry through the decision of a referendum conducted by a committee elected by the workers in the shops. But he placed two conditions: first, the Industrial Union would not give up its offensive against the bosses while the referendum was being conducted; second, Stetsky must guarantee that if the workers voted for the Industrial Union, Kaufman and the AFL leaders would not set up a new Joint Council and begin a new "reorganization" campaign. If Stetsky accepted these conditions, Gold announced, he was ready to agree in writing to the referendum proposal.

Stetsky and the Lovestoneites were stunned by Gold's reply. Stetsky knew that the AFL and the Socialist Party leaders would never consent to give up the Joint Council in the event the workers voted in favor of the Industrial Union. Stetsky's referendum proposal, never meant in good faith, had boomeranged. Instead of proving that Gold was a "tool" of outside forces, it proved that Stetsky was the tool of the AFL and the Socialist Party, and could not make a move that would go counter to their wishes.

Stetsky refused to agree to Gold's condition in regard to the referendum proposal. Gold thereupon asked that the delegates vote on the proposal that all furriers be permitted to work in any shop, regardless of whether they held cards in the Industrial Union or the Joint Council, in order to end the discrimination by the bosses. Stetsky refused to put this proposal to a vote. He insisted that the conference had no such authority before unity was effected under the banner of the AFL. But in spite of Stetsky's objections, the delegates insisted on a vote. The motion was carried, with eighteen members of the original unity conference voting for the proposal. In great anger, Stetsky announced that the Joint Council would not recognize the decision. He and his associates would withdraw from the conference.

It was 2:30 A.M. when Stetsky and other Joint Council representatives walked out of the conference at Webster Hall. But the auditorium was still filled. Stetsky, immaculately dressed, contempt for the workers written all over his face, had to pass through the crowded aisles. The furriers on both sides of the aisle, unable to restrain their hatred for this gang leader who had caused them so much suffering, rose in anger and spat all over him. Stetsky emerged a wretched sight.

The fake "unity" proposal had collapsed. But the workers who remained at the Webster Hall meeting were more determined than ever to build a powerful united front over the heads of the right-wing and AFL leaders. Under the leadership of the Industrial Union, rank-and-file unity committees conducted hundreds of shop strikes which won tens of thousands of dollars more in wages for the workers.

The offensive continued throughout the summer and fall of 1931. There was no let-up even for a single day. Every night, shop committees, elected by the workers themselves, met in the office of the Industrial Union together with the Fur Department of the union to take up complaints of the workers in the shops. The officers of the Industrial Union were authorized by the committees to carry out their decisions.

In the settlements of the July strikes, the Industrial Union insisted on the right to enter the shops to see to it that the settlements were enforced. Thereby the Industrial Union forced many employers to do away with piece work and establish week work. Many sub-contractors were forced to give up their miserable sweatshops and had to go to work to earn an honest living. Thousands of dollars in back pay were collected from the bosses who paid their workers below the minimum scale and single time for overtime. Payment for legal holidays was again established.

All this took place at a time when the wage-cutting drive of big business was in full swing throughout the country. On September 22, 1931, United States Steel Corporation, Bethlehem Steel, and Youngstown Sheet & Tube Company announced a 10 percent wage cut, effective October 1.

Two days later, the *New York World-Telegram* reported: "The movement to readjust wages inaugurated by the United States Steel Corporation became almost nation-wide today as reports from industrial centers told how other large industrial corporations were ordering wage cuts and reducing working hours."

Matthew Woll said: "I can only express great regret and profound disappointment at the action of the United States Steel Corporation." William Green also expressed "regret" and called the action "morally wrong and economically unsound."

At the fifty-first convention of the Federation in October 1931, William Green's great contribution to the fight for unemployment insurance and against wage-cutting was: "The American Federation of Labor is a bulwark against communism, and as long as the Federation functions there need be no fear."

By "communism" Green had in mind the events in the fur industry during the summer and fall of 1931. The experiences gained in these successful struggles, under the flag of the Industrial Union, re-armed the fur workers. They were on the offensive against the five-year-old AFL conspiracy that had reduced their working and living conditions. The chapter they had just opened was not to close until once again they would be a united, militant, progressive and democratic union.

CHAPTER 32

The Bankruptcy
of the Right Wing

The demoralization and decline of the New York Joint Council in 1931 brought the entire right-wing International to the verge of bankruptcy. By taxing the fur dressers of Locals 2 and 3 of Brooklyn, the only locals still able to pay their per capita, the International barely managed to remain alive.

Stetsky and six business agents handed in their resignations on October 10, 1931. Stetsky frankly admitted that "not only was the union financially bankrupt but morally ruined as well." The Joint Council had completely lost the confidence of the furriers. It was unable to stop the flow of workers into the Industrial Union or to collect dues from those who retained their paper membership in the Council.

All but two of the Joint Council delegates also submitted their resignations, stating that "the Joint Council, at this moment, cannot function any longer." The following day, without consulting the workers, Kaufman appointed himself "supervisor" of the Joint Council. He was to be assisted by a temporary committee of three International vice-presidents which was soon expanded to a "Committee of fifteen" dyed-in-the-wool right-wingers in the four locals.

Whatever remained of the Joint Council was actually administered by a group of outside Socialist leaders—Schlessinger and Dubinsky of the ILGWU, Feinstone of the United Hebrew Trades, and Vladeck of the *Jewish Daily Forward*—who pumped money into the dying organization in a vain effort to revive it. The Forward Association came through with $6,000 and the ILGWU leadership with $1,000 from that union's treasury. The United Hebrew Trades rounded up contributions from the Cap Makers, the Hebrew Butcher Workers Union, the Bakers Union, the Hebrew American Typographical Union and other right-wing unions.

Once again the strong-arm boys were hired to attack workers striking under the Industrial Union leadership. The resistance of the rank-and-file workers within the Joint Council became even stronger. With the slogan "Hands off the Furriers!" the honest workers who still remained in the Joint Council organized a Registered Rank-and-File Committee to drive out Kaufman and the "outside" masters. A large group of registered workers assembled at an open air meeting in the market and marched to the Council demanding that the organization be placed in the hands of the workers. Kaufman summoned police and had the headquarters blocked off. He warned the workers not to enter the building.

The rank-and-file opposition of the Joint Council thereupon called a meeting of all registered workers to nominate and elect a Joint Council that would truly represent the workers. Twelve hundred furriers participated in the elections held on November 4, 1931, to form a Rank-and-File Joint Council. It was the largest vote in the history of the Council since it was established by the AFL "reorganizers" in 1927. Isidore Cohen was elected chairman of the Council, William Kaiser, vice-president, Sol Wollin, secretary, and Kassel Miller, treasurer.

The newly-elected Rank-and-File Joint Council went in a body to take over the office that Kaufman had usurped. Once again Kaufman summoned the police to guard the entrance and gave strict orders that no one was to be allowed to enter. The Council promptly preferred charges against Kaufman. Kaufman retaliated by expelling the four top leaders from the right-wing union. He charged them with "planning, organizing, supporting and actively participating in a dual union." The "defendants" replied in an open letter to Kaufman: "You can accuse us of any crime you want to. But you are actually the guilty one. The furriers know your record and they will judge your charges against us accordingly."

A powerful movement was developing to build a real united front among the members of the Council and the Industrial Union. At a unity conference of representatives of the Industrial Union and the newly-elected Rank-and-File Joint Council on December 18, 1931, a United Front Committee was elected with equal representation from both organizations. A Unity Declaration, based on the program outlined by the Industrial Union, was issued to the fur workers. The committee also immediately informed the Associations and the independent employers that the members of the Industrial Union and the Joint Council would not recognize any agreements made with Kaufman. The only authorized body, the bosses were told, was the United Front Committee.

The united-front movement spread to other cities. Philadelphia furriers, members of the right-wing International, elected a committee to meet with the Industrial Union to discuss "how to bring unity among the ranks of the furriers." On November 16, 1931, Boslover Hall was filled with both left-wing and right-wing furriers to discuss unity. Even well-known right-wingers admitted that they had sacrificed their own interests in supporting the expulsion policies of the right-wing leaders. "I am largely responsible for splitting the ranks of the fur workers," Dave Schneiderman confessed. "I feel, however, that I made a terrible mistake. I endangered my own bread and butter, for the bosses took advantage of the split in our ranks, and our conditions have reached a point where it is impossible to earn a living for our families. I am, therefore, happy to announce that I will do everything in my power to restore unity in our ranks."

Shop strikes, organized by the Unity Committee, started at once in Philadelphia. In two shops, the Unity Committee won settlements that reduced the work week from forty-eight or more to forty hours. In addition, the workers received wage increases of from $6 to $10. In solidarity, the New York fur workers stopped the shop of Fox & Weissman during the strike in its Philadelphia branch.

Kaufman appealed in vain to the Philadelphia Fur Manufacturers Association to "prevail upon those two members who signed with the Communists to retract their action." He also called upon the United Hebrew Trades to pressure the workers in the right-wing local to withdraw from the united-front movement.

The efforts to break up the united front took other forms too. Jack Schneider was suddenly arrested for deportation to Roumania as an "undesirable alien." And Kaufman ran to the courts for injunctions to restrain the Industrial Union from cooperating with members of the Joint Council.

A willing court gave Kaufman a temporary injunction. But neither injunctions nor deportations, police or strong-arm squads were able to save the right wing. Agreements with Kaufman were now of little value to the bosses. On November 6, 1931, Herman Scheidlinger, the new president of the Association, informed William Green that it was absolutely essential that he meet with the Association's Board of Directors to review "the entire industrial situation, and the chaotic condition in the fur unions before the same got beyond control and made it impossible or useless for all future negotiations."

Green sent Woll and McGrady. When Woll met with the leaders of the Association, he was told quite bluntly that the right-wing union "was very weak" and "powerless" to do anything effectively.

"If the American Federation of Labor is not going to assist the Fur Workers Union," Woll reported to Green, "the Manufacturers may be forced to do business with the other group (that is led by the lefts and Communists), if they are successful in aligning with them the majority of the workers. . . ."

McGrady's report to Green was even more specific: "If the American Federation of Labor does not take control of the situation in the next week or two, the communists will capture the industry. I find that the workers generally have lost confidence in the leadership of our unions. They are not sympathetic with communism, but they are looking for militant leadership. . . ."

With these confessions of total failure before him, Green again assigned Woll, Frayne and McGrady, together with William Collins, general organizer of the AFL, to save the right-wing union from extinction.

Kaufman now announced a "mass meeting" at Bryant Hall on January 19, 1932, to make it appear that the right wing spoke in the name of the fur workers. Calling on the fur workers to "renew your spirit of the historic Carnegie Hall meeting of 1926," the United Front Committee urged them to attend the meeting. "Demonstrate to the Association that Kaufman does not speak for and is not representing the fur workers; that no agreements will be recognized by the fur workers unless signed by the United Front!"

The furriers came in thousands, densely packing the entire neighborhood around Bryant Hall. Alarmed by Kaufman, the police brought the Industrial Squad, the Bomb Squad and hordes of police both on horses and on foot. Armed with machine guns and tear-gas bombs, they beat the fur workers with clubs, and pushed and drove them from place to place. Their efforts were useless. The large mass of furriers gathered around Bryant Hall refused to retreat.

Unable to disperse the workers, the police arrested Gold, Jack Schneider and several others. But the furriers broke through the police cordon and forced the police to release the left-wing leaders.

Inside Bryant Hall there were less than one hundred people. Detectives of the Industrial Squad, assisted by strong-arm men and a group

AMERICAN FEDERATION OF LABOR

A F OF L BUILDING

Washington, D.C.,
December 7, 1931.

Mr. William Green, President,
American Federation of Labor,
A. F. of L. Building,
Washington, D. C.

Friday afternoon and Saturday morning I made a thorough
canvass of the situation myself. In brief it is this:

If the American Federation of Labor does not take
control of the situation in the next week or two, the
communists will capture the industry.

I find that the workers generally have lost confidence
in the leadership of our unions. They are not sympathetic
with communism, but they are looking for militant leadership. If the American Federation of Labor does
take control of the situation it will necessitate
somebody being on the job every day for perhaps
three months, because as soon as the American
Federation of Labor and the officers of the Fur
Workers Union commence to negotiate the new contract, the communists will start their activities
on the streets. They will hold mass meetings and
advise the workers to strike. These tactics will
of course have to be met.

The union is bankrupt financially and all their resources
for borrowing money are exhausted. Whatever money they get will
have to come from the dues the membership pays. The workers
probably will pay their dues and the manufacturers will see
that nobody works whose union card is not paid up, only if
the American Federation of Labor is in control.

Vice-President Woll, the officers of the Fur Manufacturers'
Association and the union leaders are all awaiting your decision
as to whether or not you will assign someone in to not only
help in the wage negotiations, but to direct the affairs of
the union for the next few months.

Fraternally yours,

Edw. F. M. Grady

Legislative Representative,
American Federation of Labor.

*After five years of "reorganization," McGrady adds up the
results for William Green—bankruptcy for the right wing.*

of Lovestoneites, allowed only those to enter whom they considered to
be "reliable."

The scene inside Bryant Hall was reminiscent of Carnegie Hall. Even
the "reliable" workers who were permitted to enter were in revolt. It was
almost impossible for Kaufman to speak. The furriers inside the hall demanded that the doors be opened and as many workers as possible be
allowed to come in. Many of Kaufman's henchmen realized the futility
of proceeding with the meeting. Leviche Cohen, who had been appointed by Kaufman to serve on the conference committee to negotiate
a new agreement, arose and asked: "In whose name will I speak? In
whose name will I negotiate?" He announced that he was withdrawing
from the conference committee.

Although beaten by the police and gangsters, the furriers continued
the demonstration until Ben Gold, speaking from a truck, asked them to
assemble for another meeting at the Industrial Union.

Kaufman complimented Police Comissioner Mulrooney for the assistance he had received, singling out for special praise "the following officers
of the Police Department—Inspector Walsh, Captain McDermott, Lieutenant Pyke and Jack Barry of the Radical & Industrial Squad, Captain
O'Sullivan of the 14th Precinct, Lieut. Lahey in charge of detectives of
the 14th Precinct and Detective Max Leaf of the 14th Precinct. . . ."

Reassured of cooperation by the AFL and the police, the
Association renewed the agreement with the Joint Council. Not a single
improvement was made in the expiring agreement.

Right-wing circles again exuded confidence. Bold headlines in the
Forward announced that with 754 furriers participating in the referendum, there was "an overwhelming vote in favor of the acceptance of the
new agreement."

The following exchange of letters indicates the complete bankruptcy
of the AFL union and the mockery of the new "agreement."

Herman Scheidlinger, Association president, to all Association employers, March 18, 1932: "You are instructed to direct your workers *at once*
to obtain such working cards at the office of the Union, 28 West 31st
Street. Without such working cards, the workers will not be eligible for
employment, and will not be permitted to continue to work in the shops
of the members of the Association."

Matthew Woll to William Green, March 21: "I am pleased to report
the final consummation of this Agreement and to advise you that necessary steps for the enforcement are now actively undertaken. It will, of

course, demand constant and persistent and relentless effort on the part of all to accomplish the latter end, but I am confident with the continued cooperation of our Committee, assisted whenever possible by Representative McGrady, we will successfully enforce this agreement in the fur industry."

Scheidlinger to the Association employers, April 5, after shop strikes by the resisting workers: "We have been informed by the Union that your workers have not as yet obtained their working cards and you are hereby informed that unless you direct your workers to obtain from the Union their working cards, an official complaint will be filed against you, and your workers will not be permitted to work in your shop."

William Collins to William Green, April 26, as the shop strikes continue: Though "the police have cooperated pretty well," "the employers are not living up to the agreement in the sense that they signed it." "The agreement calls for a condition where every worker must have a working card before he is employed but to be frank with you, the Mexican Army would be necessary to enforce this in the more than 1,500 shops." There are "continual factional intrigues within the Furriers Joint Council," and the Council was "gradually attempting to eliminate President Kaufman from supervising manager. . . ." Kaufman himself was "fed up with his job," and had called an emergency International Convention on May 13 "for the purpose of retiring from the International field."

Kaufman to William Green, May 6: The President of the AFL is urged to attend the emergency International convention in person. His presence is essential "to prevent the liquidation of the International." The locals in the dressing industry [Locals 2 and 3 of Brooklyn] have almost decided "to give up the International . . . and to organize a Central Body of the dressing locals only."

Matthew Woll, Hugh Frayne and William Collins to William Green, May 9: "We regret to report because of internal political affairs and group dissensions we have made practically no progress in placing the administrative affairs of the Furriers' Union on a better and more efficient working basis; indeed, we believe it is almost hopeless to accomplish anything in this direction unless other drastic measures relating to form of organization are resorted to." The Committee recommends "that the International charter should be returned or withdrawn and that Federal charters be temporarily issued to the several unions that now make up the International Fur Workers Union and until such time as it may be deemed proper to restore the International charter."

William Collins to William Green, supplementary letter, May 9: "We

AMERICAN FEDERATION OF LABOR

Executive Council.

President, William Green.
Secretary, Frank Morrison.
Treasurer, Martin F. Ryan,
400 Carmen's Bldg., Kansas City, Mo.

First Vice-President, Frank Duffy,
Carpenters' Building, Indianapolis, Ind.
Second Vice-President, T. A. Rickert,
Room 506, 175 W. Washington St., Chicago, Ill.
Third Vice-President, Matthew Woll,
Room 145, A. F. of L. Bldg., Washington, D. C.
Fourth Vice-President, James Wilson,
Second National Bank Bldg., Cincinnati, Ohio.

Fifth Vice-President, John Coefield,
Machinists' Building, Washington, D. C.
Sixth Vice-President, Arthur O. Wharton,
Machinists' Building, Washington, D. C.
Seventh Vice-President, Joseph F. Valentine,
1440 Broadway New York, N. Y.
Eighth Vice-President, G. M. Bugniazet,
1200 Fifteenth St., N. W., Washington, D. C.

A. F. OF L. BUILDING

LONG DISTANCE TELEPHONE NATIONAL 7870-1-2-3-4
CABLE ADDRESS, AFEL.

Washington, D. C.

May 9, 1932

Mr. William Green, President ·
American Federation of Labor
Washington, D. C.

RECEIVED

MAY 10 1932

Dear President Green:

  The Special Committee, selected by you for the purpose of aiding

  To meet the situation we feel that the International charter should be returned or withdrawn and that Federal charters be temporarily issued to the several unions that now make up the International Fur Workers Union and until such time as it may be deemed proper to restore the International Charter. This will give direct control to the American Federation of Labor over all local unions, which, indeed, has had to assume the burden of conducting this organization for the last five years and at the same time the money will be spent on behalf of the Fur Workers and directly handled through the channels of the American Federation of Labor.

  We need hardly indicate that early and speedy action is required if you believe our presentation and recommendations warrant a favorable response. The International Fur Workers' Union is meeting in convention in Philadelphia Thursday, Friday, and Saturday of this week and unless proper steps are taken on this occasion, we are apprehensive of ultimate consequences.

    Sincerely and fraternally yours,

    Matthew Woll, Chairman

    Hugh Frayne

    William Collins

P. S. Copy of this report has been sent to Representative McGrady.

In this letter to William Green, Woll, Frayne and Collins admit that the "reorganization" has failed completely as they recommend withdrawing the charter of the right-wing International.

would say, frankly, that 90 percent of the people in the fur industry lean towards Gold and his clique."

In less than two months between Matthew Woll's glee at the "final consummation of the agreement" and his despairing cry, "It is almost hopeless!" the revolt of the workers erupted like an earthquake underneath the AFL bureaucrats. Five whole years of AFL and Socialist Party intrigues had come to naught. Back-door agreements with the bosses—"reorganizations"—company union—strikebreaking—red-baiting—strongarm attacks—police brutality—prison sentences—plot piled on plot—everything had failed. Never was bankruptcy more abjectly demonstrated! The mass of fur workers still supported the "dead and buried" left-wing leadership. Years of hunger, terrorism, wage cuts, speedup, unemployment and suffering had proved to the workers that the left wing's path of unity and struggle was the only way to rebuild a strong, democratic union.

Memorandum, May 12, 1932, American Federation of Labor archives: "Mr. McGrady left today for Philadelphia to attend the Fur Workers Convention. Yesterday he went over with Mr. Green the recommendations made jointly by Messrs. Woll, Frayne and Collins, that the International Union should abandon its charter and the Federation take over the local unions as federal labor unions. Mr. Green does not favor that procedure."

The surrender of the International Fur Workers Union charter would have given enormous impetus to the rising rank-and-file revolt inside many other AFL unions. The dying remnants of the International had to be kept alive somehow. With this hope in mind, Green hurried McGrady and Collins off to Philadelphia to attend the emergency International Convention. They must exert "moral pressure" upon the delegates of the dressing locals "to convince them to maintain the International under all circumstances."

The emergency convention in Philadelphia recorded ruin in almost every part of the union. The condition of the Joint Council in New York was duplicated throughout the International. "Everything is in danger of being destroyed," wailed Kaufman's henchman in Toronto. "There is not even money enough for postage, that we may send mail out," the right-wing leader of Local 53 of Philadelphia wept. "Something has to be done. I cannot drag along the people with promises and good words any longer," cried the right-wing leader in Boston. Abe Rosen, right-wing manager of Local 45 of Chicago, summed up the situation in that local: "The whole local right now is in sympathy with the left-wingers, even most of the executive."

Only from the two Brooklyn fur dressing locals was the International receiving any support. They were paying double the usual per capita to enable the International to survive at all. And these locals were now complaining "we have practically had to assume the burden of conducting the union." It was time to admit that it was "impossible to make the organization function properly."

Kaufman had appointed a hand-picked Credentials Committee to make certain that "unreliable" delegates were not seated. But things did not run so smoothly. There was opposition. Left-wing delegates from Chicago, led by Abe Feinglass, other delegates from Toronto, and several from the New York Joint Council, particularly I. Opochinsky and O. Schiller, formerly Kaufman supporters, united in opposing Kaufman's dictatorial procedure. And while these oppositionists were battling the right-wing AFL leaders inside the convention hall, a delegation of rank-and-file fur workers from New York made its influence felt on the outside.

Two days before the emergency convention opened, over a thousand fur workers had demonstrated in the New York fur market demanding relief for the unemployed furriers. A committee of five workers, four of them rank-and-filers in the right-wing Joint Council, demanded of Scheidlinger, head of the Association: $10 a week for each unemployed fur worker and $3 additional for each dependent; the money for unemployed relief to be paid by the fur manufacturers; distribution of the relief fund to be placed in the hands of the furriers; free medical aid to all workers.

Scheidlinger told the committee that the Association's agreement with the Joint Council did not provide for unemployment relief. He could do nothing. The furriers' committee replied that the workers did not recognize that agreement. The Association president shrugged off their answer with the remark, "Go talk to your union."

The unemployed fur workers elected a delegation to the emergency convention to demand action against the manufacturers. Arriving at Philadelphia, the New York delegation asked Kaufman for permission to present their demands to the convention. After a hurried conference with McGrady and Collins, Kaufman stationed police at the entrance to the convention hall with instructions to keep out the entire delegation. When the workers insisted on entering, the police riot squad drove them out of the hallway and arrested four members of the delegation.

The brutal treatment of the delegation of unemployed New York fur workers threw the convention into pandemonium. Both left-wing adherents and former supporters of the machine denounced Kaufman, McGrady and Collins for conspiring with the Philadelphia police authorities against the workers. Kaufman's Credentials Committee thereupon kicked out all anti-machine delegates from New York, Toronto and Chicago.

After much effort, Kaufman, McGrady and Collins finally convinced the leaders of the two Brooklyn fur dressing locals to continue pouring their local treasuries into the International office. Kaufman declared he would no longer serve as president. Sam Mindel of Fur Dressers Local 2 of Brooklyn nominated Pietro Lucchi, business agent of the Brooklyn locals and an International vice-president, to the combined office of International president and secretary-treasurer. Acknowledging it would take a "superman" to solve the problems of the International, Lucchi reluctantly accepted and was elected.

Every semblance of democratic procedure was thrown out of the window in the election of the members of the General Executive Board. Harold Goldstein and Nathan Freiman were elected vice-presidents although they were not even delegates to the convention. No other representative from the fur manufacturing workers in New York was elected to the Board. It was composed almost entirely of representatives from the dressers and dyers locals of Brooklyn.

So completely had the right-wing union disintegrated, and so thoroughly was it discredited in the eyes of the fur workers, that only the pressure of the AFL leaders on the Brooklyn locals kept it from going out of existence. William Collins reported to William Green: "If Organizer McGrady and ourself were not present at the convention in Philadelphia there certainly would have been no convention. It would have been broken up the first day."

Only with greatest difficulty had someone been found willing to assume the presidency of an International Union that existed in name only. Kaufman was through. No one else wanted the job. Against his better judgment, Pietro Lucchi reluctantly accepted the thankless office. Actually, Lucchi was not informed of the true state of affairs of the International. "When the convention was over and I was elected President," he wrote on May 19, 1932, "I found myself with a treasury of $9.06 and about $15,000 in debts." And three months later he added regretfully: "I think I made the biggest mistake of my life when I accepted this position at the last convention in Philadelphia."

In pressuring the Brooklyn locals to keep the International going, the AFL bureaucrats had not the slightest belief that Lucchi would succeed

I think I made the biggest mistake of my life when I accepted this position at the last convention in Philadelphia — but I have nobody to blame but myself. I will, however, do everything in my power under the circumstances to pull through. I don't have to reassure you that if conditions change for the better, I will surely consider you just as well as the many other obligations which I have to meet.

Writing to Albert Roy in August 1932, Lucchi expresses his regret about having accepted the presidency of the International.

where Kaufman had failed. They were quite satisfied to have a scapegoat and looked upon Lucchi as such. "We cannot possibly see how he is going to be successful," Collins wrote to William Green immediately after the convention.

As it turned out, Lucchi was to surprise the AFL bureaucrats who could not "possibly see how he is going to be successful." He succeeded, but in a way they never dreamed of. Instead of being the scapegoat for Green, Woll, McGrady, Frayne and Collins—Lucchi was to become a leading advocate of unity. And when the Furriers Union was finally united, he became one of the builders of the powerful union that today represents the fur and leather workers.

The Second Offensive

The New York Joint Council was a shattered and broken organization. No self-respecting worker set foot in the Council's headquarters. The bulk of the membership, though formerly compelled by the bosses to register with the Council, were now members of the Industrial Union. So hateful had the right-wing organization become to the fur workers that William Collins was forced to inform William Green on May 17, 1932, "there is no one who will serve on a committee at the Joint Council headquarters. . . . The finances of the Joint Council are very low, and unless something happens within the next month they will have to close it up."

Symbolically, Charles Stetsky, the former manager of the right-wing union, committed suicide. After years of ruthless power as a leader of the strong-arm gang, Stetsky came out a beaten, broken man. Loathed by the workers and disgusted by the cynical intrigues of his "comrades," the Socialist Party leaders—Stetsky took his own life. Few indeed were his mourners.

Another suicide made news among the furriers. It was Samuel N. Samuels, the former president of the manufacturers' association. In 1920, Samuels had told the union leaders to "drown their unemployed." In 1926 and for years thereafter, he had attempted to smash the Furriers Union. He wound up in an institution for the insane, at which he committed suicide.

In June 1932, a conference was arranged by Socialist trade union leaders "to save the Furriers Joint Council," which was practically defunct.

Who was there to lead and what was there to lead? It had absolutely no influence among the workers. It had even lost the power to terrorize them with force. The conference was held in the ILGWU headquarters. David Dubinsky, Abraham Shiplacoff, Morris Feinstone and William Collins decided to place Samuel Shore, supervisor of the White Goods Workers Union, Local 62 of the ILGWU, as manager of the Furriers Joint Council. The fur workers were not consulted by these "champions" of free trade unions, these foes of "outside domination." And to add insult to injury, the Socialist leaders had picked to head the Joint Council a man

William Collins, one of the AFL reorganizers, informs Green in May 1932 that the right-wing Joint Council is but a corpse.

AMERICAN FEDERATION OF LABOR

OFFICE OF
WILLIAM COLLINS
GENERAL ORGANIZER
ROOM 1309 1440 BROADWAY
NEW YORK CITY
TELEPHONE PENNSYLVANIA 2929

EXECUTIVE COUNCIL

William Green _____ _____ President
Frank Morrison _____ _____ Secretary
Martin F. Ryan _____ _____ Treasurer
Joseph Duffy _____ 1st Vice-President
T. A. Rickert _____ 2nd Vice-President
Matthew Woll _____ 3rd Vice-President
James Wilson _____ 4th Vice-President
John Coefield _____ 5th Vice-President
A. O. Wharton _____ 6th Vice-President
Jos. N. Weber _____ 7th Vice-President
_____ 8th Vice-President

May 17, 1932.

Mr. William Green, President,
American Federation of Labor,
A. F. of L. Bldg., Washington, D. C.

RECEIVED
MAY 1 19..

Dear Sir and Brother:

Last week we were in attendance at the 10th biennial convention of the International Fur Workers Union. We sat in conference with President Kaufman and the General Executive Board

The present situation in the New York markets is very bad. First of all, there is very little work, the season being one of the worse for many years. Many of the big shops which employed fifty, sixty and a hundred people, today have about eight or ten. There is a strong suspicion that the work is being done by contractors in out of the way places and there is no method of reaching them because there is no one who will serve on a committee at the Joint Council headquarters. The finances of the Joint Council are very low and unless something happens within the next month they will have to close it up. They are functioning at the present time with four assistant

Hoping this will be satisfactory, we remain,

Fraternally yours,

William Collins.
General Organizer
American Federation of Labor.

*America during the depression.
Left, typical Hooverville shack in
which thousands had to live.
Above, Wall Street's solution for the unemployed—apple-selling.
Below, answer of thousands of American workers, led by left wing.*

More typical depression scenes. Above, one of the many thousands of breadlines that dotted the country. Below, Hooverville camp.

FSA Photo by Lee

who had no connection with the workers in the industry, a man who had been an employer himself for eight years prior to 1931!

Assuming office, Shore announced that the Industrial Union, not the bosses, was the enemy the fur workers must fight. "We must first eliminate the Industrial Union," he cried in outlining his program.

In July 1932, at the very depth of the terrible depression, the Industrial Union launched its second offensive. The campaign started with shop strikes for July increases. Before the end of the month, 150 shops had struck. In most of these shops, the Industrial Union quickly forced the bosses to raise the wages of the workers $5, $8 and $10 a week. Many firms were compelled to establish week work instead of piece work and give up their inside sub-contracting.

On July 27, the dog-skin workers went out on strike. The year before, these workers had staged the militant struggle that had practically broken the backbone of the Joint Council. Now they struck for July raises and also demanded jobs for the unemployed, no contracting, equal division of work, an unemployment insurance fund to be paid by the employers and administered by the workers, and recognition of the Industrial Union. The dog-skin strike, involving a thousand workers, completely paralyzed that branch of the trade. On July 30, the strike spread to trimming and coat shops as hundreds of workers from other shops in the same buildings joined the mass picket lines.

By the end of the first week, the whole fur market was in revolt. Over 225 shops, with thousands of workers, were on strike. Entire shops walked out. The strike wave spread so rapidly that the Industrial Union hired extra space to house the various rank-and-file strike committees.

Gangsters again tore through the fur market to smash the picket lines. But the workers, led by their fighting union, could not be stopped. When the professional underworld characters armed with guns and iron bars arrived at 29th Street and Seventh Avenue, thousands of furriers mobilized and drove the thugs out of the market. The battles raged daily, completely halting all traffic in the fur district. Several strikers were seriously wounded. But in the end the gunmen were always routed.

Suddenly, a new diversion by the Joint Council skeleton. A new charge: the Industrial Union is not permitting right-wing workers to play a part in the strikes; it is interested in getting improvements only for "Communist" workers. In reply, eight former leaders of the Joint Council—Isidor Opochinsky, Philip Brown, Oscar Schiller, Mania

Schwartz, Leviche Cohen, Motel Becker, Abraham Cherkes and Philip Milstein—now active members of the Industrial Union, declared:

"We are active in the Industrial Union. We are not Communists. We are helping with all our power to build and strengthen the Industrial Union, because it is the only union which is fighting for the workers' interests and which has the confidence of the fur workers. The Industrial Union is based upon complete democracy. All workers without exception have the unlimited opportunity and the guaranteed right to criticize the policies, tactics and the achievements of the officials. Elections in the Industrial Union, are carried through in the broadest democratic and most uncompromisingly honest fashion. We now occupy responsible, leading positions in the Industrial Union, regardless of the fact that for years we were its most bitter enemies. Our united front was carried through honorably, sincerely and fraternally. We are proud to be given the opportunity to participate in the leadership, the activities and the battles of the furriers under the fighting direction of the Industrial Union."

The Industrial Union urged all workers, right-wing as well as left-wing, to attend a special mass meeting in Cooper Union on August 10 for a complete answer to the false charges of the Joint Council officials.

DECLARATION OF THE FORMER LEADERS OF THE FURRIERS' A. F. OF L. JOINT COUNCIL

TO ALL FUR WORKERS, TO ALL NEEDLE TRADE S WORKERS AND TO THE ENTIRE LABOR MOVEMENT!

Brothers and Sisters:

Thousands of fur workers are now on strike for higher wages, for union conditions and for recognition of the Industrial Union, which was organized and is being maintained by the fur workers themselves.

Almost the entire working class is acquainted with the fact that the fur workers are being slandered, terrorized and persecuted in a most brutal and shameful manner only because they insist upon their right to belong to their own union, to carry on the

ment. We are active in the Industrial Union. We are not Communists. We are helping with all our power to build and strengthen the Industrial Union, because it is the only union which is fighting for the workers' interests and which has the confidence of the fur workers. The Industrial Union is based upon complete democracy. All workers without exception have the unlimited opportunity and guaranteed right to criticize the policies, tactics and the achievements of the officials. Elections in the Industrial Union are carried through in the broadest

the cry of "communism", "Communist Union" in order to line up the police, the courts, the A. F. of L. and all other reactionary forces against the furriers and against the Industrial Union. The truth is that the few individuals who stand at the head of the Joint Council are not interested in Socialism, A. F. of L. or Communism, or even in the labor movement. THEY ARE ONLY LOOKING OUT AFTER THEIR OWN PETTY, PRIVATE LITTLE INTERESTS—THEY ARE SEEKING SOFT, WELL PAID JOBS FOR THEMSELVES.

We, the undersigned former leaders of the Joint Council, know these people intimately, know their aims and ambitions. We have cemented a united front with the Industrial Union because we have convinced ourselves that the policies, the tactics and the personnel of the Council are the greatest danger for the fur workers and for the entire labor move-

members of the A. F. of L. union to raise a voice of protest against the outrage that is being perpetrated upon the fur workers.

Down with the hand of strike-breaking that comes out under a Socialist or A. F. of L. Label! Down with the Joint Council!

For the Unity of all workers, irrespective of color, race or political creed!

LONG LIVE THE INDUSTRIAL UNION!

(Signed)

ISIDOR OPOTCHINSKY   LEVICHE COHEN
PHILIP BROWN   MOTEL BECKER
OSCAR SCHILLER   ABRAHAM CHERKES
MANIA SCHWARTZ   PHILIP MILSTEIN

Former leaders of the A. F. of L. Joint Council now active and devoted members of the Furriers Industrial Union

Thousands of fur workers packed the hall. They heard Ben Gold declare that the success of the strike movement was based on the united front of right-wing and left-wing furriers in the struggle for better conditions. In the discussion a number of former right-wing supporters spoke. One declared: "In the last two weeks, I have learned more than in all my years in the Joint Council." He admitted that it had been difficult for him to join the Industrial Union, for he had swallowed the right-wing propaganda of "Communism" and "Moscow agent" hurled against the militant union. Before he left the Joint Council, he had approached the Industrial Union and asked permission to investigate "to see if everything that the Industrial Union says is true."

"I have since attended fifty shop meetings and have become convinced that the Industrial Union is conducted democratically and that the workers themselves are the leaders in their strike. I was present when twenty-five settlements were made and I saw for myself that in every case the union won higher wages and union conditions for the fur workers—for all furriers, right-wingers and left-wingers alike."

More hundreds of furriers joined the strike after the enthusiastic Cooper Union meeting. The strike wave spread like wildfire through the fur market. The picket lines grew larger. On August 11, the workers of all fur shops at 333 Seventh Avenue, 150 West 30th Street and 305 Seventh Avenue struck. In the next few days, all workers in other buildings, 345 Seventh Avenue, 240 West 30th Street and 242 West 30th Street downed their tools and joined the strike. Eighty of the largest shops were located in these three skyscraper buildings. On August 10, there were about 250 shops on strike; the following day close to 300; and the next day the number had already risen to 360.

It was no easy matter to close down a building like 150 West 30th Street. The police station was only a few doors away. Large bodies of police and detectives were always on hand. The main office of the Holmes Protective Agency was actually in the same building. Private detectives and special policemen stood guard watching every person who entered and left. Yet, on August 13, this immense building, like others in the market, stood empty. Mass picketing broke through every barrier.

It was a masterful strategy evolved to fit the organizational problems and needs of the workers. Out of individual shop strikes grew the dog-skin section strike. Out of the dog-skin strike grew building strikes. And out of building strikes grew whole block strikes. Important sections of the trade were completely shut down. The entire fur trimming division was paralyzed. Many of the largest shops of the manufacturers' association were seriously affected.

Yet, not even the best strategy would have produced such tremendous results without the fundamental policy of the left-wing movement—rank-and-file conduct of the strike. Rank-and-file workers—white and Negro, men and women, old and young—were the hall chairmen, secretaries and committees. Rank-and-file workers conducted shop meetings, organized buildings and blocks, conducted mass picket demonstrations, participated in the organization department and settlement committee. The strikes, in short, were being led by the furriers themselves. In many cases, they were sparked by the young, fighting dog-skin workers. When there was no money to hire a decent strike hall, these dog-skin workers sold soda and ice cream and turned over the proceeds to hire a strike hall.

Furriers told reporters: "It's the spirit of 1926! We are going to strike to the finish; until the bosses are forced to recognize our right to organize into a real union and not a company union."

On August 8, Henry Rosen, president of the Trimming Association, sent an ultimatum to the Furriers Joint Council. If it could not within ten days get the striking workers back or keep the shops operating with other workers, the Trimming Association would consider its agreement with the Joint Council no longer in effect and would negotiate with the Industrial Union for settlements.

Joint Council leaders, headed by McGrady, stepped up their efforts to fill the shops with scabs. They ran to the district attorney and demanded that "legal steps be taken against the Communist officials of the Industrial Union." They pleaded for larger police contingents and mass arrests.

But the strike wave continued to roll on. Individual members of the Fur Trimming Association settled with the Industrial Union. Letters of appreciation from whole shops listed the gains they had won.*

---

* The following letters, written in the depths of the depression, were typical:
"We, the workers of M. Kasarsky & Co., 345 Seventh Avenue, at a shop meeting held on Friday, August 12, decided to express our appreciation of the work done by the Industrial Union. The Industrial Union has won the following demands for the workers—$3 to $10 weekly increase in wages, equal division of work, no discrimination, recognition of the union."

Again: "We, the workers of Newfield & Weiss, 150 W. 30th Street, on strike under the leadership of the Fur Department of the Industrial Union, enthusiastically accept the settlement made for our shop on the basis of which we receive increases ranging from $5 to $10 per week.

"The negotiations carried on by the Industrial Union together with our shop

On August 17, after 117 shops had already settled with the Industrial Union, the Trimming Association asked the Industrial Union for a conference. It was an historic occasion. Five years before, the AFL "reorganization" had taken place. Three years before, the Fur Trimming Association had broken its agreement with the left-wing union. Now, the Trimming Association was again forced to deal with the union chosen by the workers.

The conference between representatives of the Trimming Association and the Industrial Union lasted all night. The bosses fought tooth and nail for the same agreement they had with the Joint Council. The changes insisted upon and won by Gold indicate the difference in policy between the Industrial Union and the Joint Council. The clause that the union should help strengthen the Association and the Association should help strengthen the union was kicked out altogether.

The clause that the only function of the shop chairman was to collect dues—out. In its place came a new provision that there should be a shop chairman and a shop committee in every shop who would be jointly responsible for taking up *all* shop questions. Collection of dues was left entirely out of the agreement. The left-wing leaders depended upon the workers to pay dues voluntarily and not under compulsion of the employers.

The clause which dealt with the vicious working card system—out. Also thrown out was the old provision that initiation fees of new members should be decided by a committee of two bosses, two representatives from the Joint Council, and Dr. Abelson, the impartial chairman.

Overtime, unlimited under the old agreement, was now limited to only two hours a day, and that only when all places in the shop were filled. Moreover, workers were to get time-and-a-half for all overtime.

---

committee for our demands and the gains won by us are convincing proof that the Industrial Union is fighting in the interests of the workers, and is winning substantial gains which will raise the conditions of the workers not only in our shop but in the trade as a whole."

The furriers of the Clarkfield and Schechter shop wrote: "Before the Industrial Union called us out on strike we got wages that were much lower than the scale. After the strike was settled through Max Kochinsky, a representative of the Industrial Union, we got the following raises: Sam Fox, an operator got his wages raised from $35 to $45; M. Fisher, an operator, got his wages raised also from $35 to $45; Dave Charney, a nailer, got his wages raised from $35 to $45; A. Clarfield, a nailer, wages raised from $35 to $45, and Sammy Shertzer, a finisher, wages raised from $35 to $40."

The main provisions of the new agreement, in addition to those referred to above, included:

1. Forty-hour, five-day week.
2. Week work instead of piece work.
3. A new minimum scale of wages.*
4. At least one unemployed worker to be taken into every shop.
5. Payment for seven legal holidays.
6. Equal division of work.
7. No discrimination against Negro workers.
8. Equal pay for the same work for Negroes, women and youth.
9. No contracting.
10. Within thirty days after the agreement had been ratified by both parties, a conference should be called to establish an unemployment insurance fund, to be paid by the employers.

Four thousand strikers from four hundred shops had won wage raises ranging from $4 to $15 a week, plus the other important gains provided for in the new agreement. All this at a time when AFL labor bureaucrats were insisting that it was impossible to make advances in a depression period and that workers had to take wage cuts.

Over four thousand furriers enthusiastically ratified the settlement by unanimous vote. The Cooper Union hall proved too small to hold the entire outpouring of workers. Manhattan Lyceum had to be used to accommodate the overflow.

When Joseph Winogradsky, chairman of the Cooper Union meeting, introduced Gold to present the settlement report, a tremendous ovation burst forth from the workers. For fully fifteen minutes, they stood cheering, applauding and singing songs. Workers ran down the aisles with bouquets of flowers presented in the name of their shops to the leader of the victorious battle.

There were tears in the eyes of the furriers as Gold recounted the long and bitter struggle against the bosses and their agents since 1926 against the terrible conditions the Socialists and AFL leaders had brought about in the shops. Then the entire audience roared with delight as Gold re-

---

* $50 and $60 a week for first-class cutters; $41.80 for first class operators and $35.20 for second-class operators; $39.60 for first-class nailers and $33 for second-class nailers; $38.50 for first-class finishers and $30.80 for second-class finishers. The scale for floor (unskilled) workers, hitherto unorganized and slaving unlimited hours for $8 and $10 a week, was now set at $18 a week.

minded them: "The bosses' association swore they would never negotiate with a left-wing union. They have changed their policy, however. They spoke like gentlemen to us. It is a pleasure to deal with the manufacturers who are licked."

The backbone of the "reorganizers'" conspiracy was broken. The AFL company union lay paralyzed. The strong-arm men had been routed by the mass defense of the workers. The Trimming Association had been forced to recognize the Industrial Union. It would only be a matter of time before the coat manufacturers' association would also have to yield. Already, close to 150 members of the big Association, more than half of its membership, had been forced to settle with the Industrial Union. The key to the victory, Gold concluded, was the unity of the workers.

The victorious furriers staged a victory parade. As they filled the strike halls and mobilized for the march, hundreds of police arrived in the fur market. They denied a permit for the march, but when they were told that the strikers would march in any case, they were forced to yield. Thousands of jubilant fur workers started their march up Seventh Avenue, with thousands of other needle trades workers cheering from sidewalks and shop windows.

Suddenly, the police cancelled the permit. At 27th Street and Seventh Avenue, a large army of police met the marchers. Policemen began swinging their clubs to disperse the workers. As it became clear that the police were trying to incite bloodshed, the workers shouted: "Do not permit the police provocation." "Back to the strike halls."

Like disciplined soldiers, they marched back to mass meetings at the strike halls. Resolutions were adopted denouncing the police and the right-wing Joint Council. Then the strikers returned victoriously to their shops.

The Industrial Union's campaign rolled on. Other independent and Association shops were struck. Fur dyeing shops and fur "pointers" were organized. The fur "pointers" were then entirely unorganized. Their work, gluing silver hairs into fox skins to imitate silver fox, was difficult and back-breaking. Most of the pointers were young girls who worked sixty and seventy hours a week on piece work, earning the miserable wage of $7 to $10. Of five hundred fur pointers who answered the Industrial Union's strike call, only three were earning as much as $12 a week. After a two-week strike, the fur pointers won an agreement which abolished piece work, established week work, and set up a minimum wage scale of $20 for a forty-four-hour week.

From June to September, 1932, the Industrial Union settled 868 shop strikes. These included 250 Trimming Association shops, 389 independent shops, 204 coat manufacturers' association shops and 25 fur pointing shops. The increase for thousands of workers amounted on the average to $6.50 a week.

These amazing achievements were won by the Industrial Union against all odds during the worst period of the depression, when sixteen million workers were jobless. The Industrial Union was clearly the dominant factor in the fur industry. In October 1932, Pietro Lucchi fittingly declared: "As far as the Joint Council is concerned—there is no activity there whatsoever at the present time. The only ones left in the office are Brother Begoon and Schindler. The New York Joint Council is practically out."

The Industrial Union now prepared itself for the enforcement of the agreement in the shops. Complaints were increasing in number since the drive started. The furriers felt free to complain to the Industrial Union without fear that the boss would fire them as "troublemakers." The Industrial Union increased its staff to seven organizers and established a complaint department. Among the staff members were Jack Schneider, Joseph Winogradsky, Maurice H. Cohen, Herman Paul, Sol Wollin, Max Kochinsky and Harry Greenberg.

Inspired by the remarkable gains of the furriers, workers in the other needle trades began to organize under the leadership of the Industrial Union. Effective struggles were conducted for wage increases, shorter hours and union conditions. Among those who conducted successful strikes were the sheepskin workers of Boston and Lynn; the South River, New Jersey, dressmakers; the shirt makers of Bradford, Connecticut; and the knitgoods workers.

"The brilliant victory of the union in the fur trade," wrote William Z. Foster, the leader of the great Steel Strike of 1919 and head of the Trade Union Unity League, "shows that by developing the united front and taking up the struggle for the interests of the workers it is possible to defeat the attacks of the bosses and to unite the workers in one class struggle union. The victory of the fur workers is of outstanding importance not only in the needle industry but in the entire labor movement. It has shattered the theory that the workers can not carry on successful struggles in times of crisis."

CHAPTER 34

The Struggle
for the Unemployed

Just as it fought for wage increases, shorter hours of work and better conditions in the shops, so too the Industrial Union was the outstanding trade-union fighter for relief to the unemployed. A survey made by the Industrial Union in 1932 showed that around two thousand furriers were unemployed even at the height of the season. Many of these workers had been out of work for two whole years.

Because of the unprecedented economic crisis, the 1932 season was shorter than usual. For a few months almost all furriers were totally unemployed. Even those furriers who worked during the full season found it difficult to live through the slack period. Those who had worked only a few weeks or part time were, like millions of other unemployed, faced with starvation.

The spread of finishing-contracting during the Stetsky-Kaufman regime in the Joint Council had thrown many finishers out of jobs. Instead of keeping the finishers in the shops at union wages, many fur manufacturers "gave out" finishing work to contractors—usually two or three partners who worked eighty to ninety hours a week—who might hire one or two finishers from the outside. Working piecework, these workers earned very little in spite of long hours of toil. Vicious as the practice was, the fur bosses, who got their work done for half the cost, were determined to maintain it. Particularly so, since other needle trades unions "legalized" it in their agreements.

The Industrial Union had campaigned from the start for complete elimination of the contracting evil, in order to maintain union conditions in the manufacturing shops and to enable many finishers to get jobs in union shops. In the fall of 1932, after its successful second offensive, the Industrial Union was in a position to go more deeply into the problem: investigating which manufacturers gave out work to finishing contractors and how much of such work was being done; surveying the number of workers employed in contracting sweatshops, their wages and hours of work; and checking each manufacturing shop to eliminate the phony excuse that there was "no room" for finishers there.

The Industrial Union then launched a drive against the contracting shops. Shop strikes, and enforcement of the union agreements in the organized shops, forced scores of contracting shops to close. Many jobs at union wages and hours were thereby obtained for finishers in the manufacturing shops. While the problem was still far from being solved, and it required the constant vigilance of the union to expose the almost unlimited tricks used by the bosses to contract work, an important beginning was made.

The Industrial Union also fought for relief for those who were without jobs. In accordance with the provision of the agreement with the Trimming Association, the Industrial Union opened conferences for an unemployment insurance fund for the fur workers. Heated arguments went on for two weeks. In the end, the Trimming Association agreed to set up a fund to which each boss would contribute one percent of his payroll. While no contribution to this fund came from the workers, the fund would be administered solely by the workers. The agreement also provided that if unemployment continued the following July, the employers would contribute another one-half percent to the fund.

Although it was not adequate to meet all needs of the unemployed workers, this one percent fund made labor history. The Fur Department of the Needle Trades Workers Industrial Union, affiliated to the Trade Union Unity League, was the first organization of organized labor in the United States to force the employers to pay for an unemployment fund administered by the workers themselves. Many a fur worker and his family was literally kept alive by this fund during the months that followed. It spearheaded the demand for Federal Unemployment Insurance which became the battlecry of millions of unemployed American workers.

Organizing an Unemployed Council, the Industrial Union also spurred the drive for city relief for unemployed and destitute furriers. Appearing in mass formation before the relief authorities, ready to fight for their demands, the organized unemployed furriers forced them to cut through the red tape and increase the meager relief allowances.

Many a bitter fight established a healthy reputation for the Unemployed Council at the various home relief bureaus. On December 29, 1932, a delegation demanded of Welfare Commissioner Taylor that he increase relief allowances 7 percent, and allow cash payments for rent. The Commissioner brusquely dismissed the petition and ordered the delegation to leave. Day after day, mass demonstrations and picket lines were set up at his office—two weeks later, the Commissioner gave in and granted the demands.

With forty-three relief precincts to be covered at short notice, the Unemployed Council soon acquired an efficiency that was appreciated equally by the workers and the authorities. News that a furrier faced eviction quickly brought a mass demonstration to the vicinity. A report that an unemployed worker was having difficulty obtaining relief brought a mass delegation to the relief bureau. The Unemployed Council was particularly effective in assisting Negro workers, who often found themselves discriminated against by bigoted authorities.

Scores of cases of workers receiving eviction notices were fought out by the Unemployed Council. Workers forcibly moved out of their homes by police, notified the Unemployed Council and had their furniture promptly moved back in. Relief bureaus delinquent in providing cash rental payments, were forced to speed up their work and provide the necessary payments. It is significant that not one family of a worker who registered a complaint with the Industrial Union's Unemployed Council was ever evicted!

These achievements on the unemployment front—like those on the strike front—were won only through constant mobilization and struggles by masses of workers. Many a fur worker was as severely beaten in these unemployed struggles as in battle against police and strong-arm men on the picket line.

A reporter for the *New York World,* investigating police brutality during one unemployment demonstration, quoted witnesses who "saw women struck in the face with blackjacks, boys beaten by gangs of seven and eight policemen, and an old man backed into a doorway and knocked down time after time, only to be dragged to his feet and struck with fist and club. They saw detectives, some wearing reporters' cards in hat bands, many wearing no badges, running wildly through the crowd, screaming as they beat and kicked those who looked to them like Communists. They saw women thrown down by the crowd, and knocked over by the horses. . . They saw men with blood streaming down their faces dragged into the temporary police headquarters and flung down to await the patrol wagons to cart them away."

Beatings and arrests did not halt the struggles of the unemployed throughout the country. The demand for compulsory unemployment insurance gained such tremendous support among American workers that even the gentlemen on the AFL's Executive Council were finally impressed. On July 23, 1932, the *New York Times* reported: "Unable to withstand the rapidly mounting tide of sentiment for compulsory unemployment insurance, evidenced by a flood of communications from local unions, city central labor bodies and State Federations of Labor, the executive council of the American Federation of Labor abandoned today its traditional opposition to the proposal, which has been denounced by labor leaders since the days of Samuel Gompers as 'the dole.' "

Unfortunately, the leaders of the AFL did little to implement the action of the Executive Council. It was left to the rank-and-file workers themselves to press the demand for unemployment insurance on Congress. In the fall of 1932, a nation-wide Hunger March on Washington was organized for the starving unemployed. The New York District of the Needle Trades Workers Industrial Union elected forty delegates, and Ben Gold was chosen as leader of the Eastern division. Following an enthusiastic send-off in the Bronx Coliseum, the Hunger Marchers left for Washington to present their demands to Congress.

The Hunger Marchers paraded through several cities on their way south, like a disciplined, well-organized army. But they were told that in Wilmington, Delaware, the domain of the Dupont munitions and chemical dynasty, they would not be permitted to parade. The press, the pulpit and city administration had conducted such an insidious campaign against the movement, that the Hunger Marchers were even warned against leaving their trucks while in the city.

Ben Gold asked reporters to transmit the answer of the Hunger Marchers to Boyd, the Wilmington Chief of Police, and Black, the Superintendent of Public Safety: "Neither police nor hired gunmen will stop us. There are twelve hundred united and determined Hunger Marchers in our column, and they are not going to permit anyone to rob them of their right to parade peacefully through the streets of an American city." "We will fight to the last ditch," said Carl Winter, one of the leaders of the march.

On To Washington!

Demand Winter Relief and Unemployment Insurance at Expense of the Government and Employers!

Forward to Mighty, United Struggles Against Hunger In Every Town and Neighborhood!

HELP ELECT AND SEND THOUSANDS OF WORKERS' DELEGATES IN A

NATIONAL HUNGER MARCH

To Opening of Congress December 5th

Fellow Workingmen and Women of the U. S.:

The fourth consecutive Winter of mass misery and hunger is approaching!

The lives of millions of workers and of their families are in danger!

Only the united mass struggle of all who suffer from and are threatened by mass unemployment and the deliberate hunger policy of the multi-billionaires and their government, can save the destitute masses from indescribable suffering and actual death.

More than sixteen millions of us are already to-ally jobless. Less than 15 per cent of the employ-

greedy hold upon the vast storehouses of food and clothing for want of which, we, our wives and children die.

In the effort to force us into silent submission to their hunger program, the bosses and their government have unleashed all their forces of violence and terror. They are conducting a ruthless, murderous war against the hungry masses. Within the last twelve months, a score of workers have been murdered on the streets of Chicago, Cleveland, Detroit, and the National Capitol—Washington. Many more have been maimed and wounded, gassed and trampled by their hired police and military. Hoover, the Chief Executive of the Wall St.

On the afternoon of December 2, 1932, the marchers reached the city limits of Wilmington. A delegation, headed by Gold, went ahead to negotiate with the police authorities for the parade to pass through. Boyd and Black refused permission. As the army of Hunger Marchers approached, left their trucks and formed a powerful column, the city officials, surrounded by squads of policemen, grew pale. "We are going to parade," Gold said calmly. "Go ahead," the officials answered this time.

The unemployed marched. They paraded proudly through the streets. They were unshaven and underfed. But they held their heads high, ranks closed, and sang working-class songs. Between songs they chanted "Negro and white, unite and fight."

The population of the city poured into the streets to greet the marchers. Crowds stood in deep rows all along the streets, hundreds in each block. Many cheered and applauded.

At a garage on the corner of Front and Madison Streets, about 800 of the Hunger Marchers stopped for the night. Another group of about 200 was sent to the Italian Labor Lyceum. A third group consisting of about 150 women and 100 men went to the Polish Club, a building that was formerly a Catholic Church.

At nine o'clock, when most of the marchers had settled down on the floor for a peaceful night's rest, a street meeting took place outside the church building. Several of the leaders of the march attempted to tell the crowd the aims of the unemployed. Police were everywhere. Trucks with mounted machine guns and policemen armed with sawed-off shotguns surrounded the church. They moved in to disperse the audience of the local citizens gathered in front of the speakers. As the police began to push into the crowd, several dozen Hunger Marchers surrounded the speakers, to protect their leaders. The bluecoats became enraged. This was something they had not expected. They had never seen the mass defense methods used by the fur workers in New York City against police attacks on their picket lines.

The police pushed the marchers back from the porch into the church. The marchers entered the hall and barricaded the doors. Even when the police finally broke through and forced their way into the kitchen, the aroused women forced them to retreat. "The women fought like tigers," said the *Wilmington Press* the following morning.

Suddenly the windows crashed, and tear gas bombs were thrown in. As they exploded, the big hall was filled with gas. Weak and choking, the 250 marchers, most of them women, were finally forced to leave through a side window. As they came out, the police advanced, guns and clubs drawn. One policeman threatened to shoot. A woman marcher's courageous reply caused him to put his gun back, but the police charged with their clubs. A fierce battle ensued as the Hunger Marchers defended themselves. Four policemen were carried off to the hospital. Twenty-three marchers, the first the police could lay their hands on, were arrested. Among these was Ben Gold.

The moment the police surrounded Gold, they ran berserk. Superintendent Black recognized him as the determined spokesman for the marchers. Like madmen, the police swung their clubs again and again over Gold's head and body. Other policemen rushed to the attack on the defenseless prisoner until Gold was beaten into unconsciousness. Even then the police continued the brutal beating until, giving him up for dead, they threw his limp body into the patrol wagon.

The marchers who remained returned to their "night's lodging." The hall was a wreck. The floor was covered with glass. The doors were splintered. The chairs were broken. Three-fourths of the marchers who reassembled in this shambles bore bruised faces, lacerated skulls, welts on their backs and shoulders. Tears still ran from smarting eyes. But the indomitable marchers grimly exulted: "We have stood our ground! We have shown the workers of Wilmington that we will not be stopped. We will carry out the will of the workers who elected us to the Hunger March."

Hundreds of workers gathered to see the Hunger Marchers come out of the church the following morning. Parading in orderly ranks despite their injuries, singing militant songs, they left the church and mounted the trucks. "Hold the fort for we are coming!" And on the trucks, the signs blazed: "ON TO WASHINGTON FOR UNEMPLOYMENT INSURANCE."

Meanwhile, brought from the jail to a hospital, Ben Gold slowly recovered from his injuries. Ironically charged with "assault," Gold was found guilty in a jury trial which was surrounded by all the prejudice and hysteria whipped up in this stronghold of the Dupont interests. He was sentenced to 40 days in jail and a $50 fine. Unfortunately, the appeal to the higher court was not filed in time. About a year later, Gold actually served forty days in prison in Delaware. His crime? He had fought for relief for the millions of unemployed American workers and their families!

Unemployment insurance, the demand of the Hunger Marchers, became a key plank in Franklin D. Roosevelt's New Deal program and was adopted as the law of the land during his administration. The Battle of Wilmington in December 1932 and the gallant fight of the Hunger Marchers in Washington and throughout the nation, dramatized this great struggle. They could put Ben Gold in jail, but they could not imprison the idea for which he and many other militant fur workers had fought.

CHAPTER 35

Morris Langer, Martyr of Labor

Several thousand workers were employed in fur dressing and dyeing shops in New York and nearby towns. The industry was made up of several sections, depending on the type of fur skins each shop worked on. The rabbit dressing and dyeing shops were the largest single group in this branch of the industry. In these shops common rabbit skins, imported from many lands, were dressed and dyed into lustrous furs that closely resembled beaver, seal, ermine, leopard and other expensive pelts.

The employers in the rabbit shops extracted enormous profits through the most inhuman exploitation of their workers. The work week was as long as seventy, eighty and ninety hours. Earnings even for these intolerable hours were as little as $12 to $18 a week. Moreover, the work was done in dark, damp cellars of dilapidated firetraps. Skin infections from dangerous dyes, asthma, rheumatism and other crippling diseases were common ailments among the workers. The employers callously refused to supply either gloves or other protective equipment.

The rabbit dyeing shops were almost completely unorganized. Even during the war years, when the fur dyeing industry expanded enormously as a result of the decline in the importation of dyes from Germany, the right-wing leaders made no attempt to use these favorable circumstances to organize the dye shops. From 1915 to 1932, despite the expenditure of thousands of dollars, the right-wing leaders were able to organize only three shops—Basch Company (Lamb), Chappell (Hudson Seal) and Alaska (Lamb).

The right-wing AFL International did have some rabbit dressing shops under contract, but even in these the large body of floor workers, the least skilled, were not in the union. The rabbit dressers had for years been largely under the control of Kaufman and his lieutenants, Moe Harris and Jack Shulman.

While heavy assessments were levied for "organizing pruposes," the open shops remained unorganized, new open shops sprang up, and conditions in the organized shops deteriorated rapidly. In accordance with the AFL's widespread policy during the depression years, the right-wing leaders of the rabbit dressers accepted big wage cuts and speedup demanded by the bosses. They even reinforced such policies with the "practical" theory that the only way to fight the competition of the open shops was to reduce wages in the organized shops.

On the eve of his resignation from the International, Kaufman, with Harris and Shulman, agreed upon a 25 percent wage cut in renewal of an agreement for the rabbit dressers in October 1931. In addition, the new agreement gave the employers the right to throw out the older workers. When the workers in some shops refused to accept this new agreement, they were locked out. The workers promptly struck to save their jobs and conditions. Moe Harris informed the workers in the rest of the shops that they had a perfect right to do the scab work which their employers brought in. The strikers protested to Kaufman, but their protest was completely ignored.

With scabbing officially sanctioned by the right-wing leaders, the strike ended in a smashing defeat for the workers. None other than Kaufman himself signed the new agreement which reduced the wage rate (piece work) from $2.15 per hundred skins to $1.60. The agreement also permitted the employers to discharge seventy older workers. Such were the results of the "practical" methods of the right-wing leaders.

In June 1932, the rabbit dressing employers summarily announced another wage cut. Of twenty shops, employing about six hundred workers, eighteen were controlled by the AFL International, with Moe Harris holding sway as virtual dictator. Convinced that the right-wing leaders would do nothing for them, the workers appealed to the Industrial Union for assistance.

The Dressers and Dyers Department of the Industrial Union, under the leadership of Manager Morris Langer, immediately launched a drive to force the bosses to rescind the wage cut. Fearful that the Industrial Union would make inroads in their shops, the bosses quickly surrendered.

Having defeated the wage cut, the Industrial Union now called on the fur dressers to strike for wage increases. Under Langer's leadership, a number of shops walked out and won raises. As more and more workers went over to the Industrial Union, the union drew up demands and presented them to the employers for an agreement. The demands were rejected. The workers voted to strike and the battle was on.

Fourteen rabbit dressing shops struck militantly for five weeks. In spite of the efforts of Moe Harris to supply scabs, the strikers paralyzed the trade so completely that the employers were finally forced to grant all their demands. The agreement signed with the Industrial Union won a wage increase of 23 percent; * the forty-hour week; payment for eleven legal holidays (including May First); a 3 percent unemployment insurance fund paid by the bosses and administered by a committee of workers; equal division of work; and no discrimination against Negro and young workers. Through the strike, moreover, the unorganized floor workers were organized and received a 20 percent increase in wages.

So powerful was the effect of the splendid strike that in the four nonstriking shops still controlled by Moe Harris, the bosses were forced to give the same raise to the fleshers and pullers (the floor workers remained unorganized in these shops).

During the strike, the Industrial Union started a drive to organize the fur dyeing shops as well. The workers in the Moose Fur Dyeing shop in Brooklyn joined the strike. When it was over, the Industrial Union won recognition by the employers; withdrawal of a wage cut; a $2 wage increase; hours of work reduced from fifty to forty-four a week; equal division of work; and a 3 percent unemployment insurance fund.

The Industrial Union now turned its attention to the important dressing and dyeing shop of Vande Weghe in Paterson, New Jersey.

The Vande Weghe firm had moved from Brooklyn to Paterson in 1919 to escape union organization. For thirteen years it remained an open shop. Highly skilled workers in the Vande Weghe shop earned only $12 for a fifty-hour week. Incredible as it may seem, young workers received the starvation wage of eight cents an hour. Negroes earned even less!

On September 15, 1932, the Industrial Union, under Langer's leadership, called a strike in the Vande Weghe shop. All workers in the shop, Negro and white, responded to the strike call. Determined to break the

---

* The price for working on white furs was raised from $1.85 per hundred to $2.65 per hundred. The price for working on Australian rabbits was raised from $1.50 to $1.85 per hundred. On the average, this raise amounted to more than $10 a week.

strike, the open-shop firm used all means at its disposal. And they were many. The Paterson police and courts cooperated. The Chamber of Commerce, which feared that victory in this strike would encourage the thousands of textile workers in the same town to revolt, exerted all its efforts to help Vande Weghe.

The strikers were terrorized by the police and plainclothesmen. Many were arrested for no reason whatsoever—dragged out of their beds in the dead of night and held for hours at the police station. Few were fortunate enough to escape severe beatings.

The militant strikers received help from other members of the Industrial Union, and from the International Labor Defense, the Workers International Relief, the Women's Council of Paterson, International Workers Order branches, the Communist Party, the Young Communist League and other progressive organizations. Many Paterson workers of other industries reinforced the picket lines. The tenants of houses in which the scabs were quartered were so moved by the mass meetings held in front of their buildings that they refused to pay their rent until the scabs were moved out. The New York fur workers played an important role in helping to win the strike. In shop after shop they refused to work on skins dressed by the scabs of Vande Weghe, a sharp contrast to the scabbing permitted in dressing shops controlled by Kaufman and Harris.

After twelve weeks of bitter strike, the Paterson strikers won a complete victory. The contract signed by the Industrial Union won a forty-four-hour week, an increase of $2 a week for week workers, a 10 percent increase for pieceworkers, a 3 percent unemployment insurance fund, recognition of the union, equal division of work, and a pledge to stop all discrimination against Negro workers.

News of the Vande Weghe victory quickly spread to fur dressers and dyers in Gloversville, Newark, Brooklyn, Manhattan, Bronx and other localities. There were twenty-four nationalities in the fur dressing and dyeing industries, including Italians, Jews, Latin-Americans and Negroes. All understood the common language of struggle. They knew that the Vande Weghe victory could be repeated in their shops.

Seventy workers in the Iceland shop struck first. After a few days of strike, they won a wage increase of $2 a week, reduction of working hours from fifty to forty-four hours, and a 3 percent unemployment insurance fund. The next day, forty workers in Kofsky's shop struck. Within a few days they obtained the same settlement as the Iceland shop. Next, the Superior shop struck and won, followed by the Mendoza shop.

In Gloversville, Brooklyn, Newark, the same story was repeated. From January 1 to February 10, 1933, the Fur Dressers and Dyers Department of the Industrial Union organized twenty-seven shops and won similar agreements.

One strike was particularly significant. The Chappell shop was under an agreement with the right-wing union. A few days before the expiration of the agreement in February 1933, the firm demanded a 25 percent wage cut. The workers insisted that unless the bosses signed an agreement similar to those in the Industrial Union shops, they would strike. In defiance of the workers, the right-wing leaders agreed with the firm on a partial wage cut. The workers promptly called the Industrial Union to lead them in a strike. The right-wing leaders did everything they could to break the strike. But after three weeks, the employers were forced to yield and signed an agreement with the Industrial Union. The wage cut was rescinded. The workers won a $2 increase and all other points of the Industrial Union contract.

Having organized many former open-shop centers of the fur dressing and dyeing industry, the Industrial Union now launched a campaign to organize the chief hold-outs in the industry—A. Hollander & Sons, J. Hollander, and Philip Singer, located in Newark, New Jersey. Morris Langer headed this drive.

Morris Langer's whole life was an example of militancy, courage and devotion to the working class. A worker since the age of twelve, he experienced all the hardships of workers in the dressing and dyeing shops. As a Communist, he devoted his life to the struggle to improve the workers' conditions. Modest, unassuming and fearless, he was respected and admired by all workers, left-wing and right-wing.

As one of the leaders of the struggle against the corrupt officials of the right-wing International, Langer was expelled from the International early in the AFL "reorganization." The members of Local 25 defied the intimidation of the International and a court injunction, and re-elected him manager. When the Industrial Union was founded, Langer became one of its outstanding leaders. It was largely due to Langer's great organizational ability and devotion that the fur dressers' and dyers' campaigns had been so successful. He also led demonstrations of the unemployed and on one occasion was arrested for heading a relief demonstration in Newark, but the protests of the Newark workers forced the court to free him. It was natural that Langer should be selected for the important task of organizing the Newark open shops.

Conditions in the three big open shops in Newark were unbearable. The workers of A. Hollander & Sons and J. Hollander, for example, were earning $6 to $10 for sixty to seventy-two hours of work under the usual unsanitary conditions that prevailed in the dressing and dyeing shops. The shop of Philip Singer was no better.

It was against such conditions that the workers of the big plants walked out on strike on February 22, 1933. Under the leadership of the Industrial Union, they demanded the return of previous wage cuts and a wage increase, shorter hours, protection against the poisonous dyes, recognition of the union, and an unemployment insurance fund.

The Newark police immediately came to the employers' assistance. They roped off seven blocks around the strike-bound plants and prohibited mass picketing. The strikers broke through the police cordon and battled scabs in hand-to-hand encounters. Meanwhile, the New York fur manufacturing workers showed their solidarity by refusing to work on the skins coming from the Hollander and Singer plants.

It will be recalled that in the 1915 strike against A. Hollander & Sons, strikebreaking gunmen shot and killed two strikers. The same kind of terrorism was now employed against the strikers in 1933. On Sunday, February 26, Natale Bolero, a leading young striker, 24 years old, was murdered in cold blood by an armed thug who sought Bolero out far from the scene of the strike and shot him to death. Rocco Cappo, Bolero's murderer, was arrested and found guilty of murder by a jury. The judge gave him only twelve years in prison.

The courts were not so lenient when it came to arresting and imprisoning the strikers. One after another, injunctions were issued against the workers of the Hollander plants. Strikers who insisted on their right to picket were dragged off to jail.

The cold-blooded murder of the young Hollander striker aroused all workers in the fur industry. On March 1, ten thousand furriers massed on 29th Street between Seventh and Eighth Avenues in New York, and staged a one-hour protest strike. Busloads of delegates from the dressing and dyeing shops in Paterson, Bayonne and Newark participated in the demonstration. In fur dressing and dye shops in Gloversville, Fairlawn, Bayonne, Paterson and Newark, the workers also responded to the call of the Industrial Union and stopped work in a one-hour general strike. Even the workers in Brooklyn shops controlled by the right-wing Locals 2 and 3 answered the call.

Large delegations of fur workers came to pay their respects and to honor the murdered striker as his body lay in state in Newark. When the funeral ceremony was over, the Hollander strikers at Bolero's grave solemnly pledged to continue the struggle until the Hollander plants were organized.

Three weeks later, the murderers struck again. At seven o'clock in the morning on the 22nd day of March, 1933, Morris Langer walked out of his home in the Floral Hill section of Chatham, New Jersey, and got into his car to drive to the strike headquarters in Newark. It was only by accident that Langer's two young children were not with him at the moment, for it was his custom to drop them off at school. On that morning, fortunately, they had not yet entered the car. When Langer pressed the starter, a bomb, planted beneath the hood of the automobile and connected with the ignition, exploded violently. Langer fell unconscious, his leg ripped off and his body torn to pieces.

Langer was rushed to the Overlook Hospital, his body soaked in blood. As soon as the news of the shocking tragedy reached the strike headquarters, strikers of the Hollander and Singer plants flocked to the hospital to try to save their leader's life. Many sat for two whole days and nights at the hospital awaiting their turn to give blood. Specialists were brought in by the Industrial Union to assist the doctors of the Overlook Hospital. But all efforts to save Langer were in vain. On March 26, 1933, the heroic leader of the fur dressers and dyers passed away. He was only 38 years old, leaving a grief-stricken wife and two daughters.

Langer's body was brought to the Newark headquarters of the Industrial Union. There, surrounded by an honor guard of Hollander strikers, he lay in state until five o'clock in the afternoon. After a demonstration at Military Park, the workers accompanied the body of their fallen leader to New York.

That same evening, Langer's body was carried through the streets of the New York garment center and afterwards to the headquarters of the Industrial Union. While the body remained in the union headquarters, attended by an honor guard of active union members and representatives of workers' organizations, thousands of sorrowful workers came to pay their last respects to their leader who was murdered for his devotion to the working class.

The Industrial Union called on all fur and needle trades workers to attend Langer's funeral: "Let us with more determination carry on the struggle conducted by Langer against the fur dressing and dyeing open-shoppers. Through this mass funeral let us express our condemnation of the cold-blooded murder of these workers and share our solidarity with the strikers."

When the funeral procession began, 28th Street was so solidly packed that no traffic could pass. Ten thousand workers gathered outside the Industrial Union building to hear the speakers on the balcony pay tribute to Langer. Tears flowed unashamedly down their cheeks as they heard Langer's widow call upon the workers "to cement their ranks and to continue the struggle for which my beloved husband gave all his years."

The funeral procession moved along Seventh Avenue, through the garment center, until 40th Street, then across town and over the Queensboro Bridge to the cemetery in Long Island. Five thousand workers took part in the procession, many more thousands lining both sides of the streets. The Hollander strikers, torn with grief, carried Langer's picture.

In the hall of the Industrial Union, another picture of Morris Langer was placed on the wall. The sign beneath it said: "WE WILL REMEMBER MORRIS LANGER BY BUILDING A GREATER UNION."

CHAPTER 36

Lepke-Gurrah

The dastardly murder of Morris Langer was a link in the vast chain that connected anti-labor employers, right-wing Socialist union chiefs and the most notorious of all gangs of underworld criminals. The links of this chain spelled out the most savage terror weapon of all—MURDER.

Throughout the 'twenties, the fur workers and other needle trades workers had been plagued by gunmen and sluggers used by bureaucratic Socialist union leaders to maintain their positions of power. Many a militant fur worker to this day carries the scars and wounds inflicted by mobsters wielding knives, lead pipes and bludgeons. Some even paid with their lives for defending their union and their right as working men. When the left wing attained leadership, the underworld characters, protected though they were by Tammany police, were driven out of the fur market by the rank-and-file workers organized in mass defense committees, and it seemed for a while that the worst stage of gangsterism had passed. But the bombing of Langer in March 1933 was the signal that a new orgy of violence and bloodshed was about to be loosed against the fur workers and the Industrial Union.

Out of the welter of gangs that preyed upon the workers for the past dozen years had emerged the underworld empire of Lepke-Gurrah, more powerful and far-reaching than all that had gone before—combining professional thieves, cutthroats, bootleggers, opium smugglers, racketeers and murderers.

Louis (Lepke) Buchalter and Jacob (Gurrah) Shapiro started their underworld careers in the Brownsville section of Brooklyn by preying on pushcart peddlers. Later, the two mob chieftains spread their operations to Manhattan and particularly to the garment center, where they worked as strong-arm men for the bureaucrats in the needle trades unions. At the same time, of course, they furnished the bosses with professional strikebreakers and hoodlums to break up picket lines. In times of strike, Lepke and Gurrah were on the payroll of the unions and the bosses, pocketing huge sums of money from both.

Lepke and Gurrah became fixtures in the ILGWU, the Amalgamated and other needle trades unions. They helped put through the AFL "reorganizations" against the revolting workers of the ILGWU. They were the power behind Abe "Knockout" Beckerman in the Amalgamated.* The gangsters and the right-wing union leaders pocketed whole union treasuries without ever bothering to give an account to the membership.

Lepke and Gurrah entrenched themselves strongly in the men's and ladies' clothing industries. Some employers willingly took them in as partners, assuring themselves of protection against strikes led by the left-wingers. Others resisted, but were soon brought into line when their shops were struck by the gangster-controlled union, their goods were drenched with acid, and they themselves were maimed for life. So powerful did Lepke and Gurrah become in the clothing industry that they actually owned many large shops and even financed many employers.

The tentacles of the Lepke-Gurrah gang reached into other industries as well. They controlled the pocketbook industry, fish markets, chicken markets, almost all the food industries and many more besides. When "Knockout" Beckerman was thrown out of the Amalgamated in 1931, the Lepke-Gurrah racket expanded into the fur dressing industry. The dressing and dyeing of furs is a service industry. Fur skins, owned either by dealers or manufacturers, are dressed and dyed at a stipulated price by fur dressing and dyeing firms. To snatch control of the industry, Lepke, Gurrah and Beckerman combined with a group of employers and set up a racket known as the Fur Dressers Factor Corporation. Another outfit, the Protective Fur Rabbit Dressing Association, was organized along the same lines for the rabbit dressing industry.

* So great was the scandal that Sidney Hillman, president of the Amalgamated, was eventually forced to oust the mobsters with the aid of the district attorney. Lepke and Gurrah, and "Knockout" Beckerman, were pushed out of the Amalgamated in 1931. Beckerman was expelled on charges of graft and corruption.

About the time that the racket was being organized, Morris Kaufman, the right-wing Socialist president of the AFL International, gave up his position in the union. He became manager of one of the Muskrat Divisions of the Fur Dressers Factor Corporation. Sam Cohen and Harry Yurman, two of his lieutenants, were also taken into the corporation.

Sluggers and thugs of the Lepke-Gurrah gang "visited" fur dressers and fur dealers and laid down the law. Thereafter they were to pay a stipulated price for every skin dressed, and pay it promptly every Friday to a representative of the Factor Corporation and the Protective Association. They were to give skins for dressing only to firms approved by the corporations. The fur dressers were no longer to do business with dealers. They had to become "members" of the corporations, from whom they would receive a stipulated number of skins each week to be dressed at the price ordered by the racketeers. No dresser could handle more than the number allocated to him by the corporations.

The racket yielded huge fortunes for the gang. For each skin handed out to be dressed, the racketeers set aside a few cents for themselves. With the Protective Fur Rabbit Dressing Association alone handling between twenty and thirty million rabbit skins each year, the "take" amounted to a fortune. The leaders of the racket allocated to themselves the largest share of the skins to be dressed. Dressing prices were raised 30 to 60 percent after the racket was organized. It was estimated that the racketeers netted close to $10,000,000 a year.

Naturally, the racket could only operate through a reign of terror. Dealers resisted the higher prices and the orders to ship only to members of the corporation. Many smaller fur dressers resisted the payment of initiation fees and the percentage rake-off extorted by the racket. Even some fur dressers who were assured by the racket of higher prices and prompt collections, refused to join. They foresaw that the racketeers would arbitrarily reduce their prices, or raise their own "cut," or take over their businesses completely.

The opposition did not last long. If mere threats failed to bring them around, any or all of several possibilities lay in store for them. They would be attacked by the gangsters, and beaten or stabbed. Acid would be thrown into their eyes. Acid would ruin the skins in their shops. "Stink bombs" would be exploded, ruining their merchandise and establishments. Fire would suddenly break out in their shops. Their places of business would be dynamited. Their shops would be struck or their workers quit without notice.

If such warnings still proved unavailing, the resisting dealer or dresser faced outright murder. The racketeers bombed the Waverly Fur Dressing establishment, killing an innocent night watchman. They bombed the Acme Fur Dressing Corporation, the Hunts Point Fur Dressing Corporation. They threw acid into the faces of Jay Joseph and M. Liebman, fur merchants. They stabbed Albert Williams. The list is staggering. Broken heads, arms and legs, knife wounds in the back or stomach, eyes blinded by acid, shops destroyed by bombs or fires, marked the bloody trail of the racket. The chain of outrageous atrocities committed by the racketeers in the fur industry, under the very eyes of the Police Department, is unmatched for ruthlessness and brutality in criminal annals.

The fur dealers and employers in the fur dressing shops were clubbed into submission. In mortal fear of their lives, they bowed to the murderous gang rule. Conniving with some and intimidating others, the Lepke-Gurrah gang and the others established a syndicate that dominated the fur dressing industry, controlling a business estimated at $170,000,000 a year.

From the fur dressing industry, the racketeers planned to spread into the fur manufacturing field, which offered even more lucrative possibilities. The gangsters and the right-wing union leaders working with them well remembered their plunder of this section of the industry in the 1920 strike and the years up to 1925.

But one great obstacle stood in the way of the racket's control of the fur dressing trade and its spread to fur manufacturing—the Industrial Union. To control the industry, the racket needed also to control the union.

The leaders of the right-wing locals in the fur dressing trade either submitted to the racketeers out of fear for their lives, or joined them outright in their nefarious operations. Right-wing leaders even saw in the racket an opportunity to "unionize" the open shops through the racket itself. The gang needed "unionized" shops with which to bludgeon resisting employers. It was a natural "set-up."

The union was a source of gravy to Lepke and Gurrah too. They plundered the union's treasury for all it had. The members of the right-wing locals had no idea of the entire conspiracy. They were neither consulted nor heeded. The dues and "organizing" taxes they paid went straight into the racketeers' pockets. The racketeers extorted so many thousands of dollars from the treasuries of Locals 2 and 3, that even these locals, financially the strongest in the AFL International, were reduced to virtual bankruptcy.

No victim of the racket dared complain to the authorities. Police, law enforcement authorities and influential politicians were either paid off or too frightened to tangle with the powerful mob leaders. Anyone who complained to the authorities was considered as practically signing his own death certificate. It seemed as if nothing and no one could stop the all-powerful racket.

No one except the Industrial Union!

As the Industrial Union developed its successful organizing drives in the fur dressing and dyeing industry in 1932, the racketeers were confronted with the fact that it was now the Industrial Union that was the dominant factor in the industry. Frank Buchner, treasurer of the Protective Fur Rabbit Dressing Association, later admitted that after the right-wing union had lost control over the fur dressing shops, the fate of the racket depended on whether or not the Industrial Union would be willing to cooperate. The racketeers were ready to "do business" with the Industrial Union. They were quite willing to recognize the Industrial Union in all shops and even grant concessions to the workers in Industrial Union shops in the form of increased wages. All the Industrial Union had to do was to call strikes where and when ordered by the racketeers and play along with the underworld set-up. Unfortunately for Lepke and Gurrah, the leaders of the Industrial Union were not "practical" men—they refused to do business with racketeers. Even more unfortunately for the racketeers, the leaders and members of the Industrial Union also refused to be terrorized by gangsters.

The first inkling the Industrial Union leaders had of the sinister underworld forces behind the phony Protective Fur Rabbit Dressing Association came during a meeting at the Governor Clinton Hotel late in 1932. The president of the "Protective Association," Samuel Mittleman, and the New York secretary of the Industrial Union, Irving Potash, met to discuss the terms of a contract between the union and the Association. Suddenly, Jacob (Gurrah) Shapiro walked into the room, and Mittleman rose to introduce him to Potash.

Potash, recognizing the gangster, asked Mittleman what he was doing at the meeting. "Well, we'll be together," the president of the Protective replied.

"I'll have nothing to do with Shapiro," Potash snapped angrily. "My dealing is with you."

"You will have to deal with Mr. Gurrah," Mittleman declared in a threatening voice, "because Mr. Gurrah *is* the Protective."

Potash stood his ground and insisted that he would not deal with Gurrah. Finally, Mittleman winked to Gurrah and asked him to leave for a few minutes. Gurrah left, but before leaving, he turned to Potash and said: "Potash, you will have to deal with me whether you like it or not."

Like other militant leaders and active workers of the left wing, Irving Potash had gone through many a fierce battle with the Lepke-Gurrah sluggers in the years past. In 1930, while Potash was leading a strike at 333 Seventh Avenue, the workers were suddenly set upon savagely by a mob of Lepke-Gurrah goons wielding knives. Seven workers, including Potash, were severely wounded. One worker had his entire cheek sliced off. The victims were rushed to the old New York Hospital.

Bathed in blood, Potash was first given up as too far gone for medical treatment. The doctor lifted his shirt, shook his head solemnly and moved on quickly to the others. Miraculously, however, none of the wounds had penetrated to any vital organ and Potash recovered.

The scars on Potash's back smarted when Mittleman tried to get him to talk to Gurrah. But he was not frightened by gangster threats. He knew that in every encounter with the Lepke-Gurrah mobsters, the furriers had always come out on top. The furriers had paid in blood for a clean and democratic union. They were going to have that union no matter how many battles they would have to fight against the underworld gang.

It was shortly after this meeting that Morris Langer conducted the strike against A. Hollander & Sons in Newark. Samuel Mittleman paid Langer a visit. The president of the Protective Association demanded that Langer order the members of the Industrial Union out of the shops in Gloversville. The racketeers wanted to punish those firms who refused to sign with the Protective Association or the Fur Dressers Factor Corporation.

Langer turned Mittleman down flat. He told him the Industrial Union was not a partner to any racket. The Gloversville workers were receiving union wages and all other union conditions, and the Industrial Union would not call these shops on strike.

"Don't be too wise," Mittleman warned Langer.

For his devotion to clean trade unionism, Langer paid with his life. There was plenty of evidence that the racketeers had a hand in Langer's murder. After Langer's death, Mittleman warned Ben Gold, Irving Potash, Julius Weil and Sam Burt they would meet the same fate as Langer. "You people," Mittleman told Gold and Potash, "should be more practical and avoid things like that in the future. You know that back of this Association [the Protective] are Lepke and Gurrah and they're not playing with toys." When Weil, an officer of the Industrial Union, resisted efforts of the racketeers to put fur dressing shops in Gloversville out of business, Mittleman warned him: "You seem to be as stubborn as Langer. See that you don't get the same thing."

Sam Burt, who took Langer's place as manager of the Industrial Union's Fur Dressers and Dyers Department, was also threatened by Mittleman: "There was a man who did not want to listen, and he doesn't listen any more. If you don't listen, you won't be able to listen any more either."

Then followed this conversation:

Mittleman: "No matter how many lessons you get you still don't understand and still don't have any brains. Maybe you would like to meet the boys?"

Burt: "No."

Mittleman: "These boys take care of things their own way."

Burt: "Who do you mean?"

Mittleman: "Well, Lepke and Gurrah. Do you think for a moment that if not for Lepke and Gurrah we would be able to keep all the members in the Association and be able to maintain the high prices in the market."

Although all of this evidence was made available to the police and the district attorney, the murderers of Langer went unpunished.

Events were rapidly shaping up for a life or death battle of the Industrial Union against the racket. The final links in the chain were even then fitting into place.

On January 17, 1933, Ben Gold requested a conference with the representatives of the Associated Fur Coat and Trimming Manufacturers Association to discuss a labor agreement between the Association and the Industrial Union. Four days later, the Associated indicated it was ready to meet the union's Conference Committee at the Pennsylvania Hotel. After six years of ceaseless struggle against the militant left-wing union, the big association was forced to reach this decision because of pressure from its members and because of the total collapse of the right-wing Joint Council.

The AFL-Socialist Joint Council was breathing its last. It had no money to pay the electric bill or for coal to heat the deserted office. The "boys" were compelled to play cards by candlelight. Begoon was hard-pressed "to find ways and means to either keep this office or a smaller one going."

Suddenly, a miracle occurred. The pall of gloom lifted from the premises of the Joint Council. The Associated refused to give in to the demands of the Industrial Union and the conferences were disrupted.* New life began to stir again in the Joint Council. The lights went on. A telephone was installed. A stenographer was engaged. Business was starting up.

It was later ascertained that the Associated collected funds from its employer members to fight the Industrial Union. Harry Begoon and Nathan Freiman, officers of the AFL Joint Council, suddenly opened a special banking account.

Busy conferences were taking place at the AFL headquarters in Washington. Samuel Shore, David Dubinsky's agent in the furriers' situation, and other right-wing Socialists met with William Green, Matthew Woll, Edward F. McGrady and William Collins for a new and decisive attack on the Industrial Union. Pietro Lucchi, president of the International Union, was not informed of these conferences. On April 5, 1933, William Green wrote to Lucchi and urged him to launch a "campaign immediately." Green informed Lucchi that "Organizer Collins will be assigned to help you, to advise with you and to represent the American Federation of Labor in cooperating with you in all the organizing work in which you may be engaged."

"I repeat again," Green closed his letter, "in all your work, please rely upon the cooperation and support of the American Federation of Labor."

Writing to Samuel Shore on April 5, Green informed him of the letter he had sent to Lucchi. "I wrote this letter, as you will recall, in conformity with an understanding reached at the conference held at my office today."

On Monday, April 24, 1933, an article in *Women's Wear* announced that "the American Federation of Labor has definitely decided to enter the labor situation in the fur manufacturing field and to enforce its contract." The article disclosed that the Associated had broken off conferences with the Industrial Union as soon as assurances were received that the AFL was ready "to step back into the picture." An agreement already existed between the Associated and the right-wing union, the

---

* Two of the main demands of the union involved in the disruption of the conference were: unemployment insurance paid for by the employers and administered by the workers, and equal division of work.

article continued, but due to the paralyzed state of the Joint Council it had never been enforced.

Then, the article significantly noted: "Just how to enforce this agreement, of course, becomes a problem for the International, but observers assert the manufacturers are apt to regard this as a problem that merely needs the application of what is termed with a wink, 'strenuous persuasion.' "

And the headline of the article: "A.F. OF L. TO ENTER LABOR SITUATION. Right Wing Group Attempts Realignment of Fur Workers. Drive Starts This Morning."

That same morning, April 24, an example of "strenuous persuasion" occurred which rocked all New York.

A few minutes before ten o'clock that morning a well-dressed woman entered the Industrial Union's building at 131 West 28 Street. She came up to the second floor, where the Fur Department was located. Approaching Jack Schneider, one of the organizers, she asked for a "working card" for the shop of Fox & Weisman. The well-dressed woman's visit aroused suspicion. For one, it was never the practice for furriers to ask for "working cards" from the Industrial Union when they received jobs. This procedure was only followed in the Joint Council—where the working card system had been installed in order to force workers to register with the right-wing union. And second, the shop of Fox & Weisman, for which the woman requested a "working card," happened to be one of the few shops still controlled by the Joint Council and not by the Industrial Union.

It became clear later that the purpose of this woman's visit was to "case" the layout of the office and ascertain where the leaders of the Industrial Union were meeting. Something must have gone wrong with the plans, for before she could flash a signal, all hell broke loose.

A few minutes after ten o'clock, fifteen armed gangsters—revolvers, knives and lead pipes in their hands—tore into the lobby of the building. Some fifteen or twenty workers, men and women, most of them older workers, were seated in the lobby. An aged pretzel-vendor, carrying his wares in a large basket, had just entered and was standing near the door. The clerical employees of the union were at work in a row of offices, separated from the lobby only by a wood-and-glass partition.

The gang of armed thugs rushed onto the floor and immediately opened fire upon the unarmed workers. Some swung lead pipes and blackjacks, wounding several of them.

N. Y. Daily News Photo

What was left of the gangsters who attacked the Industrial Union headquarters on April 24, 1933. Workers themselves beat them off.

Irving Potash

New York Post *editorial praising Irving Potash and Samuel Burt for their courage in presenting the testimony that clinched the government's case against the racketeers, Lepke and Gurrah.*

Samuel Burt

New York Post
Nov. 11, 1936

A Labor Victory Over Racketeering

It is important that the precise significance of the Federal Court convictions of Louis ("Lepke") Buchalter and Jacob ("Gurrah") Shapiro be understood.

There is a danger the man-on-the-street will carry away only the confused impression that the trials had something or other to do with crooked labor unions.

The danger is, therefore, that the Lepke and Gurrah convictions will hereafter come to be cited as examples of labor-union racketeering, happily ended in the courts. We are told that is happening already.

The truth is that the Lepke and Gurrah convictions are outstanding examples of racketeering *ended by courageous coöperation of trade union leaders with the United States prosecutor.*

Lepke and Gurrah were convicted of racketeering in the rabbit skin industry largely on the testimony of Irving Potash, assistant manager of the joint council of the International Fur Workers' Union and of Samuel Burt, manager of the Fur Dyers Union, Local 88.

These two filled in the outlines of the Government's story of how Lepke and Gurrah had terrorized both labor and employers in the fur industry, gaining effective control of the rabbit fur trade, amounting to $10,000,000 a year.

The courageous testimony of Potash and Burt gave backbone to the Government's case. It directly linked these two gangsters with the notorious Protective Fur Dressers Corporation, which dominated the industry.

Potash and Burt have set examples to other unions with house-cleaning problems on their hands. It should be a matter of pride to the labor movement that it has done what local law enforcers were never able to do; that it has helped break the amazing immunity enjoyed by these two thugs for so many years.

The Lepke-Gurrah convictions are labor's pride, not labor's shame. It will be a pity if enemies of union labor are allowed to broadcast the opposite impression.

WOMEN'S WEAR DAILY, MONDAY, APRIL 24, 1933

A. F. OF L. TO ENTER LABOR SITUATION

Right Wing Group Attempts Realignment of Fur Workers

Drive Starts This Morning — Most Plants at Present Not Operating to Any Great Degree

The American Federation of Labor has definitely decided to enter the labor situation in the fur manufacturing field and to enforce its contract with the Associated Fur Coat & Trimming Manufacturers, Inc., it was learned in authentic circles. In fact, the first steps toward such a move were scheduled for today.

This morning, as if in anticipation of this move, larger crowds of workers than usual were present in the fur district

No official comment could be had this morning from the right wing union as to the truth of the report, but it was learned unofficially in right wing circles that the report was substantially correct.

Officials of the Associated Fur Coat & Trimming Manufacturers, Inc., this morning and Saturday declared they had no knowledge of the situation, and suggested that the American Federation of Labor would know better than anyone else whether they would enter the labor situation.

It was pointed out that the American Federation of Labor is a party with the International Fur Workers Union to the agreement with the Associated, and that perhaps they might feel bound to enforce the terms of the agreement.

No one could be reached for comment at the local headquarters of the American Federation of Labor this morning.

While the trade believed that a drive was scheduled to commence this morning, in authentic circles it was learned that this was not to be the case, but that definite action would be taken later.

Because of the fact that employment is at a low ebb in the fur manufacturing industry at this time of the year, some of the trade were of the opinion that no drastic measures such as a lockout would be affected because while a lockout in ordinary times would be a drastic step, at this time of the year, it would mean nothing. Hence, it was believed in manufacturing circles that the right wing group will insist that any worker employed by a member of the Associated have an International card.

Just how to enforce this agreement, of course, becomes a problem for the International, but observers assert the manufacturers are apt to regard this as a problem that merely needs the application of what is termed with a wink, "strenuous persuasion."

The action by the A. F. of L. follows months of discord in the fur trade between the workers and the employers, during which the Associated went so far as to negotiate with the left wing group on the theory that they were perfectly willing to deal with any group that represented the workers.

These negotiations broke off, and since that time the Associated has been trying to get the A. F. of L. to step back into the picture.

The AFL re-enters the fur situation, and Women's Wear *predicts that "strenuous persuasion" will be used on the furriers.*

Shirley Koretz, the switchboard operator, immediately plugged in the phone upstairs to the second floor where Ben Gold and other union leaders were meeting and gave the alarm. "Gangsters! Gangsters!" she screamed into the phone, until she was sure the warning was heard. Moe Feinblatt, who worked in the bookkeeper's office, rushed to the fire-escape and shouted at the top of his lungs: "Gangsters! Gangsters!"

One of the gunmen, a big knife in his hand, ran into the office occupied by Miss Koretz. He pulled out all the phone connections and demanded, "Where is Ben Gold?" Not receiving a reply, he slashed at the telephone wire just behind the switchboard, thinking it the outside connection. Miss Koretz, still at her post, plugged in quickly and called the police even as the armed thug was running around, slashing other wires and cursing. Her duty done, she ran behind the metal safe to protect herself from the gangster's attack.

All this took but a few moments. During this time the workers in the hall were too stunned to rally. The gangsters continued shooting, beating the workers with iron pipes, and smashing the windows of the offices.

Then things began to pop. The leaders of the Industrial Union, alerted by Miss Koretz' calls, rushed down from the second floor and took on the gangsters. Workers who heard Moe Feinblatt's shouts rushed in from the street and jumped into the fray.

Simultaneously, word flashed through the market that "Ben Gold has been knifed." It was as though a great siren had sounded. Thousands of workers hastily dropped their tools and poured out of the shops. In a matter of minutes, they came pouring into the union headquarters from all directions. By the hundreds they came bounding down side streets and along Seventh Avenue.

Police also came running, but the workers rushed into the union building ahead of them. They caught the gangsters as they were fleeing from the defenders inside. The gunmen opened fire wildly. One fur worker was murdered on the spot. The gangsters' wild crossfire even mowed down one of their own number. Then the workers let them have it.

It was all over in less than fifteen minutes. Six gangsters lay unconscious on the sidewalk in front of the union hall. The others fled for their lives in all directions to escape the wrath of the fur workers.

Fifteen innocent workers were wounded by the gunmen. A bullet fired into the stomach of Harry Gottfried resulted in his death five months later. About 50 years of age, Gottfried left a wife and three children.

Two gangsters were slain in the attack, one by a stray bullet from the gun of another thug, and the other by a policeman. Seven gangsters were arrested and arraigned in the homicide court on the charge of assault in the first degree. Their records revealed many previous arrests, mostly for carrying lead pipes and knives in areas where strikes were going on.

The following day every New York newspaper carried pictures of the six gunmen lying prostrate on the sidewalk in front of the Industrial Union headquarters. The anti-union gutter journals snidely labeled the picture, "Victims of red riot waiting for the ambulance!" Some papers observed, regretfully, that the underworld characters were "inexperienced gangsters."

But nothing could conceal the magnificent heroism the fur workers displayed in defending their union and their union leaders, which evoked the respect and admiration of the workers everywhere. Three days before the attack, the Industrial Union had issued a bulletin warning the fur workers that new conspiracies were being plotted against them. The bulletin also served notice on the conspirators that the furriers would give them the answer they deserved. "They will pay for every drop of workers' blood spilled by their gangsters."

On Monday, April 24, the fur workers met the gangsters and made them pay. Thereafter, not even the dreaded Lepke-Gurrah gang dared to show their faces again in the fur market. It was a lesson the gunmen never forgot.

The fighting furriers—men and women, Negro and white, young and old—were more fearless, more loyal, more devoted to their union than ever. What enemies could ever conquer such workers?

CHAPTER 37

The Real Racket-Busters

The public scandal of gangs of gunmen attacking in broad daylight, shooting, knifing, killing and crippling workers, was too spectacular to be squashed. On the basis of testimony of union leaders and members, the seven gangsters arrested after the invasion of the union headquarters were tried and convicted. But the leaders who planned and ordered the criminal attack were still at large. The authorities took no action whatever to unearth these culprits. On the contrary, they tried to cover up for them by labeling the murderous gang attack just "another incident" in the fur market.

Law enforcement authorities were reluctant to probe deeply into the attack on the Industrial Union. The Lepke-Gurrah racketeers bought protection from policemen, judges and Tammany politicians. A real investigation would lead to the very heart of the racket and expose one of the most shameful scandals in New York history. The role played by fur bosses' associations, right-wing labor leaders and the officialdom of the American Federation of Labor would be uncovered. The article in *Women's Wear* on the very morning of the attack was quite pointed. So worried were AFL officials by this article that they quickly asserted that the Federation did not plan to re-enter the fur situation, maintaining that "the New York furriers' situation is purely a local affair." However, Green's letters, hitherto secret, belie that statement.

The Industrial Union, however, was determined to bring the leaders of the racket before the bar of justice. It issued hundreds of thousands of circulars, pamphlets and press statements exposing the racketeers to the government authorities and to the public. At scores of street meetings, it publicly revealed the crimes of the racketeers. The governmental authorities were literally forced to act against the Lepke-Gurrah gang.

Two days after the gangster attack, the Industrial Union sent a letter to Governor Herbert Lehman, District Attorney Crain and Police Commissioner Bolen. The letter, signed by Ben Gold and Irving Potash, charged: "This criminal attack upon our organization is part of a general plan to extend and implant within the fur manufacturing industry a form of racketeering that is already prevalent in some of the other branches of the industry. . . It is because of the refusal of our organization to submit to the will of the racketeers that the attack was made. We have proof to show that the same bosses and racketeer organizations which are responsible for murdering Bolero and Langer are also responsible for the criminal attack on our union last Monday. . ."

Gold and Potash insisted: "We demand, therefore, the right to bring all our proof which will show that the criminal attack was part of the conspiracy of racketeers to become the rulers in the fur industry. The plan was originated by a group of manufacturers, leaders of the American Federation of Labor and racketeers who are seeking to destroy our union and to hinder the possibility of the workers improving their working conditions. We protest very sharply against any attempt of government officials to hinder the investigation of the facts of this entire situation."

Prodded by the Industrial Union, the district attorney began to move a bit. On April 28, Abraham Beckerman, the right-wing Socialist "hero," was arrested along with four officials of the Fur Dressers Factor Corporation.

Further than this, the authorities refused to go. The racket seemed to be immune from the law. Lucchi informed a right-wing International official on May 12: "As far as the riot which occurred a few weeks ago in the communist headquarters—I am happy to inform you that none of our members were even questioned."

The indictment of Beckerman and the other officials of the Fur Dressers Factor Corporation did not stop the racketeers. Not at all concerned about the authorities, and certain that no employer would risk his life by speaking up, the Lepke-Gurrah gunmen and their allies were doing business as usual. New threats were made on the lives of the leaders of the Industrial Union almost daily. Samuel Mittleman again demanded that the union withdraw workers from shops in Gloversville to put employers out of business. He even demanded that the union contribute substantial sums of money for the purpose of bombing these plants. On August 1, 1933, Mittleman called Irving Potash and gave him final notice. If he failed to comply with the demand of the racketeers, he would "receive the same treatment as Langer."

Once again the Industrial Union demanded that the authorities go after the racketeers. In letters to District Attorney Thomas C. T. Crain and to federal, state and local officials, the union listed "several outstanding atrocious incidents." It notified them that "the union has declared war upon the racketeers and will continue an endless struggle until they are fully and completely eliminated from the industry." The letter gave a detailed description of the terror instituted by the racketeers, cited specific examples of bombings of fur dressing shops, the killing and stabbing of individuals, the shooting of Gottfried, and the murder of Morris Langer. It accused the racketeers of threatening leaders of the Industrial Union with Langer's fate if they persisted in refusing to comply with the racket's demands. It charged that despite the information already made available by the union, there had been "no disposition on the part of the authorities to take any definite action against the continuance of this form of murderous, criminal conduct in disregard of life and property."

"In view of the seriousness of the situation," the Industrial Union concluded, "we expect that immediate action be taken on your part. You will find us ready and willing to furnish all details available to us in order to initiate this investigation."

The Industrial Union mobilized the workers themselves. Mass protest demonstrations against racketeering and underworld control over the needle trades industry were held in Union Square. All workers, left-wing and right-wing supporters, were urged to unite their ranks "to drive the gangsters out of the needle trades and to fight those who are responsible for bringing them into the industry." Special defense corps were established to protect the union headquarters and leaders. The fur workers let the underworld racketeers know that although they might buy Tammany politicians and intimidate merchants and manufacturers, the terror against the union must end.

The gangsters knew from experience what this warning meant. Although Lepke and Gurrah and their gunmen continued to threaten members and leaders of other unions with death, they gave the fur market a wide berth. They did not dare to be seen there. The picture of six gangsters lying unconscious on the sidewalk outside the headquarters of the

**CALL OF THE NEEDLE TRADES WORKERS INDUSTRIAL UNION
TO ALL**

NEEDLE TRADES WORKERS

**Forward to the demonstration against racketeering and underworld
control over the Needle Trades Industry!**

FURRIERS — CLOAKMAKERS — DRESSMAKERS — MEN'S TAILORS — MILLINERY —
KNITGOODS AND WHITE GOODS WORKERS — CUSTOM TAILORS AND ALL OTHERS!
RIGHT WINGERS AND LEFT WINGERS!   NEGRO AND WHITE!
ORGANIZED AND UNORGANIZED WORKERS!
**LET US TAKE UP THE STRUGGLE TO DRIVE THE RACKETEERS AND GANGSTERS FROM THE
NEEDLE TRADES INDUSTRY!**

PARTICIPATE IN THE TENS OF THOUSANDS IN THE

PROTEST DEMONSTRATION

Sat. May 13, 1 o'clock at Union Square

Sisters and Brothers:

The murderous attack upon the NEEDLE TRADES WORKERS INDUSTRIAL UNION in an attempt to kill the leaders, following right upon the heels of the fatal bombing of Morris Langer, must

cloak and dressmakers as well as other needle trades workers in struggle for better conditions.

NEEDLE TRADES WORKERS:

We must continue the struggle against the

The Industrial Union mobilizes the workers against gangsterism.

Industrial Union remained fresh in their minds. For the first time in the history of the widespread Lepke-Gurrah rackets, a union had given fierce battle and driven the gangsters out of the industry. What the police and detectives, the district attorney, the courts, the Department of Justice and other state and federal officials were unable or unwilling to do, the Industrial Union had done. Although it later became fashionable for publicity-seeking political aspirants to pose as "racket-busters," the Industrial Union leaders and active members were the real racket-busters that broke the back of the racket.

As a result of the union's relentless pressure, the authorities were finally forced to act. The repeated public charges of the union could no longer be pigeonholed. For several weeks, the Federal Bureau of Investigation conducted a secret investigation of fur racketeering. Despite daily threats from the gangsters, Gold, Potash, Schneider, Burt, Winogradsky and other Industrial Union leaders boldly presented detailed facts to the government investigators on the scope and manner of the racket's operations.

On November 6, 1933, a Federal Grand Jury handed down three indictments. The first indictment named the Fur Dressers Factor Corporation and Carl Mansini, its president; the Associated Employers of Fur

Workers, Inc., and Abraham Beckerman, its general manager; the Allied Muskrat Dressers' Corporation, the International Fur Workers Union, Locals 2 and 3, and Pietro Lucchi, International president, Morris Reiss and Isaac B. Hertzberg of Local 2.

The second indictment, affecting the rabbit skin trade, named the Protective Rabbit Fur Dressing Association and Samuel Mittleman, its president; twenty-four firms, and nine individuals including the "Socialist" leaders Sam Cohen and Morris Kaufman. Among these nine defendants named were Louis (Lepke) Buchalter and Joseph (Gurrah) Shapiro.

But the third indictment was an astounding document to all familiar with the heroic battle of the Industrial Union to smash the racket. The third indictment was against the Needle Trades Workers Industrial Union in its branches relating to the fur trade, and twenty-eight leaders and rank-and-file members of the union. Among those indicted and arrested were: Ben Gold, Irving Potash, Jack Schneider, Joseph Winogradsky, Sam Burt, Julius Weil, Max Kochinsky, Herman Paul, Morris Angel, Maurice H. Cohen, Gus Hopman, Al Weiss, Mark Boerum, Louis Hyman, and Sol Wollin.

Thus, the very men who had battled the racketeers, the very men who had forced the Federal investigation by their public charges and had supplied the facts that exposed the operation of the racket—were now indicted. This third indictment, significantly, did not and could not charge the Industrial Union leaders with racketeering. It charged them with violating the Sherman Anti-Trust Act by calling strikes in Newark and other cities, thereby interfering with "interstate commerce." The Sherman Anti-Trust Act, passed sixty years before and amended by the Clayton Act, specifically provided that it did not apply to unions conducting strikes for wage increases and improved working conditions. It was intended to be used against the big monopolies, not against labor.

"As far as we can see it," Irving Potash indignantly protested, "the only charges against us are of union activity. Union organization work we will never give up."

Ben Gold protested bitterly: "The murderers of Morris Langer are free. The murderers of Harry Gottfried are free. The murderers of Natale Bolero are free. Twenty-eight leaders of the Industrial Union are indicted and in danger of being sent to prison because they organized and are leading the furriers in a struggle for better conditions, because they dared to fight the exploiters, racketeers and cutthroats."

So transparent was the union-busting character of the indictment of the Industrial Union leaders that the authorities did not dare bring it to trial in 1933. But it was not quashed. It was carefully kept on file for seven years, to be brought out when the Department of Justice and the employers thought the atmosphere was ripe to twist the anti-trust law into an instrument to smash unions. And even then the United States Court of Appeals had to throw the case out.

Undoubtedly the anti-trust indictment of Industrial Union leaders was intended to sidetrack the investigation of the racket into a drive against militant trade unionism. Unquestionably, too, it was calculated to terrorize left-wingers from further exposing the influential connections of the racketeers. However, the Industrial Union leaders could not be sidetracked or intimidated. Having driven the Lepke-Gurrah gangs out of the fur market, they now provided the testimony that finally placed Lepke and Gurrah behind bars.

In 1936, the government finally brought trial against Lepke and Gurrah. The case was airtight—but the government could not find witnesses with the courage to step forward and testify. Thousands of people had enough on Lepke and Gurrah to convict them, but were afraid to speak up. Potential witnesses, victims of the racket, died mysteriously. There were "accidents." Some vanished. Others knew that to speak up in court was to invite a bullet in the back or a suit of concrete at the bottom of the river.

Some witnesses did testify on racketeering in food, garment, trucking, cleaning and other industries. They even told of being terrorized into paying tribute to "protective associations." But all studiously avoided mentioning the dreaded names of Lepke and Gurrah. The *New York Times* pointed out: "None of the witnesses identified the defendants Lepke and Gurrah as their assailants." Again: "Neither of the witnesses . . . linked Buchalter or Shapiro to the corporation's activities."

At this point the fur workers' leaders, defying all threats, came forward fearlessly. Irving Potash and Sam Burt testified in court. For three days, from October 27 to October 30, 1936, Potash and Burt exposed the racketeering in the fur industry, mentioned Lepke and Gurrah by name, showed their connection with the racket, and brought to light their murderous activities against the union and against employers who had refused to comply with their orders.

The clear-cut testimony of Potash and Burt provided the vital missing link for the prosecution. Their testimony clinched the convictions and put Lepke and Gurrah behind prison bars. It smashed the Lepke-Gurrah

rackets not only in the fur industry, but in food, garment and other industries as well. Many unions, now freed from the domination of the
Lepke-Gurrah gang, benefited by the testimony of the furriers' leaders.

When the Lepke-Gurrah appeal came before the higher courts, U. S.
Solicitor General Robert H. Jackson declared: "The resentment of appellants' counsel against these two [Irving Potash and Samuel Burt] can
be easily understood when it is remembered that they were the persons
who gave the most damaging testimony against appellants."

Commending Potash and Burt for their courageous testimony, the
New York Post declared in an editorial on November 11, 1936:

"A LABOR VICTORY OVER RACKETEERING

"It is important that the precise significance of the Federal Court
convictions of Louis ('Lepke') Buchalter and Jacob ('Gurrah') Shapiro
be understood.

"There is a danger the man-on-the-street will carry away only the confused impression that the trials had something or other to do with
crooked labor unions. The danger is, therefore, that the Lepke and
Gurrah convictions will hereafter come to be cited as examples of labor-
union racketeering, happily ended in the courts. We are told that is
happening already.

"The truth is that the Lepke and Gurrah convictions are outstanding
examples of racketeering ended by courageous cooperation of trade union
leaders with the United States prosecutor. Lepke and Gurrah were convicted of racketeering in the rabbit skin industry largely on the testimony
of Irving Potash . . . and of Samuel Burt. These two filled in the outlines of the Government's story of how Lepke and Gurrah had terrorized
both labor and employers in the fur industry, gaining effective control
of the rabbit fur trade, amounting to $10,000,000 a year.

"The courageous testimony of Potash and Burt gave backbone to the
Government's case. It directly linked these two gangsters with the notorious Protective Fur Dressers Corporation, which dominated the industry. Potash and Burt have set examples to other unions with house-
cleaning problems on their hands. It should be a matter of pride to the
labor movement that it has done what local law enforcers were never
able to do; that it has helped break the amazing immunity enjoyed by
these two thugs for so many years.

"The Lepke-Gurrah convictions are labor's pride, not labor's shame.
It will be a pity if enemies of union labor are allowed to broadcast the
opposite impression."

The Achievement of Unity

CHAPTER 38

The Blue Eagle

"Workers shall have the right to organize and bargain collectively through representatives of their own choosing, and shall be free from interference, restraint or coercion of employers of labor, or other agents. . ." These were the opening words of the famous Section 7A of the National Industrial Recovery Act which was signed by President Roosevelt on June 13, 1933.

The National Industrial Recovery Act authorized the setting up of Codes for every industry. Pressure of the mounting millions of jobless workers forced a provision in the NRA Codes to limit the work week. And the rapidly increasing number of union struggles by the workers compelled recognition in the NRA of the legal right of workers to organize in unions of their own choosing.

At the same time, big business interests put into the NRA sweeping provisions that permitted them to fix prices, restrict production and engage in other monopolistic practices banned by the anti-trust laws. Profits of the big corporations rose sharply under the NRA. General Motors, for example, increased its profit from only $169,979 in 1932 to $83,214,000 in 1933.

Both the wording of Section 7A and its administration by Code Authorities (with a Blue Eagle as the symbol) did not hinder anti-labor employers from setting up company unions. In fact, during the first six months of the NRA the number of company unions in existence rose from 313 to 2,975, the highest number in the history of American labor.

The right of workers to belong to the union of their own choosing was publicly demanded by the AFL during the drafting of the NRA. In practice, this was the very same elementary right that William Green and other AFL officials insisted on denying to the fur workers.

On May 22, 1933, William Green publicly announced another AFL campaign against the fur workers, and assigned William Collins to the task. The following day, Dudley Field Malone, lawyer for the Joint Council, informed the press that he had promised the manufacturers to "exterminate the Communists" with the aid of the police. And the day after that, the *New York Times* reported: "A campaign to rid the fur industry of all Communists and Left Wing labor organizations will be started by the American Federation of Labor with the aid and support of the city administration and the Police Department, it was announced last night at a meeting of the Associated Fur Coat and Trimming Manufacturers Association. . . With the aid of additional uniformed policemen, detectives, and members of the industrial squad . . . a distribution of pamphlets will be begun. . . With the support of the police they expect to 'purge' the industry completely."

Notices were posted in all Association shops that every worker would have to show an AFL union card beginning May 25. Two Joint Council officials tried to distribute a leaflet to this effect in the fur market. As the company union representatives walked down Seventh Avenue, guarded by mounted policemen, police on foot, detectives and the Industrial Squad, a loud chorus of boos rose from the workers crowding the streets. From hundreds of windows in the tall buildings the workers in the shops joined in the booing. The *Day* reported that the noise was "so loud that it could be heard from one block to another."

Tearing the leaflets handed them into tiny scraps, the furriers flung them back into the faces of the two right-wing agents. Then they formed a moving picket line around the two men. Mounted police drove into the mass of workers to scatter them. But the furriers did not move. The line continued until the police advised the right-wing agents it would be safer for them to leave. They departed, accompanied by a heavy guard of police and detectives. Five thousand furriers followed them and staged a demonstration right at the very doors of the Joint Council.

So frightened were the bosses by this demonstration that only twenty-two shops dared try to force their workers into the AFL. Some bosses even wrote out their own checks to pay for registration cards in the Joint Council. The workers tore up the checks, ripped down the notices from the walls, and walked out on strike. Within two days, the bosses were running to the Industrial Union for settlements. They had to pay the workers for time lost while they were striking, agree to make payments to an unemployment insurance fund, and recognize the right of the workers to belong to the Industrial Union.

A letter from Herman Scheidlinger, president of the Association, again ordered the employers to demand AFL registration cards from the workers. He assured them that if the workers struck there would be plenty of police on hand. Strong-arm men, too, helped the bosses. With the police calmly looking on, they forcibly pulled the workers down from the shops and tried to drag them to the Joint Council headquarters. The workers put up strong resistance every inch of the way.

By June 5, the terror in the fur market impelled Norman Thomas, the Socialist Party leader, to protest the actions of the Socialist Joint Council leaders. "Even though I am still investigating the matter," he declared, "I can state that I condemn any so-called attempt of Mayor O'Brien and the police to organize workers."

The City Central Committee of the Socialist Party, however, by a vote of 53 to 16, upheld the stand of the right-wing leaders in conspiring with bosses and police to compel the workers to join the AFL Joint Council. They warned Socialist leaders not to copy Thomas' efforts to ascertain the true facts without first "gaining the party's approval."

Failing, despite these efforts, to bludgeon the workers into registering, the AFL union next went to court for an injunction against both the Association and the Industrial Union. The Association actually pleaded with the judge to grant such an injunction ordering every fur worker into the Joint Council.

The whole thing smelled to high heaven. In the words of Norman Thomas, who was still investigating the battle in the fur market, the Joint Council "got funds somehow—our committee did not discover how —to carry on and to get an injunction, *uncontested by the bosses,* the first and principal provision of which was to prevent the bosses from hiring members of the left wing." Years later it was made public that the funds referred to came from the employers themselves and were paid weekly to Begoon to keep the AFL Joint Council alive.

Under questioning by Louis Boudin, lawyer for the Industrial Union, the AFL officials had to admit that the furriers belonged to the Industrial Union. The Joint Council existed only on paper.

At the same time, over seven thousand fur workers signed affidavits swearing that they had voluntarily become members of the Fur Department of the Needle Trades Workers Industrial Union. The judge was forced to recognize that the vast majority of the furriers belonged to the Industrial Union and the injunction case was thrown out of court.

On June 23, 1933, ten days after the NRA became the law of the land, Pietro Lucchi, president of the International, wrote to a right-wing official: "I am confident that this recovery bill will be helpful to us. Things look brighter now than in the past."

Hearings were to take place for a Code for the fur industry. Even though the Joint Council did not dare answer the Industrial Union's challenge to produce a hundred bona fide members, the NRA administrators were ready to recognize the Council as the representative of the fur workers.

In this situation, a group of public-spirited civic leaders decided to speak out to demand trade union democracy. A "Citizens Committee to Investigate Conditions in the Fur Industry" was established in July 1933. It included Professor Horace M. Kallen of the New School for Social Research (chairman); Thyra Samter Winslow, author (secretary); Theodore Dreiser, author; John Chamberlain, associate editor of the *Saturday Review of Literature;* Kyle Crichton, editor of *Scribner's Magazine;* Lucille Copeland, of the Conference for Progressive Labor Action; Rabbi Benjamin Goldstein; Professor Jerome Michael of Columbia University Law School, and other distinguished citizens.

The committee held public hearings for two weeks. It sent invitations to the employers and their associations, to Roger Baldwin, the impartial chairman under the agreement between the Trimming Association and the Industrial Union, to representatives of the Joint Council, and to representatives of the Industrial Union. All were invited to testify.

Not a single representative of either the Joint Council or the Associated was willing to appear. Consequently, the committee was compelled to examine the claims of the Joint Council and the Associated set forth in their applications to the court for an injunction. The committee studied the entire court record, along with published statements and interviews.

The committee heard the testimony of leaders of the Industrial Union; of several former officers and members of the Joint Council; of Emil K. Ellis, spokesman for the Trimming Association; and of Roger Baldwin, the impartial chairman.

The committee's conclusions laid "special stress on the evidence of Mr. Emil K. Ellis and Mr. Roger Baldwin, who are not parties to the conflict but have a definite interest in the maintenance of peace and effective organization in the Fur Industry."

The Citizens Committee's public finding declared:

"That the great majority of the workers in the fur industry of New York City are members of the Fur Department, Needle Trades Workers Industrial Union.

"That this union is a strong, effective organization, willing and ready to keep its agreements by enforcing discipline among its members and meeting all other obligations involved in collective bargaining, while the Joint Council has proved in these respects unsatisfactory.

"That although this union is customarily called 'The Left Wing,' its members belong to all kinds of political parties, and that membership in the union does not impose political faith or any political affiliation whatsoever.

"That the charge of 'Communism' is being used only to discredit the Union in the public mind, and to provide a fictitious excuse for vitiating the authority of its officers, breaking its organization and driving away its members, by threats and intimidations.

"That the present disorder in the Fur Industry is due to a collusive activity toward this end by the Manufacturers' Association and the Joint Council.

"That, to further this end, the Manufacturers' Association and the Joint Council entered into a collusive arrangement whereby an injunction was obtained by the Joint Council restraining the Manufacturers' Association from employing any persons or other than members of the Joint Council, inasmuch as the application for injunction was granted also for the same reason. That the injunction, if continued, would by legal duress compel members of the Industrial Union to affiliate themselves with the Joint Council.

"That workers have, in fact, been beaten and intimidated into joining the Joint Council.

"That numerous assaults on members of the Union have been committed by paid gangsters and that the gangsters have been represented in court by attorneys for the Joint Council or the manufacturers or both.

"That such assaults have been committed with the knowledge of the police, and that the police have made no efforts to prevent them.

"That the Fur Industry in the City of New York is today suffering a reign of terror which threatens the fundamental right of the workers as employees and as citizens.

"That the just and equitable application of the National Industrial Recovery Act makes it necessary and desirable to establish the preferred affiliation of the workers of the Fur Industry.

"That under the terms of the Act, affiliation in a Union must be voluntary and uncoerced, the free choice of the worker."

The Citizens Committee then recommended that an impartial tribunal conduct a referendum among the fur workers to determine the proportional representation of the Joint Council and the Industrial Union before the National Recovery Administration.

The report of the Citizens Committee fully substantiated the charges of the Industrial Union against the Associated, AFL officials and the Socialist Party.

While the NRA stalled and the right-wingers waited for the government officials to rescue them from bankruptcy, the Industrial Union moved ahead. At the same time that it was presenting the demands it wanted included in the NRA Code, the Industrial Union won July raises averaging $5 a week. It conducted a series of struggles to enforce union conditions in 90 percent of the shops. The minimum scales were enforced. The unemployment fund was collected. Overtime work was stopped in hundreds of shops, enabling about two thousand unemployed workers to get jobs.

On August 9, a jammed meeting of shop chairmen and shop committees was held at Webster Hall by the Industrial Union. At this meeting and again at a giant mass meeting at Cooper Union the following week, a resolution was unanimously adopted that *all shops in the fur industry work thirty-five hours a week beginning September 1, at the same pay as forty hours.*

Six hundred shops—coat, trimming and independent—went out on strike for the thirty-five-hour week under the leadership of the Industrial Union. They returned to work only when their employers agreed to this at no reduction in pay. The Industrial Union started conferring with the Trimming Association as a whole on this question. Meanwhile, hundreds of employers, including members of the Associated (coat Association) yielded. The Industrial Union's prestige grew even greater. The left-wing leadership had won the forty-hour-week in 1926. Now it took another giant stride ahead. The demand for the thirty-five-hour week spread into the remaining shops in the fur industry.

After a hurried meeting between the leaders of the Joint Council and the Associated, the manufacturers' association came to a hard decision. It announced it was signing the "blanket" Code (tentative NRA Code for all industries until each industry adopted its own) with a thirty-five-hour week beginning September 5. By this maneuver, the Associated hoped to stop the march of the Industrial Union and perhaps keep the Joint Council alive.

To the workers in the market and in the shops, it was clear. The battles of the Industrial Union on the picket line had forced the Associated to concede the thirty-five-hour week. The Trimming Association had to grant it directly to the Industrial Union. The fur pointing shops, persian "plate" shops, and retailers had to follow suit, with substantial raises in wages as well.

The right-wing International was gasping for breath. In October 1933, it paid per capita to the AFL on 455 members! It appealed to Dubinsky for aid, but the latter was unwilling to throw more money down the drain.

The right-wingers then brought back Isidore Cohen to manage the memberless Joint Council. A roar of derision rose from the market when the fur workers learned about it. Isidore Cohen, the man who said you could not run a union without gangsters and who had been kicked out back in 1917!

Morris Stein, a vice-president of the International, privately appealed to the other officers to face the grim facts. "Our International controls Locals 2 and 3 and a few more insignificant locals. . . The Industrial Union controls about 99 percent of the furriers in New York. . . The Industrial Union succeeded in organizing the thousands of dyers who were never organized before . . . won for the furriers wage increases, a thirty-five-hour week, an unemployment insurance fund. . . The task and duty of the officials of our International Union is to make every effort to get together with the thousands of Fur Workers who belong to the Industrial Union. . ."

But the other voices still spoke louder in the right-wing camp.

In October 1933, Edward F. McGrady was appointed Assistant Secretary of Labor in the Roosevelt Administration, as well as representative of organized labor on the staff of General Hugh Johnson, NRA chief. The fur workers were certainly not consulted about these appointments. The fur bosses and the right-wing leaders, however, rejoiced. *Women's Wear* noted: "Mr. McGrady is a familiar figure to the needle industries because of his activity in assisting the International Ladies Garment Workers Union and the International Fur Workers Union in their fights against Communist domination of their unions."

Early in December, some two months later, the Fur Trimming Manufacturers Association and the Associated Fur Manufacturers were in conferences with the Industrial Union for a new agreement.

At about the same time, a hearing was conducted by NRA officials in Washington for a retail fur code. At the hearing, Pietro Lucchi, president of the AFL International, sat beside Deputy Administrator Howard. McGrady was there advising the Administration on procedure. It was scarcely a surprise, therefore, when Administrator Howard ordered Special Commerce Department Police to eject fur workers who represented the Industrial Union.

A few days after the NRA hearing in Washington, the Associated and the Trimming Association suddenly broke off conferences with the Industrial Union. They announced that they were entering into a contract with the Joint Council.

The Industrial Union immediately alerted the fur workers to defend their working conditions and their union. It warned them against another deal between the bosses and the AFL union.

"All the furriers must unite in order to resist and smash these conspiracies on the part of the bosses together with their scab agencies," the Industrial Union urged. "All the furriers must unite to defend their union and their living standards. Raise your voice in mighty protest against these new conspiracies. Be prepared to answer the call for a determined and uncompromising struggle against these bandits! Together we will defeat them in the struggle just as we have done in the past."

On December 29, 1933, at the NRA hearing in Washington for a code for the fur manufacturing industry, two hundred fur workers attended on behalf of the Industrial Union. Ignoring warnings of guards, the furriers staged a demonstration protesting the use of Section 7A by the fur bosses to force workers to register in the Joint Council against their will. Gold informed the Code authorities and all present at the hearings that the fur workers would fight every attempt to force them into a union picked by the bosses.

"The furriers will fight against the conspiracies," Gold declared. "The furriers will fight to maintain their economic gains and for the right to belong to their union. If the NRA administration will not carry out Section 7A, the furriers will do so themselves, for no one can drive the furriers to belong to a union they do not want."

The following week, at a huge mass meeting at Cooper Union, three thousand furriers vowed that they would never recognize any agreement between the two Associations and the Joint Council. A showdown battle between the employers and the Industrial Union appeared imminent.

At this point, the fine hand of Edward McGrady made itself felt again. Object: to behead the fur workers' leadership, thereby clearing the way for the AFL!

The phony "assault" conviction in Wilmington against Ben Gold for leading the Hunger March, was now before the judge for final sentence. Wilmington officials were prepared to accept Gold's counsel's plea for a suspended sentence, especially since it was urged by the American Civil Liberties Union.

"We have known Ben Gold for a number of years," the Civil Liberties Union wrote to the Wilmington authorities, "as an able trade union leader whose reputation in his industry and this community is excellent. We can see no purpose served by jailing a man of his standing for so slight an offense and in a state where he does not reside. We trust that the Court will take a liberal view of the case and will grant the motion made in Mr. Gold's behalf."

The judge was about to suspend sentence. Suddenly a letter arrived from Assistant Secretary of Labor Edward F. McGrady. Unlike the American Civil Liberties Union, McGrady saw a "purpose" in having Gold jailed. He informed the judge that "Gold is a menace to society and should be behind bars." The judge sentenced Ben Gold to forty days in jail. Gold was immediately put behind bars. Before he entered the Newcastle Workhouse, Gold transmitted a message to the fur workers, brought back by Charles Nemeroff, assistant national secretary of the Industrial Union: "I send my heartiest greetings, and whether I am there or not, continue the struggle, redouble your energies. I am sure we will be victorious."

With Gold imprisoned, the leaders of the two employers associations and the AFL moved swiftly to conclude an agreement. Hugh Frayne was to draw up the agreement. Matthew Woll would countersign it. Just two days after Gold was jailed, a worker walked into the office of the Industrial Union with the news that the bosses and the AFL leaders were meeting at the Hotel New Yorker to sign an agreement behind the backs of the workers.

In five minutes, several hundred workers were at the Hotel New Yorker, only a few blocks from the Industrial Union office. They stormed into the lobby, climbed up to the third floor, and dashed into the conference room. Hugh Frayne later described it as "one of the wildest demonstrations I have ever witnessed."

Heatedly, the fur workers informed the assembled employers that

unless the workers' committee participated in negotiations, there would
be no conference. "We come to see to it that Section 7A is carried out,"
one fur worker declared. "We believe that wherever questions about the
fur workers are being negotiated they should be represented either by
themselves or by elected representatives. We will not permit scab agents
to represent us."

The police arrived with the manager of the hotel. "Who rented this
room anyway?" they inquired. "I did," answered Dr. Paul Abelson, "and
these roughnecks [pointing to the fur workers] have no business here."

The workers said: "We will not leave here until these fakers leave."
The police answered by clubbing them mercilessly, raining blows on their
heads and faces. Not giving way, the workers fought the police to a
standstill. Finally, the police suggested a compromise. A committee of
the workers would be allowed to remain in the room if all the others left
peacefully.

At the request of their own leaders, the workers left, waiting in the
lobby while their committee remained in the conference room. By this
time the hotel was in such turmoil that the manager of the hotel decided
there would be no more conference. He ordered everybody to get out,
including bosses and right-wingers and Hugh Frayne.

Apparently the employers and right-wingers met secretly later the
same night. For the very next day the newspapers announced that the
Joint Council had just concluded an agreement with the two associations.
"Mr. Pietro Lucchi, president of the International Fur Workers Union,"
the press release continued, "pointed out that with the consummation of
this contract, the Communist Needle Trades Workers Industrial Union,
which is an opposition union to the American Federation of Labor, is
definitely removed as a factor in the Fur Industry."

The Industrial Union warned the employers: "The Joint
Council is an organization without members . . . a small group of racketeers and underworld types working in conjunction with a handful of
Lovestoneites. . . The Industrial Union will defend to the utmost the
basic right of the workers to belong to a union of their own choosing. The
Industrial Union will defend the gains of the workers and will see to it
that the bosses live up to all the conditions that the furriers have won
through their long and heroic struggles."

The bosses were reminded that the murder of five furriers in the past
year in the attacks on the Industrial Union "did not bring about the rule
of the Joint Council over the fur workers." These attacks were beaten

back by the united resistance of the furriers, and any "new bloody venture" would suffer the same defeat.

The Industrial Union exposed the new "agreement" signed by the paper union with the employers and mobilized the fur workers for the inevitable struggle ahead. The fur workers were especially indignant over the action of the Joint Council in scuttling the Industrial Union's proposal for the thirty-hour week.

At the hearing on the fur code in Washington in December 1933, Ben Gold had presented powerful arguments for the thirty-hour week in the fur industry, proving that the thirty-five hour week had not alleviated the widespread unemployment. The bosses had speeded up the work, and were obtaining the same production as in the forty-hour work week. Even Goldstein and Begoon, representing the Joint Council, had supported the Industrial Union's demand for the thirty-hour week at the NRA hearings. Now, three days after Gold was jailed, along came the Joint Council with a contract giving up the fight for the thirty-hour week.

In January 1934, the American Civil Liberties Union asked the NRA National Labor Board to conduct a referendum among the New York fur workers to determine who was to represent them in negotiating with employers. With Senator Robert F. Wagner of New York acting as chairman, the National Labor Board invited the employers, the Industrial Union, and the Joint Council to a hearing in Washington on a referendum. Meanwhile, pending a final decision, the Board issued a temporary order to maintain the status quo as of January 31, before the agreement between the two associations and the Joint Council went into effect. The National Labor Board hearing was held February 1-3, 1934.

"We feel that our workers are all faithful to the American Federation of Labor, that they want to be led by their leaders representing the American Federation of Labor," John Rompapas, labor manager for the Fur Manufacturers Association argued. If the workers were allowed to choose their leaders and their union in a referendum, chaos would result, Rompapas declared. "My people [the manufacturers] will not allow their workers to create chaos in their shops. They would rather close shop and call it a day." This was the fur manufacturers' conception of democracy.

"To hold a referendum," argued Samuel Markewich and Samuel Null, attorneys for the AFL International, "would be destructive of the very idea of trade unionism in this country, for, assuming for the sake of argument that the Needle Trades Workers Industrial Union would have a majority in such a referendum, the minority would not and could not possibly submit to the leadership of the Needle Trades Workers Industrial Union." This was the AFL conception of democracy.

Senator Wagner was amazed at these unprincipled attacks on the referendum proposal by the men who claimed to be fighting for democracy in trade unions. The following are excerpts from the record:

Samuel Null (lawyer for the Joint Council): "No election will do any

JANuary 30, 1934

National Labor Board,
    Washington, D. C.

Gentlemen:

    Permit me, as Labor Manager representing fur manufacturers in the City of New York who for the last eight years are working under a Collective Agreement with the Greek Fur Workers' Union Local 70 of the International Fur Workers Union affiliated with the American Federation of Labor, to express my doubt as to the rights of employees to choose their representatives at will because of Section 7-A of the National Industrial Recovery Act. If the workers in our shops, because of individual like and dislike for certain leaders, choose to change their leaders, a chaos will result and the Union will have to be divided into smaller unions, thereby creating an industrial chaos in our industry.

    If we have to take Section 7-A of the N.R.A. without reserva-

    In closing permit me to inform your Board that my people will not allow their workers to create chaos in their shops. They would rather close shop and call it a day. But, before they do so, they

John Rompapas expresses the manufacturers' idea of democracy.

Samuel Markewich reveals the AFL's conception of democracy.

To order a referendum at their request or behest would be construed by the average worker as a stamp of approval by the government on the leadership of the Needle Trades Workers Industrial Union, which, in the opinion of

    All of this we are stating to you for the purpose of showing you the injustice and the utter futility of a referendum between two contending and irreconcilable elements.

good. The struggle between us and the Industrial Union in the fur trade is the struggle between two philosophies. The Industrial Union is filled with Communism which does not enter into the spirit of Americanism."

Senator Wagner: "The aim of our Recovery Board is to create industrial democracy. Do you have another answer to the problem, if not an election?"

Judge Panken, well-known Socialist leader and lawyer (representing the Joint Council): "An election is dangerous because it may become a revolution against the contract which the manufacturers concluded with the Joint Council. The Council can conclude an agreement even when it represents only 5 percent of the workers and force this agreement and decision on the other 95 percent of the workers."

Senator Wagner: "But that does not mean democracy. That means fascism."

Finally, throwing up his hands in disgust, Senator Wagner asked the employers and the right-wing union officials:

"You claim that the fur workers do not belong to the Industrial Union. You insist that they belong to the Joint Council. If they really do belong to the Joint Council, then they will vote for the Joint Council and you have nothing to fear."

The bosses and the right-wing union officials were stumped. They had to admit that their real reason for opposing the referendum was their complete certainty that the Industrial Union would be overwhelmingly chosen as the representative of the fur workers.

Behind prison bars in the Newcastle County Workhouse, Ben Gold analyzed the referendum hearings in Washington:

"Why do they insist upon their policy of dictatorship and why do they oppose real trade union democratic forms for the widest possible opportunities for the masses to express their wishes and desires? The employer, Mr. B. Dretel, at the hearing before the National Labor Board answered this question very clearly and concretely by informing the Board that the employers cannot buy our representatives but they can and they do buy the right-wing leaders, and because of this, they, the employers, don't like our Needle Trades Workers Industrial Union. This is very simple and very explanatory. . . . It therefore logically follows that the few bureaucratic leaders of the Socialist-AFL together with employers stand for very little democracy in the unions and for complete dictatorship of the few corrupt bureaucrats. The close merger between the two is a life necessity for both, for the employers and for the corrupt leaders."

More than two weeks passed after the hearings in Washington before the National Labor Board announced its decision. Enormous pressure was exerted on Senator Wagner to abandon all plans to hold a referendum. Telegrams from national and local AFL leaders poured into the Senator's office. James C. Quinn, secretary of the Central Trades and Labor Council of Greater New York and Vicinity, telegraphed Senator Wagner: "In the establishment of code for fur industry, the Central Trades and Labor Council of Greater New York and Vicinity are opposed to any recognition being given to those employees in fur industry who are under the reign and rule of the leaders opposed to the recognized labor unions having charters from the American Federation of Labor. If the outlaw group receives recognition and support it will mean disruption and chaos in other industries and for other recognized legitimate unions. We are opposed to any recognition being shown to the outlaw group or their leaders, as they are also opposed to the principles of the American form of government."

The brazen objections to a democratic election were too much for Senator Wagner to swallow. On February 15, the Board ordered a referendum among the New York fur workers to decide whether they wished

Writing from prison, Ben Gold analyzes the referendum hearings.

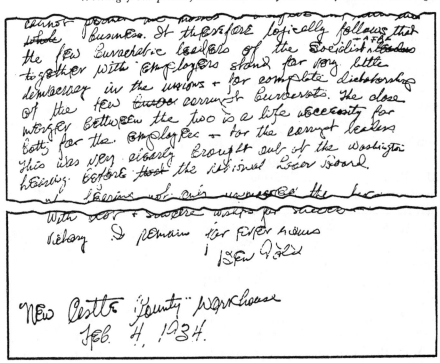

to be represented by the International Fur Workers Union or by the Needle Trades Workers Industrial Union. Details were postponed until the Board conferred with representatives of the two unions involved.

But the referendum was never held. Pressure against it continued from the AFL. As late as May 11, 1934, the National Labor Board drew up detailed provisions for a referendum to be conducted by a committee appointed by the Board. But still nothing came of it. Lucchi informed the Board that the right-wing International was "unalterably opposed to a referendum at this time." Green assured Lucchi that he would give the matter his "most careful attention." The Labor Board, giving Green its "most careful attention," abandoned the referendum entirely!

While the National Labor Board was stalling and delaying, the bosses began to lock out workers who refused to register in the Joint Council. The Joint Council right-wingers and the Lovestoneites supplied scabs to replace workers discharged for refusing to register in the Council. The police and underworld characters played their usual roles of terrorizing and intimidating the fur market. The campaign of violence was climaxed by the kidnapping and torture of Jack Schneider, courageous leader of the fur workers. Schneider was beaten and slugged by detectives until he lost consciousness. When he was finally released, he was in a critical condition, his body a mass of bruises and his head covered with gashes.

The Industrial Union prepared for the picket line battle to safeguard the rights and conditions of the furriers. Greeted by thousands of needle trades workers at the New York Pennsylvania Station on February 23 upon his release from prison, Ben Gold was carried on the shoulders of the workers down Seventh Avenue to the headquarters of the Industrial Union. He told the furriers that now was the time for action, not speeches. He called upon them to smash the latest conspiracy of the bosses' association and the Joint Council.

Shop strikes started immediately. By the end of March, 150 shops had settled with the Industrial Union. The bosses were compelled to recognize the Industrial Union as the workers' representative, to increase wages to the minimum scale previously established, to pay up all money owed the unemployment fund, and to reinstate with back pay all workers discharged for refusing to register in the Joint Council.

Thus, even before the season began, with most shops still not working, the furriers demonstrated their strength on the picket line. Once the season began in earnest, the Industrial Union ripped to shreds the paper agreement signed by the Associations and the right-wing leaders. By the end of August, four thousand strikers had the industry at a standstill. The Joint Council right-wingers could not even muster a handful of scabs despite the frantic demands of the bosses. Even the strong-arm gang refused to work for the Joint Council until they received the "back pay" due them. The minutes of the Industrial Union's Fur Trade Board ironically record: "As strange as it may seem, gangsters that were formerly employed by the Joint Council went as far as to engage lawyers, also sent messengers to our Union, to take up their fight for the back pay that is due them from the Joint Council."

The agreement of the Joint Council and the bosses was cracking at the seams. The two employer associations fought each other furiously. Each accused the other of failing to enforce the agreement with the Council. The coat manufacturers charged that the trimming manufacturers were employing members of the Industrial Union and contributing to its unemployment insurance fund. The trimming manufacturers, on the other hand, charged that all coat manufacturers, "except maybe 25 or 30 shops, negotiated with the Industrial Union."

The strikes called by the Industrial Union deepened the split between the two associations. The strikes in August paralyzed 126 leading trimming shops. The struck firms saw their business going to their competitors. Their panic increased even more when members of the Associated stepped in to chisel their customers away too.

The Trimming Association presented the Associated (coats) with an ultimatum: either hold a referendum in the industry to determine which union the workers want, or both associations should discharge all members of the Industrial Union. The Associated refused to accept either proposal. Even if 98 percent of the furriers chose the Industrial Union, they declared, they would not negotiate with it. Nor would they agree to discharge workers who refused to register with the Joint Council, for this would confront them with dozens of strikes at the height of the season.

By the end of August, the Trimming Association was forced to sign an agreement with the Industrial Union. "Our members would have been ruined had the strike continued," the Trimming Association announced.

The agreement provided recognition of the Industrial Union; a thirty-five-hour week; an unemployment insurance fund of one-and-a-half percent of the weekly payroll, administered exclusively by a committee of the workers; no contracting; equal division of work during four months; four-week trial period for new workers; and eight paid legal holidays. For the first time, the bosses recognized the right of the unskilled floor workers, the most exploited group in the trade, to belong to the union.

Even the *New York Times* was forced to admit that four thousand workers in the fur trimming shops, members of the Industrial Union, had won a resounding victory in the agreement negotiated between "the left-wing organization and the Trimming Manufacturers Association."

The agreement was a shattering blow to the AFL International. In desperation the right-wingers concocted a plan to force the trimming manufacturers to break the agreement or face destruction.

Samuel Markewich, attorney for the right-wing International, wrote to Matthew Woll:

"I do not hesitate to say that the Association must be destroyed if we want the [International] union to survive. I have given this matter a great deal of thought. I have talked with Mr. Lucchi and some of the other officials in the union and I believe that the only practical solution of the entire subject is by the establishment of a union label . . .

"If you can get the AFL Council to request the Executive Board of the International Ladies Garment Workers Union to instruct their officials and Shop Chairmen that no fur trimmings, not bearing the International label should be attached by them to garments in their shop, it will go a long way towards rebuilding the [International] Fur Workers Union; because, as you can see, these fur trimmers, if they want to get the label, will have to employ our men, and if they don't get the label, most of them will go out of business as they deserve to be . . ."

According to this plan, employers who refused to join with the right-wing leaders in "liberating" their workers, were to be driven out of business.

"I am in complete accord with the suggestion contained in your letter of September 15th," Woll answered Markewich. "I need hardly affirm I will be more than happy to contribute my aid . . ."

But nothing came of this new plan. The Fur Trimming Manufacturers Association remained in existence. The Industrial Union enforced the agreement in the shops. Many members of the Associated now had to deal with the Industrial Union on an individual basis, granting the same conditions enjoyed by the fur workers in the trimming shops.

The January statement of the Joint Council that the "Industrial Union . . . is definitely removed as a factor in the fur industry," was, like the celebrated rumor of Mark Twain's death, "slightly exaggerated."

CHAPTER 39

The Picture

outside of New York

After a year of hearings, conferences and correspondence, the NRA fur manufacturing code went into effect in May 1934. For months, the right-wingers had been assuring those fur workers over whom they still exerted some influence, that "as soon as the code will be signed things will be better," and that through the code "they would be able to sustain themselves decently."

The reverse actually happened. The NRA code completely ignored the fur workers' demands for the thirty-hour week, equal division of work, an unemployment fund, and minimum wage scales for the fur industry. The Code legalized overtime and the worst evil in the trade—contracting.

The NRA's fur dressing code was equally bad. The employers had agreed with the Industrial Union that the minimum wage scale in the agreement should be specified in the code. But behind closed doors, this understanding was repudiated and the code omitted all mention of a schedule of minimum wages for skilled workers. The low minimum wage of sixty-five cents per hour for unskilled workers set by the code was applied also to the skilled workers whose minimum wage in the union agreement was $1.65 an hour.

Under the NRA codes, speedup increased in the shops, contracting and sub-contracting became more widespread, wages were cut and unemployment rose. Moreover, even the codes, as adopted, were not enforced. Some employers claimed exemption from them as "retailers." Others moved their shops to out-of-town areas where there were no enforcement

434

agencies; they operated day and night, paying workers as little as $8 and $10 a week for fifty and sixty hours' work. Still others were permitted by lax code authorities to violate the provisions of the codes at will. Wherever there was reliance upon the codes, the workers' conditions deteriorated sharply.

Fur Dressers Local 2, a right-wing local, consisted of the fleshers who dressed mink, fox, ermine, beaver, persian lamb and other costly fur skins. Very skilled craftsmen, they were the most highly paid workers in the fur dressing industry. Significantly, Morris Reiss, Local 2's business agent, complained to William Green in the spring of 1934 about the operations of the code:

"Since then the open shops, which previously constituted 15 percent of the industry, have grown so that now they are about 50 percent of the industry. The minimum of 65 cents per hour for unskilled labor has been used as a guide by the employers, and the tendency is to hire skilled workers on that basis.

"Employers who still employ union help tend to do as much of the work as they can themselves, week-ends and nights, with the help of relatives. Others tell their help they cannot pay them at all, and permit them to contract out some of the work and get what they can out of it. All this for the purpose of evading the hour and wage provisions of the code and the standards arrived at by agreement, with the result that weekly earnings for the workers are now $12 and $15 a week."

Widespread corruption existed in the enforcement of the Fur Code. Documentary evidence and sworn affidavits of witnesses submitted by the Industrial Union proved that manufacturers were shielded who were violating the fur code of the NRA as well as the union agreement.

A statement signed by B. Dretel, an employer, on September 6, 1934, affirmed that he had been promised "that if I would stop the merger with the Trimmers and steer my Association into the Associated in a month I could operate my out-of-town factory just as I wished without fear of interference from the Code Authority."

Reliance of the right-wingers on the codes, as an automatic solution for the workers' problems, quickly turned out to be a bitter illusion in their few remaining locals. So confident had the right-wing leaders been that the code would usher in the millenium that they even signed agreements with the employers providing that conditions set forth in the codes would "automatically" replace those already in existence. The result was that in the shops in Chicago, St. Paul, Minneapolis and Boston, controlled by the right-wing International, the workers were compelled to put in a forty to forty-four hour week.*

Members of Locals 52, 57 and 71 of St. Paul and Minneapolis were moved to complain to Lucchi: "To us it seems strange that a local affiliated with the International shall be allowed to enter into an agreement to work 40 and 44 hours per week when we are all asking for 30 and 35 hours."

In Cleveland as soon as the code was signed, the employers began to reduce wages. First-class cutters were immediately cut from $50 to $45, and operators from $40 to $37.60.

Complaints were submitted by the right-wing leaders to NRA officials. They were promptly filed and forgotten. "We have put a complaint to the NRA for the last two and a half months and we have had no reply," one official in Buffalo wailed. Another finally admitted: "It seems it's no use to file any more complaints with the NRA. I have been filing complaints since last year, but up-to-date no action has been taken."

The International office in New York was deluged with letters from the few locals it had. They were hard-pressed to meet the rising protests of the workers.

"Mr. Lucchi, our whole crowd is clamoring for action and results," wrote Joseph Schmitt of Local 56, Buffalo. "This looks like the showdown."

"I fear that we may not be able to hold this local together much longer," Louis A. Liebowitz wrote from Local 95, Hartford. "They are losing their hope and confidence in us and the International. I might say that there is some talk of the Industrial Union."

"The people here are becoming disgusted," declared Sam Butkovitz of Local 30, Boston. "They claim that if the union can't help them they don't need a union."

"I really don't know what else to write," Hyman S. Schechter of Local 50 in Baltimore pleaded. "The members are so impatient."

Lucchi could only write that "as the government approved it [the code] we had to do the best under the circumstances." Or: "I am sorry to learn that the workers in your locality have become impatient. Please try to explain to them that we are doing everything possible to see that the code should be enforced, but of course everything takes time."

---

* On June 7, 1934, Jack Mouchine, Local 45's business manager, admitted to Lucchi that "every shop was working on Saturday, some of them forced our people to work 48 hours. Just to rub it in—the scale of wages (minimum) was outrageously violated."

Ben Gold photographed with his wife shortly after his release from prison in Wilmington, where he served a forty-day term arising out of the Hunger March. Sadie Gold's father was Harris J. Algus, progressive chairman of the N. Y. Joint Board who died in 1922.

A mass demonstration of fur workers outside Industrial Union headquarters, January 31, 1934, protesting a new attempt of the bosses and AFL leaders to force them into registering with the company-union Joint Council.

N. Y. Daily News Photo

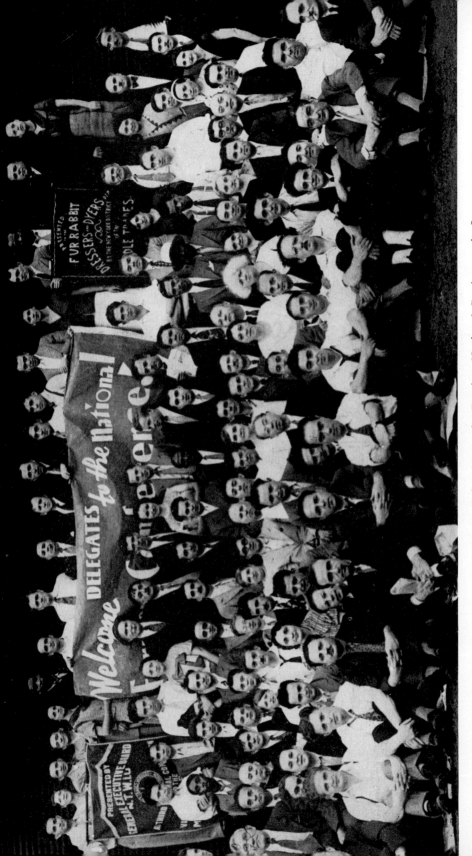

Delegates to the Furriers National Conference in June 1934, one of the important events leading to the achievement of unity.

Appealing to Colonel Harry S. Berry, deputy NRA administrator, Lucchi wrote: "The average [fur] worker has lost all faith in the Code, in the NRA and in the government, and most of them are fast becoming followers of Communist agitators. . . . It is my humble opinion that you owe the duty not only to the industry and to the workers, but as a sacred duty to the NRA and to the government, to bend every effort in giving the skilled workers a decent minimum wage schedule as the only way of checking cut-throat competition now prevailing in the industry and in stopping the workers from turning to Radicalism. A great states-man once said that the only way to make a Conservative out of a Radical is to give him something to conserve. I have given up hope of getting a wage for the workers which may give them something to conserve but if you can help them get a meagre living, there would still be hope of saving them from Radicalism."

The Industrial Union followed an entirely different policy. It had never entertained any illusions that a paradise would prevail in the fur shops once the NRA codes were adopted. The Industrial Union did not rely on appeals to the good-will of employers or government of-ficials to secure decent conditions for the workers. It relied on militant struggles conducted by the workers themselves to wrest concessions and improved conditions from the employers. While fighting for the best pro-visions it could get in the NRA codes, it never forgot that workers win increases, shorter hours and other gains only through the strength of the union.

The successful struggles of the Industrial Union increased its follow-ing and influence among the fur workers all over the country. At the same time it tried to unite the ranks of the furriers everywhere for joint struggles.

In Detroit, under the leadership of the Industrial Union, the furriers succeeded in tying up the greatest part of the trade. Gains of 30 to 60 percent were registered in wages. A thirty-five-hour week and other union conditions were established.

In Los Angeles, the Industrial Union organized the majority of the furriers and in a militant strike, won the thirty-five-hour week, substan-tial wage increases, and an unemployment insurance fund.

In Cleveland, the local of the right-wing International won the thirty-five hour week with the active assistance of the Industrial Union.

In July 1934, the Industrial Union and the AFL International local in San Francisco united their ranks, and, under the leadership of Frank

Brownstone, head of the Industrial Union, organized every one of the open shops in the city, winning a 10 percent wage increase and the thirty-five-hour week.

In August and September, a united front strike in the rabbit dressing trade in Brooklyn resulted, despite the obstructing maneuvers of the right-wing leaders, in a nearly 100 percent increase in wages. The solidarity and unity of the rank and file in the Brooklyn strike was the fruit of months of tireless activity on the part of the Industrial Union to unite the workers in the fur dressing shops. Only a few shops remained in operation. The strike, a tribute to united front action, won an increase in rates for fleshing rabbit skins from $1.10 to $2.10 per hundred. Ten cents for every hundred skins was paid by the employers to the unemployment insurance fund. The fund was to be administered by a joint committee elected by members of the Industrial Union and the locals of the International Union.

In every contract negotiated by the Industrial Union, the workers won wage increases; equal pay for Negro and white workers; equal pay for women and men; provision for an unemployment insurance fund to be paid by the employers and administered by the workers; and severe limitations on overtime and contracting.

Strikes conducted by the Industrial Union in this period in two fur centers, Philadelphia and Chicago, were especially significant.

The International Union had absolutely no more influence among the fur workers of Philadelphia. In the fall of 1933, paralleling the successful campaign of the Industrial Union in New York, the Philadelphia fur workers mobilized for the fight for the thirty-five-hour week. To block the Industrial Union, the fur bosses met with Samuel Rudow, the manager of a men's clothing contractors' association, and decided to sign an agreement with the right-wing International Fur Workers Union.

On August 22, Rudow wrote to Louis Shaffer, the labor editor of the *Jewish Daily Forward,* to complete the deal:

"I have decided to write to you on this particular subject, as I really do not know who else to write to.

"I had the occasion of meeting the President and other active members of the Furriers Manufacturers Association in Philadelphia, and after a discussion with them, on the present prevailing conditions in their industry, and in the country generally I have practically gotten them to agree to get together with the Furriers International Union, and sign a market agreement with them.

"I also pointed out to them the necessity of signing up with the Furriers International before the Communists will get ahold of them and disturb the whole market for them.

"Will you please get in touch with someone in the Furriers' International, and have them get in touch with me, so that I can arrange a conference for them. Needless for me to tell you my feelings in these questions, I always have been and will always be interested in our movement above all."

A fine combination: the bosses, the contractor, the Forward *and the AFL union. Nobody bothered to consult the workers.*

Philadelphia Men's Clothing Contractors Ass'n
210 Commonwealth Building
12th & Chestnut Streets
PHILADELPHIA, PA.

EPHRAIM BROWNSTEIN, Pres.
MARIO RANIERI, Vice-Pres.
HARRY COHEN, Secretary
ISADORE PINCUS, Treasurer

SAMUEL RUDOW, Manager

August 12,1933.

Executive Committee:
N. D'ALONZO
J. PALADINO
I. FARBMAN
H. MARCUS
CHAS. JASKY
M. EISENBERO
J. MINTZER
M. FORMAN
PH. KATZ
WM. KASLOW
I. BARRIS

Mr. Louis Shaffer,
Labor Editor,
Jewish Daily Forward
175 East Broadway
New York, N.Y.

My dear Mr. Shaffer:

I have decided to write to you on this particular subject, as I really do not know who else to write to.

I had the occasion of meeting the President and other active members of the Furriers Manufacturers Association in Philadelphia, and after a discussion with them, on the present prevailing conditions in their industry, and in the country generally I have practically gotten them to agree to get together with the Furriers International Union, and sign a market agreement with them.

I also pointed out to them the necessity of signing up with the Furriers International before the Communists will get ahold of them and disturb the whole market for them.

Will you please get in touch with someone in the Furrier's International, and have them get in touch with me, so that I can arrange a conference for them. Needless for me to tell you my feelings in these questions, I always have been and will always be interested in our movement above all.

Yours very truly,

Samuel Rudow

Manager
PHILADELPHIA MEN'S CLOTHING CONTRACTORS ASS'N.

Responding eagerly to the call of the Industrial Union, the Philadelphia furriers declared a general strike early in September 1933, for the thirty-five-hour week and other union conditions. The strike committee received able assistance from Joseph Winogradsky, manager of the Industrial Union's fur department. This effective leadership and the magnificent spirit of the strikers completely paralyzed the fur industry in Philadelphia. Despite the four-way arrangement they had banked on, the bosses had to settle with the Industrial Union.

The Industrial Union was recognized, the work week was set at thirty-five hours, an unemployment insurance fund was set up, and a guaranteed minimum wage was provided corresponding to the contract between the Industrial Union and the New York Trimming Association.

The situation in the right-wing Local 45 in Chicago had changed from bad to worse in the course of the depression. The opposition of the honest workers became more and more pronounced. The right-wing leaders of the local had more than they could handle.

In the summer of 1932, Abe Rosen decided "not to run again for business manager on account of extreme nervousness due to internal trouble." The next choice was Mike Muky, a former president of the local. It soon appeared that he was "incompetent to fulfill the position." When Muky broke down, the right-wingers, in desperation, brought in an outsider, named Daniel E. Smith. Rosen described Smith as "energetic, cold-blooded, has lots of *influence* (in the full meaning of the term) . . ."

```
This we aim to prevent and to the end to hold your own——
In as much as we hate to have an out side men at the head of our org
anisation , there is no other alternative-
We have the man, sufficiently known in the labor movement in Chicago
energetic, cold blooded, has lots of influence(in the full meaning
of the term) to have his decisions carried out, he would command the
respect of both the manufactors and workers-
What we need most right now is discipline and for any member inirin-
```

Chicago right wing gets "cold-blooded" character to run local.

On January 3, 1933, Rosen asked Lucchi to issue credentials to Smith empowering him to act as the International Representative in Local 45. "We can not, as there is no way for it," Rosen explained, "submit that man to an election as he is not a member." On February 1, 1933, Smith received his credentials.

Soon the right-wingers were imploring Lucchi to take away the credentials. Smith kicked the right-wing leaders out of Local 45's headquarters into the street, and proceeded to take whatever he could from the local's treasury. After the treasury was exhausted and the landlord was threatening to evict the local for non-payment of rent, Smith went to Abe Feinglass of the Industrial Union and offered to sell him Local 45 for $200. Turned down by Feinglass, he made the same offer to the right-wingers and was bought off. "We have tried all last week to raise money in order to eliminate them," Rosen wrote to Lucchi on March 28, 1933.

After Smith, the right-wingers brought in Jack Mouchine as business manager. Writing on April 8, 1933, Mouchine admitted that his predecessors had sold out to the bosses. With the aid of the Industrial Squad, the Jewish Federation and the *Forward,* Mouchine was planning to crush the rank-and-file revolt led by the left wing.

To this day, the mention of Jack Mouchine evokes a vivid picture in the memories of the Chicago fur workers. His "ethics" as a labor leader

Sell-outs to the bosses, reliance on the Industrial Squad and the Forward *characterize the work of the right wing in Chicago.*

The trade is very dull, the trimming bosses employ very few people, and as Mike Muky neglected to sign them up last year they are now running open shops. Lucas pulled one shop and apparently was offered ten dollars from the boss so he sent them right back to work. I do not want to take any action on them now as the spring season is nearly ended, but if left alone they will keep

There is a handful of militant communists who are harassing the people, using the same old phrases; crooks gamblers, and etc. I am determined not to engage in any fights. The first move they make, the 'Industrial squad' will get them. We can't afford to be kicked out of this building; it is too hard to get headquarters. At the next Board meeting we will expel about fifteen of them for calling outside meetings and not answering summonses

question, but I have to meet bills and have fares and nickels with which to telephone. The Jewish Federation in cooperation with the Forward paper has given us $75, and that has saved us so far. Let us hope that through Roosevelt's program the wheels of industry will soon move onward and our trade will again be a dominant factor in the labor movement.

All the Boys wish to convey to you their faith in your leadership and as for myself I want you to feel that you have in me a loyal friend and an ardent supporter.

Fraternally yours,

Jack Mouchine
Business Manager Local #45

are best described in a letter that he himself sent to the International office on June 7, 1933: ". . . the Needle trades [Industrial Union] decided to call a strike on an open shop by the name of Krammers in the heart of the loop. The people which were all non-union were prevented from going to work and started parading in front of the building. *We couldn't afford* to let them gain even one shop, although it was an open shop and we got in touch with Mr. Krammer telling him that the strike was illegal because not called by us, that we alone were a bona fide organization affiliated with the AFL and we gave Krammer's lawyer a few leads in order to get an injunction. The judge, D. Sullivan, wouldn't issue an injunction unless proof was given him that the Furriers Union, Local 45, didn't call that strike. I was subpoenaed in court and without violating the ethics of the Labor movement I convinced the Judge that an in-

Mouchine reveals how he "ethically" broke a left-wing strike.

junction should be granted. Subsequently the shop went back to work on its former status. . . ."

Mouchine's management of the Chicago local proved no more successful than his predecessors'. He resigned in the summer of 1935, complaining that he was "on the verge of a breakdown."

In the summer of 1934, the Industrial Union, under the leadership of Abe Feinglass, organized the Evans Fur Company of Chicago and signed an agreement providing for a thirty-five-hour week and a wage scale equal to that in New York. Even the right-wingers admitted the importance of this victory. Joe Indes, who succeeded Jack Mouchine as manager of the AFL Local 45, wrote that "the lefts were able to build a very strong unit in Chicago because of this shop. . . . The feeling in Chicago is, whichever union has Evans—that one is the only one that can survive. The entire Association in Chicago does not employ more than the single shop of Evans."

The Evans Company suddenly broke its contract with the Industrial Union. Locking out sixty-three workers, it took in eight scabs furnished by the right-wing leaders. It obtained a ruling from the Labor Board that the eight scabs constituted the workers of the shop, and signed an agreement with the AFL local which provided a forty-hour week from January to August, and forty-five hours from August to January. The weekly wages of operators were cut by $5; nailers, $3; and finishers $3.50 to $4.50. In addition, the agreement restored the right of the company to fire workers at its own discretion.

The militant strike of the Evans workers continued under the leadership of Abe Feinglass, assisted by Irving Potash, who came from New York to help the Chicago furriers. It won the admiration of workers all over the country. The strikers were beaten by police and gangsters and arrested again and again. But they did not flinch. On the contrary, they introduced new tactics in strike strategy. They carried on a telephone campaign that tied up the company's wires. Women strikers went into the company's store, chained themselves to posts and urged customers to boycott the firm; when they were dragged out to the waiting police wagons, showers of strike circulars descended from the windows. A picket line of the children of the strikers was another outstanding feature.

Faced with this determined struggle, the Labor Board was forced to reconsider the situation in the Evans Fur Company. It appointed a special board of three persons to hold a hearing. Sixty-three affidavits produced at the hearing in January 1935, made it clear that the workers wanted the Industrial Union to represent them. The Board was compelled to rule that all sixty-three workers had a right to their jobs and that the Industrial Union contract was still in effect. The vote was two to one in favor of the Industrial Union. The lone negative vote was cast by John Fitzpatrick, head of the Chicago Federation of Labor.

Fitzpatrick was the "labor" representative on the special board. He was supposed to be impartial in the dispute. His "impartiality" in the Evans case was described in his own letter to Pietro Lucchi on July 18, 1934: "I had a conference with the representatives of Local Union No. 45 and of course we will be glad to cooperate with them in any way possible. There is only one concern here with which they feel they may have difficulty, and that is the Evans Fur Company, which seems inclined to give preference to Communists, in order to keep the Fur Workers divided. We discussed ways and means to overcome this kind of opposition to your local, and I hope they will soon be able to report to you a union agreement with the Evans Fur Company."

Even after the Labor Board's decision, the strike continued. The Evans Fur Company was finally forced to capitulate and restore its contract with the Industrial Union. The fur workers regained the thirty-five-hour week and the wage scales that had existed under the agreement with the Industrial Union.

"Impartiality" of Fitzpatrick, AFL arbitrator in Evans case.

The right-wing conspiracy in Chicago and the militant strike of the Chicago furriers had far-reaching effects. In addition, it brought the name of Abe Feinglass, the able young leader of the strike, to the attention of fur workers all over the country.

Born in Bessarabia in 1910, the son of working class parents, Feinglass emigrated to Chicago in 1920. His father was already known as a leading rank-and-filer in the Amalgamated Clothing Workers Union. After completing high school, Feinglass was determined to study medicine. He went to work in a fur shop at the age of 16 to earn the funds he needed for college. He worked in the shop during the day, and attended college at night. Joining the union in 1926, he devoted whatever time he could spare to aiding the local progressives in their fight against the right-wing machine.

In 1930, Feinglass met Ben Gold for the first time. That meeting was the turning point in his life. Thereafter, abandoning his study of medicine, he devoted himself completely to the struggle for a democratic furriers' union in Chicago. He organized a left-wing group in the local and led in the struggles of the unemployed. He became the target of weekly attacks by the right-wing strong-arm squads and by his resistance won the respect and admiration of the Chicago fur workers.

In 1932, Feinglass was elected a delegate to the International Convention in Philadelphia. Kaufman refused to recognize him as a delegate. Feinglass fought so vigorously for his rights that he was assaulted by Edward McGrady right on the convention floor. Feinglass returned blow for blow. Impressed by Feinglass' spirit, McGrady later proposed that he leave the left wing and line up with the AFL. McGrady promised him a rich reward. Feinglass turned him down flatly.

Expelled by the International without charges or trial upon his return to Chicago, Feinglass turned to building the Industrial Union. Under his leadership, the Industrial Union grew, organized unorganized shops, and won wage increases and better conditions for the Chicago fur workers. The victory in the Evans strike climaxed two years of effective work by the Industrial Union under Feinglass' leadership.

In the course of these struggles all over the country, the Industrial Union achieved united action in many locals. A unity conference was called in New York on June 22, 1934, attended by delegates from seven different cities. The 124 delegates at this conference repre-

sented over seventeen thousand organized workers. Two locals of the
right-wing International participated officially at the conference—Local 3
of the fancy fur dressers of Brooklyn, one of the largest locals in the International, and Local 86 of Cleveland. Organized groups from other
International locals also took part in the conference, and agreed to work
with the Industrial Union in all future struggles for improved conditions.

Rank-and-file delegates from every city and branch of the trade spoke.
Summing up, Ben Gold urged the fullest mobilization of the fur workers everywhere in united struggles to bring conditions in out-of-town
areas up to the level won in New York. Gold showed how the reliance
of the right-wing leaders on the NRA codes, particularly in the out-of-
town areas, had led to betrayal of the workers' interests.

"A powerful organization," Gold emphasized, "responsibility, discipline, militant action, resistance, struggle—that is the only code and the
best code for the furriers and for all the workers."

The conference welded the fur workers into a national front of struggle. A United National Committee of twenty-three members, elected by
the conference, began immediately to establish contacts with fur workers
all over the country, including those who were members of the right-
wing International. In Brooklyn and Cleveland, the United National
Committee led the workers of both the Industrial Union and the right-
wing locals to strike victories and won important improvements in their
conditions.

As the year 1935 opened, some of the right-wing officials themselves
were beginning to realize the futility of the policies they were pursuing.
Answering the complaints of San Francisco workers about their miserable conditions of work, Pietro Lucchi, president of the International
Union, said: "I must say quite frankly that the only way you can improve your conditions is through a powerful union. I am afraid that all
of us put too much faith in the NRA, the Code Authority and the Code
itself. The only time you obtain results through this medium is when
they know that you are organized 100 percent."

The crying need of the fur workers was—unity!

CHAPTER 40

The Pressure for Unity

The year 1934 went down in history as a year of militant struggle that produced deep reverberations in the entire American labor movement. The San Francisco general strike, organized in sympathy with the striking longshoremen on the Pacific Coast, lasted from July 17 to July 20, and involved over 125,000 workers. The textile general strike in September lasted about three weeks until it was suddenly called off by the union leaders, even though the strikers had gained none of their basic demands. Involving about a half million workers, it was the largest strike in a single industry the country had ever known up to that time.

All told, about a million and a half workers were involved in the strike wave of 1934. The militancy of these strikers, conducted in the face of bitter opposition from the AFL bureaucrats, was especially significant. The growing hostility of the workers to the AFL bureaucracy was intensified by the activities of the Federation leaders during these strikes. While workers were being killed in cold blood by police, troops and national guardsmen, William Green, Edward F. McGrady and other AFL leaders were denouncing the strikers as "subversive Reds."

To all demands of the rank and file, William Green answered that the most important problem facing American labor was "to make war" on Communism. The bitterness of the workers found expression at the 1934 AFL convention in San Francisco. For the first time in many years, there were delegates who came from the factories—delegates who were not bureaucratic officials, removed by years of pie-card positions from the

447

conditions of the workers. Many were delegates from federal locals *—
the rank-and-file beginnings of unionization in the hitherto unorganized
mass production industries of steel, auto, rubber, cement and the like.

These rank-and-file delegates demanded that the Federation abandon
its antiquated craft union structure and organize the unorganized workers into industrial unions, regardless of skill or craft. By openly railroad-
ing any resolution which smacked of militancy, the bureaucracy hoped to
stifle this rank-and-file revolt. But with John L. Lewis, president of the
United Mine Workers, largest Federation affiliate, supporting the demand for industrial unionism in the mass production industries, the first
step was taken. The convention, at least formally, resolved that "the
executive council is directed to issue charters for national and international unions in the automotive, cement, aluminum, and such other mass
production industries as in the judgment of the executive council may
be necessary to meet the situation."

The masses of new workers who had entered the Federation since 1933 were demanding a militant policy of struggle. This upsurge of a militant rank and file in the AFL seriously alarmed both the
union bureaucrats and the leaders of big business. The big corporations
had depended on government officials, company unions, and leaders of
the AFL and the Socialist Party to keep the workers in check. Indeed,
certain industrialists were repeatedly reminded "that they *must* have the
good will and help of responsible labor leaders in order to protest against
the irresponsible organizers." These "responsible labor leaders" were
"opposed to strikes, and their influence, on the whole, is against strikes."

Disillusioned with the NRA, the men at the bench had broken through
and engaged in struggles of nation-wide proportions. The labor chiefs,
battling fiercely to defend the interests of big business, were being rebuffed by the workers. New methods were sought by big business to
counteract this—methods like Hitler's in Germany and Mussolini's in
Italy. Fascist organizations, backed and financed by monopoly interests
in Wall Street, came into existence all over the country. Dedicated to
smashing unions, to exterminating all but "100 percent Protestant, pure
white Americans," and to persecuting all progressives—the Ku Klux
Klan, the Silver Shirts, the Khaki Shirts, the Blue Shirts, the Black
Legion, etc., etc., openly declared war upon the American working class.

* The federal labor unions were kept directly under the AFL national office
control until they could be distributed around to the various craft international
unions.

As the year 1934 drew to a close, the number of lynchings of Negroes, kidnappings and murders of militant workers, lawless attacks on unions and strikers, rose alarmingly. A conspiracy of terror and murder stalked through the land to smash the labor and progressive movement. The Ku Klux Klan was revived to "go after" radical strikers, Communists, Negroes and Jews. The Black Hundreds were organized to break the San Francisco general strike and to raid workers' organizations, homes and strike relief kitchens. The Order of '76 was secretly organized and began to cooperate with paid Nazi agents in the distribution of anti-Semitic propaganda. The United States Fascists, Inc., was organized in Newark, New Jersey, and announced its intention of wiping out Communists, Socialists, Anarchists and all other radicals. The White Legion was organized in Birmingham, Alabama, and immediately proceeded to raid the homes of miners and other strikers. Father Charles E. Coughlin organized a National Union for Social Justice with a demagogic program of pronounced fascist leanings.

To the Jewish workers, the rise of American fascism held out an even worse threat than slavery. The openly-proclaimed goal of fascist organizations in the United States was Hitler's goal of death and extermination of the Jewish people. "No Jew left in these United States," the American fascists cried. "Hitler is not going to finish that work," the organ of the Silver Shirts screamed. *The finish of it comes right here in America.*"

Fur workers were fully aware of the growing menace of fascism in the United States. At every meeting of the Industrial Union, the leadership and the workers discussed the revolt of the rank and file against the bureaucrats of the American Federation of Labor, the strikes of workers in dozens of industrial centers, and the efforts of reactionary forces to smash these militant struggles. Although deeply involved in their own battles, the furriers mobilized support for the workers of San Francisco and of the entire Pacific Coast, of Milwaukee, Toledo, Minneapolis, and of dozens of textile centers in the South and other parts of the country.

In February 1934, the world was thrilled by the heroism of the Austrian workers who defended themselves on the barricades against the attacks of the Mussolini-backed Dollfuss government. As soon as the news reached this country, the Industrial Union proposed a united front of all needle trades workers to send help to the Austrian workers. The right-wing officials ignored this appeal. However, the needle trades workers, Socialist and Communist, jammed the huge open air meetings called

NEEDLE TRADE WORKERS!

of all Political Shades and Opinions -- Negro and White -- Men and Women

CLOAKMAKERS, DRESSMAKERS, FURRIERS, MEN'S CLOTHING WORKERS, MILLINERY, KNITGOODS AND WHITE GOODS WORKERS, AND ALL OTHER NEEDLE TRADE WORKERS!

Sisters and Brothers:—

The toiling masses of Austria are fighting on the barricades in a life and death struggle against the hordes of the Fascist dictator, Dolfuss, who is attempting to destroy their conditions, their freedom and their very lives.

We, the workers of America, irrespective of political belief and opinion, must mobilize immediately and organize a mighty united front to assist the workers of Austria in their struggle against reaction, oppression and Fascism; in their struggle for freedom and bread.

The armies of the capitalist countries, France, Italy, Germany and the others, are at the threshold of Austria ready to assist the capitalists of that country to

A call to help the Austrian workers in their anti-fascist fight.

by the Industrial Union. They stopped work at three o'clock on the afternoon of February 16, 1934, and marched with banners and placards to Madison Square Garden to demonstrate their support of the workers in Austria.

Three months later, the right-wing officials rejected an invitation from the Industrial Union to hold joint May Day celebrations. This did not stop Communist and Socialist needle trades workers from marching together in the May Day parade holding high their banners which proclaimed the need for unity against fascism.

The Industrial Union made a determined effort to end the fratricidal strife in the fur trade. It vigorously proposed the formation of a united, militant Furriers Union to be part of the American Federation of Labor. In open forums and in weekly bulletins distributed in the market, the question of unity was discussed with the workers again and again.

"With reaction on the march everywhere, with fascism rearing its ugly head in our own country, we must try more than ever before to remove every obstacle in the way of unity of all fur workers," said Ben Gold at a mass meeting of furriers in Webster Hall on February 20, 1935.

By unity, Gold pointed out, the Industrial Union meant the entrance of the left-wing union into the AFL International as a body with full and equal rights and with full trade union democracy.

After Gold's report, over twenty-five rank-and-file workers spoke from the platform. Although all were in full agreement with Gold's analysis of the need for unity of all fur workers in one organization, many were worried about associating with the American Federation of Labor. As at many meetings called by the Industrial Union, they expressed their distrust and suspicion of the right-wing leaders. They feared new intrigues and betrayals at the hands of those who had caused them so much grief in the past eight years. In reply, Gold agreed that the workers had good reason to feel concerned about entering the AFL. They had constant reminders on their heads and bodies of the reactionary policies of the Wolls, Greens, McGradys and other Federation leaders. Nevertheless, he urged them to remember the tremendous upsurge of rank-and-file opposition to this leadership and its policies. It was with these rank-and-file members of the AFL, and not with the bureaucracy, that the furriers would be uniting. The problem was the interests of the workers and how best to defend them.

Gold's report and recommendation were carried unanimously. The meeting voted to work for uniting the Industrial Union with the AFL International, for one union in the fur industry.

The Industrial Union's letter proposing a conference between the two unions to achieve unification was addressed to the International over the signatures of Joseph Winogradsky, manager, and Ben Gold, general secretary-treasurer. The letter, first in a long series of communications on the subject of unity in 1935, follows in part:

"For the past ten years thousands of fur workers, members of the former Joint Board of the Fur Workers Union and since 1929 members of the Fur Workers Industrial Union, have been forced to carry on a struggle against your Joint Council in order to defend their fundamental rights as workers and as union members. . . You will agree that the bosses, and more recently the NRA have taken advantage of this division in the ranks of the fur workers to advance their own greedy interests. . . We do not at present desire to go into the basic causes of this struggle . . . because we want to avoid prolonged and unnecessary debates, and to eliminate even the slightest possibility for any misrepresentation that might in any way confuse and defeat the purpose of this communication.

"The purpose of this communication is to make an honest, sincere and straight-forward attempt to persuade you to make every conscious effort to do away with the criminal struggle between our union and the Joint Council. . . Therefore we directly appeal to you and propose that a conference between the representatives of the Fur Workers Industrial

Union and the Joint Council shall be called for the purpose of merging both unions into one AFL union on the basis of a definite program, conducive to the interests of the fur workers and approved by them. . . We desire to emphasize that this is the most reasonable and practical manner in which such a purpose can be achieved. . . We propose that you designate a small committee to meet with a similar committee of the Industrial Union to work out the details for the larger conference. . ."

For several days there was no official answer to this frank bid for unity. The leaders of the Joint Council finally issued a leaflet that bristled with denunciations of the Industrial Union. The Joint Council charged that the Industrial Union was seeking unity because of "secret orders" from the Communist Party. Much was made of the fact that in the spring of 1934 the Trade Union Unity League, to which the Industrial Union was affiliated, had dissolved as a separate body.* Rejecting the proposal for a unity conference, the Joint Council said: "Why this play with conferences. It is commonly known that there is an established, bona-fide and recognized Furriers Union that is affiliated with the American Federation of Labor—the International Fur Workers Union—where the doors are wide open for the fur workers to come in as equals among equals. To build another Furriers Union within the AFL is totally impossible and entirely unnecessary."

The Industrial Union lost no time in answering. Point by point it ripped apart the oft-repeated red-baiting arguments by which the Joint Council justified its rejection of the unity proposals.

"Will you [Council leaders] please tell us," the Joint Board asked, "who authorized you to reject our proposal for a conference. Did you consult the fur workers about it? Did you call together your own few members to consult them? Just think of it, without the consultation or the advice of the fur workers, you, four or five people, took it upon yourselves to carry out the orders of the bosses to reject our proposal. . .

"In your reply you state that the Communist Party has issued an order to our union to unite with you into one AFL union. Let us assume for one moment that your statement is correct. . . Then, gentlemen of the Council, it would be the duty of each and every honest worker to greet the Communist Party in its struggle for workers' unity. However, you know very well that it was the furriers themselves who, at a mem-

---

* The actual dissolution of the TUUL did not occur until March 1935. What happened in the spring of 1934 was that the TUUL voluntarily disbanded its affiliates and instructed them to enter the AFL, there to spur on the organizational campaign.

While blocking all moves for unity, the right-wing International actually represented a total membership of only 2000, as indicated in this receipt for per capita paid to the AFL.

bership meeting in Webster Hall after a thorough discussion, unanimously voted to invite you to a conference. . ."

The Industrial Union repeated its proposal for unity. It called for the establishment of one AFL union in the industry on the basis of: elimination of gangsterism and clique control; full democracy with free speech and free criticism; no discrimination and no blacklisting of workers; equal rights for Negro workers; a determined struggle against contracting, against wage cuts and speedups; and a joint struggle of all fur workers for better conditions in the trade. The Industrial Union rejected the idea that the workers join the Council individually, because this would mean "discriminations, inevitable misunderstandings, continuation of the old and new conflicts, fresh struggles, divisions and splits, which provide fertile soil for cliques, clique rule, corruption and gangsterism."

"Why are you opposed to a conference with the workers' representatives?" the Industrial Union inquired. "Are you afraid to face the masses? If you prove at the conference that you honestly and sincerely intend to help to unite the forces into one union, then there is no reason why you should be afraid to meet the masses at a conference. There is no other way."

Despite the obstruction of the right-wing leadership, the agitation for one union continued. On March 6, 1935, *Women's Wear* reported that a conference was about to be held by representatives of the two unions. It was a false alarm. Nevertheless, many telegrams and letters from furriers all over the country poured into the International office congratulating the right-wing leaders for their willingness to attend a conference with the Industrial Union. Lucchi dispatched telegrams to all locals on

March 8 dispelling this expectation. "No conference will be held with their representatives as stated in *Women's Wear* March Fifth," he wired.

That same day, Winogradsky and Gold, in the name of the United National Committee of Fur Workers, formed by conference of the Industrial Union and AFL locals in June 1934, issued a call to all fur locals to elect delegates to a national conference to be held in New York City on March 29, 1935. All problems facing the fur workers in the United States and Canada would be discussed. Above all, a plan of action to bring about one union in the trade would be formulated and put into operation.

The combination of events—rising pressure of the workers for unity, exposure of the Joint Council's leaflet rejecting the unity proposals, the *Women's Wear* announcement, the telegrams from local unions of the International, and the call of the United National Committee for a national conference—forced the right-wing leaders to call a membership meeting at the Rand School on March 13. A strong-arm committee at the door saw to it that no "undesirable" workers were admitted. All but three members of a committee from the Industrial Union were turned back. Of these, only one was allowed to speak.

A few days later, a leaflet headed, "A CHALLENGE," appeared in the market over the signature of the Joint Council.

"1. All furriers . . . who sincerely want to build one powerful union should come into the American Federation of Labor without discrimination or difficulties.

"2. The Industrial Union should be immediately liquidated.

"3. Democratic elections should be held under the supervision of the fur workers in which thousands of fur workers should participate in order to choose their leaders. We, on our part, pledge ourselves to cooperate and support wholeheartedly the administration that would be elected.

"Will the leaders of the Industrial Union accept the challenge of our Union?"

This challenge was immediately answered by a mass membership meeting of the Industrial Union. Twelve hundred fur workers at Irving Plaza Hall unanimously endorsed Gold's proposal to accept the challenge on the following basis, which was communicated to the Joint Council:

A joint committee composed of ten workers elected by the Joint Council and ten by the Industrial Union should be authorized to carry through the unification of the furriers in one union within the American Federation of Labor. The joint committee should carry out all elections of officers within thirty days after it began to function. The committee should be dissolved immediately after the elections. During the thirty days, until the elections, the joint committee should manage the affairs of the fur workers.

"Should the leaders of the Joint Council reject this proposal," Gold declared, "we will build our union stronger than it ever was before, fight more intensely for better conditions, destroy the contracting system and through further struggles in the shops for better conditions, bring about one union in the trade. The fur workers always wanted unity and they want it now. Anyone who fails to utilize all possibilities to bring about unity is committing a crime against the interests of the workers."

The Joint Council made no reply. It was the end of unity negotiations so far as the right-wingers were concerned. Much to their disappointment, their "challenge" had been accepted. Since they were afraid to go through with it, they kept quiet.

In their private correspondence, the right-wingers were anything but quiet. Letters and telegrams kept pouring into the International headquarters from leaders of right-wing locals all over the country. Many members demanded that delegates be elected to the National Unity Conference in New York City on March 29. Others demanded that the International leaders meet with the representatives of the Industrial Union to establish unity.

On March 18, the secretary of Local 3 in Brooklyn wrote to Lucchi: "I am directed by a unanimous decision of the members at the last regular membership meeting to convey to you our endorsement of the proposal made by the Fur Workers Industrial Union. . . . The establishment of one Union in the fur industry is of the greatest importance, not only to the fur manufacturing workers, but to the dressers and dyers as well. Our bosses are attacking our Union standards, conditions, and wages with the same forces as they are attacking the fur manufacturing workers. The establishment of one Union will certainly make our organization stronger and easier for us to conduct a unified campaign for Union conditions and the organization of the open shops. We hope that you will act in the interests of our members by accepting the proposal of the Fur Workers Industrial Union for one Union in the industry."

Albert Roy of Montreal urged Lucchi to support unity with the Industrial Union. "We may have some differences if they join," he wrote, "but it would bring activity in our Union and you know that there is more work to be done with ten of those fellows than with our 325

Fur Floor Workers' Union, Local No. 3
I. F. W. U. of U. S. and C.
957 WILLOUGHBY AVENUE

BROOKLYN, N. Y., March 19, 1935, 193

Mr Pietro Lucchi,
General President,Secretary,
International Fur Workers Union.
9 Jackson Avenue,
Long Island City. N.Y.

Dear Sir & Brother:

   I am directed by a unanimous decision of the members
at the last regular membership meeting to convey to you our
endorsement of the proposal made by the Fur Workers Industrial
Union for a conference between its representatives and the
representatives of the New York Furriers Joint Council and the
International Union for the purpose of working out a plan for
merging the two Unions into one Union inside the International.
Our members without a dissenting vote, decided that we urge upon
the Officers of the International, as well as the Joint Council
to accept this proposal which we believe will bring about one
Union in the fur industry.

Floor Workers Local 3 appeals for the formation of one union.

members. If they are smart enough to take the control, well let them have it."

Lucchi replied to all locals warning them not to elect delegates to the National Conference. The Industrial Union, he charged, "is not a trade union in a genuine sense, but rather a branch of the Communist Party, and in reality the Communist Headquarters." The International would enter into no "dealings, negotiations or conferences whatsoever with groups who are openly or in disguise connected with political parties."

Ben Gold summed up the attitude of the right-wing leaders: "Why do these gentlemen set themselves like a stone wall against unity, when, by merging with the Industrial Union, the International could become a powerful union in forty-eight hours? As they are today they have no members to speak of, no leadership, no prospects, and no possibilities for existence as a union.

"Fourteen thousand stalwart workers, experienced in every phase of union activity, with a developed rank-and-file leadership of hundreds of workers, such as few other unions can boast of, would immediately join the International. Such a blood transfusion would overnight bring into being a mighty organization of workers within the International that would be able to deliver even more telling blows against the manufacturers in the interests of the workers.

"The Socialist leaders are simply afraid that the thousands of furriers would get rid of them as soon as they had a chance to vote as members of the International, and would overwhelmingly elect left-wing and Communist leaders. Therein lies the main obstacle to unity of the furriers."

Many of the International's locals flatly rejected the leadership's command to boycott the National Unity Conference. The San Francisco local, typical of others, telegraphed Lucchi: "We have carefully considered your letter and it is our opinion that you are wrong in your attitude. Continued division in the ranks of the fur workers will only hurt us. We urge you to go to the conference and make every possible effort to come to an agreement to merge both unions so as to unite the workers in an effective fight to improve our working and living conditions."

San Francisco workers urge the International to accept unity.

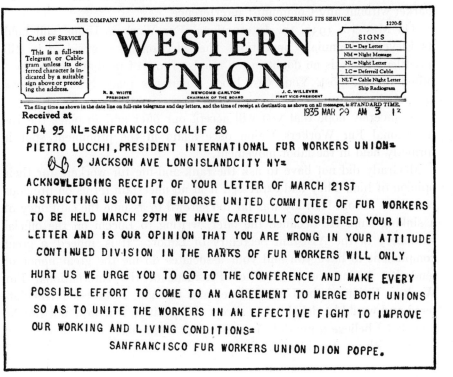

THE COMPANY WILL APPRECIATE SUGGESTIONS FROM ITS PATRONS CONCERNING ITS SERVICE

1220-S

WESTERN UNION

CLASS OF SERVICE

This is a full-rate Telegram or Cablegram unless its deferred character is indicated by a suitable sign above or preceding the address.

R. B. WHITE
PRESIDENT

NEWCOMB CARLTON
CHAIRMAN OF THE BOARD

J. C. WILLEVER
FIRST VICE-PRESIDENT

SIGNS

DL = Day Letter
NM = Night Message
NL = Night Letter
LC = Deferred Cable
NLT = Cable Night Letter
Ship Radiogram

The filing time as shown in the date line on full-rate telegrams and day letters, and the time of receipt at destination as shown on all messages, is STANDARD TIME.

Received at   1935 MAR 29 AM 3 12

FD4 95 NL=SANFRANCISCO CALIF 28

PIETRO LUCCHI,PRESIDENT INTERNATIONAL FUR WORKERS UNION=
    9 JACKSON AVE LONGISLANDCITY NY=

ACKNOWLEDGING RECEIPT OF YOUR LETTER OF MARCH 21ST
INSTRUCTING US NOT TO ENDORSE UNITED COMMITTEE OF FUR WORKERS
TO BE HELD MARCH 29TH WE HAVE CAREFULLY CONSIDERED YOUR I
LETTER AND IS OUR OPINION THAT YOU ARE WRONG IN YOUR ATTITUDE
CONTINUED DIVISION IN THE RANKS OF FUR WORKERS WILL ONLY

HURT US WE URGE YOU TO GO TO THE CONFERENCE AND MAKE EVERY
POSSIBLE EFFORT TO COME TO AN AGREEMENT TO MERGE BOTH UNIONS
SO AS TO UNITE THE WORKERS IN AN EFFECTIVE FIGHT TO IMPROVE
OUR WORKING AND LIVING CONDITIONS=
            SANFRANCISCO FUR WORKERS UNION DION POPPE.

Neither Lucchi nor any of the other top leaders of the right wing attended the National Unity Conference. But many delegates from the International locals did. Together with the delegates from the Industrial Union, they voted to call a convention in May 1935 to organize an independent Fur Workers International Union which should direct and coordinate the activities of the furriers throughout the United States and Canada. It would be held at the same time that the right-wing leaders and their handful of supporters were convening the Eleventh Biennial Convention of the International.

The Socialist leaders had thus far refused to accept the only logical basis on which unity could be established. Yet so deplorable was the state of affairs within the International Union that on April 16, 1935, Lucchi made the following proposal to McGrady:

"Last month when I was in Washington with brothers Begoon and Goldstein, we had a discussion with you in regard to the New York situation. At the present time, more than ever before, do all concerned feel that there is a golden opportunity for success. Under the proper management and stimulation the Joint Council could once again control the fur market without any Communist interference.

"On May 16, 1935, the International Fur Workers Union will hold its Eleventh Biennial Convention. The selection of a president is still unsettled. There is no doubt in the minds of any of us that you are best suited for the post. Your vast labor experience places you far above anyone else. . .

"I sincerely hope that you will accept our offer and so place the International Fur Workers Union once again in the prominent spot it formerly held in the labor movement."

McGrady did not have to ask the rank-and-file fur workers for their opinion of him. They had expressed it in no uncertain terms on previous occasions. Also, McGrady was far too shrewd to assume the captaincy of a sinking ship. He declined the offer, writing to Lucchi on the official stationery of the Assistant Secretary of Labor: "It is, indeed, a great compliment to have you and your associates do me the great honor of tendering to me the position of President of the International Fur Workers Union of the United States and Canada. I confess I feel flattered and would be delighted to accept this position if it were not for the fact that I believe it my duty in these great trying days of reconstruction to stay with my President. . ."

DEPARTMENT OF LABOR

OFFICE OF THE ASSISTANT SECRETARY

WASHINGTON

April 17, 1935

Mr. Pietro Lucchi
General President-Secretary
International Fur Workers' Union
9 Jackson Avenue
Long Island City, New York

My dear Mr. Lucchi:

It is, indeed, a great compliment to
have you and your associates do me the great honor
of tendering to me the position of President of the
International Fur Workers' Union of the United
States and Canada.   I confess I feel flattered
and would be delighted to accept this position if
it were not for the fact that I believe it my duty
in these great trying days of reconstruction to
stay with my President and to offer, feebly though
it may be, my contribution in this great adventure.

If the time comes in the future when
it is felt I am no longer needed by this Administration
I will be very glad to discuss with you the possibility of enlisting in the service of the International
Fur Workers' Union for the purpose of bringing about
a better day and a better life for all of the men and
women within this industry.

Sincerely,

EDW. F. McGRADY
Assistant Secretary

*McGrady, refusing to accept the captaincy of a sinking ship, re-
jects the right-wing offer to make him International president.*

In the third week of April, Ben Gold left New York to visit all International locals. The purpose of the trip was to win the support of the membership of the right-wing locals for the Industrial Union's struggle for unity. Everywhere Gold went—Boston, Chicago, Toronto, Cleveland, Montreal, St. Paul—the furriers flocked to hear him. Members of the right-wing locals sat side by side with the members of the Industrial Union in the crowded halls where the meetings were held.

Gold told the workers how the Industrial Union had accepted the Joint Council's challenge, how the right-wing leaders had refused to go through with their own program. He warned the workers that unless they applied pressure on the right wing, the furriers would remain split.

Gold dwelt at length on the serious grievances of the fur workers and showed why unity was necessary before they could be remedied. He described the spread of the contracting evil and the open shops under the NRA, mass unemployment, speedup, and lack of security on the job. He pointed out that thousands of furriers were unorganized, and illustrated how this weakened the efforts of the organized fur workers to secure improvements.

The rapid rise of fascist organizations in the United States, Gold emphasized, made unity of the workers a matter of life and death for the labor movement. He urged the furriers to remember the mistakes of the leaders of the German working class who had refused, in the face of Hitler's rise to power, to achieve unity with millions of Communist workers. The concentration camps were filled with men and women who were paying for this tragic mistake. Unless the American workers learned from this experience and took steps to unite their ranks, they would suffer the same agony.

There was only one conclusion the members of the International locals could draw from Gold's addresses—that those who opposed unity were indifferent to the needs of the fur workers. By the time Gold completed his tour of the International locals, the sentiment for unity was at such a fever pitch that not even the staunchest supporters of the right wing dared oppose it. In every local Gold visited, a resolution was adopted demanding that the forthcoming International convention take immediate steps to establish one union in the fur trade.

Joe Indes wrote Lucchi from Chicago: "In as much as our delegates are leaving Chicago to attend our Convention, it is imperative for the writer to explain the reasons motivating the presentation of our Resolution. . . The trade is at a standstill and our membership is discouraged and hungry. They have been led to believe that through the merger there would be plenty of jobs and better conditions. This sentiment has crystalized to such an extent, that our staunch active members are for 'One Union.' The resolution that will be presented at the convention was carried without a dissenting vote, not exactly unanimously but no votes went on record against the same."

The right-wing machine in Chicago could not prevent the unanimous adoption of the unity resolution. Even "reliable" right-wing supporters were clamoring for unity. If they continued to reject the Industrial Union's unity proposals, the leaders of the International were faced with a final rank-and-file revolt. Whatever membership was still left in the AFL union, except for a handful of Lovestoneites and die-hard right-wingers, would move into the Industrial Union. The right-wing leaders had to decide: give up existence altogether or join with the Industrial Union in creating one union in the fur trade.

Chicago right-wing leaders admit that the workers want unity.

CHAPTER 41

One United Union

Two conventions and one union. These words spelled unity.

On May 15, 1935, the convention of the Fur Workers Industrial Union opened at Irving Plaza in New York City. Delegates representing fourteen thousand fur workers in New York, Brooklyn, Newark, Philadelphia, Chicago, Detroit, Cleveland and Los Angeles were present. They came from fur manufacturing shops, fur dressing and fur dyeing plants. Their militant struggles had won tremendous advances in working conditions—wage raises, shorter hours, and unemployment insurance funds.

While listening to the reports and outlining a program for future struggles, the delegates in New York anxiously awaited news from Toronto where the Eleventh Biennial Convention of the International Union opened on May 16. What stand would that convention take on unity?

Reports from Toronto by Irving Potash, the Industrial Union's on-the-spot observer, were not encouraging. The Socialists and the Lovestoneites were doing everything possible to prevent unity. A number of rank-and-file delegates were battling vigorously for one union, but they were unable to make headway. Determined to encourage these pro-unity forces, the Industrial Union's convention sent Ben Gold and Abe Feinglass to Canada. The delegation joined Potash with instructions to do everything possible to achieve unity.

In Toronto, the right-wing leaders still seemed to be rushing headlong to suicide for the organization. The lengthy report of the General Executive Board was mainly a bitter attack on the Industrial Union.

462

The report's only reference to the subject of unity was an attack on the Industrial Union's proposal for a merger of the two unions. This was characterized as "a scheme on the part of the Communist Party to capture the Union." After the report was submitted, Morris Stein of Local 3, an International vice-president, asked: "How can we have unity and peace with all this slander and all these lies?" None of the right-wing leaders answered.

Telegrams pouring in to the convention demanded unity. Locals, shops and individual workers instructed the delegates to "bring back unity and solidarity," and "go on record to amalgamate both unions into one international affiliated with the American Federation of Labor." Many resolutions were sent in, pointing out that fascism, "the bitterest and most dangerous enemy of the workers and of the labor movement," was making "tremendous headway in Europe" and was "already beginning to show its head in the United States." All fur workers, "no matter what may be their differences on political or other views," must unite their forces.

Nevertheless, on the morning of May 18, the last day of the convention, the right-wing leaders introduced a different kind of "unity" resolution. It proposed a merger of the International Fur Workers Union with the International Ladies Garment Workers Union. Instantly, Delegate Stein was on his feet. "This resolution," he cried bitterly, "is a shameful one. You came to this convention to build a powerful union of fur workers, and you are flirting with the International Ladies Garment Workers Union. This is because you came with the purpose of opposing unity." Stein's protest was ignored. The resolution was adopted.

The time was 11:25 A.M. It seemed that in a few hours the convention would adjourn without taking a stand on uniting the fur workers. Suddenly, the delegates learned that the committee from the Industrial Union—Ben Gold, Irving Potash, and Abe Feinglass—was waiting in the lobby.

Several delegates proposed that they be permitted to enter the hall and participate in the proceedings. This proposal was rejected by the International officers. But the majority of the delegates, including many right-wing leaders, moved into the lobby to greet Gold, Potash and Feinglass. Only a handful of die-hard Socialists and Lovestoneites remained in the convention hall. The "unofficial" convention was now actually taking place in the lobby. Here the most important business of the convention was going on.

Gold told the delegates that this was their opportunity to stop the destructive internal warfare in the fur trade and build one union. If the International convention adjourned without carrying out the rank-and-file demand for unity, the Industrial Union's convention, still in session in New York, would launch a campaign to organize every fur worker into an independent international.

Pietro Lucchi held a brief conference with Ben Gold on the spot. He told Gold that he, too, was convinced that unity was the only choice now remaining for the International. He assured Gold that he personally had no intention of destroying the organization to please the Socialist Party leadership, the *Forward,* and the Lovestoneites.

"I think you are sincere," Lucchi remarked to Gold. "I am sorry that I cannot let you into the convention, but that does not seem to matter since you practically have the whole convention with you here in the lobby. I want to assure you that I will work for unity if you will work with me."

"Do you want to work with me?" Lucchi asked after a pause.

"If you are sincerely in favor of unity, I will work with you," Gold replied. "You have my word."

"That's enough for me," Lucchi answered. "I am going back inside to fight for unity."

Gold and Lucchi shook hands on this pledge, cheered by the crowd in the lobby. The cheers resounded within the convention hall where the few Socialists and Lovestoneites sat scattered among the empty seats. They knew these cheers doomed their efforts to prevent unity.

Gold left immediately for New York to report to the Industrial Union's convention that a major obstacle to unity had been overcome. His meeting with Lucchi was a decisive turning point in the movement for one union. Significant elements in the right-wing leadership were sick of bloody warfare against the fur workers. They were weary of carrying the ball for the bosses and the officialdom of the American Federation of Labor and Socialist Party.

Before the International convention adjourned, a unity resolution was adopted. Admitting that "fratricidal struggle in New York, where eighty percent of the fur industry of the United States and Canada is concentrated, has so weakened the International that the smaller centers stand isolated, unprotected and make them more vulnerable to the attacks of the employers," the unity resolution decided "to make every possible effort to achieve unity and one union which will be affiliated with the American Federation of Labor." It called for liquidation of the Industrial Union, and assured all fur workers, members of the Industrial Union or unaffiliated, that they would be taken into the Joint Council of the International Fur Workers Union "as full-fledged members," with "full democratic rights and privileges of membership." The resolution instructed the incoming G.E.B. to reinstate all members formerly expelled as soon as they applied to rejoin.

Finally, the resolution set up an International Convention Unity Committee of seven members, five from different locals of the International and two from the Joint Council. This Committee was to have the full right to establish unity among the ranks of the fur workers. The Committee was to call upon the Industrial Union to disband; then register the fur workers into the Joint Council, and arrange for an election.

Several of the delegates objected strongly to obvious omissions in the Unity Resolution. They argued that the fur workers would be suspicious of a unity committee on which there were no representatives of the Industrial Union, and that the absence of a specific date for elections would strengthen these suspicions. They also objected to a section in the resolution which authorized the Unity Committee, if it found it necessary, to ask the AFL to designate someone to assist the Committee as chairman. This would open the door for last-minute sabotage of the unity negotiations.

Lucchi urged the delegates to waive their objections and to accept the proposed unity resolution as a compromise. He admitted that many of the objections to parts of the resolution were justified. But he reminded the delegates that it was necessary to have agreement among different elements in the International leadership. Under the circumstances, it was the best that he could achieve. He pointed out, for example, that originally it was proposed that the President of the AFL should designate the chairman of the Unity Committee. Upon Lucchi's insistence, this clause had been dropped.

Lucchi's plea revealed that a clear-cut resolution without these weaknesses would have caused the secession of the faction led by Begoon. The secessionists would then have demanded recognition from the AFL and the Federation leadership would have been only too eager to bestow the International's charter on a secessionist group.

By preventing the secession and persuading Begoon and his group to accept the compromise unity resolution, Lucchi played a decidedly constructive role. And by agreeing to abide by the convention's decision, Begoon also made an important contribution. He knew very well that the Forward Association would never forgive this step, and that he would be subjected to vicious attacks. Nevertheless, he decided to line up with the forces seeking unity.

The unity resolution was finally adopted by an overwhelming vote of the delegates. An International Convention Unity Committee was elected consisting of Michael M. Mandl of St. Paul and Minneapolis, Albert Roy of Montreal, Hyman Kalmikoff of Local 2, Brooklyn, Samuel Butkovitz of Local 30, Boston, and Harry Begoon, Simon Kass and Harry Simon of the Furriers Joint Council.

The Convention proceeded to elect a new G.E.B. and International officers. The democratic procedure, of course, would have been to wait for the conclusion of the unity negotiations, and then, at a united convention, elect new officers to lead the International.

Lucchi, it must be said, was quite reluctant to accept the nomination for another term as International president. He told the delegates why he finally agreed to continue in office: "Up to about half an hour ago, my mind was not made up. I stated frankly to all the delegates who asked me this question during the Convention and prior to coming here that unless we will be able to unify the forces of the International, I will not accept. Upon noting the splendid attitude taken by all the delegates in the resolution adopted not long ago, I made up my mind and I say to you at this moment that I do accept the nomination as President and I promise that if my health permits, to leave no stone unturned for the benefit of all the fur workers regardless where they may be."

The news of the actions taken at Toronto reached the Industrial Union's convention on May 18. Some left-wing delegates urged a point-blank rejection of the unity program outlined at Toronto. To their long-standing suspicions of the right-wingers was now added sharp criticism of the wording of the Toronto resolution. But Gold pointed out that to reject the proposal would only play into the hands of those who would like to see the unity movement upset at this critical stage. He regarded the Toronto unity resolution as a decisive victory for the forces fighting for one union. If the Industrial Union failed to utilize the opportunity offered by this change in the right-wing's position, it would in effect be prolonging the split at the expense of the workers.

The Industrial Union's convention accepted the unity proposal adopted at Toronto. It did, however, protest the election of new International officers before the vast majority of the united fur workers could express their choice. It insisted that the International Unity Committee should meet with a similar committee elected by the Industrial Union's convention to work out a plan for unity. Should this fall through, the newly-elected G.E.B. of the Industrial Union would proceed to build an independent international of fur workers.

Events in the New York fur market persuaded the International's Unity Committee to meet with the representatives of the Industrial Union. The Industrial Union fought on two fronts simultaneously: it fought for unity with the International; at the same time it conducted new struggles in the shops for better conditions. While the right-wing leaders debated whether or not to confer with what they still called the "Communist dual union," the Industrial Union called sixty shops out on strike against contracting and for wage increases.

Realizing that the Industrial Union meant business, the International's Unity Committee sat down around a conference table on May 31, 1935, with Ben Gold, Joseph Winogradsky, Irving Potash, and T. Berg, the committee representing the Industrial Union.

Speaking for the Industrial Union, Gold announced that the unity resolution adopted at Toronto was acceptable as a basis for unity. In order to put the resolution into practice, he proposed eight modifications and additions. Registration of Industrial Union members into the Joint Council should be taken care of by a joint committee. Members holding good-standing books in the Industrial Union from May 1935 should pay only four weeks' dues to receive an International Union book; those who were not in good standing and those who did not belong to any union should pay $3 initiation. Unemployed members and old furriers should be taken in for a smaller fee. From the first day of the registration a joint committee representing both unions should attend to the complaints and grievances from shops. A joint committee should administer the finances during the period of registration. A mass meeting should be called to inform the fur workers that unity was established. All expelled members should be taken into the International Union within three days after they made application for reinstatement. The election of new officers for the New York Joint Council should take place within one month.

Although the International's Unity Committee refused to give an immediate answer to these proposals, the first conference in itself marked an important advance towards unity. The very fact that the right-wing leaders were willing to confer with representatives of the Industrial Union indicated more than anything else that they were sincerely seeking peace.

After several conferences, the International's Unity Committee agreed to embody the most important proposals of the Industrial Union into the original unity plan adopted at Toronto. Initiation fees were set at $3.25. Elections for the Joint Council were to take place within forty days after the official dissolution of the Industrial Union and after a majority of the members of the Industrial Union had joined the Joint Council. Expelled members would be reinstated within seven days after their applications were received. All members of the Industrial Union could enter the Joint Council either through their shops or individually, thus enabling them to enter as an organized body. The staff of the Joint Council would be enlarged to attend to all complaints during the registration period; three leaders of the Industrial Union were added to the staff of the Joint Council—Jack Schneider, Herman Paul and Gus Hopman.

This compromise plan was submitted by the Industrial Union to a mass meeting of fur workers in Cooper Union on June 12. Many meetings had been held in Cooper Union since the bloody civil war had started in the trade. None was more important than this meeting. Here would be given the answer to the question in the minds of the whole labor movement: will one united furriers' union finally be established?

"This was a serious meeting," a fur worker wrote to William Green, in an effort to persuade the president of the Federation to support the movement to establish one union in the fur trade, "a meeting of great importance to the fur workers. This meeting was to become history in the American labor movement. It was a meeting to make history in the lives of the fur workers. It was a meeting of hope. Considering the fact that the night was a terribly hot one, thousands of people jammed into an auditorium that hardly has any ventilation, perspiration running down from the faces of all the thousands of people present, considering all these facts I must add that in spite of all these handicaps the meeting was conducted in a real honest-to-goodness American fashion, as befits real Americans and that is what the majority of the fur workers are, 'real Americans.' The furriers realized the seriousness of the evening and they gave their individual attention to the events of the evening. . . .

"As to Ben Gold. That he is liked by the furriers there is no doubt. He is the straw that the furriers grasped when they thought they were sinking. Somehow they have held on to him since. . . . The furriers appreciate the good that they believe Gold has done for them and being grateful, they stick to him."

It was truly with "undivided attention" that these thousands of perspiring furriers listened to Ben Gold's analysis of the question before

them. Gold reminded the furriers that although the Industrial Union had
controlled the vast majority of the shops and workers, it had been the
first to propose unity. It believed that the organized power of the fur
workers would be much greater if one union was established in the trade.
This did not mean that after unity was achieved, the furriers would have

The call for the historic meeting at which unity was approved.

TO ALL FURRIERS!

SISTERS AND BROTHERS:

WHAT IS YOUR POSITION ON THE ESTABLISHMENT
OF ONE UNION?

**Shall we accept the terms which the International Unity Committee agrees to, or shall
we reject those terms?**

YOU WILL MAKE YOUR DECISION THE COMING

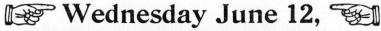 **Wednesday June 12,**

RIGHT AFTER WORK (5 O'CLOCK) AT THE BIG

COOPER UNION MASS MEETING
8th STREET & FOURTH AVENUE

We are convinced that you are aware of the extraordinary importance of this problem.
It concerns the livelihood of the thousands of fur workers and their families. It concerns
the possibility of stopping the strife that has been going on for ten years and the possibility
of creating one furriers' union.

FUR WORKERS! DO YOU GRASP THE IMPORTANCE OF THIS
MASS MEETING?

YOUR DECISION AT THE COOPER UNION MASS MEETING WILL BE STRICTLY
CARRIED OUT. That is why every fur worker is called upon to come to this important and
possibly historic meeting at Cooper Union the coming Wednesday.

Fur Workers: Come to this mass meeting under all circumstances. Participate in the discussion and in the making of the decision on the most vital
question of one union.

ALL SHOP CHAIRMEN ARE CALLED UPON AND INSTRUCTED TO INFORM
THE WORKERS IN THE SHOPS OF THE IMPORTANCE of ATTENDING the COOPER
UNION MASS MEETING.

The unemployed as well as the employed must attend the meeting. Remember: At this great meeting you will be called upon to make the most important decision in ten years.

FORWARD TO THE COOPER UNION MEETING!
COME IN MASSES! COME ON TIME!
REMEMBER: WEDNESDAY, JUNE 12th, 5 O'CLOCK, AT COOPER UNION!

General Executive Board
Indt. International Fur Workers Indust. Union
Ben Gold, Chairman
Joseph Winogradsky, Manager, New York

smooth sailing. The bosses would look for new ways to block their advance. But without having to divert so much of their energy to the internal struggle, the fur workers would quickly defeat any new attacks.

Gold outlined the latest plan proposed by the International's Unity Committee, and which demands of the Industrial Union had been accepted by the right-wing leaders. The omissions in the International plan were not decisive and should not stand in the way of a unanimous vote in its favor. Before the workers voted, Gold continued, they should remember that proposals on paper guaranteed nothing in themselves. The furriers must not rely on miracles; they themselves must do the work necessary to cement unity.

At 9 P.M. on June 12, 1935, the thousands of fur workers at Cooper Union voted unanimously to accept the recommendation of the leadership of the Industrial Union. Without a dissenting vote, they dissolved the Industrial Union, and agreed to register as members of the International Fur Workers Union.*

The Industrial Union warned the fur workers against countless rumors that were flying fast and furious in the market. There was a good reason for this warning. Already the *Forward* and other newspapers were circulating reports that unity would never be achieved because of the opposition to a merger of the two unions by the leaders of the AFL. On June 9, the *Forward* had reported that William Green was preparing to "suspend the Fur Workers Union if they unite with the Communists." Two days later, *Women's Wear* declared that "some person who is very close to William Green" stated that the Federation would not permit the unification of the two unions.

These reports were not just rumors. On June 4, 1935, John Fitzpatrick, president of the Chicago Federation of Labor, wrote to William Green: "Considerable effort has been and is being made to merge Local Union No. 45 of the I.F.W.U., and the organization composed of Communists. We have consistently resented any such moves and have served notice on Local No. 45 that they cannot maintain an affiliation with the Chicago Federation of Labor if they accept as members of their local this group of Communists, the so-called 'Industrial Fur Workers Union.' Can you advise us as to what is being done in New York City in this matter and if Local Union No. 45 accepts these Communists whether we will be required to continue this organization in affiliation with the Federation?"

* In April 1935 the Industrial Union dressmakers had entered the ILGWU. They were not taken in as a body, but were treated individually as new members.

Green answered: "We will support you and your associated representatives of the Chicago Federation of Labor in refusing to afford representation to the local union of fur workers in the event it merges with the communists. . . . Local unions which compromise with the communists, merge with them and accept them into membership ought to be, should be, and must be denied representation in central bodies until they purge themselves of communist membership and of the acceptance by implication of communist philosophy. We are following in New York the policy herein enunciated. Be assured that we will maintain this policy without change."

To reverse the unity decision of the leaders of the International Fur Workers Union, Matthew Woll, on Green's instructions, called a conference in his office on June 18. The conference was attended by David Dubinsky, Sidney Hillman, Pietro Lucchi, William Collins and Woll himself. Woll, again acting on Green's instructions, promised Lucchi that the Federation would extend "all assistance possible" to the International if it broke off the unity negotiations and repudiated the merger with the Industrial Union. Similar assistance would be forthcoming from the Amalgamated Clothing Workers and the ILGWU.

Pietro Lucchi stood his ground. He refused to betray the fur workers. Neither promises of financial assistance nor threats of expulsion from the Federation had any effect on him. He told Woll, Collins, Dubinsky and Hillman that the International convention had acted in favor of unity. On the basis of this decision, plans to establish one union had already been accepted by the fur workers and were being put into operation. Under no circumstances, Lucchi declared bluntly, would he violate this decision.

For several hours, pressure was brought to bear on Lucchi to force him to reverse his stand. But to no avail. Reporting to William Green directly after the conference, Woll noted sadly:

"It is thus apparent that the International Fur Workers Union has capitulated to a procedure which may again result in Communistic control and domination by the Communistically led group. . . .

"It is the opinion of Representative Collins and I that we might as well let the Communists know directly that insofar as the American Federation of Labor is concerned we have not altered our attitude of irreconcilable hostility toward the Communists even though the Communists have changed their tactics and are now endeavoring to bore from within under one pretense or another. Even though we are unable to guide or direct the furriers' unions by reason of lack of strong leadership and depressed trade conditions, there is no sound reason why we should compromise our attitude and associate with them. Such a relationship cannot long continue and of course it is a relationship designed to destroy trade unionism as conceived and as carried out through the teachings and practice of the American Federation of Labor. I have requested President Hillman and President Dubinsky to advise you of their respective conclusions so that you may be fully advised and from different sources.*

"P.S. Since dictating the foregoing report I have carried out your instructions of advising the International Fur Workers Union that we would not recognize any local unions admitting Communists into their organization."

"I feel very strongly about this matter," replied Green on June 19. "We cannot tolerate a situation which means the control and domination of the International Fur Workers Union by the Communists. We should prevent the development and existence of such a situation rather than to wait until such a situation had been created before taking drastic action."

It is clear that the reactionary officialdom of the AFL viewed the establishment of one union in the fur trade as the most serious defeat it had sustained over a period of years. Nowhere had the AFL leaders devoted so much time, energy and money as in the efforts to keep the fur workers divided and fighting among themselves. After ten years of intrigue, the leaders of the AFL were now forced to admit defeat. They had accomplished nothing. The bosses had enjoyed a Roman holiday and increased their profits at the expense of the workers. They had held back the total organization of the fur industry. But the main aim of the AFL was defeated.

It is noteworthy that in the entire correspondence of William Green and Matthew Woll opposing the unity movement, there is not a single reference to the desires of the fur workers themselves.

The final blast against unity was delivered by Woll on June 19. "The American Federation of Labor," he threatened, "will not countenance any such action . . . no 'united front' [is] in harmony with the philosophy of the American Federation of Labor."

A day later, over six thousand fur workers attended an overflow meeting at the Manhattan Opera House in New York, and formally entered the "united front." Unanimously, they approved a resolution of "wholehearted approval of the work of the unity committee." Amid thunderous

---

* In a statement to the press, Dubinsky tried to give the impression that he had nothing to do with the attempt to persuade Lucchi to retreat on the issue of unity.

AMERICAN FEDERATION OF LABOR

Executive Council.

[officer roster illegible]

LONG DISTANCE TELEPHONE NATIONAL 3070-1-2-3-4
CABLE ADDRESS, AFEL.

A F OF L BUILDING

Washington, D.C.,

June 18th, 1935

RECEIVED
JUN 19 1935

Mr. William Green, President,
American Federation of Labor,
A. F. of L. Building,
Washington, D. C.

Dear President Green:

A conference was held this morning on the subject of the International Fur Workers' Union. The conference was attended by President Dubinsky, President Hillman, President Lucchi, the Presidents of two of the New York Local Unions of furriers, Representative William Collins and myself.

It developed in this conference that the International Fur Workers' Union, at its recent convention by definite resolution agreed to reinstate all former expelled members and officers and that forty days thereafter a new election would be held in the New York Local Unions. It further developed that local plans had proceeded so far under this convention action that it is difficult, if not impossible for the officers of the Fur Workers' Union to interfere with this procedure. It would thus seem that former expelled Communists are to be re-admitted without question or restraint.

It is thus apparent that the International Fur Workers' Union has capitulated to a procedure which may again result in Communistic control and domination by the Communistically led group.

Considering all ascertainable facts the Conference seemed of the opinion that it would be well to let the situation rest at present with the statement recently issued by you in Chicago, that is, the statement to the effect that the Chicago Federation of Labor was justified and is directed not to recognize the Local Union of Furriers if Communists were admitted and that the same course will be followed in New York City and elsewhere. It was believed by this declared policy of the American Federation of Labor that all Central Labor Unions and State Federations of Labor would be guided accordingly and without further direct instructions on your part.

I have requested President Hillman and President Dubinsky to advise you of their respective conclusions so that you may be fully advised and from different sources.

With kindest personal regards, I am,

Cordially and fraternally yours,

[signature] Matthew Woll

W:H

P. S. Since dictating the foregoing report I have carried out your instructions of advising the International Fur Workers Union that we would not recognize any local unions admitting Communists into their organisation.

AFL leaders never give up the fight—to split the union.

applause, Pietro Lucchi declared in answer to Green and Woll: "I am hopeful . . . that all furriers . . . will realize the stupidity of division in our ranks, of continued fratricidal conflict, either inside or outside our organization, and will henceforth conduct themselves as genuine trade unionists in the face of the employer class. Any other conduct will be denounced as acts against the best interests of the workers in the fur industry. I will and must carry out the will of the fur workers and abide by the unity decision of the Toronto Convention one hundred percent. We are not interested in what parties the workers belong to."

On June 27, Green and Woll received their final answer. Ben Gold and sixteen other leaders of the Industrial Union were reinstated into the International Fur Workers Union.*

In Chicago, the fur workers gave their answer to John Fitzpatrick. The members of Local 45 and those of the Industrial Union jointly hailed the achievement of unity in New York and took steps to establish one union in their own city.

Six weeks after the registration of Industrial Union members started, the formerly defunct Furriers Joint Council boasted a membership of eight thousand fur workers. Six business agents were added to the Council's staff—three from the right wing and three from the left wing—to supervise one thousand former Industrial Union shops that now came under the control of the Joint Council.

Preparations were now made for the election of a new administration in the New York Joint Council. The membership was to elect a manager, an assistant manager, a secretary-treasurer, twelve business agents and thirty-five Council members.

On July 27, a membership meeting nominated candidates and decided that the Election and Objection Committee should consist of the Unity Committee, plus four former members of the Industrial Union. The four members elected at this meeting were: Mencher, Kravitz, Katz and Brenner. The Election and Objection Committee set Tuesday, Wednesday and Thursday, August 6, 7 and 8, as the dates for the election.

The left wing had the support of the overwhelming majority of work-

---

* No action was ever taken by the Federation leadership to carry out their threats against the International Fur Workers Union. After a quarterly Executive Council meeting on August 10, 1935, Green was asked whether any action had been taken in regard to the International's admission of the Communists. Green answered: "I cannot divulge our thoughts on the subject until then [the October Convention]." No action was taken at this convention.

THE COMPANY WILL APPRECIATE SUGGESTIONS FROM ITS PATRONS CONCERNING ITS SERVICE

1220-S

WESTERN UNION

CLASS OF SERVICE

This is a full-rate Telegram or Cablegram unless its deferred character is indicated by a suitable sign above or preceding the address.

R. B. WHITE
PRESIDENT

NEWCOMB CARLTON
CHAIRMAN OF THE BOARD

J. C. WILLEVER
FIRST VICE-PRESIDENT

SIGNS

DL = Day Letter
NM = Night Message
NL = Night Letter
LC = Deferred Cable
NLT = Cable Night Letter
Ship Radiogram

The filing time as shown in the date line on full-rate telegrams and day letters, and the time of receipt at destination as shown on all messages, is STANDARD TIME.

Received at

CB893106   NL 4 EXTRA=CHICAGO ILL 17   1935 JUL 17 PM 10 46

MINUTES IN TRANSIT

PIETRO LUCCHI,PRESIDENT INTERNATIONAL FUR WORKERS UNION OF

UNITEDSTATES AND CANADA=9 JACKSON ST LONGISLAND NY=

MASS MEETING OVER TWO HUNDRED FIFTY WORKERS UNANIMOUSLY

ACCEPT PROPOSALS UNITY COMMITTEE BASED ON TORONTO CONVENTION

FOR ESTABLISHMENT OF ONE UNION IN CHICAGO DECISION TO BEGIN

IMMEDIATELY TO REGISTER IN LOCAL FORTY FIVE TO BUILD ONE

STRONG UNITED UNION WHICH WILL BE ABLE TO CARRY ON A FIGHT

FOR IMPROVEMENTS OF FUR WORKERS CONDITIONS AGAINST

CONTRACTING SPEED UP AND FOR INCREASES OF WAGES AND THIRTY

FIVE HOUR WEEK MEMBERSHIP UNANIMOUSLY PLEDGES SUPPORT AND TO

BUILD LOCAL FORTY FIVE LONG LIVE UNITY OF THE FUR WORKERS

LONG LIVE OUR INTERNATIONAL FUR WORKERS UNION OF THE

UNITEDSTATES AND CANADA OF THE A F L=

LEW GOLDSTEIN   ORGANIZER ABE FEINGLASS MANAGER.

The Chicago fur workers unite and prepare for common struggles.

ers. It could have swept every elected position. But to maintain and cement unity in the ranks and in the leadership, the left wing entered a unity slate for only half of the officers to be elected. It recommended the election of the right-wingers to the remainder. The left-wing slate consisted of Ben Gold for manager; Maurice H. Cohen, Julius Fleiss, Gus Hopman, Max Kochinsky, Herman Paul, Jack Schneider and Joseph Winogradsky for business agents; and eighteen candidates for Joint Council delegates.* The left wing did not contest the posts of assistant manager or secretary-treasurer.

* Anton Emeneth, William Kaiser were the left-wing candidates from the cutters local; Mark M. Boerum, Philip Brown, Philip Glantzman, Hymie Greenberg, Isidor Opochinsky, Mania Schwartz, Louis Tellis and Sol Wollin, operators local; Leviche Cohen, Sam Davis, Lucas Premice and Sam Resnick, nailers local; Harry Berkowitz, Mary Fleishman, Clara Meltzer and Ida Thal, finishers local.

Opposing the left-wing slate, the old-guard Socialists, Lovestoneites and other groups combined to put forward their own candidates for all positions. Headed by Harold Goldstein as candidate for manager and Benjamin Baraz and Mike Intrator, Lovestoneites, as candidates for business agent, the anti-left-wing slate was endorsed by various groups which called themselves "Furriers Trade Union League," "Furriers Socialist Group," "Furriers Progressive Group," and "Furriers Unity Group." These groups had no substantial following among the fur workers. They usually were organized at gatherings attended by six or less workers. Strangely enough, they seemed to have plenty of funds to flood the market daily with thousands of leaflets. The employers distributed the same leaflets to the workers in the shops.

The anti-left-wing candidates unleashed a barrage of red-baiting propaganda. They charged that the election of Gold and other left-wingers would spell disaster for the furriers. They tried to frighten the furriers with predictions that the union would be outlawed by the AFL if left-wingers were elected.

The *Day,* supporting the anti-left-wing candidates, argued that Gold should withdraw his candidacy for manager. Morgenstern, a writer for the *Day,* sounded alarms that "his [Gold's] position as manager will bring about such a political situation in the Furriers Union which will create more trouble than the entire thing is worth."

David Dubinsky appealed to the fur workers to defeat the left-wing slate if they wanted to be "saved." The election of the left-wing candidates, Dubinsky wrote in the *Forward,* would antagonize the leaders of the AFL and force them to take disciplinary action.

The day before the election, an unsigned cartoon-leaflet was distributed, picturing a figure in Moscow giving orders to the leaders of the American Communist Party who, in turn, were giving orders to Ben Gold. "Don't vote for candidates that take orders from Moscow," the scurrilous leaflet appealed.

Inspired rumors circulated through the market that the election of left-wing candidates would split the union. To clarify the issues, Gold addressed a personal appeal to the furriers. Stressing above all the preservation of unity of all fur workers in the International Fur Workers Union, Gold demolished the rumors and threats.

There would be only one union in the fur trade, Gold assured the fur workers. He called upon them to vote for the left-wing candidates. Every pledge made by the left wing to the fur workers in the course of the past ten years had been kept. They had obtained the forty-hour week in 1926 and other improvements in conditions. When the crisis began, and wages were being cut in every industry, the left wing had upheld with all their power the wage scales of the furriers. They had cleaned out the gangsters and racketeers. They had won an unemployment insurance fund paid by the bosses. They had obtained the thirty-five-hour week in 1934.

"Now we tell you," Gold wrote, "that we will safeguard the integrity of our one union with all our strength, ability and energy and if necessary with our blood. And you may rest assured that we will fulfill this promise just as we have fulfilled all the other promises we have made to you.

"We assure every fur worker and the entire labor movement that if we are elected, a short time after election we will fortify our union and place it on such a sound and solid foundation that neither the bosses nor any other enemies, nor the devil himself will be able to disrupt the unity in our ranks.

"Where will we get the power to fulfill this promise? My answer is, we will do it with the invincible might of the thousands of fur workers! We will do it with your support, with your trust, just as we have demonstrated in the past ten years our ability, with your aid, and fulfilled programs and plans in a manner that called forth the admiration of the entire working class movement and the consternation of our enemies. Nobody will dare deny the truth of this statement."

Gold's stirring appeal was endorsed by five hundred shop chairmen of the largest and most important fur shops who urged all fur workers to vote for the left-wing candidates.

For three days, seventy-five hundred workers went to the polls and cast their votes. It was the greatest vote ever cast in a furriers' election up to this time. Even then some three thousand furriers who wanted to vote could not do so. The Greek furriers did not participate because their transfer to the AFL union was not yet completed. In addition, a large number of fur workers who paid the registration fee to the Joint Council had not yet received approved receipts and were thus prevented from voting. The vast majority of these workers unable to vote were former members of the Industrial Union. Nevertheless, the left-wing candidates won an overwhelming victory. Ben Gold was elected manager over Harold Goldstein by a vote of 5,029 to 1,944. All seven left-wing candidates for business agent were elected by large majorities, Jack Schneider leading the list with 4,978 votes, Herman Paul second with 4,493 votes, Gus Hopman third with 4,316 votes and Joseph Winogradsky fourth with 4,211 votes. Every left-wing candidate for Joint Council delegate was elected. Moreover, all right-wing candidates on the left-wing slate were elected, although with lower votes than the left-wing candidates. Benjamin Baraz, the Lovestoneite leader, was the only anti-left wing candidate voted in. He received 2,083 votes for business agent, next to the lowest vote cast for any candidate. Hyman Sorkin and Harry Begoon were elected assistant manager and secretary-treasurer respectively by the Joint Council, the offices on the ballot left vacant by the left wing.

August 15, 1935, was a gala day in the fur market—a day of excitement and festivity. That afternoon the fur workers celebrated another milestone in their history. The installation of the new administration of the Joint Council was to take place. This was no ordinary meeting. Ten years of bitter warfare were officially closed. A new era of internal peace had begun.

Immediately after work, throngs of workers poured out of the fur shops and headed for the Manhattan Opera House. Within half an hour, four thousand furriers had filled every corner of the auditorium while other thousands waited in the street, listening to the proceedings broadcast by loudspeakers.

The large rostrum of the Opera House was covered with flowers. Messages greeting the new administration and hailing the unity of the fur workers were stacked in a huge pile on a table.

At 5:25 P.M., Pietro Lucchi opened the meeting. He was enthusiastically greeted by the fur workers who appreciated his forceful stand for unity despite the terrific pressure exerted by AFL leaders. In opening the installation ceremonies, Lucchi delivered a brief but moving speech. He referred to the bitter strife and struggle that had marked the past ten years, and pointed out that all this now belonged to past history. "The only benefit we can derive from those bitter struggles," he said amidst enthusiastic applause, "is a firm conviction that the only ones who can profit from a civil war among the workers are the bosses and the exploiters of labor." The applause mounted as Lucchi declared that Communists, Socialists and workers of other political beliefs must work together in a union to be successful in the struggles for better conditions.

Finally, Lucchi turned to Ben Gold. "I have known you for a great many years," Lucchi said as he shook Gold's hand. "I know your abilities and I know of your devotion to the cause of the workers. I wish you a successful administration and so long as you will continue to have the interests of the workers at heart, I promise you, both individually and as president of the International Fur Workers Union, my undivided loyalty and support."

After the installations, Gold was called on to speak. The entire audience rose to greet him, and for several minutes the Opera House shook with applause and cheers. There on the platform stood the beloved leader who had led the fur workers successfully through all these years of struggle against incredible odds. Under his leadership, the fur workers had blazed new trails for the labor movement, emerging victorious in their heroic battles for a clean, militant, democratic, united union.

The fur workers assembled in the Manhattan Opera House also knew that with Gold in all these struggles was a collective leadership of sincere, courageous and militant left-wingers—Irving Potash, Jack Schneider, Joseph Winogradsky, Maurice Cohen, Sam Burt, Gus Hopman, Sam Resnick, Max Kochinsky and others. Each one of these men was a great leader in his own right. They honored them as such.

When the applause finally ceased, Gold began his address. Fifteen years later, it has lost none of its significance.

Gold pointed out that the main principle of a trade union must be the full rights of all members, regardless of their political opinions and their political affiliations. He pledged that there would be no discrimination against any member of the union because of his political views.

This did not mean that there should be no politics in a union. The economic struggles of the workers could not be separated from the struggles on the political front. The unions had to conduct their own politics in opposition to the politics of the employers. Workers could have their own political beliefs, but they would find in the union a basis for common action against the employers on both the political and economic fronts.

The main tasks that now confronted the fur workers were: to create a better understanding and full unity among all elements in the union; to cement the ranks of the workers and to strengthen the union; to guard carefully all the points in the present agreement; to do away with contracting and speedup; and to win for the furriers a truly decent wage and a right to their jobs.

The fur workers could not think only of their own problems and their own conditions. They were part of the American labor movement and they had to make their contribution to the basic struggle that was developing inside the ranks of organized labor.

"Our aim is to utilize our united forces to fortify our AFL International Fur Workers Union so that it may serve the well-being of the fur workers and their families. At the same time, we endeavor with all our power and ability to strengthen all of the AFL unions and assist the AFL in the organization of the unorganized workers. A strong and fighting AFL is a vital necessity to enable the workers to resist the attacks of the organized employers in their working and living conditions and to enable the workers to defend their organizations and their democratic rights to strike, picket and organize. The tragic example of Hitlerism in Germany and fascism in Italy, where trade unions were destroyed, where the rights of the workers are trampled upon, where the living conditions of the workers are becoming more unbearable from day to day, and where the working class is suppressed in a most brutal and murderous manner—these examples show how necessary it is for the workers to smash every attempt of the fascists to capture power in the United States. For this we must have a healthy, powerful and united AFL. To achieve this we have been striving to realize unity not only among the furriers, but also in every trade where the ranks of the workers have been split and divided.

"We have achieved this unity among the furriers. Let this unity become a model for all workers and teach them that men and women of all shades of political opinion can unite their ranks to achieve a full and happy life for themselves and their children."

Old-line AFL and Socialist leaders scoffed at the unification of the Furriers Union. They predicted that left-wingers and right-wingers could never work together. They prophesied that political differences would soon split the union again. They were doomed to disappointment.

The achievement of unity marked the crumbling of a dam that had long been holding back the fur workers' full strength and vigor. So much of their energy had had to be diverted towards the battle for their democratic rights that they had been unable heretofore to apply their total strength to the struggle to organize the entire industry and to secure ever-improving working conditions and true job security. When that stream of energy was unleashed by unity, outworn conceptions that were by-products of reactionary AFL policies were smashed overnight.

The unity that was now achieved in the Furriers Union—the devotion of the workers for their leadership—the experience that had come from ten years of the most bitter struggle in the history of the American labor movement—the courage and militancy of the fur workers—these were the guarantees that complete organization of the fur industry was a matter of but a very short time.

CHAPTER 42

Reconstruction

Unity had been achieved. But in many locals, internal problems still paralyzed the union and prevented it from reaping the fruits. In some locals, there still remained dishonest, grafting officials. In others, incompetents were entrenched in leading positions. And in the International Union itself, the officers, organizers and General Executive Board were those elected by the right wing at the Toronto convention. The left wing, which had produced such outstanding leaders as Ben Gold, Irving Potash, Joseph Winogradsky, Jack Schneider, Sam Burt, Abe Feinglass, Frank Brownstone and others, still had no place in the G.E.B.

Complaints continued to pour into the International office. Minneapolis asked that "proper leadership" be furnished the local to help it "to organize the workers in the shops." The workers complained that Mike M. Mandl, the business agent, "does not show sufficient interest to be of any value to the fur workers in Minneapolis. . . . He has been lax in attending our meetings, and he has given us no organizational assistance. He thinks Minneapolis is hopeless, and a person with that frame of mind cannot be successful to organize our city."

I. Lutterman, the business agent of Local 53, was certain "that it will be almost impossible to set the Philadelphia workers in motion."

In Somerville, New Jersey, the organizer abandoned the workers in the midst of a strike. They complained to the International in October 1935: "We are left without a leader. After four months of this strike we are getting no place, and the men are getting tired of it all. Also of see-

481

ing things being done wrong. . . . If you wish to keep the union here you had better send us a leader as the men are getting discouraged and will go back to work. SO PLEASE DO SOMETHING."

"Please do something," was also the appeal of Winnipeg workers to the International. Working fourteen to sixteen hours a day, they could not earn more than $14 a week. The best mechanic received only thirty cents an hour. A Winnipeg local of the International had been organized in July 1935, and an organizational campaign started. In spite of the bosses' terror and blacklisting, the workers flocked into the union. All preparations were made for a general strike, which awaited only the signal from the union. Max Federman, the G.E.B. member and leader in Toronto, refused to go to Winnipeg to help the workers. He was fearful that "this situation would shape out nicely in favor of the Industrial [Union] organizers for them to take over the Union after I leave."

Federman's sabotage undermined the organizational campaign in Winnipeg. The secretary of the local wrote to the International three months later, "because of the fact that the general strike was not called and the organizers had no full authority to take such steps, the fur workers in the city have been very much disillusioned and discouraged, and the terror and blacklisting in the trade has increased."

Unable as yet to play a decisive role in International matters, the left-wingers concentrated on strengthening the united organization in New York. Although the new administration of the Furriers Joint Council came into office when the season was already well under way, it launched an extensive campaign for improvement of conditions in the shops. It took aggressive action to stop overtime work, obtain July raises, enforce wage scales, collect back pay due the workers, abolish contracting, return runaway shops to New York, and wipe out many evils that sprang up during the years of internal warfare.

Resisting employers soon discovered that the Furriers Joint Council was no longer an impotent body. In the four-and-a-half months from August 1935 to January 1936, the Council demonstrated what a united union could accomplish. Close to five thousand complaints were adjusted in favor of the workers. Four hundred sixty-three shop strikes were successfully conducted. More than a hundred contracting firms went out of business. Three hundred open shops were signed up. The sum of $128,-473 was collected for the workers from the manufacturers, including over $50,000 for the unemployment insurance fund, and thousands of dollars for wage raises. Systematic educational, cultural and recreational activities were undertaken by the Council. About one thousand fur workers registered for classes, for a band, chorus, dramatic group and other activities.

Hundreds of active rank-and-file workers, shop chairmen and building committees participated in the work of reconstructing the union. Their activities extended into residential sections of the city. They ferreted out contractors and compelled them to give up their sweatshops. And their campaign against the out-of-town runaway shops became the talk of the labor movement.

During the years of internal struggle, the New York bosses set up open shops in small towns in eastern Pennsylvania and New Jersey. Local Chambers of Commerce offered them cheap factory rentals and a supply of unorganized, low-wage workers. In these out-of-town shops, workers received as little as $15 for a sixty to eighty-hour week. All needle trades unions suffered from this ever-growing out-of-town evil.

The new administration of the Joint Council organized an out-of-town department. It located every out-of-town sweatshop and made connections with key workers in these shops. Upon the call of the union, many skilled New York workers in these out-of-town shops returned to New York. Shops were soon closed down in Portchester and Elmsforth, New York, in Washington, New Jersey, and in Greenwich, Connecticut. The runaway shop of Greenberg & Tarnoff in Quakertown, Pennsylvania, was struck. The firm had to return to New York, reinstate all its New York workers and operate its shop only in New York.

The runaway Kost Fur Shop in Easton, Pennsylvania, employing 160 workers, was struck by the Joint Council. A contract was signed providing a substantial wage increase, the thirty-five-hour week, and an unemployment insurance fund paid by the company.

In its drive against out-of-town shops, the Joint Council worked closely with the fur dressing and dyeing locals. In the rabbit industry alone, at the beginning of 1936, more than half the skins were produced by non-union labor out of town at incredibly low prices.

A campaign of Locals 85 and 88, under Sam Burt's leadership, merging with the drive of the Joint Council, unionized all runaway fur dressing and dyeing shops in Pennsylvania. Bayonne Fur Dressing & Dyeing at Whitehaven, Queens Fur and United Fur Breeders in Bethlehem, Van Dye Way at Copley and other out-of-town shops were forced to sign union agreements. The union established the thirty-five-hour week, the closed shop, and raised wages—in many cases actually doubling the former level.

The agreement of the Furriers Joint Council expired at the end of the 1935 season. At first the employers replied to the union's demands by presenting counter-demands: return to the forty-hour week, reduce the number of paid holidays, abolish the unemployment insurance fund. The union mobilized to meet this attack. Gold, manager of the Council, warned the manufacturers: "The fur workers are courageous and experienced fighters. If it is absolutely necessary to remind the bosses of 1926 to soften their hearts and to loosen their purse-strings, then the Union is ready. The leadership of the Union is the same as in 1926, and with more experience." The employers, impressed by the union's preparations, backed down and withdrew their counter-demands.

The union, for its part, had not yet completed the process of consolidation it was engaged in. Under these circumstances, the union sought to obtain a peaceful settlement with substantial improvements and utilize the next two years to gather its full strength. After several conferences, the union won a 10 percent increase in the minimum scale; * six months equal division of work instead of four; reduction of new workers' trial period from five to four weeks; stronger job security provisions for shop chairmen; no more than two bosses permitted to do production work; women workers to be paid the wage of first-class work; hand sewers (mostly women) to have the same minimum scale as first-class operators; and other improvements.

The agreement ratified, the Joint Council immediately launched an energetic campaign to make certain the conditions were actually carried out. Even in the slack period, when there was little work in the trade, the bosses were forced to abide by every provision of the agreement. By prompt handling of complaints, holding frequent shop meetings, calling and settling shop strikes, reinstating discharged workers, stopping contracting shops and bringing out-of-town shops back to New York, the union saw to it that the bosses could no longer violate the agreement without punishment.

The Organization Department, composed of honest, loyal and tried trade union members, worked eighteen hours daily, seven days a week. Again hundreds of active rank-and-filers, shop chairmen and building

* The new scale of wages with the 10 percent increase were as follows: cutters, first class, $56; cutters, second class, $48; squarers, $48; nailers, first class, $44; nailers, second class, $36; operators first class, $46; operators, second class, $39; finishers, $42; tapers and stayers, $34.

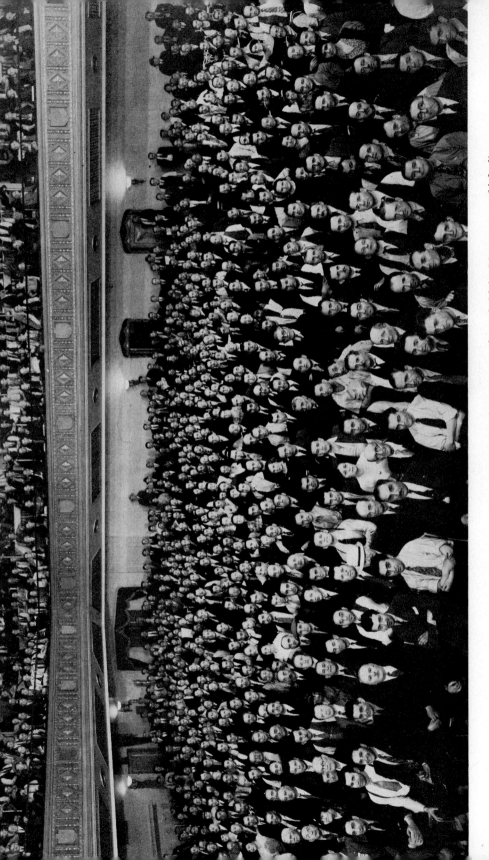

One of the historic mass meetings, held in May 1935, which discussed ways and means of establishing one union in the fur trade.

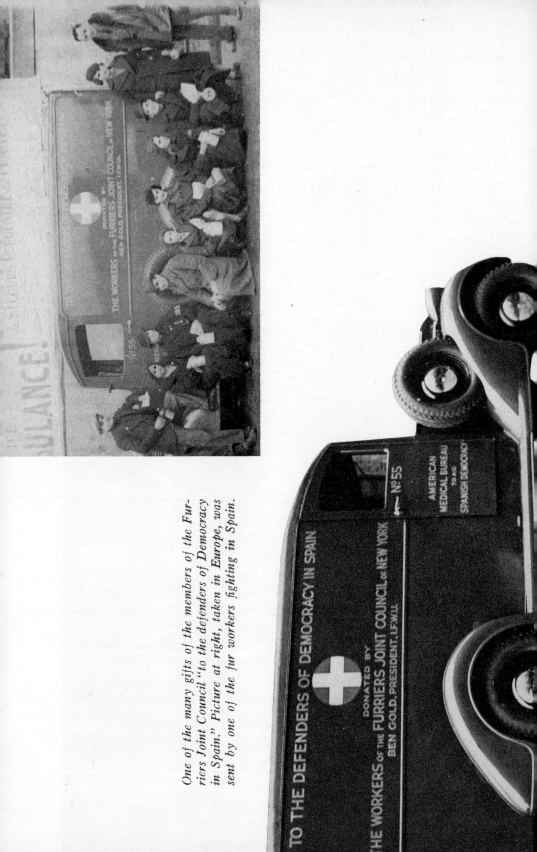

One of the many gifts of the members of the Furriers Joint Council "to the defenders of Democracy in Spain." Picture at right, taken in Europe, was sent by one of the fur workers fighting in Spain.

committees participated in the work. They set a record of achievement unparalleled in the history of the Furriers Union.

During ten months of activity, the union held 3,483 shop meetings, adjusted 11,988 complaints, conducted over 800 successful shop strikes, struck 298 contracting shops, brought about the liquidation of fifteen out-of-town shops and organized the largest shops in Easton, Pennsylvania, reinstated 716 discharged workers, placed 623 unemployed workers on jobs, eliminated 71 phony "partner" arrangements, signed 501 new agreements, and won $11,670 in weekly wage increases. The total amount of money collected for the fur workers from the employers during these ten months was $217,858.

At the beginning of 1936, when the new agreement was signed, the fur workers received a 10 percent wage increase. In June, many workers received raises of $3, $4 and $5 a week. Then in July, thousands of furriers won July raises of $3 to $20 a week. Every furrier saw the results of a united union in his pay envelope.

It came as no surprise, therefore, that the united administration of the Joint Council was overwhelmingly re-elected to office in the summer of 1936. Over six thousand union members participated in the elections. They gave 5,144 votes to Gold as manager, 4,829 to Potash as assistant manager and 4,607 to Begoon as secretary-treasurer, all three running unopposed. All twelve business agents endorsed by the left wing were elected. Jack Schneider received the highest vote (4,629) for business agent.

The record of the fur workers in the struggle against fascism at home and abroad is a record that justified pride on their part and the respect of the entire country. When the imperialist war lords of Japan invaded Manchuria in 1931, the first act of World War II, the furriers were alert to the menace to world peace that was involved and adopted resolutions denouncing Japanese aggression and boycotted Japanese goods.

Two years later, Hitler's appointment as Chancellor of Germany started the bloody march of Nazi conquest and terror. To strike back at Hitlerism, the fur workers boycotted German products. German-made cutters' knives, machine needles and other tools disappeared from the trade. Leaders of the union, cooperating with Jewish and other antifascist organizations, scoured fur factories and fur dealers' establishments for German furs. The fur workers also obtained a provision in their agreement that no furs or supplies processed or produced by Nazi Germany would be used in a union shop. The fur workers, moreover, really enforced the boycott against Hitler. When several large fur merchants obtained skins from Nazi Germany, the fur workers called them to task. Huge fines were levied on these employers and contributed directly for the relief of anti-fascist refugees. The Joint Boycott Council of the American Jewish Congress and the Jewish Labor Committee praised the union for "the splendid part" it played in enforcing the boycott against Nazi Germany.

An outstanding demonstration of the fur workers' hatred of fascism and unwavering battle for democracy was the election conducted by Fancy Fur Dyers, Local 88, in the year 1936. One of the candidates for the office of union organizer was Lyndon Henry, a Negro.

Born in Kingston, Jamaica, Lyndon Henry came to the United States in 1924. For three years he worked as a fur dyer in the Federal Fur Dyeing Company in New York City. Forced to leave because of discrimination against Negroes, he worked for the next five years at all sorts of jobs. In 1932, he returned to his former job in the Federal Dyeing Company. In January 1933, the firm announced a wage cut of $1 a week. Just at that time, the Industrial Union's campaign to organize the dyeing shops was in full swing. When the workers at Federal were approached, they immediately went on strike.

Henry took a leading part in the strike. He was not at all convinced that the Industrial Union was different from other unions, which openly discriminated against Negroes. To his great surprise, Irving Potash and Morris Langer, who represented the Industrial Union in the negotiations with the Federal Company, asked the strikers to elect a Negro worker to the negotiating committee. The strikers hailed the proposal and selected Henry to represent them.

With Potash's and Langer's assistance, Henry negotiated a successful settlement of the strike. The wage cut was rescinded. The workers received a $2 weekly increase and other gains. Henry was elected chairman of the shop. In 1936, having demonstrated his ability, he was nominated for organizer of Local 88.

In 1935, Mussolini had invaded and conquered defenseless Ethiopia. Lyndon Henry militantly denounced the fascist aggression. The moment it was announced that Henry was a candidate for office in Local 88's election, pro-fascist Italian papers in New York called upon the Italian workers to defeat him. The members of the local, the overwhelming majority of them of Italian descent, scorned the fascist propaganda and elected Lyndon Henry as manager.

The furriers were accustomed to bringing flowers to an installation meeting. But at the Joint Council installation meeting on August 5, 1936, the flowers were missing. The Joint Council had urged that instead money be contributed for the anti-fascist fighters in Spain. The shop chairmen brought more than $2,000 to the meeting and decided there to raise $5,000 to help the brave Spanish people. The Joint Council advanced the money the very next day to the Spanish anti-fascist fighters.

In addition to contributing regularly to aid the Spanish anti-fascists, the furriers volunteered work on their own time to manufacture thousands of warm fur jackets, gloves and caps for the fighters in Spain. They flooded Congress with petitions urging the lifting of the unjust embargo which prevented the legally-elected Spanish government from buying war equipment and other necessities of defense.

The greatest contribution of the fur workers to help the Spanish people defend themselves against the armies of Hitler and Mussolini was the enlistment of more than fifty fur workers in the International Brigade to fight against fascism in Spain. The furriers hailed these union brothers as heroes. And never to be forgotten was the great sacrifice of those members of the union who died in Spain that democracy might live in the world—Maurice Jellin, Philip Spector, and John Tremule, fur dyers. To their memories the fur workers have never ceased paying tribute.

Among the most courageous and heroic fighters in Spain were many members of the newly-organized union of floor workers. Commonly referred to as "floor boys," the floor workers were young, energetic and of every nationality. The largest groups were Jewish, Negro, Italian and Greek.

Six days a week, from seven in the morning until seven in the evening, the unorganized floor boys labored at the most menial work. In the fur market, they scurried in and out of buildings at full speed with packages or bundles of fur skins under their arms. In the shop, they swept floors, wetted and stretched skins, carried heavy nailing boards to and from the tables, bundles from cutter to operator and operator to nailer—a human conveyor belt in the fur shops. Some, especially Negro floor boys, had to clean toilets and washrooms besides their work in the shop. The average pay for their long hours of toil was $8 and $10 a week.

After working hours, the bosses would often make the floor boys do work for which mechanics got $60 and $70 a week. Frustrated and disillusioned by hardships of the depression period, many floor boys fell prey to arguments of employers that this was the way to become skilled mechanics and receive higher pay and better working conditions. In this way, the bosses very profitably used the unskilled floor workers against the skilled mechanics.

The floor boys eventually learned that their chances of becoming skilled craftsmen in the already over-crowded industry were slight. If they wanted decent wages and working conditions, they would have to organize a union and fight on the picket line just as the older skilled craftsmen had done.

But would the older workers help the floor boys organize? Most unions, in keeping with the traditional policy and practice of the AFL, were indifferent to the problems of young, unskilled workers. Many AFL unions actually placed barriers in the way of the youth when they did try to organize.

The Industrial Union had achieved some results in 1933 and 1934.* But it was not until one union was established that a real organizing drive among the floor boys got under way. In the autumn of 1935, a committee of floor boys met with Ben Gold, manager of the Joint Council. Gold assured the young workers that the Council would back them to the hilt. He warned them that there would be no ready-made union. The employers would not easily yield their hitherto unchallenged authority to deal with floor boys as virtual slaves. The employers would use intimidation, police, courts and blacklisting. The floor boys would have to be ready to fight it out on the picket line in spite of arrests and terrorism.

The floor boys' committee began its work on a modest scale. A temporary organizing committee was designated. Headed by Leon Straus as organizer, the committee included Herbert Kurzer, Seymour Atlas, Ira Gordon, William Wasserman, Bernard Woolis, Bernard Stoller, Max Bronsnick, Al Bland, Willie Bass, Joe Nicosia, Al Lutsky, Tom Jasper and Bernard Goldfine. Weekly dues were set at fifteen cents.

The son of working class parents, Leon Straus was studying at New York University when he was forced by depression conditions to leave day college. He went to work as a shipping clerk in a dress shop, continuing his studies at night. Straus' parents were members of the dressmakers union. He first devoted himself to the task of organizing shipping clerks

---

* Some floor boys won increases of $3 to $5 a week and the five-day week as a result of the Industrial Union's organizing campaign.

in the dress industry. Later he found a job as a floor boy in a fur shop.

Selecting the busiest firms, the union committee tackled the shops one by one. Their demands were: $18 minimum pay for a forty-four-hour week; no overtime. In consultation with Gold, Potash and other Joint Council leaders, the committee won raises and agreements shop by shop. By October 1935, the newly-organized Fur Floor Boys and Shipping Clerks Union had four hundred dues-paying members.

When the firm of Greenberg & Tarnoff refused to meet the union's demands in December 1935, twelve floor boys struck. The fur market saw its first picket line of floor boys. All day long other floor boys joined the picketing. The news spread to every building. The boss settled! Working hours were cut from sixty and seventy to forty-four. Each floor boy received his $4 increase.

With the opening of the new season in 1936, the floor boys stepped up their organizational work. In a six-week drive ending July, over seventy shops were organized. On one day alone fifty shops in one building at 214 West 29th Street were struck. By noon all of the bosses had settled, granting the floor boys a forty-four-hour week and a $3 weekly wage increase.

The strike of twenty-three floor boys employed by Feshback & Ackerman symbolized the whole struggle of the floor boys for better working conditions. The bosses immediately tried to bring in scabs. But the hard-fought strike remained solid. A continuous picket line was maintained in front of three building entrances. Mass picketing was organized. Thousands demonstrated along the entire length of Seventh Avenue during lunch hour. The strike won the attention and support of every worker in the fur market and of thousands of other young workers in the city.

Every day pickets were arrested—twelve, fifteen, twenty-three at a time. On August 9, the police charged the mass picket line and arrested Leon Straus and two other leaders of the union. The following day, the police rushed the picket line and herded thirteen floor boys into the lobby of the building at 333 Seventh Avenue. The union immediately held a mass meeting at the corner. Many hundreds of workers responded to Leon Straus's call for a mass picket line. The line extended from one end of the street to the other. The police could not break up the demonstration.

Over one hundred floor boys were arrested in the next few days. Mass picket lines were broken up by the police every day—and promptly re-formed by the workers. Every attack strengthened the determination of the strikers to win. Production in the shops came to a standstill. The fur mechanics had remained at their jobs, doing their own work. But they refused to touch any floor boys' work despite all pressure of the bosses. In the third week of the strike, the fur workers went out on a one-day sympathy strike. The bosses settled. Each floor boy won a $4 raise. The forty-four-hour week was established. The floor boys' union was recognized.

A wave of organization brought hundreds of new members into the union. All dogskin manufacturing shops were struck simultaneously. Then in one building after another, up and down Seventh Avenue and into the side streets, uniform wage and hour conditions were established. Modeling itself after the Joint Council, the union involved the rank and file to check and enforce the agreement scrupulously.

The successful organization of these most exploited, unskilled young workers in the fur trade was an object lesson to young and unskilled workers in all industries.

Imbued with an enthusiasm for and devotion to the union, these young people were to make signal contributions in many struggles of the fur workers thereafter. Soon the names of Leon Straus, Bernard Woolis, Herbert Kurzer, Max Bronsnick, Tom Jasper and other floor boys' leaders were to be known and respected throughout the labor movement.

The Greek fur workers, it will be remembered, were first organized in 1925 by the united-front administration headed by Ben Gold. In the 1926 strike, the Greek workers fought heroically on the picket lines, and proved themselves militant strikers. After the strike, when the fight against the Joint Board was launched by the International, the Greek Fur Manufacturers Association organized a company union, called the "Brotherhood." They recruited scabs and learners for membership in the "Brotherhood" and packed open shops with notorious characters.

The Greek Branch of the Joint Board conducted several drives to organize the open shops. At the same time, the Greek members of the Joint Board won over the better element of the "Brotherhood" and persuaded them to join the Joint Board. In 1927, a majority of the "Brotherhood" voted to dissolve and join the Greek Branch of the Joint Board.

At this point, the right-wing International officials stepped in and chartered the company union as Local 70. During the eight years of internal struggle that followed, the conditions won by the Greek fur workers in 1925 and 1926 were completely wiped out.

The company-union leaders of Local 70 bitterly opposed unity. They remained in touch with AFL officials. On July 29, 1935, Matthew Woll reported to William Green: "It is a pleasure to know that this local union [70] which has always been antagonistic towards the Communists is still maintaining its position notwithstanding the attitude assumed by the International Fur Workers Union."

The Joint Council was anxious to achieve close cooperation with Local 70. Although Local 70 was a separate local, not affiliated to the Joint Council, many Greek fur workers worked in Joint Council shops. Without mutual cooperation, conflicts and misunderstandings were bound to arise.

The leaders of Local 70, however, were determined to utilize the separate existence of their local to disrupt the organizational work of the Joint Council. Their splitting activities continued. An outstanding example was the case of the workers of Silverman & Green in the fall of 1935. The firm, under contract with the Joint Council, employed a number of Greek finishers, members of Local 70. The employers forced the Greek finishers to work below the union scale or to "kick back" part of their wages. The shop was struck by the Joint Council and the workers were instructed to picket. Immediately, George Margiolas, business agent of Local 70, called together the Greek finishers, escorted them back to the struck shop and instructed them to return to work. All this was done without the knowledge or approval of the Joint Council. The Council again called the workers out. The strike continued until the Council collected $1,690.11 for the workers for payment below the scale and an additional $1,038.94 for loss of time during the strike. The Council preferred charges against Margiolas for "improper conduct as a Business Agent of the Union."

In January 1936, the Joint Council struck the Kost Fur Company in Easton, Pennsylvania, as part of its campaign against the out-of-town open shops. In the midst of the strike, John Apostol, president of Local 70, and other leaders of the Greek local called the strikers together. They warned them against placing any trust in the officials of the Joint Council on the ground that "Ben Gold and Irving Potash are Communists." They then advised the strikers how they could get more strike relief than was coming to them. The strikers, however, sent Apostol and his gang packing. The General Executive Board was asked to investigate the actions of Apostol and other Local 70 leaders.

When the G.E.B. met in April 1936, it received a petition signed by a large number of members of Local 70. The petition denounced the leaders of the local for circulating "racial and anti-Jewish propaganda

. . . which serves to split the Greek fur workers from the Jewish and other fur workers in New York City and enables the bosses to force non-union conditions upon the Greek fur workers." The Greek workers urged that Local 70 be affiliated to the Joint Council "because in this manner, the Greek workers will have the protection of the 13,000 organized within the Joint Council."

A committee of the G.E.B. attempted to straighten out the controversy between Local 70 and the Joint Council. The officials of Local 70, however, insisted upon their right to issue an unlimited number of books to new members. They demanded that the new members be placed in the Joint Council shops despite the fact that many furriers were unemployed. At the same time, the officials of Local 70 refused to concern themselves with the unbearable conditions in the Greek shops. They recognized contractors. And when the Joint Council called strikes, they escorted Greek finishers back to shops. They demanded that Local 70 remain a separate union.

Charges were preferred against John Apostol and other leaders of Local 70 by members of the local's Executive Board. The evidence proved that Apostol and his clique, in concert with the bosses, had woefully ignored union conditions in the Greek shops; that they tolerated wage payments far below the minimum scale, in some cases as low as $18 per week; that they permitted unlimited overtime without overtime pay; that they had refused to call shop meetings for a period of eight months; and that they ignored complaints about agreement violations brought to them by the workers.

All G.E.B. members but one, Max Federman of Toronto, voted to suspend John Apostol as an International vice-president. Federman, it was soon to be learned, had good reason to support Apostol's practices.

Charges were preferred against Apostol and eleven other officials of the local. The membership meeting of Local 70 elected a trial committee which investigated the charges and conducted a public trial. The accused were removed from office with the unanimous approval of the membership and new elections ordered.

A progressive slate headed by Theodore Johnson, president, Louis Hatchios, secretary, Nick Apostolides, treasurer, and John Vafiades, organizer, was swept into office on December 18, 1936, the first honest election in Local 70's history.

The Apostol clique rushed to William Green for help to recapture control of Local 70. They appealed to the courts for an injunction. The

All above officers are old timers, right wingers, and loyal to the American Federation of Labor. The meeting was attended by the largest number of voters, almost three times the largest amount of voters we had at previous elections, and each and every one of those elected won by a very large majority.

The Unity activities between the International Fur Workers Union of U. S. & C. and the other organization caused an irregularity in our market, still we hope that the conditions will be clarified, and we believe that with the precious advices and support of the American Federation of Labor, to whose principles Local 70 adheres we will be able to pull through from our present difficulties.

Reassuring you of our loyalty, we are,

Fraternally yours,
GREEK FUR WORKERS UNION LOCAL 70,

John Apostol
President,

Steve Poulos
Secretary.

Mr. William Green, President,
American Federation of Labor,
American Federation of Labor Building,
Washington, D. C.,

Dear President Green:

I was delighted to receive copy of the letter sent me which you received from the Greek Fur Workers Union Local 70.

It is a pleasure to know that this local union which has always been antagonistic towards the communists is still maintaining its position notwithstanding the attitude assumed by the International Fur Workers Union.

Fraternally yours,

Matthew Woll

Matthew Woll is "delighted" to learn that the Apostol clique in Greek Local 70 is "loyal" to the AFL's policy of disunity.

Greek bosses' association refused to deal with the newly-elected officers of Local 70.

But the fate of the clique was sealed. Their injunction suits were thrown out of court. William Collins, assigned by Green to help the Apostol clique, discovered that there was nothing he could do. Six strikes in major shops broke the resistance of the Greek employers. In March 1937, the Greek manufacturers' association was compelled to recognize Local 70.

The outcome in Local 70 offered proof that the International of 1936 was not the International of the tragic days of the internal struggle. Although late to act decisively in the situation, the International had acted with firmness when it finally saw the need to do so.

Additional evidence of the emerging strength and influence of the International was its action in the unbearable situation in Chicago's Local 45. For over a year-and-a-half after unity, the Chicago workers sent complaints to the General Executive Board. In January 1937, the G.E.B. was finally forced to take action. A special committee from Chicago reported that two unions existed in practice in the city despite the official unification. Jack Mouchine refused to let anyone "interfere" in shops where he was the business agent. In these shops, which he regarded as his personal property, the furriers worked forty hours a week instead of thirty-five. Complaints of the workers were completely disregarded. The bosses in these shops were enjoying a field day.

Unable any longer to tolerate this scandalous situation, the International sent Harry Begoon to Chicago to investigate the situation. Supported by the International, Local 45 took steps to rid itself of Mouchine. Despite Mouchine's threat to form a separate union, a local meeting decided to suspend the business agent, pending trial. A committee was elected to examine the charges and give Mouchine a fair and impartial trial. Mouchine was summoned to appear before the committee to answer the charges. Instead, he sent a letter tendering his resignation. His resignation was not accepted, and the committee proceeded with the trial. They found Mouchine guilty of all charges and decided that he should stand suspended from membership for a period of not less than ten years. The recommendation was immediately approved by the local.

Following the ouster of Mouchine, the local, under Feinglass' leadership, immediately organized a number of open shops. Union conditions were enforced in all of the shops for the first time since unity. The local membership increased to eight hundred. The Chicago Fur Manufacturers Association was forced to grant the workers a thirty-five-hour week, substantial wage increases and other improvements. The local also organized the fur dressers and dyers of Chicago, winning union recognition and a contract.

As the year 1937 opened, thousands of New York fur workers looked forward with joy and enthusiasm to a great holiday—the twenty-fifth anniversary of the Furriers Union. Twenty-five years had passed since the fur workers laid the foundation of the union in 1912 with the great strike that had lasted thirteen weeks and aroused the admiration of the entire labor movement. During the many years thereafter while the New York fur workers were battling to build a militant and democratic union, they had never doubted that the American labor movement would eventually recognize the necessity for adopting a progressive trade union program. Their evaluation was correct. Now on the occasion of their twenty-fifth anniversary, they were rewarded with the reawakening and rejuvenation of the progressive labor movement. They could ask for no better reward.

CHAPTER 43

The Fur Workers
Join the CIO

The fur workers had received a remarkable schooling during their years of militant struggles for a democratic union. Out of their struggles emerged an understanding of the need for industrial unionism, trade union democracy and unity within the ranks of the workers regardless of race, color, religious or political beliefs. The achievements of the first two years of unity further strengthened their belief in these basic principles.

Millions of workers in the unorganized mass production industries were learning the same truths in their own way and were demanding organization. The open-shop shackles of the AFL bureaucrats' craft-union policies could no longer hold them back. Leaders of ten AFL unions, headed by John L. Lewis, formed the Committee for Industrial Organizations in the fall of 1935. The fur workers joyfully greeted the new movement as one of the greatest events in the history of the American labor movement and a powerful blow against the bankrupt policies of the AFL.

No sooner was the CIO born than the AFL Executive Council began a systematic campaign against the ten unions. The chief accusation of the AFL bureaucrats against the CIO was that it was "Communistic" and inspired by Moscow. Under the same banner of anti-Communism, the Morgans, duPonts, Fords and other economic royalists were doing everything in their power to defeat CIO organizing drives in the mass production industries. Once again the top leaders of the AFL proved themselves allies of the most reactionary anti-labor groups in the country.

496

Meanwhile, the CIO accomplished what the AFL had been neither willing nor able to achieve in half a century. Rejecting the red scare and red-baiting in favor of unity of all workers despite political and other differences, the CIO in less than two years organized one and one-quarter million unorganized, exploited and oppressed American workers into militant industrial unions. In 1937, the CIO could point to victories in basic industries like steel, auto, rubber, electrical, radio, textile and marine, which spoke much louder than theoretical debates of AFL leaders.

In the midst of the organizing campaign, while conducting successful strikes of the newly-organized workers, the CIO was ordered by the AFL Executive Council to dissolve by June 3, 1936. Believing the organization of the unorganized to be more important than preserving the vested interests of the AFL bureaucrats, the CIO ignored this ultimatum. The AFL Executive Council thereupon threatened to suspend the ten CIO unions. A minority group, declared William Green in justifying this autocratic threat, must accept "majority rule."

At numerous mass meetings, the fur workers protested the red-baiting of the AFL leadership against the CIO and the expulsion threats. The fur workers called upon the AFL leaders to cease their war against the CIO and to cooperate with the CIO unions, as was their duty to the American workers.

Speaking at the convention of the New York State Federation of Labor late in August 1936, Irving Potash voiced a fervent plea against the impending suspension of the ten CIO unions by the AFL Executive Council. Potash pointed out that "these unions have waged great and successful battles, that they greatly improved and advanced the union standards of their members, thereby pulling up trade union standards generally throughout the country, that they brought hundreds of thousands of new members into the folds of the AFL. . . . Is it their crime that they proceeded to organize these workers along industrial lines, the only way these workers in the basic industries can be organized, and in accordance with the mandate given to the Executive Council of two successive conventions of the AFL?"

"A great deal has been said," continued Potash, "about democratic procedure, majority rule and family quarrels. These are all questions of vital importance. But I say it is a far cry from democratic procedure and majority rule when sixteen men, with due respect to their wisdom, take upon themselves the grave responsibility of suspending ten International Unions and over one million loyal members of the Federation."

Potash's plea was endorsed by the fifty delegates at the state convention who called upon the AFL Executive Council to lift the suspension order. The appeal was lost on the dictatorial bureaucrats in the AFL leadership. By a vote of 13 to 1, the Executive Council ordered the suspension of the ten CIO unions with their 1,156,862 members.

To make certain that the suspensions would be upheld, the Executive Council put them into effect before the AFL convention met. Had these unions been represented at the convention, the Executive Council could not have mustered the required two-thirds majority.

Representing the International Fur Workers Union at the 56th annual AFL convention at Tampa were Pietro Lucchi, Harry Begoon and Samuel Mindel. The three fur delegates voted with the majority at Tampa to uphold the Executive Council's suspensions. Practically every local in the International, however, repudiated this action of the three delegates.

In 1937, one after another, the principal CIO unions were undemocratically expelled from the AFL. The Furriers Joint Council was already cooperating with the CIO unions in the American Labor Party. In the Presidential election of 1936, the fur workers had joined with the members of the CIO unions in campaigning to re-elect President Roosevelt, who was attacked by the big business Liberty Leaguers as a "Communist," just as AFL leaders were attacking the CIO.

There was little room for doubt that at the Twelfth Biennial Convention of the fur workers at Chicago in May 1937, the fur workers would take their stand squarely with the CIO, the new progressive and militant body of organized labor.

The Eleventh Biennial Convention of the International Union in Toronto had reported fewer than three thousand members. The united International came to Chicago two years later with a paid-up membership above thirty thousand, with forty-three locals in twenty-three cities. The New York fur manufacturing industry was literally one hundred percent organized. In the dressing and dyeing branch of the industry, the only open-shop fortress still remaining was the Hollander Company. During the two years since Toronto, the International had organized and chartered thirteen new locals in ten different cities. Fancy Fur Dyers Local 88 of New York had increased its membership by a full thousand new members within nine months. Chicago Local 45 had doubled its membership.

The main increase in the strength of the International, however, was in the Furriers Joint Council of New York. International President

Pietro Lucchi greeted the New York fur workers on their twenty-fifth anniversary: "I have no hesitancy in stating that due to the marvelous accomplishments in the New York field, the International was able to attain unparalleled organization heights all over the country."

On the eve of the convention, the members of the New York Joint Council adopted a resolution by a huge majority greeting the CIO and urging the International "to fight for unity in the American labor movement on the basis of the program of the CIO."

The members of many other locals all over the country took a similar stand. When the delegates gathered in Chicago, telegrams poured in from locals throughout the country advocating affiliation to CIO. The report of the G.E.B., however, urged that industrial unionism could best be achieved within the AFL. The CIO issue was not to be decided until the fourth day of the proceedings.

During the first three days of the convention, major attention was paid to reports of the union's activities. A detailed campaign was projected to win job security for the fur workers, to abolish the employers' power of arbitrary discharge, and to organize the unorganized shops—especially Hollander. The Fur Floor and Shipping Clerks Local 125 was officially chartered.

On Friday morning, May 21, the convention was addressed by a representative from the CIO, Nicholas Fontecchio, district director of the Steel Workers Organizing Committee, headed by Philip Murray. Plunging directly into the red-baiting attacks on CIO by leaders of the AFL, Fontecchio pointed out that the issue at stake in the struggle was neither majority rule nor "Communism" but the building of a labor movement which would work and fight for all workers and make America what it should be. The only crime the CIO was guilty of was the "crime" of organizing the unorganized workers who were living in virtual slavery. "If that is a crime that we are committing, we are going to continue to commit that crime," Fontecchio declared amidst the cheers of the delegates.

"We are charged with being Communists, yes Communists," he continued. "In the early days of labor progress, labor leaders were charged with being anarchists. Later we were charged with being socialists. Now, then, the slogan of the day is 'Communist.' I do not know what Communism is. But, if organizing labor, making a laborer and his wife and children happy, making America a better place to live in—is Communism, then I am a Communist.

"Furthermore, fake patriots are putting out statements that we are foreign agitators. . . . If we would organize fascism here, we would be National American patriots would we not? That is the idea of William Randolph Hearst, and the *Chicago Tribune* and the rest of them, but because we are organizing real labor unions here for the benefit of labor in this country, we are foreign agitators, and we are Communists. We take no offense at those things, because we know where these statements come from."

That evening, Irving Potash introduced the resolution on CIO adopted by a majority of the Resolutions Committee and sponsored by fifty-four delegates: "Your Committee approached this problem in the light of the greatest task confronting the trade union movement of America, namely, the task of organizing the millions of unorganized workers in the basic industries and improving their conditions. We consider this task most urgent for the preservation of the trade union movement and for successful resistance to the reactionary and fascist forces that seek to destroy the labor movement, wipe out its gains, and deprive the people generally of their democratic and civil rights."

The resolution condemned the AFL Executive Council for refusing to recognize the inspiring success of the CIO, for illegally suspending ten CIO unions with a membership of over a million, and for creating disunity in the ranks of organized labor.*

"To be true to the progressive and militant traditions of our Union,

---

* The chief weapon used by the AFL leaders in blocking the CIO's organizing drives was to paint the CIO as "communistic" in origin and in operation and to picture the CIO leaders as "Reds" in intimate connection with Moscow and who followed instructions laid down by Joseph Stalin. "These hypocritical, insincere, conscienceless agents of Moscow are trying to use the labor movement as a revolutionary vehicle," the AFL bureaucrats proclaimed. Anti-Semitic epithets were also hurled against the CIO.

A striking example is the appeal made by President A. O. Wharton of the International Association of Machinists in a letter dated April 20, 1937: "Since the Supreme Court decision upholding the Wagner Labor Act, many employers now realize that it is the Law of our Country and they are preparing to deal with labor organizations. These employers have expressed preference to deal with A.F. of L. organizations rather than Lewis, Hillman, Dubinsky, Howard and their gang of sluggers, communists, radicals and soapbox artists, professional bums, expelled members of labor unions, outright scabs and the Jewish organizations with all their red affiliates.

"We have conferred with several such employers and arranged for conferences later when we get the plants organized. The purpose of this is to direct all officers and all representatives to contact employers in your locality as a preliminary to organizing the shops and factories."

and to the traditional fraternalism among all needle trade unions, this Convention must take its place by the side of militant and progressive trade unions of America, particularly the United Mine Workers."

The Resolutions Committee recommended that the convention go on record for the affiliation of the International Union to the CIO, and for the incoming G.E.B. to extend all possible moral, financial and organizational support to the CIO's organizing campaigns.

On the section of the resolution calling for affiliation with the CIO, a minority report submitted by Samuel Mindel of Local 2 subscribed "unqualifiedly to the principles, tenets and methods of the CIO," but opposed immediate affiliation. It recommended instead that the convention instruct the incoming G.E.B. to designate a committee "to call upon both factions and urge them for the good of the labor movement in general to lay aside their animosities and personal ambitions and meet jointly and make every effort to unite, recognizing equally the need for industrial as well as craft unionization."

Full and free discussion by the delegates followed the submission of the majority and minority reports of the Resolutions Committee. Every delegate who wished to speak had an opportunity to express his views. It was a significant example of trade union democracy in action.

Ben Gold made the major speech in favor of the majority report. He expressed his great happiness at the fact that not a single delegate had voiced opposition to the program, activities and struggles of the CIO. But he pointed to the inconsistency of lauding the CIO and then in the next breath arguing, "Let us not affiliate."

"Why not?" Gold asked. "If you agree with the program of the CIO, if you agree that this program expresses the needs and desires of the American toiling masses, then why don't you want to lend your support and aid this movement of the American labor masses?"

The basic issue, Gold argued, was whether the fur workers could continue to lend their support to the AFL when it was weakening the struggles of the American workers. For years the furriers had dreamed of the day when they would see masses of American workers flocking into the trade unions and battling against the steel, auto, rubber barons and other monopolists.

"The mass movement is here," Gold cried. "Now that it is developing, you of the minority say, 'We dare not join it.' Will you remain in the camp that fights it? Will you remain in the camp that wants to defeat it? Will you remain in the camp that wants to destroy it? . . . .

"Our strength does not lie in the great numbers we have. We are comparatively speaking, a small union. But our strength lies in our militancy, in our devotion to the sacred principles of the aggressive class struggle. And the first moment that you give up that militancy, the first moment that you move away, you turn back from this progressive movement and slink down to the reactionary camp, you are signing the death warrant of your union! . . . . I urge you—let us join the progressive labor movement; let us fight on for the emancipation of the labor movement."

After several others spoke, Lucchi called for a vote. Before placing the vote, Lucchi praised the CIO but refused to endorse affiliation. He made it clear, however, that no matter how the convention voted, the unity of the fur workers would remain intact. "No matter what confronts us after this decision, we will be able and courageous enough to meet the situation."

The recommendations of the Resolutions Committee that the convention endorse the CIO and empower the incoming G.E.B. to extend all possible moral, financial and organizational support to the CIO's organizing campaigns—were carried unanimously. On the recommendation calling for affiliation with the CIO, a roll-call was taken. Several of the delegates, as their names were called, announced that, convinced by the discussion, they were changing their votes from opposing to supporting affiliation.

Lucchi voted "yes" without further statement. Mindel and Giabrielli of Local 2 voted for affiliation in order that "there should not be any division in our ranks." Begoon at first abstained, but as he saw the sweep for affiliation, he changed his mind and voted "yes."

The final vote for affiliation was 94 in favor, 4 against, and 3 abstentions.* Potash moved the adoption of the resolution in its entirety. The motion was carried.

---

* One of the four votes against affiliation was cast by Michael M. Mandl of Minneapolis. After the vote, Mandl declared that he did not want the delegates to feel "that because I voted against the proposition that we are not going to go along." When he returned to his local, he would see to it "that we work along in harmony with the International Fur Workers Union."

Soon after he returned to the twin cities, however, Mandl informed Frank Morrison, secretary-treasurer of the AFL, that he wanted to take the St. Paul and Minneapolis locals out of the International and bring them into the AFL. "Kindly advise what can be done and oblige," Mandl wrote. Morrison sent Mandl an application form for an AFL charter for the twin cities locals. But Mandl discovered that none of the fur workers would follow him out of the International, and he abandoned the plan.

The following afternoon, the convention saw another display of unity in operation. Pietro Lucchi nominated Ben Gold for president of the International. He was unanimously elected. Lucchi was then nominated by Gold for secretary-treasurer of the International. He, too, was unanimously elected.

The new G.E.B. reflected the spirit of unity. Left-wingers and right-wingers, Communists and Socialists, sat together on the incoming Board. Gold and Lucchi, Begoon and Potash, Mindel and Burt, Butkovitz and Winogradsky, Feinglass, Vafiades and Roy—here were men who had fought each other over a period of more than ten years uniting to assure the continuous improvement in the living standards of the fur workers.

"Let me assure you, delegates," Gold declared on receiving the gavel as newly-elected president, "that as president of the International, I will do everything in my power to further that unity and to help all of us to understand one another, to help one another, to cooperate and develop mutual understanding, and to cooperate in the most harmonious manner so that the fur workers, the members of our Union, and the entire labor movement will be proud of our Union."

On this note Ben Gold closed the first convention held after unity. As its last act, the convention voted to set up a memorial for the three fur workers, Maurice Jellin, Philip Spector, and John Tremule, who had died heroically in Spain in the cause of democracy and freedom.

Two weeks after the convention, the new G.E.B. contributed $10,000 to the CIO for organization work. In the letter accompanying the check, Ben Gold wrote to John L. Lewis: "Permit me to assure you that our organization appreciates fully the invaluable work of your Committee, and we pledge wholehearted support in your struggles to accomplish the great task of the CIO."

The Furriers Union kept its pledge. Time and again the union threw its resources fully into the struggle to build the CIO and to aid in achieving its progressive program. The CIO gladly accepted this support. When the fur workers joined the CIO, they were not asked to submit affidavits on their political views. They were invited to join a modern, progressive labor movement and to participate in organizing the unorganized and creating a better life for the American workers. Democrats, Republicans, Communists and Socialists, men and women of all races, creeds, color, religion and nationality joined hand in hand to achieve this program of labor.

CHAPTER 44

The Fruits of Unity

For twenty years, Hollander, "the Ford of the fur industry," had operated his dressing and dyeing plants on a company union basis. Ten successive conventions of the International had adopted resolutions to unionize the plant. Four fur workers, including the beloved Morris Langer, had lost their lives in battles to organize Hollander. But every attempt had failed.

The International leadership understood fully the resistance the Hollander firm could muster against the union. Employing some two thousand workers, it was the richest and most powerful concern in the industry. It was influential in political circles, especially in New Jersey. The workers were under the control of company union agents.

Nevertheless, after the 1937 convention, the united International leadership made the organization of Hollander the order of the day. A detailed plan of action was worked out. Sam Burt and his entire staff of officials and active rank-and-file committees concentrated upon the factory in Long Branch. Organizers Myer Klig and Herman Paul, with the help of Burt, Mike Hudyma and a committee of Local 85, were assigned to the important plant in Middletown. Two separate committees were assigned to the Newark plant. One visited workers at their homes; the other carried on organizational work within the Newark plants.

A campaign was also begun among the workers employed in the firm's Montreal plant. Several groups were organized to contact the workers in the plant and at their homes.

The entire staff of the New York Joint Council, under the leadership

504

of Manager Irving Potash, Assistant-Manager Joseph Winogradsky, and Secretary-Treasurer Harry Begoon,* was alerted for the forthcoming struggle. John Vafiades and the staff of Local 70 alerted the furriers working Hollander skins in Greek shops. New York would be one of the most important battle fronts. At the same time, the International wired the General Confederation of Labor in France for organizational assistance in the factory Hollander operated in Paris.

The preparations on every front were reminiscent of 1926. Rank-and-file committees worked with the union leadership. The workers participated in every discussion, worked out the demands, elected their executive boards and shop chairmen. In a few weeks, the union made the first dent in the supposedly impregnable non-union fortress of A. Hollander & Son.

While the union was preparing for a decisive battle, it also made an effort to obtain a peaceful settlement. The union's strategy was not to declare a general strike against all Hollander factories at one time. As the first step, the union struck only one plant, in Long Branch. This was to be the springboard for action in the other plants, if and when a general strike would be necessary.

The Hollander firm was amazed by the response of the Long Branch workers. Earning as little as twenty-seven cents an hour and working sixty to seventy hours a week, the Long Branch workers struck militantly. Their courage and determination had an excellent effect upon the workers in the other Hollander factories.

While the strike was going on at Long Branch, the union concentrated its best forces at the Middletown plant, one of the most important of the firm's far-flung factories. Under the local leadership of Howard Bunting and Ruth Siegel, hundreds of workers joined the union. The more militant workers addressed meetings and called for action. Appeals of a local priest to the workers to stay away from the union were in vain. It was certain that upon the union's call, the Middletown workers would respond one hundred percent.

In New York, the fur workers served notice that Hollander must recognize the union and improve the conditions of his workers. At a membership meeting at Manhattan Opera House, the members of the Joint Council unanimously voted full power to the Council to call a stoppage in the fur trade in support of the Hollander strikers. Fifteen hundred

---

* After Ben Gold was elected International president, Potash, Winogradsky and Begoon were elected at a general membership meeting on June 2, 1937. All three were re-elected at a general election on July 14 and 15, 1937.

shop chairmen endorsed this decision. Workers of fifty New York fur shops refused point-blank to work Hollander skins. Unless there was a settlement, Hollander-dyed furs would not be worked on.

By the second week in June, the campaign to unionize the Hollander factories was developing rapidly to the point of a general strike. A conference of the New York locals was called, attended by representatives of the Joint Council, Locals 2, 3, 48, 70, 77, 85, 88 and 89. The conference unanimously decided to raise a strike fund of $100,000. Other locals of the International throughout the country also mobilized to contribute their share.

As in the 1920 and 1926 general strikes, Motty Eitingon, president of the fur-importing firm of Eitingon-Schild, intervened in the dispute. A practical business man and a man of liberal views, Eitingon knew that a strike in the Hollander plants would throw the entire industry into confusion and chaos. Eitingon's business in the fur industry amounted to millions of dollars annually, and would suffer considerably if the struggle between the union and Hollander was allowed to run its course.

Eitingon finally succeeded in bringing his friend, Michael Hollander, head of the big firm, to the conference table with the union. Conferences went on for several weeks.

On June 28, even as conferences with Hollander were going on, ten thousand fur workers gathered in a giant demonstration at 29th Street and Seventh Avenue. They served notice on the fur manufacturers that Hollander's failure to come to terms would bring a shutdown of the entire New York fur industry.

On July 5, the union scored a victory in another branch of the fur dressing industry. After a five-day strike, fifteen hundred members of Locals 2, 3, 4 and 122, under the leadership of Samuel Mindel, aided by the Joint Council and Local 70, organized six open shops in the fur dressing industry. The fleshers, floor workers, pluckers and chauffeurs won a closed shop contract, wage increases ranging from 50 to 60 percent, thirty-five-hour, five-day week,* and a provision in the agreement that no factory could move beyond the five or six cent fare limit.

Not even Hollander could resist any longer the mounting pressure of the united union. With a general strike imminent, A. Hollander & Son, the biggest fur dresser and dyer in the United States and the largest fur

* The chauffeurs, who had only recently been organized into Local 122, won a reduction of hours from about 65 to 37½ and a wage increase of about 40 percent, or a minimum scale of $40 for drivers and $30 for helpers.

ALL OUT FOR THE
HOLLANDER DEMONSTRATION
Today

TO ALL FUR WORKERS:

Your International and your Joint Council call upon all the fur workers to assemble on 29th Street and 7th Avenue Today, Monday, at 5 P.M., right after work.

Come in the thousands. March directly from your shop to 29th Street and 7th Avenue right after work.

Today the fur workers, fur dressers and fur dyers will demonstrate their protest against the miserable conditions in the shops of A. Hollander & Sons.

Today the mighty army of fur workers will serve notice upon Hollander that he must recognize the Union and improve the conditions of his workers.

Today we call upon you to demonstrate your solidarity and support to the strikers of A. Hollander & Sons.

The strike of the Hollander workers is OUR strike. It is our duty to help them win a Union and Union conditions. By helping the Hollander workers, we are also helping ourselves.

The leaders of our International and the leaders of our Joint Council and of the other locals of our International will address you at this great demonstration.

Let every furrier like a soldier respond to the call of the Union.

ALL OUT TODAY—MONDAY—at 5 P.M. to 29th Street and 7th Avenue.

International Fur Workers Union of U. S. & C.

BEN GOLD, President   PIETRO LUCCHI, Secretary-Treasurer

FURRIERS' JOINT COUNCIL OF NEW YORK
Irving Potash, Manager

FUR DRESSERS' UNION, LOCAL 2
Sam Mindel, Manager

FUR FLOOR WORKERS' UNION, LOCAL 3
Philip Silverstein, Manager

LAMB & RABBIT DRESSERS' UNION, LOCAL 85
Mike Hudyma, Manager

FUR DYERS' UNION, LOCAL 88
Sam Burt, Manager

FUR CHAUFFEURS & HELPERS UNION, LOCAL 122
Joe Franks, President

GREEK FUR WORKERS UNION, LOCAL 70
John Vafiades, Organizer

New York fur workers are rallied to aid the Hollander strikers.

company in the world, signed an agreement with the International Fur Workers Union on July 6.

The agreement covered six Hollander plants, three in Newark, and one each at Middletown and Mt. Vernon, New York, and Long Branch, New Jersey. All Long Branch strikers were to be taken back to work without discrimination.

The agreement provided complete recognition of the union; closed shop; thirty-five-hour, five-day week; time-and-a-half for overtime; security on the job; equal division of work; no discrimination for union activities; sanitary conditions; and an increase in wages ranging from $7\frac{1}{2}$ to 15 percent—the lower paid workers receiving the higher increase.

Among the congratulatory telegrams which poured into the International office was one from John L. Lewis, president of the CIO. Lewis wired Ben Gold: "Congratulations on your splendid agreement with Hollander firm. May your fine progress continue."

The twenty-year campaign to organize the Hollander plants had succeeded in less than two months after the first united convention, the first fruit of unity.

The union opened offices in Newark, Long Branch and Middletown, and issued four charters to the Hollander locals—Locals 130, 135, 140 and 145. The workers joined the locals and then elected officers and departmental shop chairmen. A number of workers, influenced by the Middletown Republican machine, at first abstained from joining the union. The union exposed the anti-labor methods of the Republican machine and won over these workers.

In their local communities, the Hollander locals won a place as leaders of progressive social, cultural and political activities. They took an active part in the building of the American Labor Party. The Middletown local subsequently gained state-wide recognition for its part in defeating the notorious, red-baiting Congressman Hamilton Fish for re-election. The Newark local similarly engaged in energetic activities against the dictatorial machine of Jersey City's Mayor—"I am the law"—Hague.

The 1937 convention had decided to unite all fur dressing and dyeing locals of New York and vicinity into one Joint Board. With the Hollander campaign successfully completed, the International called a conference of eight dressing and dyeing locals—2, 3, 88, 80, 85, 89, 59 and 48—to lay the foundation of a real Joint Board. Each local was to manage its own financial affairs and its own local affairs. One staff of business agents and organizers would be elected by the locals under the supervision of the Joint Board and its manager.

Spokesmen for Local 2 rejected the proposal. Arguing that their local autonomy would be interfered with and that the economic conditions of the members of Locals 2 and 3, the best in the International, might be affected adversely, these locals refused to join the Joint Board.

Without compelling Locals 2 and 3 to join, the G.E.B. granted Locals 80, 85, 88 and 48 a Joint Board charter. Organized on November 16, 1937, with about three thousand members, the Board was composed of an equal number of delegates from each of the four locals. At the first meeting of the delegates, Sam Burt was unanimously elected manager. Under the leadership of Manager Burt, Mike Hudyma and Lyndon Henry, the Joint Board immediately proved its worth by organizing new sections of the industry, improving the living standards of its members, increasing wages in all shops, doubling and tripling earnings in newly-organized shops, winning shorter hours and other gains.

A fairly typical example was the case of workers employed by fur dealers, fur storage and auction houses. Before the Joint Board was formed, these workers were totally unorganized. They received $14 for a sixty-hour week. In July 1938, after an organizing campaign initiated by the Joint Board, these same workers were earning between $22 and $45 for a forty-hour week. They also won time-and-a-half for overtime, a minimum of one week vacation with pay, ten days' sick leave with pay in any one year, pay for ten legal holidays, and a guarantee to the workers of full-time employment fifty-two weeks a year.

The united Furriers Union still had the problem of ridding itself of corrupt elements. The leadership of the Joint Board discovered that Henry Caravella, a business agent of Local 80, was on the weekly payroll of the Mendoza Fur Dyeing Company. They brought the issue directly to the local membership. Caravella was immediately ousted.

A serious situation was uncovered in Toronto. Max Federman, in control of the Toronto locals and a leading light in the Socialist and Left-Workers Zionist Party, filled the local union offices with his followers. By pitting Jewish and Gentile fur workers against each other, Federman retained power over the Toronto union.* His followers got the best

---

* Federman saw to it that the Jewish and Gentile fur workers in Toronto were split apart into separate locals. Locals 35 and 65 consisted of Gentile fur workers and Locals 40 and 100 consisted of Jewish fur workers.

jobs in the trade, but rarely paid union dues or assessments. Towards the end of 1937, President Gold received detailed charges of serious irregularities perpetrated by the Toronto union leadership.

Gold appointed Vice-Presidents Begoon and Winogradsky to conduct an investigation. When Begoon discussed the state of affairs with Federman, he was assured that everything was in perfect order. Begoon and Winogradsky investigated the union books and interviewed Executive Board members of Locals 40 and 100. They were astounded at the widespread theft, graft and corruption which they discovered, including forged signatures on checks of the union's Unemployment Fund and misappropriation of money. Officers of Locals 40 and 100 helped themselves to union funds without consent or knowledge of the membership. Begoon and Winogradsky preferred official charges against Federman before the International Sub-Committee.

Federman, who had done everything in his power to obstruct the investigation, quickly set up a local "trial committee," composed of his supporters, to exonerate him. His hand-picked "trial committee" included a contractor and two men who were not members of the union. The chairman was Federman's closest friend. The trial committee, of course, white-washed Federman. They recommended expulsion of all union members who testified against him, including some of his own supporters.

A special membership meeting was called by the International. President Gold came to address the meeting. When the workers protested at the meeting against the committee's report, Federman's supporters began to slug the workers in the presence of Gold, Begoon, Winogradsky and Organizer Klig. To prevent serious injury to the workers, Gold adjourned the meeting. The G.E.B. expelled Federman by unanimous vote. At subsequent meetings of Locals 40 and 100, Federman, Simon Littman, Greenspan and others were expelled.

Federman formed a dual union and received a charter from the AFL. When Federman asked the AFL Toronto District Labor Council to seat the delegates from his dual union, the Toronto Council referred the matter to its Executive Committee. The Executive Committee, by unanimous vote of the Council, made a thorough investigation of the case. Its report was unanimously accepted by the AFL Toronto Labor Council on April 7, 1938. The report of this impartial committee of responsible leaders of the Toronto Labor Council exposed the system carried on by Federman and his gang.

"In general, we must state at the outset," the Executive Committee of the Toronto Labor Council wrote, "that the facts disclosed and estab-

lished to us, show that there existed in the affairs of the locals 40 and
100, of the International Fur Workers Union in Toronto, a situation so
deplorable that participation in the inquiry and in the presentation of
this report constitutes a distressing, although a necessary duty."

Top AFL officials, however, continued to recognize Federman and to
render him financial support. Pietro Lucchi and Samuel Mindel visited
William Green to discuss the matter. The AFL President assured them
that after he studied the report of the Toronto Council he would withdraw support from Federman. Green failed to live up to his pledge.

Under the leadership of Organizer Myer Klig, a Joint Board of all
Toronto locals was organized. The racial antagonism between Gentile
and Jewish fur workers, fostered by Federman, was eliminated. Trade
union democracy was introduced and practiced in all Toronto locals. The
honest, democratic union that emerged in Toronto began immediately to
repair the damage caused by the Federman administration. It enforced
union conditions in the shops and developed a campaign to organize the
remaining open shops.

"Honesty of our leaders is an uncompromising principle of the progressive trade union movement," commented President Gold on the ousting of Federman. "That is the law in our International."

That was the law in 1938. It is still the law in the International Union.

The activities of AFL officials against the fur workers were
by no means confined to Toronto. In Seattle, Washington, the newly-
organized Fur Workers Local 49 was conferring with the employers for
an agreement in June 1937. At the first conferences, the employers
granted recognition of the union and closed shop. It was certain that
agreement would soon be reached on the question of wages and hours.
Suddenly, officials of the AFL interfered and insisted that the employers
sign a contract with the AFL, even though Local 49 produced affidavits as
bargaining agent signed by the overwhelming majority of the Seattle fur
workers. Behind the AFL attack stood the dictatorial head of the Team-
sters Union, Dave Beck, the Chamber of Commerce, and the Mayor of
Seattle, John Dore.

Local 49 began intensive preparation for a strike. The high spirit of
the workers compelled the employers to conclude a settlement with the
union, providing a closed shop; no discharge; equal division of work;
minimum wage scales with considerable wage increases; 37½-hour week
until the end of 1937, thirty-five-hour week beginning 1938; and time-
and-a-half for overtime. The settlement was approved by the fur workers.

But before the settlement was approved by the Association, a committee of AFL officials induced the employers to repudiate their agreement. The AFL committee stopped off shops to force the workers into the AFL. The Seattle furriers replied with a general strike which paralyzed the industry.

It was a bitter strike. The strikers, many of them women, fought bravely. But they could not defeat the combined forces of the employers, the scabs, the Mayor, the police department and the AFL officials. Upon the Mayor's orders, police arrested the peaceful pickets. The strikers were warned that if they returned from jail to the picket line, the police would send them to the hospital. In the tenth week, the strike had to be called off. The workers were forced to return to work under an AFL contract which gave the bosses a forty-hour week and no improved conditions. In some shops the wages of the workers were actually reduced. In spite of this defeat, a number of furriers, led by Alberta George, maintained the local and remained loyal to the International.

The 1937 economic "recession" hit the fur industry early. In June, the wheels of the manufacturing trade began to slow down. New orders were not forthcoming. Many orders were cancelled. Very few buyers came to New York. The majority of the manufacturers were loaded with much stock. There was a general feeling in the trade of an oncoming economic depression. The employers seized this opportunity to inform the Joint Council that the July increases would not be granted in 1937.

The Joint Council replied with an intensive mobilization for July increases. Scores of shops were called on strike. Every employer received notice that unless a satisfactory July increase was given, his shop would be struck. The union's firm action forced the employers to retreat. The union obtained July raises for 6,128 workers in 708 shops, amounting to $33,095 weekly.

The employers struck back that fall by discharging thousands of fur workers, a practice permitted under the old agreement. The employers' objective was to demoralize the ranks of the workers just when conferences for a new collective agreement would begin.

The Council took the offensive at conferences of shop chairmen and active workers, open forums of unemployed workers, local meetings and membership meetings at which the aims of the employers were exposed. At the same time, the Council launched another drive against reviving contracting sweatshops, for strict enforcement of union conditions in the shops, against wage reductions and against overtime.

The Unemployment Committee of the union fought on the relief front. Under the committee's guidance, militant action was applied by the workers themselves to obtain city relief for the increasing number of unemployed furriers. As a result of the work of the Committee on Unemployment, over one thousand furriers received relief from the city during the months August to October, 1937. Despite the dozens of dispossess notices, there was not a single eviction. Lunches for school children, eye-glasses, shoes and many other provisions were obtained for needy workers.

Unemployment developed rapidly in many industries. At a CIO conference in November 1937, John L. Lewis declared vigorously: "One of the great principles for which labor in America must stand is the right of every man and women to have a job, to earn a living, if they are willing to work. . . . If the corporations which control American industry fail to provide them with that job in their management of industries' affairs, then there must be some power, somewhere in this land of ours, that will go over and above and beyond those corporations with all their influence and power and provide a job and insure the right to live for that American."

In the year following the Chicago convention, the unified International grew rapidly to forty-five thousand members, an increase of fifteen thousand. Nine new locals were established. Everywhere the International locals—manufacturing, retail, dressing and dyeing—despite the hardships of the economic crisis not only maintained their positions but also recorded substantial achievements. In Philadelphia, Atlantic City, New Haven, St. Paul, Los Angeles, Cleveland, Minneapolis, Detroit, Boston, Providence and other cities, shops unorganized for over thirty-five years signed closed shop contracts with wage increases.

These achievements were due in no small part to the splendid corps of International organizers who covered the country, organizing the fur workers everywhere and helping the locals win new and improved agreements. Myer Klig, Frank Brownstone and Abe Feinglass worked tirelessly and effectively to build the International. These men, appointed to the posts of International organizers at the recommendation of President Gold, soon achieved a most remarkable record of successful strikes as well as peaceful negotiations.

Typical was the story in Minneapolis. The city had been a dark spot on the map of the International for over seventeen years. The loss of a strike in 1920 resulted in complete liquidation of the local. The fur workers were left entirely at the mercy of their employers.

It was not until 1933 that a small group of furriers were again chartered as Minneapolis Fur Workers Local 71. The employers, having enjoyed the open shop for so many years, were determined not to recognize the union. A number of shop strikes resulted only in verbal understandings which proved meaningless in the shops. The bosses still maintained the open shop. Largely because of the incompetence of the business agent, Mike M. Mandl, the union was unable to compel the employers to live up to their promises. In July 1937, Myer Klig was assigned to organize the fur workers of Minneapolis. No better man could have been selected.

Born in Russia, Myer Klig had migrated to Canada at the age of seventeen. For several years he held odd jobs. He was a farm hand, a welder's assistant, a railroad section gang worker. In 1925, an operator in a Winnipeg fur shop, he plunged into union activity. Although only a few men then held fur union cards, Klig immediately joined, and started to organize the shop. He soon became secretary of the Winnipeg local and took a leading part in the 1926 strike. He continued his work in the fur trade until 1930, when he began a period of six years' work organizing Canadian dressmakers, furniture workers, lumberjacks, miners and other workers. In 1936, he returned to the fur trade. After the 1937 convention, the G.E.B. appointed Klig to the post of International organizer on President Gold's recommendation.

Minneapolis was Klig's first assignment. He set to work at once with an organizing drive. Shop meetings were held, non-union furriers visited and special meetings called. Within two weeks, the membership of Local 71 had greatly increased. Most of the shops were organized 100 percent, each with a shop steward.

The speed of the organizing drive convinced the employers that this time the fur workers meant business. If the employers resisted, the union was preparing for a strike. The employers concluded that peaceful negotiations with the union would be the better part of valor.

After several conferences, a collective agreement was signed between Local 71 and the wholesale, retail and department stores.* The Minneapolis workers obtained a closed union shop; wage increases of $3 to $10 per week; thirty-five-hour week; time-and-a-half for overtime; mini-

* For almost a year, the firm of Schlamp & Son, the largest retail shop in Minneapolis, refused to recognize the union and continued to operate a company union shop. In June 1938, however, the firm was compelled to sign an agreement with Local 71 similar to the one in effect with the other employers of Minneapolis.

mum scales for all crafts; six paid legal holidays; and equal division of work.

Within one month, without a strike, the Minneapolis workers had won conditions that they had been unable to secure in seventeen years. The Minneapolis drive was but one example of Myer Klig's untiring organizing work and negotiating ability. In the Hollander strike, in the organization and negotiations of Machinists Local 150, in Montreal, Toronto and as far away as Duluth, Minnesota, Myer Klig's services recorded gain after gain for the fur workers.

Another leading organizer on the International's staff was Frank Brownstone. Brownstone was born in Bessarabia in 1904. His parents died when he was only one and one-half years old, and he was reared by his grandmother. At the age of ten he went to work on a tobacco plantation. In 1921 he came to the United States. Following a series of jobs in textile factories and laundries, Brownstone obtained work in a fur shop in New York as a learner. He became an operator, but was prevented from joining Local 5 when he refused to pay $125 in graft to the strong-arm men who controlled the issuance of union books during the right-wing administration. In 1925, when Ben Gold became manager of the Joint Board and cleaned out the strong-arm men from the union's executive committees, Brownstone became a member of Local 5.

An active rank-and-filer and TUEL member, Brownstone was soon elected chairman of his shop. He distinguished himself as a member of the organization committee during the 1926 strike, and was one of the men singled out for immediate expulsion during the AFL "reorganization" in 1927. Brownstone refused to register with the right-wing Joint Council, and in 1928 went to the Pacific Coast where he worked in fur shops in San Francisco and Los Angeles. Returning to New York in 1929, he became an active figure in the Industrial Union. A year later, he went back to California, and, as a representative of the Industrial Union, began a drive to organize the open shops. Under his leadership, right-wing and left-wing fur workers in San Francisco united their ranks in the AFL local and conducted successful strikes to organize the industry and improve the workers' conditions. The San Francisco local, under Brownstone's leadership, became a spearhead of the drive for unity among fur workers all over the country. It was inevitable that soon after unity was achieved Brownstone would rise to prominence as a leader of the International.

Assigned by President Gold to organize one open-shop center or weak local after another, Brownstone's able work made itself felt in Atlantic City, Philadelphia, Washington, New Haven, Providence, Hartford and other cities. Atlantic City Local 75 had been smashed in 1931. Brownstone organized these shops again within a few weeks' time and won thirty-five-hour agreements, wage increases, ten paid holidays, no discharge, time-and-a-half for overtime and closed shop.

The Philadelphia local was strengthened, new shops organized and agreements signed with many improvements. New Haven, hitherto open shop, was organized by Brownstone. Contracts were won after a short, successful strike. Providence Local 92, was also organized by Brownstone. Defying all threats against "dangerous outside agitators," the local won its first agreement after a one-week strike, removing the threat of open-shop competition from nearby Boston.

Locals which had existed for years only on paper were transformed literally overnight. They won collective agreements guaranteeing the closed shop, a shorter work week, time-and-a-half for overtime, paid holidays and equal division of work.

A letter received in August 1937 by Irving Potash, manager of the New York Joint Council, from the Pittsburgh Fur Workers Local 69 tells its own story: "With the aid of Brother Joseph Winogradsky, the Pittsburgh Fur Workers Union was able to conclude successfully an agreement with seven Pittsburgh department stores.* The negotiations were the shortest in the history of the department store negotiations, and a great deal of this speed can be attributed to Brother Winogradsky's excellence as a negotiator and his splendid understanding of our problems. In the name of our Local, I would like to have you convey our thanks to the Joint Council for relinquishing Brother Winogradsky's services to help the Pittsburgh fur workers."

In the first six months of 1938, Abe Feinglass, in charge of the Mid-Western District which included Illinois, Wisconsin, Minnesota, Missouri, Michigan and Ohio, traveled sixteen thousand miles to help the locals in the area organize the unorganized fur workers, and win effec-

---

* The agreement, considered by Pittsburgh trade unions as a magnificent achievement, provided for the following conditions: the firms agreed to employment of union members only; equal division of work; gradual increases up to the minimum wage scale inside of one year; 40-hour, 5½-day week; vacations with pay; six legal holidays with pay; two weeks' trial period instead of eight as before.

A mass picketing demonstration during the 1938 strike. In the

Testimonial from shop chairmen of the Joint Council to President Ben Gold (above) after 1938 strike.

Mass demonstration of fur workers during the employers' lockout which preceded the 1938 general strike.

tive agreements. He established an impressive record of achievement.

In St. Louis, the fur workers, under Feinglass' leadership, forced the employers to grant them security on the job and a closed shop. In St. Paul, Feinglass aided the workers to replace an antiquated, twenty-year old agreement with a new contract that provided a closed union shop, thirty-five-hour week, equal division of work, seven paid legal holidays, wage increases of $2 for every worker, and time-and-a-half for over-time.* In Cleveland, Feinglass helped the members of Local 86 defeat the employers' efforts to establish a company union. They obtained agreements with the largest independent firms, heretofore unorganized, with a 25 percent wage increase and other important gains.

In every city he visited, Feinglass, like all the other International organizers, made it a cardinal principle to involve the workers themselves in the actual building of the union, in preparations for a strike, and in conducting negotiations with the employers.

At great mass meetings at the Hippodrome and the Hotel Center in November and December, 1937, the New York fur workers adopted their demands for the new collective agreement. Over ten thousand fur workers attended these meetings.

The New York Joint Council presented seventeen proposals to the manufacturers for inclusion in the new agreement. The chief demands were job security; a 25 percent increase in the minimum wage scales; a thirty-hour, five-day week; automatic July increases; three additional paid holidays; a sick relief fund; prohibition against runaway shops; and abolition of speedup.

The CIO Regional Office endorsed the furriers' demands, pointing out that they were "calculated to eradicate evils of long standing in the fur industry and to provide the workers with a measure of security on the job which they have a right to expect from the industry." The demands deserved "the endorsement of all fair-minded people."

At the conferences held during December and January, the Association rejected all demands of the union, including the demand for job security. The employers even advanced counter-demands to reduce the wage scale and to legalize the contracting system. Every conference ended with the employers' stubborn "No." Undoubtedly, the employers had decided that conditions were ripe for smashing the union in open battle.

* The scrapped agreement provided, among other points, that the president of the employers' association would be the "impartial arbitrator" of all disputes

A vast number of fur workers had been unemployed for months. The union's finances were limited. There was every indication that the economic recession would continue. Some employers counted on their ties with contracting and out-of-town shops. And finally, the employers depended on a new split in the union's ranks similar to 1926. Like the AFL leaders, they were convinced that it was impossible for a union to win a strike during an economic depression. They decided to provoke a strike.

The arrogant stand of the fur manufacturers paralleled the conspiracy of big business to defeat the social reforms of Roosevelt's New Deal and to smash the CIO. Known as the "Sit-Down of Big Business," the conspiracy of big business contributed to the sharp decline in industrial production and increase in unemployment in 1937. Putting the brakes upon reviving industry, it was calculated to throw the country into a panic and force the Roosevelt Administration to withdraw its progressive legislation. Because of the "Communistic" Roosevelt government and the "Communistic" CIO, big business hypocritically charged, industrialists had no "incentive" to keep their factories in operation.

The leaders of the fur manufacturers' association opened battle by locking out the fur workers on February 11, 1938. It was the accepted rule in the labor movement that a union must answer a lockout with a general strike. The fur manufacturers planned to exhaust the union's funds and the workers' meager resources during the early months of the year, and after a long strike, force the fur workers to accept the old agreement with changes for the worse.

The union leadership, however, adopted novel tactics to meet the attack. It did not call a general strike. Wherever possible, it convinced individual employers not to lock out their shops. For the remainder, the union leaders proposed that only firms that locked out workers be declared on strike. A general strike was meanwhile postponed. This policy, it was stated frankly, would preserve the strike fund and the energy of the workers, for the moment when the employers would have to make their samples.

The policy of delayed strike action, despite the employers' lockout, amazed the entire labor movement. It was something new. It could be carried out only with a most mature, experienced, disciplined and united membership. It was like commanding your own entrenched army not to return fire while the enemy artillery fired salvo upon salvo and his battalions advanced steadily toward your own positions. Confident of the support of the mass of fur workers, the union leaders were determined not to strike until they "could see the whites of the enemy's eyes." It was a brilliant strategy, brilliantly executed. The lockout by the manufacturers was fought, but not in a manner to deplete the union's treasury. The strike fund was carefully husbanded for the strategic counterattack, seven weeks later. Events proved this to be one of the most important factors responsible for the success of the strike that followed. Gold, Potash, Winogradsky, Schneider and the other leaders of the union had correctly gauged the situation and provided the labor movement with another outstanding example of daring, resourcefulness and experienced leadership in meeting the employers' attacks.

This unique policy was submitted to the fur workers for their approval. A small clique of Lovestoneites and some right-wing Socialists, still fighting against unity in line with editorials in the *Forward,* charged that this meant betraying the fur workers. They insisted that the union answer the lockout with a general strike. At the same time, in public circulars, they informed the bosses that the union had little money prepared for a strike. Much to the disappointment of the employers, the fur workers overwhelmingly rejected the maneuvers of the disruptionists and approved the delayed-action policy.

The union machinery was organized from the very first day of the lockout. As the locked-out workers came to the strike halls, they assembled in their designated places. Building captains registered every worker. Shop and building meetings were held. Picketing against the locked-out shops began immediately.

A complaint department, an information bureau, an investigation committee were set up. Every worker, locked out or not, was assigned his special task and responsibility. The thorough organization and discipline displayed from the first day of the lockout was the product of long experience in past struggles. The hall chairmen, Jack Schneider and Gus Hopman, and the rank-and-file committees, had the complete confidence of the workers.

The leadership of the lockout situation was in the hands of the General Strike Committee elected by the membership. Ben Gold was chairman; Harry Begoon, vice-chairman; Irving Potash, secretary; Pietro Lucchi, chairman of the out-of-town committee; Nathan Freiman, chairman of the independent shops settlement committee; Joseph Winogradsky, general hall chairman and chairman of Royal Windsor; Frank Brownstone, chairman, Manhattan Opera House; Gus Hopman, chairman, Irving Plaza; Mark Boerum, in charge of designers and patternmakers; Herman Paul, in charge of organization and out-of-town committees.

On February 15, Mayor Fiorello LaGuardia invited the union and the Association to a mediation conference. Several days before the lockout, the Association had rejected a conference proposed by the State Mediation Board. The leaders of the Association were not interested in a public airing of the issues. Under strong pressure because of the union's unexpected strategy, the Association leaders were compelled to reverse themselves and attend the conference.

The Association leaders demonstrated the same uncompromising attitude in the conference with Mayor LaGuardia and the State Mediation Board that they had displayed toward the union. To justify retaining their arbitrary power of discharge, the Association spokesmen raised the bogey of out-of-town competition. The union spokesmen exploded their argument by proving that every important fur center in the United States and Canada was unionized, all operating under agreements providing for equal division of work and no discharge. Association leaders decided not to attend any more conferences called by the State Board.

On March 31, after seven weeks of lockout, the General Strike Committee called a general strike. The fur workers responded magnificently. The strike machinery went into high gear. Shop, building and block committees began to function. Daily, systematic picketing of shops was carried on, supervised by rank-and-file committees composed of experienced, loyal and militant fur workers. Night picketing was conducted by the special Shop Committees. Shop chairmen meetings and mass meetings of the strikers were held regularly in every strike hall.

The response of the Greek workers to the general strike call was a sight to behold. In all its eleven-year history under the old, corrupt administration, Local 70 had never called a strike. Now, every single Greek manufacturing shop was shut tight. Even the foremen, foreladies, and the salesmen stopped working. Fifteen hundred Greek workers registered in the strike halls. The Greek workers had their own committees. Their strike machinery was so well organized that almost 100 percent of the strikers picketed daily. The militancy and discipline of the Greek strikers was a tribute to the new, progressive leadership of Local 70.

Women members of the Joint Council and of Local 70 distinguished themselves in the strike. A Women's Committee of the most active and union-conscious women fur workers was organized. This committee had its own specific strike duties, including investigations of suspected shops and home work. Thousands of women strikers were on the picket line daily for five and six hours at a stretch. The women organized their special demonstrations in the fur market and put out a women's strike bulletin. When needed, they were at the union hall six o'clock in the morning, ready for strike duty. They were in the forefront of every mass demonstration.

The strike activities of the floor boys proved invaluable. Locked out along with the skilled mechanics on February 11, they modeled their tactics after the strategy of the Joint Council. Under the leadership of Leon Straus, two thousand floor boys answered the general strike call. Side by side with their older union brothers, they reported twice daily at the union halls for roll call, marched their shifts on the picket line. In the General Strike Committee, in every strike hall, in every block, building and organization committee, the youthful floor boys performed their duties with outstanding enthusiasm and spirit, earning the respect and admiration of the skilled workers.

The designers employed in fur shops were now organized. Under supervision of Joint Council member Sol Chakrin, they met in their own strike hall and remained out for the duration of the strike. Patternmakers, employed in hitherto open shops supplying the fur trade, joined the strike. George Kleinman and Max Cohen, both Joint Council members, were assigned to organize and assist these workers. They struck in the second week of the lockout, picketed militantly and stayed out until the fur workers' strike ended.

The spirit and organization of the 1938 strike reminded veterans of 1926. From early morning to late at night, mass picket lines formed in front of each building in the market. Huge demonstrations wove in and out of the fur district. Mass meetings of thousands of strikers were held in the streets. Through the night, Saturdays and Sundays, committees of hundreds of loyal and tried rank-and-file workers patrolled the length and breadth of the market. Never was there such a complete stoppage of work in the fur industry as during this strike.

The Council's Educational Committee transferred all its activities into the strike halls. On alternate afternoons the furriers listened to lectures on developments in the strike, on health, and on current economic and political topics. On other afternoons they heard famous actors, singers and musicians from Actors Equity, the Hebrew Actors Union, the Musicians Union, the Teachers Union, the New Theatre League and other groups who willingly performed without compensation.

A lecture on lifting the embargo against Loyalist Spain culminated in thousands of post-cards to the State Department. When Barcelona was ruthlessly bombed by Hitler's and Mussolini's planes, the strikers spontaneously collected funds for an ambulance to be sent to Spain as a token of their solidarity with the Spanish people. Despite their own straits, the strikers collected over $1,500 in pennies and nickels for Spain.

In many respects the 1938 strike differed from the 1926 strike. All International officials and G.E.B. members made notable contributions to the strike. They helped in determining the policies, addressed mass meetings of strikers and shop chairmen, and were in constant consultation with the strikers' leaders. When the Lovestoneites and other disruptionists tried to sabotage the strike by agitating the strikers to demand large sums in strike benefits, men like Samuel Mindel, Harry Begoon and Pietro Lucchi, all known as right-wingers, publicly exposed these agents of the bosses. The *Forward* continually damned Begoon and other Socialists in the union leadership as traitors who had sold themselves to "Communists." But these men proved during the 1938 strike that they owed allegiance only to the fur workers.

In 1926, leaders of the AFL had collaborated with the bosses and the right-wing officials of the International, sabotaged the strike and tried to sell out the workers in the back-door agreement signed in Washington. In contrast, the CIO gave its fullest support to the 1938 strike. John L. Lewis, president of the CIO, pledged financial support and was ready to endorse a loan of $50,000 for the union at a crucial moment of the strike. Following militant and progressive policies, CIO leaders in those days supported the struggles of workers in all industries to defend and improve their conditions.

Thanks to the progressive administration of Mayor LaGuardia, the police refrained from making the type of wholesale arrests of peaceful pickets that they had practiced in the past strikes. Picketing demonstrations were not broken up. No heads of strikers were split by police clubs in this strike. The detectives of the Industrial Squad, whose specific duties had always been to blackjack the strikers, did not dare to do so this time. Nor did the employers dare to hire professional sluggers, as during the Tammany administration.

The general strike was settled on May 26, 1938. The struggle had been hard, the victory of the workers was all the sweeter. The most important gain was seasonal job security, the best attained by the New York fur workers to that date. The six months' period of equal division of work in the previous agreement had been split by a period when the employers could discharge without cause. The equal division of work period was now extended to eight consecutive months. The mid-season discharge period was completely eliminated. (The workers said a "zipper" had closed the job security period for the full season.)

In addition the strikers won a two-week trial period for new workers, something new in the trade; a 10 percent increase in the minimum scale; an automatic collective July increase; * assurance of employment for elderly workers; limitation on productive work by bosses while thousands of furriers were unemployed; the right to refuse to work on skins coming from scab shops or from Nazi Germany; and stiffer penalties for violations of the agreement, especially in the cases of contracting or "kick-back."

These important gains were now added to every gain won by the furriers during the twenty-five years of the union's existence, such as abolition of contracting, prohibition of overtime and pay for legal holidays.

For the first time in any needle trade industry in New York City, the young, unskilled workers were included in an agreement together with skilled craftsmen. The collective agreement covered the members of the Fur Floor and Shipping Clerks Local 125. They won a closed shop, a minimum scale of $18 a week, forty-hour week, nine paid holidays, automatic July increases, and eight months' equal division of work with no discharge.

The designers and patternmakers, organized in one local union, also won their first agreements with significant gains from their respective employers.

The great victory of the New York fur workers after the fifteen-week struggle was a magnificent achievement. As in the 1926 general strike, the furriers pointed the way to the American workers. The victory in 1938 showed American workers throughout the country not only how to defend past gains, halt wage cuts and anti-labor offensives, but also how to win higher wages and other gains from the employers even in a time of economic crisis. In a telegram to the union, John L.

---

* For many years the furriers had been forced to strike for their July raises. In many shops the workers lost a week's work or more because the bosses refused to grant the July increase. In many shops, too, the workers were forced to strike because the boss refused to grant the July increase to one or two workers. In the 1938 agreement, the July increase was recognized and would be given to each and every employed worker without the necessity of shop strikes.

Lewis wrote: "Just heard of your splendid victory. The CIO wishes to extend to yourself and members congratulations for your fine work. The settlement in your industry will go a long way in stopping the downward trend of wages. Yours for continued success."

What a contrast between the treachery of William Green in the 1926 strike and the encouragement of John L. Lewis in 1938!

The united International Union chalked up a remarkable record of organizational achievements in 1937 and 1938. The organization of Hollander, the Joint Board of Fur Dressers and Dyers Unions, the many localities organized for the first time and weak locals revitalized, the successful general strike of New York fur workers—all were proof of the new strength of the union. Unity and collective leadership—guarantees of full democratic rights to all members, regardless of their religious or political beliefs—election of officials and organizers based upon honesty, sincerity and ability—produced outstanding results. The wage increases, shorter hours and other improvements gained by the fur workers were all the more significant because they were won in the midst of an economic recession and severe unemployment. The fur workers were indeed reaping the full fruits of their hard-gained unity.

The Fur and Leather Workers
Join Hands

CHAPTER 45

A Grim Story of Betrayal

In the spring of 1917, a group of leather workers employed in Newark tanneries approached the Fur Dressers and Dyers Union and pleaded to be organized. These tannery workers told a pitiful story of working sixty and seventy hours a week for $7 to $10.

Moved by the tragic plight of these leather workers, the Newark fur local wrote to Frank Morrison, secretary-treasurer of the AFL, asking for jurisdiction to permit them to organize tannery workers. Secretary Morrison threw cold water upon the suggestion. Leather workers employed in the tanneries, he wrote, were organized in local unions directly affiliated to the AFL. No national organization, he added, had jurisdiction over that branch of the industry at that time.

The request of the Newark tannery workers to be organized by the fur dressers and dyers union was both logical and practical. The work of fur dressers and dyers was similar in many respects to that of leather tanners. Many of the processes of dressing fur skins were almost identical with tanning leather hides. Dyeing of furs was also similar to coloring of hides. A principal difference was that tanning involved an unhairing process while dressing carefully preserved the fur. In some leather plants, the workers were also engaged in dressing fur skins. Many fur dressing and dyeing workers were also employed in leather tanning shops. On sheepskin, the processes in both fur and leather plants were so similar that jurisdiction over sheepskin tanning shops had in fact been assigned to the International Fur Workers Union back in 1913.

Obviously, it was to the interest of the workers that all workers on fur skins and leather hides be organized in one union. The narrow craft-union policies of the AFL Executive Council kept these workers apart. Unfortunately, the result was that the leather workers remained unorganized for many years.

The manufacture of leather is a complicated process that requires years of training, experience and skill. A government survey even as late as the 1930's pointed out: "The amount of work done by hand in tanneries is still considerable. Hardly any of the machines in use can be called automatic, and almost every process involves some manual skill. The stock is easily damaged by unskillful handling, and at some stages it deteriorates rapidly if not pushed with due promptness through the routine of manufacture. A high premium is consequently put on skill and training."

In spite of the high degree of skill required in the industry, the leather workers for over one hundred years were compelled to work under the most miserable conditions. They worked long hours for low pay. Unsanitary conditions in the tanneries were shocking. Thousands of leather workers were poisoned and their health undermined by the dangerous chemicals, noxious fumes, polluted air and filthy materials. The death rate from anthrax was highest among tannery workers. Industrial accidents made it one of the most dangerous of all occupations. And the leather workers never knew the meaning of job security.

Although tannery workers had engaged in militant strikes as far back as the 1830's, they were defeated time and again in their efforts to build a union. At best they won only temporary gains. The unions they set up crumbled after a year or two under attacks of the employers.

Under the Knights of Labor, the tannery workers succeeded in the 1880's in organizing most of the tanneries in New England and in Newark, New Jersey. They won higher wages, shorter hours and union recognition. But when the national leadership of the Knights of Labor abandoned their original militant and progressive policies, the organization disintegrated. The leather workers re-formed their ranks into unions affiliated with the American Federation of Labor. Again the fighting spirit and militancy of the leather workers were completely undermined by leaders who abandoned the policy of struggle and advocated "cooperation with employers."

Some AFL officials maintained themselves in power by establishing a complete dictatorship over small, ineffective leather workers' unions. Many locals ceased to exist altogether. Those that managed to remain alive, had only a small fraction of the workers in the leather industry. The vast majority were either driven out of unions by employers' offensives or withdrew in disgust with a leadership that did nothing to improve their conditions.

A United Leather Workers International Union was formed in July 1917 through the amalgamation of the practically defunct United Leather Workers on Horse Goods, the Travelers Goods and Leather Novelty Workers International Union, and several local unions of tannery workers affiliated directly to the AFL.* The total membership of the new union was thirty-two hundred. Its leaders optimistically predicted that fifty thousand leather workers would soon be brought into the organization. It was an idle boast. The top leaders of the United Leather Workers were the same men who had misled the leather workers on horse goods for so many years. William E. Bryan, the bureaucratic president of the United Brotherhood of Leather Workers on Horse Goods, was president of the new union. He continued his policy of cooperating with the employers at the leather workers' expense.

Coming into existence during the First World War, the new union should have made progress. The leather industry was rapidly expanding. Orders from the United States Government and the Allies gave even the declining saddlery industry a new lease of life. With sky-rocketing living costs, a wave of trade union organization swept many industries.

The new union also grew rapidly, increasing its membership to 11,700 in 1920. But this growth was not achieved through organizing. Through an arrangement with the U.S. War Department, most of the new members were handed to the United Leather Workers on a silver platter. To win support for the war among workers and to prevent strikes for higher wages and decent working conditions, the War Department signed an agreement with the leadership of the United Leather Workers. There were to be no strikes. In return, the War Department ordered all manufacturers of army leather supplies to sign contracts providing for the eight-hour day, time-and-a-half for overtime, and general wage increases. The union itself did not deal directly with the employers. It signed an agreement with the War Department. The War Department then signed contracts with the leather manufacturers which stipulated that the workers receive certain improvements in working conditions.

* The United Leather Workers International Union of America was formed in Peabody, Massachusetts, in 1915 to organize the tannery workers, but it never affiliated to the AFL. It was primarily a New England union.

While the union increased its membership, it was by no means stronger. The leather workers knew that the employers made concessions to the workers as a temporary wartime expedient, to be taken back at the very first opportunity.

The post-war period proved that the United Leather Workers was built on quicksand. The war contracts expired. The employers immediately wiped out every concession they had been forced to grant the workers. The union did nothing to halt the employers' wage cutting. Its membership rapidly vanished. By 1923, it was down to two thousand. Two years later, it had only 1,460.

The incompetent leaders of the United Leather Workers were completely bewildered. Bryan, the president, could not explain "the basic reasons which have induced thousands to forsake the union and become one of the army of non-unionists." "Nothing has been found that has any influence with leather workers," declared John J. Pfeiffer, the secretary-treasurer.

The union leaders blamed the workers. They were foreign-born. They were content to remain slaves to the bosses. They spoke too many languages. There were too many nationalities. They were simply unorganizable. The leather workers had a different opinion. They openly blamed the union leadership for its incompetence and wrong policies.

The leather workers, as was demonstrated time and again, were militant enough. In 1920, the leather workers of Oshkosh, Wisconsin, struck against wage cuts and their employers' effort to restore the open shop. The employers immediately obtained an injunction from Judge Burnell forbidding picketing. The strikers defied the injunction. Several were arrested and fined, but returned at once to the picket line. The next day they were arrested again. This time they were sentenced to jail for thirty days. Other pickets took the place of the jailed strikers. They informed Judge Burnell that even if he imprisoned all the pickets, their wives, sisters and sweethearts would still keep the picket line going.

The determined fight of the strikers won the support of other labor unions. A parade by the trade unions of Oshkosh protested the imprisonment of the strikers.

The jailed strikers sent a message to the trade unionists and citizens of Oshkosh. "Greetings: The strikers imprisoned in the county jail wish to express their gratitude for the sympathy you have shown them by parading through the streets and near the county jail of Oshkosh. We wish to assure you that we will not quit until the management of the company is ready to deal with us in a spirit of fairness through our chosen representatives."

Pictures of the leather workers in jail were sold all over Wisconsin at ten cents each, the funds thus collected going as relief to the strikers. In Oshkosh alone, two thousand photographs were sold on Labor Day.

Judge Burnell was finally compelled to amend his injunction, allowing the leather workers to picket. The strikers now turned to the national leaders of the United Leather Workers for help.

Instead of aiding the strikers, President Bryan advised them to go back to work on the company's terms. It was impossible to win strikes, Bryan told the Oshkosh strikers. "The employers' associations are attacking the labor union forces on all fronts." If they smashed the leather workers' conditions and destroyed their union, it would not be the result of the employers' doings but of "the workers themselves acting under impulses that seem to have succeeded reason and good judgment."

Again and again, the leaders of the United Leather Workers repeated this refrain. Whenever the membership, driven by desperation, struck against lockouts and wage cuts, they received long lectures from President Bryan beginning with the statement that "the conditions confronting labor at present are beyond the influence or control of the officers or members of the unions." He advised them "to accept the terms of the employers, rather than the alternative of witnessing the hunger and perhaps starvation of women and children dependent upon them for the necessaries of life."

Attacked by the employers and their agencies in local, state and national government, and unaided by the leaders of their union, the leather workers went down to defeat in strike after strike. Many were forced to sign "yellow-dog" contracts. Others were driven into company unions. Still others, disgusted with the leadership's policies, quit the United Leather Workers.

In 1920, the union had had a large membership in Philadelphia, mainly workers in the glazed kid industry. Under Mike Brown, autocratic local secretary and business agent, the membership dwindled to the vanishing point. Brown ran the local like a private business. Rank-and-file leather workers proved that Brown was short in his accounting. (The exact amount could never be determined since the records were destroyed.) The top leadership of the United Leather Workers refused to prosecute Brown. Instead, they made a deal whereby Brown could pay back about $1,200 in monthly installments. President Bryan himself admitted that he did nothing when he learned that the workers "were compelled to contribute to him [Brown] out of their wages to meet his obligation to the Union," and that the only reason the workers paid was that "no glazer can get work or hold a job unless he is 'OKd' by Brown."

When the post-war economic crisis was over and so-called prosperity returned, Bryan again held that conditions were not ripe for an organization drive. The workers were not in the frame of mind for militant struggles, he argued, for they were concerned with saving up money to buy stocks. Instead of learning strike methods, Bryan advised the leather workers that "they must study investments as a practical problem."

This was addressed to leather workers who were earning forty cents an hour and taking home after a full sixty-hour week exactly $24.

The leaders were deaf to all appeals to organize. Not a single union convention was held after 1920. Frank Morrison, secretary of the AFL, was informed in 1929 that the union saw "no reason for holding a convention." Morrison's only comment was: "Thanks for filling out the blank advising that there is no convention in sight at the present time."

Instead of organizing the unorganized leather workers, Bryan and his aides spent months conspiring and planning to raid other unions. They

The leaders of the AFL United Leather Workers claim that there has been "no reason" to hold a convention in nine years.

Owing to the depressed conditions in the leather industry for the past nine years and the consequent broken spirit of the workers there has been no reason for holding a convention, hence none has been held since July 1920. At the present time there is nothing that a convention could do to change present condition. The work of organizing is being pushed just as rapidly as possible with the limited means at hand.

The eastern members of our General Executive Council have been called together in New York City for to-morrow November 10th. Working on Sunday as a protective measure.

Things are beginning to look brighter and we hope to show good results ere long.

With best wishes, I am

Fraternally yours

Gen'l Sec'y-Treas. Pfeiffer

RECEIVED NOV 1 2 1929

ANSWERED NOV 13 1929

tried to persuade the top AFL officials to order the International Pocket Book Workers Union to hand over its members to the United Leather Workers. The Pocket Book Workers Union, Bryan insisted in a letter to William Green on August 3, 1925, was "composed largely of communists," and only a conservative leadership like that of the United Leather Workers should be entrusted with the "dangerous and acute problem" of controlling these workers.*

"The future of the United Leather Workers Int[ernational] Union," Bryan wrote to Green on December 9, 1925, "rests primarily upon the organization of Tannery Workers, and Travellers Goods workers, but, for some unknown reason the workers in these industries are most difficult to organize, and more difficult to control and keep within the union after chartered. To an extent we can account for this: The foreign element predominates in the tannery and [is] composed of people from the most backward countries of Continental Europe. . . . The [Travellers Goods] industry is largely controlled by Jews, also the workers in the principal centers are of this nationality in the great majority. They have been organized a number of times, but, each time have gone to pieces through radical visionary action at inopportune times, and because of the inborn trait of the Jewish race to give as little as possible for value received. . . ."

William Green did not rebuke Bryan for this vicious attack on the Polish, Italian, Ukrainian, Irish, Jewish and other foreign-born workers in the leather tanneries and luggage shops. In typical fashion, Green joined Bryan in blaming "the indifferent and apathetic attitude of the workers" for the decline of trade union membership.

The United Leather Workers finally started an organizing campaign in 1926 among tannery workers in several cities. After three years of the widely-advertised drive, with much expense for organizers paid out by the AFL Executive Council, all the union could show was five hundred members in Philadelphia (out of four thousand workers); twelve in Camden (out of thirteen hundred); one hundred fifty in Wilmington (out of nineteen hundred); and twenty-five in Newark (out of three thousand). The rest were either totally unorganized or members of company unions.

The picture in the New England tanneries was no better. In January 1929, the United Leather Workers International Union of America, an

---

* In January 1929, the International Pocket Book Workers Union combined with the United Leather Workers and became part of it for a few years.

United Leather Workers
INTERNATIONAL UNION

AFFILIATED TO THE AMERICAN FEDERATION OF LABOR

General Officers

WM K BRYAN
General President.
616 Walsix Building,
Kansas City, Mo

BERNARD G QUINN,
Genl. Vice President.
3628 North 10th St.,
Philadelphia, Pa

I GORDON,
Genl Vice-President.
4634 Indiana Ave.
Chicago, Ill

JOHN J PFEIFFER,
Genl Secy-Treas.,
610 Walsix Building,
Kansas City Mo

Members General Executive Council

P P MALONEY
Keansburg, N J
WM F ALTERMAN,
707 Cedar Springs St.,
Dallas, Texas
J W TRAPP,
104 Bryant Street.
Los Angeles, Cal.
WM TRIPP,
707 A Accomac St.,
St Louis, Mo
JOHN A GRANT,
38 N Franklin St.,
Wilmington, Del
ROSH CARR,
360 N Harrison St.,
Wilmington, Del.

GENERAL OFFICE
608-9-10 WALSIX BUILDING

Kansas City, Mo., Dec, 9, 1925.

Mr. Wm. Green, President
American Federation of Labor,
Washington, D.C.

Dear Sir and Brother :-

I am in receipt of your letter transmitting a copy of the report made to you by Organizer Marks of his visit to Philadelphia, Pa. and Wilmington, Del. I note no addressed

The future of the United Leather Workers Int. Union rests primarily upon the organization of Tannery Workers, and Travellers Goods Workers, but, for some unknown reason the workers in these industries are most difficult to organize, and more difficult to control and keep within the union after chartered. To an extent we can account for this: The foreign element predominates in the tannery industry and composed of people from the most backward countries of Continental Europe, the industry never has been organized to any great extent, for some years there was a charter from the A.F.of L. exclusively covering this industry, but it was surrendered because of failure to perfect a lasting organization. Likewise, there was for some years an outstanding charter covering the Travellers Goods line, this industry is largely controlled by Jews, also the workers in the principal centers are of this nationality in the great majority, they have been organized a number of times., but, each time gone to pieces through radical visionary action at inopportune times, and because of the inborn trait of the Jewish race to give as little as possible for value received, they promote secession and independent movements in order to retain the per capita tax they would otherwise be obligated to pay the International Union.

the way to avoid the inevitable result, unless, the United Leather Workers International Union can live and function.

With my highest personal regards, I remain

Fraternally yours

W E Bryan
General President.
United Leather Workers International Union.

WEB/WEB

W. E. Bryan, president of the United Leather Workers, reveals his prejudice against Jewish and foreign-born workers in this letter to William Green as he attempts to explain away the complete failure of the AFL union to organize the leather industry.

independent union, had a total membership of fifteen hundred tannery
workers, all of them in Massachusetts. About six hundred were in Salem
and Peabody, between three and four hundred in Lowell, less than two
hundred in Woburn, and about three hundred were scattered about in the
tanneries of the Massachusetts North Shore.

In Massachusetts alone there were more than ten thousand unorganized workers in the leather tanneries. Many of these workers were forced
to belong to company unions. In the Midwest and on the Pacific Coast,
no organization whatever existed.

Unorganized and completely at the mercy of the tannery bosses, the
leather workers were unable to resist the brutal effects of the great depression. The employers callously slashed their wages and reduced their
living standards still further. Between 1930 and 1932, the vast majority
of the employed leather workers suffered four wage reductions of 10 percent each. The top wage of a skilled leather worker (if fully employed,
which the vast majority were not) was $23.74 for a fifty-five-hour week.
Unskilled workers earned $14.98 for the same number of hours. Women
workers earned an average of 27¼ cents an hour, or $10.52 a week. An
investigation in 1932 of the leather goods industries in Massachusetts
by the State Minimum Wage Commission revealed that wages varied
between $10 and $13 a week.

To rally the leather workers against further wage cuts, a member of
St. Louis Local 66 of the United Leather Workers wrote a stinging letter to William Green in April 1931, demanding action. "I firmly believe
that the time of being a conservative has been passed," he argued, "and
that we will have to assert ourselves to offset this strangling of Labor that
is being put into effect by the Captains of Industry." He proposed
that "mass meetings should be held throughout the Nation protesting
against any further reductions of wages whereby many now working are
all but objects of charity."

In his reply, William Green read this leather worker a long lecture.
How dare he imply that the AFL was not exerting heroic efforts to resist
wage cuts. "Last week," Green wrote, "I issued a statement in opposition to wage reductions. . . . In addition, I delivered a Movietone address in the Pathe News Service last week in opposition to reduction in
wages." Totally exhausted by his exertions in speaking for Movietone,
Green continued: "Your suggestion that mass meetings be called for the
purpose of protesting against reductions ought to be submitted to your
own International President."

Nothing was further from W. E. Bryan's thoughts than calling mass meetings against wage reductions. He was busy with other matters, such as helping the employers break a strike of the Surpass leather workers in Philadelphia. "I am advised the Federation has issued a document," Bryan wrote to Frank Morrison, "dealing specifically with the activities, policies, etc., of the Communists in this country. . . . Having made good use of the 'Red Invasion' [another pamphlet issued by the AFL] with the Tanners in the Glazed Kid Industry. . . . please send me *first class mail* 100 copies of this [new] Communist document."

The conditions under which thousands of tannery workers in small isolated communities worked and lived are revealed in a sworn affidavit by Mrs. Nellie Gardner, widow of a worker in the Elkland Leather Company of Elkland, Pennsylvania.

"My husband, a tanner, was employed by the Elkland Leather Company for sixteen years. During that time he never received any pay checks except twice, and one of these was for 5 cents and the other in the amount of 2 cents. All other wages he earned were deducted by the Elkland Leather Company to pay his bills at the company store.

"On two or three occasions, as near as I can remember, I accompanied my husband to the tannery store office and talked with Mr. William Ord-

Bryan distributes anti-Communist literature in an effort to break a strike of the Surpass leather workers in Philadelphia.

way, manager of the company store. We asked him to let us have a part of my husband's wages in order to carry a small policy of life insurance. We wanted to pay $1.50 a week premium on life insurance. But Mr. Ordway did not consent and said that he must take his store bill out of my husband's wages first. When my husband died he left no life insurance, as we were unable to carry any.

"During my husband's illness I never was able to get any groceries at the company store. They refused to allow me credit. The Elkland Leather Co. did employ my son-in-law, Cecil Youngs, but they took my husband's bill out of my son-in-law's wages and made deductions for about 18 months after my husband's death until his bill was paid in full and until my son-in-law quit working there. During the eighteen months my son-in-law drew no pay checks at all."

Elkland Leather Company agents did not even hesitate to dictate to the workers in the tannery how they should vote. "When Roosevelt was running for president against Hoover [in 1932]," a worker wrote, "the bosses carried a box around in the plant and took the votes. When the boss came to my job and asked us if we wanted to vote, we told him how we were going to vote, which was Roosevelt. The boss told us if Roosevelt would get to be president the plant would no doubt shut down."

Lloyd Bennet, tannery worker born and raised around Gowanda, New York, worked at the Moench Tanning Company. On his job, he handled formaldehyde and inhaled poisonous fumes:

"I used to vomit often and I couldn't eat. My teeth crumbled. I always felt tired, and I felt there was something wrong with me. But you know how it is, I couldn't give in for fear of losing my job.

"They never told me to be careful when I handled the formaldehyde. I had to pour it from the bottle directly into the pail with the finish with my bare hands. The ceiling is low . . . and there is no ventilation . . . and I had to work on it all day long . . . and the tray containing the finish is open.

"On January 15, 1932, I dropped at the machine on the floor and collapsed."

The workers in many tanneries suffered the tragic effects of poisoning from handling dangerous chemicals used in tanning. The workers were not provided with arm-length rubber gloves, rubber overalls or boots. Proper exhaust systems were not installed. Fresh-air rest periods were not allowed. Gas masks were not provided for certain especially dangerous operations. And poisonous materials were used that should have been legally banned. What legal prohibitions there existed, were cynically ignored. And instead of organizing the tannery workers and leading them in struggle to end the terrible conditions in the plants, the president of the United Leather Workers was busy distributing anti-Communist literature!

The statistics of the number of leather workers who died from the poisonous, corrosive and explosive chemicals used in the tanneries are still too fragmentary to tell even a partial story.* Occasionally the newspapers would report the gruesome fate of leather workers like that of the two tanners in Peabody, Massachusetts, who died in 1932 after sweating blood from their pores. But usually the wealthy tanners exercised enough control over the press to keep such stories out of the papers.

After a careful study of the tanning industry in the early 1930's, Horace B. Davis reported: "More than once, men sent to clean out old vats used in connection with tanneries have succumbed to the noxious fumes of hydrogen sulfide and died before they could be rescued. At the Hess & Drucker tannery in Newark, five men were overcome in this way in May 1933. In one western tannery the experience was so common that every time the tanning vats were cleaned out it was expected the bones and hair of some poor devil would be found at the bottom. Nearly every tannery can tell of some mysterious explosion which injured or killed certain workers some time in the past."

This was the bitter fruit of years of betrayal by AFL leaders who were primarily concerned with helping the leather bosses fight "communism" and collaborating with them at the expense of the workers' sweat and blood.

A picture showing workers in a leather tannery scraping the flesh off the inside of the hide appeared in *Fortune* magazine in the early 1930's. The caption under the picture read, "NO AESTHETE'S JOB." The editors of the business magazine, part of the Luce chain, added the following comment: "To this wet and stinking job the workers have apparently become inured."

The day was not far off when the leather workers would also show the bosses and the smug editors of the commercial press how to end many of the miserable conditions under which they were compelled to work.

---

* An article in *Industrial Hygiene* for July 1925 listed forty-two occupational diseases in tanning. "We believe," wrote the author, "that this industry has a greater variety of occupational hazards than almost any other one."

CHAPTER 46

The National Leather
Workers Association

On March 21, 1933, the 250 Agoos tannery workers of Lynn, Massachusetts, went out on strike demanding a wage increase and a cut in hours. Quickly workers of other tanneries in Lynn joined them. The strike spread up the North Shore. Five hundred workers walked out at Amdur Limon in Danvers; 150 at Thayer Foss; 30 at Pearse Leather; and 120 at Kirstein in Peabody. Then the strike movement swept through Salem and into the Woburn-Winchester area.

Upwards of five thousand workers joined the struggle. On March 24, a parade of strikers one-quarter of a mile long marched through the Peabody leather district. Other leather workers joined the swelling ranks. The parade ended at the Peabody City Hall where the workers took a pledge "to stick together and fight for our rights."

At first the leather bosses were not too worried. "The strikers are made up of several nationalities," the *Peabody Times* observed in explaining the employers' attitude, "and a break on the part of any one of them might precipitate a rush back to the jobs by all. In the past, jealousy between these racial groups has made it possible to 'play one against the other' and so control the situation." And again: "The strikers are in no position to withstand a prolonged strike, and the lure of a good week's pay is going to be strong."

Despite these predictions, the workers' ranks held solid. Soup kitchens were set up. Money and other support came from various nationality groups in the community and from people in every walk of life. "Food aplenty is being donated," a newspaper reported early in April, "and a list of the donors would be a long and comprehensive one."

The Massachusetts State Board of Arbitration stepped into the picture on March 28. Forty manufacturers met with the State Board and made it clear that while they were willing to grant a wage increase and a forty-eight-hour week, they would under no circumstance deal with the union "even if they have to close their plants and go out of business." The strikers replied immediately that they would not return to work except as a recognized union.

The battle reached the showdown stage. Scabs were imported and made ready for action. Police were alerted. The leather bosses in Peabody, Danvers and Lynn inserted advertisements in the newspapers announcing that they were opening their plants on Monday, April 17, "to deal individually with our employees . . . but refuse to recognize the union, which has been fomenting trouble in shops where workers are perfectly satisfied."

At a mass meeting, the strikers answered the manufacturers' threats with a call for a monster parade. Speaking in favor of the proposal, one striker, who had several dependents, declared: "I remember other strikes, when the manufacturers issued the same statement, which didn't mean a thing to us working men." Without a union, he pointed out, many of the strikers would be blacklisted in all leather shops.

"It was surprising the number of strikers who echoed his sentiments," wrote one reporter after the mass meeting. "The strikers appeared to be a determined bunch of men and women and although they are anxious to get back to work, they are willing to suffer if they can win their point which is recognition of the union."

Mayor Sullivan of Peabody denied the union a permit for the parade. The following day, tear gas made its first appearance in Peabody. Strikers were gassed and clubbed when they tried to keep the scabs out of the plants. Twice again in the next few days the police hurled tear gas bombs into the strikers' mass picket lines. Six strikers were arrested for stopping scabs from entering the B. E. Cox factory.

Public resentment against the importation of strikebreakers and the police terror was expressed in petitions to Mayor Sullivan by the Polish Mutual Benefit Society and by 220 Greek merchants, proprietors and citizens. The petition urged that "an immediate stop be put to the most inhumane practice in the civilized world—strikebreaking."

Meanwhile, individual leather manufacturers signed with the National Shoe and Leather Workers Union. On April 27, the remaining manufacturers sat down with a committee of twelve strikers and negotiated a contract which the workers approved on May 2. Union recognition was won, though not the closed shop. Strikers were guaranteed their jobs. The workers failed to gain a general wage increase or shorter hours, but adjustments on jobs gave many workers $5 to $8 a week increases.

Strike activities had been directed by a committee of the leather workers in each city, two from each shop. At the meeting which

Reports in Peabody and Salem newspapers, April and May 1933, indicate the militant character of the leather workers' strike.

Manufacturers Unite To Break Leather Strike

All Shops To Open Doors Next Monday; Strikers Invited Back At Highest Wage Scale In Industry

Mass Meeting of Strikers Voted Against Return Except As Organized, Recognized Union; Trouble Likely Next Week If Workers Split Up

Following nearly three weeks of failure in getting together the strikers and manufacturers, during which time the public has been on the anxious seat awaiting settlement of the strike which has effected several thousand workers, the meeting in Boston Wednesday with the State Board of Arbitration resulted in another deadlock. The manufacturers are now taking the initiative and are determined to break the strike. They are issuing a call to their employees through the local papers today, pointing out the fact that the shops will be opened Monday, and that the men are invited back under a standard minimum scale of wages, based on a 48 hour week. They further state that men not reporting for work Monday

TEAR GAS BOMBS ARE USED TO ROUT STRIKE CROWDS IN PEABODY

Donnell Gets Bodyguard and Permit to Carry Pistol; Received Threat; Tear Gas Saved a Riot on Street Car; No Settlement Yet

For the first time since the leather strike was called in the North Shore district, more than three weeks ago, police on duty in Peabody were forced to use tear gas in an effort to quell uprisings on two occasions yesterday afternoon and again this morning, when strikers menaced workers and strike breakers.

Fresh signs of violence on the part of the strikers came to light last evening with the reports that Atty. S. Howard Donnell, Peabody's first mayor, and former district attorney of Essex county, had been threatened. Last evening Atty. Donnell permit to carry a revolver after receiving a telephone threat on his life. Atty. D the interest Leather com Shoe & Lea has been att strike. The have come a had made it bring conten against offic Police Ch serve Patrolm as bodyguar

SIX TAKEN BY POLICE IN YESTERDAY'S RIOT IN PEABODY STRIKE

Bottles, Bricks and Stones Heaved at Autos ikebreakers; No One Injured; e Trouble at Ipswich

er of a riot- other strike ccurred late strikers let bricks and rrying strike ut of Hardy

hields were missiles and re struck by juries being monstration of five strik- sympathizer. f Chief Ed- more police already has ng near Cox's howed that o fully cope ged forward made their as follows: f 42 Turner had just got through speaking to the strikers who again filled Peabody City hall yesterday afternoon, about refraining from violence, but evidently the strikers had their own ideas as to handling strike breakers and when they lined up on Central street at the junction of Hardy, which runs in back of the B. E. Cox factory, they were all prepared to greet the workers when they appeared.

The first worker to make his appearance was a

Man on a Bicycle

who turned into Central amid some booing but who was not molested However, when the automobile calvacade made its appearance and started up Central street the crowd let loose and the air was filled with flying things and the sound of crashing glass, which was not only due to the smashing of windows and windshields but also to the breaking of milk bottles as they smashed on

LEATHER WORKERS GO BACK TO SHOPS TODAY FOLLOWING AGREEMENT

Strike Which Affected More Than 5000 in 32 Factories Settled When It Entered Sixth Week; Union Is Recognized

As swiftly and momentous as it began nearly six weeks ago, the disastrous strike to the leather industry in the North Shore district came to a sudden end yesterday when striking leather workers at afternoon mass meetings held in Peabody and Lynn voted their approval of the agree business, for if the work had not been cleaned up the employes will be able to start in where they left off.

The strike, which effected upwards of 5000 leather workers and 32 plants in Salem, Peabody, Danvers and Lynn, was settled late yesterday afternoon when the new agreement was accepted ratified the settlement, the workers set up the National Leather Workers Association as an independent union. Locals were immediately organized in Lynn, Peabody, Salem, Danvers and Woburn. Headquarters were established in Peabody.

The National Board of the National Leather Workers Association met in Peabody on July 6, 1933, and elected the following officers: president, Joseph H. Foster; secretary-treasurer, Daniel J. Boyle; and vice-president, Frederic J. Doherty. Joseph F. Massida was the general organizer.

The union expanded. In July 1933, it chartered a local in Wilmington, Delaware. In the late fall, it chartered Local 26, for the nearly one thousand employees of Winslow Bros. and Smith in Norwood. A short, bitter strike followed in Norwood.

Imported thugs beat up pickets and innocent townspeople in the South Norwood area where the leather workers lived. "Their belligerent appearance," the *Norwood Messenger* observed, "aroused great resentment among the strikers and also from many neutral citizens." Company "guards" took over the streets of Norwood. When they were not shoving pickets around, they patrolled the streets in prowl cars, trailing the strikers, seeking to provoke and intimidate them. On December 5, 1933, the *Norwood Messenger* reported: "While women and children fled from the scene, screaming in terror, three carloads of guards from the Winslow tannery yesterday morning engaged in a wild melee on Washington Street, South Norwood. Several heads were broken as the men swung clubs wildly and apparently without care in the selection of their victims."

When the strikers tried to defend themselves, the Norwood and state police swung into action against them. The battle raged over an eighth-of-a-mile stretch. A score of men and one woman were taken to the police station. No company guards were arrested.

Even while the fiercest battle of the strike was being waged by company thugs and police against the strikers and their sympathizers, a compromise pact was signed by representatives of the tannery and the union. The agreement, conceding recognition of the union by the company, was ratified that same evening by the battered but victorious strikers.*

News of the history-making strikes in the Massachusetts leather industry spread to Gloversville, New York. About twenty-one

---

* The demand for increased wages was to be settled by discussion. The scale agreed upon was the same as that prevailing in the Peabody tanneries.

FIRST STRIKE VIOLENCE AT WINSLOW TANNERY

—:—

Workers In Cars And Bus Stoned As They Leave Plant Last Night. Two Men And Girl Bystander Injured. Strikers Issue Statement Setting Forth Their Position.

—:—

With the strike at the local tanneries ready to enter its second week its status remains about the same, with neither the strikers nor employers ready to concede anything beyond their original proposals. In the meantime the first violence has occurred, with one man being sent to the hospital for attention, another man requiring the attention of a physician, and a small girl being trampled and badly cut. The girl is the daughter of a striker.

The trouble of
private cars con
Winslow plant
crowd of

TANNERY STRIKE

—:—

WILD OUTBREAKS MARK STRIKE DAY

UNION IS RECOGNISED AND WAGE SCALE TO BE SETTLED

—:—

Will Probably Follow That Prevailing In Peabody Plants Of Same Type. Plant To Close For Week Preparing For The Resumption Of Normal Production.

—:—

COPS AND STATE
ICE AID LOCAL FORCE

CROSBY DEFENDS POLICY
OF HIRING GUARDS

Blames Manager For Lack Of Protection. Says Chief Suff.
an Hindered By Superiors In Maintaining Order. Men
May Still Return To Work At Company's Terms

en Grounds And Strikers Yesterday Morn-
ts Outbreak In Afternoon Near Tannery.
re Arsenal

Even while the fiercest battle of the whole period was being waged
on Walpole street Tuesday afternoon between state and local police,
and strikers and their sympathisers, a compromise pact was signed
by representatives of the tannery and the union, and the strike came
to an end that evening, when the actions of the union

Norwood Messenger *headlines in November and December 1933 tell the dramatic story of the leather workers' bitter struggle.*

hundred workers were employed in the tanning of leather, about thirty-five hundred in the cutting and making of gloves, besides those that worked at home, and about two thousand additional workers were employed in industries which were very closely related to the glove industry.

When the Massachusetts leather workers struck in March 1933, only about two hundred glove workers were organized into an AFL union.* The tannery workers were not organized at all. There was only one local union in the community which stood out. Its members had the best conditions and the highest wages in the industry. They were the rabbit dressers who dressed skins used in fur-lined gloves. The rabbit dressers had been organized by the Fur Department of the Industrial Union.

* The majority of the glove workers remained aloof from the AFL because they still remembered the strike of 1912, led by the AFL, which they lost because while the cutters struck, the operators remained at work.

In July 1933, Lewis Solomon organized one hundred fifty fur liners into the Industrial Union. They struck for four weeks. Despite the united front of the fur bosses and the glove manufacturers, they won union recognition, a 50 percent increase in wages, recognition of shop committees, and equal division of work.

This victory spurred the tannery workers to organization. Led by Clarence Carr, a militant tannery worker, and assisted by the fur organizer, Lewis Solomon, six hundred tannery workers formed the Independent Leather Workers Union of Fulton County. When the employers refused to meet their demands and declared a lockout, the tannery workers answered with a general strike.

The strike took place in October and November, when temperatures in the foothills of the Adirondacks go down to fifteen and twenty below zero. In spite of these hardships, and in defiance of injunctions prohibiting picketing, two thousand Gloversville leather workers surrounded the tanneries with mass picket lines for eight weeks. They militantly defied gas attacks and clubbings by the police and three hundred sworn deputies.

On November 23, one thousand leather workers and several hundred rabbit dressers and fur liners surrounded the tannery of Richard Young. They held the boss and scabs inside the plant for eight hours. The boss was forced to wave the white flag and sign a truce closing the factory for the duration of the strike.

Tannery bosses spent thousands of dollars in an attempt to break the strike. Full-page advertisements in the Gloversville press denounced the union and the strikers as "Communist." The union invited the tannery bosses to debate the issues in the strike at a public mass meeting with Clarence Carr and other members of the union. The challenge went unanswered.

After eight weeks of bitter struggle, the workers won recognition of the shop committees; an increase in wages ranging from 15 to 30 percent; and the right to collective bargaining. From six hundred members that the union had before the strike, the membership grew to sixteen hundred. The tanneries in Gloversville operated on a union-shop basis, although until 1937 the union functioned as an informally recognized bargaining unit.

Close fraternal ties were maintained between the National Leather Workers Association and the Independent Leather Workers Union of Fulton County.

Fifty-one delegates attended the first national convention of the National Leather Workers Association, representing workers from four locals—Local 20 in Lynn, Local 21 in Peabody, Local 22 in Woburn, and Local 26 in Norwood.

Its first year brought the National Leather Workers Association many victories. It won strikes, and gained new members. It won the union shop in negotiations with the newly-organized employers' association—the Massachusetts Leather Manufacturers Association. Its membership rose to seven thousand.

But already there were serious weaknesses in the union. Little progress had been made outside of Massachusetts. Within the Bay State itself at least sixteen important tanneries remained non-union. South and west of Massachusetts, the union had no influence to speak of. This weakened the union's bargaining position with Massachusetts leather manufacturers who kept prodding the union to "bring up the wage scales in competing districts to a standard more comparable to that of Peabody."

Moreover, the Massachusetts employers paid little attention to agreements. Many members of the National Leather Workers Association were discriminated against in the plants because of union activity.

The influence exerted over the union by Joseph F. Massida, general organizer, was a very serious weakness in the organization. The union's constitution gave Massida considerable power. Massida ranted and raved in speeches against the bosses and the bankers. But in deeds he systematically stifled the militancy of the leather workers. He would allow employers to provoke the workers into ill-prepared strikes, after which he would often hold the strikers back from taking action against the efforts of the bosses to break the strike.

In July 1933, the National Leather Workers Association chartered a local in Wilmington. Within a few weeks, the local was reported to have enrolled eleven hundred members, with five hundred additional applications on hand. Massida came down to supervise the organizational work. He stirred up the workers for immediate strike action, though many urged that a strong organization be built before any demands were made on the employers.

On July 18, a strike was called at the Amalgamated Leather Company, one of the largest kid-leather tanneries in the country. Only three hundred of the eleven hundred workers of the factory joined the strike. The strikers were militant. Massida, however, docilely submitted to police orders that only a couple of pickets be at the mill gates. As a result, scabs came and went freely.

The outcome was tragic. After three months, the union conceded defeat. The strike was called off. The Wilmington local rapidly lost its membership and withdrew from the National Leather Workers Association.

The wave of organization which coincided with the formation of the CIO brought many leather workers into the National Leather Workers Association. In August 1936, Local 27 was organized in Newark, New Jersey. In May 1937, Local 29 was formed in Girard, Ohio.

Both of these locals were born in struggle. The Newark local, headed by the young militant, Tom Galanos, was at one time Branch 80 of the AFL United Leather Workers. In July 1936, while still an AFL local, the union called a strike at A. J. Crowhurst & Sons in Belleville, New Jersey. Although the local had been paying a per capita tax of fifty-five cents per member to the national office of the United Leather Workers, it received no financial assistance from the union during the strike. On the contrary, President W. E. Bryan reminded the local that it had fallen behind one month in its per capita payment since the strike started. Bryan threatened that if the local did not immediately pay its per capita, he would start court action to collect it. Enraged by this indifference to the plight of the strikers, the Newark local pulled out of the AFL.

The Newark local then affiliated with the National Leather Workers Association, which sent down Organizer Massida to help the Crowhurst strikers. He proved to be more of a liability than an aid. After an inflammatory harangue, Massida urged the strikers to return to work, present their demands once again to the bosses, and then, if they were turned down, go out on strike again. The strikers spurned his advice and voted to continue.

On September 2, 1936, the Crowhurst strikers won the first written agreement in the modern history of Newark leather workers. It was a tremendous victory. Before the strike, the workers earned from $10 to $16 for a fifty-four-hour week. Now they received $22 for a forty-hour week and time-and-a-third for overtime.

Local 29 was born in the midst of a sit-down strike at the Ohio Leather Company at Girard, Ohio. Georgia-born Augustus J. Tomlinson, leader of the strike, had been a steel worker and had participated in the great steel strike of 1919. In 1933, he returned to work in a tannery, obtaining employment at the Ohio Leather Company. After a nine-day sit-down strike had demolished its company union, the Ohio Leather Company was ready to negotiate with the strikers. The agreement was the first union contract for leather workers in the entire area.

Following the successful strike, the workers in the plant affiliated with the National Leather Workers Association as Local 29. Tomlinson was elected to represent the local on the union's National Executive Board.

Despite such expansion outside of Massachusetts, the National Leather Workers Association still failed to advance. The locals did not receive adequate guidance from national headquarters to withstand the mounting attacks of the employers. The tanners banded together in regional and national associations with the principal objective of crushing the union.

Company unions were set up in almost every open shop to combat the National Leather Workers Association. The company union at Goniprow, in Lynn, formed in 1934 to break Local 20's strike, was a typical example. Six years later, Joseph Montejunas, president, and Roger McCarthy, secretary of the company union, revealed in sworn affidavits that the so-called "Leather Workers Protective Association" was a front through which the Goniprow Company and the company union each separately obtained injunctions preventing the strikers from picketing. (Officers and members of the National Leather Association were subsequently fined $1,475 under this injunction.) The "agreement" and "by-laws" of the company union were prepared by the company and subsequently signed by company union officials who were not even permitted to read their contents. Union meetings, held on company property and on company time, were dominated by company foremen. Company union elections were engineered fraudulently by company executives. Ballot boxes were stuffed and ballots numbered with invisible ink so that any worker who voted contrary to the employer's wishes was subject to discrimination.

As in other open shops, Goniprow workers were also threatened that attempts at organization would mean shutting down the plant. Workers in the organized plants were continually told that work would be shifted to open shops in other areas. An account in the Winchester press in 1936 gives an example of the effect of such threats: "With the threat of liquidation hanging over their heads, most of the strikers of the Beggs & Cobb tannery in Winchester returned to work this morning. . . . For hours after the conference involving the management, the workers, the union and state and federal labor experts had been concluded, workers in a mass meeting could not decide whether to return or not. But when Edwin L. Fisher, chairman of the Board of Arbitration and Conciliation, announced the company threatened to liquidate unless the men returned to work today, most of them voted to return."

The National Leather Workers Association was powerless to meet these threats. They became entangled in dealings with the State Labor Board, and often found their hands tied in the face of open strikebreaking by the tanners.

In Newark, where a militant leadership existed headed by Tom Galanos, the local was hard pressed to retain its members in the face of repeated lockouts by the employers. Frequent strikes—at least fifty-six strikes and one hundred and twenty-one weeks of shut-down between August 1936 and November 1939—drained the local's resources and made regular dues collections impossible.*

Labor Board cases dragged interminably in the courts while the tannery bosses smashed the workers' organizations. Discharged and blacklisted workers waited for years to be rehired while their cases went through tortured and prolonged hearings and appeals. Company unions were ordered dissolved, but new ones were established by the bosses while appeals from Board decisions piled up in the courts. Most of the union's time and money were consumed in Labor Board cases and appeals.

In May 1937, at its fourth annual convention, the National Leather Workers Association voted to affiliate with the CIO. In joining the CIO, the union looked forward to great advances. Several local unions of leather workers had previously been taken in by other CIO unions.**

* During this period, the local did not enjoy six consecutive weeks without a strike or lockout in one of its shops. Many of these strikes were among the most bitterly-fought of the period, the bosses importing gangsters from New York to aid the police in beating up strikers.

** The Grand Haven and Whitehall, Michigan, Leather Workers local, formerly in the AFL United Leather Workers, affiliated in May 1937 to the United Automobile Workers of America. In a letter to all members of the United Leather Workers, the Michigan workers explained why they had left the AFL union:

"We, the employees of the Eagle Ottawa Leather Company at Grand Haven, Michigan, and of the Whitehall, Michigan, tannery operated by the same company, were forced to go on strike on September 16, 1936. The strike was called because of the employer's, Julian B. Hattan, President of the Eagle Ottawa Leather Company, using discrimination in discharging employees discovered to be members of Local 81 of Whitehall and Grand Haven.

"During the ten-week strike, the only assistance received was $35 from a sister local from the United Leather Workers International Union. Our organ-

In June 1937, imbued with the spirit of the early, militant CIO, the National Leather Workers Association tackled the Elkland Leather Company, by its own admission "the largest sole-leather plant in the world." Elkland, in Tioga County, Pennsylvania, was a typical company-dominated town, controlled lock, stock and barrel by the tannery which employed one thousand of the community's three thousand inhabitants. The Elkland Leather Company, paying an average wage of less than $18 a week, deducted from pay envelopes for bills at the company store, for rent, for electricity (it owned the "Elkland Electric Company" which sold power generated by the tannery itself!), for water, coal, paint and medical services. The company also owned about 108 houses which it rented to the workers. These shacks stood in swamp land, with pools and stagnant water on all sides. A family of four lived in one room with no gas, electricity or water.

For years there had been no organized protest by the workers. In 1933, a young townsman, Lowell Bostwick, returned from beyond the hills with the new, enlightened message of unionism. He spoke to the workers and finally sent for an AFL representative from Philadelphia. On the day the United Leather Workers organizer arrived, the company laid off one hundred men. The next day another hundred men were laid off. The company served notice that it would shut the plant down unless the organization of its workers was abandoned. A committee composed of a banker, merchant and doctor called upon the AFL organizer and pleaded with him to cease his efforts, that the community could not live without the tannery, the town would be in darkness as the plant produced the electric current, etc.

---

izer, Louis J. Hart, of the AFL deliberately placed the future destiny of all our members in the hands of a Citizen's Committee. This committee, having no knowledge of the issues existing between the employee and employer, settled the controversy in the usual Citizen's Committee manner. The settlement made no provision for union recognition or collective bargaining. The organizer recommended acceptance of the Citizen's Committee's settlement. A written copy of the settlement was not submitted to the Local, but was informed, by Mr. Hart, that union recognition had been won and that there would be no discrimination.

"The organizer's explanation and recommendation was accepted and it was voted to declare the strike ended. One month thereafter the local was furnished with a copy of the terms of the settlement only to discover that it had been betrayed. The officers are the victims—they have not been returned to work. The employer made promises in said agreement which he had no intention of keeping."

The organizer finally disappeared, declaring his life had been threatened. Rumors floated through the town that he had been paid off by the company and the citizens' committee. Bostwick was fired.

Early in 1937, the workers again realized that the only way for themselves and their families to achieve a semblance of human dignity was through organization. Word was sent to the National Leather Workers Association for organizers. Led by Lowell Bostwick, the new organizers began the slow, tedious process of setting up a union.

The company immediately showed its claws. Hysterical handbills were plastered throughout the town charging the union with "Communism." If the union gained control, the plant would close down. "And if such occurs, Elkland will become just another ghost town, a wide place in the road that once boasted the largest sole-leather tannery on earth."

On June 26, the men struck for a wage increase, the forty-hour week and union recognition. The strike was solid. The next day the company went into battle. The notorious Burns Detective Agency sent plug-uglies from Philadelphia; local men were deputized. Policemen, deputy sheriffs, foremen and straw bosses began systematic canvassing of strikers' homes. Individual strikers were hustled down to the Justice of the Peace who hurriedly signed them up in the company's Elkland Leather Workers Association, Inc., for anywhere from twenty-five cents up to $3—or nothing if the workers could not pay. The *Philadelphia Record* reported:

". . . Over the week-end more Burns Operatives, crudely disguised in farmers' costumes such as Tioga County never saw before, pulled into town and were sworn in as borough policemen. More deputies were sworn in, and the union charges some of them were company employees, paid by the company.

"Mobs headed by Allen [company union leader] and addressed by Williams [company lawyer] gathered in the streets and threatened CIO men. Sheriff Metcalf [political pal of Senator Owlett, chief counsel for the company] swaggered about the streets, menacing CIO men with arrest.

"Credit at the company store immediately was cut off to the strikers. The company took out of the next pay the entire bill, even in cases where there were agreements that bills be paid off at so much a week. All merchants in town except one quickly followed suit. Threats were made that those strikers living in company houses would be evicted.

"Over and beyond threats of physical violence, the economic pressure was terrific. Most of the employees were in debt to the company store. All a man had to do in the past was to be ill a couple of weeks, or be laid off in a slack season, and he was in the clutches of the company store forevermore. On their pay, few of them ever catch up completely.

"Spasmodic violence flared in the town that week. Six strikers were arrested, and a seventh sought with a warrant. The Sheriff invaded the Backes home, early one morning, though he showed no warrant, and searched every bit of it, including a room in which a young woman and a 16-year-old girl were sleeping.

"The six men arrested were held by Justice of the Peace Irons in higher bail than they could raise. The arrested strikers were put 3 in a cell—in cells with only two bunks so that all through the night one had to stand; it was the beginning of a reign of terror against the men who dared to strike in Elkland. . . ."

Later Elkland learned that the Burns army had been financed with town funds. They had been hired by Mayor W. G. Myers (foreman of the outside crew in the plant) on the ground that an "emergency" existed.*

After fourteen months the strike was broken. Despite the unprecedented terror, the strikers were brave and militant enough. But they were betrayed by their leaders.

One night Bostwick, the National Leather Workers organizer, received a message warning him that if he remained in Elkland his body would be found on a hillside some dawn. The strikers pleaded with their organizer to remain. "Let's go out in the hills and fight it out," they cried. "We want to defend the union. We want to defend the strike. We can win!"

Bostwick ran away. He deserted the strike and the men who had fought so bravely for so many months. The goons and thugs, the stool-pigeons, the scabs and the company union stepped up the attack. The spirit left the strikers. They were starving. Finally, they acknowledged defeat. Many were blacklisted. The others returned to the plant disheartened and disillusioned with unions.

The tragedy of Elkland was a terrific setback for the National Leather Workers Association. It was besmirched by the cowardly

---

* The information was revealed during a Labor Board hearing into charges that the company violated the Wagner Act by using unfair labor practices. The burgess, William G. Myers, first testified that hiring of the Burns detectives was authorized by the borough council. But when it was shown that the Council's books failed to show minutes of any such meeting, Burgess Myers blurted out: "All right. I hired them myself. I have the authority to do it without vote of the Council." Three of the five Councilmen were employed by the company.

betrayal of its organizer. And the incompetent leadership supplied by other NLWA organizers did not sustain the leather workers' respect for the union.

In June 1937, Local 30 began a sit-down strike at McNeely Price in Philadelphia. Militant and courageous, the strikers fought doggedly to win their demands. But the NLWA leadership completely mismanaged the strike. The negotiations and the numerous court actions which arose were poorly handled. The struggle dragged on for over two years until it disintegrated. During this period, the ineffectual strike hampered organization throughout the entire district. As late as April 1939, the NLWA confessed that "until this situation [at McNeely-Price] is cleared up, the Philadelphia area has had a tendency to be held back in organization of leather workers." In his recent study, *Union Policies in the Leather Industry,* the Rev. Leo Cyril Brown points out that the mismanagement of the McNeely-Price strike "became evidence to unorganized leather workers of the inefficiency of the union."

Strong employer opposition in 1938 involved the National Leather Workers Association in costly, fruitless strikes. The union's leadership had never learned the art of settling disputes to the advantage of the workers without resorting to strikes. And the strikes often took place at the time chosen by the employers, not by the workers.

Organizing activity slowed down to a walk. During the existence of the Massachusetts locals, practically no new organization was carried on after the general strike of 1933. Membership declined from nine thousand in 1937 to less than six thousand in 1939. In the six years, 1933-1939, only one general wage increase was won—5 percent.

After six years of existence, the National Leather Workers Association had only eleven locals, most of them in a small area in Massachusetts. Other than Newark and Girard, the rest were paper locals with a handful of members. They were under constant attack by the employers. They had poor working conditions in the shops. They could not defend their members and were losing ground rapidly. Most of the locals could hardly bring a quorum to a meeting. Some had no headquarters. Few, if any, of the officials had any organizational ability. Some were dishonest.

In short, the National Leather Workers Association was rapidly falling apart. It's treasury was practically bankrupt. It was powerless to win improvements for its members. Even in the few organized shops the bosses told the union that they would not renew contracts because non-union shops were creating unfair competition.

Company unions and the spy system kept down the standard of the leather workers. Their wages averaged about sixty-one cents an hour and as low as forty cents in the South. (This average included the skilled workers.) The leather workers knew nothing of paid holidays, paid vacations, minimum rates, reporting-time pay, free boots, aprons and gloves, grievance machinery, job security or health insurance.

The leather bosses accumulated fortunes through their exploitation of the miserably underpaid workers. But the workers were suffering the worst working conditions in the country. Many were forced to kick back part of their meager pay to the foreman or the bosses, to work for nothing in the foremen's and bosses' homes, cutting lawns and doing odd jobs. In many areas, the cellar workers, with a large percentage of Negroes, were regarded with contempt and considered as condemned to a life of miserable exploitation under the most unhealthy working conditions of any industry.

An entirely new day dawned for the leather workers in May 1939. In that month the leather workers merged their organization with the fur workers and became part of the International Fur & Leather Workers Union.

CHAPTER 47

Merger of
Fur and Leather

In January 1938, Newark tannery workers wrote to Ben Gold, president of the International Fur Workers Union, expressing their gratitude "for the time and effort you spent in helping us to negotiate a settlement in the Crowhurst strike, which was in its fourth month when you came to our assistance."

"It was your assistance and cooperation," the letter continued, "which enabled us to end this strike, which began as a lockout, in its fifth month, with better conditions than we had when we were forced out. . . . The bosses at first took a provocative attitude, knowing the conditions of our union and the lack of work in the industry. They quickly changed when they learned that we had asked for and gotten the support of the International Fur Workers Union."

The furriers had always been famous for their aid to other unions. Even in the midst of their own struggles, they found the time and money to aid brother unions under attack. Furriers brought money inside auto plants to assist the sitdown strikers of the UAW. They gave financial assistance to unions in steel, auto, maritime, shipbuilding, farm equipment, packinghouse, transport, furniture, mine, food and many other industries. Most of the new unions organized after the rise of the CIO were assisted in their struggles by the members and leaders of the International Fur Workers Union.

The furriers responded eagerly and gave freely of their time and money to help the struggling leather workers in Chicago, Newark, Brooklyn, Gloversville, Gowanda and other leather centers.

554

"They [the bosses] quickly changed when they learned that we had asked for and gotten the support of the International Fur Workers Union." The word got around to the entire membership of the National Leather Workers Association. The lesson was obvious. When they were backed by a powerful national organization with leadership experienced in organizing, negotiating and strike struggles, the leather workers could force the employers to grant their demands.

In April 1938, on the eve of the fifth annual convention of the Leather Workers Association, Local 21 of Peabody instructed its delegates to urge the union to appeal to the International Fur Workers Union for the merger of the two organizations. The proposal won enthusiastic support among the delegates. They had just listened to a report from the union's national organizer and attorney which had made it clear that the National Leather Workers Association faced the dismal prospect of losing what little it had and being ultimately destroyed by the open-shop employers. The union was so seriously handicapped by the lack of funds that it had not been able to finance proper handling of its cases before the National Labor Relations Board. Small wonder that the delegates endorsed the resolution proposed by Local 21, and voted to invite a representative from the International Fur Workers Union to address their convention.

The idea of uniting the fur and leather workers into one union was not a new one. As far back as 1917, the Fur Workers Union had raised this question with the AFL. Since many operations in dressing and tanning shops were almost identical, amalgamation would make it possible to solve both jurisdictional and organizational problems in a way that would strengthen the position of the workers in both leather and fur.

On Sunday evening, May 1, 1938, the regular order of business at the convention of the National Leather Workers Convention was suspended in order that the delegates might hear an address by Vice-President Irving Potash of the Fur Workers Union. Potash informed the delegates, "We have the finest example of American democracy in practice, a single fraternity of men and women of all races, religions and political beliefs, freely exchanging ideas and sinking differences of religious beliefs and political convictions in a common cause—the betterment of the life and welfare of the fur workers."

He told them of the working conditions achieved by the furriers. Discussing the difficulties facing the leather workers, he declared that the obvious need of the hour was unification, and the launching of a nation-wide campaign to organize the entire industry. The finances of the leather workers' union were insufficient. However, a merger of the leather and fur workers would solve this problem. The proposal, Potash assured the delegates, would be welcomed by the fur workers, for it was a logical extension of the principle of industrial unionism. He proposed that the question of amalgamation be discussed by committees representing both unions.

At the conclusion of his address, Potash was tendered an ovation and a rising vote of thanks. The delegates then empowered the incoming National Executive Board to work out a satisfactory plan for a merger of the two unions and submit it to a referendum vote of all locals of the National Leather Workers Association.

The merger did not come about automatically. There were forces in the National Leather Workers Association who dreaded the idea. Some were afraid of losing the petty jobs they held. Others argued that the leather workers would be "swallowed up" by the fur workers. Still others spread anti-Semitic propaganda and red-baited the Furriers Union.

Meanwhile, the fur workers continued to aid the leather workers in their battles. With the help of the Chicago Fur Workers Union, the tannery workers of Local 43 won their first victory, a contract with the Huch Tannery Company of Chicago. The workers won a closed shop, 10 to 22½ percent increases in wages, pay for seven legal holidays, equal division of work, and one and two weeks' paid vacation.

Fur and leather workers in many centers extended their contacts through joint activities. Leather workers involved in strikes or lockouts appealed to the fur workers for assistance. The leather workers saw that trade union democracy was the every-day practice among the fur workers and not merely a hypocritical slogan to be violated by corrupt bureaucrats.

On March 18, 1939, a joint meeting of the National Executive Board of the National Leather Workers Association and the Sub-Committee of the International Fur Workers Union unanimously adopted a plan for the merger of both unions. The amalgamated organization would have two divisions, fur and leather, each with its autonomous and democratic rights carefully preserved. Each division would elect its own officers, manage its own finances. The executive boards of the two divisions would constitute the full executive body of the combined International Union.

Irving Potash and Daniel J. Boyle, secretary-treasurer of the leather union, went to Washington and presented the merger plan to CIO President John L. Lewis for approval.

On March 21, 1939, John Brophy informed the two unions that the CIO was "very glad to give its full approval to the proposals for the merger of the International Fur Workers Union and the National Leather Workers Association. . . . We feel that this merger will be a great contribution to the organization of the unorganized workers in the industries under the jurisdiction of the enlarged union. Many thousands of unorganized workers, particularly in the leather industry, are waiting and eager for the benefits of industrial organization. . . . Best wishes for a successful career to the new International Fur and Leather Workers Union."

The referendum vote on the merger took place in April 1939. Forty-five hundred members of the National Leather Workers Association in Peabody, Lynn, Norwood and Woburn, Massachusetts, in Philadelphia and Curwensville, Pennsylvania, Newark and Hoboken, New Jersey, and in Brooklyn, New York, cast their votes by secret ballot.* For several weeks before the referendum, the open-shop bosses and their agents deluged the leather workers with stories that a vote for the merger would be a vote for "Communism." In Peabody and Lynn, stooges of the bosses planted a red flag near the headquarters of the union and announced they would replace it with an American flag only if the merger was rejected.

Some of the National Leather Workers Association's local leaders joined in the red-baiting, Jew-baiting and furrier-baiting. They realized that the organization of thousands of leather workers in a democratic, progressive trade union would spell the finish of their jobs and corrupt practices that would inevitably be exposed.

Some leather workers had honest doubts about the success of the merger. But these leather workers were in a distinct minority. In spite of all the red-baiting, in spite of all the attacks and threats, the vast majority of the leather workers stood firm. The majority agreed with the sentiments expressed by one Irish-Catholic leather worker at a mass meeting in Peabody: "I believe that the merger is for the good of the leather workers, and that we should bury all religious and political differences for the greatest benefit of every worker in the leather industry. I have seen the men who represent the fur workers and I am convinced that through their militant leadership in behalf of their membership, they

* Locals 43 of Chicago and 44 of Gowanda, New York, did not participate in the referendum since they had already voted to affiliate with the IFWU and had been accepted by the fur workers' union as part of the International.

are proving themselves to be better Americans than the bosses who force the leather workers to live on the very edge of poverty."

The merger was carried by an overwhelming vote of more than two to one.

On the sixth day of the fur workers' Thirteenth Biennial Convention in Atlantic City, 1939, the Committee on Officers' Reports recommended the merger to the fur delegates. The committee, headed by Samuel Mindel of Local 2, predicted that the merger "will serve the best interests of both the fur and leather workers and will make possible the organization of many thousands of unorganized leather workers, improve the economic conditions of both fur and leather workers, and advance the interests of the entire organized labor movement."

There were opponents to the merger in the ranks of the furriers, too. They led off the debate. They argued that the union could not afford to take away strength from the fur workers and throw it on the side of the leather workers; the merger would strain the union's finances, members would have to pay many taxes and assessments; it would be impossible for a small organization like the Fur Workers Union, with limited resources, to organize the giant leather industry with its million-dollar corporations; Jewish organizers of the Fur Workers Union would not be able to organize an industry composed mainly of non-Jewish workers. If the leather workers had to be organized, they said, let the CIO do it.

"Give the leather workers $25,000 as a contribution," said one delegate. "Your conscience will be satisfied."

The supporters of merger tore these arguments to shreds. "All bosses are alike," Jack Schneider insisted, "no matter if they employ workers on fur garments or in mines or otherwise. . . ."

The argument that Jewish organizers would not be able to organize non-Jewish workers was ridiculous, Abe Feinglass declared. "Outside of New York City, the majority of the members of the [Fur Workers] Union are non-Jewish, and they have been organized through these organizers." Moreover, within the ranks of the leather workers there were plenty of Irish and other non-Jewish leather workers capable of doing organizational work.

"The leather workers are militant workers," argued John Vafiades. "They have not had the experienced leadership that would give them the proper guidance. They did not have the experience that would use proper tactics and strategy in organizing thousands of unorganized workers."

"Let us leave the finances out," cried Howard Bunting of Middletown.

"If we believe in the American labor movement, then there is only one thing left. Forget finances, but mark down in your hearts that you are going to have the spirit and the initiative to go out and organize these workers that they may have the same benefits that we do."

Ben Gold conceded that the problem of obtaining finances to organize the leather industry was important. But the union would find the means to solve the problem.

"Our union is not very large. Financially, we were never rich. But our union is in possession of one kind of precious capital thanks to which we are placed in the category of one of the most powerful organizations in the labor movement. That capital is our great, well-trained, disciplined and devoted membership."

And the leather workers, Gold declared, would add to that "precious capital." "They are as good workers and as loyal trade union men as all workers in this country and just as good as the furriers. They will help you, providing you do the proper work." In turn, organization of the leather workers would strengthen the entire union.

By a vote of 100 to 8, the convention approved the merger. The International Fur & Leather Workers Union of the United States & Canada was born.

The fraternal delegates from the leather workers carried home a vivid memory of how a democratic trade union functioned. They had heard reports dealing with wages and conditions won for the workers, activities and achievements of the organization. At every session, they heard fur workers freely expressing their opinions on each of these issues. Each delegate presented his point of view, whether it agreed or differed from that of the majority. Delegates were repeatedly urged by President Gold to voice their opinions and to voice their disagreements if they had any. Now the fraternal delegates from the leather workers' union knew what Gold meant when he told the delegates: "The greatest achievement of our International is the trade union democracy that we have." Now they knew what Samuel Mindel meant when he said of President Gold at the very opening of the convention: "For two years I have worked on this General Executive Board under the guidance of a leader who is not a 'Fuehrer.' He has demonstrated to me and to every other officer of this Board his sincerity, his honesty, his integrity, his tolerance of every man's opinion, regardless of any political view that he might have."

The convention's decision on the merger was submitted to the fur locals for final approval. Only a small group of Lovestoneites and diehard followers of the *Jewish Daily Forward* opposed the merger. "For our Union to involve itself in new expenses in strange territories is criminal," their leaflets in the fur market charged. The bulk of the fur work-

dent for assistance on the International. For our Union to involve itself in new expenses in strange territories is criminal. Instead of helping the leather workers let us better help our own locals; let us help our own unemployed. But this is not all. We all hope that some day will bring about unity between the A. F. of L. and the C. I. O. These songs of unity were heard loudly at the convention in Atlantic City. But the jurisdiction question which is already the stumbling block to unity will be raised in the case of our own merger with the leather workers and instead of helping unity this merger will be a hindrance to unity.

Fur Workers! demand that we tend to our own business and stop running after new fields. We have

The Forward *group and Lovestoneites who were opposed to unity now cynically denounce the merger with the leather workers.*

ers scoffed at these obstructionists. The locals ratified the proposal by an almost unanimous vote. The merger was now an accomplished fact.

For the first time in their history, the leather workers were in a position to tackle the enormous task of organizing the entire industry. For the first time in their history, the leather workers were part of a powerful national union, big enough, strong enough and experienced enough to see the task through to a successful conclusion.

CHAPTER 48

Laying the Foundation in Leather

Any student of the labor movement must conclude that organizing the leather industry was one of the most difficult tasks ever undertaken by a trade union. The employers were rich, and influential in politics. In many small towns they dominated the whole community, including the banks, stores, public services and city officials. Leather tanneries scattered at great distances all over the country were literally infested with company unions and spy systems. Complaints to the Labor Board were held up by years of red tape.

Ninety percent of the industry was unorganized. Defeat after defeat had been suffered by the leather workers in almost all shops. Militant strikes of the workers had been brutally broken. Blacklists and humiliation still rankled in the memories of the workers. The AFL had betrayed them again and again. Hardly a single tannery existed where an AFL organizer had not at one time taken the workers' initiation fees and then skipped town. Inexperienced officials and some downright crooked organizers had abandoned the leather workers in the midst of struggles. Defeatism and pessimism greeted the organizers of the International Fur & Leather Workers Union in every open-shop plant.

On top of all other difficulties, the new union began its organizing campaign at a time when a wave of reaction was sweeping the nation. The witch-hunting Dies Committee was snooping into unions. "Shackle organized labor!" was the cry of big business and the controlled press. From poll-tax Congressmen and stooges of monopolies came the hue and cry against unions. Anti-labor bills filled the Congressional hopper. The De-

561

partment of Justice prosecuted union leaders, among them furriers, for violating "anti-trust" laws. And an economic recession again gripped the country, with many factories shut down or working part time and thousands of leather workers unemployed.

No other union wanted to undertake the job of organizing leather. Practically the whole labor movement had concluded it could not be done. Some union heads even told the IFLWU organizers: "Don't spend your money. Don't waste your energy. It's impossible!"

The more difficult the task was, the more determined the fur workers' leaders were that the job *must* be done. No great fund was on hand, but enough was available to make the start. Far more important was the tremendous wealth of experience and ability accumulated by the fur workers' leaders and organizers in the course of twenty years of continuous struggles. Steeled and tested in great battles, they had proved themselves able to surmount incredible odds and emerge victorious. They were masters of organizational and strike tactics. They enjoyed the confidence and support of a trained army of union fighters—the furriers. The democratic union they built rolled up new strength with each new member. And included in all their calculations was the deep-rooted conviction that with their help and guidance there would emerge from the ranks of the militant leather workers themselves new leaders of the union.

The campaign to organize leather began slowly. Pending strikes had to be brought to a successful conclusion. Expiring agreements had to be renewed with improvements without permitting the employers to force unnecessary strikes upon the union, if possible. Cases before the Labor Board and the courts had to be fought through. And most important of all, a new approach was needed to organize the open shops, methods and organizers that would convince the oft-disillusioned tannery workers that this union was going to do the job.

President Gold, the Executive Board and the staff of organizers mapped out the campaign, step by step. Within a few months, the first results of the merger could already be seen.

"The merger is already bearing fruit," Thomas Dino, president of the Hoboken Leather Local 34 wrote to Gold on July 4, 1939. With the help of Organizer Myer Klig, the bitterly-fought strike against R. Neumann Leather Co. of Hoboken was ended with an agreement providing exclusive bargaining rights, an increase of $2 on the minimum wage scale, five legal holidays with pay, a forty-hour week, and other improvements.

The Surpass agreement was renewed in Philadelphia, covering over nine hundred workers, and automatically doubled the union membership. The employer's demand for a wage cut was defeated. Nevertheless, the local was told that unless competitive shops were organized and paid the same wages, Surpass would not deal with this union again.

The Swoboda agreement in Philadelphia was renewed shortly after, on the same terms as Surpass. An agreement specifying the preferential union shop was signed between Local 30 and the Dungan-Hood Company on November 1, 1939, following a Labor Board election in which the majority of the workers voted for Local 30 as their sole collective bargaining agency.* Two months later, Local 30 won an election at Hubschman's despite intimidation of the company agents who spread rumors that the company would close up the plant and that every worker would lose his job. With Frank Brownstone in charge of the drive, the Hubschman workers gave Local 30 a two to one majority. The union agreement signed early in 1940 ended an open-shop record at the plant of over fifty years.

With the help of organizer Abe Feinglass, the Kittel strike in Chicago was settled with a 10 percent wage increase, closed shop, forty-hour week and other gains. This marked the first successful leather strike in the Chicago area in more than thirty years.

With Klig's assistance, the Brand agreement was concluded in Brooklyn with a 5 to 14 percent wage increase, forty-hour week, time-and-a-half for overtime, and other improvements.

The Huch Leather Co. of Chicago attempted to provoke Leather Local 43 into a premature strike. A short time before the contract expired, the company discharged a worker without just cause. A month before the expiration of the contract in September 1939, the company notified the union that it would not agree to the same terms and would sign only an open-shop contract. The firm stopped soaking hides. With thirty more days of operation under the contract, the company expected to complete

---

* Local 30 also defeated the attempts of the almost defunct AFL leather union to undermine the IFLWU agreements. The decision was handed down by the Philadelphia Common Pleas Court, May 7, 1940, dismissing the AFL application for an injunction against Local 30 and against the Dungan-Hood Company, which was under contract with Local 30. After reviewing the facts that Local 30 had twice won Labor Board elections in the Dungan-Hood plant and that the contract in effect in this shop was in full accord with the law and with trade union usage, the court dismissed the case and placed the burden of paying all court cases upon Local 64 of the AFL United Leather Workers Union.

all work in process, lay off more workers each week and effect a complete lockout when the month was over.

Guided by Abe Feinglass and Lew Goldstein, Local 43 telegraphed the firm that the discharge of workers and cessation of operations were violations of the agreement. Unless the company agreed to an immediate conference, the union would feel free to take action to protect the interests of the workers. The wire gave the employer exactly one hour to make up his mind.

Its plan upset by this prompt union action, the firm agreed to an immediate conference. A new agreement was concluded after three successive days of negotiations. The discharged worker was reinstated with back pay for time lost. A two-year closed shop contract was concluded, providing wage increases of 6 to 20 percent, forty-hour week, time-and-a-half for overtime, double time on Sunday, one week vacation with pay and other improvements.

A core of loyal, experienced, hard-working and self-sacrificing organizers under the direct supervision of Ben Gold, carried the union's message from one end of the country to the other, from leather center to leather center. Myer Klig, Frank Brownstone and Abe Feinglass constituted the leaders of the staff in the field. Day and night, six and seven days a week, they devoted their time and energy and organizing ability to help break the chains of fear and intimidation with which the open-shop companies bound the leather workers. They built strong and active locals which were in a position to speak for all the workers in the industry.

To this leading staff was added a group of young, new organizers, picked wherever possible from the ranks of the workers in the shops. Their weekly pay was low. Expense accounts were sharply limited. Their work was hard, sometimes actually punishing. But they stuck to the work with a zeal that could only come from sincere devotion to the workers. Gold and the other union leaders knew that it would take time to build a capable, experienced organizational staff in leather. A new organizer who showed promise was patiently taught by the more experienced members of the staff. And as in fur, the union leadership insisted that every leader of the leather division, from the local organizer to the highest official, had to be honest and incorruptible.

Shortly after the merger, the union received letters from many leather workers and small-businessmen accusing Joseph F. Massida, former organizer for the National Leather Workers Association now working in the IFLWU's leather division, of borrowing money while in the field. At its October 1939 meeting, the Executive Board of the Leather Division elected a committee of its own board members to investigate these complaints. The committee made a personal investigation in the Hoboken-Newark area and in the Elkland area, obtained numerous affidavits and presented its report to the next meeting of the Leather Division Executive Board. The Board decided unanimously that Massida had conducted himself in a manner unbecoming an officer of the union and discharged him from his duties and position in the union. It gave Massida thirty days' time to make arrangements for complete repayment. "There is no room in the Leather Division of the International Fur & Leather Workers Union or in the trade union movement," the Executive Board announced, "for such persons who betray the trust and responsibilities imposed in them by the membership of the union."

The action taken in the Massida case convinced many leather workers that the Fur and Leather Workers Union was honest, progressive and democratic. It helped to win their confidence and trust.

The leather bosses tried frantically to stop the organizing drive. They reorganized their old company unions. When IFLWU organizers appeared on the scene, they suddenly became very generous and gave the workers a few more pennies. Their paid agents and the anti-labor press circulated vicious rumors and red-baiting propaganda against the union. They threatened to shut down their plants and go out of business.

These anti-union tactics failed to stop the IFLWU's forward march. One after another, leading open-shop citadels toppled before the organizing drive. The example of Worcester richly illustrates the skill, perseverance and sound organizing methods used in surmounting all obstacles faced by the union drive. In August 1939, Frank Brownstone began organizing the workers of Graton & Knight Leather Company in Worcester, Massachusetts.

Worcester was an industrial city of about two hundred thousand population. Major industries in Worcester and the surrounding areas—steel, wire, fabricated metals, machine building, textile, shoes, leather, grinding abrasives, envelope manufacturing, etc.—employed thousands of workers. But most of the Worcester plants were unorganized. CIO unions such as steel, textile, shoe, clothing, mine and toy workers, and AFL building trades and ladies' garment workers unions had attempted organization in this area, but few had attained any substantial degree of success. Strikes were broken and the unions compelled to retreat. Since 1910 there had not been a major strike won in the city, and the total trade union membership in this huge industrial community was less than seven thousand. Throughout New England, Worcester was known as an open-shop center.

Graton & Knight produced processed and finished leather, belting, shoe welting, hydraulic packings, washers, casings and other leather products for industrial use. The firm had been in business since 1851. It had subsidiaries in London, England; Hamilton, Ontario; and Milwaukee, Wisconsin. It had a capital of over $4,500,000. During the First World War, Graton & Knight had employed as many as twenty-five hundred workers manufacturing exclusively for the United States Government. In 1939, it employed about six hundred workers in Worcester.

The company had never been organized. In the last attempt at unionization in 1921, an ill-starred four-week strike failed. About half of the workers employed in 1939 had been in that strike and the memory of that bitter defeat still lingered. To overcome the pessimism felt by many workers and to safeguard against premature exposure and consequent company discrimination, Brownstone adopted methods directly contrary to the inflammatory soap-box speeches of Massida.

He contacted the first workers in their homes, one by one. After a number of interviews, Brownstone gradually overcame their hesitation, broke down their pessimism and won their confidence. Each time he visited Worcester, new contacts were made. Small groups of workers were brought together in meetings. An organizing committee of the workers themselves was set up. In a few weeks, as the circle of organization grew, a local union organizer was put on full time. Through meetings of small committees and groups of contacts, sentiment for unionization was developed. Committees were set up for each department. Special attention was paid to key departments and those where the greatest resistance was encountered. Every phase of the work was carefully planned. Nothing was left to chance. The workers saw that an experienced organizer was guiding them, backed by a strong national organization.

Hasty actions were avoided. Not even a leaflet was issued in the beginning of the drive. When it was possible to bring ten people together, they met secretly in the local organizer's home. The next time, they met in a fraternal club. The next time, they rented a larger club hall.

After twenty-five workers were signed up, an organizing committee of these workers was set up to do house-to-house canvassing at night. It took courage to do this in Worcester, but the workers were learning and were acquiring confidence in the union. Special language committees concentrated on each nationality. Finally, when the union felt itself well-entrenched, editions of the leather section of the *Fur & Leather Worker* in different languages were distributed in front of the plant and in a house-to-house canvass.

In the short period of two months, the overwhelming majority of the workers in the plant had joined the union. Public mass meetings were held, and the union aroused so much stir among the workers in the plant that the company was no longer able to single out a few leading militants for discrimination.

To counteract the union, the company announced a 5 percent wage increase. The union made capital of this increase as the first gain won by the union, pointing out how much more would be gained with a union contract. The enthusiasm and confidence of the workers grew rapidly.

On October 4, 1939, Local 46 of the International Fur & Leather Workers Union was officially chartered, already a functioning local union. In mid-October, the union formally proposed a collective bargaining conference. Knowing that the majority were already in the union and that more were joining daily, the company shrewdly did not challenge the union's right to represent the workers. Had it done so, the union would have won an election by such an overwhelming vote that its bargaining position would have been even stronger.

Just about this time, in response to an appeal for organization from shops in the Atlantic Seaboard area, Organizer Frank Brownstone was assigned to launch the leather drive in Philadelphia, Camden, Wilmington and other cities. When the conferences began with Graton & Knight on October 27, Myer Klig came in to conduct the negotiations.

The conferences between the union and Graton & Knight turned into an epic of labor negotiations. For eight months negotiations went on, in the course of which it became apparent that company representatives were bent upon provoking a strike before the union had fully mobilized and prepared the workers. That this scheme—not at all unusual in leather industry history—backfired, was due largely to the skill and understanding of the union spokesman, Myer Klig. The union's policy was first to exhaust every possible effort to reach a peaceful settlement. If a strike became necessary as a last resort, the workers must know that all peaceful efforts had failed and must be fully prepared to fight it out on the picket lines as the only way left to them.

Jay Clark, the attorney for Graton & Knight, had been the negotiator for the employers in the 1937 strike of the steel workers against Reed &

Prince of the same city. Clark's own "court stenographer" had recorded minutes of every word spoken during the prior negotiations. When the steel workers struck, the company applied for an injunction. Attorney Clark produced minutes of a supposedly derogatory remark about courts made by a provoked union official during negotiations. The injunction was granted. The picket line was broken by police armed with full equipment. The strike had to be called off.

Understanding on points in the Graton & Knight agreement that could have been reached in a few hours, required days, weeks, even months of grueling argument and negotiation. And Mr. Clark's stenographer took down every word.

Despite every calculated attempt by the company and its attorney, Klig refused to be provoked. Month after month negotiations went on, with conferences every few days. Gradually, through the sheer inexhaustible patience and perseverance of the union negotiators, a few preliminary points were agreed upon. These included recognition of the union; job security and seniority; forty-hour week; time-and-a-half for overtime; double time for Sunday work; one week vacation with pay; reopening after six months; and other points.

But even with these concessions, the Graton & Knight workers still had no written agreement. At a conference held in May 1940, the union proposed that a clause be inserted that veterans from the shop retain seniority and be re-employed upon their return. Clark insisted that ex-servicemen be re-employed only if there was sufficient work and if they could prove they were still efficient and able.

Clark's arrogance aroused the workers. Many of them were veterans of the First World War. They took the veteran issue into veteran organizations and to the public generally. They demanded disbarment proceedings against the attorney for trying to undermine the rights of veterans.

Meanwhile the union mobilized the workers for a final showdown with the company to put an end to the stalled negotiations. Confronted with a fully-aroused membership, after eight and one-half months of stalling, Graton & Knight finally signed the agreement with the IFLWU on July 12, 1940.* At the insistence of the union representatives, the company posted a notice the same day putting vacation with pay into effect for 1940. The Worcester agreement was the first in the country obtained by any union which protected the serviceman.

* In March 1941, Local 203 of the IFLWU organized a subsidiary of Graton & Knight in Cudahy, Wisconsin—the Scherer Leather Co., employing 250 workers.

Leather Merger Ratified

Leather Local 34 Wins 14-WeekNeumannStrike

Hoboken, N. J.—After a bitterly fought strike of 14 weeks against the R. Neumann Leather Co., an agreement providing exclusive bargaining rights, an increase of $2.00 on the minimum wage scale, 5 legal holidays with pay, a 40-hour week, and many other important provisions was won by the Hoboken Leather

Convention Decisions Backed By 45 Locals; Gold Hails United International

New York City--"The almost unanimous endorsement of the Convention decisions by our International locals," declared President Gold in a statement to the
...e of inspiration and encouragement. There is no
...bt in my mind that both the fur and leather workers will
...n a great deal by the merger of the two unions into the In-
...national Fur and Leather Workers Union."

Goniprow Landslide Names IFLWU. 114-18

Lynn, Mass.—In a dramatic climax to the sensational expose of the illegal metho...

Surpass Contract Best Leather Gain

Philadelphia, Pa.—The best agreement in the history of the Philadelphia leather Local 30 and the Surpass ... crew meeting at Lithuania... ment runs until August 1, ... ers employed in the Surpass pl... Outstanding gain of the new...

CHICAGO WINS CLOSED SHOP FROM HUCH CO.

Leather Local 43 Balks Firm's Efforts To Provoke Strike; Sweeping Gains Won By Negotiation

PEABODY SIGNS 9 SHOPS DURING 1-MONTH DRIVE

...eds Organizational

Local 30 Wins Pay Increases At Hubschman

Ayer Majority Chooses IFLWU In N.L.R.B. Poll

U.S. Court Outlaws Greenebaum Co. Union; Orders Reinstatement 3 IFLWU Members With Back Pay

Chicago Upsetting the plans of Chicago...

Leather Local 30 Enrolls Majority At Harvey Plant

Leather Local 30 Signs Two Philly Shops; 10% Raises

Philadelphia—Two ... plants were added to the s... the past month in the orga... Leather Division Conventio... the Densten Hair & Felt an... was announced by Infernal 'stone.
Under the agreement ... ploying approximately 1 ... workers, the union won...

Graton-Knight Signed; Worcester Hails Victory

Worcester, Mass.—After 8 and one-half months of protracted ne... ...ations, the agreem... ...ight Leather Comp... ...nt was hailed by

Philly Signs Dungan-Hood; Pay Boosted

Philadelphia.—A 1-year preferential shop

Goniprow Co. "Union" Exposed By Lynn Local

Lynn, Mass.—The most sensatiol scandal

Typical headlines in the Fur & Leather Worker *from July 1939 to July 1940 show the first gains resulting from the merger.*

The Worcester labor movement had watched the difficult negotiations with bated breath. At numerous times, representatives of other unions urged IFLWU officials to settle for even a minimum agreement, since any agreement would be of tremendous importance to the whole labor movement of Worcester. Up to this time no union had been able to secure an agreement in Worcester. When the contract was finally signed, every union in Worcester hailed it as a source of new hope and encouragement for the local trade union movement. The shoe workers employed at Brown Shoe Company immediately received a contract based on the Graton & Knight agreement. Workers in other Worcester plants demanded similar pacts.

Worcester was an example of how much the leather workers had gained through the merger with fur. Previous leather unions would have been provoked into a strike at a time selected by the employers, and the end would have been tragic not only for the leather workers but for the entire labor movement of Worcester. Brownstone and Klig, working under the guidance of President Gold, cracked this open shop, organized the workers and conducted the most complicated negotiations. They had opened the door for the organization of other Worcester mass production industries.

In the early part of 1940, the union tackled the Goniprow Kid Plant at Lynn. The company union at this plant had been set up to break Local 20's strike in 1934.* Its continued existence was a thorn in the side of the unionized plants in Lynn, Peabody and the surrounding area. To aid the local union in Lynn, President Gold sent in John Vafiades, manager of Greek Fur Workers Local 70 of New York.

After several weeks of intensive work, Vafiades won the confidence of the president and secretary of the company union. He convinced them that the time had come to make a clean breast of their secret connections with the company. The affidavits they submitted on company representatives stuffing ballot boxes, marking supposedly secret ballots and singling out militants for discrimination—exploded the sordid story in huge front-page headlines in the press.

The six-year-old company union was doomed. The workers flocked into Local 20 and gave it a big majority in a Labor Board election. On April 23, 1940, the company was compelled to sign the standard union shop contract with Local 20, a tremendous victory for the Massachusetts leather workers.

* See page 547.

Worcester and Goniprow were repeated in many leather centers. House-to-house canvassing, mass distribution of leaflets, bulletins and the *Fur & Leather Worker,* indoor and outdoor rallies, factory gate meetings, the complete involvement of the members, shop stewards and committeemen—featured the union's organizing drive. Committees of rank-and-file workers from distant organized plants came in to help. The union hammered away at specific grievances in each plant. Workers were signed up; department committees set up to complete the task until big majorities of the plant were enrolled in the union. Only after thorough preparations did the union go into Labor Board elections.

In contrast to the methods used previously by the National Leather Workers Association, strikes were not used as the organizing medium. Strikes were called only when all efforts at negotiating peaceful settlements had failed, and then only after the most painstaking preparations. The skill of the union's experienced negotiators usually prevented lockouts and resulted in satisfactory agreements without the necessity of striking. And every agreement raised wages, established job security and won other important gains for the workers.

In the progress of the organizing drive, the International Union's paper, *Fur & Leather Worker,* played an important role. From the first issue after the merger, the paper was used as an effective organizing instrument distributed at open-shop plants. Meeting red-baiting, anti-Semitism and anti-Negro propaganda head-on, the *Fur & Leather Worker* emphasized in issue after issue that only the enemies of the leather workers benefited from division in their ranks.

The *Fur & Leather Worker* was edited by George Kleinman, a New York fur cutter who had been taken right out of the shop and assigned to this work. Previously Kleinman had been a member of the educational committee of the Furriers Joint Council. In the 1938 general strike, he helped organize the patternmaking shops, stayed with them throughout their strike and assisted them in negotiating their agreement.

The *Fur & Leather Worker* published many thoroughly-documented exposés of conditions in open-shop tanneries, of the slums in which thousands of tannery workers lived, and of health and accident hazards in the plants. In addition, the union paper headlined every union gain, every plant organized, every election won, every strike struggle, and every wage increase.

Monthly organizing messages by President Ben Gold, written in popular style, appeared in the *Fur & Leather Worker.* Thousands of copies

TO THE UNORGANIZED LEATHER WORKER:

For YOU—
and your FAMILY!

THERE is a way out of your difficulties. You can improve your working and living conditions. You can earn higher wages. You can reduce your long working hours. You can secure your jobs. You can stop the speed-up which saps your energy and undermines your health. You can bring more happiness into your lives and into the lives of y...
sive genuine workers' union...

What can you do no...
tory? What can you do r...
What can you do now if...
at the expense of your hea...
boss moves his plant to a...

After a hard week's w...
provide your families with...
submission by bosses and fo...
union officials, company spie...
of losing your job and of be...
you're licked before you s...

The leather industr...
in the country. The tann...
facturers, speculators and...
every year. The leather in...
cent living. You earn it—...

Many times you were...
ion officials. Many times you...
"independent" union politici...
Now the International Fur &...
ing the leather workers. Our...
powerful CIO which organiz...
textile, rubber and oil worke...
ing hours, and freed them f...

WE CALL upon you to jo...
union for all leather wor...
family of millions of organi...
the call of your union. Bring...
of your factory with you into...

In recent months, thousa...
bers of our union. Follow th...

Some of President Gold's messages in the Fur & Leather Worker. *Distributed at hundreds of plants, these appeals played an important part in the successful organizing drives that followed the merger.*

—To The Unorganized Leather Worker—
LOYALTY TO YOURSELF!

THE 450 workers of E. Hubschman & Son's tannery of Philadelphia were never before organized. They were "loyal" leather workers who were kept away from the Union. They wanted higher wages, but couldn't get it. "Loyal" workers are rewarded from time to time—with wage cuts. The workers couldn't help it. They had to shut up and take it—whether they liked it or not.

A few weeks ago, these Hubschman workers joined the union. The union officials and committee...

...g the workers:
...departments;
...s that cannot
...y other gains.

...an AFL union. You didn't
...in charge. You know that
...with the bosses. That's why
...The results of CIO activities

...ers like helpless and de-
...rcy" of the bosses and
...ll such workers "loyal,"

...ars,—too many years. You
...Your bosses considered you

...ou work longer hours! Are
...ges! Do you get legal holi-
...the "loyalty" that kept you

...f and to your family? No
...ves. Even your hard boiled
...ou organize and unite your
...If when you become one of
...ERS UNION. This loyalty
...oyalty" to your boss.
Join the union

To The Unorganized Leather Worker—
YOUR BUDGET PROBLEM

WHAT is your budget for 1940?

During September, October, November and December of 1939 the leather industry was bus... But during January and February, 1940, production fell. Some plants were closed for a few weeks. Othe... worked part time. Now is the time to examine your 1940 budget.

When you work a full week you hardly get along on your low earnings. When you work part time, you're plain out of luck. You can't get along. When the factory shuts down for a few weeks, you... in dire need. Very few lea...

Suppose the leat...
pay your debts and put awa...
part time. How will y...
year to live decently...
How will you manage...
cut amusements. You'...

What do you intend...
against insecurity and star...
dren look to you for their v...

THE only practical answ...
few dollars for a rainy...
ion to fight for you. Unorg...

—To The Unorganized Leather Worker—
DON'T SELL DOLLARS FOR PENNIES!

DID you get your long expected Christmas or New Year's bonus? HOW MUCH? A hundred dollars? I'll bet you didn't even have the courage to think about such a bonus. You would have been happy with a fifty-dollar bonus. You would have compromised for a twenty-five dollar bonus. But you had to swallow much, much less than that. In some shops "kind hearted" bosses gave the workers a five or ten-dollar bill! What help will that be? None! This so-called "bonus" will not help your economic situation.

Just think for a moment and see how impractically unorganized workers manage their economic affairs. If you were well organized, if you had a powerful union, your weekly wage would have been much higher than it is at present. Your wages would be at least ten dollars higher on the average. Assume that you work only 40 weeks a year. THAT MEANS YOU WOULD EARN $400 MORE IN WAGES EVERY YEAR. Union members receive time and a half for were distributed to the unorganized leather workers in front of factories and in homes. These stirring appeals and reports of the union's struggles and victories provided ammunition for the organizers and rank-and-file committees. Much educational and political material went into the *Fur & Leather Worker* to counteract the anti-union propaganda of the commercial press.

Thousands of leather workers joined the IFLWU. The first year proved the merger a bigger success than even the optimists had predicted. In spite of economic crisis and unemployment—when other unions were hard-pressed even to maintain their positions—the Leather Division of the IFLWU made significant gains. The hopelessness and pessimism which had permeated the ranks of the leather workers disappeared. Courage and hope, a new morale and fighting spirit now imbued the membership which more than doubled in a single year. Nineteen leather locals were now in existence, and applications for charters from other localities were already on file at Leather Division headquarters.

All expiring agreements were renewed. The union organized and won agreements in hitherto open-shop tanneries. Thousands of leather workers won substantial wage increases and learned for the first time of vacations and holidays with pay, more sanitary shop conditions, free protective clothing and job security. They acquired a new voice and dignity as befitted free American workers, even in towns formerly notorious for company domination.

The local unions were strengthened and consolidated. Meetings were better attended. More workers were drawn into participation in union activities. Legislative, educational and social activities enriched the life of many locals. In some, women's auxiliaries were formed. Many locals published their own weekly and monthly bulletins.

The union won a number of important Labor Board cases and reinstated discriminated union members with back pay. Company union charges were fought through in the courts. Every Labor Board election in which the union took part was won.

The first year of the merger laid a solid foundation upon which to complete the building of a powerful union in the leather industry.

CHAPTER 49

The Acid Test

As the organizing drive in leather gathered steam, the Furriers Joint Council of New York, the backbone of the International, became the target of a constant barrage of attacks.

An attempt was made to imprison one of the most important, beloved leaders of the Joint Council, Jack Schneider. For ten years, the employers had tried desperately to put Schneider behind bars. Every time a boss was compelled to pay back-wages to his workers, or a "kick-back" racket was uncovered in a shop, or a boss was caught doctoring his books, the word went out—"get Jack Schneider." Parasitic contractors and union-hating employers—all united to "get" Jack Schneider. Fearless, energetic and incorruptible, beloved by the workers, Schneider was a pillar of strength in the union, a fact which was well recognized by the bosses.

Schneider was arrested many times before 1939, but the frame-ups never stuck. Still the employers moved heaven and earth to keep him out of the fur market. After the strike victory in 1938, Schneider was arrested on a charge of "coercion" against a scab during the strike. The prosecution relied on two witnesses. One was an employer whom Schneider had caught forcing his workers to "kick back" part of their wages. The other witness, a worker in the shop whose wages had been repeatedly raised as a result of Schneider's vigilance as business agent, was a Nazi.* He was under the influence of the foreman of the shop, a man who openly

* A few months after Schneider was convicted, this worker committed suicide.

574

proclaimed himself a fascist, and who even had the nerve to appear in the shop dressed in a Hitler storm trooper's uniform.

Five other defendants, active rank-and-file leaders, stood trial with Schneider. They were acquitted.* Schneider, the main target, was found guilty. The sentence was vengeance pure and simple. Coercion, even where true, is a misdemeanor, for which the usual sentence averages three to six months. Schneider was given the maximum sentence, three years. Three of the jurors subsequently informed the judge that although they were completely convinced of Schneider's innocence, a few hold-outs in the jury persuaded them to compromise on what they considered a relatively minor charge of "coercion."

While in jail, Jack Schneider was re-elected business agent of the Joint Council with the highest vote of all candidates—4,723 out of about 5,600 valid ballots—a vote of absolute confidence by the fur workers.

The spearhead of the next attack was the United [Greek] Fur Manufacturers Association. The Greek employers refused to live up to the settlement of the 1938 strike. In addition to violating provisions of the settlement, the United Association applied for an injunction against Local 70 and the Joint Council. In August 1939, the court denied the injunction and upheld the union.

Conferences following the court's decision ended in continued refusal of the Greek employers to sign an agreement with Local 70. In November 1939, when it became evident that further negotiations and conferences were useless, the Greek fur workers struck.

At the same time the Joint Council was engaged in a running fight with the sweatshop contractors. Operating fly-by-night shops, these contractors mainly employed members of their own families who worked day and night, Saturdays, Sundays and holidays, undermining union standards in the organized manufacturing shops. A group of these contractors had banded together under the name of Independent Fur Manufacturers Association.

With contracting outlawed by the collective agreement in the trade, the union refused to recognize these sweatshops or to sign any agreement with them. The so-called Association went to the courts repeatedly in vain efforts to force recognition from the union. Many of the contractors also boasted openly of their connections with the big Association in the trade, the Associated Fur Manufacturers.

* Samuel Mencher, Isidore Gru, Isidore Rau, Morris Lauber, and Alfred Liben were acquitted.

While the strike of Local 70 was going on, and the fight against the contractors became intensified, rumors circulated through the fur market that the government was about to prosecute the union. The old "anti-trust" indictment, issued against the union leaders in 1934, was now being dusted off.* A prosecution was being planned, right in the midst of the Joint Council battles.

Only many months later was it revealed that on June 1, 1939, H. D. Glicksman, lawyer for the Independent Fur Manufacturers' Association, had written to Morris Ladenheim, chairman of the Board of the so-called Association: "Several days ago, I was advised by Assistant Attorney Generals McGovern and Henderson of anti-trust division of New York that when the hucksters indictment is disposed of in July, their office will immediately bring to trial the indictment against Gold and the others who were indicted about the same time as Lepke and Gurrah. This fact was also confirmed by the first assistant to Thurman Arnold, Wendell Birges [Berge] on my recent visit to Washington. *The attorney general feels certain of a conviction against Gold and the others and that this will be sufficient pressure to force the union to give us the agreement we seek.* In the meantime to make doubly sure he is subpoening witnesses to get the facts ready for presentation to the Grand Jury for an indictment against the Union officials under the Sherman Anti-Trust Act. Again I have been assured that we have sufficient basis on which to obtain an indictment. I feel that the fact we have been so active has brought the attorney general's office to the point where they must bring these old indictments to trial as otherwise they will risk serious criticism."

Other sections of Glicksman's report stated that the National Association of Manufacturers "are very much interested in the situation and will give us whatever aid we require in our fight."

The prosecutions predicted by the lawyer for the contractors were soon realized. The six and one-half year indictment under the Sherman Anti-Trust Law was revived against Ben Gold, International Union president; Irving Potash and Joseph Winogradsky, Joint Council manager and assistant manager respectively; Samuel Burt, Joint Board manager; business agents Jack Schneider, Herman Paul, Maurice H. Cohen, Gus Hopman, Sol Wollin and sixteen others.

The fur workers had battled like lions against the Lepke-Gurrah racket in the fur industry. Through the courage of their leadership, the sacrifices

* See pages 412-13.

HARRY D. GLICKSMAN
Counsellor at Law

885 SEVENTH AVENUE
NEW YORK
PENNSYLVANIA 6-8088

June 1, 1939

Morris Ladenheim,
Chairman of the Board,
Independent Fur Mfrs Ass'n

Dear Morris:

Since I was requested to make a report of our recent activities to the committee, and I find that I will be unable to be present due to prior engagements, I would appreciate your reading the following report to the committee:

UNITED STATES ATTORNEY GENERAL'S OFFICE

Several days ago I was advised by Ass't Attorney Generals McGovern and Henderson of anti-trust division of New York that when the hucksters indictment is disposed of in July, their office will immediately bring to trial the indictment against Gold and the others who were indicted about the same time as Lepke and Gurrah. This fact was also confirmed by the 1st ass't to Thurman Arnold, Wendell Birges on my recent visit to Washington. The attorney general feels certain of a conviction against Gold and the others and that this will be sufficient pressure to force the Union to give us the agreement we seek. In the meantime to make doubly sure he is subpoening witnesses to get the facts ready for presentation to the Grand Jury for an indictment against the Union officials under the Sherman Anti-Trust Act. Again I have been assured that we have sufficient basis on which to obtain an indictment. I feel that the fact we have been so active has brought the attorney general's office to the point where they must bring these old indictments to trial as otherwise they will risk serious criticism.

NATIONAL ASSOCIATION OF MANUFACTURERS

This association communicated with us. Due to the fact that they were called to Chicago they promised that they would communicate with us on Tuesday for an app't for Thursday. They state they are very much interested in the situation and will give us whatever aid we require in our fight.

There are other avenues of approach and pressure which we have not as yet exploited. I feel that it is unnecessary to discuss them at this time since we have so many coals in the fire right now.

Let me again thank you fo   he trouble to which I am putting you,
                                                        very truly yours,

The conspiracy between the contractors and the government to railroad the furriers' leaders to jail is outlined in this report by the lawyer for the so-called Independent Association.

of the rank-and-file workers and the martyrdom of Langer, Bolero and Gottfried—the gangsters had been driven out of the fur industry. The public scandal had forced government authorities to take action against the racketeers. And when the Lepke-Gurrah gang was finally brought to trial in 1936, it was these very union leaders who risked their lives to testify against the gangsters in court and put them behind bars. Now, in a period of developing attacks on labor, the union leaders were being prosecuted under the "anti-trust" law.

The Attorney-General, when the matter was later called to his attention, never denied that the attorney for the contractors had been in consultation with officials in the Department of Justice before the shelf-worn indictment was revived. It should also be noted that the case against the IFLWU officials was the first of almost one hundred "anti-trust" indictments against labor unions in the period 1939-1941. The most progressive union in the country had been selected as the first target in the newest all-out drive against the trade unions.

On February 20, 1940, the trial opened in the New York Federal Court. Neither in the indictment nor in the trial were the union leaders charged with price-fixing collusion with employers, racketeering or dishonesty. The sole charge was that the defendants had entered into a "conspiracy" in 1931 to unionize fur dressing and dyeing establishments located in New Jersey. The prize evidence introduced by the government was a circular allegedly found by a police officer in the pocket of one of the defendants, a shop worker, describing the strike conducted by the Industrial Union against the fur dressing and dyeing corporation of A. Hollander & Sons of Newark, New Jersey, during which Natale Bolero and Morris Langer were killed. The alleged circular called upon the fur workers to "refuse to work on fur skins dressed and dyed by scabs."

The carefully prepared prosecution suffered some amazing upsets in the course of the trial. For several hours, William Karpouzas, a government witness, related a gruesome tale of how Ben Gold, Irving Potash and Jack Schneider met with a union committee and urged them to perform hair-raising acts of violence against scabs. His testimony about concluded, Karpouzas suddenly turned to Judge Bondy and declared tensely: "Your Honor, I want to make a statement."

A pounding silence filled the courtroom. Judge, jurymen, defendants, prosecutors, attorneys and spectators leaned forward in surprise.

"I want to make a full confession that my testimony was engineered by Mr. Soulounias and Mr. Whelan [Assistant U. S. District Attorney, and one of the three prosecutors in the case]. It was Mr. Soulounias who brought me here to testify to Whelan. I don't want to be a stooge for anybody in this case."

"Wasn't a stenographer present when I questioned you in the presence of Soulounias?" Whelan angrily asked the witness.

"Yes, but you and Soulounias did all the answering," Karpouzas replied. "Whelan said I should try my utmost to implicate Ben Gold. Soulounias told me again last Friday to implicate Ben Gold as much as I could," Karpouzas continued, turning to the judge.

"So you swore falsely today?" asked Judge Bondy.

"Yes, Your Honor," Karpouzas replied, "but I testified to what I was supposed to. He [Prosecutor Whelan] told me today during the recess to do my utmost to implicate Gold."

This confession exploded in court like a bombshell. Besides the charge of witness-coaching, it exposed Charles Soulounias, who had been twice expelled from the union as a stoolpigeon and had frequently threatened to "get even" with the union leaders. Soulounias was also one of the promoters of the so-called "American Federation of Fur Workers," chartered by the AFL to break the strike of Local 70. The company union he helped found actually signed an agreement with the Greek manufacturers abolishing many working standards that had been built up through years of struggle.

Another government witness spilled the beans on the stand. He was Frank Bader, an employer. He repeatedly accused Jack Schneider of "terrible crimes." When asked to elaborate, he cried: "Every time Jack Schneider came up to my place of business, he asked for money for the workers. If not for Jack Schneider, the workers would not have received such high wages. When I refused to give the workers an increase, Jack Schneider declared a strike." Judge Bondy asked Bader whether Schneider had ever demanded money for himself. "Never," the boss admitted, "he only wanted wage increases for the workers."

Throughout the trial, it became evident that the government authorities were determined to use the anti-trust laws to deprive trade unions of their constitutional right to strike and to organize. A witness for the government, a New York fur manufacturer named Morgan, told the court that in 1933 a strike was called in his shop after he had refused to sign an agreement with the Fur Workers Union. He also stated that approximately 85 percent of his finished products were shipped out of the state. The judge and the prosecuting attorney then held the following dialogue in open court:

Judge Bondy: "I don't see what this has to do with interstate commerce."

Mr. Henderson: "There is a strike and it affects interstate commerce."

Judge Bondy: "Does the government contend that if any man is engaged in interstate commerce and he has a strike, that this affects interstate commerce?"

Mr. Henderson: "Yes."

Judge Bondy: "Mr. Henderson, suppose tomorrow I go into the manufacturing business to manufacture some of these garments that these people make. Do you mean to say that if a labor union leader comes to me and honestly and honorably says, 'We want our union in here and if you can't take our union we will strike,'—does that affect interstate commerce?"

Mr. Henderson: "It does if the strike absolutely cripples his business."

Judge Bondy: "If it does, then every industry in the United States is subject to federal jurisdiction without any conspiracy charge."

Under this theory of the prosecutor, any union that dared to call a strike for wage increases or other improvements in working conditions could be prosecuted under the Sherman Anti-Trust Act. In fact, the mere formation of a union in more than one state would become a criminal act!

It was precisely for this unconstitutional purpose—to deprive the workers of their right to strike—that the union was found guilty. In his charge to the jury, Judge Bondy was very specific.

Judge Bondy: "I will now tell you that I have held these defendants on this theory: that I believe there is evidence in the record, on which the jury has to pass, that in 1931 there was a conspiracy TO UNIONIZE THE ENTIRE INDUSTRY, which conspiracy might have included the dyers and dressers in New Jersey. If in 1931 the jury finds that was the conspiracy, the agreement that they were going to industrialize the whole union, including the dyers and dressers in New Jersey, whom the courts have held to be engaged in interstate commerce, then the fact that they started only local strikes becomes a relevant fact as an act which they undertook to carry out in their conspiracy.

"I will also state that the operation in the court's mind is that the wrong is done when the combination is formed; they need not perpetrate the act on interstate commerce. *If they never did a thing, if they formed a combination that would be sufficient.*"

On the basis of this charge, eleven leaders were found guilty and sentenced to a total of seven and one-half years in jail.* Accepting Mr. Hen-

* The individual sentences were as follows: Ben Gold, 1 year and $2,500

Round-robin telegram sent to President Roosevelt by fur workers, demanding release of their leaders imprisoned on anti-trust charges.

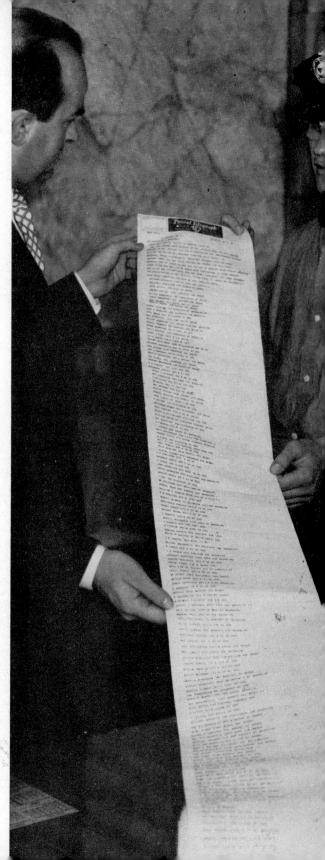

Jack Schneider, framed on an "assault" charge during the 1938 strike, is warmly greeted by his daughter Mona on release.

N. Y. Daily News Photos

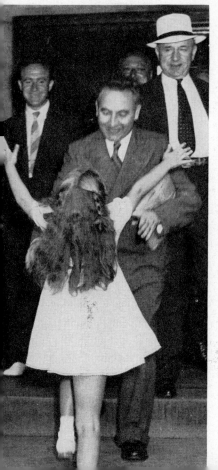

John Vafiades and Irving Potash are greeted by Gold and other leaders of the union upon their release from prison. Fourth from left is Joseph Winogradsky, released a few months before.

derson's demands, Judge Bondy imposed the maximum sentence of one year's imprisonment on four defendants, severe sentences on seven other defendants, and an aggregate fine of $7,000. Bail was set at the high sum of $48,500.

The only leniency shown was in the case of Julius Weil who, a union member in 1933, *had since gone into business*. In this one case, Mr. Henderson asked and the judge granted a suspended sentence. It was a significant commentary on the whole atmosphere of the trial.

During the very same period, a number of gigantic industrial trusts pleaded guilty or were found guilty of real violations of the Sherman Anti-Trust Act. The Drug Trust, Standard Oil of Indiana, and General Motors Corporation were let off with light fines. (General Motors paid a fine of $5,000.) A case against duPont was dropped altogether.*

The trial had not halted the militant strike being conducted by Local 70 against the Greek fur manufacturers. On May 9, 1940, as the new season opened, the Greek manufacturers' association was compelled to sign an agreement with Local 70—the best agreement, in fact, in the history of the Greek fur workers.

Six days later, the government attacked again. This time the union officials were indicted on a charge of "conspiracy to obstruct justice" in the anti-trust trial. In addition to Gold, Potash, Winogradsky and eight other defendants of the anti-trust case, the new indictment also included John Vafiades, manager of Greek Local 70, and four other Local 70 officers and members. The union charged that the "new indictment is apparently the government's answer to the victorious settlement of the six-month strike of the Greek fur workers, marking the complete collapse of the company union backed by the government's stoolpigeon witnesses. . . . Would a new indictment have been issued if the Greek fur workers had lost their strike?" the union asked.

The star witnesses against the union leaders in the second trial were Charles Soulounias, a stoolpigeon, and Leo Loukas, a contractor. Soulounias was the founder of the "American Federation of Fur Workers"

---

fine; Irving Potash, 1 year and $2,000 fine; Joseph Winogradsky, 6 months; Sam Burt, 1 year; Jack Schneider, 1 year and $2,000 fine; Herman Paul, 6 months; Morris Lauber, 6 months; Julius Weil, 9 months and $500 fine (later suspended); Al Weiss, 6 months; Julius Schwarz, 6 months; and Oscar Milief, 3 months.

* Throughout the 50 years of the existence of this law, no employer was ever sent to jail under the Sherman Anti-Trust Act.

which had signed an agreement with the Greek Association. As the trial opened, William Green issued an AFL charter to the "American Federation of Fur Workers." A fitting touch was added in the announcement that the charter would be presented by William Collins, a gentleman whose name evoked bitter memories among fur workers.

At the second trial, four defendants were convicted. The judge refused to grant bail pending the appeal and forced Irving Potash, Joseph Winogradsky, John Vafiades and Louis Hatchios to begin serving long prison sentences as soon as they were convicted.

The fur and leather workers launched a nationwide campaign to obtain the release of their imprisoned union leaders. Progressive Americans, outraged by the denial of bail, responded eagerly. Trade unionists, educators, ministers, civic leaders and thousands of rank-and-file workers rallied in protest against this travesty of justice. One hundred and fourteen AFL, CIO and Railroad Brotherhood officials wired President Roosevelt to urge the release of the prisoners. A delegation of local officials of the International Ladies Garment Workers Union went to Washington with a large petition signed by ILGWU members. The CIO's 1940 convention and other union conventions went on record for the release of the union leaders and pointed out that the union officials "were convicted solely on the testimony of the same known labor spies and anti-union sweatshop employers," and that the right to bail, permitted even to notorious criminals, was being denied to "these militant union officials with an outstanding unblemished record of honest trade unionism."

Ten thousand fur workers signed a telegram of protest to President Roosevelt. Stretching 303 feet, it took Postal Telegraph ten hours to transmit the wire to Washington. The cost of the wire was paid by individual contributions of five cents from each signer.

A gigantic petition bearing the signatures of 100,000 workers from all over the country was presented to President Roosevelt by a delegation of important trade union and civic leaders. Even from far-off Alaska came a petition signed by officials of the Juneau Mine and Mill Workers local.

A delegation of leading women trade unionists, including the wives of the prisoners, visited Mrs. Eleanor Roosevelt to plead for the freedom of the four union leaders.

The union's appeal to the higher courts won a complete reversal on the anti-trust convictions, but the "obstruction of justice" appeal was denied.* Ironically, although the anti-trust indictment was thrown out altogether, Potash, Winogradsky, Vafiades and Hatchios were compelled

* The court did reverse the conviction of Max Kochinsky in the same case.

FROM THEIR PRISON CELLS
POTASH, WINOGRADSKY, VAFIADES, AND HATIOS
ISSUE CALL TO FUR WORKERS!

FUR WORKERS:

We thank all of you for your strenuous efforts to defend us in court against the conspiracy of the bosses, contractors and provocateurs. We are certain that you will continue your efforts to free us from prison. We are convinced that the progressive labor movement will soon take up the struggle against the scum who are responsible for the frame-up against us. The history of the labor movement is full of examples of how stool pigeons and professional scabs were used to frame-up trade unions and union leaders. We are not the first to be jailed because of frame-ups, and, to our sorrow, not the last. In the present critical period, when reaction is spreading throughout the United States, progressive trade unions and their leaders are the first to be attacked by organized labor's enemies. The unprincipled provocateurs now see their best opportunity to knife the labor movement.

thieves and stool pigeons to split our Union - - our Union remained a united, strong and militant organization that carries on the daily struggle for the economic interests of thousands of fur workers and their families.

This is why employers and their agents hate us. They cannot swallow the united might and success of our Union. The employers and their numerous agents don't hide their hatred toward us. They don't even hide their desire to destroy our Union through various attacks and persecutions. This was clearly demonstrated by the fact that while we were busy defending ourselves in court, the Greek Association, together with professional scabs and labor spies, tried to organize a company union in order to weaken and split our organization. THEIR AIM IS CLEAR.

Fur workers, we call upon you to do everything in your power to beat back the attacks up-

to serve prison sentences in the very case that grew out of this trumped-up anti-trust trial.

The victory of the union in defeating the anti-trust case was hailed far and wide by the labor movement. It was a decisive factor in halting the avalanche of anti-trust prosecutions undertaken by the government against trade unions in many industries. Congratulations poured in on the union from all sides.

The commercial press had performed a vicious role during the trial. Many newspapers had the audacity to print that the union was on trial for racketeering, and featured it as "the fur racket trial." These newspapers carefully refrained from telling their readers that the union was on trial because it organized and improved the working and living standards of its members.

On threat of suit for libel, some newspapers were compelled to retract. The *New York Sun,* for example, announced that it wished to correct the idea that the union leaders had been found guilty of "racketeering": "The *Sun* desires to correct any such impression and to state that these union officials were indicted and found guilty only on a charge of violating the Sherman anti-trust law through the calling of strikes for the trade union objective of improving working conditions. The trial of the union and its officials had no relationship whatever to the crime of 'racketeering.' " *

* On July 13, 1942, the *Fur Age Weekly* published its retraction. On September 4, 1942, two years and four months after the libel was committed, the *New York Herald-Tribune* published its retraction. It was buried on an inside

Although practically all the union leadership of New York was tied up in court for months during the various trials, the leather organizing drive rolled on. In the Philadelphia area, in the Midwest, in New England and in Western Pennsylvania—the union organizers toiled day and night. New contacts, new rank-and-file shop committees, new elections, new locals chartered, new agreements with increases and union conditions.

The New England area still constituted the principal organized section of the leather division. And the bulk of the membership here was under a collective agreement negotiated by the locals in Lynn, Peabody and Woburn with the Massachusetts Leather Manufacturers Association. Norwood's agreement was also related to the over-all contract. The collective agreement was due to expire December 31, 1940. A month before, conferences for the new contract began. Following the pattern developed over a number of years, the employers rejected all union demands, prepared to stop soaking (leading to an automatic lockout) and forced the dispute into the hands of the State Labor Board for arbitration. With a strike inevitable, President Gold assigned Organizer Klig to assist the locals in their negotiations. What followed proved the effectiveness of the new methods introduced in the leather division since the merger.

When Klig arrived, conferences had already ended. The State Board had the dispute before it. Klig immediately exposed the employers' maneuvers as an evasion of collective bargaining and compelled the State Board to return the dispute to both parties for real negotiations. At the same time, to forestall a lockout, Klig obtained a written stipulation that all factories would continue soaking of hides during the negotiations. In return, the union guaranteed that in the event of a strike, all perishable stock would be removed from soak and no material would be permitted to spoil. This forced the employers to negotiate in earnest and removed the threat of a lockout which would inevitably result if the employers stopped the soaking of hides.

Negotiations were resumed under Klig's leadership. After many arduous conferences, the union succeeded in winning the best agreement the leather workers ever had. Besides wage increases that totaled $1,000,000 for the two-year period, the union obtained higher minimums, preferen-

page with the small heading: "A Correction." Quite a different treatment from the slanderous story on April 14, 1940, which was displayed very prominently under the glaring headline: "BEN GOLD GUILTY WITH TEN OTHERS IN FUR RACKET."

tial hiring, equal pay for women, reporting-time pay, wash-up periods, free protective equipment and other new improvements.

The entire leather division hailed the new agreement and Klig's role in achieving it without a strike. James J. Chenery, president of the Leather Division, declared it was "the greatest single gain" since 1933 and "indicates the strengthening of our union through organization work carried on since merging with the furriers."

The new method paid off—and paid well.

The Joint Council agreement expired in February 1941. Potash, Winogradsky, Schneider and Vafiades—the most important leaders of the Council—had been framed and imprisoned. To fill the dangerous breach, International President Gold took over management of the Council. Organizer Brownstone was assigned to the Council to strengthen its staff of business agents.

Even as conferences with the manufacturers dragged on without result, the International succeeded in renewing the agreement of the four Hollander locals with wage increases totaling $450,000. The new agreements of the Hollander workers and the Massachusetts leather workers strengthened the position of the union in New York.

The imprisonment of the Joint Council's leadership and the chartering of the AFL union among Greek fur workers emboldened the New York fur manufacturers. They not only rejected the union's demands, but presented counter-demands to cut into the old agreement. The Association arrogantly rejected even a proposal to arbitrate.

February 15, the expiration date of the agreement, came and went. Still no agreement. Their lockout in 1938 having failed, the Association now simply rejected all demands and confidently expected the union to call a strike under conditions favorable to the employers. The union, however, surprised the Association again with a startling new tactic, never before tried.

In 1938, when the fur workers were locked out, the union delayed calling a general strike for seven weeks. The crucial difference in timing helped win the strike that followed. In 1941, relying on the experience and discipline of the fur workers, the union called no general strike at all. At one mass meeting after another, the union alerted and mobilized the membership for a new form of struggle. Working without any agreement, the union enforced all conditions and maintained tight control in every shop. As the season approached and more workers returned to the shops, the union took up the fight for wage increases. Shop by shop, the union negotiated with each employer separately. When an employer refused, his shop walked out on strike. While hundreds of shops won increases, scores of others were on strike. The full pressure of the union's strength was felt by each employer. The Association, however, was left out of the situation completely. It could not dispose of grievances, settle shop strikes, or otherwise aid the employers. Many employers came to the conclusion that the Association could not help them and that they would have to settle with the union.

Without a voice in the affairs of its member employers, the Association became paralyzed. In danger of being frozen out of the picture altogether, the Association agreed to resume conferences. On May 2, 1941, a new collective agreement was concluded with wage increases, higher minimums, a longer period of division of work and other important gains.

On the day scheduled for the membership meeting to ratify the agreement, the union was suddenly notified that the Association members had rejected the contract negotiated by its authorized committee. This was unprecedented in the long bargaining relations between the Association and the union.

The union leadership met this new development with still more unusual tactics. On its recommendation, the workers ratified the employer-rejected agreement for the industry and warned the employers it would be rigorously enforced.

Completely checkmated and unable any longer to control the situation, the Association reversed itself. After another conference, it approved the agreement. A week later another mass meeting of the workers approved the final settlement.

The fur workers and their leadership had passed the acid test with flying colors. The imprisonment of its most important leaders had not stopped the Furriers Joint Council from marching ahead and winning the best agreement in its history to that date. In June of the same year, the fur workers re-elected all their imprisoned leaders with the highest vote in any election—a moving demonstration of loyalty and confidence.

When Potash, Schneider, Winogradsky and Vafiades emerged from prison, the fur workers received them like heroes, and carried them on their shoulders through the streets of the fur market in triumph.

CHAPTER 50

Building the Structure
in Leather

"Our main problem during the past year," Ben Gold told ninety-seven delegates from nineteen leather locals at the first convention of the Leather Division in April 1940, "was to break through difficulties and lay down a solid foundation upon which to build the union. This has been accomplished. The foundation is ready. Our next task is to build the structure." In the next four years the structure was built.

Waukegan, Illinois, was an open-shop town. The Fan Steel sit-down strike in 1937 had been crushed. Countless organizing drives by the AFL and CIO had been defeated. Waukegan could boast about its native son, Jack Benny, the film and radio comedian, but not about unions.

The Griess-Pfleger tannery in Waukegan employed about six hundred workers, white and Negro. It had once had a company union. The AFL had also come in and chartered a local which got nowhere. The CIO Amalgamated had tried to organize the plant but failed. Under the direction of Abe Feinglass, IFLWU organizers launched a whirlwind drive and signed up a majority in two weeks. The stagnant AFL local dropped out of the picture. Its charter members joined the IFLWU. The plant was organized before the company officials knew what was happening.

In a Labor Board election, IFLWU Local 204 won by the landslide vote of 513 to 43. When the company rejected the union's demands after long negotiations, the Griess-Pfleger workers voted almost unanimously to strike.

587

In accordance with the union's firm policy against any form of sabotage of work or damage to material in process even during strikes, the Waukegan local sent enough strikers into the plant for several days to remove $35,000 worth of leather from soak and get it into a non-perishable state. This action won wide support for the strikers from the public, including the town's two newspapers.

The strike went on for five weeks. Waukegan witnessed a new example of trade union militancy, unity and discipline. Negro and white strikers established a twenty-four-hour picket line, elected picket captains, opened a strike headquarters and set up a soup kitchen. The strike staff was headed by Abe Feinglass and, besides other IFLWU organizers, included Negro and white rank-and-file workers from the shop. The Negro workers saw by actual deeds that the union's policy of full equality for all members regardless of race, creed or color was a reality and not the all-too-usual lip service.

Fur and leather locals in Milwaukee and Chicago pitched in with funds, pickets and aid in the soup kitchen. Trade-union leaders in the area gave full assistance to the strikers. Local merchants donated 80 percent of the food for the strike kitchen. The strikers dug in for as long as it would take.

After a seventeen-hour conference in the Mayor's office on May 23, the strike ended victoriously with a general wage increase of seven cents an hour; one week vacation; free boots; forty-hour, five-day week; time-and-a-half for overtime; and many other important gains. New minimums gave some workers increases as high as thirteen cents an hour. It was the first successful strike of a labor union in Waukegan, paving the way for unions in other industries.

A few months later, the union conducted a militant strike of the Gardner pocketbook workers of St. Louis. The 120 strikers, most of them young girls, were slugged on the picket lines by squads of police—that in many cases outnumbered them two to one—so brutally that many had to be taken to the hospital for treatment. The terrorism used against the girl strikers became a national issue. In the seventh week of the strike, an agreement was reached providing for union shop and wage increases of from $2 to $5 per week.

Led by Abe Feinglass, indefatigable director of the Midwestern district, the union organized tanneries which had been open shops for decades.

The key center in the Midwest was Chicago. At the time of the merger only a handful of the workers in this big leather center were union members. The first important break in the Chicago open-shop chain was the organization of the Monarch tannery in the fall of 1941. Employing about five hundred workers, Monarch was organized and an election was won after an intensive four-week drive. After two weeks of negotiations, Local 43 concluded an agreement with Monarch, the first union agreement with a big tannery in Chicago.

In the months that followed the Monarch victory, Local 43 organized and won contracts at Hoffman-Stafford, Superior Tanning, and Guttman's, all important plants. The agreements brought wage increases, paid vacations, shorter hours, and vast improvements in working conditions. Discrimination, intimidation, and vicious company-union systems were ended. The nightmare of open-shop conditions was ended for the workers in these tanneries.

Local 43 went on to organize the huge plant of Chicago Rawhide Co. To overcome the difficulties involved in the organization of this open shop, the union carried on the most energetic and spectacular campaign. Regional Director Abe Feinglass, Organizers Frank Mierkiewicz, Robert Herbin and Lew Goldstein, and Board member Benson Burns, worked day and night for many months. Over one hundred thousand pieces of literature were distributed at the plant's gates. Special radio and sound-truck broadcasts featured the organizing drive. The pace was grueling, but the results fully justified the effort. Chicago Rawhide workers voted overwhelmingly for the IFLWU. And the AFL (the Rubber & Plastics Local of the Wine & Distillery Workers Union) was snowed under with only one vote out of every twenty-four cast.

"As Boyne City goes so goes the north country"—was the slogan of the leather workers as the drive started at Michigan Tanning early in 1941. Immediately the company circulated rumors that if the union came in it would move the plant to a section where there would be no labor trouble. Thirty-two men were summarily laid off. Management and foremen resorted to every means of coercion and intimidation. But the workers voted more than two to one for the IFLWU. In the same company's plant in nearby Petoskey, the workers were not long in following suit.

In the same manner, the IFLWU planted its banner firmly in Sault Ste. Marie, Michigan, where eight hundred Northwestern Leather workers of Local 223 won their first union agreement; in Fond du Lac, Michigan, where Local 360 organized the Fred Rueping Leather Co.; in Cincinnati, Ohio, where Local 214 organized American Oak Leather Company; in Milwaukee, Wisconsin, where the IFLWU broke wide open the biggest open shop in Midwest leather with a smashing victory at Greenebaum; in Sheboygan, Wisconsin, where Leather Local 325 organized the Armour Tannery.

The AFL's feeble contract with the American Oak Leather Company in Cincinnati had been in effect for six years with no substantial benefit to the workers. The highest wage minimum at the plant was forty-four cents an hour. The IFLWU swept a Labor Board election and within a few weeks obtained a blanket increase of ten cents an hour, a huge jump in the minimum scale, and other important benefits. Subsequent increases pyramided the wage rates to triple their former levels.

The successful organizing drive at Greenebaum in Milwaukee climaxed an eight-year struggle for collective bargaining by these workers. Back in 1934, a strike was broken and hundreds of workers fired. In 1938, another union tried unsuccessfully to organize the plant. Hundreds more were discharged.

As the IFLWU organizing drive took hold, the company gave five increases of 5 percent each, plus a holiday bonus on Thanksgiving Day, to keep the workers out of the union. Meanwhile, the union fought through and won a case in Federal Court, enjoining the company from discrimination against workers for union activity.

A new spirit of militancy and confidence imbued the Greenebaum workers as a result of the IFLWU drive. Volunteer organizing committees of militant workers were set up in key departments. The company retaliated by discharging some of the most active union members. Two of the latter, Ed Bobrowicz and Walter Black, a Negro, were put on the IFLWU staff to work with Organizer George Bradow, Local President John Churka, District Director Abe Feinglass and Leather Division President Augustus J. Tomlinson. The drive was speeded up until it reached fever pitch.

The brilliant work of the organizers, and volunteer committees of men and women, Negro and white, young and old, culminated in a two to one vote for the union in August 1942. The organization of this open-shop citadel, the largest tannery in the Midwest, was acclaimed by the entire labor movement in the Wisconsin-Illinois area.

As Ben Gold had predicted with such foresight at the time of the merger, from the ranks of the leather workers themselves had emerged organizers and volunteer workers to unionize the open-shop tanneries. Scores of Greenebaum volunteer workers, working under the guidance of experienced organizers, made the victory possible.

IFLWU Local 325 celebrated its landslide election victory at the Armour Sheboygan Tannery with a mammoth parade on August 25, 1943, followed by a meeting of six hundred leather workers in the Armory.* It was the first CIO victory in the community. Top officials of the union addressed the spirited rally, including Gold, Tomlinson, Feinglass and Leroy Gartman, secretary of Local 325 and member of the City Board of Aldermen.

Sheboygan's Mayor, Dr. William M. Sonnenburg, was moved to say at the meeting: "It was without doubt the largest demonstration of labor solidarity shown in Sheboygan in a decade. You call it a victory parade and you call tonight's meeting a victory meeting. And so they are. You have been victorious in setting up the first large union in the CIO in Sheboygan and you did it overwhelmingly; and you did it in a quiet and dignified manner . . . I know your leaders here and know them well. They obtained their experience in public relations and in leadership by serving their wards in the Common Council. This in a measure explains the confidence of the members of your organization in their leaders. As long as your leadership remains in the hands of such trustworthy and capable persons your organization will continue to be strong, prosperous and progressive."

In the short space of four or five years, the Midwest District was built. Instead of just the one functioning local in Girard and a handful of members in Chicago, the district now consisted of eighteen local unions covering thirty-five shops in nine states. Functioning organizations existed in Chicago, Waukegan, Milwaukee, Sheboygan, Detroit, Boyne City, Petoskey, Sault Ste. Marie, Holland, Alpena, Girard, Cleveland, Cincinnati, Indianapolis, Ashland, St. Louis, Red Wing, and Hazelwood.

A staff of competent, experienced organizers was developed in the process. In addition to its capable District Director Abe Feinglass, and fur organizers like Lew Goldstein and George Bradow who contributed greatly to the organization of leather, the staff now included Bob Herbin, Cliff Johnson, Frank Mierkiewicz, John Churka, Ed Bobrowicz, Phil Parr, Harold Shapiro and other able leaders. In addition, Augustus J. Tomlinson, president of the Leather Division, had moved to the important center of Milwaukee and was devoting his full time to the organizational work in Wisconsin and other areas in the district.

* The vote rolled up for the IFLWU was 602 to 46 against with 4 void and only 15 workers in the entire plant not voting. The Armour Sheboygan Tannery was the sixth successive Armour plant organized by the IFLWU.

At the time of the merger, the Leather Division had only four small locals in the Eastern Seaboard area—Local 30 in Philadelphia, a one-shop local in Hoboken, a good local in Newark organized by Tom Galanos but constantly beset by strikes, and a small local in Brooklyn. The bulk of the leather plants in the area were unorganized. The few organized shops were under constant attack by their employers.

The key to the district was Philadelphia, one of the largest leather centers in the country. Surrounded by open shops and led by thoroughly incompetent officials, Local 30 was struggling ineffectively to remain alive. A futile two-and-a-half-year strike without strikers was still technically going on at McNeely-Price. A $5,000 judgment hung over the heads of the local members. Such apathy and discouragement had set in that a quorum could not be mustered for local meetings or even for Executive Board meetings.

District Director Frank Brownstone came in to launch an organizing campaign in the Philadelphia area. He established contact with the workers in the shops only after innumerable difficulties. The petty bureaucrats in the local's office had been opposed to the merger. They regarded the influx of new workers into the local as a threat to their own positions as paid officials. And one, Charles Majerik, the chief red-baiter, was later caught stealing money from the local's treasury. Majerik agitated against the International and engaged in red-baiting and anti-Semitism to cover up his stealing. Finally, he withheld per capita payments.

When finally apprised of Majerik's sabotage, the membership of Local 30 stripped him of authority to sign checks or handle union funds. A certified public accountant was brought in to audit Local 30's books. He reported that $3,000 of the union's funds had mysteriously disappeared, that many receipts had never been recorded in the books, and that even funds contributed by the leather workers for gifts to the local's servicemen had been embezzled by Majerik. Arrested, Majerik admitted the charge and was sentenced to eighteen months in jail. As innumerable cases bear out, he was neither the first nor the last red-baiter that turned out to be a crook.

Meanwhile, overcoming the obstruction of the two local officials, the organizing drive got under way. A new spirit gradually permeated the workers in the organized shops. They began to attend union meetings. A new active leadership and a group of volunteer organizing committees was developed. Members of the local carried application cards with them constantly. They visited leather workers at their homes and contacted unorganized leather workers through churches, fraternal organizations, clubs, and other groups. Agreements at Surpass, Hubschman and Dungan-Hood were renewed with wage increases and other improvements.

New members were won every day. Workers from Burk's, Houghton's, Densten's, Keystone, Brodsky's, Gluck & Mohr, Schaeffer, Horstman's, Fishman's, Printz Leather and other big plants signed up. Spurning the disruptive activities of the AFL representatives in various Philadelphia plants, the unorganized leather workers realized that their future was tied up with Local 30 as the only union that was bringing benefits to the workers in the industry. Smashing victories in NLRB elections in tanneries and wool pulleries in the Quaker City were quickly followed by union contracts providing better wages and working conditions. Strikes were won.* By 1944, Local 30 became one of the biggest locals in the entire union. Its members had closed-shop contracts and enjoyed vastly improved working conditions, higher wages, paid vacations, holidays and many other gains.

The IFLWU also organized the unorganized leather workers all along the Eastern Seaboard area. Newark Local 27 organized Sterling Leather, Camden Tanning, Lindenoid Shoe Leather, J. Nieder, Colden's, Hahn & Stumpf, and other open-shop tanneries. Camden Local 206 organized the huge John R. Evans plant and other tanneries. Brooklyn Local 35 grew from a membership of fifty-five in 1940 to over five hundred dues-paying members in 1942. Quakertown Local 208 organized the Peabody Leather and McAdoo & Allen Welting shops.

Under Frank Brownstone's leadership as District Director, young, energetic and devoted organizers had been developed from the ranks of the leather workers themselves. In addition to the pioneer organizer of the Newark workers, Tom Galanos, the district now had Steve Coyle, Frank Di Vincenzo, Edward Incollingo, Joe Muscardo and Jim Pasquay as organizers and an invaluable group of active rank-and-file leaders in the most important shops and locals.

Wilmington, the open-shop fortress of the duPonts, was known to the fur workers as the place where Ben Gold had been beaten almost to death and then imprisoned during the Hunger March of the unemployed.** It was also known to leather workers throughout the coun-

---

* On August 5, 1941, eight hundred workers at Surpass struck. After four weeks, the strike ended in victory for the local.

** See page 387.

try for its unorganized tanneries and shockingly poor working conditions.

Every attempt to organize Wilmington tanneries had been smashed. Wrong policies and inept leadership of the AFL leather union resulted in defeat for the Wilmington workers every time they struck. The AFL failed to unite all the workers, white and Negro, Polish, Italian, native-born American, men and women. Disunity was skillfully used by the employers to play off one group against the other. And every defeated attempt to organize was followed by blacklisting, discrimination, speedup and wage cuts.

It was against this background of repeated defeats that the IFLWU drive, under the leadership of Frank Brownstone, began in Wilmington. A streamlined, rapid-fire campaign swept through the huge Amalgamated Leather plant. In the short space of two months, the plant was completely organized. The first retaliation of the company was a layoff of over three hundred workers. The attempt at intimidation failed. Union ranks held solid. In a Labor Board election, the union swept the vote by 597 to 55. Negotiations for an agreement went on for weeks until they reached a deadlock. A one-hour stoppage, followed by a half-day holiday, failed to budge the company's resistance. It became evident that no agreement would be reached. The Amalgamated Leather workers were compelled to strike.

The strike, one hundred percent effective, started on January 16, 1941. Sleet and snow and bitter cold, did not stop the twenty-four-hour picket line around the plant maintained by the strikers. It was the most militant rank-and-file battle ever seen in Delaware. Every striker was mobilized and ready for instant duty. Pickets were organized with captains in charge of each shift; squads of cars transported the strikers to the picket lines and back to the strike hall; picket captains kept careful check of the picketing. Outstanding in the conduct of the strike and the key factor in its success was the unity achieved between the white and Negro strikers. Jim-Crow, by no means a stranger in Wilmington, was an outlaw in the union hall and on the picket line. Negroes served with whites on every committee and took part with unbounded enthusiasm in every strike activity. The unshakeable devotion of the Negro workers to the union proved to be the very backbone of the strike.

Public opinion was on the side of the strikers from the start. Stalling tactics of the company during negotiations, extremely low wages paid at the plant, and the just demands of the strikers were widely publicized. Grocers, bakers, milkmen, butchers, fruit markets and many small business people contributed generously to the union soup kitchen.

A deliberate and almost fatal assault was made on the picket line calculated to create, as the press would put it, a "riot" and permit the police to step in and smash the strike. At a signal given by a police lieutenant, a scab truck loaded on company premises with leather hides, sped through an open gate and crashed into a line of women pickets. Caught in the wheels of the truck, Mrs. Nellie Gorak, one of the strikers, was dragged for a distance of more than two hundred yards before her legs and clothes became disengaged. The truck heedlessly continued to speed on its way, running down other pickets. Nearby strikers rushed over and picked up the wounded pickets. Officers in police cars laughed at the tragic scene. The strikers themselves rushed the women to the hospital. Mrs. Gorak hovered between life and death for many days. Even after she recovered, she remained crippled.

Only the strong discipline of the strikers, guided by the union leadership, avoided the trap of a collision with the police which would have endangered the strike. The entire labor movement of Newcastle County joined the strikers in a protest movement demanding the removal of the police lieutenant and the arrest of the driver.

After twelve days, with the ranks of the union solid and every provocation defeated, the strike was settled. Assisted in negotiations by Organizers Brownstone and Klig, the strikers won a wage increase, union shop and other standard union conditions.

It was the first large plant of any industry in Wilmington to secure a union shop agreement. The victory at Amalgamated Leather was followed up by the union in other Wilmington shops such as Diamond State Tanning Co., Youngco, Allied Kid, and in other tanneries in the South. Overcoming many obstacles which confront the labor movement in the South—low wages and sweatshop conditions, deep-rooted prejudice and bigotry, discrimination against Negroes, segregation, deprival of elementary civil liberties, and terrorism which union organizers repeatedly encountered—the IFLWU organized leather shops in Baltimore and Hagerstown, Maryland, and in Richmond, Luray and Iron Gate, Virginia. Union conditions were established and rates of pay were increased steadily. In twenty years, workers in Charles Walton Co. in Baltimore had received only one wage increase, a one-cent-an-hour raise. In the two years after Local 219 was organized, the workers' wages were raised twenty-eight cents an hour!

By 1944 the Atlantic Seaboard District 2 boasted eleven local unions in six states. It had locals in Newark, Hoboken, Camden, Brooklyn, Philadelphia, Quakertown, Wilmington, Baltimore, Hagerstown, Richmond and Luray. In all, fifty-three shops were under contract with the union.

District 3 (Western Pennsylvania and Upstate New York) started with one local in Curwensville which had never been able to obtain a union agreement; a local in Gowanda which had been engaged in a losing battle against a series of company unions; and an independent union in Gloversville.

The tanneries in small Western Pennsylvania towns were mainly sole-leather tanneries, located near the source of supply of tanbark.* The multi-millionaire tanneries dominated the entire life of many leather workers from cradle to grave. In some company towns, leather workers —heads of families—made as little as $14 a week, and that after they had worked for the company as long as fifteen and twenty years. In hide-bound company-town fashion, rent, groceries, and other necessities were deducted from the workers' pay envelopes before they opened them.

Sole-leather tanneries are usually owned by companies which operate more than one plant. In Western Pennsylvania there were three such chains—United States Leather (later known as Keystone), Howes Brothers, and Armour. None of these chains had ever been organized. For over fifty years these tanneries had remained open shops.

The first dent in the open-shop chains in Western Pennsylvania came in September 1940 with election victories by the IFLWU at the Franklin Tannery in Curwensville and the Mt. Jewett Tannery and Stephenson & Osborne at Mt. Jewett, all Howes Bros. subsidiaries. Curwensville Local 31 signed the first leather-union agreement in fifty years in Western Pennsylvania on November 1, 1940.

The success of the union in Curwensville and Mt. Jewett was followed up by the IFLWU in other tanneries. Wilcox Local 83 and Ridgway Local 82 won Labor Board elections and union agreements at U. S. Leather plants in their towns. The vote in Ridgway, which finished off a company union, was a test of strength for the IFLWU. Workers in un-organized leather tanneries throughout Pennsylvania were watching the election results. The victory spurred the drive for the organization of U. S. Leather at Clearfield, Salamanca and other tanneries in the state.

As in the other districts, Organizers George O. Pershing, Victor Hersh-

---

* Heavy leathers are usually tanned by vegetable agents or by a combination of vegetable and mineral agents. Light leathers are generally chrome-tanned.

field, Harry Millstone, John Russell and Phil Parr conducted the drive with the help of rank-and-file committees. Leather workers from the newly-organized plants traveled hundreds of miles on week-ends to distant towns to talk about the IFLWU to the unorganized leather workers. They told how they had improved their working conditions since they were organized. The strenuous work of the organizers and rank-and-file committees brought successive victories at NLRB elections and in the contracts that followed.

The organization of the Armour chain of tanneries was begun in 1941. Armour Leather, a subsidiary of Armour of Illinois, was one of the biggest companies in the country. The largest Armour sole-leather tannery, employing 750 workers and the key to the whole chain, was located in Williamsport. In 1935, the AFL United Leather Workers had set up a small local in Williamsport for a time. It never had more than a mere handful of workers in Wiliamsport and no contract at all for the three Armour plants in the city.

After several months of intensive organizational work, the union won a series of elections and planted the IFLWU banner at Williamsport, St. Marys, Noxen, and Gleasonton. Another election was subsequently won at Westover.

The union sewed up the Armour chain by organizing the large Armour tannery in Holland, Michigan (District 4). Contracts with important improvements were won for all plants.

Another seventy-five-year-old open shop of the sole-tanning industry in Western Pennsylvania bowed to unionism when the Eberle workers at Westfield voted in the IFLWU as collective bargaining agent despite terrific intimidation and red-baiting propaganda.

The Independent Leather Workers Union of Fulton County affiliated as Local 202, adding some fifteen hundred new members to the Leather Division. The leather workers of Buffalo joined Local 39 and won contracts. On October 29, 1941, the four-year struggle of the leather workers in Gowanda, New York, to win collective bargaining rights was ended when the Moench Tanning Co. (subsidiary of the Brown Shoe Co. of St. Louis) signed its first union agreement. The Gowanda campaign was dubbed by the press "the second toughest organizational struggle in the leather industry." It rang down the curtain on an unsavory record of company unionism sponsored by the Moench firm back in 1937.

In many towns in all districts, the IFLWU was the first union to win an agreement, thereby stimulating the organization of workers in other industries. Many leather locals became the spark plugs for the organization of the furniture, shoe, farm equipment, laundry, carbide, textile, radio and electrical workers in their communities.*

For fifty-eight years, the powerful corporation of Endicott-Johnson, the country's second largest shoe and tannery company, had resisted organization and had kept unionism out of the tri-city area of Endicott, Johnson City and Binghamton. Through complete domination of business, schools, community services, city administrations, the press and all walks of life in the area, through a host of well-placed company agents and a widely-advertised and deceptive system of paternalism, Endicott-Johnson had become one of the most notorious holdouts against trade unionism in the entire country. Repeated efforts both by the AFL and the CIO to organize this open shop had ended in dismal failure. In 1940, the firm had whipped up such anti-union sentiment through intimidation that a competitive organizing drive conducted by AFL and CIO shoe unions was decisively defeated with the vote of five to one for "no union." The workers were further humiliated by being forced to parade in a celebration in honor of the company's great victory!

To some two thousand Endicott-Johnson tannery workers, the company's so-called paternalism was not what it was cracked up to be. Favoritism in the plants deprived them of seniority and security. Many had bought their homes from the company, but they did not own the land under them. Their wages were cut whenever it pleased the management to do so. At the will of the company, they were forced to contribute 5 percent of their pay to the highly-touted medical plan that the company controlled from the nurse in the plant to the hospital in the town.

The Fur and Leather Workers Union brought the message of progressive trade unionism to Endicott tannery workers in an organizational campaign under the direction of Organizer Myer Klig. It took a whole year to carry out a carefully-planned campaign and break through the barriers built up by the company around the tannery workers and the entire tri-city area. It was the first serious challenge to the company's open-shop domination.

Each tannery was tackled individually, sole leather, upper leather, and calfskin. Each plant was organized by departments. Visiting commit-

---

* For example, in Parsons, West Virginia, Leather Local 310 organized an Armour Tannery and then organized the textile workers at the Dorman Mills. Later, the local turned these workers over to the Textile Workers Union.

tees from other locals of tannery workers came to the tri-city area and spoke to the Endicott-Johnson workers. Leaflets were distributed in different languages. House-to-house canvassing continued for weeks; one street after another was taken up and checked until every tannery worker was seen and talked to. The paternalistic system was cracked as the Endicott workers learned from the union of gains won in organized tanneries, working conditions and job security they could enjoy only through the union.

Throughout the American labor movement, especially after the AFL and CIO defeat in 1940, everyone believed that the Endicott-Johnson open-shop stronghold was impregnable. But on December 22, 1942, newspapers all over the country featured the news that the fortress had at last been penetrated. The IFLWU won the Labor Board election among twenty-three hundred Endicott tannery workers, despite the terrific resistance of the company and the most flagrant campaign of intimidation and coercion on the day of the election.

This was history. For the very first time, the workers of Endicott-Johnson had won the right to belong to a union. Excitement ran high all through the tri-city area, not only among twenty thousand Endicott-Johnson shoe workers, but also among workers at International Business Machines Company and Remington-Rand. Hundreds of workers crowded the newly-chartered IFLWU Local 285's first mass meeting.

Within a few weeks after the historic Labor Board victory, the local's membership was up to two thousand, the largest trade union local in the tri-city area.

The first union contract obtained from Endicott-Johnson by any union was signed on March 19, 1943. The leather workers won important improvements, far exceeding their previous conditions. Besides job security and higher wage rates, they obtained paid vacations, paid holidays, free protective clothing, night-shift bonuses and other gains. The medical plan, paid entirely by the company, became part of the agreement.

The organization of the Endicott-Johnson tannery workers proved that the most powerful open-shop fortresses could be broken through. It was most unfortunate that because of jurisdictional issues, the drive could not be extended at this time to include organization of the twenty thousand shoe workers. Apart from the obvious benefits it would have brought to these workers, the presence of such a huge body of unorganized workers in the plants made it difficult for IFLWU Local 285 to build a solid foundation. It remained an island of trade unionism, surrounded on all sides by the open shop.

Endicott became the largest local in District 3, which obtained contracts covering forty-five shops in Curwensville, Mt. Jewett, Port Alleghany, Ridgway, Wilcox, Westfield, Clearfield, Emporium, Elkland, Williamsport, Noxen, St. Marys, and Gleasonton, Pennsylvania; Salamanca, Ludlow, Gowanda, Buffalo, Gloversville, and Endicott, New York.

The heart of the old National Leather Workers Association had consisted of the four locals in Lynn, Peabody, Woburn and Norwood, Massachusetts. These became District 1 of the Leather Division. Worcester Local 46 was added in 1939, followed by Nashua Local 212, Lowell Local 270 and Winchester Local 295. The Lowell leather workers, organized since 1890 as an independent union known as the United Leather Workers Union of America, affiliated to the IFLWU in 1942.

Although the merger of the fur and leather unions in 1939 had been approved by a two-thirds majority of the workers, a small group of New England local officials remained hostile to the merger. The greater the progress of the union's organizational drives in the unorganized areas, the sharper their hostility became. The main center of the opposition to the International was in Peabody Local 21.

Local 21, with some three thousand members, was the largest local of the Leather Division. Internally it was torn by various groups and factions. Petty partisan politics seriously hampered the functioning of the local. Many open shops right in Peabody remained unorganized. At the large A. C. Lawrence plant, a company union flourished. Local 21 members, disgusted by constant bickering and group maneuvers, became apathetic to the union. Local meetings were usually attended by only a handful of workers. The officials used favoritism to build a machine with the prime purpose of maintaining their union positions. The bulk of the workers were actually excluded from participation in union affairs, a condition that inevitably discouraged workers in the open shops from joining the union.

The local opposition to the merger, led by James J. Chenery, then the president of the Leather Division, indulged in both open and undercover red-baiting and anti-Semitism, particularly during election periods. In 1940, the candidate of this group for business agent of Local 21, Harry Stathos, was charged with having used fraud and trickery to win the local election. The charges were investigated by a committee designated by the local. The inquiry revealed that Stathos and his associates had passed out dues-books to people who were not entitled to vote, none of whom were members of the union, and that Stathos had "threatened, intimidated and coerced . . . members and non-members of this union having knowledge of his illegal activities in the election of Local 21 on March 29, 1940." The committee concluded that "the activities in the election should shock the conscience of any decent fair-minded union man," and recommended that charges be placed against Stathos "for directing and participating in a fraudulent election in which he resorted to unethical and unfair practices so that he might be elected."

Exposed before the membership, Stathos was forced to resign. He intensified his work as a member of the anti-International group in Peabody. Indeed, this group now saw the handwriting on the wall.* The influence of the progressives in the local was growing. The growth of the Leather Division, the establishment of well-functioning locals throughout the country and the International's achievements in improving the conditions of the leather workers, embittered the clique to the point of desperation. They tried in every way to sabotage this growth. They told leather workers in open shops not to join the union since it was controlled by "Communists and Jews," and hinted that the Peabody local was soon getting out of the International. They secretly urged the Lowell independent union not to affiliate with the International, and agitated against the IFLWU in an A. C. Lawrence election, undermining the union drive.

Undoubtedly the International's democratic policy of not interfering in the internal affairs of local unions gave this anti-union group an opportunity to prolong its harmful work. The International was busy organizing the open-shop areas, building the union. The time was not long in coming, however, when the disruptive activities of this clique of self-seeking officials was bound to burst into the open. The showdown came in 1943.

The growth of the union, the organization of new locals and districts, and the joint functioning of the two divisions had reached the point where an International constitution was a necessity. Successive conventions of the Leather Division in 1940, '41 and '42 and the convention of the Fur Division in 1942 had unanimously instructed the officers to prepare such a document. Committees of the Executive Boards of the two divisions prepared a constitution which was approved by the entire International Executive Board. It was submitted to the membership of both divisions for the final referendum vote in 1943.

The International Constitution was regarded as a many-sided threat

* The clique leaders had been in close contact with Charles Majerik, secretary of Philadelphia Local 30, who was caught embezzling union funds.

by the group of oppositionists and disrupters in the Peabody local. As a most democratic body of rules governing the functioning of the union, it guaranteed basic rights to every member regardless of race, creed, color, religious or political belief. Discrimination was outlawed. Democratic election procedures were mandatory. And honesty in the administration of union officers was strictly prescribed. In addition, the very adoption of an International Constitution would cement even tighter the merger of fur and leather into one union. The union-wrecking clique in Peabody therefore furiously opposed the adoption of the constitution.

In the referendum vote, 45 locals of the Fur Division approved the constitution unanimously, only two members in one local voting against. In the Leather Division, overwhelming majorities in 35 locals approved and 7 locals voted against. Eighty-five percent of the membership of the Leather Division voted for it.

Even in Peabody, where most of the local officials campaigned bitterly against it with open red-baiting and Jew-baiting attacks, the majority of the local membership approved the constitution in a secret-ballot vote.

Completely contemptuous of the democratic decision of the majority, the clique leaders halted payment of per capita to the International and prepared to pull the local out of the International. A membership meeting to vote for secession was called for August 12, 1943.

The plot of the union-splitters did not go unchallenged. In the course of three years of continuing internal struggles for organization of the unorganized, for democracy in the union and for a strong, united International—a group of young, energetic, sincere and progressive leaders had developed. While the clique had demagogically captured practically all leading union positions except that of business agent (Imberiol Moroni), the progressives now represented the true desires of the majority of the membership for a united union. The progressives set to work apprising the membership of the plot against the union and mobilized for the August 12 meeting. That meeting became a turning point in the district's history. Out of the struggles that ensued, the young progressive leadership emerged tempered and steeled.

Instead of the usual small meeting of forty or fifty workers, mostly machine men, expected by the clique in control, the August 12 meeting became a mass meeting with over six hundred union members on hand to defend their union. The intensive red-baiting that preceded the meeting was fully exposed as the camouflage behind which the clique was moving to split the union. The indignation of the aroused leather workers, evident from the very size of the meeting, was fully apparent. James

E. Begemes, vice-president of the local, was so frightened by the size and temper of the meeting that he hastily adjourned it without discussion or vote. The clique leaders demonstratively walked out, expecting to draw the workers with them and terminate the meeting.

But the progressives were ready. Richard O'Keefe immediately leaped upon the platform, seized the gavel and asked the workers: "Do you want to adjourn?" "No!" the workers shouted. Twenty workers walked out with the clique. Six hundred remained!

The meeting continued. It condemned the splitters and urged the International Union to suspend the union-wreckers from office. District Director Isador Pickman, Richard B. O'Keefe and Business Agent Imberiol Moroni were elected as the temporary steering committee of the local until a new election could be held. Pickman and O'Keefe had worked in tanneries since early youth. Both were veterans of the 1933 strike in Peabody.

The opposition group in Peabody announced that it was setting up a new union to be known as "Local 21 of the National Leather Workers Association." They declared that the new union would be affiliated with the CIO. "Unionism or Communism! Leather Workers take your choice," the union-wreckers shrieked. With this announcement, the clique tried to seize Local 21's funds, consisting of some $27,000 in the bank and in War Bonds. When halted from so doing by court action, they charged that the merger of the leather and fur workers was illegal. The court, after a long delay, ruled that the question of the merger had been submitted to a referendum of the leather workers and "was carried by more than two-thirds vote," and that the IFLWU constitution was "legally adopted in May of 1943."

The union-wreckers were also rebuffed by the CIO. In a letter to a Peabody leather employer on August 31, 1943, the Massachusetts CIO Industrial Union Council declared "that no charter of any kind can be and will be issued by the CIO to any group other than through the International Fur and Leather Workers Union . . . which has jurisdiction over all fur and leather workers."

It was now obvious that the union-wreckers were defeated at every turn. They had been able to mislead only a small group of workers. The overwhelming majority remained loyal to Local 21 and the International. New officers, headed by Moroni and O'Keefe, were elected by the membership. International Representative Myer Klig, who had already contributed greatly to organizational work in the area, was assigned to assist Pickman, O'Keefe, Moroni, Ed Freeman and the other young leaders.

The next move of the clique, now thoroughly exposed, re-vealed their desperation and their readiness to stop at nothing in their efforts to smash the union. The United States was at war with the fascist axis. Labor recognized that this was a war for survival of democratic liberties against Hitler enslavement. The leather workers were doing their part in the war effort on the battlefront, in the shops and in defense ac-tivities, and doing it magnificently. They had heartily endorsed the union's pledge not to strike for the duration of the war. Many leather plants were busy on essential orders for the Army and Navy.

The anti-International group sneered at the union's outstanding pa-triotic war activities. Some of its leaders were "America Firsters" and one was actually campaign manager for a candidate of this pro-fascist, anti-Semitic, anti-Negro organization.

No less treacherous toward the embattled nation than to the leather workers themselves, this group called a "general strike" of Peabody leather workers on November 2, 1943. Combining coercion and intimida-tion at factory gates, particularly against women workers, with dema-gogic agitation about "Communist" domination, the clique succeeded in forcing a stoppage of work at eleven factories, some of them engaged in war production. Many loyal members of the IFLWU condemned the strike and attempted to report for work. The employers, however, co-operated with the clique by shutting these plants down.

The so-called "general strike" was a fiasco. Despite all intimidation by the union-splitters, over two thousand workers in some forty Peabody plants remained at work. Hailing this action, thousands of CIO workers in Essex County appealed publicly to members of Local 21 "to give not one inch to these Hitler-helpers" who were "calling the strike . . . be-cause they are opposed to America's war against Nazism."

In quick succession, the clique brazenly defied return-to-work orders of the Regional War Labor Board and the National War Labor Board. On November 18, 1943, the nation's Commander-in-Chief, President Franklin D. Roosevelt, ordered the strikers back to work and wired the leaders of the union-wrecking clique: "Your nation is at war. These strikes are inexcusable and constitute a defiance of the War Labor Board, a challenge to government by law and a blow against the effective prose-cution of the war. . . They must not be permitted to continue."

When the splitters defied even the President's order, army officers and troops took possession of thirteen tanneries and put an end to the force and violence of the union-wreckers. The strike collapsed.

ARMY TROOPS SEIZE PEABODY-SALEM LEATHER PLANTS TO RESTORE ORDER

NLWA Merger With AFL Due In Week

The American Federation of Labor will officially rkers Association in- n the necessary af- hton by representa-

F.D.R. Directs War Secretary To Take Over

Three Week Strike Disrupted Business Making Goods For War—Rival Unions Claim Victory In Move—Post Office Assigned As Headquarters For Army Officials—Expect All Workers To Return Monday—Thirteen Factories Under Government Control—War Labor Board Will Make Every Effort To Set-

WLB Upholds CIO In Leather Dispute

Restricts Rival Union From Soliciting Members and Collecting Dues in Plants—New Workers Can't Be Discharged

A National War La board ruling received by the office of Lieut. Curtis G. Pratt which controls leather fact pending a final action union-dispute supports

Supreme Court Upholds Decision for CIO Union

Fur Workers' Group Gets $28,000 Fund

The full bench of the state supreme bench heard the arguments last March, and word of the decision was delivered to the superior court here today.

The two unions have been engaged in a bitter jurisdictional fight since the internal dissension in the CIO ranks caused the split. The members who left the IFLWU a year ago last August revived the old National Leather Workers association and then, following a general strike in the district last fall affiliated with the AFL. It is expected that a general collec-

CIO Wins Election For Bargaining in 70 Plants

Other Facts In Salem, Peabody Area

The International Fur and Leather Workers Union, CIO, Local 21, was

Harriman Co., Wilmington Each union obtained 28 votes. The CIO

Massachusetts headlines tell how the leather workers defeated the America-Firsters who sabotaged the war against Hitlerism.

One of the most shameful episodes of the strike, reported in the *Salem News* of November 8, 1943, showed a picture of the clique leaders with the heading, "LABOR UNION LEADERS VOTE TO JOIN AFL." The caption read: "Group of officials of National Leather Workers Association in Peabody, Salem and Woburn shown at Hawthorne Hotel just before important conference with AFL chieftains after which NLWA group voted to recommend affiliation." On November 28, 1943, the Peabody *Sunday Express* reported: "Filled with admiration at the plucky fight the independent leather workers union made against the Communistic fur workers CIO union, national officials of the American Federation of Labor expressed pleasure yesterday at the action of the leather group in becoming affiliated with the AFL."

All this took place in the midst of a strike against the nation's war effort engineered by the clique against the will of the majority of workers! The AFL officials, who had publicly proclaimed support for the no-strike pledge, welcomed these wreckers as allies. Red-baiting and opposition to the war effort went hand in hand.

The affiliation of the union-splitters to the discredited AFL leather outfit cleared the smoke for many leather workers taken in by the red-baiting propaganda. They knew the AFL leather union and its treachery to the workers only too well. When the whole fight was finally climaxed by a Labor Board election, IFLWU Local 21 snowed under the dual-union AFL in 68 out of 70 shops in Peabody, Salem and Danvers. All the AFL could win was two small contracting shops employing altogether about thirty-five workers!

The overwhelming defeat of the dual-unionists and "America Firsters" demonstrated to the entire labor movement that the leather workers were unified and loyal to the International. A militant, strengthened leather workers' union had come into existence in Peabody. A large corps of active members and shop stewards participated in the union's affairs. For the first time in the local's history, the workers attended local meetings in large numbers. Real democracy prevailed. There was no more red-baiting or Jew-baiting. Union business was attended to seriously and soberly. Union educational, cultural, recreational and legislative activities, never before known in the local, now flourished. The organization was healthy. It functioned. Its officers were honest and union-conscious. The members supported them. Local 21 had become a real union, respected by the entire labor movement.

It was a union in the shops as well. So long as the clique had been in control, many of the open shops in the area remained unorganized. With the ouster of the wreckers, dozens of new shops were organized. Conditions rose to the highest point in the history of the leather workers.

No less important was the fact that out of this struggle emerged a tested and experienced leadership in the local and the district, devoted to democratic trade unionism and able to cope with all attacks against the union from within or without.

Local 21 led the way for all New England. The defeat of the union-wreckers laid the foundation for a real district organization. The struggle in Peabody tore the mask off the red-baiters and anti-Semites and exposed them as enemies of the American labor movement and the nation. The leather workers achieved a clearer understanding of the contributions of the fur workers to clean and democratic unionism. The whole International union was strengthened immeasurably.

At the first joint convention of the International union in 1944, the delegates represented 100,000 organized fur and leather work-

The tremendous struggles and achievements of the Leather Division are summarized in these typical headlines taken from issues of the Fur & Leather Worker *for the years 1940 to 1944.*

ers. At convention sessions, in the hotel lobby, in restaurants near the convention hall, one could hear the twang of the Midwest, a slow Southern drawl, quick-clipped New Yorkese, the accent of a Jewish, Italian or Polish worker, an Irishman's brogue, and the soft-tongued French Canadian. Negro and white, from all parts of the country and of every nationality, broke bread together and acted in unison, a model of progressive trade unionism.

In 1939, there were less than five thousand organized leather workers. In 1944, there were fifty thousand organized leather workers, 85 percent of the industry.

What the AFL had failed to do in fifty years, what the independent unions could never accomplish, what even the CIO in 1936, 1937 and 1938, its most militant and progressive years with its historic march through basic industry, could not achieve—the International Fur & Leather Workers Union had accomplished.

The Leather Division now had about fifty-five functioning locals in seventeen states and Canada.

But this numerical growth was only half the story. Deplorable conditions that existed in 1939 had been eliminated; wages and working standards in the organized districts had been raised to a much higher level; vacations with pay and holidays with pay, completely unknown in 1939, were established; job security in the form of seniority rights and protection against unjust discharges were universal; free protective clothing and many fringe benefits were provided in every shop under union contract. The threat of the runaway shops had been defeated.

In 1944, Augustus J. Tomlinson and Isador Pickman, president and secretary-treasurer of the Leather Division, wrote to CIO President Philip Murray:

". . . We feel that the great gains of the leather workers' union are consolidated, the democratic rights of our local unions and membership are safeguarded, and the leather division strengthened immeasurably as part of our unified International Union.

"In the growth of our union since the merger with the fur workers in 1939, we have made great progress in organizing the unorganized, raising the wages and working and living standards of our members. This was made possible by the experienced and capable guidance and assistance of the officers and members of the fur division, organizationally and financially, who have helped us build a healthy, democratic, functioning trade union organization, developed a loyal and experienced leadership among the leather workers, devoted to the progressive principles of the CIO."

The War Against Fascism

The dark clouds of war, which to most Americans loomed only on the distant horizons of fascist aggressions against Manchuria, Spain, Ethiopia, Austria and Czechoslovakia in the early and middle 'thirties, burst in full fury from 1939 to 1941. The Hitler-Mussolini fascist war machine conquered Poland, France, Belgium, Holland, Norway, Denmark, Hungary, Yugoslavia, Greece, Bulgaria and Roumania. Hirohito's imperialist armies overran China and Indo-China. Whole nations lay devastated and in ruins. The bombardment of Britain, the invasion of Soviet Russia and finally the attack on Pearl Harbor on December 7, 1941, made it clear that Hitler, Mussolini and Hirohito were bent on conquering and enslaving the whole world.

Hitler, Mussolini, Hirohito and the industrial monopolists and bankers who stood back of them were aided and abetted by powerful financial and industrial leaders of the democratic countries, not excluding our own. Big business interests in the United States played ball with the fascist tyrants during the years that preceded the outbreak of war. American bankers gave huge loans to Hitler, Mussolini and the Japanese imperialists. They helped them suppress their own people with the most barbaric brutality, and build up war machines that subjugated one country after another. Some big American industrialists, like Ford, and newspaper magnates, like Hearst, even received medals from the fascist rulers. Others, like the oil trust, entered into private agreements with German cartels, sharing inventions and formulas for important war essentials kept secret even from the United States government. Pro-fascists, including industrialists, bankers and reactionaries in Congress, extolled the virtues of the fascist murderers and advocated doing business with Hitler.

"We must stop the fascist war makers," declared a leaflet distributed by the Furriers Joint Council in 1937. "We must arouse the greatest indignation against them! We must organize the greatest protest of the American people who love peace and nurse a hatred against war and the war makers." To stop the fascist war makers, the furriers and their leaders called upon the United States to participate in a program of collective security with the Soviet Union, Britain, France, China and other nations.

In 1937, President Roosevelt issued his call to the nations of the world to "quarantine the aggressors." Unfortunately, the hopes of uniting the peace-loving nations against the danger of fascist aggression were blasted by powerful forces in Europe and in the United States who openly appeased fascism and plotted to turn the aggressors towards the East against the Soviet Union. Chamberlain and Daladier sacrificed Ethiopia, Austria, Spain, China and Czechoslovakia to the fascists. By sabotaging every effort to build up a peace bloc through an effective system of collective security, they encouraged Hitler to march on. In effect, they guaranteed the speedy approach of the war in which the United States too would be involved.

A month after the outbreak of the European War in September 1939, the second CIO convention met in San Francisco. In the report of President John L. Lewis, unanimously adopted by the delegates, the CIO declared that organized labor was "unalterably opposed to any involvement of the United States in the European war," that "preoccupation with foreign affairs must not be allowed to distract attention from unemployment and other pressing problems of internal economic insecurity," and that "the greatest contribution that can be made to the cause of democracy, peace and prosperity is through the building of the progressive labor movement."

This statement was supported by the Fur and Leather Workers Union. Within the union, it was agreed that differences of opinion should not be allowed to divide the union and divert it from its fundamental tasks.

In June 1940, after the fall of France, the CIO Executive Board unanimously adopted a statement on National Defense which announced: "We are prepared to lend practical, wholesome and feasible cooperation in any undertaking to protect this nation and prepare for national defense." The statement also asserted "in unequivocal terms that we will defend the free institutions of this Republic, under which the Declaration of

Independence and the Constitution gives us the greatest democracy on earth—a government of the people, for the people and by the people." Ben Gold, the IFLWU representative on the CIO's Executive Board, voted for the resolution, and the International Executive Board of the union endorsed the CIO's stand on June 15, 1940.

The fur workers, whose hatred of fascism became even more intense with the mounting atrocities of the conquerors, had for years fought militantly against every fascist act of aggression and savagery. They had supported the fight of the Spanish Republic against Hitler-backed Franco, boycotted Japanese and German products and supported anti-fascists in every struggle. When the United States itself was drawn into the war with the bombing of Pearl Harbor, the fur and leather workers dedicated all their energies toward the single objective: to win the peoples' war against the fascist axis.

On behalf of the International Executive Board, Ben Gold and Pietro Lucchi appealed to all fur and leather workers immediately after Pearl Harbor: "Our country calls upon us in this hour of grave need. The independence of our country, the freedom and lives of our people, are in danger. Hesitation or vacillation would be disastrous. We expect you to fulfill your duty to our country in the most honorable manner. Smash the enemy of our country, the enemy of mankind. Destroy fascism forever!"

The response of the union was immediate. Nearly one hundred wires from locals of the union in every part of the United States poured into the International office approving the International Board's call. From their prison cells, Potash, Vafiades and Schneider, victims of frame-ups, urged: "No sacrifice is too great to assure the victory of our country."

In November 1941, even before the United States was drawn into the war, the New York fur workers gave a magnificent demonstration of solidarity with the war victims of our Allied nations. At a public mass meeting in Madison Square Garden, Joseph Winogradsky, the first of the imprisoned union leaders to be released, presented two checks of $50,000 each for British and Russian war relief, raised by a voluntary assessment of the fur workers. Greek fur workers' Local 70 sent thousands of dollars through the Red Cross for relief to the starving Greeks.

The fur and leather workers' war-supporting activities after Pearl Harbor set an example of true patriotism and sacrifice unexcelled by any body of Americans throughout the land. Hundreds of union members, including organizers, business agents, local officers and executive board members, men and women, volunteered for the armed forces on December 8, 1941, the first day after the attack. All told, fifteen thousand members of the IFLWU, including 250 organizers and local officers, entered the armed services during the war. Over twenty-three hundred floor workers of Local 125, including practically all of its leaders, served in the armed forces.

Thousands of IFLWU members were cited publicly for heroism in action against the enemy. They received numerous Distinguished Flying Cross, Air Medal, Silver Star, Bronze Star, Purple Heart, Croix de Guerre and Presidential citations. Many who joined as privates returned as captains, lieutenants and non-commissioned officers.

Whether as privates or officers, the organized fur and leather workers brought with them the unusually high morale, discipline, courage and militant determination instilled by their struggles for trade union democracy and by their keen understanding of the horrors of fascism. Incomplete records show that the union suffered 980 casualties, 248 killed in action and 732 wounded.

The home front activities of the fur and leather workers, organized through the union, aroused the admiration and respect of the trade union movement and led the activities of whole communities.

On February 22, 1942, two days out of his jail cell, Irving Potash told a mass meeting in honor of the freed union leaders: "Let this union of ours be a strong weapon for winning the war, a strong weapon that will also set the example to the entire labor movement how a union organized for the welfare of the workers is also organized for the welfare of the entire nation."

"Save a soldier's life with a pint of blood!" That was the pledge of solidarity of thousands of fur and leather workers all over the country to their brothers on the battlefields. They lined up at the chapters of the Red Cross to give their blood. Mobile Red Cross units were brought into fur and leather shops as Negro and white members of the union gave mass blood donations. Joseph Gemelli of Norwood Leather Local 26 won nationwide distinction for his work in bringing thousands of blood donors to the Red Cross. In all, the members of the IFLWU themselves contributed over thirty-four thousand pints of blood to the Red Cross!

Every local in the International organized committees for war relief work. Large committees of women members and wives of union members set up Red Cross bandage-rolling stations, and knitting clubs which knitted thousands of woolen sweaters, scarves and socks for British and Soviet fighters and for fur and leather workers in the armed forces.

December 8, 1941—the fur market (above) hails the first union fur volunteers after Pearl Harbor. Right, union leaders and members at a send-off party for Newark's militant leader, Tom Galanos, and his brother John, both of whom volunteered to serve in the Army. Below, one of the many events sponsored by the union for its members in the armed forces. Sam Burt, manager of Joint Board, is in the center of the photograph.

The union's fur vest project swept across the nation. Above, a fur workers' contingent in a parade carries banners telling of the project. Below, Mayor Fiorello LaGuardia starts the New York project as President Gold and others look on. Fourth from right is Louis F. White, representing the fur manufacturers. At right, testimonial letters from Prime Minister Mackenzie King of Canada, Rear Admiral A. S. Carpenter of the U. S. Navy, and E. S. Land, Administrator of War Shipping Administration.

OFFICE OF THE PRIME MINISTER
CANADA

Ottawa, April 13, 1942.

To the Officers of Local #45,
International Fur and Leather Workers Union,
123 Madison Street, West,
Chicago, Illinois.

Sirs:

It has been brought to my attention
that the members of your Union have, with their
own labour and at their own expense, produced
many hundreds of splendid fur jerkins for the
use of the merchant seamen of the United Nations
sailing into and out of Canadian ports. These
jerkins have been sent by your members through
the British War Relief Society of Chicago to the
Navy League of Canada, which body is charged by
the Canadian Government with looking after the
welfare of the men of the Mercantile Marine.

These leather jackets give inestimable
comfort to the men who are fortunate enough to
receive the same, and I want to take this opportunity of thanking you, and through you, the
members of your Union, for their generosity in
making this gift. I want you to know that the
people of Canada are deeply appreciative of this
splendid gesture of friendship towards Canada
and of kindliness towards the men of the sea
who come into Canadian ports.

Yours sincerely,

Prime Minister of Canada.

COMMANDANT
NINTH NAVAL DISTRICT
GREAT LAKES, ILLINOIS

20 March 1944

Fur & Leather Workers Union
States and Canada, CIO,
dison Street,
llinois.

nding work of your organization in manufactur-
ets to be donated to men in the Maritime
a and in our naval forces has been called to
ion.

able undertaking on your part is an encourag-
to men in the armed forces that the people back
lly appreciate the hardships under which they
ny times.

extend to you thanks and congratulations, and may
ain your goal of 50,000 jerkins in 1944.

Sincerely yours,

A. S. CARPENDER
Rear Admiral, U. S. Navy.

WAR SHIPPING ADMINISTRATION
WASHINGTON

September 3, 1943

AIL

ur Vest Project
ar Emergency Board
035 South Hill Street
Los Angeles, California

The War Shipping Administration appreciates the cooperative
action of the War Emergency Board of the Fur Industry in supplying
fur vests to American merchant seamen and the seamen of our Allies.

We should like to thank the Southern California Branch particularly for the 5,000 vests which have been distributed through
the United Seamen's Service to seamen and officers on the West Coast.

Many individual letters of appreciation have been received
by the War Shipping Administration from merchant seamen who have been
provided with fur vests by your organization. The warmth and protection afforded by these vests have been of the greatest assistance to
the men on winter voyages in the North Atlantic.

It is especially gratifying to know that your organization
intends to continue its work of distributing fur vests for the duration of the war. Your pledge of continued cooperation will be appreciated not only by the War Shipping Administration, but also by the
officers and men of the Merchant Marine as well.

Sincerely yours,

*The leather workers' deerskin proj-
ect aided soldiers in the arctic cli-
mate. Skins brought in by hunters
stored and processed by volunteer
leather workers, including women.*

Typical union contributions to war relief agencies.

IFLWU contribution of a hospital wing for Chinese guerrilla fighters brings warm acknowledgments from Wendell Willkie and Mme. Sun-Yat-Sen, widow of Chinese Republic's founder. Chou En-Lai, noted leader of Chinese people, is in center of photo.

THIS HOSPITAL WING SPONSORED and MAINTAINED BY INTERNATIONAL FUR & LEATHER WORKERS UNION U.S.A.

3 Hsin Tsun
Liang Lu Kou
Chungking
November 30, 1942

Mr. Ben Gold
President
International Fur & Leather Workers' Union
New York City, U. S. A.

Dear Mr. Gold,

I am writing to thank you and the International Fur and Leather Workers' Union for the gift of US$7,000 made through the China Aid Council and our China Defence League to finance the building and first year's operation of a new wing of the International Peace Hospital founded by Dr. Norman Bethune in the Wutai area, behind the Japanese lines in North China.

The men and women fighters whom the money will help are peasants who have taken up arms for the defence of their homes and workers from the Shansi anthracite mines, the Peiping-Hankow, Tatung-Puchow and Taiyuan-Shihchiachuang railways who operated these enterprises when they were ours, and who are fighting to win them back for China now that they are in the hands of the enemy. In five years these men and women have forged themselves into an army which the forces of aggressive Fascism, with their officers trained in military academies and their arms produced by a national industry geared entirely to war, have been unable to drive from its mountain bases, an army whose members not only fight but use their workers' skill to sabotage the enemy's communications and to make their own weapons in numerous mobile arsenals.

These fighters understand a workers' gift. They know the kind of people it comes from, because they are the same kind of people as themselves. They will accept it as it is given, as a hand stretched in warm greeting and support from one sector of the people's front against Fascism to another.

Soon you will have their own thanks, and their story of how your gift has been applied in the common fight.

With greetings to all your members,

Yours sincerely,

WENDELL L. WILLKIE
15 BROAD STREET
NEW YORK

July 27th, 1942

My dear Mr. Gold:

I have just learned of the $5,000 contribution which was made by the International Fur and Leather Workers Union toward the maintenance of a hospital in China. I was also happy to learn that your Union has undertaken to continue support of a fifty bed wing of the hospital.

I can't begin to tell you how delighted I was to hear of your generous gesture and hope that you will tell the members of your Union how much I personally appreciate this fine contribution. It is certainly a great cause and one in which we are all proud to participate. I know that your action and your expression of willingness to stand by for the duration will warm the hearts of our heroic Chinese allies.

Cordially,

Above, *a great mass demonstration in the fur market during a war bond drive.* Right, *Liberty Ship contributed by the IFLWU is named for Joseph Weydemeyer, early German-American fur organizer.*

Banner awarded by the War Emergency Board of the Fur Industry.

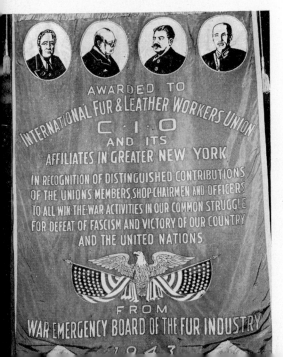

U. S. Government's tribute to President Gold for "excellence of performance" in war effort.

THE UNITED STATES OF AMERICA

In behalf of

The Army, the Navy, the Marine Corps

and the Coast Guard of the

UNITED STATES OF AMERICA

the

New York City — USO — Joint War Appeal

awards to

Ben Gold

this *Certificate of Achievement* for

EXCELLENCE OF PERFORMANCE

during its 1942 Fund-Raising effort

Chairman

NEW YORK, July 4, 1942

Typical IFLWU member contributions to the war effort: Above, *Norwood—Joseph Gemelli, record recruiter of blood donors, at right;* above right, *Milwaukee women volunteers;* right, *Chicago blood donors.*

Union contribution to the Red Cross acknowledged by leather manufacturer.

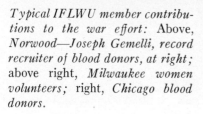

Below, Furriers Joint Council blood drive organized by Jack Schneider.

FURRIERS JOINT COUNCIL CIO MEMBERS GIVE 1000 PINTS OF BLOOD TO SAVE A THOUSAND FIGHTERS

Special committees raised funds and contributed thousands of packages of cigarettes to British and Russian War Relief. At the same time, these committees sent thousands of Thanksgiving and Christmas gift packages and cigarettes, candy and shaving kits to the union's servicemen.

Shop chairmen in fur shops and union stewards in leather plants pitched in during the War Loan Drives, canvassing the workers and selling bonds outright or taking pledges for payroll deductions. In every War Loan Drive, the fur and leather workers dug deep in their pockets, exceeding the government goal set for workers and almost doubling their assigned quotas. Together, the union and the membership bought War Bonds amounting to $42,633,887. One of the Joint Board's Negro members, James Tabbanor, invested his life savings of $5,000 in War Bonds. There were many similar examples.

Each year of the war, the fur workers and every District of leather workers adopted voluntary assessments for war relief. Besides contributing numerous ambulances and trucks to the Red Cross, the United States Army and to Allied relief agencies, the membership contributed directly through the union over two million dollars to the Red Cross, U.S.O. British, Russian, Chinese, French and other Allied war relief agencies.

Medical supplies and operating equipment contributed by the union found their way to almost every battlefront. A hospital room was donated for Leningrad. A hospital wing was contributed to China's heroic guerrilla fighters. Perhaps the most stirring expression of appreciation came in a letter to President Gold from Madame Sun Yat-sen, widow of the Chinese people's great leader. Madame Sun wrote of the fur workers' contribution to the Chinese people: "These fighters understand a worker's gift. They know the kind of people it comes from, because they are the same kind of people themselves. They will accept it as it is given, as a hand stretched in warm greeting and support from one sector of the people's front against Fascism to another."

On the production front, too, the IFLWU membership earned distinction. At least twenty-six union shops—leather, fur and mechanical—received Army-Navy "E" awards. Over eighty-eight union plants were awarded the Minute Man flag. In plants producing war orders for the government, the leather workers initiated important proposals which resulted in the elimination of waste in increased production of leather for war. J. H. Jordan, president of the Griess-Pfleger Tanning Company of Waukegan, Illinois, publicly commended IFLWU Vice-President Feinglass and the workers' committee for their contribution.

"The result of your work and action," he wrote, "undoubtedly will be a better understanding, cooperation and feeling as well as a great production of a better quality product to be used by our soldiers. It was a great patriotic move and policy on your part."

The American Oak Leather Company of Cincinnati lauded the work of the labor-management committee established at its plant: "The work done by the Committee has unquestionably been beneficial to the war effort, the Company and the workers. . . . We wish to compliment the Committee for the unselfish manner in which they have given their time and their energy to the matters which have come before them."

One of the outstanding war contributions of the fur workers was the unique undertaking to produce fur vests for the servicemen and the merchant marine. In the fall of 1941, Local 45 launched a campaign to make fur-lined jerkins for British sailors who patrolled the Atlantic sea lanes. The Chicago fur workers contributed their labor without compensation, working mainly at night. At about the same time, Montreal Locals 66 and 67 also established a fur vest project.

In all, sixteen projects were created throughout the country by committees of the local unions in cooperation with the principal employers in the industry. The largest was set up in New York City by the War Emergency Board of the Fur Industry, an organization composed of representatives of the union and all the fur employer associations.* Under the direction of Jack Schneider, the New York fur vest project was turned into one of the largest fur shops in the city. It had facilities for over seventy-five cutters, operators, nailers, finishers and floor workers. It was staffed by volunteer workers from the shops who took turns to keep up a steady flow of fur vests.

Mayor Fiorello LaGuardia started the machines whirring at the New

---

* The organization embraced the entire fur industry of New York City, including the twenty-eight manufacturers' and merchants' associations. The New York Joint Council, the Joint Board, Locals 2, 3, 4, 120, 122, 125 and 150, and Locals 130, 135 and 140 and 145 were all part of this joint labor-management organization.

President Ben Gold and Louis F. White, president of the manufacturers' association, were co-chairmen of the War Emergency Board. Irving Potash, manager of the Joint Council, and Louis Fenster, representing the manufacturers, were co-chairmen of the Fur Vest Project. Joseph Winogradsky, assistant-manager of the Joint Council, and George I. Fox, representing the fur dealers, were co-chairmen of the War Bond Committee. Michael Hollander was chairman of the War Chest Committee of the War Emergency Board.

York project and President Ben Gold sewed the first fur vest. The Mayor declared: "You fur workers are to be congratulated for initiating something that stars in the entire labor movement. By contributing your time and labor to make these fur vests you have demonstrated that labor can make an additional contribution to our government's war effort."

Fur vest projects were also sponsored by local unions in Boston, Philadelphia, Milwaukee, Easton, Pittsburgh, Los Angeles, Cleveland, San Francisco, Toronto, Detroit, St. Paul, Minneapolis and Duluth. The project became the talk of the armed forces and the nation. Thousands of women contributed their fur garments to help produce the vests.

A hundred thousand garments was the quota that the fur workers set for themselves. Some twenty thousand fur workers contributing over 150,000 hours of volunteer labor, actually produced a total of 119,701 vests. Packed in cartons, they were distributed to the United States Navy and to American, British, Russian, Norwegian and other Allied merchant seamen that plied the shipping lanes of the seven seas.

The value of these fur vests was best expressed by the men of the merchant marine who, in the face of death, manned the ships that delivered the implements of war to the armed forces and to our Allies. Rear Admiral E. S. Land, administrator of the U. S. War Shipping Administration, wrote: "Many individual letters of appreciation have been received by the War Shipping Administration from merchant seamen who have been provided with fur vests by your organization. The warmth and protection afforded by these vests have been of the greatest assistance to the men on winter voyages in the North Atlantic."

In recognition of the patriotic and constructive contributions of the union, its members and officers towards the successful win-the-war activities on an industry-wide scale, the War Emergency Board of the Fur Industry twice gave awards to the union in the form of a banner and a plaque. The inscription on the banner reads: "Awarded to the International Fur & Leather Workers Union, CIO, and its affiliates in Greater New York in recognition of distinguished contributions of the union membership, shop chairmen and officers to all win-the-war activities in our common struggle for defeat of fascism and victory of our country and the United Nations."

Members of the Leather Division also made a unique contribution to the war effort. At a District 3 Council meeting in Pennsylvania, H. L. "Pete" Parsons, a Local 209 delegate, proposed the salvage of deerskins, usually wasted by hunters, to relieve a serious shortage of deerskin leather. This leather, warmer than all others, was urgently needed for the manufacture of trigger-finger gloves used by the army in Arctic climates, where a second gained in pulling the trigger of a gun saved many lives.

Through their volunteer labor, members of the Leather Division in Pennsylvania and New York succeeded in salvaging thousands of deer hides. The deerskins were collected at the various tanneries, storaged and processed through IFLWU members' voluntary labor, and shipped to tanneries in Johnstown and Gloversville, New York, where they were sold to provide leather for army gloves.

The Deerskin Salvage campaigns produced a total of four thousand skins. Proceeds from the sale of these hides were used to purchase two ambulances and a mobile canteen for the U. S. Army, the American Red Cross and the Soviet Red Cross. Army officers, Red Cross representatives, employers who represented management in the deerskin project, and local civic leaders, were unanimous in praise of District 3's effort to aid the war. Mr. Van Santon, head of Karg Bros., declared: "You are deserving of the highest praise and warmest thanks from those who will benefit from your gift. This was made possible by your fervent spirit of Americanism which at all times dominates your organization."

In carrying out the union's slogan, "Fight the War on All Fronts," the IFLWU locals joined with other unions and other groups in their communities to fight the isolationist and defeatist propagandists. In every city and town, IFLWU local unions were in the forefront in mobilizing the entire population for the war effort and unmasking the pro-fascist supporters of Hitler, Mussolini and Hirohito.

The *Fur & Leather Worker,* edited by George Kleinman, reflected the union's all-out campaign to win the war against fascism. It fought anti-Semitism and Jim Crow as hindrances to the war effort and as agencies for helping the Axis by disrupting national unity. It exposed fifth column-ists in American economic and political life and demanded stern action against them. It fought red-baiting and Soviet-baiting as the main dangers to a speedy victory and a lasting peace. Its news reports on the contributions of fur and leather workers in other countries to the struggle against the fascist axis stimulated the members of the union to increase their own contributions to the war effort.* Backing every win-the-war

* The *Fur & Leather Worker* carried full reports of the anti-fascist activities of Charles Michels, the secretary of the Fur and Leather Workers Union of France and Deputy to the French Parliament from the Seine District. An out-

measure of President Roosevelt, the *Fur & Leather Worker* sought to arouse mass support for the Commander-in-Chief so that he would be able to resist the demands of those who would prevent him from carrying through policies necessary to speedy victory.

The International Convention in May 1944 unanimously endorsed the re-election of President Roosevelt. The four hundred delegates, including Republicans, Democrats, American Labor Party members, Communists and Socialists, without a single dissenting vote, placed the IFLWU squarely behind the "draft Roosevelt for a fourth term" campaign. The decision was later approved by the entire membership.

Intense political action campaigns were carried on by every single local and district council. Mass meetings rallied the workers and their friends to re-elect Roosevelt. Special committees of fur and leather workers canvassed among foreign-language-speaking voters to bring out a huge registration vote, and to pile up a large FDR vote. Every single member of the International Executive Board went on record for Roosevelt's re-election and joined actively in the campaign.

"We consider our war record," the Board declared in its report to the Sixteenth Biennial Convention, May 1946, "one of the most glorious chapters in the history of our union. We are proud to represent a membership that rose to the occasion, that understood the issues involved in this great bloody world tragedy, that realized the importance of supporting our government and the United Nations with everything at their command in order to win this great people's war.

"We mourn the loss of our members who sacrificed their lives on the battlefields to save mankind from the clutches of the barbaric Nazis. We bow our heads to our union heroes . . .

"We will do everything in our power to assist the progressive forces of our country and of the world in the great struggles ahead and we will take all necessary measures to guarantee that the great sacrifices of the people shall not have been in vain."

---

standing leader of the Resistance Movement, Michels was executed by the barbarous Nazi conquerors in revenge against continued resistance by the French population in occupied France. At its 1944 convention, the IFLWU paid tribute to Michels' memory and voted to prepare a suitable plaque in his honor.

The January 1943 issue of the *Fur & Leather Worker* carried detailed reports of the heroism of Soviet fur workers in lifting the siege of Leningrad. In August 1943, the paper carried a report of the activities of the Leather Workers Union of the USSR in the war against the fascists.

CHAPTER 52

Wartime Collective
Bargaining

In spurring the union's war activities, President Ben Gold always insisted: "At the same time, we continue to build our organization, organizing the unorganized and improving the working and living conditions of the workers, so that we can make our greatest and most effective contribution to the successful prosecution of the war and achieve victory over fascism."

As a leading progressive trade union, the IFLWU wholeheartedly supported the no-strike pledge of labor for the duration. Conscious of the great stakes involved in the war against Hitlerism and of the vast sacrifices of American and Allied soldiers and sailors, the fur and leather workers lived up scrupulously to their no-strike pledge.

Unfortunately, there were employers in both the fur and leather industries who, placing profits above everything else, sought to take advantage of the workers' patriotism. Aware that the union would not resort to strikes, these employers arrogantly refused to recognize the union's just demands despite wartime living costs.

Wages were frozen by an Executive Order which was also supposed to freeze the cost of living. But while wages were in practice rigidly controlled, heartless profiteering and black market shortages cut into the workers' living standards. The Little Steel Decision of the War Labor Board in May 1942 permitted wage increases only to a limit of 15 percent over January 1, 1941. During the same period and the months that followed, the cost of living actually rose far above that amount. Meanwhile industrialists and war profiteers piled up billions in profits.

Still abiding by its no-strike pledge despite these difficulties, the Fur and Leather Workers Union carried on a persistent and skillful struggle to win improvements for its membership. Utilizing every avenue of patient and experienced negotiations, it obtained wage increases and improved working conditions to the uttermost limits of War Labor Board regulations. This was particularly important in the leather shops. Although wages of the leather workers were increased, over-all rates were still too low, especially considering the high cost of living.

The union had to solve other important wartime difficulties too. Many of its experienced organizers were inducted into the armed forces. As new organizers or executive board members replaced draftees, they themselves were called up and had to be replaced. Thus the union was compelled to carry on the increased activities of an expanding organization and to meet the unusual problems of wartime collective bargaining with a seriously reduced staff of organizers.

In spite of these difficulties, the union recorded some of the most outstanding gains and organizational victories during this period.

In January 1943, the Furriers Joint Council of New York won a precedent-shattering agreement for the fur workers. The two-wage system, which had existed in the trade for the past forty years or more, was suspended for the period of the war emergency. Wages were to be kept at the highest levels of the busy season throughout the year. By eliminating the annual slack season wage cut-back, the wages of every fur worker were increased many hundreds of dollars each year. This was the most ingenious use of the Wage Stabilization Order to the advantage of the workers. Fur workers in Chicago and other centers achieved a similar understanding.

The wages of the fur workers were also sharply increased by reclassification of jobs, merit increases, transfer of workers to better lines and higher paying shops, bonuses, and other means.

Added to steady work and overtime, these gains pushed up the general level of wages of the fur workers all over the country. In addition, the union won hospitalization, sick benefit and life insurance plans, additional paid holidays and vacations with pay.

In the leather industry particularly, the IFLWU organizers became skilled in every War Labor Board rule and regulation. They explored every opportunity to raise wage rates and improve conditions in the shops. With bulldog tenacity, they added gain upon gain to their agreements: equal pay for women workers; spot increases; Christmas and year-end bonuses, many in the form of War Bonds; vacations with pay; paid holidays; special rates for work on larger hides; second and third shift bonuses; hospitalization, sick benefit and life insurance plans; free boots, shoes, aprons, gloves, raincoats, etc.

Of the large number of War Labor Board cases fought through by the union, a few examples will suffice. It took nearly a year to get an increase for pullers at Horstmann's in Philadelphia of one-half cent per skin. But Local 30 never gave up. On January 11, 1944, the Review Committee of the Regional War Labor Board finally approved the increase, with a year's retroactive pay to January 28, 1943.

When the first union contract was signed by Local 310 and the Ashland, Kentucky, plant of A. C. Lawrence in March 1943, it provided three weeks paid vacation for those employed twenty years or more. The usual one and two week vacation provisions were approved by the War Labor Board. But the third week was denied. Nothing daunted, the union appealed. The Board denied its appeal. The union appealed a second and third time. These appeals were also denied. The union stuck to it and filed a new application. At last the Board ruled in favor of the union on January 4, 1944. Its ruling made the third week of vacation retroactive to March 1, 1943.

Joint Board Fancy Fur Dyers Local 88 and Chicago Leather Local 43 shared the honors of being the first IFLWU locals to win agreements with health insurance plans in the fall of 1943.

Local 88 won an agreement with the Fur Dyers Trade Council and the Fur Dyers Guild, establishing a sick and death benefit fund paid by an employer contribution of 2 percent of the payroll. Full administration of this fund was under the sole auspices of the union. The plan included $1,500 death benefits; $500 additional in the event of accidental death; $250 to $500 dismemberment; $16.50 weekly up to thirteen weeks for sickness and accident; maternity benefits up to six weeks; $4 daily up to thirty-one days hospitalization; up to $20 for operating room, X-ray, etc., and $150 for surgical fee.

Trail-blazing agreements were concluded at the same time with the Monarch Leather Company and Hoffman-Stafford in Chicago by Local 43 providing important hospitalization and life insurance benefits. Benefits in the Monarch agreement, the cost of which was to be paid 75 percent by the company, included: $1,000 life insurance; $1,000 for accidental death; $10 weekly sick benefit; $3 daily allowance for hospital room; $15 for anaesthesia, operating room, etc.; $150 for surgical expenses. The Hoffman-Stafford hospitalization and insurance benefits, paid 75 percent by the company, were even higher.

Fur Dyers Local 88 and Leather Local 43 made the beginning. The other locals energetically pressed demands for health insurance benefits. Gradually, they became a part of every agreement. In many cases, the employers paid the entire cost right from the start. Eventually all agreements provided for full payment by the employers.

Early in the war, the union leadership launched a drive to achieve one hundred percent organization of the Canadian fur industry. Concentrating first on Montreal, the union developed a staff of capable organizers, organized practically every fur manufacturing shop and built up the largest local in the history of the fur workers of that city. Wage scales and working conditions were sharply lifted. Next the union completed the organization of the dressers and dyers, making Montreal one of the best-organized centers in the industry.

From Montreal, the union's campaign, directed by Organizer Myer Klig, moved on to Winnipeg. In 1926, as a worker in a fur shop, Klig had taken an active part in the general strike of that year, defeated by the employers. Ten years later, in 1936, Winnipeg Local 91 had conducted a bitterly-fought strike which lasted over a year. Over one hundred arrests took place. Five strikers were sentenced to jail for terms of from two to four months. The fur strikers won wide public support,* but they were unable to carry through to victory. The strike was defeated and the local smashed.

Many of the most skilled mechanics left Winnipeg for fur centers in the East. Others were compelled to open small shops of their own. The city was left without a sufficient number of skilled workers, for years stunting the growth of the fur industry in Winnipeg.

In October 1943, after a rapid-fire organizing drive by Klig, Local 91 was re-established. Without a strike, the union signed closed-shop contracts with sixteen fur manufacturing firms, including the largest fur shops in the city. Through skillful negotiations, Klig convinced the manufacturers that it was to their own interest to recognize the union and provide decent conditions as the only means to retain skilled fur

* For the first time since 1919, when the historic general strike of all workers of Winnipeg, including the police, took place, a general demonstration of the Trade and Labor Council was held. This time it was in support of the Winnipeg fur strikers.

workers in their shops. The victory in Winnipeg brought to a successful conclusion a twenty-six-year struggle.

Less than a year later, the Montreal local climaxed a thirty-year struggle to achieve a closed union shop, winning in addition average increases of 20 percent in the minimum scales, vacation with pay, an eighth paid holiday and health insurance paid by the employers.

At the war's start, only a minority of the Canadian fur workers were organized. By the end of the war, almost every important fur center in the Dominion was operating under a union contract. From small, impotent and impoverished locals, there had emerged a sound, progressive and influential union.

The drive to the South also spurted forward during the war. Most of the Southern tanneries were sole-leather plants. This branch of the industry had the lowest wage rates. And by far the lowest pay and worst working conditions in the sole-leather industry existed in the South. In some Southern plants, wages were as low as forty cents an hour as late as 1941. Racial prejudice was skillfully used by employers to divide the ranks of the workers and prevent their organization. Jim-crow, poll tax and discrimination always ended up with less wages for all the workers, white as well as Negro, sub-standard working conditions and the complete absence of job security.

In the South, as in the North, IFLWU policy in organizing was based on full and equal rights for all members of the union, Negro and white, regardless of religious or political belief. Both white and Negro workers were drawn into participation in the union's activities. Only by unifying the rank and file for the common benefit of both was the union able to organize plants, win elections and sign agreements with substantial increases and improved conditions.

Advances toward the South had already been made by three Districts. The Atlantic Seaboard District had organized plants in Delaware, Maryland and Virginia. District 3 organized the Armour tannery in Parsons, West Virginia. The Midwest District expanded into Ashland, Kentucky, and Hazelwood, North Carolina. At the 1944 Convention, the union decided to drive ahead in the South, concentrating on North Carolina, where the principal tanneries were located.

On August 24, 1944, ninety Negro and 114 white workers employed at the Transylvania Tanning Plant in Brevard, North Carolina, went to the polls to vote in an NLRB election. For weeks preceding the election, they had been subjected to a veritable reign of terror. They had been barraged by every anti-union shell in the arsenal of union hatreds conceivable in this little mountain town. Anti-union incitements were printed in the form of full-page paid advertisements in local newspapers by a so-called "Citizens Committee of Transylvania County." Race hatred was played upon. The citizenry was incited to violence against the union organizers. AFL organizers were brought into the picture in the hope of preventing the swing to the IFLWU.

But throughout the entire period of organization Negro and white workers displayed the finest type of solidarity. And on election day, they gave a strong majority vote to the IFLWU.

The union's campaign in Brevard was repeated in Sylva, Rosman, Asheville, Andrews and Winston-Salem, North Carolina, and in Newport, Tennessee.

The Fur Division of the union also launched a drive to organize the fur trappers of Louisiana. Several thousand trappers, in the marsh and bayou areas along the Louisiana coastline, made their living trapping muskrats, mink and other wild animals each winter. In the summer, they worked as fishermen. Trapping on millions of acres controlled almost exclusively by a huge New York fur company, the trappers received only 35 percent of the sale of the hides. The trappers had to provide their own equipment, traps, boats, shelter and living needs. Whole families worked in the marshlands during the trapping season, including wives and children.

The unorganized trappers were completely at the mercy of those who controlled the land. The trapper had no voice in the sale of the hides, in determining their real value, or in the grading of quality (a slight variance in quality sharply reduced the price of the pelt). While the lordly landholders amassed a fortune out of their toil, many of the trappers were compelled to exist on only a tiny fraction of the wealth they produced. Their living conditions were of the crudest nature. For months they were out in the marshlands, living in primitive huts without heat, water or lights. In most areas there were no roads. Where there were roads, there were no bridges. Travel was by boat. Deprived of schooling, most adults as well as children could neither read nor write. Descendants of French and other early immigrants, the trappers were known as Cajuns and spoke mainly French dialect.

Extraordinary difficulties were encountered in organizing the fur trappers. Language, distance, means of travel and absolute company control were barriers to be overcome. In addition, the fur trappers were suspicious of all unions because of their tragic experiences with AFL unions. Money paid by the trappers as initiation fees and dues had disappeared while AFL local officials suddenly bought homes and land.

Organizing fur trappers became a long uphill struggle. Locals were established in a number of parishes. Even as the fight for recognition was carried on, the union took up the battle for summer school terms for trappers' children away from the towns during the winter trapping season, for roads and other community needs. The union also won a number of important public struggles that gave added protection to the trappers' fishing rights during the summer season.

In organizing the leather industry, the IFLWU also brought unionism to hitherto unorganized luggage and other finished leather shops in Detroit, Los Angeles, St. Louis, Cincinnati, Milwaukee, Montreal, Winnipeg and other cities.

Fifteen hundred luggage workers of Chicago were members of an AFL union. They were ruled with an iron hand by their manager, Samuel Laderman. Although the manager's salary amounted to almost $10,000 a year, the luggage workers' wages even during wartime averaged only $22 a week! Many shops were unorganized. In union shops, conditions were miserable. Provisions of the agreement were not enforced. Grievances of the workers were ignored. At union meetings, the workers dared not complain. Those who spoke up risked immediate loss of their jobs. Finances of the union were not accounted for. Dues and assessments were paid aplenty, but there was no explanation of where the money went. Any worker who dared question or criticize was branded a "Communist," the usual reply of every bureaucrat.

After eight years of such conditions in the shops and such "unionism," the Chicago luggage workers revolted. Unable to oust Laderman within their own International, no matter how often they brought charges, the workers, led by Business Agent John Wesolowski, petitioned the IFLWU for a charter.

Unwilling to intervene in the affairs of the AFL local, disgraceful as they were, the IFLWU agreed to consider a charter only if the entire local wanted it. In a Labor Board election in July 1945, the workers gave their reply. Without exception, every shop (of some thirty) gave an overwhelming vote for the IFLWU. Laderman was unable to win a single shop. In some shops the AFL did not get even one vote!

Chicago Luggage Local 415 was then chartered by the IFLWU. A new era of honest trade unionism opened up for the Chicago luggage workers.

Elections became democratic. Union members began to participate in the local's activities. Finances were accounted for. Workers came to meetings. Complaints were welcomed and attended to.

Within six weeks after it was chartered by the IFLWU, Local 415 won the best agreement in its history, with wage increases, job classifications, health insurance paid by the employers, two weeks paid vacation after three years work, a sixth paid holiday, and other important gains. In this one IFLWU contract, the workers won more than in all their previous eight years in the AFL. Most important of all, the Chicago luggage workers' revolt won democracy in their union! *

While organizing the leather industry and developing the campaigns in Canada and the South, the International did not neglect the work of continuing the organization of the fur industry in centers all over the country. Boston Fur Local 30 achieved one hundred percent organization. Detroit Local 38 organized Newton Annis, the largest and oldest open-shop manufacturing establishment outside New York, and unionized the rest of the Detroit fur shops. St. Paul Locals 52 and 57 organized a fur dressing and dyeing shop in the city which had operated for thirty years as an open shop. Local 72 of Washington, D.C., organized H. Zirkin & Sons, knocking out the AFL's company union in that shop.** Chicago Local 45 organized more than a dozen new shops. Local 70 in New York completely eliminated the AFL dual union from Greek

---

* Shortly after the Chicago luggage workers joined the IFLWU, the entire luggage workers' local in Montreal left the AFL, and by an overwhelming vote decided to join the IFLWU. The background for this decision is a repetition of the story in Chicago.

** The struggle to organize Zirkin's went back to 1937, when the AFL helped break a strike of Local 72. On October 4, 1937, Isidor Gartenhaus, president of Local 72, sent the following letter to Frank Morrison, secretary-treasurer of the AFL: "Our union has conducted a strike against H. Zirkin and Son for the past 6 weeks. Zirkin has made every effort by intimidation, hiring of scabs, etc., to break our strike. But we are carrying on to this day. . . . About two weeks ago he told one of the strikers to come back and join a union which 'he' is organizing. We have an affidavit to that effect. We are now informed, much to our surprise and to the shame of the entire labor movement, that the AFL has issued a charter to Mr. Zirkin's privately organized company union. We believe that no honest trade unionist would countenance such strike-breaking activity on the part of the AFL. It will be to the everlasting disgrace of the Central Labor Union of Washington and to the Executive Council of the AFL if a halt is not put to the efforts on the part of unscrupulous officials to charter company unions."

fur shops. Local 87 of Los Angeles organized twenty new shops. The New York Joint Board organized newly-opened shops and completed the organization of several runaway shops.

The outstanding organizational victory of the union in fur during the war years, however, was the achievement of job security by the New York fur workers. When the Furriers Joint Council agreement with the fur manufacturers' association expired in February 1944, this was the principal demand of the union. To win it during wartime, when the union was pledged not to strike, required a new kind of strategy and struggle that lasted fifteen months.

For thirty-two years, since the union was organized in 1912, the New York fur workers had been unable to win job security. The first dozen years of the union's existence, it had been held back by one misleader after another. Thereafter the union had been split for eight years. Only after unity was established under democratic and progressive leadership, was the union able to take serious steps toward attaining the long-denied job security.

As a result of the victorious 1938 strike, the period of no-discharge had been extended to eight consecutive months. In 1941, it was increased to nine months. And now in 1944, while pressing other demands also, the union was determined to win full job security.

Conferences with the Association quickly revealed that the employers were contemptuous both of the union's demands and of the necessity to reach a peaceful settlement because of the war emergency. The bosses flatly refused to give ground on any demand, and even put forth counter-demands to deprive the workers of some former gains. As union spokesmen argued the need for job security, one employer hunched back in his chair and declared: "If I don't like the 'rats' at one dealer, I go to another. This is a free country." Another employer, hearing the union leaders describe the increase in the cost of living, sneered: "Tell the workers to eat vegetables instead of meat." A third employer displayed his "patriotism" by replying: "National unity? I don't know what you're talking about."

The stubborn attitude of the employers' association was fortified by the knowledge that the fur workers had pledged the government not to strike for the duration. As the agreement expired with conferences deadlocked, one employer gleefully gloated: "This [the no-strike pledge] is the end of the union."

"This is not the end," President Gold told eighty-five hundred fur

Top Season Wage Secured

N.Y. Workers Stop Slack Period Cuts

New York—Wages of the New York fur manufacturing

Wilmington Leather Local 201
WINS EQUAL PAY FOR WOMEN AT AMALGAMATED TANNERY

Wilmington—Equal pay for equal work—and no ifs or buts, especially since the War Labor Board has met its seal of approval on it.

IFLWU Signs First Contract With Hollander In Montreal

Montreal—Signing of Montreal dressing and dyeing major outposts of unorganized banner of the IFLWU. An among the outstanding gains won in the agreement. Headed by the meats organizer

Waukegan Leather Local 204
Gains Closed Shop, Checkoff Spot Raises Totaling $28,000

Waukegan, Ill.—Winning a closed shop and checkoff for the first time in real of its contract with the Greiss-Pfleger tannery, Leather Local 204 also obtained crenses totaling $28,000 for 261 workers and a $10 Christmas bonus for the plant. and the Chri gained after tives and the bonus, which under the W bonuses previ continued to b

LEATHER LOCALS WIN NEW GAINS, VACATION IN MASSACHUSETTS

d agreement of Leather Locals 20 nds and Woburn respectively ha

Mass. Leather

WAR LABOR BOARD OK'S GAINS WON IN CONTRACT RENEWAL

Win At Asheville Plant—108 to 64

Asheville, North Carolina, May 9th—Workers of the Hans Rees' Sons tanners gave IFLWU CIO Local 285 a big majority vote of 108 to 64 in a National Labor Relations election here, repudiating the AFL which held a contract with this plant for the past four years.

Toronto
Win 4 More Fur Shops; Obtain Raises Up to $7

Fur manufacturing workers of four more ed the Toronto Fur Workers Union, IFLWU, raises which ranged up to $7 a week in their

Pittsburgh Fur Local 69
Sets Precedent In Winning Sick & Death Benefit Fund

Pittsburgh—Setting a precedent for the entire IFLWU, Fur Local 69 won the establishment of a Sick and Death for the first

An esti and a 5c an hr all night shi

Ballston Spa Goes IFLWU—155 to 67

its first victory in the town when the dressing and dyeing industry

Montreal Signs 3 More Dressing, Dyeing Shops

Montreal—With the inspiring and historic Canadian conference of all IFLWU them, the Montreal fur work the road to carrying out it convention decision to organ the Canadian dressing and dy ing industry 100%, when they w their first union contracts at thr Montreal dressing and dyeing

Peabody Local 21
WLB OK'S PAY BOOSTS SECURED AT 4 PLANTS

Peabody—War Labor Board approval has been received for in

UNION SECURITY, FREE MEDICAL, VACATION, HOLIDAYS AWARDED E-J WORKERS BY WLB PANEL

Endicott, N.Y.—The War Labor Board Panel has sustained most of the union now pending between IFLWU Local 285 and the Endicott

Two Chicago Leather Pacts First To Gain Sick & Death Benefits, Hospitalization

Chicago—Trail-blazing agreements that are an example to the entire labor movement have just been concluded with the Monarch Leather Co. and Hoffman-Stafford Co. providing important hospitalization and life insurance benefits

Montreal, Toronto Contracts Provide Raises, Vacations Health Insurance Benefits

Announcement of the two new agreements has be solely headed everywhere M and Hoffman-Stafford com ers have set an example that

Winnipeg Is Unionized!

ion organizing drive, the IFLWU has organized and signed contracts cluding the large factories of Neaman's and Reich's Fur Co., it was

Union Shop, 10% Won By Montreal

Montreal—Climaxing a 26 year struggle, IFLWU Locals 66 and 67 made history when they secured their first union shop clause in their new collective agreement with the employers of this city. A three month deadlock in negotiations, which threatened develop into a strike because f the employers' current refusal to grant the workers' demands, was broken with the assistance of IFLWU President Ben Gold

Fur Dyers Loc. 88 Wins 2% Sick And Death Fund Agreement Provision

dent-setting victory was won by Joint Board Fancy Dyers of the Fur Dyers Trade Council and the Fur Dyers

Locals 2, 3, & 4 Win 15% Wage Increase

NEW YORK—Members of Locals 2, 3 and 4 employed by the Fur Dressers Guild of their weekly earning

Vacation And Health Insurance Won In Los Angeles Fur Shops

Los Angeles, Cal.—A vacation and health plan

Joint Board Local 80
5c WAGE HIKE FOR RABBIT DYERS APPROVED BY WLB

New York—The War Labor Board has approved a flat 5c an hour wage increase for 600 members of Local Joint Board Manager Sam B the wage increases are retroactive to April 3, 1943, for time workers and to August 1 for piece workers. Total back pay received by the workers approximately $10 The increase, in addition to raising the time workers 5c an hour

Second North Carolina Tannery Votes IFLWU

Job Security, Vacations Granted By WLB Panel For New York Fur Workers

Fond du Lac Concludes First Union Contract With Important Gains

NEW MASS. LEATHER AGREEMENT GAINS INSURANCE, 2 WEEKS VACATION, RAISES

Wartime contract gains as featured in Fur & Leather Worker.

workers jammed into Manhattan Center on February 20, 1944. "It is just the beginning."

The union did not propose to fight it out with the employers through strike action. To prevent the employers from locking out the workers, the union submitted the dispute to the War Labor Board. A panel was set up consisting of Maurice London, representing industry, Richard Seller of the American Newspaper Guild, representing labor, and Dr. Harry J. Carman, Dean of Columbia College, a member of the New York Board of Higher Education and one of America's leading historians, representing the public. Dr. Carman was chairman of the panel.

Hearings on the dispute began on April 4, 1944. At the very outset, the Association attorney served notice upon the panel that he did not recognize its authority and that the Association would not abide by a decision of the War Labor Board. For four weeks the War Labor Board panel conducted hearings, Association leaders mustering every argument and threat to confuse the issues, intimidate the Board and defeat the union's demands.

Employers and "experts" engaged by them, during many hours of deceptive testimony, claimed that the high craft skills required to make fur coats made it impossible for any but the employers themselves to judge the competency of the workers. Expensive furs could be ruined, they argued, if the workers had job security. The union's spokesmen—Ben Gold, Irving Potash, Joseph Winogradsky and Jack Schneider—made short shrift of every false argument. Their cross-examination of the witnesses tore their "facts" to shreds.

Scores of witnesses were examined. Documentary evidence was submitted. The union produced unchallengeable records accumulated during eight years to support its case. When the panel was through with the hearings, every member visited manufacturing establishments, personally studied the process of production, the work of the various crafts, the skill of the workers, the methods of labor and all other matters pertaining to the dispute.

On July 20, 1944, the panel recommended to the Regional War Labor Board that complete job security be granted, with an extended period of equal division of work, and vacations with pay ranging from one to two weeks. On the union's demand for health insurance, the panel recommended that the union and the employers continue to negotiate for the establishment of a health insurance fund. The employers' counter-demands were rejected.

As soon as the recommendation of the panel was made public, the Association replied that it would refuse to abide by it. It did not matter to the leaders of the employers' organization that the panel had pointed out specifically that "rankling disputes in one industry, if allowed to become festering sores, may possibly affect adversely employee-employer morale throughout the land." Nor that it was "beyond the comprehension that a labor dispute involving an industry of this size and importance in the New York area could not possibly spread to other industries or other workers."

While the New York Regional War Labor Board was considering the panel's recommendation for final approval, the usual procedure before it became a binding decision, the union representatives were shocked to learn that something had gone amiss. Although approval of panel recommendations was the normal procedure for Regional Boards, in this case the Board suddenly appeared to be ready to reverse the panel recommendation.

The union learned that an opponent of the panel's recommendation was exerting pressure upon the panel chairman, Professor Carman, and other Board members. This pressure was being exerted through Dr. Paul Brissenden, economics professor at Columbia University and one of the most influential members of the Regional War Labor Board. Dr. Brissenden, it was learned, had introduced Professor Carman to Dr. Paul Abelson, formerly the impartial chairman of the fur industry. Professor Carman was not informed that Abelson had been removed from his position as impartial chairman because of the union's protest concerning certain of his official acts. Nor did Brissenden inform Professor Carman that during the dispute between the union and the Association he continued to have an undisclosed connection with the employers. Dr. Abelson, introduced as an "impartial" expert, exerted his efforts to influence Professor Carman's decision against the union, and even requested that the chairman of the panel should not make his decision public until he (Dr. Abelson) could review and approve it!

As the recommendation of the panel proved, and unlike other members of the Board, Dr. Carman refused to be influenced by Dr. Abelson or any other outsider. Dr. Carman steadfastly decided the issue on the merits of the case. Dr. Abelson and Brissenden, however, had exerted influence on other members of the Board, which was now about to change the panel recommendation in favor of the Association.

Upon discovering this, the union confronted Dr. Thomas Norton, chairman, and Walter Gellhorn, member of the Board, with the sordid facts. The union declared that in order not to disrupt the whole process of wartime arbitration of labor disputes, it would not make a public exposé of the shenanigans in the case—but on condition that the improper aspects of the case be erased. Dr. Norton and Mr. Gellhorn, therefore, decided to pass the case to the National War Labor Board without decision. A "Confidential Memorandum" to the National War Labor Board in Washington, dated September 15, 1944, declared: "Dr. Brissenden readily acknowledges that he did suggest a conference between the Panel Chairman and Dr. Abelson and that, as the other Public Members were previously informed by him, he himself subsequently conferred with Dr. Abelson concerning some of the issues in dispute between the parties."

The "Confidential Memorandum" also stated frankly that "the views expressed by Dr. Abelson did unquestionably affect the judgment of some of the Public Members [of the Regional War Labor Board]." It, therefore, concluded that the Board was no longer in a position to make any decision in the dispute.

In Washington, the case went before the usual division of the National War Labor Board, consisting of one representative each of the public, labor and management. This division considered the case on the further briefs of the parties but without oral argument. Suddenly, the union was advised by the union representative on the division that the division had decided to return the case for decision to the Regional War Labor Board. Such a decision made no sense in that the Regional Board had already put itself on record as disqualifying itself; it was as if an appellate court had sent a case back to a trial judge after the trial judge had refused to pass on it because of improper influences brought to bear upon him.

It was obvious that some influence was again at work on behalf of the manufacturers' association within the National War Labor Board itself. Nathan Witt, the union's attorney, took the matter up directly with Chairman William H. Davis. Davis called in the members of the division, had them withdraw their decision to return the case to the Regional Board, and had the case set down for full argument before the full National Board. On November 11, 1944, the National War Labor Board rendered its decision. The panel recommendation on job security was upheld. However, the workers were denied the second week vacation which was part of the original panel recommendation.

The union promptly signified its acceptance of the order. The Association, however, defied the War Labor Board. After all the finagling on its behalf to subvert the whole system of wartime arbitration, the Association now asserted the Board was "without power or authority" and that the decision was "unacceptable and uncompliable!"

When the War Labor Board informed the union that it had no means to force compliance upon eight hundred employers in the manufacturers' association, the union replied: "You make the decision. We'll carry it out!"

During all these months, since February 15, 1944, the workers had worked without any agreement at all. The union had nevertheless maintained a most thorough-going check on conditions in the shops. Every complaint had been attended to, even without an agreement. Now that the War Labor Board had rendered its decision, the union made all necessary preparations to enforce the decision.

At the January 1945 meeting of the International Executive Board, the Fur Division took the first step by establishing a million dollar defense fund to back the Furriers Joint Council. The New York fur workers taxed themselves a day's pay. Every section of the Fur Division pledged its share of the million dollars at once. The Leather Division Board members unanimously voted their full support and declared that an attack upon any part of the union was an injury to the whole union. The leather workers would not stand by idly while the furriers were fighting down the employers' defiance of the government board's order!

A showdown fight was shaping up. The furriers were determined that job security—their long-sought demand—must become a fact.

Dealing with each employer individually, the union began by collecting one week vacation pay for every worker for the year 1944. This was the first vacation pay ever received by New York fur workers.

In February 1945, the union concluded an agreement with the New York Retail Furriers Association, covering 250 establishments. This contract embodied job security, vacation pay, and all other points of the Labor Board's decision.

During the same weeks, the union signed about five hundred contracts with independent shops, including all points in the agreement.

At the same time, by an intensive campaign within the ranks of the employer members of the Association, the union succeeded in convincing many employers that the Association was following an irresponsible course, heedless of the nation's war effort. Many employers were dissatisfied with the shameful spectacle of the Association defying the government. Some even began to form a new association.

As the busy season approached, the union served notice on the Association. The agreement must be signed and it must embody the Labor Board's decision! With the Association still adamant, the union called a mass meeting of all fur workers for Tuesday morning, May 22, 1945. The final decision would be made at the meeting.

On the day before the scheduled meeting, out-maneuvered, divided, exposed before the public, and faced with a hopeless struggle—the Association gave up! After working fifteen months without an agreement in a display of strength and discipline unexcelled by any group of workers anywhere, the furriers had won their agreement. And with it, their dream of many years—job security!

On May 22, at 8:30 A.M., the workers of all Association shops gathered in front of their respective buildings in the fur market. Led by their shop chairmen, they marched in a body to Manhattan Center.

At the jam-packed meeting, Gold and Potash reported the final settlement with the employers. The new agreement, to run until February 15, 1948, conformed to the directive of the National War Labor Board issued November 14, 1944. It specified equal division of work for ten months each year, the remaining two months to be designated as sample production months. During the sample production months, equal division of work would be practiced if possible. But in any event, at the end of the two-month sample period, *all the workers of the shop must be recalled and equal division of work resumed for the next ten months.*

The agreement also provided for one week vacation with pay, retroactive for the year 1944. It was also understood that negotiations would continue for health insurance and retirement systems to be paid by the employers. (The two funds, totaling 2½ percent of the payroll and paid entirely by the employers, were actually started in 1946.)

The settlement was approved unanimously by the ten thousand workers gathered in and around Manhattan Center. The New York fur workers had upheld their no-strike pledge despite all the employer defiance. Yet they had emerged victorious after this remarkable fifteen-month struggle.

It was fitting that job security was won exactly ten years after the ranks of the fur workers were united. The results of that unity were now evident to every member of the union, both fur and leather workers. They were evident in the growth of the union, in the number of members, in the number of locals, and in the strength of the organization.

A powerful union stood ready to face the new problems and new struggles that were inevitable in the post-war years.

CHAPTER 53

The Post-War Wage Drive

With the death of President Franklin D. Roosevelt on the eve of victory over the Hitler axis, Harry S. Truman became President. The New Deal, which had been virtually suspended during the war emergency, was now scrapped altogether. Powerful business interests moved swiftly to cash in at the expense of the people. The cost of living rose. Black market operators, speculators, and profiteers made a mockery of OPA "ceiling" prices. Profits of the trusts were pushed to unprecedentedly high levels. At the same time earnings fell drastically because of elimination of overtime work. Unemployment, which had vanished only during the war years, now reappeared. War industries discharged millions of workers. More millions were out of work for months during reconversion of factories to peacetime production. Hundreds of thousands of women and Negro workers, who had succeeded in obtaining jobs in industry during the war, were cast on the scrap heap of the jobless. Still others found themselves working only part time in industries hit by declining purchasing power of the mass of consumers.

In the fall of 1945, six weeks after V-J Day, the IFLWU launched its post-war drive for wage increases, particularly for the leather workers. The first step, outlined by the International Board and approved by special conferences in every district, was a national one-day stoppage in the leather industry. The first such action ever undertaken in the industry, this was to be a demonstration of union solidarity to prepare the ground for the wage drive.

On November 15, 1945, in 250 plants which produced the bulk of the leather in the United States, sixty thousand members of the Leather Division of the IFLWU stopped work almost to a man. In disciplined ranks, these men and women in sixty-two cities, Negro and white, paraded jubilantly through the streets to their union meeting halls. Leather production for the entire nation was at a standstill. Not a hide was processed. Local after local wired the International of its complete turnout.

November 15, 1945, was a symbol to the leather workers—a symbol of their strength and determination, a symbol of their coming of age as a nation-wide progressive union. In the months that followed this national stoppage, the leather workers of every district obtained wage increases ranging from fifteen cents an hour upward.*

A fifteen-cents-an-hour raise won for six thousand New England leather workers in January 1946 set the pace for the entire leather industry in the union's first-round drive. In every district, in every shop, negotiations were pressed. Through peaceful negotiations, backed by a thoroughly mobilized membership, the locals obtained fifteen cents, seventeen cents, eighteen-and-a-half cents an hour more in their pay envelopes. But other contracts, with similar gains, were won only after strike action. Some strikes were brief, like the one-day strike at Hubschman's in Philadelphia. Others, as in Newark, were long and bitter: ten and one-half weeks at Hahn & Stumpf and Goliger's, ten weeks at Colden, five weeks at Lindenoid, and four and one-half months at Star Leather. Every strike, short or long, was won.

The major challenge to the union in the first-round wage drive was at the plants of the American Hide & Leather Company in Lowell, Massachusetts, and in Ballston Spa, New York.

The Ballston Spa plant was organized by the IFLWU in the spring of 1945. A seven-week campaign, directed by Organizer Bernie Woolis and Clarence Carr, president of Gloversville Local 202, ended on May 22 in a nearly three-to-one vote for the IFLWU. A preliminary contract, concluded in September 1945, left wages and other conditions open for further negotiation. It was to take a bitter struggle, conducted jointly

* The very announcement of the stoppage played a part in the victorious conclusion of the seven-week strike at the John R. Evans plant in Camden, New Jersey. This was the first strike of the union after V-J Day. The employer had provoked the strike, which was a test of strength for the union as a whole. The strike ended victoriously on November 5, ten days before the stoppage, with the signing of a contract providing an initial 7½ cents-an-hour wage increase, a down payment on the first round.

with the workers of the Lowell plant, before the Ballston Spa workers completed their first union agreement.

In the spring of 1946, all other leather workers in the area of the two plants obtained a fifteen-cent increase. Months of negotiations with American Hide failed to bring about a settlement. On March 6, 1946, eight hundred workers at Lowell and Ballston Spa walked out, determined that both plants must win settlements at the same time.

The company concentrated its attack on the newly-organized local in Ballston Spa, where there was a long history of broken independent and AFL unions. The company planned to reopen Ballston Spa on an open-shop basis and use it as a club against the older and larger local at Lowell. It counted on starving out the Ballston Spa workers, splitting their ranks, bribing some to act as strikebreakers, and finally calling in the AFL to break the strike.

The carefully worked-out company strategy was defeated. All the union-busting tricks were tried. The company made a partial offer to divide the ranks of the strikers. A back-to-work movement was tried by appeals to individual workers. The company tried to set the community against the strikers. But each maneuver was anticipated—and foiled. A powerful bond of solidarity among the strikers was forged in the struggle. The workers in Lowell and in Ballston Spa pledged to fight it out together. As a token of the solidarity between the two groups of strikers, the Ballston Spa workers contributed $250 from their strike fund to the Lowell workers who, according to Massachusetts law, could receive no unemployment insurance benefits while on strike.

The strike at Ballston Spa, led by Organizer Bernie Woolis, the young veteran who had formerly organized both fur and leather workers, proved to be one of the most militant and best organized strikes ever conducted in the leather industry. The long picket lines never faltered or wavered. The entire community was aroused in support of the striking leather workers. Funds and food for relief came from other locals in the district, from other unions in the area, from the organized farmers and even from a group of Ballston Spa storekeepers who recognized that higher earnings of the workers advanced the interests of the community. The merchants established a fund of $1,000 for strike relief at the beginning of the strike, an unprecedented action in that town.

Characteristic of every IFLWU struggle, the Ballston Spa strikers kept up their fight on every front. The strikers mobilized the village for support of important legislative measures which would advance the interests of the entire community. At every strike meeting, some important bill or political issue was acted upon, such as FEPC, the sixty-five-cents-per-hour minimum wage bill, opposition to the Ball-Burton-Hatch bill to cripple the Wagner Labor Act, and support for the Murray-Wagner-Dingell Bill for federal health insurance. In the fight for extension of OPA, the striking workers distributed leaflets at every factory gate in town, urging the workers to wire their Senators to save price control. At tables on street corners, hundreds of signatures were gathered on petitions issued by the local. The strikers sent a telegram to Governor Thomas E. Dewey demanding removal and prosecution of the police officers responsible for the slaying of the Ferguson brothers, Negro veterans, in Freeport, Long Island. The intensive activities of the strikers on the picket lines, in the streets and at union meetings, raised their morale and fighting spirit to the highest pitch.

In the fifth month of the strike, the company played its trump card. An official of the AFL United Leather Workers suddenly came into Ballston Spa to recruit strikebreakers. He let loose an orgy of red-baiting against the IFLWU and offered strikers sums of money to join in a back-to-work movement.

The Ballston Spa strikers ran the AFL strike-buster out of town. They answered the company with a demonstration of labor solidarity never before witnessed in that community. Hundreds of delegates of CIO, AFL and Railroad Brotherhood locals of the area, including delegations from IFLWU Locals 202 of Gloversville and 285 of Endicott joined in the Ballston Spa demonstration.

Starting at nine o'clock with mass picketing at the struck plant, a parade that was four blocks long wound through the center of the town. It went on to the Mayor's home, and then back to the plant gate for a mass meeting. Speaker after speaker pledged all-out support to the strikers and condemned the strikebreaking efforts of the AFL leather union officials.

In the sixth month, their spirit and determination even higher than during the first six weeks of the strike, the strikers won their agreement.* The Lowell workers won a general increase of fifteen cents an hour retroactive to December 31, 1945. The Ballston Spa workers won the same raise and additional spot adjustments, two paid holidays, health insurance paid by the company (as was already the practice in Lowell), and other important benefits.

The American Hide & Leather strike was proof to other employers that

* Myer Klig and Isador Pickman negotiated with company officials for four weeks.

it was a costly proposition to challenge the Fur and Leather Workers Union. The great six-month strike and the victory won by Lowell and Ballston Spa convinced other employers that it was more practical for them to settle with the union. Most of the leather workers in the remaining plants won first-round increases through peaceful negotiations.

The fur workers, too, scored impressive victories. In almost every case, the fur workers were able to win first-round increases and other gains through peaceful negotiations. When a strike was necessary, it usually lasted only a few days.*

On April 10, 1946, fourteen thousand members of the Furriers Joint Council of New York won a triple-headed victory—wage increases ranging from seventeen-and-a-half to forty cents an hour, and health insurance and retirement funds paid entirely by the employer.**

Fur locals all over the United States and Canada followed the wage pattern set by the New York Joint Council. Pittsburgh members of IFLWU Local 69 received wage increases including substantial retroactive back pay. Increases averaging 17½ percent were won for its members by Local 71 of Minneapolis. Locals 66 and 67 of Montreal won increases averaging 18 percent in the minimum wage scales and a 10 percent general increase for those earning above the minimum. Local 53 of Philadelphia won a 12½ percent raise. Local 85 of the New York Joint Board won raises as high as $1.25 per hour at five shops. Wage increases ranged from $3.49 to $9.50 per week in Duluth; seven-and-a-half cents an hour in Winnipeg; 18 to 20 percent for every fur worker in Chicago. Four Hollander plants received increases up to eighteen cents an hour. Workers in New York fur dressing shops received increases totaling approximately $1,200,000 annually.

From April 1945 to June 1946, according to an exhaustive study made by Labor Research Association, the "real earnings" of factory workers had declined 18 percent as the result of a drop in weekly earnings and the rise in cost of living. And this was even before

---

* Typical was the 14 percent over-all increase on the prevailing rates ($8.75 to $15 a week) won by Los Angeles Fur Local 87 in July 1946 after a three-day stoppage affecting the entire fur industry. Fur Local 180 in Muskegon, Michigan, won an 18½ cents-an-hour raise after a five-day strike.

** The employers would pay 1½ percent of the total payroll as a sick insurance fund for the fur workers and one percent of the total payroll for the old age retirement fund.

the death of OPA. Between June 30 and September 15, 1946, the cost of food alone shot up over 30 percent. Coffee went up thirteen cents a pound, butter eleven cents and meat nine to fifteen cents.

The big trusts and monopolies were reaping a harvest. (The rise in meat prices in September 1946 alone took about $756,000,000 a year more out of the workers' pocketbooks and put it into the pockets of the meat trusts.) Big business stood on the peak of the highest profits in the

NEW YORK WORLD-TELEGRAM
January 2, 1948

THE NEW YORK TIMES
December 21, 1947

Food Price Index Goes to New High

The continued rise in foodstuffs lifted the Dun & Bradstreet whole-sale food price index for Dec. 30 to $7.24, a new peak. This is a sharp rise above the $7.11 a week earlier. The most recent index represents an increase of 16.6 per cent above the corresponding date a year ago when the index stood at $6.21.

The Dun & Bradstreet whole-sale food price index represents the sum total of the price per pound of 31 foods in general use. It is not a cost-of-living index.

INDUSTRY PROFITS AT RECORD LEVELS

Net Incomes of 247 Companies Included in Survey Up 89% in First Nine Months

TOTAL   IS $1,807,372,339

These reports in the press show how big business profits rose as the cost of living was jacked up during the post-war years.

history of the United States. The billionaire corporations and their agents in Congress and the administration were not satisfied even with that. They murdered OPA altogether. They then removed the wartime excess profits tax (in the name of "free enterprise"), but maintained high war-time tax rates on wage earners.

Senator Taft cynically declared that the people should "eat less." President Truman went Taft one better. When the demand arose to re-establish price control, he told reporters that he considered price control as "methods of a police state."

The 1946 Convention of the IFLWU stepped up the fight for wage increases to meet the rising cost of living. At the same time, the Convention launched an intensive political action campaign for PAC candidates for Congress and state legislatures.

A large number of IFLWU officials ran as candidates in both the primaries and elections. Joseph Prifrel, Jr., of St. Paul and Luverne Noon of Minneapolis were elected to the Minnesota State Legislature. The outstanding Congressional campaigns of IFLWU officers were those of Edmund V. Bobrowicz, IFLWU organizer in Milwaukee, and Richard B. O'Keefe, manager of Leather Local 21.

Bobrowicz, candidate for Congress in the fourth Congressional district in Milwaukee, received 45,065 votes against 49,164 for the victorious Republican candidate. O'Keefe rolled up 33,776 votes on the Democratic line in the Salem Congressional District, traditionally Republican, against his opponents' 77,033.

The Milwaukee battle aroused nation-wide interest. After Bobrowicz had won the Democratic nomination, the Democratic Party chose to throw the election to the Republicans by running as an independent the very man whom Bobrowicz had defeated in the primary. Democratic and Republican party officials, the National Association of Manufacturers, and the anti-labor press concentrated their attacks on Bobrowicz throughout the campaign. And the same press which slandered and red-baited him refused to sell Bobrowicz an inch of space for an advertisement to answer these slanders. Rather than permit a union official to win, the Democratic machine sabotaged Bobrowicz's campaign, split the vote and threw the election to the Republican.

In the fall of 1946, as prices kept skyrocketing, the union outlined its second-round drive at a special wage policy conference of IFLWU leaders. The union's first-round struggles had been reinforced by the simultaneous wage fight carried on by practically all CIO unions. CIO organizations had conducted militant wage struggles in steel, auto, maritime and other industries. To break the backbone of any new wage struggles, anti-labor forces now concentrated on splitting the CIO.

Spearheading the drive were the same monopoly forces and their bi-partisan servants in government who were driving toward a new world war. This drive of American imperialists toward a third world war was speeded by Winston Churchill's infamous speech at Fulton, Missouri, early in 1946 in which he demanded not only a "get tough policy with Russia", but also the creation of a western bloc of nations against the Soviet Union. Churchill's policy of preparing for war against Russia was hailed by American big business interests and their bi-partisan agents in the government. While concentrating sharp attacks upon organized labor, these reactionaries intensified their drive to smash the unity of the

United Nations and plunge this country into war against Soviet Russia. Having already destroyed the unity of the United Nations, these same forces were now determined to smash the unity of CIO and convert the militant organization into an instrument to carry through their policies.

The 1946 convention of CIO was preceded by a hysterical red-baiting campaign in the big-business-controlled press, urging witch-hunting purges of progressives in CIO. Recognizing that labor's struggles all over the country would be set back by any split in CIO, representatives of IFLWU consistently fought for unity on the basis of progressive policies. President Ben Gold served on the special six-man committee set up by CIO to deal with these questions at the convention.

The efforts of reaction to split CIO were defeated when the committee adopted a compromise resolution. It unanimously reaffirmed the unity that existed within the organization and again dedicated "our efforts to win economic security and social justice and to unite our movement against the forces of reaction and the enemies of democracy" as the basic policy of the CIO.

The CIO convention went on record emphatically for substantial wage increases and called upon labor to mobilize for the coming wage struggles. It condemned anti-Semitism and discrimination against Negroes; demanded a housing program to meet the needs of the American people; called for a drive to organize the unorganized with the intensification of the CIO's campaign in the South; urged American labor to rally to resist the anti-labor legislation being pushed by the Republicans in the 80th Congress. Without mincing words, the CIO convention urged a return to the progressive policies of the late President Roosevelt for unity among the three great wartime allies—the United States, Great Britain, and the Soviet Union. It recorded its firm opposition to peacetime military conscription, expressed its wholehearted support for the World Federation of Trade Unions, and called for relief, rehabilitation and reconstruction in war-torn countries, but emphasized "that under no circumstances should food or any other aid given by any country be used as a means of coercing or influencing free but needy people in the exercise of their right of self-government." Condemning the world-wide race for ever mounting armaments as a threat to world peace, the CIO convention called for "a fulfillment of the agreement between the big powers of the complete demilitarization, utter destruction of all vestiges of Fascism in Germany and in Japan, and in the complete elimination of the cartels which furnished the economic base for Hitler's and Hirohito's military aggression."

As the 80th Congress opened, dominated by a Republican majority, the IFLWU launched its second-round wage drive. The pattern for the leather industry was again set by the New England District. In January 1947, Locals 20, 21, 22 and 26 renewed the Massachusetts collective agreement with fifteen-cents-an-hour wage increases, an additional paid holiday, and a health insurance fund paid by the employers.

Leather locals in every district swiftly followed suit in their negotiations. In practically all plants in District 1, the 1947 wage increase was fifteen cents an hour. Hospitalization, sick benefit and insurance were extended to additional shops.

In addition to wage increases ranging up to twenty cents an hour in some plants, District 2 won six and seven paid holidays in 96 percent of its contracts renewed in 1947. Practically every agreement provided for two weeks paid vacations and health insurance paid by the employers.

District 3 won wage increases in all but one of its locals ranging from twelve-and-a-half to nineteen cents an hour. Additional paid holidays, improved vacations, and health insurance featured every one of the contracts renewed in the district.

Wage increases in District 4 in 1947 ranged up to fifteen cents an hour in luggage and up to eighteen-and-a-half cents an hour in tanneries. All shops but one were now covered by hospitalization and insurance, and some shops even won three weeks paid vacation.

Wage raises in the newly-organized Southern District, District 5, ranged from ten to twenty cents an hour.* District 5, with nine functioning locals in the South, secured a total of $400,000 in wage raises in the second-round drive.

In May 1939, the leather workers throughout the country had been earning an average of sixty-three cents an hour. In April 1947, even before the IFLWU's second-round drive was completed, the United States Commissioner of Labor Statistics reported that the leather workers earned an average of $1.20 an hour. In exactly eight years, the wages of the leather workers on the average had doubled.

The fur locals kept pace with the leather locals in the second-round wage drive and even went higher. Some fur locals won hourly increases

---

* This first Southern District of the IFLWU was organized at an all-day convention, June 8, 1947, when sixty-three delegates, Negro and white, met in Asheville, North Carolina, and adopted a fighting program for advancing the interests of the Southern leather workers. John Russell was elected District Director.

of twenty-five to fifty cents, totaling in a number of cases up to $25 a week. The New York Joint Council also won a second week paid vacation in the retailers' agreement, and in the pattern shops, in addition to collective increases of $9 a week, a third week vacation and the thirty-five hour week. The Montreal fur workers in many shops obtained $2 to $10 weekly increases although no agreements expired during this period. Winnipeg fur workers won wage increases of $3.50 per week and Toronto fur workers, $5.80 per week.

With few exceptions, every agreement in both fur and leather was renewed as a result of peaceable negotiations. But it took a hard-fought, militant two-week strike with round-the-clock picketing during bitter cold weather for Leather Local 27 to win a second-round increase ranging from $5 to $7.50 a week at P. Joyce Co. in Newark. It took five weeks of a 100 percent solid strike before the firm of H & P in Johnstown, New York, decided to settle with Local 80 and grant an increase of seven-and-a-half cents an hour. A solid two-and-a-half week strike won increases of seven-and-a-half to twelve-and-a-half cents an hour and improved vacations for Local 213 workers at Monarch Trunk Co. in Los Angeles. Leather Local 205 in Oshawa, Canada, registered a sweeping victory in its second-round drive after practically nine weeks on the picket line in front of Robson Leather Co. Ltd. The workers' solid ranks won them increases for day workers up to twenty-three cents an hour, fourteen cents an hour for pieceworkers, and four paid holidays.

The bi-partisan cold war policy adopted by the Truman administration was beginning to show its fangs at home as well as abroad. In scuttling Roosevelt's peace program and New Deal policies at home, the bi-partisan movement of Democrats and Republicans paved the way for the most ferocious attacks on labor. More than 250 anti-labor bills were introduced in the 80th Congress. These bills called for repeal of the Wagner Act, repeal of the Wages and Hours Law, repeal of the Norris-LaGuardia Anti-Injunction Law, revision of the Anti-Trust Law to make it apply to unions, outlawing of the closed shop, compulsory arbitration, the Ball-Burton-Hatch "ball and chain" bill, etc. The most immediate danger to the organized labor movement came from one of the most vicious of these union-busting measures, the Taft-Hartley "Slave Labor" Bill.

The front page of the April 1947 *Fur & Leather Worker* carried a full-page appeal by President Ben Gold calling the fur and leather workers throughout the nation to action against the open-shoppers'

Camden 7-Week Strike Won; New Contract Provides 7½c Increase, Union Security

Camden — The seven-weeks strike of 600 John R. Evans workers was concluded victoriously with the signing of a contract providing 7½c an hour wage increase, union maintenance of membership clause and other important...

$500,000 Back Pay Won For 4 Armour Locals; Increases Retroactive To July, 1944

Wage increases to meet the skyrocketing cost of living, improved vacation plan...

60,000 Leather Workers In Nation-Wide Stoppage Demand 30% Wage Increase

Sixty thousand members of the Leather Division of the IFLWU stopped work almost as one man from the A... ber 16 in a history-making demonstra...

$175 BONUS, 6c INCREASE WON BY IFLWU LOCAL 214 AT AMERICAN OAK LEATHER

Local 30 Wins 10c to 17½c Raise At Swoboda And Int'l Shoe Plants

Philadelphia—Pressing th...

MASSACHUSETTS LEATHER WORKERS WIN 15c AN HOUR WAGE INCREASE!

Pittsburgh Fur Workers Win $7.50 to $10 Weekly Increases

Pittsburgh—Fur workers of this city, members of I.F.L.W.U. Local 89 received wage...

One Day Strike At Hubschman's Wins 15c Raise, Closed Shop; Pay Upped 21c Since V-J Day

Philadelphia—A 15c an hour raise, clo...

New Raise Averages 18%; Pay Uped 22½c An Hour In Past Eight Months

Peabody — A 15c an hour raise won for 6,000 New England leather workers by the International Fur & Leather Workers U...

Atlantic City Local 75

Increases of $20 and $25, Retirement Fund, 2nd Week Vacation Won At Gettleman

Wilmington Local 201
INCREASES TOTALING 17½c AT AMALGAMATED LEATHER

Worcester Local 46
18½c Raise Won At Graton-Knight

Boyne City and Petoskey Tannery Workers Obtain 16c Raise, Other Gains

Increases Obtained In All Chicago Leather Shops Ranging From 15c Up To 24c An Hour Since V-J Day

Chicago—The intensive drive launched by the union to w...

IFLWU Gives $50,000 To Steel Strikers, $25,000 To Auto; Relief Tops $100,000

With contributi... ing steel workers an auto workers topp... the list over one h... dred thousand dollars to...

L. A. LUGGAGE STRIKE WINS 10c-12½c RAISE, VACATION

NEW 16c RAISE AT RAWHIDE BRINGS POST V-J TOTAL TO 24c

Joint Board Dressers & Dyers
Local 85 Wins Raises As High As $1.25 Per Hr.(!) At Five Shops; Vacation Obtained In Other Shops

Furriers Joint Council & Local 125

N.Y. Fur Workers Win Up-To-40c Raise, Health Insurance, Retirement Fund

New York — Fourteen thousand fur manufacturing workers of New York, members of the Furriers Joint Coun... cil and Fur Floor & Shipping Clerks Loc...

15c INCREASES WON BY LOCAL 30 IN SEVERAL PHILADELPHIA PLANTS

IFLWU Wins In South
1st UNION CONTRACT AT PARSONS, W. VA. UPS RAISE TO 16c

CHICAGO LOCAL 415
Wages In 6 Luggage Shops Brought Up To 17½c an Hour; 7 New Shops Organized

15c Across Board Adjustments In New Fond du Lac Contract

Milwaukee Greenebaum Plant Wins 15c Hourly Raise; Total Since V-J Day Boosted To 21c

$15-$50 A WEEK RAISES OBTAINED BY FUR LOCAL 45

Four Hollander Plants Receive Increases Up To 18c An Hour

Chicago Joint Board Picnic Draws Over 1,500 Fur And Leather Workers

LOS ANGELES GENERAL STRIKE WINS $8.75 TO $15 RAISE

MONTREAL CONTRACT RENEWED WITH 10% TO 18% INCREASES

LOWELL, BALLSTON SPA WIN 167-DAY STRIKE!

167-day strike against the American Hide & Leather Co... Spa Local 410 began their triumphant march back into the plant...

15c-18½c RAISES WON BY LOCAL 80 AT DYERS' SHOPS; STRIKE ON IN MIDDLETOWN

Locals 2, 3, & 4
New Increases In Fur Dressing $1,200,000 Yearly

Joint Board Locals 85 and 46
Rabbit Dressing Shops Win 10% Increase, 5% Fund For Health, Vacation, Retirement

3 Strikes Won, 1 More Goes On At Newark, 5 Contracts Renewed, Raises Up To 17c

2-Week Vacation Won By Furriers Joint Council In Retailers Agreement

3 NEW HAMPSHIRE LOCALS
WIN THIRD ROUND INCREASE

UNION WINS VICTORY IN TRAPPERS' CASE; RIGHT TO ORGANIZE UPHELD!

NEW YORK FUR WORKERS STRIKE VICTORY!

New York — The five-week lockout and general strike of 10,000 New York fur workers ended May 7, with a victorious settlement pro...

15c Increases Won In New Col Massachusetts Contract; Oth

Headlines dramatically show the tremendous scope of the IFLWU's post-war wage drives.

offensive against labor and the people: "Unite with the workers of the AFL, the RR Brotherhoods, Independent Unions, unorganized workers and with the people in your community to break the backbone of brutal reaction in our country. In every state, city and community devote all your energy and experience to bring about unity of labor and the people and to defeat the onslaught of reaction . . . Act Now! Let there be no delays! Let your deeds speak louder than words. Defeat Reaction!"

Responding to Gold's appeal, fur and leather locals throughout the country mobilized their membership in one of the most intensive campaigns in their history. Five thousand members of the New York Furriers Joint Council, the Joint Board and Local 125 paraded through the city carrying their union banners and placards saying, "LINCOLN SAID AN ENEMY OF LABOR IS AN ENEMY OF THE NATION" and "FUR VETS FOUGHT FASCISM, NOW WE FIGHT ANTI-LABOR BILLS." Others said, "WE WON HEALTH AND RETIREMENT PLANS AND WE WILL KEEP THEM." The marchers wound up their parade with a large outdoor rally in the fur market. Here thousands of fur workers signed postcards to their Senators demanding that the anti-labor bills be defeated.

"The enactment of this contemplated legislation," CIO President Philip Murray declared of the Taft-Hartley Bill, "is the first real step toward the development of fascism in the United States."

Denunciations of the Taft-Hartley Bill, however fierce, were not enough. When it came to action, the leaders of the AFL and CIO, including Murray, were sadly wanting. Millions of American trade unionists, whose instant mobilization would have compelled Congress to vote down the Taft-Hartley Bill, remained completely inactive. Only the most progressive union leaders, and scattered rank-and-file groups, rallied the workers for mass demonstrations of protest.

As the vote on the bill came nearer, with labor's protests only feebly felt, Ben Gold urged at a CIO Executive Board meeting that a one-day or even a one-hour general stoppage of all CIO members be called. Murray adamantly refused.

The monopolists and open-shoppers, on the other hand, mobilized every resource and pressure to push the bill through. On June 23, 1947, their agents in Congress passed the Taft-Hartley Law.*

* Written by corporation lawyers, the Taft-Hartley Law, among other things, outlaws the closed shop; reduces to paper the effectiveness of the union shop or maintenance of membership; requires a sixty-day notice before strikes; restricts welfare and insurance funds and requires employer participation in their administration; enables bosses legally to intimidate the workers through em-

Typical scenes during the historic November 15, 1945, stoppage of leather workers: Chicago, Peabody, Newark and Philadelphia.

Scenes from some of the famous strikes of leather workers in the post-war drive for wage increases. Top, picket line of Hubschman, Philadelphia, workers during the victorious four-week strike in April 1949. Center, picket-line demonstration at Graton-Knight in Worcester in July 1948. Bottom, picketing in the Ballston Spa strike against American Hide & Leather.

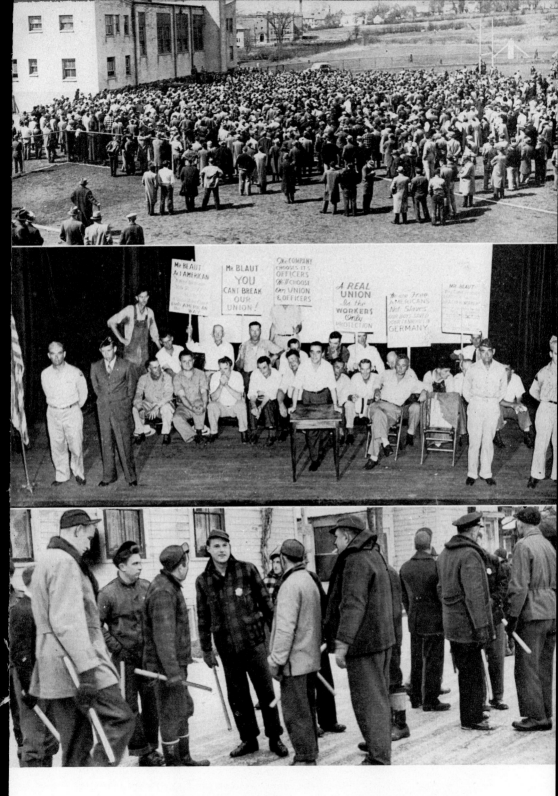

Top, *a mass meeting of Local 21 in Peabody in April 1949 during a one-day holiday.* Center, *International Organizer Bernie Woolis addresses a meeting of Luray strikers.* Bottom, *imported goons deputized to help break the Gloversville strike.*

General Executive Board of the International Fur & Leather Workers Union elected at the Seventeenth Biennial Convention in May 1948. Bottom row: Leon Straus, Samuel Burt, Augustus J. Tomlinson, President of the Leather Division, Ben Gold, International President, Pietro Lucchi, International Secretary-Treasurer, Isador Pickman, Leather Division Secretary-Treasurer, Irving Potash and Joseph Winogradsky. Second row: Frank Bertolini, Richard B. O'Keefe, Samuel Mindel, Oscar Oberther, Abe Feinglass, George B. Grigsby, Clarence Carr, Samuel Mencher and Jack Schneider, Assistant Manager Furriers Joint Council*. Third row: Tom Galanos, John Churka, Michael Donahue, Henry McInnis, Donald Fish, Michael Costin, Lyndon Henry, John Russell, Julius Berger, and Mike Hudyma. Fourth row: George Kleinman, Fur & Leather Worker Editor,* Howard Bunting, Frank Mierkiewicz, George O. Pershing, Myer Klig, Frank Brownstone, Stephen Coyle, Edward Incollingo, Joseph Bruno, Samuel Leibowitz, International Organizer,* and Irving Stern, Assistant Editor of the Fur & Leather Worker.*

*Not a member of the Board

Photo by Fred Hess & Son

The vote on the bill in Congress gave American labor an insight into the true nature of the bi-partisan coalition to destroy labor's hard-won gains. In the vote in the combined two houses of Congress, 273 Republicans voted for it and only 14 voted against; 126 Democrats voted for it and only 93 against. In the House of Representatives, the overwhelming majority of both Republicans and Democrats were for the bill. Only a handful of progressive Democratic Representatives and one American Laborite, Vito Marcantonio, fought bitterly against its adoption.

President Truman vetoed the bill. Beyond vetoing it, he did nothing to mobilize the Senators of his own party to support his veto. Moreover, as soon as the bill was passed, the President announced that he would enforce it. And his appointments to the new National Labor Relations Board, including the viciously anti-labor Robert Denham, a Republican, as General Counsel, guaranteed that it would be enforced in keeping with the wishes of the monopolists.

The IFLWU's Executive Board denounced the Taft-Hartley Law as "vicious, fascist legislation" aimed at "complete destruction of the trade union movement." The union refused to cooperate with the Taft-Hartley Law or submit disputes to the Taft-Hartley Labor Board.

"Instead, our International Union will utilize the full organizational strength of our union and our membership to defend our wages, our job security, our collective bargaining rights and union conditions, as well as the constitutional and democratic rights of each and every member of our organization."

The Board's decision was unanimously endorsed by conferences in every district. Delegate after delegate rose to blast the Taft-Hartley NLRB trap set for labor and to pledge wholehearted support for the International Board's resolution to by-pass the NLRB and to work for the repeal of the Taft-Hartley "Slave Labor" Act.

The 1947 CIO convention unanimously pledged "an increasing campaign against the un-American conspiracy which has produced this Act."

---

ployer organizations, vigilante outfits, supervisors and foremen; penalizes unions for "restraining or coercing" scabs or strikebreakers; outlaws "secondary boycotts"; penalizes so-called "feather-bedding"; makes unions liable to damage suits by employers for acts never authorized or approved by them; outlaws political expenditures by the union in any federal primary or election, and even bans any mention of political candidates or their records in union newspapers, pamphlets or leaflets; to use the Labor Board, officers of the local and the International must file sworn affidavits that they are not "Communists" and do not believe in the "purposes or objectives" of the Communist Party.

Summing up the intent of the Taft-Hartley law, the CIO labeled it as "a triumph of repression . . . a direct step toward fascism." Fully aware that the organized labor movement would be mortally injured if it submitted to the slave labor law, the convention unanimously declared: "We cannot and will not acquiesce in a law which makes it a crime to exercise the rights of freedom of speech, freedom of press, freedom of assembly. We would betray a fundamental heritage of political liberty if we allowed ourselves to be gagged by the law."

While speaking loudly for the resolution and piously avowing their determination to fight the Taft-Hartley Law, many CIO leaders were in fact ready to embrace it. In rapid succession Emil Rieve (Textile), Walter Reuther (Auto), Jacob Potofsky (Amalgamated), and other CIO union heads surrendered ignominiously to the law they had so eloquently denounced as fascist and un-American. Philip Murray was not long in following their example.

The AFL leaders, on the other hand, with few principles left to strip, turned their backs openly on the American workers and almost immediately accommodated themselves to the deadly shackles of the Taft-Hartley Act. With David Dubinsky, the so-called Socialist, in the lead, the AFL Executive Council turned somersaults, crawled and groveled in their haste to live up to big business' dictates to unionism.

Contemptuously disdaining this betrayal of the workers, John L. Lewis of the United Mine Workers declared on the floor of the AFL convention: "Are our leaders to be the first to put their tails between their legs and run like the craven before the Act? It is a sorry sight that the great host of workers in our organization are being led across the plains by such fat and saintly asses."

The first Taft-Hartley blow against the IFLWU was struck by the powerful Endicott-Johnson Company in the summer of 1947. Endicott Local 285, with some fifteen hundred tannery workers, represented only one tenth of E-J's employees. The rest, shoe workers, were almost completely unorganized. Forced to grant to all its workers every concession won by the tannery workers of Local 285, E-J was determined to destroy the tannery local. The Taft-Hartley Law was just the weapon the company had been waiting for.

The agreement of Local 285 was due to expire on June 1, 1947. In the spring of that year, fully aware of the isolated position of the tannery local, the IFLWU started a joint drive with the CIO Shoe Workers Union to organize the fifteen thousand E-J shoe workers. Before the drive was able to penetrate the open shops, E-J counterattacked. It refused to renew the agreement with Local 285 and let loose a wholesale red-baiting attack against the union. At the same time, in violation of the agreement still in effect, it discharged three leading union officers from their jobs in the tannery.

The newspapers, radio speakers, the Chamber of Commerce, the politicians, the superintendents and foremen and the company stooges, the chosen favorites of the company's paternalism—all joined in the frenzied red-baiting chorus. For days and weeks, the newspapers were filled with smear attacks against the union, its officers and leaders. Eight-column streamers, front page headlines, long articles shrieked—"Red! Red! Red!"

The union was suddenly unable to rent an office or meeting hall. Union organizers distributing leaflets were arrested as violators of a village ordinance which had repeatedly been declared unconstitutional by the United States Supreme Court. In all, forty-nine arrests were made of union organizers and members distributing leaflets. The arrests were appealed. After long delays, the ordinance was again declared unconstitutional. The cases were dismissed and the police officer made a written apology to the arrested organizers and members and to the union.

After all the intimidation, coercion and red-baiting, the company challenged Local 285 as not representing the majority of the workers. Simultaneously, the company announced a 15 percent increase on base rates for all tannery and shoe workers and promised a pension system.

In the early part of May 1947, before the Taft-Hartley Bill had been voted upon in Congress, Local 285 demanded a Labor Board election. The company refused. While the Labor Board delayed, the company applied for an injunction in Federal Court against the NLRB. When the union had this injunction thrown out, the company stalled by applying for a new injunction.

By the time the NLRB set the date for a hearing, the Taft-Hartley Act had been passed. However, the amendments to the Wagner Act made by the Taft-Hartley Law were not to go into effect until August 22, 1947. The Labor Board representatives cooperated with E-J by notifying the union that the hearing had again been postponed. The Board representative unashamedly informed the union's attorney that the joint Senate and House Labor Sub-Committee, whose chairman was the notoriously anti-labor Senator Ball, had intervened to postpone the hearings and make an election impossible. The election was never held. It was the first example of Taft-Hartleyism in action.

With the shoe drive ineffective, the union refrained from calling a strike of the minority that was organized. The company had been forced to give a wage increase and institute a pension system. The union decided to make a temporary retreat, biding its time for the moment when all E-J workers could be drawn into the struggle. A solid core of E-J workers, members of Local 285, remained loyal to the union despite all company intimidation.

On the day the Taft-Hartley Law was enacted by Congress, some New York fur manufacturers literally danced for joy in their shops. "It's the end of the union," they gloated. Accordingly, it was not surprising that conferences for renewal of the agreement in February 1948 quickly became deadlocked. A new battle was shaping up.

During the war years and immediately thereafter, the Furriers Joint Council had succeeded in raising the fur workers' wages to an average of $3 an hour, and maintaining the busy season wage all year 'round. In addition, the union had won complete job security, no discharge, paid vacations, health insurance and retirement funds. Encouraged by the enactment of the Taft-Hartley Law, the fur manufacturers were now determined to cut wages and restore the right to discharge any worker they didn't like.

The two-wage system for busy and slack seasons had been suspended during the war. The employers now sought to gain their ends through the resumption of the two-wage system. They demanded a free hand to deal with each worker separately at the end of the busy season. The boss would tell the worker how much he would pay during the slack season. If the worker didn't like it, he was out. In one stroke, therefore, the bosses would both be able to cut wages all they wanted during the slack season and get rid of the militant union workers. The bosses' demand became known throughout the market as a discharge and wage cut "package."

The two-wage system had existed in the fur industry for several decades. The union agreed to the resumption of the two-wage system but refused to give up the workers' job security or submit to the employers' ideas of what the slack season wage should be. The union was determined to safeguard both the wages and the job security of the workers.

Conferences between the union and the Association continued on the understanding that the union would not call a strike and the association representatives would not lock out the workers. The negotiations were to go on until a settlement was reached.

Suddenly, Irving Potash, manager of the Joint Council, was arrested by agents of the Federal Bureau of Investigation and held without bail for deportation. At the same time, in violation of the understanding that had been reached, the bosses' association announced that it would lock out the workers.

Potash had come to the United States as a young boy with his parents, before World War I. At an early age, he became active in the labor movement. When he reached maturity and repeatedly applied for citizenship papers, they were denied him because of his labor activities. It was not until 1948—on the eve of the manufacturers' lockout—that an attempt was made to deport him.

Attorney-General Tom Clark ordered Potash held without bail on Ellis Island. To force the granting of bail, Potash joined in a hunger strike together with other trade union and political leaders who were being similarly detained. At the bail hearing, the district attorney admitted in court that he did not charge Potash with any criminal or unlawful act. Moreover, Potash's many war citations for distinguished services and contributions to the war effort were introduced in court. Federal Judge Bondy ordered Potash released on bail. A few weeks later Federal Judge Goldsborough in Washington granted an injunction on Potash's application, ordering the Attorney-General not to proceed with the deportation hearing on the grounds that it was being done in violation of the law.*

On Friday, April 2, the employers locked out the fur workers. For three weeks the lockout continued. The union mobilized its forces and organized a complete strike apparatus. At the same time, the International union raised a fund of half a million dollars to add to the Joint Council's defense fund. On Monday, April 26, a general strike was declared. Ten thousand fur workers kept the picket line solid throughout the fur district. It was one of the most disciplined and effective strikes in the history of the union. Meanwhile, conferences with the employers continued.

On May 7, two weeks after the general strike began, the bosses surrendered. The Association withdrew its "package". The union won its demand that the two-wage system would operate without discharges and that the union had the right to intervene on behalf of the workers in determining what the slack season wage should be. In addition, every fur

---

* The United States Supreme Court later held in a similar case that Judge Goldsborough's ruling was correct and that the Department of Justice had to revise its procedures for hearings in deportation cases.

worker was to receive a wage increase in June 1948. The new June increase would be added to the prevailing weekly wages which averaged
about $105 for the thirty-five-hour week. A second week paid vacation
after three years of work was to go into effect in 1951. In addition to
retaining all previous gains of the workers, including the no-discharge
clause, the union won other important provisions in the new agreement.

The victorious settlement was approved by a jam-packed mass meeting
of the striking fur workers at the St. Nicholas Arena. The terms were
identical on all major points with the proposals made by the union
before the lockout. The employers, despite the Taft-Hartley Law, had
suffered a crushing defeat. The five weeks of lockout and strike were a
demonstration of the unity and fighting spirit of the fur workers and the
strength of the union. The workers returned to the shops triumphant.

A new struggle unfolded as June rolled around. Defeated
in the strike, the employers now tried to refuse the increases that were
to be given in June 1948. With shops walking out where necessary, the
union obtained increases in every shop, averaging $8.50 a week for the
skilled crafts and $4.50 for the floor workers.

Stymied in its efforts to block the increases, the Association arbitrarily
declared that the agreement was no longer in effect and applied to the
courts for an injunction against the union. Under the Taft-Hartley Law,
it also sued the union for $5,000,000 damages. In fact, the Association
even demanded that the workers be forced by court order to return the
increases they had already received!

Shutting down its "labor department," the Association refused to
adjust disputes with the union. The union thereupon proceeded to deal
with each boss independently. Every dispute was adjusted peacefully.
There were no more shop strikes. To the dismay of the Association
leaders, some bosses even became convinced that they could get along
better with their workers and the union without the Association.

At the court hearing, the union proved that the bosses had arbitrarily
broken the contract. Supreme Court Justice Bernard Botein denied the
Association's request for a temporary injunction and he suggested arbitration. The Association gave its usual answer—no! When Judge Botein
refused to order the Association to live up to the agreement, the union
appealed to the higher court for such an order.

The employers had been defeated in their lockout. The
June increases had been won despite their opposition. Their efforts to

nullify the contract and obtain an injunction had failed and now, as the union's appeal for an order enforcing the agreement was pending in the higher court, a new force entered the picture to aid the fur manufacturers in their battle against the union—the United States Congress.

The Taft-Hartley Congressional Committee, officially called the "Special Sub-Committee on Education and Labor," suddenly instituted a so-called investigation into the affairs of the union. For public consumption, the committee was supposed to investigate "Communist" activities in the fur industry. It soon became obvious that the investigation's main object was to split and undermine the union, and to help the employers deprive the workers of the union wages and conditions won through so many years of struggle and sacrifice.

Special "investigators" for the committee worked for weeks preparing the attack. They secretly interviewed fur employers and their agents. They lined up a group of anti-union employers and the worst sweatshop contractors to be witnesses against the union. For the finishing touches, the committee also had on hand two stool-pigeons.

For five days beginning September 8, 1948, Congressmen Max Schwabe (Republican—Missouri) and Wingate Lucas (Democrat—Texas) had their "star" witnesses on parade.* With full congressional immunity at such hearings against libel suits, the union-hating contractors and stool-pigeons spewed forth vicious and sensational stories about the union. The newspapers and radio commentators dutifully broadcast these slanders. The headlines proclaimed: "UNION DRIVES SMALL SHOPS OUT OF BUSINESS!" "RIGHT-WINGERS LIQUIDATED AND EXTERMINATED BY COMMUNIST LEADERSHIP!" "UNION CAUSES FORCE AND VIOLENCE IN FUR INDUSTRY!" "WORKERS COMPELLED BY UNION TO CONTRIBUTE FUNDS TO HENRY WALLACE!" "BEN GOLD CONTROLS UNION ELECTIONS!" "UNION REFUSES TO ADMIT VETERANS TO MEMBERSHIP!"

Association representatives, groveling before the Congressional committee, pleaded with the Congressmen to make the Taft-Hartley Law even stronger. They bemoaned the fact that there was no opposition group to split the union as in years past.

The legitimate employers, however, refused to join in the smears against the union. Among these employers were some of the largest in the industry. The refused to sully themselves with falsehoods. They gave facts: the union lived up to its contracts; although the union leaders were "determined" to win better conditions, they "leaned over back-

* Congressmen Schwabe and Lucas were appointed to conduct the hearings by Congressman Fred Hartley, co-author of the Taft-Hartley Act.

wards" to honor their agreements. These employers gave unreserved praise for the honesty and integrity of the union leaders. One after another testified to the fact that the union was a responsible, honorable organization. Typical was the statement of Mr. Ballon, attorney for I. J. Fox, one of America's leading fur manufacturers, who had had contractual relations with the union for years: "I have dealt with a lot of unions apart from this furriers' union. During the war I served in that capacity in the Army, and I have done a lot of work in the field of labor relations. I consider this union a very dynamic union. They have been very strong bargainers and negotiators, but I hope I never have any less trustworthy people to deal with in the course of settlement of grievances, or in trying to work out what I consider a fair and practical solution of a problem that may come up, either under the administration agreement or if we reach a bottleneck in the course of negotiations. I have found the people who represent this union in the course of their negotiations in my opinion very statesmanlike in the handling of labor relations."

Such employers were quickly dismissed by the committee, and all that came through in the monopoly-controlled press all over the country was the refrain of "force and violence," "exterminated," "strikes," "driving small shops out of business," "Communists," etc.

On the last two days of the hearings, Ben Gold and fourteen other IFLWU leaders testified.* Every leader of the union stood up firmly against all efforts of the two Congressmen to split and divide the ranks. Every leader of the union, regardless of his political beliefs, defended the union ardently, asserted the democracy that existed within the organization, and reaffirmed the tremendous benefits the workers had derived from the union's policy of unity. Before they finished, the malicious tales of the stool-pigeons and union-hating contractors had exploded. Lie after lie crumbled as the union leaders revealed the truth to the committee. The whole attack on the union boomeranged. When the principal witness for the union, Ben Gold, had given the committee an outline of the

---

* In addition to Gold, the leaders of the union appearing at the hearing included: International Secretary-Treasurer Pietro Lucchi, International Executive Board members Sam Mindel, Sam Burt, Joseph Winogradsky, Lyndon Henry, Frank Bertolini and Sam Mencher; Furriers Joint Council Local 101 Manager Jack Schneider, and Local 125 Manager Herbert Kurzer; Joseph Karass, president of Local 2; Frank Magnani, business agent of Local 3; Tom Maestri, business agent of Local 122; Ida Langer, widow of the martyred organizer, Morris Langer, and now Furriers Joint Council member; and George Kleinman, editor of the *Fur & Leather Worker*.

great struggles of the fur workers for a democratic union, the Committee Chairman, Schwabe, declared that the "Committee is fortunate in having such an intelligent and forthright witness."

Gold challenged the right of the committee to inquire into his personal political philosophy. In a rapid give and take with Congressman Lucas, he proudly told the committee that he had been a Communist for over twenty-five years. "Everybody knows that," Gold declared. "The press knows that. I have never denied it, and I will never deny my principles, my affiliations, and my philosophy. I take my Americanism seriously, Congressman Lucas, and will fight to the death for this democratic country and its free institutions."

In spite of the bias and prejudice of the committee, and particularly of Congressman Lucas, ample evidence, *documentary evidence,* established the fact that the union policy was democratically determined by the membership; that the general policy was set by the Convention and the Executive Board was authorized to carry out this policy; and that the union was operated wholly on the democratic basis of freedom of speech, freedom of thought and freedom to offer criticism as provided in the constitution. One of the most moving statements on this question was made by Lyndon Henry, Negro organizer of Fancy Fur Dyers Local 88. Looking straight at the Southern Congressmen, Henry declared:

"I am myself a member of an oppressed people. My people, the Negro people, have been victimized and discriminated against in the most undemocratic fashion, in industry, in agriculture, in political affairs and in the civic and social life of their communities, North and South, especially in the South. I have felt the abominable abuses of Jim Crow and the dread of the horrors of lynchings. As a Negro, I know the full meaning of the word democracy, because I have felt its absence and violation.

"I have come to Washington with my colleagues, and no decent hotel will give me accommodations—in the capital of the nation. My colleagues are quite willing to put up with me; they do not see any difference; they are all human beings. *Why do we not investigate things of that sort?* My very position in this union in which the Negroes are in a minority is proof that democracy is not just a word in this union but is practiced. In this union, the provisions of our constitution and the tradition of this leadership of no discrimination against any individual because of his race, color religion or political belief, means exactly what it says. In this union, I emphasize, there is complete equality of job opportunity for Negroes and they are not relegated only in the services of menial jobs.

"If more proof be needed, I call to the attention of this Committee the fact that I have been elected and re-elected as a member of our International Executive Board by democratic vote at our International Conventions, and that other Negroes share that privilege and honor with me. I defy this Committee or any other body to point to any other union or any other kind of organization in which greater democracy is adhered to and practiced."

The appearance in person of such right-wingers as Lucchi, Mindel, Karass, Bertolini, Magnani disproved the charges of "liquidation and extermination." "We work together," declared Pietro Lucchi, as he told the committee how the union leadership functioned to build the union. "There is no domination," Sam Mindel, manager of Fur Dressers Local 2, testified. ". . . my experience has been with the present leadership of the International from Ben Gold down; they have never interfered with our political beliefs; they have never come down to our union and instructed us how to vote; they have never denied us the right to criticize. . . ."

The union leaders punctured the lie that the present leadership of the union repeatedly called strikes in the fur industry, by proving that this leadership had never precipitated a single general strike. In 1926, 1938 and 1948 it was the bosses who *locked out* the workers!

They proved that "force and violence" came into the industry only when gangsters were brought in by the employers to beat up strikers and smash the union. When the union succeeded in driving the gangsters out of the fur market, there was no more "force and violence."

They blasted to smithereens the charge that the union had refused to admit veterans to membership by describing the outstanding contributions of the union to the war effort and by offering proof that the union had welcomed thousands of returning veterans into its ranks.*

They smashed the lie that workers were compelled by the union to contribute funds for the Progressive Party by proving that every contribution for political activity was strictly voluntary. That, it was definitely established, was *law* in the union.

They proved that union elections were all by secret ballot, conducted by an election committee elected by the members, and supervised by International Executive Board members from different locals. As for the claim that Gold interfered with the voting, Samuel Mindel, who previously supervised many Joint Council elections, declared he never saw him there at all.

* A telegram signed by 753 members of the union who were veterans of World War II blasted the charge as "an outright lie."

One of the most vicious falsehoods of the sweatshop contractors was the charge that fines paid by employers for violating the agreement were a racket for the union. Mr. Rosenberg, president of the manufacturers Association, had to admit that the fines were set by the impartial chairman after the violation was proved; that it went into a joint fund of the Association and the union; that representatives of both organizations must sign checks, and that payments out of the fund were exclusively for sick workers and charitable organizations.

Once again the Fur and Leather Workers Union had set an example for all trade unions. The attackers of the union were exposed. Their attempts to smear and besmirch the organization were reduced to a shambles by the factual evidence presented in a calm, resolute and straightforward manner by the union. The union's record was unassailable. It had proved that it had one objective—a better living for its members and a democratic America for them to live in. By refusing to knuckle down to the Taft-Hartley Law, it had done its best job for its membership. "A non-compliance union has us licked," cried one employer to Congressman Schwabe.

The frank, truthful and courageous manner in which the union officials testified at the hearings and defended their union made a strong impression even upon the Congressional Committee members. In one of the most remarkable documents ever published by an avowed anti-labor Congressional body, the Committee itself was forced to pay an inverted tribute to the union's leadership. In its report to the House on January 1, 1949, the Committee admitted that "the wage scales of the fur workers are as high or higher than any other industry, and the union is largely responsible for increasing the wage rates and lowering the hours of work to their present standard." * Dealing with the efforts of the fur employers to smash the union, the Committee declared that "it was the employers' use of every means for union-busting and subjugation, including physical violence, that created the opportunity for the present type of officers to take over the leadership of the workers."

In December 1948, five judges of the New York Appellate Division unanimously upheld the Furriers Joint Council's position in the dispute with the New York fur manufacturers. The judges ordered the

---

* The standard referred to was the average weekly wage of fur manufacturing workers estimated at $105 for craft workers for a work-week of thirty-five hours. Cutters ranged from $110 to $200; operators from $90 to $175; nailers, $85 to $125; finishers, $80 to $110. These were the highest wage rates in the country.

fur manufacturers to abide by the agreement and to "adjust, mediate and arbitrate" all disputes as demanded by the union.

Even before the ink on the court order was dry, the Association was already defying it. It told its employer members that they could cut wages freely on January 1, and that any worker who did not like it could be fired. Employers who guided themselves by these instructions of the Association tried to cut wages as much as $40 and $50 a week. When the workers indignantly rejected these cuts, they were ordered out of the shops in violation of the agreement. During the first week of January 1949, about seventy-five shops were locked out.

While conferences to end the dispute dragged on without result, the union succeeded in settling the lockout with each firm individually. The workers were all reinstated without wage cuts, at the full busy season wage.

Deserted by its own members, the Association was finally compelled to submit to arbitration. The arbitrator, Dean James M. Landis, upheld the basic contention of the union. He ruled that the employers who attempted to impose arbitrary wage cuts in January, or to fire workers who disagreed with proposed cuts, had violated the collective contract.

The much-disputed two-wage system did not go into effect until 1950. Late in 1949, the union and the Association finally agreed upon the two-wage formula. The slack season wage (when very few workers were employed) was set at 11 percent below the busy season wage, which was to be resumed on June 15, 1950. Floor workers, the least skilled and lowest paid workers in the shop, received the busy season wage all year 'round. In actual practice, the few shops that were working in January 1950 adjusted their slack season wage at an average of 7 percent below the top wage of the busy season. In many cases, the adjustment was about equal to the June 1948 increase won by the union as a "cushion" for the two-wage system.

The two-wage system was thus re-established with every safeguard demanded by the union. The job security of the workers remained unaffected. The amount of the off-season wage differential was determined by collective bargaining. The busy season wage is resumed in June.

Every attack and maneuver of the employers in two years of continuous struggle had been defeated. The general lockout and strike, shop lockouts and shop strikes, injunction cases, damage suits, arbitrations, court orders—out of it all the Furriers Joint Council emerged the unquestioned victor, a tribute to the discipline and loyalty of its members and the ability of its leaders.

CHAPTER 54

The Struggle Goes Forward

Four hundred and eighteen fur and leather workers assembled in Atlantic City on May 16, 1948, for the Seventeenth Biennial Convention. The most critical political issues confronted the labor movement and the whole nation. The fate of the American people hung in the balance. The "cold war" policy, the enactment of the Taft-Hartley Law, inflation, and attacks on civil liberties were warning signals of an emerging fascism.

Events since the death of President Roosevelt had convinced many fur and leather workers that both major parties were lined up against labor and the people. The Republicans and Democrats had joined in smashing price control, enabling the big corporations to reap stupendous profits at the expense of the people. The majority of both Republicans and Democrats had voted for the Taft-Hartley Act. President Truman's veto, unsupported by any attempt to mobilize even his own Democratic Congressmen and Senators to sustain it, had proved itself merely a vote-catching gesture. In May 1946, Truman broke the railroad workers' strike and demanded legislation to enable the government to draft strikers into the army. Then he used the Taft-Hartley law to obtain strikebreaking injunctions against the miners, who were fined with the staggering sums of $700,000 in 1947 and $1,400,000 in 1948.

Soon after V-J day, President Truman adopted the "get tough" policy put forward by leading Republican spokesmen like Hoover, Dulles and Vandenberg. When Winston Churchill in a speech at Fulton, Missouri, issued the call for war against our former ally, Soviet Russia, Truman sat on the platform and applauded. In March 1947, he announced the Truman Doctrine. Billions of dollars, ammunition and military equipment were shipped to the Greek royalist government, the Turkish fascist government (the "neutral" ally of Hitler during World War II), and to the reactionary Chinese Kuomintang regime headed by Chiang Kai-shek. Civil wars were encouraged in these distant lands. Fascist governments were propped up by American ammunition. Thousands of union leaders were imprisoned and executed in Greece and Turkey. The American-supported Greek government decreed the death penalty for strikers.

The Marshall Plan, which followed the Truman Doctrine, was put forward as a humanitarian plan to feed the hungry people of Europe and help them in their efforts at rehabilitation. The fur and leather workers, like all decent Americans, heartily supported a sincere effort to feed the hungry people of the war-ravaged European countries. They urged all possible assistance in rebuilding the ruined homes, farms, industries and cities of the liberated nations. Indeed, an IFLWU delegation went to Europe in the fall of 1946, visited seven war-torn countries, and distributed approximately $100,000 in cash relief. Part of this money was given for direct relief to orphan institutions, youth training schools, refugee groups, etc. Part was given through the local trade union movements to launch a cooperative tannery and shoe factory in Cerignola, Italy, and a cooperative clothing factory in Breslau, Poland.

Like millions of other American workers, the fur and leather workers soon discovered that the Marshall Plan was a false bill of goods. Using food and other relief paid for by American taxpayers, it was employed by American bankers and corporate monopolies as a political weapon to intervene in the internal affairs of the European countries in favor of reactionary governments and against labor and the democratic forces. The trusts and cartels in Europe were being revived, even in Germany. The very Nazi industrialists and bankers who built up Hitler were being restored to power. Wall Street was being helped to seize control of the basic industries in the Marshall Plan countries. The workers in those countries suffered steadily worsening conditions, inflation and unemployment. Their trade unions were attacked and their strikes broken by government troops.

At the same time, under State Department pressure, the CIO turned its back on its own resolutions which had demanded complete demilitarization and utter destruction of all vestiges of fascism in Germany and Japan and the breaking up of cartels and Nazi control in industry. Although the CIO conventions had specifically emphasized that under no

Hitler Aides Ruling Bavaria; Germans Cool to Democracy

The New York Times

NOVEMBER 30, 1949

By DREW MIDDLETON
Special to The New York Times.

MUNICH, Germany, Nov. 23—"It is very important to rec-ognize that renazification has left Bavaria largely in the hands of those who controlled it under Hitler." This is not the statement of a Communist agitator or an excitable tourist. It is contained in a detailed and balanced report prepared for the Office of the Land (State) Commissioner for Bavaria by one of that official's chief subordinates and his staff and it is only one of many of the blunt statements in this document emphasizing the return of the former Nazis to power.

In Bavaria, however, the movement called renazification by United States officials has been more open than elsewhere and approval by the state Government more outright.

Ex-Nazis in Government

Special to The New York Times.

MUNICH, Germany, Nov. 23—Here is a table showing the number of former Nazis now employed in Bavarian Ministries' and their administration:
(As estimated by U. S. Military Government directors and advisers)

Ministry	Employes	Total Former Nazis	Per Cent Former Nazis
Economics	No figures available		
Education and Religion	168*	10	6
Finance	15,000**	9,150	60
Food, Agriculture and Forestry	1,918	1,468	77
Interior	5,229	1,016	19
Justice	924‡	752	81
Labor	11,919	2,646	22
Transport	191	34	18
Total	35,349	15,076	43

* Excluding school teachers employed by the Ministry
** Estimated
‡ Including only the judges and prosecutors, not the administrative personnel.

This newspaper report shows one of the major results of the bi-partisan foreign policy—revival of fascism in Germany.

circumstances should food or any other aid to any country be used to interfere in the people's rights of independence and self-determination, CIO leaders endorsed the Marshall Plan.

The Fur and Leather Workers Union Convention in 1948 unanimously denounced the Truman Doctrine and Marshall Plan. Using the identical language formerly expressed by CIO, the convention declared that relief should not "be used as a means of coercing free but needy people in the exercise of their rights of independence and self-government or to fan the flames of civil warfare." In place of the war-breeding Truman Doctrine and Marshall Plan, the convention urged large-scale relief to the European countries through the United Nations, particularly to those countries devastated by Hitler's armies.

The "bi-partisan" policy of the Republicans and Democrats had destroyed the New Deal coalition of labor and the common people which had existed in the Democratic Party during President Roosevelt's administration. This powerful coalition time and again had defeated the attacks of the giant monopolies, labeled by President Roosevelt as the "economic royalists." The labor-Roosevelt coalition had brought into being progressive New Deal legislation that enriched our country and broadened our democracy. But now President Truman and the majority of Democrats lined up with the Republicans to smash the New Deal coalition. The "bi-partisan" policy was leading toward fascism and a new war. The IFLWU convention therefore hailed the almost single-handed fight conducted by Henry Wallace, former Vice President of the United States, to restore Roosevelt's policies in government. To advance the interests of labor, to protect our democracy and preserve world peace, the convention endorsed the new-born Progressive Party and Henry Wallace, its Presidential candidate.*

Reporters who had attended many conventions—AFL, CIO and other organizations—declared that at no convention within their knowledge had there ever been such a display of genuine democratic procedure which both permitted and encouraged the fullest discussion of any and all problems by the rank and file. This was in sharp contrast to the picture in the Steel Workers Union convention from which many reporters had just come. At the steel convention those who disagreed with the administration had literally to beg for a chance to say something and then they risked abuse, booing, threats and interruptions. One opposition delegate was beaten up outside the convention hall after daring to speak in opposition to President Philip Murray on wage policy.

At the IFLWU convention, President Ben Gold addressed repeated pleas to delegates urging them not to hesitate to speak if they disagreed. "Just mark 'opposed' on your slips of paper, and I'll guarantee you the floor," he said. The writer, who attended every session of the convention as a guest, heard delegate after delegate express his great pleasure at the democratic manner in which the convention was conducted. Richard B. O'Keefe of Peabody Local 21, who spoke in opposition to endorsing the Progressive Party, declared in a proud voice: "I think that we have the best, fightingest, progressive, democratic union in the country. The membership of Local 21 and New England think and holler as loudly as they can that our union is the best in the country."

The long discussion on the Progressive Party was not perfunctory. A number of delegates subsequently arose to say frankly that their views were deeply influenced by the discussion. In the end, the convention went

* All but two members of the International Executive Board—Richard B. O'Keefe and Julius Berger—were in favor of the Third Party and Henry Wallace as its Presidential candidate.

On these four pages are a few IFLWU leaders mentioned in this book. Above, Myer Klig, George O. Pershing, Frank Brownstone, Ben Gold, Abe Feinglass, John Russell, Isador Pickman.

Augustus J. Tomlinson   Pietro Lucchi   Isador Pickman

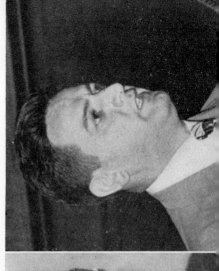

Ben Gold

Staff of the Furriers Joint Council. Seated: *John Demelis, Hyman Richman, Jack Schneider, Irving Potash, Joseph Winogradsky, Harold Goldstein, Murray Brown.* Standing: *Isidore Gru, Morris Breecher, Jack Hindus, Sam Resnick, Harry Jaffe, Max Brons-* *nick, Bernard Stoller, Samuel Freedman, Max Kochinsky, Leon Shlofrock, Oscar Ward, Joseph Morgenstein, Julius Fleiss, Herbert Kurzer, Steve Leondopoulos, Maurice H. Cohen.*

Photo by Tommy Weber

Samuel Wittel

Richard R. O'Keefe

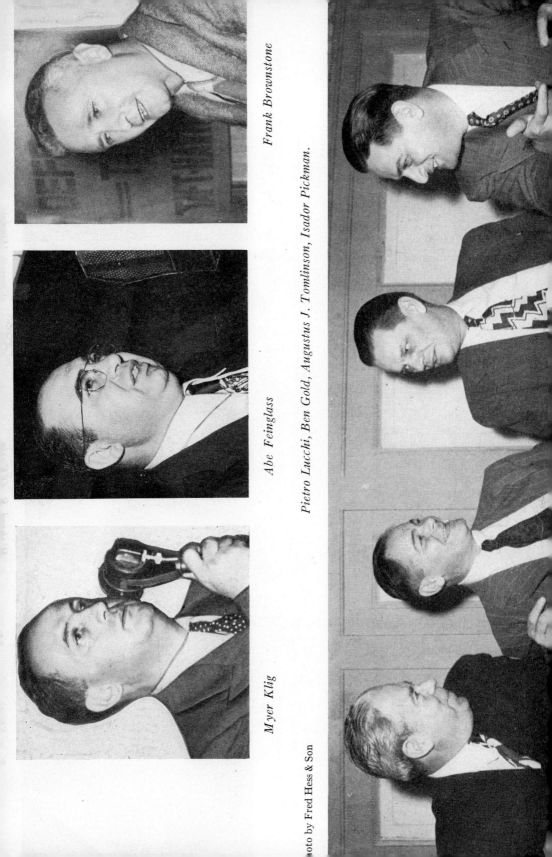

Frank Brownstone

Abe Feinglass

Myer Klig

Pietro Lucchi, Ben Gold, Augustus J. Tomlinson, Isador Pickman.

Photo by Fred Hess & Son

Photo by Fred Hess & Son

Jack Schneider, Irving Potash, Ben Gold, Joseph Winogradsky, Sam Burt.

Lyndon Henry

Samuel Leibowitz

George Kleinman

on record by an overwhelming vote endorsing the new party and candidates Henry Wallace and Senator Glen H. Taylor. At the same time, the resolution sharply emphasized the "right of every worker in our International Union to vote and act on political issues in accord with his own convictions and conscience."

Large sections of the fur and leather workers campaigned energetically for the Progressive Party. They made up one of the staunchest battalions in Henry Wallace's "Gideon's Army." Despite the small vote for the Wallace ticket, the Progressive Party had made a tremendous contribution to labor and the nation. It established a third party organization and got on the ballot in a majority of states. It brought to the fore the real needs of the people. The deep-rooted stirring aroused in the ranks of the common people by the Progressive Party led President Truman to make demagogic promises for peace, repeal of Taft-Hartley, civil rights, housing and a host of other measures demanded by the people. Once re-elected, Truman's pledges remained uniformly unfulfilled.

Intimidation, terrorism, and unbridled red-baiting attacks were employed against the Progressive Party in the 1948 elections. The Wallace vote, small as it was, signified an active revolt on the part of America's most progressive citizens against the betrayals of both the Democratic and Republican Parties.

The situation in the leather industry in 1948 and 1949 was not very favorable for new rounds of wage increases. Unlike workers in steel, auto and certain other industries, many leather workers worked part time for many weeks. Some were completely unemployed for months on end. The sole leather industry, seriously affected by growing use of substitute materials, was hit worst of all, a number of plants shutting down altogether. The union-busting Taft-Hartley Law, coupled with the red-baiting hysteria in which even CIO and AFL leaders engaged, encouraged anti-union employers in the leather industry. Moreover, the fact that many CIO unions like auto, steel, textile, shoe and clothing did nothing to secure wage increases for their members stiffened the resistance of the leather employers to the IFLWU's demands. A report in the *New York Times* of November 27, 1949, reveals the abandonment of the wage fight, typical of many CIO unions: "Because of the financial condition of the industry, leaders of the CIO Textile Workers Union have decided not to seek wage increases and pension benefits in the first half of 1950 for 90,000 workers in New England and Middle Atlantic woolen and worsted mills. *This marks the third time since woolen and worsted wages were increased in February, 1948, that this division of the union has waived its contractual right to present demands . . ."*

Instead of leading the textile workers in struggles to improve their working and living conditions, Rieve, Baldanzi and other leaders of the Textile Workers Union, like many other CIO leaders, were spending their time and the workers' money in red-baiting and raiding sister unions.

In the face of the serious economic conditions in the leather industry and the capitulation of many CIO unions to the employers, the IFLWU nevertheless energetically pressed its third and fourth-round wage drives. At the end of 1949, it went on to start the fifth round.

The New England District was the pacemaker for the leather division in the third and fourth-round drives. Third-round increases were obtained in 1948, ranging from eleven-and-a-half to fourteen cents an hour plus two additional holidays for approximately eight thousand New England tannery workers.*

Following generally the pattern set in New England, all other districts completed the third round with increases ranging from seven-and-a-half to fifteen cents an hour. Fur workers won an average of $15 a week during 1948. Additional paid holidays, increased vacations, life and health insurance systems paid by the employers, and other important gains were also won. Even the sole leather plants, with the most difficult economic

---

* When New England leather workers won their third-round wage increase of ten cents an hour in January 1948, they raised their wages 114 percent above the average wage at the time of the merger of the fur and leather workers in 1939, exclusive of all other gains. A comparison of the working conditions of the four locals covered by the collective contract, shows these remarkable improvements achieved in nine years:

	1939	1948	Percent Increase
Average wage, all workers	70¢	$1.50	114%
Minimum wage, women	40¢	1.05	138%
Minimum wage, men, dry depts.	54¢	1.15	113%
Minimum wage, men, wet depts.	62½¢	1.32½	113%
Paid holidays	one	five (six in Norwood)	
Paid vacations	none	one and two weeks	
Nightshift premiums	none	5¢ and 7½¢	
Insurance	none	$1,000 life	
Sick benefit	none	$12.50	
Hospitalization	none	Blue Cross	

In 1949, wages, holidays and insurance benefits were increased again. Nor is this list of improved working conditions complete by any means. Space does not permit discussion of every gain won in shop conditions.

situation to contend with, obtained average increases of ten cents an hour. The only local that failed to obtain a third-round increase in 1948 was Gloversville Local 202, confronted by extraordinary problems.

The IFLWU made great strides forward in Canada during these years. In Montreal, Toronto and Winnipeg, the IFLWU set the pace for all trade unions, winning increases of thirteen and fourteen cents an hour in addition to other contract improvements. Winnipeg, for example, with fourteen cents an hour, led all other unions including railroad, packers, clothing, machinists and steel. During this period, the Canadian fur and leather workers carried on intensive organizational work, attaining the highest union membership in their history.*

The IFLWU was the only industrial union in New England to break through for a general fourth-round wage increase in 1949. District 1's fourth-round victory came after five months of intensive and difficult negotiations with the Massachusetts Leather Manufacturers Association. Anxious to exhaust every possible means to obtain a peaceful settlement, the union nevertheless set up a five-hundred-man strike committee and mapped detailed preparations for all eventualities should the employers persist in their refusal to grant the workers' demands. With a strongly disciplined and fully alerted membership, the union was able to enforce all union conditions although compelled to operate for three months without an agreement.

Negotiations virtually broke down on April 18, 1949. A strike seemed inevitable. Strikes started in a number of shops where some employers had stopped soaking in violation of the understanding with the union. To back up the union's conference committee, Local 21 members took a one-day holiday. The settlement was achieved on the day of the stoppage. Highlighting the gains won in the two-year contract were a 4½-cents-an-hour across-the-board general wage increase, with retroactive pay for the month of January, and an additional holiday with pay, making a total of six paid holidays.

The Atlantic Seaboard, Midwest and Southern Districts, all handicapped by the fact that most CIO unions scrapped the wage fight, also came through with fourth-round increases in 1949. Increases generally ranged from five cents up, in some cases as much as twelve-and-a-half cents, and fringe benefits. About half the sole leather workers of Western

* The Canadian District of the IFLWU was founded on October 16, 1948, at a conference in Montreal attended by 107 delegates representing nineteen locals from Vancouver to Quebec. Robert Haddow was named Canadian Director of the IFLWU.

Pennsylvania had won their fourth round by the end of 1949, with negotiations still going on in the remaining locals.

Local 223 at the Northwestern Leather Co. in Sault St. Marie, Michigan, was the first union in the entire country to win a fifth-round wage
increase. By January 1950, the start on the fifth round had also been
made by the IFLWU in Chicago, Philadelphia and other cities.

Most of the gains in the third, fourth and fifth-round wage
drives were won without strikes. Many months of difficult negotiations
were required to win fourth-round wage increases, an old age pension
plan and two paid holidays for the workers at the four Hollander plants.

It took seven months of patient negotiating and a one-week stoppage
in Toronto for members of Fur Local 58 to win the fourth round. Everywhere the local unions were engaged in conferences, meetings, rallying
the membership, fighting back against wage cuts demanded by the employers, combating speedup, demanding increases and other benefits.

It required a hard-fought four-week strike at Hubschman's in Philadelphia to win a fourth-round across-the-board package increase of eight
cents an hour in 1949. It took a militant six-week-long strike by Leather
Local 221 members in Ontario to win an eight-cents-an-hour across-the-
board fourth-round hike. A bitter twenty-six-week strike of five hundred
Kirstein workers—the longest strike in the history of District 1—was
necessary to win the same increases already obtained by all other New
England tannery workers. But outstanding in the battles of 1948 and
1949 were Luray, Worcester, and Gloversville.

Luray is a tiny town in central Virginia. Cradled between
high hills near beautiful caverns, it has only one factory, a leather tannery. Back in 1940, when the IFLWU came in, the wages at the tannery
were only twenty-eight to forty cents an hour. In the spring of 1948, they
were three times that, but still the 250 Luray tannery workers needed a
raise in pay to meet the high cost of living. For three long months, they
pointed out to Mr. Blaut, the boss of Virginia Oak Tannery, that the cost
of living was soaring and that in practically every other tannery in the
country, the workers had received an increase. But Blaut had only one
answer—no! He rejected mediation. He rejected arbitration. He was out
to smash the union.

The strike was called on May 28, after a unanimous vote by the 250
workers. All hell broke loose on that very day. Governor Gregg Cherry
rushed in at the request of the firm with state troopers. They patrolled

the area as if a war was on. Unable to recruit scabs from among the Luray townspeople, who were almost solidly behind the strikers, the firm imported drunkards and 'teen-agers from forty and fifty miles away. The scabs were driven through the picket lines by troopers at breakneck speed in trucks and jeeps, endangering the peaceful pickets at the five plant gates.

In the second week of the strike, Blaut got a temporary injunction from the local judge, Ford. The testimony in favor of the union by the president of the businessmen's association, the deputy sheriff, and other leaders of the community were all disregarded by the court in granting the injunction. Seven strikers were hailed before Judge Ford on false charges. He put them under $1,000 "peace" bonds for each.

The strikers, typically kindly, law-abiding folk, were slow to anger; but once aroused they were ready to go the limit. Now the tannery workers burned with a deep wrath. One of the leading members of the strike committee declared that "before going back to work without a contract, I would crawl out of the state on my hands and knees." The International Union sent financial, organizational and moral aid to these courageous workers. Locals in District 2 forwarded funds collected to supply food and milk to the families of the strikers.

Blaut and his hirelings were getting desperate. Despite the daily scab-herding by the company in far-off communities, the tannery had had no success in resuming the production of suitable hides for shipment. The company and its hirelings wanted a stronger injunction. They sought ways to provoke "violations." They wanted to throw the union leadership into jail, to weaken the ranks and bust the strike.

In the ninth week of the strike, the Luray workers were enraged to learn that the CIO Regional Director was cooperating with the company to break the strike. He had gone directly to Blaut and opened negotiations without consulting the strikers. Then he went to the local leaders of the union over the heads of both the strike leaders and the International officials, and urged them to call off the strike and accept the settlement he had worked out with the company. The strikers turned him down flat. But this official nod from the CIO encouraged Blaut to intensify his drive to break the strike. The CIO took no action against the injunction, failed to protest the use of troopers for scab-herding or the persecution of the strike leaders, and did not contribute a cent to the strikers' relief.

At the company's request, Judge Ford issued a sweeping injunction against the union. Only three pickets were allowed. Severe, incredible restrictions were placed on the right of the strikers to assemble peacefully anywhere in the neighborhood. Later, Judge Ford was compelled to disqualify himself as prejudiced.*

In November, in keeping with the scheme of company representatives,** twenty-six strikers were framed on charges of "violating" the injunction. The case was heard by the new judge, Crosby. The hearing went on for weeks. The chief of police, Harry Farrar, and the policeman, Everett Baker, both Blaut's witnesses, had observed the picket line, and were compelled to admit that there had been no violence. Blaut's managers and stoolpigeons swore to "mass picketing," but on questioning had to admit that there were never more than three pickets at the plant gate.

Despite all of this evidence, Judge Crosby found the twenty-six strikers guilty. He singled out the two union organizers, Bernie Woolis and Ike Kostrow, for special punishment, sentencing them to a year imprisonment plus a $500 fine on Kostrow and a $250 fine on Woolis. The rest, he sentenced to two to nine months' imprisonment, but suspended sentence and put them on "probation" up to one year.***

Faced with a virtual reign of terror, the strikers fought on bravely. But it was impossible to win out against such tremendous obstacles. In April 1949, the eleven-month struggle of the Luray leather workers was called off. Many of the strikers were blacklisted, and those who were taken back in the plant were forced to accept drastic wage cuts and humiliating working conditions. They had lost this battle, but at terrific cost to the employer. Other leather bosses learned that it was wiser to

---

* Judge Ford's disqualification came after the union's attorneys confronted him with the following compromising facts: (1) Judge Ford was the former lawyer for the tannery; (2) Judge Ford's nephew was the lawyer for the tannery; (3) Judge Ford shared a law office with the lawyer for the company; (4) Judge Ford was a personal friend of Mr. Blaut, owner of the tannery.

** By a rare accident, Abe Brubaker, Sheriff of Page County, and Robert Huffman, the County Clerk, overheard the plan for the conspiracy. Testifying in court, the Sheriff and the County Clerk told how they overheard a telephone conversation on June 15 in which Mr. Robertson, the company attorney, was told by two plant managers that the strike was "very effective; this injunction we have up here is no good. We want one with teeth in it." Robertson then said: "We must get these boys heavily penalized and in jail before we can break this union. . . . Have them do something to make the judge mad . . . try to get specific violations."

*** At the close of the hearing, Blaut's lawyer demanded that Judge Crosby impose a fine on the union, "heavy enough and large enough" that in the event they did not pay the fine, the court should "order the union dissolved" and should "prohibit and ban" the union from the state of Virginia! But this proposal was too raw even for Judge Crosby.

settle peacefully with their workers than to pay the price of such a challenge. The union in Luray was compelled to retreat, but it vowed to reform its ranks at the earliest possible moment.

An eighteen-week strike (June 8—October 8, 1948) of 550 leather workers at Graton-Knight in Worcester, preceded by months of fruitless negotiations, was remarkable for the discipline and loyalty of the strikers, and their resistance to every company effort to split their ranks. The company had fastened its hopes on exhausting the strikers, starving them out, weakening their morale, splitting them internally by red-baiting propaganda. But the strikers defeated every attack. Other locals in District 1 came through with moral, organizational and financial support to the strikers. Rather than exhaust the defense fund of the union, more than half the strikers took any other job they could get, picking apples, road-work, construction gangs and even the most backbreaking and low-paid work. They nevertheless reported at every strike meeting and turned out for demonstrations on the picket line.

Around the sixteen-acre plant was a picket line—twenty-four hours a day. Up to two hundred strikers held that line, rain or shine. Delegations of pickets from all over New England helped man the line. From Peabody and other locals, IFLWU members and officers marched with their striking G & K brothers on the picket line.

A strike committee of seventy, constantly in touch with the membership, constantly giving heart to the strikers, was at the core of the battle. Strike meetings were practically one hundred percent attended. The rank and file decided the issues. And the rank and file carried on with their own activities. Every strike meeting began with a one-hour show, with home-talent providing the entertainment.

It was obvious weeks before the settlement that the company was licked. (In August, President Gold told the strikers, "You have already won your strike.") Nevertheless, Graton-Knight did not give up the ghost until it had suffered a series of decisive defeats, until the strikers had proved that nothing the company might do could break the strike.

The final knockout blow was administered on September 13 when the workers contemptuously rejected a six cents offer by a vote of 455 to 43 in a secret ballot poll conducted by the State Board. After that the game was up and the company was compelled to settle. It came through on October 8, 1948, with a ten-cents-an-hour increase, with five of the ten cents retroactive for nine weeks from April 1 to June 8 when the strike started; two additional paid holidays in the contract year; four hours reporting time; and a one-year agreement. It was a complete victory for the Worcester workers and a lesson to all employers in the industry.

In October 1948, a committee representing the leather workers in Gloversville, New York, members of IFLWU Local 202, opened negotiations with the Tanners Association for a wage increase. Pointing out that every other group of organized leather workers the country over had received the third round and practically all a fourth round of wage increases, the leather workers in Fulton County asked for a third-round wage increase.

Conferences dragged for many months. At each conference the tanners turned a deaf ear to the committee's arguments. The Tanners Association offered to renew the contract without a raise. They even praised the union for maintaining peaceful relations since 1933. They lauded the union leadership and Clarence Carr, its president, for the responsible manner in which the organization conducted its business. All the tanners insisted on was that Local 202 should give up its demand for a raise.

The union made one proposal after another to settle the dispute peacefully. In answer to the tanners' plea of poverty, it proposed to settle only with those whose financial condition was unquestionably sound. The tanners refused. When the State Mediator proposed arbitration, the tanners hastily rejected it. To every fair proposal the answer of the tanners was an arbitrary, blunt refusal.

On June 29, 1949, Mr. Myers, the spokesman for the Tanners Association, sent the union a letter offering to extend the agreement eighteen months—if it would not ask for a wage increase. The leather workers rejected the proposal and repeated their demands for wage increases and other improvements in working conditions.

On July 15 the tanners gave their answer. Employers in eighteen tanneries locked out the members of Local 202. A broad rank-and-file policy committee, headed by Clarence Carr, was elected by the workers to direct the strike. Bernie Woolis, IFLWU organizer, was assigned to help them.

A terrific red-baiting campaign was loosed against the strikers. For sixteen years the employers had been dealing with this same union. As late as June 29, the Tanners Association had offered to renew the agreement with this union for eighteen months, but without an increase. Now, the union suddenly was "disloyal." Screaming advertisements appeared in the press crying "Communism" and "subversive," signed by the very same tanners who a day before were ready to sign a no-raise contract with the union. With the picket lines around the eighteen plants solidly manned by determined strikers, the tanners tried in vain to reopen the plants. Widely-advertised back-to-work movements brought no results. Company unions, set up by various tanners for the occasion, were shunned by the strikers. The employers now turned to the AFL to do their dirty work.

On August 25, a meeting was held at the Yates Hotel in Syracuse, about a hundred miles from Gloversville. The meeting, arranged by Jack Forster, the $12,000-a-year "labor" relations expert of the Tanners Association, was attended by eight tannery employers and their hirelings, eleven leather workers whom the bosses considered to be "loyal" workers, and organizers Walsh and Schrier of the AFL United Leather Workers Union. The meeting mapped out the plan for the AFL to enter the picture and break the strike.

But the employers made a serious blunder. Unknown to the bosses, there were a couple of good union men present. Through them, the union had been alerted. When the employers, their supposed stooges, and the AFL organizers left the hotel, the union's photographers were on hand to snap pictures. The next day, in huge advertisements, the union announced that the bosses had been "caught in the act" of illegally trying to set up a company union with an AFL label. The bosses' only answer to this exposé was more red-baiting: they were only trying to break the hold which the "Communist Union" maintained over the workers by "terror and intimidation."

The union proposed an election by the city administration, the state conciliation board, the federal mediation service, or any other similar agency, to let the workers decide by secret ballot whether they wanted Local 202 or not. The tanners shrieked that only a NLRB election would be "legal." This was the tanners' idea of democracy, an election in which Local 202 would be off the ballot for having refused to comply with the vicious Taft-Hartley Act, while a union brought in by the employers would be on the ballot.

The tanners and the AFL petitioned the NLRB for an election. To enable the strikers to defeat this maneuver, President Gold advised Local 202 that it could disaffiliate from the International, return to the independent status it had held up to 1940, comply with the Taft-Hartley Act, and ask for a place on the ballot in the Taft-Hartley Board election. Gold proposed this in order to expose completely the lying propaganda of the tanners and put an end to all their subterfuges. The Gloversville strikers voted reluctantly to follow his advice. After the vote, the union's officers filed the required affidavits and the union applied for a place on the ballot.

The decision of the strikers was a terrific setback to the schemes of the Tanners Association. They had never dreamed that the union would comply. They knew that the now-independent union would sweep any election. They now exerted every possible influence on the Taft-Hartley Labor Board, through Congressmen and other forces, to keep the union off the ballot though it had filed the Taft-Hartley affidavits. The Taft-Hartley Board readily accommodated the tanners. Disregarding all previous rulings of its own Board, it disqualified the independent union.

With the exposure of the AFL-tanners' scheme, and aware of the deep-rooted hatred of the workers for the discredited AFL, the tanners turned in desperation to the CIO for help to break the strike. Among the men paid by the bosses to split the ranks and break the strike was Leonard Gray. A loyal union man and striker, Gray submitted reports to the union on everything he did and heard, told how the employers brought the CIO Textile Workers Union into a company union deal after they saw that not a single honest worker would have anything to do with the AFL outfit.*

In many ways, the NLRB election in Gloversville on December 9, 1949, was the most unusual in American labor history. Perhaps for the first time in labor history, the bosses and their allies pleaded with the strikers to "vote for a union!" They had in mind, of course, the two unions certified to appear on the ballot—the CIO Textile Workers Union or the AFL Leather Workers, who were both attempting to smash the six-month strike of the Gloversville workers. A vote for the AFL Union or the CIO Textile Workers, the employers declared in full-page advertisements and in letters to the workers, would result in immediate reopening of the shops and a contract. A vote for "no union," the only way the workers could express their support for their own union, would mean the shops would remain closed. The press, many church officials and the CIO Textile Workers Union echoed the tanners' threats. Jack Rubinstein, head of the CIO Textile Union's phony "leather division," delivered red-baiting speeches over the radio and inserted ads in the press urging the strikers to vote for "a Right Wing Union," the "Leather Division of the Textile Workers Union, Right Wing CIO."

On the day before the NLRB election was held, the *Leader-Republican* of Gloversville and Johnstown came out with a prediction that Local 202's "obituary will be written December 9, the aftermath of a death brought about by ballots, not words." The next day the paper had to eat its words. The vote was 536 for "no union," 180 for the Textile Workers, and 144

---

* Gray's report, published as a paid advertisement by the union two days before the NLRB election, created a sensation in Gloversville.

for the AFL. "The result is a victory for Carr & Company's Independent Union," the *Leader-Republican* wept. "It is a defeat for the Tanners."

Following the election, the union succeeded in breaking the solid front of the Tanners Association when one shop, McKay's, signed a contract for wage increases ranging from 13½ cents to 31½ cents an hour, and opened operations on January 3. But the other seventeen tanners were still determined to smash the union. Not only were they assured of continuing support from the AFL and the CIO Textile Union, but they also set up a new company-union outfit, and announced a grand reopening of the struck plants on January 25, 1950.

On the day of the scheduled "return to work," a reign of terror gripped the cities of Gloversville and Johnstown. Some three hundred club-wielding police, deputized thugs and goons took over the two cities and held it in a strikebreaking siege. Most shameful of all, at the very same time, national CIO representatives were joining hands with the deputized goons, with union-smashing employers, anti-labor local politicians, and the boss-controlled press in an effort to smash this bitterly-fought strike.

On or about January 20, John Sutliff and Willard Bennett, workers in Karg's Tannery, a struck shop, met with area representatives of the CIO, John J. Maurillo, CIO sub-regional director of Syracuse, and Peter Aversa, a former official expelled by the Farm Equipment Union. Allan Haywood, CIO vice president and director of organization, was informed

Ads in the Gloversville papers show how the bosses and the CIO Textile Workers Union united to break the leather workers' nine-month strike.

of these meetings. Under the direction of CIO representatives, Sutliff led thirty men back to work through the picket line.

On February 9, the scabs at Karg's tannery sent a letter to the strikers informing them that they "are back at work because they have the assurance that by doing so they can become affiliated with a strong National Right-wing Union that will issue them a charter." The strikebreaking groups told the workers: "By returning to work Monday you can save your job, end this useless strike, and become a member of a sound National Right-wing Union . . ."

On February 10, apparently timed to coincide with the attack of CIO officials, men and women on peaceful picket lines in front of the seventeen strike-bound plants were tear-gassed, clubbed and arrested in a brutal terror drive. The armed thugs, backed by an overwhelming array of force, crashed the picket lines to run in scabs. The wife of a striker, Mrs. Clayton Sweet, suffered a concussion from the clubbing of a policeman. Other strikers' wives, including Mrs. Clarence Carr, were assaulted as they stood by their husbands on the picket lines. Many pickets were arrested on framed charges.

Spokesmen for the CIO cooperated in the brutal assault on the picket lines. They urged the striking workers to return to work, and men going in to scab in the struck shops were immediately signed up into the CIO with the assistance of the employers.

In its issue of February 25, the leather industry magazine, *Leather and Shoes,* informed the tannery employers all over the country: "Fulton County tannery strike due to take on new twist. National CIO expected to declare war openly against Independent Leather Workers Union, former International Fur and Leather Workers Union, CIO, affiliate which still receives financial and organizational aid from IFLWU." The magazine also pointed out that the back-to-work drive was "launched with full knowledge of Philip Murray, CIO President."

On March 2, the anti-labor papers in the Fulton County area blazoned out the news that Allan Haywood had granted a charter to the men who had gone in to scab in the struck shops. The charter to the "United Tannery Workers Union" had been approved by Philip Murray. With the knowledge and approval of Murray and Haywood, while the overwhelming majority of the strikers were battling it out on the picket lines, the national CIO had granted a charter to scab shops where conditions won in seventeen years of union struggle were eliminated. Workers forced back into these shops faced wage and rate cutting, longer hours, speedup, intimidation, coercion and even "yellow-dog" contracts.

Exhausted by eight months of the most bitter battle ever fought by any group of leather workers, their families suffering many hardships, beaten up by police and armed thugs, and split by the strikebreaking intervention of the AFL and CIO unions, groups of workers were finally forced back to work. The independent union, although receiving full organizational and financial assistance from the IFLWU, was compelled to call a retreat. In most shops, it had no alternative but to tell the remaining workers that their strike had been broken by CIO and that they must get back into the shops whatever the conditions. Some shops, as this is being written, voting almost unanimously in secret ballot, decided to continue the fight on the picket lines. Even those workers forced back because of the strikebreaking of CIO remained loyal to the union, waiting for the first opportunity to resume the battle.

For the tannery employers, the nine-month battle exacted a terrific cost. It is doubtful whether they ever would or could undertake another such fight which ate up the profits of years of operation and cost them two seasons of shut-down.

Whatever the final outcome, the struggle of the heroic tannery workers of Gloversville and their leaders will forever remain an epic in the history of American labor.

The shocking role of CIO in breaking the Gloversville strike brought into full view the extent of the shameless betrayal of the American workers by CIO leaders since they abandoned the CIO's original progressive policies. It fully rivals the notorious practices followed by AFL leaders for many years, of which the fur workers had such bitter experiences in the 1920's and 1930's.

For more than ten years after its birth, the CIO had fired the imagination of American labor. Despite the sabotage of the AFL leadership, which undemocratically expelled the original CIO unions, millions of American workers had responded to the clarion call to organize militant, progressive and democratic unions in the mass production industries on an industrial union basis. In a few years, sparked by the CIO, American organized labor made greater progress than in all the preceding fifty years of the AFL. The CIO became the spearhead in the mobilization of the American people behind President Roosevelt and the New Deal.

The achievements of the CIO flowed directly from the progressive policies and basic democracy which prevailed within the CIO. Again and again John L. Lewis, guiding spirit and president of the CIO at its founding, pointed out that the morale and strength of the CIO depended upon the great principle of democracy, of equality for all workers regardless of differences among them. At the first constitutional convention of the CIO in October 1938, Lewis declared: "I say to my fellow countrymen, and I say to the rich and influential and wealthy . . . you cannot strike down in this country through the use of your influence, great as it may be, a powerful movement of the workers of this country under the banner of the CIO, who stand for equality of protection to any group, any minority, any religion that exists here in our country."

But even as Lewis was speaking, the agents of "the rich and influential and wealthy" were working inside the CIO to divide the ranks of the workers, weaken the CIO, and undermine its ability to defend the workers' interests. Right-wingers like Rieve, Baldanzi and members of the Association of Catholic Trade Unionists, even when Lewis was at the helm of CIO, tried to split the coalition between men and women of different political beliefs and to provoke a fight inside CIO against Communists, left-wingers and progressives. But they were afraid to do so openly. So hostile were the vast majority of delegates at CIO conventions to red-baiting that the Rieves, the Baldanzis and the ACTU did not dare to expose themselves.

As soon as Philip Murray succeeded Lewis as president of the CIO, the disrupters came out of the woodwork and began to apply pressure on Murray to abandon the basic principles on which the CIO was built. For a period of time, Murray maintained a center position between the left and the extreme right in the CIO and used his authority to maintain unity based upon CIO's original policies. Every convention of the CIO continued along a progressive road, hammering out a democratic and constructive program. Unity was maintained in the ranks in spite of pressure and attacks from both the direct and concealed agents of the open-shop employers.

"Let no one create conflict within this movement," President Philip Murray stated at the 1946 CIO convention in an obvious rebuke to the sinister forces inside the organization who were making the fight against Communists, left-wingers and progressives their primary object. At the same convention, in a reply to an address by the late Alexander F. Whitney, President of the Brotherhood of Railroad Trainmen, Murray said: "I should say to you at this moment that this mighty organization, the CIO, is not going to be divided by anybody. It has been a united movement and will continue to be one throughout its existence, I hope . . . We have our divisions of opinion and we, I suppose, in the years to come, will be susceptible to divisions of opinion. That is mighty healthy. If we were all united in the sense that we had one opinion on every subject I imagine that we might become a little rusty. That of course is what has happened to our ancient friendly enemies in the other house of labor. Their thinking has become corroded, and their seats are leaden because they are of heavier weight . . ."

An even stronger endorsement of the fundamental principles upon which the CIO was founded and grew was made by President Murray at the steel workers' convention in 1946. "We ask no man his national origin, his color, his religion or his beliefs," he declared. "It is enough for us that he is a steel worker and that he believes in trade unionism . . . Our union has not been and will not be an instrument of repression. It is a vehicle for economic and social progress . . . As a democratic institution, we engage in no purges, no witch-hunts. We do not dictate a man's thoughts or beliefs. Most important of all we do not permit ourselves to be stampeded into courses of action which create division among our members and sow the disunity which is sought by those false prophets and hypocritical advisers from without who mean us no good."

And at the 1947 convention of the United Automobile Workers, Murray reaffirmed the autonomy of CIO affiliates: "We never determine the course of action of our affiliates . . . They are sovereign, autonomous unions, and in matters of great moment we got together and we considered and advised with each other, but in the end we left the ultimate decision to each of the international unions for important policy decisions. There is a reason for that. I hope the day never comes in the history of the CIO when it shall take upon itself the power to dictate or to rule or to provide by policy methods of dictation and ruling that run counter to the very principles of true democracy."

The final word on democracy within CIO was laid down, apparently, at the CIO convention the same year. Murray declared: "They have in the constitution of the American Federation of Labor, and they have within the structure of their policy-making, power in the heads of that organization, the power to expel unions when they don't comply with the decrees of the people who occupy positions of authority at the top of the American Federation of Labor.

"The CIO in those days resented that idea. At its first constitutional convention held in Pittsburgh in 1938, they were careful to incorporate a provision which prevented officers of the National CIO or the National Executive Board in power to expel. Repeatedly since that time, questions have developed within the Council of CIO. Questions of a more or less serious nature, but the CIO has the framework within its own democratic institutions to resolve these issues without resort to the use of the sword or the axe. We decreed in 1938 that each union affiliated with the Congress of Industrial Organizations should and must exercise certain autonomous rights, and those rights could not be abridged by dictum issued by the President of this organization or by its Executive Board. And we have acted accordingly ever since. Therefore, the affiliated unions attached to this organization, exercise the greatest possible degrees of autonomy. That is a democratic process."

But even as Murray so solemnly paid tribute to the fundamental principles of union autonomy, democracy and unity, the Great Betrayal was already in the making.

Significant changes had taken place in a number of important CIO unions. R. J. Thomas, the middle-of-the-road head of the Auto Workers, was defeated by the right-wing Walter Reuther. Reuther ousted progressives and left-wingers from their positions in that union and used the full strength of the UAW to influence CIO towards a reactionary policy. In the Steel Workers Union, Philip Murray had also eliminated progressives and left-wing organizers who had made a decisive contribution to organizing the steel union in CIO's early years. In the third largest CIO union, the United Electrical, Radio and Machine Workers, James B. Carey, CIO secretary and darling of the ACTU, tried to seize control. Repeatedly defeated by the UE membership, he carried his disruption to the point of splitting the union.

In the battle to defeat the Taft-Hartley slave labor bill, CIO leaders had contented themselves with denunciations and resolutions of protest. They resisted all pleas of the progressives for an all-out mobilization of the workers, including Ben Gold's proposal for a one-day national stoppage. When Taft-Hartley became law, CIO leaders piously repeated their condemnation of this "step in the direction of fascism," and then turned right around and embraced it. Instead of fighting Taft-Hartley, they shamelessly used this bosses' weapon to raid, disrupt and split the progressive unions. To cover their shocking treachery, CIO leaders laid down a smokescreen of the most unbridled red-baiting.

Great changes were simultaneously taking place in the country as a whole. President Truman and the Democrat-Republican "bi-partisan" coalition had embarked on the cold war. Fifteen to twenty billion dollars for military preparations was included in each year's budget. Munitions makers were handed fantastic profits. Peacetime conscription was enacted for the first time in the nation's history.

As the Truman Doctrine was broadened out into the Marshall Plan and the Atlantic Pact, the State Department and other government agencies increased their pressures upon the trade union movement. Leaders of the AFL and CIO blossomed out as Marshall Plan enthusiasts. Dispatched on missions to split the powerful trade unions in the European countries, they did their utmost to sell the Marshall Plan to the workers there.

The parallel in policy between government and CIO leaders in internal union affairs is too startling to be overlooked. The Administration developed the red-baiting hysteria—CIO joined it. The Administration launched witch-hunts and purges—CIO did too. The Taft-Hartley Law required a "non-Communist" oath—so did the CIO. And so on.

President Truman broke the strike of the Railroad Brotherhoods in May 1946. In swift succession came the murder of OPA, the Taft-Hartley Law, peacetime conscription, government "loyalty" purges, the betrayal of every post-war pledge and the total abandonment of Roosevelt's progressive policies. Nevertheless, CIO leaders turned the CIO and its PAC into a political appendage for the Administration. Their slavish and cowardly role in supporting Truman in the 1948 Presidential election provided ample testimony of how far CIO leaders had deserted the progressive principles which had characterized that organization.

The first signs of the changes in CIO were already noticeable at its 1946 convention in Atlantic City. The trend became more pronounced at the Boston convention in 1947. At Portland, in 1948, the break was out in the open. By the time of the Cleveland convention in 1949, the transformation was complete.

The 10th Constitutional CIO Convention at Portland in 1948 was marked by hysterical red-baiting. In violation of democratic procedure, progressive delegates were heckled, booed, hissed and cat-called. They were told that they must either support the political dictates of the top officialdom or "clear out" of the CIO. Not only did President Philip Murray do nothing to halt the booing and hissing of minority speakers, but he actually encouraged this repulsive spectacle.

Having accepted the role of cold-war "labor statesmen," CIO officials dropped the fight for higher wages, the organization of the unorganized, particularly in the South, the struggle against the Taft-Hartley Law, for the civil rights program pledged by the Truman Administration, for housing, health and peace.

The IFLWU International Board rejected "as dictatorial" the resolution on political action adopted by the Portland Convention which deprived the International unions of their autonomy and abolished the democratic right of their members to make decisions. The IFLWU Board also rejected that portion of the wage resolution adopted by the Portland Convention which put "reasonable profits" for the employers before wage increases for the workers; condemned raids carried on by right-wing CIO unions against progressive CIO affiliates; resented and rejected the Reuther dictatorship formula of "accept or get out"; and deplored the undemocratic procedure displayed at the CIO convention, which deprived delegates of their freedom of speech, freedom of thought and the right of minorities to express disagreement. "If permitted to continue and spread throughout the CIO unions," the Board warned, "it will destroy the strength and prestige of CIO which, until now, distinguished itself as a progressive, democratic and militant federation of trade unions —a bulwark and spearhead of democracy in our great country."

Unfortunately, these words were lost upon the top leaders of the CIO. Throughout the months following the Portland Convention, the red-baiting, raidings and invasions of the democratic and autonomous rights of affiliated unions continued at an ever increasing pace. Instead of fighting for wage increases, the CIO leaders raided and crippled sister unions.*

The complete change in CIO policies was sharply demonstrated by its withdrawal from the World Federation of Trade Unions. The WFTU had been founded at the close of the war against the Hitler axis by the trade union centers of the Allied and liberated nations. CIO enthusiastically helped found the WFTU and proclaimed it a "bulwark for world peace." Sidney Hillman was the leading CIO representative to the WFTU. Upon Hillman's death, Philip Murray appointed CIO Secretary James B. Carey to represent CIO at the WFTU meetings. As the cold war was stepped up by the State Department, Carey's chief function at WFTU meetings became to split the world labor organization, and to split European trade union movements, the same role he was carrying on within the UE. In early 1949, Carey and Murray withdrew the CIO from the WFTU. This action was contrary to previous CIO convention decisions. It was taken without even consulting the CIO Executive Board, typical of the CIO leadership's new conception of democracy.

During the same period, top CIO officials endorsed the North Atlantic

---

* Typical of the new tactics of CIO leaders were the Steel Workers Union's raids on organized shops of the Mine, Mill and Smelter Workers Union in Alabama. Maurice Travis, secretary-treasurer of the MMSW, was slugged and blinded in one eye by goons employed in the steel workers' raid.

Military Pact. This action, too, was taken without consulting the CIO Executive Board and contrary to all previous peace and disarmament resolutions of CIO conventions.

The moral bankruptcy of the majority of CIO leaders was finally established by their joining with William Green, Matthew Woll, David Dubinsky and other completely discredited AFL leaders to set up a dual international labor body. Red-baiting, splitting and war propaganda were the main props of the new organization. Gone with the wind were CIO's once-loud pronouncements of international labor solidarity and world peace. The change was now complete.

When the eleventh CIO convention opened Monday, October, 31, 1949, at Cleveland, American workers faced a crucial situation. Some five million were completely jobless and ten million were working only part time. Unemployment was steadily increasing. The cost of living was still extremely high. Necessities of life were beyond the reach of the worker's budget. Decent housing within the means of the average worker was still an unfulfilled dream. Speedup was rampant in the plants; the speedup in steel and auto was described by a recent delegation of British workers as "inhuman." In many industries employers were openly attempting to cut wages. Hundreds of thousands of steel workers and a half million coalminers were out on strike. Big business, piling up fantastic profits, was displaying increasing arrogance and a studied disregard of the workers' rights or needs.

The leaders of the Democratic national administration and the majority of Democratic and Republican congressional representatives were callously repudiating their commitments to the American people. Instead of anti-poll tax, anti-lynching, anti-Jim Crow legislation, the people were given mounting anti-Semitism, continued denial of equality to the Negro people, and savage attacks against civil liberties of racial and political minority groups. Instead of repeal of the Taft-Hartley Act and re-enactment of the Wagner Act, the people were given new reactionary labor legislation containing the same provisions as the Taft-Hartley Act with a change merely in the name of the sponsors. Instead of a program of peace and the building of the United Nations, the people were given increasing appropriations of billions of dollars for armaments at home, the arming of western Europe under the North Atlantic Pact, rebuilding of Nazi cartels in western Germany, credits for fascist regimes of Franco Spain and Greece, and the dismal prospect of the annihilation of civilization in atomic warfare.

Anti-labor newspapermen, movie cameramen, radio commentators, reporters and columnists descended like vultures upon the Cleveland Auditorium where the CIO was to meet. They did not come to report how the CIO would deal with the crucial issues facing American labor and the American people. They were there to report the dismemberment of the CIO. For months preceding the Cleveland Convention, the big-business press had advised the CIO leaders to purge and expel unions, to squelch and crush the militants. Now the reporters, cameramen and commentators were on hand to flash the news that the advice of the anti-union press had been taken.

On the very first day, in his opening address, President Philip Murray singled out the "issue" for the convention to deal with—Communism. Not a word about the half million coalminers out on strike. Not a word about Taft-Hartley, about the high cost of living, about wages, about discrimination, about civil liberties and the Bill of Rights. Not a word about the fact that the CIO's basic program to organize the unorganized was stagnating; that the campaign to organize the workers in the South had so far been a failure in spite of the fact that millions of dollars had been poured into that drive. The only issue facing American workers, Murray shouted, was Communism!

The Officer's Report was distributed that same day. Not a word in it about the fact that the CIO had made no effort to carry out its own resolutions to struggle for wage increases, although it was admitted that some CIO unions actually took wage cuts. Significantly, only two CIO unions were mentioned as having won wage increases. Both were left-wing unions—the International Fur & Leather Workers Union and the International Longshoremen's Union under the leadership of Harry Bridges.

Only one portion of the Murray report was read in its entirety. But that was the highlight of the report. In it, the minority group of unions that opposed raiding and political dictation were slandered, called foes of labor, reactionaries of the left, and accused of retrogressive dictatorship, hostility to CIO and strikebreaking! Delegate Isador Pickman, secretary-treasurer of the Leather Division, took the floor on behalf of the Fur and Leather delegation in opposition to this section of Murray's report. Proudly and vigorously he asserted the record of the union, pointing out that the contracts and gains of the fur and leather workers were second to none. "When trade union democracy is recognized, there is no reason for disunity in CIO," he concluded. All that the committee chairman, O. A. Knight of the Oil Workers, could answer was, "The Fur

Workers as such have not been mentioned in the report." The right-wing majority mechanically approved the report.

The following day, the most tragic, fateful day in all CIO history, the Constitution Committee proposed amendments to CIO's Constitution. As they were read, they sounded strangely like the legislation of the notorious 80th Congress. Like Taft-Hartley (once denounced as "diabolical" and "fascist" by CIO), they proposed to bar Communists from CIO's Executive Board. They even went further than Taft-Hartley, proposing a catch-all that would bar anyone who followed "policies and activities directed toward the achievement or purposes of the Communist Party."

In an impassioned, stirring plea for democracy and unity in CIO, Ben Gold attacked the undemocratic amendment to CIO's Constitution. He urged unified action on the real issues confronting the workers—wages, hours, conditions; demanded to know why not a single resolution dealt with the miners' strike; hammered away at the undemocratic, disruptive character of the proposed amendment, and pointed out that "the majority rules only as long as it carries out the basic principles of democracy and among these basic principles is that you cannot deprive the minority of its rights and its expression of opinion. Once you do that, you are destroying the morale and strength and power of this great organization." But neither Gold's plea nor those of other minority spokesmen had any effect. After several hours of red-baiting tirades, the amendment was adopted.

On the third day, the Convention buckled down to the only "work" scheduled for this Convention—expulsions! The Constitution Committee proposed that the CIO Executive Board be authorized to remove any Board member it found guilty of violating the new, undemocratic amendment to the Constitution and to expel a whole union from the CIO on the same ground. Then came the resolution to expel the United Electrical, Radio and Machine Workers of America. There was neither charge, trial or hearing of the case. The trumped-up resolution declared that the 500,000-strong UE did not support the Marshall Plan, did not support the Atlantic Pact, and that leaders of the UE supported Henry Wallace in the 1948 Presidential election. All charges were political. Not a single one dealt with economic questions.

Delegate Pietro Lucchi, secretary-treasurer of the IFLWU, pleaded for unity and against the expulsion of UE. "I fought with the lefts for ten long years," he reminded the delegates. "What happened during those ten years? The fur workers and the union paid very, very dearly. Only the employers profited. . . . I do not want to see the electrical workers and their union suffer the same way. I do not want to see their union wrecked and their gains and conditions destroyed." But Lucchi's argument was of no avail. The expulsion of UE was voted. A dual-union charter for electrical workers was handed to James Carey, CIO secretary-treasurer who led the secession movement in UE. The next day, the Farm Equipment Union was expelled and its jurisdiction handed over to the Auto Workers.

With these two unions expelled without a hearing and the ground laid for the expulsion of other militant, progressive unions, the Convention for all practical purposes was finished. No discussion on wages, unemployment and many other important issues. The orgy of red-baiting and witch-hunting continued down to the very last day of the Convention. A new pattern was introduced in the election of CIO Executive Board members. At previous conventions, the delegation of each International union, in alphabetical order, would nominate its representative. When all nominations were in, all would be voted on at one time. But now the nominations were not in alphabetical order of the unions, and each nominee was voted on separately. The names of the right-wing unions were called first. All the right-wing union nominations were approved. Then came the minority group of unions, those who fought for unity and democracy, against the expulsion policy.

Augustus J. Tomlinson, president of the IFLWU Leather Division, announced in a loud and firm voice: "By unanimous decision of the delegation from Fur & Leather, I am proud to nominate as our union's representative on the CIO Executive Board—the President of our Union, Ben Gold." There was an awkward moment of silence. Then Murray announced that he refused to receive the nomination. Ten unions made their nominations. Ten times Murray machine men read prepared objections from little slips of paper passed to them.

Soon it was all over, the orgy of red-baiting, the Convention of name-calling, attack and disruption, the most disgraceful spectacle in all labor history. A new course had been charted for the once great, democratic and progressive federation of unions—the road of the Greens, the Matthew Wolls and the Hutchesons, the road of bureaucracy, surrender and bankruptcy. Where that road was leading to was revealed only a few months after the disastrous Cleveland Convention. On January 28 and 29, 1950, an American Legion-sponsored "anti-Communist" conference was held at the Astor Hotel in New York City. James B. Carey, secretary-treasurer of the CIO, shared the platform with NAM spokesmen and a wide assortment of labor-haters—men like William Randolph Hearst, Jr., and Rep. Jack Tenney of California, main figure in the state's "Little Dies Committee." In his speech to the infamous gathering, Carey, as quoted in the *New York Herald Tribune*, said: "In the last war we joined the Communists to fight the fascists; in another war we will join the fascists to fight the Communists."

"He [James B. Carey] was speaking not only as an individual but as a CIO official," an unnamed CIO leader declared in an interview with the New York *Compass* on February 1, 1950.

And on March 23, 1950, James Carey reaffirmed his "join with the fascists" speech at the regular monthly meeting of the Philadelphia CIO Industrial Union Council. Carey distributed to some fifty CIO delegates attending the meeting mimeographed copies which he said quoted accurately his New York speech. He himself marked in pencil the paragraph containing the declaration which he confirmed having made. This read: "Yes, we would join with Fascists in order to fight, in a war, Communists."

Unity with fascists! Such is the trail's end of the new road taken by the leaders of CIO.

As this is being written, four more progressive unions have been expelled by the CIO Executive Board.* The "hearings" were conducted behind closed doors "guarded" by goons and Washington City police at the headquarters of the CIO. Only a limited number of rank-and-file members were admitted. Only limited time was allotted for a few officials of the International unions involved. The atmosphere around the CIO "trials" was reminiscent of the notorious witch-hunts of the un-American Committee. Two of the four "trials" were presided over by Emil Rieve of the Textile Workers Union ** who, during the debate on the expulsions at the CIO Convention blurted out: "I have waited for this opportunity for a good many years."

The final decision will not be made at such undemocratic "trials." In the end, it will be the workers who will decide. For, as the members of the International Fur & Leather Workers Union have declared at meetings of the International Executive Board, the Furriers Joint Council, the Joint Board, the various districts and locals: "The CIO was created by the millions of American workers. It belongs to the workers.

---

* The unions expelled were the United Office & Professional Workers; United Public Workers; Food, Tobacco & Agricultural Workers; and Mine, Mill & Smelter Workers.

** Jacob Potofsky, president of the Amalgamated Clothing Workers, presided over the other two.

NEW YORK HERALD TRIBUNE,

SUNDAY, JANUARY 29, 1950

James B. Carey, chairman of the International Union of Electrical, Radio and Machine Workers, C. I. O., told the gathering

"In the last war we joined with the Communists to fight the Fascists; in another war we will join the Fascists to defeat the Communists.

Statement by CIO Sec'y-Treas. James B. Carey indicates where recent policies of CIO are leading—unity with fascists for war.

It is not the property of a few leaders. It is now the duty and the obligation of every single member of the CIO to fight to restore democracy in the CIO and put the control of its policies back in the hands of its membership. In this manner the militancy, the fighting spirit, the progressiveness of the CIO can and must be rebuilt, to enable the CIO to resume its rightful place in the forefront of the people's onward march for peace and democracy."

As this is written, the fur and leather workers are gathering for the Eighteenth Biennial Convention of their Union. With a history of struggles unparalleled by any group of American workers, the fur and leather workers emerged as one of the most militant, progressive and democratic unions in the country. Perhaps the most important of all the lessons learned by the fur and leather workers is that of unity.

Only a united labor movement, following the path of democracy and solidarity, can lead the whole nation forward to peace, progress and security. And such unity depends both on an honest, tested, devoted leadership and on the democratic participation of the rank and file in every phase of the union's life.

More than once in the past thirty-eight years, the eyes of the labor movement were focused on the dynamic struggles of the fur and leather workers. There is no doubt in this writer's mind that the struggles and achievements of these workers will again provide a brilliant example for all trade unions—a beacon light for the American working class.

Conclusion

The closing chapter of this history of the fur and leather workers is written, but their story begins anew.

From time immemorial, the ceaseless struggles of those who toil have stamped mankind's strivings for freedom and security. The unquenched thirst for a fuller, better life spurred the masses of exploited and oppressed everywhere to take their destiny into their own hands and climb painfully upward to new heights of grand achievement.

In modern times, it is the organized labor movement whose struggles spearhead the fight for democracy, for liberty and for progress. The William Greens, Matthew Wolls and David Dubinskys of the AFL and their more recent imitators within the CIO try to paralyze the struggle of the workers and stifle their outcry for freedom. The struggle against these misleaders of labor is an integral part of the struggle against the exploiters and oppressors.

The story of the fur and leather workers is a unique and brilliant chapter in the history of the American working class. Long after the labor fakers are buried and forgotten, the dynamic struggles and achievements of the fur and leather workers will command respect and admiration and will be studied for the rich lessons they teach all labor.

The success of the struggles of the fur and leather workers was no accident. Definite policies, democratic and progressive aims and methods brought about these results. They are fundamental and enduring principles for trade union organizations. Among them are:

685

Unity of all the workers in a clean, democratic union which guarantees and practices full and equal rights to all members and bars discrimination because of race, sex, creed, color, religious or political beliefs or affiliations.

A militant policy of constant struggle for the improvement of the workers' conditions and for the protection of their democratic rights.

A rank-and-file-controlled union in which the membership has and exercises the opportunity to full participation in all organizational political and financial affairs of the union.

A tested, incorruptible, fearless and responsible collective leadership, democratically elected on the basis of proven integrity, ability and loyalty to the progressive principles of democratic trade unionism—a leadership with full faith in the rank and file and enjoying the confidence and trust of the workers.

A progressive policy, supported by energetic activities, on all economic, political, legislative and social problems that directly or indirectly affect the rights and well-being of the workers.

Some unions are older than the fur and leather workers union. Others have larger memberships. Some unions may possess one or another characteristic enumerated above. But it is the union which possesses them all that is best able to serve its membership and the labor movement as a whole.

Such a union is the International Fur and Leather Workers Union.

Giant struggles loom ahead. Powerful forces of reaction seek to obliterate the liberties of the people, to crush the labor movement and particularly its most progressive sections. An organized hysteria will attempt to throw the labor movement into a state of chaos. Disunity and division within the ranks of labor will be artfully cultivated through red-baiting, prejudice, falsehood and bigotry. Every trade union which stands up for a better life for its members, a life of plenty, health and security in a peaceful world, will be labeled as "Communist" and "un-American." Every liberal, democratic or progressive thought will be hounded and persecuted. Every struggle for better working conditions will face police clubs, machine guns and tear gas, arrests and bloody battles on the picket line.

But deep-rooted and indestructible are the forces of the common people. Out of every struggle the people emerge stronger and clearer, a step nearer to victory. For truth and justice and progress are on the side of the people. Their triumph is inevitable.

> "The people learn, unlearn, learn
> A builder, a wrecker, a builder again,
> A juggler of shifting puppets.
>   In so few eyeblinks
>   In transition lightning streaks,
> The people project midgets into giants,
> The people shrink titans into dwarfs.

> "The honorable orators, the gazettes of thunder,
> The tycoons, big shots and dictators,
> Flicker in the mirrors a few moments
> And fade through the glass of death
> For discussion in an autocracy of worms.

> "While the rootholds of the earth nourish the majestic people
> And the new generations with names never heard of
> Plow deep in broken drums and shoot craps for old crowns,
> Shouting unimagined shibboleths and slogans,
> Tracing their heels in moth-eaten insignia of bawdy leaders—
> Piling revolt on revolt across night valleys,
> Letting loose insurrections, uprisings, strikes,
> Marches, mass-meetings, banners, declared resolves,
> Plodding in a somnambulism of fog and rain
> Till a given moment exploded by long-prepared events—"

From *The People, Yes* by Carl Sandburg

SOURCES

CHAPTER 1

BOOKS AND PAMPHLETS. John R. Commons and Associates, *History of Labor in the United States,* New York, 1918, vol. I, pp. 607-08; Herman Schleuter, *Die Anfaenge der deutschen Arbeiterbewegung in Amerika,* Stuttgart, 1907, p. 131; Philip S. Foner, *History of the Labor Movement in the United States,* New York, 1947, pp. 107-08, 221.

NEWSPAPERS AND MAGAZINES. *Working Man's Advocate,* Nov. 3, 10, 1832; *National Laborer,* Apr. 23, May 7, 28, Oct. 1, 15, Nov. 10, 1836; Apr. 25, 1837; *New Yorker Staatszeitung,* Mar. 23, 26, 1853; *New York Tribune,* Mar. 2, 6, 1854, Apr. 8, 1864; *New Yorker Democrat,* Oct. 31, Nov. 2, 1860; *New York Herald,* Nov. 6, 1857, Apr. 8, 1864; *Fincher's Trades' Review,* July 2, Oct. 29, 1864; *The Hat, Cap and Fur Trade Review,* June, 1877, p. 234; Apr. 1881, p. 188, Oct. 1, 1885, p. 238, June, 1886, p. 804, May, 1886, pp. 746-47; *New Yorker Volkszeitung,* Apr. 17, May 29, June 29, July 6, 10, Aug. 28, Sept. 11, 1882, Feb. 12, 1883, Feb. 13, 20, Mar. 13, Apr. 10, 24, June 5, July 13, 20, 27, Aug. 24, 1885, Jan. 8, 11, Feb. 19, Apr. 22, 26, May 5, 1886; *Salem Gazette,* Apr. 19, 20, 1886.

CHAPTER 2

BOOKS. Horace B. Davis, *Shoes: The Workers and the Industry,* New York, 1940, pp. 209-11.

NEWSPAPERS AND MAGAZINES. *Hat, Cap and Fur Trade Review,* May, 1886, pp. 746-47, June, 1886, pp. 804-05; *New Yorker Volkszeitung,* Apr. 22, 28, May 5, 6, 7, 13, 14, 1886, Nov. 9, 1887; *New York Times,* May 1, 2, 4, 5, 13, 14, 1886; *Chicago Tribune,* May 1, 2, 5, 1886; *Salem Gazette,* Apr. 19, 20, July 13-20, Aug. 12, 1886.

688

CHAPTER 3

MANUSCRIPTS. *American Federation of Labor Archives:* Hugo Koch to Samuel Gompers, Apr. 27, 1904, March 12, 20, Apr. 3, 19, 1906; C. E. Carlson to Samuel Gompers, May 1, 1905, Mar. 12, 1906; Emil P. Johnson to Frank Morrison, May 2, 1906; A. V. McCormack to Samuel Gompers, June 2, 1906; A. V. McCormack to AFL Executive Council, Oct. 3, 9, 1908; A. V. McCormack to Frank Morrison, Sept. 29, 1909, Mar. 15, Apr. 3, 1911; Louis Cassler, Jr. to Samuel Gompers, Mar. 11, 1908; Arthur Kahn to A. V. McCormack, Sept. 22, 1908; "Official Report of Proceedings of the First Annual Convention of Fur Workers of United States and Canada," Apr. 1904, pp. 1-13, typewritten copy attached to letter of Hugo V. Koch to Samuel Gompers, Apr. 27, 1904.

BOOKS AND PAMPHLETS. B. Weinstein, *Di Idisher Unions in Amerika,* New York, 1929, p. 442. *Sixth Annual Report of the Board of Mediation and Arbitration of the State of New York,* Albany, 1893, pp. 81-94; *Constitution of the International Association of Fur Workers of U. S. & Canada,* as adopted April 4, 1904.

NEWSPAPERS AND MAGAZINES. *Hat, Cap and Fur Trade Review,* Oct. 1886, p. 230, June 1, 1887, p. 210, *Fur Trade Review,* Feb. 1891, p. 56, Apr. 1891, pp. 142, 145, Sept. 1891, p. 373, Oct. 1891, p. 421, Apr. 1892, p. 153, May, 1892, pp. 195, 219, June, 1893, p. 299, Sept. 1899, p. 442; *New Yorker Volkszeitung,* Feb. 14, Oct. 22, Nov. 19, 1888, July 14, Aug. 12, 13, 25, 1890, Aug. 14, 1893, Dec. 13, 1894, July 3, 1895, Jan. 22, Apr. 30, June 10, 12, July 3, 4, 11, 25, 1896; *Arbeiter Zeitung,* Jan. 27, 1895; *Furriers' Journal,* June 1905, pp. 1, 2, 4-5, 7, 11-12, Aug. 1905, p. 6; Oct. 1905, pp. 1, 4, 6; *New York Times,* Apr. 15, 1892, Sept. 15, 1907; *New York Tribune,* Sept. 17, 1907; *Jewish Daily Forward,* Sept. 15-17, 24, 1907.

CHAPTER 4

MANUSCRIPTS. *AFL Archives*: Chas. L. Conine to Frank Morrison, Dec. 12, 1901; Chas. L. Conine to Samuel Gompers, July 8, Sept. 20, 1901; John J. Pfeiffer to Frank Morrison, Sept. 30, 1902, Nov. 21, 1907, Apr. 19, 1910, May 1, Sept. 22, 1911; John J. Pfeiffer to Samuel Gompers, Feb. 27, 1903, Jan 24. Apr. 19, 1910; C. H. Turner to Frank Morrison, Mar. 28, 1907; H. H. Spruykel to Frank Morrison, Apr. 28, 1908; Frank C. Stumpf to Frank Morrison, Oct. 4, 1903; Edward J. Baker to Samuel Gompers, Mar. 7, Apr. 29, May 28, June 21, 1910; Samuel Gompers to Edward J. Baker, June 8, 1910; W. E. Bryan to Samuel Gompers, June 6, 14, 1910. *U. S. Department of Labor Archives*: Chas. L. Conine to William Sackett, 1900.

BOOKS AND PAMPHLETS. Davis, *op. cit.*, pp. 212-13; *Constitution of the Amalgamated Leather Workers Union of America*, Olean, New York, 1901; *Convention Report of the Amalgamated Leather Workers Union, 1906*, pp. 17-18.

NEWSPAPERS AND MAGAZINES. *John Swinton's Paper*, Apr. 18, 1886, May 8, 22, June 12, July 31, 1887; *Leather Workers Journal*, Sept., 1900, pp. 16, 131, Oct., 1900, pp. 27, 46, Nov., 1900, pp. 58, 61, 65, Dec., 1900, p. 89, Feb., 1901, p. 132, May, 1901, p. 193, July, 1901, p. 246, Sept., 1901, p. 62, June, 1902, p. 293, July, 1902, pp. 330-31, Oct., 1902, p. 83, Dec., 1902, pp. 151, 163, Jan., 1903, p. 192, Feb., 1903, pp. 247, 269, 272, May, 1903, p. 454, June, 1903, p. 510, Sept., 1903, p. 1, Jan., 1904, pp. 277, 299-316, Feb., 1904, pp. 361-63, July, 1904, p. 702, Aug., 1904, p. 795, Sept., 1904, pp. 8-9, 29-30, 31, Oct., 1904, p. 92, Dec., 1904, p. 7, Mar., 1905, p. 328, Oct., 1906, p. 93, Nov., 1906, p. 176, Jan., 1907, p. 322, Mar., 1907, p. 452, May, 1907, pp. 52, 550, 569, 583-84, July, 1907, pp. 677, 687, 720, Aug., 1907, p. 767, Sept., 1907, pp. 13-14, 32, Dec., 1907, p. 225, Jan., 1908, pp. 270-271, Mar., 1908, p. 35, May, 1908, p. 487, July, 1908, 594-95, Aug., 1908, pp. 698-99, Sept., 1908, pp. 36, 102, Nov., 1908, p. 150, Jan., 1910, p. 269, May, 1911, pp. 406-07, July, 1911, p. 496; *Amalgamated Leather Workers Journal*, Sept., 1903, pp. 10-11.

CHAPTER 5

MANUSCRIPTS. *AFL Archives*: Frank Morrison to A. V. McCormack, Mar. 30, 1911.

BOOKS AND PAMPHLETS. Weinstein, *op. cit.*, pp. 144, 198-99, 446-51; Louis Levine, *The Women Garment Workers*, New York, 1924, pp. 144-95.

NEWSPAPERS AND MAGAZINES. *Fur Trade Review*, June, 1892, p. 36, March, 1910, June, 1912, pp. 66-67; *Ladies Garment Worker*, vol. III, no. 4, Apr. 1912, p. 13; *New Yorker Volkszeitung*, May 13, 1912; *New York Times*, June 18, 22, 23, 24, July 28, Aug. 28, Sept. 9-10, 1912; *Jewish Daily Forward*, Jan. 8, June 12, 13, 16, 20-21, 30, July 2, 9-10, 11, 17, 18, 20, 21, 27, 28, Aug. 1, 2, 4, 5, 7, 9, 15, 17, 22-23, 28, Sept. 1-7, 9-10, 1912; *New York Call*, June 13, 16, 19, 20-22, 25, 27, 28-29, July 17, 19, 24, 25, 28, Aug. 1-6, 9, 16, 21, 22-23, Sept. 4-5, 9-10, 1912.

CHAPTER 6

MANUSCRIPTS. *AFL Archives*: A. V. McCormack to Frank Morrison, Apr. 10, 1912; Samuel Gompers to Samuel Korman, July 3, 1913; A. W. Miller to Frank Morrison, Aug. 16, 1913, July 11, 18, Aug. 28, Sept. 12, 19, 26, Oct. 3, 31, 1914; Samuel Korman to Frank Morrison, Feb. 18, 1914; Hugh Frayne to Frank Morrison, Sept. 3, 1914. *International Fur Workers Union Archives*: A. W. Miller to A. V. McCormack, Dec. 17, 1913; A. W. Miller to Samuel Korman, Aug. 7, Oct. 2, 24, 25, 26, 27, 29, Nov. 3, 9, 11, 12, 18, 21, 26, 1914; A. W. Miller to Dr. Leo Mannheimer, Feb. 18, 1915; A. W. Miller to Andrew Wenneis, June 22, 23, 26, July 21, Sept. 16, 17, 18, 21, 24, 1916; A. School to Joint Board Furriers Union of Greater New York, Aug. 19, 1914; Furriers Union to A. School, Aug. 20, 1914; Leslie Cohen to Isidore Cohen, Oct. 3, 1914; Otto J. Piehler to A. W. Miller, Oct. 10, 1914; A. W. Miller to Otto J. Piehler, Oct. 3, 1914; S. Schacher to A. W. Miller, Aug. 14, Sept. 3, 7, 16, 1916; Charles Gmeiner to Samuel Korman, Nov. 30, 1915; "Record of the first meeting of the Furriers Convention held in the Typographical Temple, 423 G Street," typewritten copy; "Constitution of the International Fur Workers Union," typewritten copy.

BOOKS AND PAMPHLETS. Levine, *op. cit.*, p. 199.

NEWSPAPERS AND MAGAZINES. *New Yorker Volkszeitung*, Oct. 22, 1912; *New York Post*, Mar. 4, 1912; *New York Times*, Sept. 4, Oct. 9, 1914, July 4, Aug. 13, Sept. 14, Oct. 4, Nov. 27, 1915, Jan. 20, Sept. 10, 13, Dec. 11, 27, 1916; *Chicago Tribune*, Oct. 30-Nov. 2, 1915; *Newark Times*, April 13-21, 1915; *Jewish Daily Forward*, Oct. 23, 1912, June 16, 19, 1913, May 9, 1914; June

20, 1916; *Fur Trade Review*, Apr., 1912, p. 68, Nov. 1914, p. 2.

CHAPTER 7

MANUSCRIPTS. *IFWU Archives:* Charles Gmeiner to A. W. Miller, Jan. 15, 1916; Robert Schwartz to Andrew Wenneis, Apr. 22, 1917; Abe Heck to Samuel Korman, Sept. 19, 1915; Joseph Zoyance and others to A. W. Miller, May 15, 1917; Montreal Fur Workers to Andrew Wenneis, July 11, 20, 1917; Paul Smith to A. W. Miller, Apr. 10, 1916; Herman Dorfman to A. W. Miller, Mar. 22, 1917; A. W. Miller to Hugh Frayne, Feb. 15, 1916; Dr. Louis J. Harris to A. W. Miller, July 26, 1917.

NEWSPAPERS AND MAGAZINES. *Fur Trade Review*, Sept., 1915; Dr. Louis L. Harris, "A Clinical and Sanitary Study of the Fur and Hatters' Fur Trade," *Monthly Bulletin of the Department of Health, New York City*, Oct., 1915; *Jewish Daily Forward*, May 28, Aug. 26, 1916, Feb. 24-28, March 12, 16, 1917; *Women's Wear*, Dec. 17, 1916; *The Fur Worker*, Nov. 2, 1916, Mar. 13, 20, Apr. 17, 1917.

CHAPTER 8

MANUSCRIPTS. *AFL Archives:* Henry F. Hilfers to Samuel Gompers, Jan. 15, 1918. *IFWU Archives:* A. W. Miller to Andrew Wenneis, May 2, 5, 7, 9, July 11, Aug. 14, 18, Sept. 30, Oct. 19, 22, 23, 1917; A. W. Miller to G.E.B., Jan. 18, 1918; A. W. Miller to Sub-Committee, G.E.B., Feb. 20, 1918; Andrew Wenneis to A. W. Miller, June 29, 30, July 8, Sept. 22, 1916, Sept. 11, 19, Oct. 22, 23, 1917; Andrew Wenneis to Charles Gmeiner, Apr. 8, 26, 1918; Andrew Wenneis to Fur Workers Locals, Sept. 19, 1917; J. A. McEwan to Andrew Wenneis, Mar. 5, 1918; Louis A. Harvey to Andrew Wenneis, Apr. 22, 1918; Louis A. Harvey to Henry F. Hilfers, June 1, 1918; Louis A. Harvey to A. Hollander & Sons, May 15, 1918.

BOOKS AND PAMPHLETS. Lewis L. Lorwin, *The American Federation of Labor*, Washington, 1933, pp. 142-46.

NEWSPAPERS AND MAGAZINES. *The Fur Worker*, April, Aug., Dec., 1917, Feb., Mar., Apr., 1918.

CHAPTER 9

MANUSCRIPTS. *IFWU Archives:* Morris Kaufman to Andrew Wenneis, Nov.

19, 1917, June 19, 1918; Andrew Wenneis to Charles Stetsky, Jan. 28, 1919; Andrew Wenneis to B. Lederman, Dec. 12, 1919; B. Lederman to Andrew Wenneis, Dec. 15, 1919; I. L. Epstein, "Facts about the St. Paul Locals nos. 57 & 58"; "Testimony taken at the Investigation of conditions existing in St. Paul, carried out by a committee of the G.E.B. in the city of St. Paul, Jan. 9, 1919"; Simon Schacter to Andrew Wenneis, Mar. 17, 1919; J. Millstein to Andrew Wenneis, Mar. 22, 1919; Chas. Stetsky to Andrew Wenneis, Feb. 20, Mar. 6, 1919; Simon Schacter, "Regarding the Leaflet 'Furriers' Attention,'"; Simon Schacter to Rosen & Son, June 10, 1919; Simon Schacter, "Important considerations for our convention"; Andrew Wenneis to Samuel Leibowitz, May 9, 1919.

BOOKS AND PAMPHLETS. "Report of the Fourth Bi-Annual Convention of the International Fur Workers Union, Chicago, June 2 to 7, 1919," pp. 156, 165-66, 190, 203*ff*., 241-43, 271.

NEWSPAPERS AND MAGAZINES. *The Fur Worker*, Nov., 1917, Feb., July, Sept., 1918, Jan.-Sept., Nov., 1919, Mar.-May, 1920; *New York Times*, Jan. 28-29, 1919; *Jewish Daily Forward*, July 15, Sept. 10, 29, Oct. 22, Dec. 6, 1918, Jan. 14, 31, Feb. 1, 3, 4-5, 8, Mar. 28, Apr. 28, May 25, 1919, Apr. 1, 2, 26, May 25, 1920.

CHAPTER 10

MANUSCRIPTS. *IFWU Archives:* Meyer London to Andrew Wenneis, July 12, 1920; H. F. Somins to Andrew Wenneis, June 28, July 23, 1920; David Mikol to Andrew Wenneis, Aug. 12, 22, Oct. 13, 25, 1920; Charles Gmeiner and O. Shachtman to Andrew Wenneis, May 19, 1920; Andrew Wenneis to O. Shachtman, Nov. 24, 1920; Morris Kaufman to B. Lederman, Aug. 7, 1920; Furriers Strike Bulletin, No. 3, Nov. 30, 1920; "Report of the Proceedings of the Fifth Biennial Convention of the International Fur Workers Union, Phila., June 5th to 10th, 1922," pp. 323-24, mimeographed copy; "Proceedings of the Convention of the International Fur Workers Union, Boston, Nov. 7-9, 1925, "vol. I, pp. 75-80, 214.

NEWSPAPERS AND MAGAZINES. *The Fur Worker*, March-July, 1920, Dec., 1920, Jan.-Feb., 1921 (Jewish edition); *Women's Wear*, Sept. 29, 1919, July 8, 1920, Jan. 7, 14, 1921; *New York Call*, May 18, July 28-30, Aug. 17, Sept. 19, Oct. 11, Dec. 17, 1920; *New York Times*, July 28-29, 1920; *Freie Arbeiter Stimme*, Feb. 5, 1921; *Fur Trade Review*, Sept.-Oct. 1920; *Jewish Daily For-*

ward, Apr. 1, 2, 26, May 18-25, June 2, July 28-30, Nov. 30, Dec. 22, 1920, Jan. 12, 14, 1921.

CHAPTER 11

MANUSCRIPTS. *IFWU Archives:* B. Lederman to Andrew Wenneis, Jan. 5, Mar. 14, 1921; O. Shachtman to Andrew Wenneis and Morris Kaufman, Jan. 17, June 19, 1921; G. Domes to Andrew Wenneis, Feb. 25, 1921; Morris Kaufman to Andrew Wenneis, Aug. 23, 1921, Apr. 23, 1922; telegram signed by Morris Kaufman, Mar. 11, 1921; Morris Kaufman to Albert Roy, Feb. 25, 1922; Morris Kaufman to Joint Board Furriers Union, Dec. 19, 1921, Feb. 1, 1922; Morris Kaufman to A. Brownstein, Jan. 23, 1922; Andrew Wenneis to G. Domes, Apr. 4, 1921; Andrew Wenneis to Morris Kaufman, May 10, 1921; O. Shachtman to Andrew Wenneis, Apr. 19, 1921; R. Barth to Andrew Wenneis, Apr. 22, 1921; Andrew Wenneis to members of the International Fur Workers Union, May 4, 1921; "To the Joint Board in the matter of Samuel Cohen, Oct. 1921"; A. Brownstein to Morris Kaufman, Jan. 18, 27, May 10, Aug. 3, Nov. 23, Dec. 30, 1922; Executive Committee of Local 15 to Andrew Wenneis, Jan. 17, 1922; Executive Committees of Locals 1, 5, & 10 to the International Fur Workers Union, Jan. 16, 18, 19, 1922; Andrew Wenneis to A. Brownstein, Feb. 9, 1922; Leaflets issued by the Joint Board and by the Welfare Club, Mar., 1922; A. Lewitz to Joint Board Furriers Union, Mar. 22, 1922; Sam Cohen, L. Weiser, Wm. Weiner to Sub-Committee of the G.E.B., Mar. 29, 1922; N. Lutsky to Andrew Wenneis, Apr. 8, 1922; undated letter, Charles Stetsky to Morris Kaufman; Charles Stetsky to Morris Kaufman, Sept. 1, 22, 1922; Philip Silberstein to Andrew Wenneis, Dec. 20, 1922; Andrew Wenneis to Max Suroff, Dec. 22, 1922; Pietro Lucchi to G.E.B., Jan., 1923; Fred Feigenbaum to Morris Kaufman, Apr. 10, 1921; Jack Scherles to Morris Kaufman, June 5, 1921; Frank A. Currie to Andrew Wenneis, Jan. 5, 1921.

NEWSPAPERS AND MAGAZINES. *The Fur Worker,* Feb.-Mar., 1921 (Jewish edition); Jan.-Mar., 1922; *The Worker,* Apr. 29, 1921; *Women's Wear,* June 16-18, 1922; *Jewish Daily Forward,* Jan. 5, 16, 17-22, Mar. 19-20, Apr. 15, 1922, Jan. 6, 1923; *Freiheit,* Jan. 6, Feb. 5, June 9, Sept. 22, Oct. 12, 1922, Apr. 10, 1923, Mar. 8, 1924.

CHAPTER 12

MANUSCRIPTS. Correspondence of the American Fund For Public Service, New York Public Library: David J. Saposs to Roger Baldwin, Mar. 19, 1923.

BOOKS AND PAMPHLETS. William Z. Foster, *The Bankruptcy of the American Labor Movement,* New York, 1922, pp. 23, 24, 54; William Z. Foster, *American Trade Unionism,* New York, 1947, pp. 54-57; Louis Levine, *op. cit.,* pp. 125-26.

NEWSPAPERS AND MAGAZINES. *The Fur Worker,* Dec., 1920; *Labor Herald,* Mar., 1922, pp. 6-7, Sept., 1922, p. 5; Mar. 1923, p. 20; *Freiheit,* Dec. 5, 1922.

CHAPTER 13

MANUSCRIPTS. *IFWU Archives:* "Statements of Dr. Moissaye J. Olgin and Morris Kaufman in investigation re publication against Furriers Union"; "Proceedings of mass meeting, March 17, 1922, in Webster Hall," typewritten copy in Yiddish; copy of resolutions adopted at the Manhattan Lyceum meeting, March 17, 1923; Minutes of the objection committee of Local 15, June 16, 1923; Fannie Warshafsky, Lena Greenberg, J. Winogradsky, Lena Bremer to Andrew Wenneis, June 22, 1923; A. Wenneis to Warshafsky, Greenberg, Winogradsky, Katz, Bremer, June 22, 1923; Election and objection committee of Local 5 to Sub-Committee, no dates; Harry Kravitz to Andrew Wenneis, no date; Andrew Wenneis to Harry Kravitz, June 27, 1925; "Proceedings of Mass meetings in Webster Hall," Dec. 5, 1923, Jan. 5, 1924, typewritten copies in Yiddish; Statement of Lena Greenberg, J. Winogradsky, Max Suroff, Lena Bremer and Esther Polansky in the matter of charges preferred against Samuel Cohen by B. Gold; Morris Kaufman to AFL Labor Weekly News Service, Feb. 2, 1924; "Memorandum of terms agreed upon by the union and the Association, Feb. 2, 1924." *AFL Archives:* Morris Kaufman to Chester Wright, Apr. 12, 1923.

MAGAZINES AND NEWSPAPERS. *Furriers Bulletin,* published by the Furriers section of the TUEL, No. 2, 1923, *Freiheit,* Feb. 28, Mar. 9, 12, 14-16, Apr. 6, May 2, 10, 15, Dec. 14, 15, 17, 18, 21, 22, 23, 25, 27, 28, 30, 1923, Jan. 3, 1924; *The Fur Worker,* Sept., 1923, Feb.-Mar., 1924, *Jewish Daily Forward,* Mar. 8, 18-19, Dec. 21-23, 1923; *The Worker,* Mar. 31, 1923; *New York Times,* Mar. 18, 1923.

CHAPTER 14

MANUSCRIPTS. *IFWU Archives:* Charges of N. Markoff against B. Gold, Jan. 10, 1924; Joseph R. Brodsky to Joint Board

Furriers Union, Jan. 3, Feb. 7, 1924; A. Brownstein to B. Gold, Feb. 4, 1924; Minutes of Joint Board meeting, Mar. 25, 1924; Proceedings of meeting in Webster Hall, Mar. 24, 1924, typewritten copy in Yiddish; "Report of Proceedings of Sixth Biennial Convention of the International Fur Workers Union, held at the Morrison Hotel, Chicago, Illinois, May 12-17, 1924," pp. 124-25, 148, 155, 162-63.

MAGAZINES AND NEWSPAPERS. *Nodel Arbeiter*, April, 1924, p. 7; *Freiheit*, Apr. 16, May 26, 1924, Aug. 14, 1925; *Daily Worker*, June 3, 1924; *Jewish Daily Forward*, May 25, 1924.

CHAPTER 15

MANUSCRIPTS. *IFWU Archives:* Morris Kaufman to Philip Silberstein, May 29, 1924; Morris Kaufman to J. Millstein, Feb. 9, 1925; Morris Kaufman to Joint Board Furriers Union, May 21, 1925; Charles Stetsky to Morris Kaufman, 10/22, 1923; Andrew Wenneis to Morris Kaufman, Dec. 4, 1925, night letter; Frank Staub, Ph. Stefanesko, Harry Yurman, Harry Begoon, M. Kleeger, Ph. M. Brown, W. Weiner to G.E.B., Dec. 19, 1924; Andrew Wenneis to A. Brownstein, Feb. 19, 1925; B. Gold to Andrew Wenneis, Mar. 4, 1925; "To the Members of our New York Locals, 1, 5, 10 and 15," no date; A. Brownstein to G.E.B., no date; Request of Local 10 to G.E.B., Jan. 3, 1925; Testimony of Morris Dermer, Jan. 2, 1925; "Testimony taken at a Joint Meeting of the Special Committee of the International Fur Workers Union and a Special Committee of the Joint Board Furriers Union, April 15th, 1925"; J. Millstein to Andrew Wenneis, May 11, 1925; Testimony in the investigation of A. Rosenthal; A. Rosenthal to the G.E.B., May 25, 1925; Joint Board Fur Workers Union, Examination of Books and Records, 1922, 1923, 1924, 1925, Report of Progress.

NEWSPAPERS AND MAGAZINES. *Freiheit*, Feb. 9, June 3, 6, 7, 12, 1924, Apr. 23, May 22, 25, 27, 1925; *The Fur Worker*, Mar., 1924, Apr., May, 1925.

CHAPTER 16

MANUSCRIPTS. *IFWU Archives:* A. Wenneis to Election Committee Local 5, July 9, 1925; Andrew Wenneis to Charles Gmeiner, July 20, 1925; Harry Begoon to Andrew Wenneis, July 16, 1925; Pencilled report of a telephone conversation with Meyer London, Saturday, Aug. 1, 1925; Minutes of Conference in the Fur Industry,

July 8, 1925; "Proceedings of the 1925 Convention of the International Fur Workers Union," vol. I, pp. 258-59, 264-65, vol. II, pp. 406-07, 660-61, typewritten copy; Samuel N. Samuels to Joint Board Furriers Union, June 23, 1925.

BOOKS AND PAMPHLETS. Jack Hardy, *The Clothing Workers,* New York, 1935, pp. 40-41; Joel Seidman, *The Needle Trades,* New York, 1942, pp. 158-62.

NEWSPAPERS AND MAGAZINES. *Women's Wear,* June 24, 30, July 7, 8, 9, 10, 16, 22, 23, 27, 28, Nov. 3, 5, 1925; *Jewish Daily Forward,* June 22, July 7-8, 10, 11, 26, 1925; *Freiheit,* June 24, July 22, 28, 29, Aug. 11, 26, 29, Sept. 22, Nov. 5, 1925; *The Fur Worker,* July, Nov.-Dec. 1925; *Daily Worker,* June 25, July 7, Sept. 31, Nov. 5, 10, 13, 1925; *Workers' Monthly,* Aug., Nov., 1925.

CHAPTER 17

MANUSCRIPTS. *IFWU Archives:* Emile Perrault to Hyman Sorkin, July 3, 1925; Emile Perrault to O. Shachtman, June 17, 1926; Report of Albert Roy to G.E.B. (1925); Albert Roy to Ben Gold, Aug. 4, 1925; Charles Stetsky to Morris Kaufman, Aug. 12, Sept. 2, 1925; Audit of Books of the Joint Board Furriers Union by Stuart Chase for the Labor Bureau, Inc., Mar. 1, 1926, p. 3; Morris Kaufman to J. Millstein, June 25, 1925; J. Millstein to Morris Kaufman, Aug. 8, 21, 1925, telegrams; Andrew Wenneis to Geo. H. Ritzheimer, Oct. 6, 1925; "Proceedings of the International Fur Workers Union, American House, November 9-17, 1925, Boston, Mass.," 2 vols., typewritten copy, vol. I, pp. 30, 36, 121-24, 161-72, 175-82, 197-99, 206, 207, 217, 231-32, 240-70, 274, 285-94, 358-59, 393-96, vol. II, 400, 404, 411-12, 427-28, 476-77, 565-68, 608-78, 681-90, 694-96; "Supplementary Report of the General Executive Board referring to the New York Situation," 32 pp. *AFL Archives:* "Investigation by the American Federation of Labor into the 1926 Furriers Strike," pp. 37-38, 130-66.

NEWSPAPERS AND MAGAZINES. *Freiheit,* Aug. 16, 24, 29, 31, Sept. 17; *Women's Wear,* Sept. 2, Nov. 13, 1925; *The Fur Worker,* Aug., Oct., 1925; *Daily Worker,* Sept. 2, Nov. 14, 16, Dec. 16, 1925.

CHAPTER 18

MANUSCRIPTS. *IFWU Archives:* I. Winnick to O. Shachtman, Dec. 10, 1925; Paul Abelson to O. Shachtman, Jan. 25,

1926. *AFL Archives:* "Investigation by the American Federation of Labor into the 1926 Furriers Strike," pp. 18-30, 39, 57, 134.

BOOKS AND PAMPHLETS. William Z. Foster, *American Trade Unionism,* pp. 91-110; "Our Demands and their Significance," pamphlet issued by Joint Board Furriers Union.

NEWSPAPERS AND MAGAZINES. *Women's Wear,* Nov. 18, 1925, Jan. 5, 12, 13, 22, Feb. 2-3, 5, 16, 25, Mar. 29, 1926; *Jewish Daily Forward,* Feb. 3-4, 5-6, 12-14, 1926; *The Fur Worker,* Nov.-Dec., 1925, Jan.-Mar. 1926; *Federated Press Labor Letter,* Mar. 31, 1926; *Jewish Morning Journal,* Jan. 25, Feb. 5-6, 1926; *Fur Age Weekly,* Dec. 7, 21, 1925, Jan. 18, Feb. 1, 1926; *Freiheit,* Jan. 12, 26, 29, Feb. 12-14, 16, 1926; *Daily Worker,* Feb. 17, 1926; *New York Times,* Apr. 3, 1926.

CHAPTER 19

MANUSCRIPTS. *IFWU Archives:* I. Wohl to Ben Gold, Feb. 26, 1926; I. Winnick to J. Bowman, Mar. 15, 1926; I. Winnick to I. Beckman, Mar. 11, 1926; I. Winnick to O. Shachtman, Mar. 4, 1926; I. Winnick to H. Sorkin, Mar. 19, 1926; telegram; I. Beckman to I. Winnick, Mar. 10, 1926; O. Schachtman to Ida Weinstein, Apr. 22, 1926; William Green to O. Shachtman, Mar. 30, 1926. *AFL Archives:* Morris Kaufman to William Green, June 22, Aug. 11, 1925; William Green to Morris Kaufman, June 24, Sept. 3, 1925; Hugh Frayne to William Green, June 17, 1925; William Green to Morris Sigman, June 24, 1925; Abraham Baroff to William Green, Aug. 5, 1925; Abraham Baroff to Frank Morrison, Sept. 16, 1925; "Investigation by the American Federation of Labor into the 1926 Furriers Strike," pp. 7, 11-12, 13-14, 15-18, 30-52.

NEWSPAPERS AND MAGAZINES. Newspaper clippings in American Civil Liberties Union Collection, State Clippings, vol. IV, 1926 (New York-West Virginia), New York Public Library; *The Central Furrier,* March, 1926, p. 69; *Fur Age Weekly,* Feb. 1, Apr. 5, 1926; *Women's Wear,* Feb. 25, Mar. 6, 24-26, Apr. 16-17, 1926; *Jewish Daily Forward,* Feb. 22-27, Mar. 6-9, 9-11, 14-17, June 23, 1926; *New York Times,* Feb. 23, Mar. 9, 1926; *Freiheit,* Feb. 19, 23, Mar. 5, 6, 1926; *Daily Worker,* Mar. 5, 8, 9, 12, 1926; New York *Daily News,* Mar. 9, 1926.

CHAPTER 20

MANUSCRIPTS. *IFWU Archives:* O. Shachtman to Joseph Ryan, Apr. 14, 1926;

O. Shachtman to S. Butkowitz, Apr. 22, 1926. *AFL Archives:* O. Shachtman to William Green, Apr. 13, 19, 1926, telegrams; Frank Morrison to O. Shachtman, Apr. 13, 1926, telegram; William Green to O. Shachtman, Apr. 14, 1926, telegram; Agreement, New York, April 19, 1926, signed by William Green and Hugh Frayne.

NEWSPAPERS AND MAGAZINES. *Women's Wear,* Apr. 15-17, 20, 22, 1926; *New York Times,* Apr. 16, 22, 1926; *The Fur Worker,* Apr. 13, 1926; *The Day,* Apr. 17, 1926; *Freiheit,* Apr. 15, 16, 1926; *Daily Worker,* Apr. 21, 22, 1926; *Fur Age Weekly,* Apr. 19, 1926.

CHAPTER 21

MANUSCRIPTS. *IFWU Archives:* Ben Gold to O. Shachtman, Apr. 30, 1926; J. Bowman to O. Shachtman, Apr. 30, 1926; J. Bowman to I. Wohl, Apr. 29, 1926, telegram; J. Millstein to O. Shachtman, Apr. 22, 26, May 5, 1926; O. Shachtman to Joseph Bearak, Apr. 30, 1926; Isaac Wohl to Maurice Cohen, May 5, 1926. *AFL Archives:* Hugh Frayne to Samuel N. Samuels, Apr. 9, 1926; Samuel N. Samuels to Hugh Frayne, Apr. 20, 29, 1926; Samuel N. Samuels to William Green, Apr. 22, 1926; William Green to Samuel N. Samuels, Apr. 21, 23, 1926; Hugh Frayne to William Green, May 3, 1926.

NEWSPAPERS AND MAGAZINES. *Women's Wear,* Apr. 20, 21, 22, May 3, 8, 11, 1926; *Daily Worker,* Apr. 22, 27, May 1, 5, 7, 1926; *New York Times,* Apr. 22, May 4, 1926; *The Fur Worker,* Apr. 29, 1926, May 1926; *Fur Age Weekly,* May 3, 10, 1926; *Freiheit,* May 7, 1926.

CHAPTER 22

MANUSCRIPTS. *IFWU Archives:* J. Beckman to O. Shachtman, May 17, 1926; O. Shachtman to J. Beckman, June 5, 1926; Frank A. Currie to I. Wohl, May 4, 1926; I. Wohl to Frank A. Currie, May 15, 1926; O. Shachtman and I. Wohl to Amalgamated Clothing Workers, May 13, 1926, telegram; Ben Gold to O. Shachtman, May 18, 1926; Paul Abelson to O. Shachtman, June 10, 1926; O. Shachtman to William Green, June 14, 1926; William Green to O. Shachtman, June 15, 1926. *AFL Archives:* I. Winnick to William Green, May 17, June 1, 1926; R. Lee Guard to I. Winnick, May 18, June 2, 1926; Hugh Frayne to Frank Morrison, June 7, 1926.

NEWSPAPERS AND MAGAZINES. *New York Times,* May 20, 23-24, June 3, 13-16, 1926; *Women's Wear,* May 14, 20, 23-24, 26, June 5, 9-10, 11, 15, 1926; *Federated Press Labor Bulletin,* May 26, 1926; *The Fur Worker,* May, 1926; *Jewish Daily Forward,* May 24-25, June 14-20, 1926; *Daily Worker,* May 15, 29, 30, 1926; *Freiheit,* May 25, 26, June 2, 4, 7, 11-16, 1926.

CHAPTER 23

MANUSCRIPTS. *IFWU Archives:* O. Shachtman to the Sub-Committee, Aug. 23, 1926; Aaron Gross to I. Wohl, Nov. 24, 1926; O. Shachtman to I. Wohl, Aug. 16, 1926; J. Millstein to O. Shachtman, Aug. 5, 12, 1926; I. Wohl to I. Isrealson, Oct. 28, 1926; I. Wohl to I. Winnick, Nov. 1, 1926; O. Shachtman to Chas. Gmeiner, Oct. 7, 1926; O. Shachtman to William Green, Nov. 12, 1926; Irving I. Isrealson to I. Wohl, Sept. 24, 1926; I. Wohl to Irving I. Isrealson, Sept. 29, 1926; S. Butkowitz to O. Shachtman, Dec. 23, 1926; I. Wohl to Mr. Greenberg, Nov. 17, 1926; Morris Langer to Sub-Committee, G.E.B., Dec. 1, 1926; Milton Corbett to International Fur Workers Union, Jan. 28, 1927; O. Shachtman to J. Millstein, Aug. 12, 1926. telegram; J. Millstein to O. Shachtman, Aug. 25, 1926; O. Shachtman to J. Millstein, Aug. 27, 1926; Irving I. Isrealson to O. Shachtman, (Sept.) 1926; O. Shachtman to Irving I. Isrealson, Oct. 1, 1926; William Green to O. Shachtman, July 23, 1926, Jan. 13, Feb. 1, 1927; Hugh Frayne to O. Shachtman, July 23, 1926; William Green to Secretaries of Fur Workers Local Unions, Mar. 14, 1927; Walter M. Cook to International Fur Workers Union, Mar. 27, 1926; Walter M. Cook to I. Wohl, Oct. 7, 1926; Ben Gold to I. Wohl, Dec. 30, 1926; Ben Gold to Sub-Committee, G.E.B., Feb. 1, 1927; O. Shachtman to Joint Board Furriers Union, Mar. 3, 1927. Mar. 14, 1927. *AFL Archives:* O. Shachtman to William Green, Nov. 12, 1926; I. Wohl to Matthew Woll, Nov. 22, 1926; William Green to Charles Stetsky, Aug. 23, 1926; Ben Gold to William Green, Aug. 5, 1926; "Investigation by the American Federation of Labor into the 1926 Furriers Strike," pp. 4, 37-39, 66-123, 139-84; O. Shachtman to William Green, Jan. 8, 1927; William Green to Edward F. McGrady, Feb. 9, 1927; Matthew Woll, Hugh Frayne, and Edward F. McGrady to William Green, May 7, 27, 1927; Edward F. McGrady to Edgar Wallace, Feb. 23, 1927; Edgar Wallace to Edward F. McGrady, Feb. 25, 1927; O. Shachtman to Ed Wallace, Feb. 26, 1927; Edgar Wallace to E. R. Mosbury, Feb. 28, 1927.

BOOKS AND PAMPHLETS. Jack Hardy, *The Clothing Workers,* pp. 48-49.

NEWSPAPERS AND MAGAZINES. *Freiheit,* July 16, Aug. 18, 19, 27, 29, Sept. 12, 14, 16, 21, 23, 24, 27, Oct. 11, 15, 26, 27, 1926, Feb. 26, Mar. 2, 1927; *The Fur Worker,* Aug.-Sept., Dec., 1926, Jan.-Feb., 1927; *Jewish Daily Forward,* Dec. 22, 1926.

CHAPTER 24

MANUSCRIPTS. *IFWU Archives:* Letter of A. I. Shiplacoff and M. Feinstone, Mar. 18, 1927; Harry Begoon to Chas. Gmeiner, May 2, 1927. *AFL Archives:* Matthew Woll, Hugh Frayne and Edward F. McGrady to William Green, May 7, 10, 1927. *American Civil Liberties Union Correspondence,* New York Public Library, Library vol. no. 329, pp. 173-74, 179-80, 185-86, 188, 229-33: Frank P. Walsh to Ann Washington Craton, Apr. 5, 1927; Account of interview with Forrest Bailey on morning of Mar. 26, 1927; Morris Sigman to American Civil Liberties Union, Mar. 26, 30, 1927; Arthur Garfield Hays to Morris Sigman, Mar. 31, 1927.

BOOKS AND PAMPHLETS. Jack Hardy, *The Clothing Workers,* pp. 129-30.

NEWSPAPERS AND MAGAZINES. *New York Times,* Jan. 16, 17, 19, Mar. 19-21, 24, 31, Apr. 1, 2, 5, 9, 11-14, 19-22, 24, 27, 28, May 20, July 22, 1927; *Freiheit,* Mar. 8, 10, 11-14, 18, 19-21, Apr. 14, 19-22, 24, 26, 28, May 2, 20, July 27, 1927; *Jewish Daily Forward,* Mar. 11-14, 1927.

CHAPTER 25

MANUSCRIPTS. *IFWU Archives:* Morris Langer to O. Shachtman, Apr. 1, 1927; O. Shachtman to Hugh B. Reilly, May 23, 1927; Harry Begoon to Consolidated Dressing Corp., May 17, 1927; Photostatic copy of bail record of Ben Cohen; Morris Langer to G.E.B., July 1, 1927. *AFL Archives:* Matthew Woll, Hugh Frayne and Edward F. McGrady to Hon. Joseph A. Warren, May 31, June 10, 1927; Edward F. McGrady to Hon. Joseph A. Warren, June 3, 1927; Matthew Woll, Hugh Frayne and Edward F. McGrady to Mayor James J. Walker, June 11, 1927. *American Civil Liberties Union Correspondence,* New York Public Library, Library vol. no. 329, pp. 396-97: Norman Thomas to Forrest Bailey, June 28, 1927.

NEWSPAPERS AND MAGAZINES. *New York Times,* June 10-13, 15, 16, 25, July

7-20, 1927; *Daily Worker,* June 2, 4, 6, 13, 14-16, 18, July 1, 4, 15, 21, 1927; *Freiheit,* May 27, 30-June 1, 3, 6, 7, 10, 27, July 1, 5, 12, Aug. 2, 1927; *New York Telegram,* June 6, 1927; *New York Herald-Tribune,* June 7, 1927; *New York Evening Graphic,* June 9, 1927; New York *Daily News,* June 28, 1927; *New York Evening Post,* June 24, 1927; *New York Sun,* June 25, 1927.

CHAPTER 26

MANUSCRIPTS. *IFWU Archives:* Matthew Woll, Hugh Frayne and Edward F. McGrady to O. Shachtman, Apr. 21, 1927; "Report of the Proceedings of the Eighth Biennial Convention of the International Fur Workers Union, held at Washington, D. C., June 13 to 18, 1927," pp. 1-2, 10, 11, 18-19, 62-68, 72-74, 81, 86-94, 99-105, 109, 121-23. *AFL Archives:* Matthew Woll, Hugh Frayne and Edward F. McGrady to William Green, May 7, 1927; O. Schachtman to Frank Morrison, May 15, 1927; Letter of Joint Board, Toronto Fur Workers Union, Locals 35, 40 and 65 to William Green, May 30, 1927.

NEWSPAPERS AND MAGAZINES. *New York Times,* June 15, 1927; *The Fur Worker,* July, 1927; *Daily Worker,* June 14, 15, 17, 18-21, 1927; *Freiheit,* June 14, 15, 17, 18-20, 1927.

CHAPTER 27

MANUSCRIPTS. *IFWU Archives:* Declaration of the newly-elected G.E.B. to our Local Unions, and all fur workers of the United States and Canada, June 25, 1927; "An open letter from the Unity Conference Committee of the International Fur Workers Union,"; F. C. Cribben to Harry Begoon, Sept. 2, 1927; Harry Begoon to F. C. Cribben, Sept. 22, 1927; Harry Begoon to Frank A. Currie, Sept. 9, 1927; Harry Begoon to Jack Millstein, Jan. 26, May 28, 1928; George Pearlman, Local 30, Herman Feigel, Local 3, to Harry Begoon, Mar. 7, 1928; George Pearlman to Harry Begoon, Mar. 10, 1928; N. Dorfman to Sam Ferrari, Mar. 8, 1928; Harry Begoon to Harry L. Landy, Mar. 17, 1928; Harry Begoon to the Locals of the International, Mar. 17, 1928; George Pearlman to Sub-Committee, G.E.B., Mar. 28, 1928; Harry Begoon to Joseph Bearak, Mar. 30, 1928; Charles Weiss to Sub-Committee, May 3, 1928; Sam Burt to Harry Begoon, June 7, 1928; Joseph Dordick and J. Greenspan to Harry Begoon, June 12, 1928; Charles Weiss to Harry Begoon, June 12, 1928; Harry Begoon to Arthur Foucher, May 22, 1928; Harry Begoon to George Pearlman, June 5, 1928; Captain T.

Matsuda to Harry Begoon, May 25, June 1, 1928; Harry Begoon to Captain T. Matsuda, May 29, 1928; Harry Begoon to Matthew Woll, Sept. 7, 1927; A. Shiplacoff and I. Feinstone to members of Committee for Preservation of Trade Unions, Oct. 21, 1927; William Collins to Edward F. McGrady, Jan. 3, 1928 attached to Edward F. McGrady to Harry Begoon, Jan. 4, 1928; Simon Felperin to Harry Begoon, July 10, 1928; Edward F. McGrady to A. I. Shiplacoff, July 6, 1928; Letter of A. I. Shiplacoff, July 11, 1928; Archives of Furriers Joint Council of New York: Edward F. McGrady to James Quinn, May 7, 1928; Report of Charles Stetsky covering the activities of the office, Oct. 18 to Oct. 24, 1927. *AFL Archives:* Hugh Frayne to William Green, Sept. 14, 1927; F. C. Cribben to Frank Morrison, Sept. 2, 1927; Edward F. McGrady to Frank Morrison, Sept. 24, 1927; The Committee of Fifty to William Green, Feb. 4, 1928. *American Civil Liberties Union Correspondence,* New York Public Library, Library volume no. 329, pp. 145-47, 151-52, 360-361: Ben Gold to Sacco-Vanzetti Liberation Committee, July 8, 1927; Abraham Shiplacoff to American Civil Liberties Union, July 8, 1927; Adolf Wolff to Civil Liberties Union, July 9, 1927.

NEWSPAPERS AND MAGAZINES. *New York Times,* July 17, 1927; *Women's Wear,* July 27, 1927; *Daily Worker,* July 20, 21, 1927, Mar. 21, 23, June 6, 22, July 5, Nov. 10, 1928; *The Fur Worker,* Jan. 1928; *Freiheit,* July 8, 16, 19, 1927; Mar. 8, June 27, 1928.

CHAPTER 28

MANUSCRIPTS. *IFWU Archives:* Executive Board of Fur Rabbit Dressers Local 58 to Harry Begoon, Oct. 10, 1928; Harry Begoon to Corn Exchange Bank, Oct. 22, 1928; Harry P. Grages to Harry Begoon, Aug. 23, 1928; Harry Begoon to Harry P. Grages, Aug. 27, 1928; Samuel Brooks, Secretary, Fur Manufacturers Association of Philadelphia, to Local 53, Sept. 8, 1928; Harry Begoon to Mr. McGrady, Sept. 12, 1928; Harry Begoon to Frank A. Currie, Aug. 23, 1928. *Archives of the Furriers Joint Council of New York:* Report of Charles Stetsky to Joint Council for period, July 23-Aug. 11, 1928. *AFL Archives:* The Committee of Fifty to William Green, signed by Wolf Beiner, chairman and Saul Shelly, Secretary, Feb. 4, 1928; William Green to Wolf Beiner and Saul Shelly, Feb. 14, 1928; Matthew Woll, Hugh Frayne and Edward F. McGrady to William Green, Aug. 27, 1928.

BOOKS AND PAMPHLETS. Joel Seidman, *The Needle Trades*, pp. 167-68; Jack Hardy, *The Clothing Workers*, pp. 49-50; *Report of the National Organization of the ladies garment workers, to the First Convention for the Establishment of our new Union, December 28, 1928, to January 1, 1929*, pp. 23-24, 58-59, 59-60.

NEWSPAPERS AND MAGAZINES. *Women's Wear*, July 15-17, Sept. 22, 1928; *The Fur Worker*, *Aug. 1928; Daily Worker*, May 15, June 23, 30, July 2, 12, 17, Aug. 6, 13, 15-17, Sept. 21, Dec. 28, 1928-Jan. 4, 1929; *Freiheit*, Aug. 5-17, 1928.

CHAPTER 29

MANUSCRIPTS. *IFWU Archives:* William Green to Harry Begoon, Feb. 4, 1929; Harry Begoon to Mary Milligan, June 25, 1929; Harry Begoon to Frank A. Currie, July 12, 1929; Harry Begoon to Mike M. Mandl, Aug. 15, 1929. *Archives of the Furriers Joint Council of New York:* Minutes of Joint Council entitled, "Report of Activities of Office for Twelve Months beginning December, 1928 and ending November, 1929"; Norman Thomas to Comrade Stetsky, May 14, 1929; Chas. Stetsky to Roger Baldwin, May 27, 1929; Chas. Stetsky to James J. Walker, May 28, 1929; Chas. Stetsky to Grover A. Whalen, May 28, Aug. 8, 1929; Roger Baldwin to Charles Stetsky, May 29, 1929; Manifesto issued by Charles Stetsky, Apr. 26, 1929. *AFL Archives:* Edward F. McGrady to William Green, Dec. 1, 1928; Feb. 2, 1929; Harry Begoon to William Green, May 11, 1929; Harry Begoon to Edward F. McGrady, May 7, 1929; Charles Stetsky to William Green, May 11, Aug. 13, 1929; William Green to Matthew Woll and William Collins, May 14, 1929; William Green to Joseph P. Ryan, May 14, 1929.

NEWSPAPERS AND MAGAZINES. *Women's Wear*, June 25, 1929; *The Communist*, July, 1928, pp. 421ff; *Daily Worker*, June 7, July 3, 23, 1929; *Freiheit*, June 14, 19, 20-24, July 23, 1929; *Revolutionary Age*, Nov. 1, Dec. 15, 1929; Jan. 1, 1930.

CHAPTER 30

MANUSCRIPTS. *IFWU Archives:* Harry Begoon to Charles Gmeiner, July 30, 1929; Resolution of Local 45 Executive Board, Feb. 9, 1930; Frank G. McDonagh to Morris Kaufman, Dec. 12, 1930; Harry Simon, etc., to International Fur Workers Union, Sept. 27, 1930; Harry Cohn to Morris Kaufman, Mar. 26, 1930; Morris Kaufman to B. C. Vladeck, Feb. 12, Mar. 25, 1930; Morris

Kaufman to Samuel N. Samuels, Mar. 25, 1930; Samuel N. Samuels to Morris Kaufman, Mar. 26, 1930; Morris Kaufman to Furriers Joint Council of New York, Mar. 14, 1930; Charles Stetsky to Morris Kaufman, Mar. 7, 1930; Matthew Woll to Morris Kaufman, Apr. 3, 1930; Joe (Bearak) to Morris Kaufman, Apr. 22, 1930; Matthew Woll and Edward F. McGrady to Morris Kaufman and Charles Stetsky, May 12, 1930; Morris Kaufman to Joseph Bearak, June 5, 18, 1930; Joseph Bearak to Morris Kaufman, June 5, 21, 1930; Morris Kaufman to Charles Stetsky, June 23, 1930; Charles Stetsky to Morris Kaufman, July 3, 1930; unsigned letter marked Business Agent to Dr. Paul Abelson, July 7, 1930; H. Schindler to the Hebrew Sheltering & Immigrant Society, Apr. 1, 1931; Morris Kaufman to M. M. Mandl, Aug. 13, 1931; Harry Cohn to Morris Kaufman, Mar. 26, 1930; "Report of the Proceedings of the Ninth Biennial Convention of the International Fur Workers Union. . . Held at Montreal, Canada, January 13 to 18, (inclusive) 1930," pp. 19-20, 56, 241, 254-57, 290, 313. *AFL Archives:* Charles Stetsky to Matthew Woll, March 31, 1930.

NEWSPAPERS AND MAGAZINES. *American Federationist*, Nov. 1930, pp. 1363-70; *The Fur Workers' Hope*, Nov. 1930, Jan. 1931; *Women's Wear*, July 22, 1929; *Jewish Daily Forward*, Apr. 15, 19, 1930; *Freiheit*, Dec. 9, 1929, July 4, 1930.

CHAPTER 31

MANUSCRIPTS. *IFWU Archives:* Morris Kaufman to Edward Mulrooney, June 30, 1931; Morris Kaufman to workers of Meyrowitz & Zeigman, July 7, 1931, telegram; Morris Kaufman to Mike Mandl, July 21, 1931. *Archives of the Furriers Joint Council of New York:* Minutes of special meetings of the Joint Council, July 14, 18, 25, Sept. 15, 26, 1931; Minutes of meeting held at the Rand School July 30, 1931. *AFL Archives:* Edward F. McGrady to William Green, July 20, 1931.

NEWSPAPERS AND MAGAZINES. *New York Times*, Mar. 2, June 1, 2, 25, Sept. 19, Oct. 2, 19, 1930; Sept. 23, 24, 1931; *Women's Wear*, June 26, July 10, 20, Oct. 2, 1931; *American Federationist*, Oct. 1930, p. 1200; *Daily Worker*, Oct. 15, 1930; Feb. 2, July 10, 17, 31, 1931; *Freiheit*, Mar. 18, Apr. 8, June 24-25, 29, July 10, 15, 17, 18, 24, Sept. 16, 18-19, 24, 25, 30, Oct. 3, 1931; *Labor Herald*, July, 1923, p. 11; *The Needle Worker*, Sept. 1930, July-Aug. 1931, Jan.-Feb. 1933, pp. 5-7; *Revolutionary Age*, Aug. 8, Sept. 19, Oct. 10, 1931.

CHAPTER 32

MANUSCRIPTS. *IFWU Archives:* Morris Kaufman to Joseph Bearak, Oct. 1, 1931; Morris Kaufman to M. M. Mandl, Sept. 15, 1931, Apr. 14, 1932; Morris Kaufman to S. Butkowitz, Oct. 1, Nov. 21, 1931; Morris Kaufman to G. Rhodes, Dec. 3, 1931; Sol Wollin to Morris Kaufman, enclosing copy of the charges, Dec. 1, 1931; William Green to Morris Kaufman, Nov. 13, 1931; Morris Kaufman to Edward F. Mulrooney, Jan. 20, 1932; Morris Hillquit to Morris Kaufman, Dec. 31, 1932; Geo. Sparks to Morris Kaufman, Apr. 13/32; S. Butkowitz to Morris Kaufman, Apr. 15, 1932; J. Bowman to Morris Kaufman, Apr. 2, 1932; H. Grossman to Morris Kaufman, Mar. 14, 1932; J. Littman to Morris Kaufman, July 8, 1932; Abe Rosen to Morris Kaufman, May 4, 1932; Morris Kaufman to G. Blumenfeld, Apr. 15, 1932; Pietro Lucchi to Albert Roy, May 19, Aug. 24, 1932; Proceedings of the Tenth Biennial Convention of the International Fur Workers Union, May, 1932, pp. 4-5, 28-29, 131-48. *Archives of the Furriers Joint Council of New York:* Charles Stetsky to Joint Council, Oct. 10, 1931; Minutes of meetings of the Joint Council, Oct. 12, 1931, Mar. 23, May 3, 1932; Harry Kopp to Furriers Joint Council, Feb. 1, 1932. *AFL Archives:* Edward F. McGrady to William Green, Dec. 7, 1931; Matthew Woll to William Green, Mar. 21, 1932; William Collins to William Green, Apr. 26, May 17, 1932; Morris Kaufman to William Green, May 6 1932; Matthew Woll, Hugh Frayne, and William Collins to William Green, May 9, 1932; Memorandum, dated May 12, 1932, initialed RLG.

NEWSPAPERS AND MAGAZINES. *Jewish Morning Journal,* Oct. 14, 1931; *New York Times,* May 9, 1932; *Jewish Daily Forward,* Mar. 8, 17, 1932; *Daily Worker,* Nov. 26, 1931, May 6, 7, 31, 1932; *Freiheit,* Oct. 27, 30, Nov. 7, 12, 13, 18-20, Dec. 3, 5, 16, 17, 18-19, 20-21, 1931, Jan. 20, Mar. 18, 23-25, 28-30, May 16-19, 1932.

CHAPTER 33

MANUSCRIPTS. *IFWU Archives:* Pietro Lucchi to Mike M. Mandl, Oct. 7, 1932; Pietro Lucchi to Samuel Butkowitz, Oct. 20, 1932. *AFL Archives:* William Collins to William Green, May 17, 1932.

NEWSPAPERS AND MAGAZINES. *Women's Wear,* June 21, 28, July 1, Aug. 4, 12, 18, 1932; *The Needle Worker,* Dec. 1932, p. 9; *Daily Worker,* June 18, July 18, Aug. 1, 4, 8, 11, 16-17, 18, 19, 20, 22, 23, Oct. 13, Dec.

31, 1932; *Freiheit,* June 21, 22, 27, July 12, Aug. 4, 11, 12-17, 19, 21, 22, 23, 24, 26, Sept. 8, 9, Nov. 18, 1932.

CHAPTER 34

BOOKS AND PAMPHLETS. Bruce Minton and John Stuart, *The Fat Years and the Lean,* New York, 1940, pp. 257-58; *The Furriers Convention Bulletin,* May, 1935, p. 9.

NEWSPAPERS AND MAGAZINES. *The Needle Worker,* Dec. 1932, pp. 8-9; Jan.-Feb. 1933, pp. 7, 16-17; *Daily Worker,* Oct. 5, Dec. 17, 1932, Jan. 13, 1933; *Freiheit,* Aug. 26, Nov. 19, 1932.

CHAPTER 35

NEWSPAPERS AND MAGAZINES. *The Needle Worker,* Jan.-Feb. 1933, pp. 10-11, Mar.-Apr. 1933, p. 8; *Daily Worker,* Mar. 2, July 18, 1932, Feb. 28, Mar. 2, 3, 6, 28, 1933; *Freiheit,* Aug. 21, 24, Sept. 29, 1932, Jan. 22, 25, Mar. 3, June 8, 23, 1933.

CHAPTER 36

MANUSCRIPTS. *IFWU Archives:* Petro Lucchi to Samuel Butkowitz, Feb. 16, 1933. *AFL Archives:* William Green to Pietro Lucchi, Apr. 5, 1933.

BOOKS AND PAMPHLETS. Ben Gold, *Who are the Murderers?* New York, 1933, pp. 4-5, 14-15.

NEWSPAPERS AND MAGAZINES. *New York Times,* Apr. 25, 1933, Oct. 27-29, 30-31, 1936; *Daily Worker,* Feb. 18, Apr. 25-26, 1933; *Jewish Daily Forward,* Apr. 25, 1933; *Women's Wear,* Apr. 24-25, 1933; *Freiheit,* Apr. 25, Sept. 28, 1933; *The Needle Worker,* Jan.-Feb., 1933, p. 2.

CHAPTER 37

MANUSCRIPTS. *IFWU Archives:* Pietro Lucchi to Mike M. Mandl, May 12, 1933.

NEWSPAPERS AND MAGAZINES: *New York Times,* Nov. 7, 1933, Oct. 27-Nov. 1, 1936; *Women's Wear,* Nov. 7, 1933; *Daily Worker,* Apr. 26, 28, Aug. 4, 1933, Oct. 27-Nov. 1, 1936; *Freiheit,* Apr. 29, 30, Aug. 4, 1933.

CHAPTER 38

MANUSCRIPTS. *IFWU Archives:* Pietro Lucchi to Albert Roy, June 23, 1933; Pietro

Lucchi to M. M. Mandl, June 23, 1933; Pietro Lucchi to Frank Dowd, Sept. 1, 1933; Pietro Lucchi to David Dubinsky, Oct. 7, 1933; Pietro Lucchi to S. Butkowitz, Oct. 28, Nov. 24, 1933; Pietro Lucchi to Harry Begoon, Oct. 2, 1933; Pietro Lucchi to Edward F. McGrady, Jan. 3, 1934; Pietro Lucchi to Dr. Leo Wolman, Dec. 6, 1933; Pietro Lucchi to Robert F. Wagner, Feb. 2, 1934; Pietro Lucchi to Augusto Belanca, Mar. 29, 1934; Samuel Rudow to Louis Shaffer, Aug. 12, 1933; Frank Morrison to Pietro Lucchi, Sept. 28, 1933; M. Rosenman to International Fur Workers Union, Sept. 28, 1933; Lena Greenberg to International Fur Workers Union, Sept. 28, 1933; Morris Stein to Pietro Lucchi, Oct. 22, 1933; John J. Mulholland to Pietro Lucchi, Feb. 10, 1934, enclosing copy of telegram sent to Robert F. Wagner by James C. Quinn, Feb. 6, 1934; Alan R. Stuyvesant to Pietro Lucchi, Mar. 31, 1934; S. Markewich to Matthew Woll, Sept. 15, 1934; Matthew Woll to S. Markewich, Sept. 17, 1934; Jack Mouchine to Pietro Lucchi, Jan. 30, 1934. *Archives of the Furriers Joint Council of New York:* Irving Potash and Joseph Winogradsky to the members of the Associated Fur Manufacturers and the Fur Trimming Manufacturers Association, Jan. 30, 1934; Minutes of the Fur Trade Board, Apr. 4, Sept. 26, 1934; Summary of Report of Activities of Fur Workers Industrial Union. *AFL Archives:* Pietro Lucchi to William Green, Jan. 19, June 5, 1934; Hugh Frayne to William Green, Feb. 8, 1934; John Rompapas to National Labor Board, Washington, D. C., Jan. 30, 1934; Samuel Markewich to William Green, enclosing memorandum, Feb. 3, 1934; "Provisions for Referendum in the Fur Industry in New York City, May 11, 1934"; Pietro Lucchi to National Labor Board, May 24, 1934; William Green to Pietro Lucchi, June 5, 1934. *American Civil Liberties Union Correspondence,* New York Public Library, library volume no. 653, p. 270: American Civil Liberties Union to Mr. Louis L. Redding, July 24, 1933. *In possession of Mr. Charles Nemeroff:* Ben Gold to the Furriers Trade Board, office staff and to all furriers, New Castle Workhouse, Feb. 4, 1934; Ben Gold to Charles (Nemeroff), undated letter, New Castle Workhouse.

NEWSPAPERS AND MAGAZINES. *American Federationist,* Jan. 1934, pp. 28, 42; *The Needle Worker,* Sept. 1933, pp. 9, 15, Dec. 1933, Jan. 1934, pp. 12-13, Feb.-Mar. 1934, pp. 18-19; *New York Times,* May 24, 1933, Feb. 16, Sept. 5, 1934; *The Day,* Mar. 25, 1933; *Women's Wear,* Aug. 4, Oct. 14, Dec. 31, 1933; Jan. 2, 13-15, 1934; *Daily News Record,* Oct. 10, 1933; *New York Evening Post,* Jan. 22, 1934; *Jewish Daily Forward,* Sept. 7-8, 1933; *Daily Worker,* Mar. 25,

May 25, 26, July 8, 21, Aug. 8, Sept. 8, 9, Oct. 28, Dec. 16, 26, 1933, Jan. 29, Feb. 24, Mar. 23, May 14, July 4, Oct. 2, 22, Nov. 20, 30, 1934; *Freiheit,* May 25, 26, 30-June 5, 20, 27-30, July 13, 19, 23, 26, 27, Aug. 10, 16, 18, Sept. 15, Nov. 18, Dec. 18, 1933, Jan. 4-6, 21, 23, Feb. 1, 3-4, 5, Sept. 22, 1934.

CHAPTER 39

MANUSCRIPTS. *IFWU Archives:* Pietro Lucchi to Jack Mouchine, Jan. 26, 1934; Pietro Lucchi to S. Butkowitz, Apr. 28, June 21, 1934; Pietro Lucchi to Col. Harry S. Berry, Sept. 15, 1934; Pietro Lucchi to M. M. Mandl, Jan. 23, 1935; Alvin Friedman to Pietro Lucchi, Jan. 2, 1935; Sylvester Zaccaria to Pietro Lucchi, Oct. 8, 1934; Joseph Schmitt to Pietro Lucchi, Aug. 14, 1934; Louis A. Liebowitz to Pietro Lucchi, June 7, 1934; S. Butkowitz to Pietro Lucchi, June 20, Sept. 24, 1934; Hyman S. Schechter to Pietro Lucchi, Aug. 20, 1934; Ellen M. Schroeder to Pietro Lucchi, Oct. 20, 1934; Albert Roy to Pietro Lucchi, Sept. 6, 1934; Jack Mouchine to Pietro Lucchi, June 9, 1934; Joe Indes to Pietro Lucchi, Jan. 21, 23, 1935; John Fitzpatrick to Pietro Lucchi, July 18, 1934; Pietro Lucchi to San Francisco Local, Jan. 6, 1935; Pietro Lucchi to M. Federman, Sept. 25, 1934; National Industrial Recovery Administration, Hearing by Special Fur Commission of the Research and Planning Division, N.R.A., Held in New York City, November 24, 1934, vol. II, pp. 268-69, typewritten copy.

NEWSPAPERS AND MAGAZINES. *Furriers' Bulletin,* July 1934; *Daily Worker,* June 4, July 2, Aug. 23, Sept. 3, 28, Oct. 3, 15, Nov. 20, 28-30, 1934; *Freiheit,* Jan. 5, 1934, Jan. 26, 31, 1935.

CHAPTER 40

MANUSCRIPTS. *IFWU Archives:* Pietro Lucchi to David Dubinsky, Nov. 21, 1934, Apr. 16, 1935; Pietro Lucchi to Edward F. McGrady, Jan. 3, 1934; Pietro Lucchi to Alvin Friedman, Mar. 20, 1935; Pietro Lucchi to H. Feigelman, Apr. 2, 1935; Pietro Lucchi to Joe Indes, Mar. 8, 1935; H. Feigelman to Pietro Lucchi, Mar. 18, 1935; Albert Roy to Pietro Lucchi, Nov. 12/34; San Francisco Fur Workers Union to Pietro Lucchi, Mar. 29, 1935; Edward F. McGrady to Pietro Lucchi, Apr. 17, 1935; Joe Indes to Pietro Lucchi.

BOOKS AND PAMPHLETS. *Labor Fact Book,* vol. II, New York, 1934, pp. 180-81; *Labor Fact Book,* vol. III, New York, 1936, pp. 145-86; Bulletins Nos. 1-7, issued by the Fur Workers Industrial Union, Jan.-Feb. 1935.

NEWSPAPERS AND MAGAZINES. *New York Times,* Aug. 19, 1934; *Daily Worker,* May 2-3, Oct. 24, 29, Nov. 8, 1934; Feb. 23, 28, Mar. 20, 1935; *Freiheit,* May 2-3, 1934; Feb. 28, Apr. 27, 1935.

CHAPTER 41

MANUSCRIPTS. *IFWU Archives:* Pietro Lucchi to H. Feigelman, Apr. 2, 1935; Pietro Lucchi to Michael M. Mandl, June 13, 1935; Copy of speech by Pietro Lucchi at Installation Ceremonies, Manhattan Opera House, Aug. 15, 1935; "An Important Appeal to all Fur Workers by Ben Gold," four-page bulletin. *Archives of the Furriers Joint Council of New York:* leaflets issued by the Independent International Fur Workers Industrial Union, listing the names of shops on strike; "Declaration to the Fur Workers by the G.E.B. of the Independent International Fur Workers Industrial Union." *AFL Archives.* Nathan Tepper to William Green, June 20, 1935; John Fitzpatrick to William Green, June 4, 1935; William Green to John Fitzpatrick, June 7, 1935; Matthew Woll to William Green, June 10, 11, 18, 1935; William Green to Matthew Woll, June 7, 19, 1935; Matthew Woll to David Dubinsky, June 12, 1935; Matthew Woll to Pietro Lucchi, June 12, 1935; William Collins to William Green, June 17, 1935.

BOOKS AND PAMPHLETS. *Report of the Eleventh Biennial Convention of the International Fur Workers Union held in Toronto, Canada, from May 16th to May 18th, 1935,* pp. 21, 26, 63-65, 111, 117, 164-65, 210-11, 221; *Report of the Twelfth Biennial Convention of the International Fur Workers Union . . . held in Chicago, Illinois from May 16th to May 22nd, 1937,* pp. 62-63; *Furriers Convention, Information Bulletins,* Nos. 1-2, May 16, 17, 1935.

NEWSPAPERS AND MAGAZINES. *New York Times,* June 20-21, 28, 1935; *The Day,* July 25, 1935; *Jewish Daily Forward,* Aug. 6, 1935; *Daily Worker,* June 28-29, July 24, Aug. 5, 7, 1935; *Freiheit,* May 17, 19, 20, June 1, 14, July 28, 30, Aug. 7, 9, 10, 16, 1935.

CHAPTER 42

MANUSCRIPTS. *IFWU Archives:* Miss Ellen H. Ruff to Pietro Lucchi, May 23, 1935; M. M. Mandl to Pietro Lucchi, Aug. 29, 1935; I. Lutterman to Pietro Lucchi,

Aug. 9, 31, Sept. 5, 1935; Ben Gold to Pietro Lucchi, Aug. 29, 1935; H. Sorkin to Pietro Lucchi, Nov. 11, 1935; S. Butkowitz to Pietro Lucchi, Sept. 16, Nov. 12, 1935; M. Federman to Pietro Lucchi, Sept. 27, 1935; Fillipo Trippanera to Pietro Lucchi, Oct. 21, 1935; "Organizational campaign of the Winnipeg Furriers" by W. M. Litvin, Sect'y Local 91; M. L. Bergstein to Pietro Lucchi, Aug. 30, 1935; W. M. Litvin to Pietro Lucchi, Nov. 26, 1935; Letter signed by Winnipeg workers to the G.E.B., July 17, 1935; Ben Gold to Pietro Lucchi, Dec. 18, 1935, Jan. 20, 1936, enclosing photostatic copy of "Statement of Easton Furriers," dated Jan. 15, 1936; Ben Gold to O. Schachtman, Jan. 10, 1927; Pietro Lucchi to Greek Fur Workers, Local 70, Dec. 20, 1935, Aug. 13, 1936; Pietro Lucchi to John Apostol, Oct. 15, 20, 1936; Harold Bernzweig and Leo Mandelblatt to Pietro Lucchi, Oct. 4, 1935; Notarized letter of J. Metaxas and Geo. Baltas to G.E.B. *Archives of the Furriers Joint Council of New York:* Minutes of Meeting, Joint Council, Mar. 16, 1937. *AFL Archives:* John Apostol and Steve Poulos to William Green, July 17, 1935; Matthew Woll to William Green, July 29, 1935; Steve Poulos to Matthew Woll, Feb. 24, 1936; Matthew Woll to Steve Poulos, Mar. 10, 1936; William Green to William Collins, Dec. 12, 16, 1936; William Green to Steve Poulos, Dec. 12, 1936; Steve Poulos to William Green, Dec. 11, 1936, telegram.

BOOKS AND PAMPHLETS. *Report of the Twelfth Biennial Convention of the International Fur Workers Union, . . . 1937,* pp. 66-67, 69-75, 76-77, 81, 82, 98-99; *Floor Boys Organize,* New York, June 15, 1940, pp. 5-7.

NEWSPAPERS AND MAGAZINES. *Furriers' Bulletin,* Jan., Feb., Apr., July 15, 27, Sept. 1, Oct. 1936, Jan. 15, Apr. 1, 1937; *Daily Worker,* July 23, Sept. 18, 1934, Jan. 15, May 20, June 8, 25, July 1, 2, · 18, 22, 29, Aug. 3, 10, 11, 1936, Jan. 2, Feb. 20, May 15, 1937; *Freiheit,* Dec. 8, 10, 14, 1935.

CHAPTER 43

MANUSCRIPTS. *AFL Archives:* M. M. Mandl to Frank Morrison, July 8, 1937; Frank Morrison to M. M. Mandl, July 13, 1937. *Archives of the Furriers Joint Council of New York:* Minutes of meetings of Joint Council, Oct. 9, 20, 29, Nov. 10, 1936.

BOOKS AND PAMPHLETS. J. Raymond Walsh, *CIO, Industrial Unionism in Action,* New York, 1936, p. 215; *Report of the Twelfth Biennial Convention of the Inter-*

national Fur Workers Union, ... 1937, pp. 20-21, 102-05, 212-17, 255-57, 269-72, 277-82, 334.

NEWSPAPERS AND MAGAZINES. *Furriers' Bulletin,* Sept. 1, Oct., 1936, May 15, 1937; *Daily Worker,* Aug. 31, May 17, June 4, 1937.

CHAPTER 44

MANUSCRIPTS. *AFL Archives:* Maurice Wax to Frank Morrison, May 19, 1938. *Archives of the Furriers Joint Council of New York:* Minutes of Joint Council meetings, June 22, Aug. 31, Sept. 21, Oct. 11, 19, Nov. 3, 1937. *IFWU Archives:* Sam Burt to Pierto Lucchi, Sept. 30, 1935.

BOOKS AND PAMPHLETS. *Text of the Report of the Executive Committee of the Toronto Trades and Labour Council upon investigation conducted by it, re the Furriers Union in Toronto; Report of the Twelfth Biennial Convention of the International Fur Workers Union . . . . 1937,* pp. 100-01 334; *Proceedings Thirteenth Biennial Convention, International Fur Workers Union . . . May 7th to May 14th, 1939, Atlantic City, N. J.,* pp. 71, 79-82, 83, 84, 85, 97-99, 100-01, 102, 103, 110-15, 127, 137-38, 142-48, 159, 160, 180-81.

NEWSPAPERS AND MAGAZINES. *New York Times,* Feb. 12, June 27, 1938; *Jewish Daily Forward,* Aug. 1, 1937; *Furriers Joint Council Bulletin,* July, Aug., 1937; *The Fur Worker,* June-July, Aug.-Sept., Dec. 1937, Jan.-Mar., June, July, Sept., Dec. 1938, Mar., 1939; *Daily Worker,* June 2, July 6, 7, 1937.

CHAPTER 45

MANUSCRIPTS. *AFL Archives:* Louis A. Harvey to Frank Morrison, June 23, 1917; Frank Morrison to Louis A. Harvey, June 27, 1917; Frank Morrison to J. O. Walsh, July 31, 1918; W. E. Bryan to members of General Executive Council, United Leather Workers International Union, Dec. 4, 1925; O. Wolinsky to William Green, July 21, 1925; W. E. Bryan to William Green, Dec. 9, 1925, Apr. 26, 1926, Feb. 13, 1929. William Green to W. W. Bryan, Dec. 11, 1925; John J. Pfeiffer to Frank Morrison, Dec. 28, 1928, Nov. 9, 1929; Frank Morrison to John J. Pfeiffer, Dec. 31, 1928, Nov. 14, 1929; Alexander Mark to William Green, Dec. 17, 1925, Feb. 1, Mar. 6, 1926; W. E. Bryan to Frank Morrison, Jan. 29, 1927, Sept. 7, 1929; Frank Morrison, Jan. 31, 1927; J. M. Richie to William Green, Dec. 12, 1928;

Henry F. Hilfers to William Green, Dec 6, 1928; Frank H. McCarthy to William Green, Jan. 25, 1929; Joseph B. Watley to William Green, Apr. 7, 28, 1931; William Green to Joseph B. Watley, Apr. 9, May 1, 1931.

BOOKS AND PAMPHLETS. Horace B. Davis, *Shoes: The Workers and the Industry,* pp. 114, 118, 156-57, 214.

NEWSPAPERS AND MAGAZINES. *Leather Workers' Journal,* Aug., 1917, p. 385, June, 1920, p. 309, Oct., 1920, pp. 14-15, Jan., 1921, pp. 110-11, July, 1925, p. 1, May, 1926, p. 101, Sept. 1926, p. 92; *The International Pocket-Book Worker,* Jan. 1929, p. 5; *Fur & Leather Worker,* May, Dec. 1939, Jan. 1940; *Fortune,* Feb. 1935.

CHAPTER 46

MANUSCRIPTS. *International Fur and Leather Workers Union Archives:* "First National Convention of the National Leather Workers Association, April 27-29, 1934"; "Second Annual Convention of the National Leather Workers Association, Norwood, Mass., April 26-May 5, 1935"; "Report of the National Executive Board, National Leather Workers Association, fiscal year ending April 24, 1935"; "Proceedings of the Third Annual Convention of the National Leather Workers Association held in Woburn, Mass., April 24-May 5, 1936"; "Fourth Annual Convention of the National Leather Workers Association, Peabody, Mass., April 3-May 2, 1937"; "Proceedings of the Fifth Annual Convention, National Leather Workers Association, held at Copley Square, Boston, Mass., April 29-May 2, 1938"; "6th Annual Convention, National Leather Workers Association, Lynn, Mass., April 28-30, 1939"; Agreement between A. J. Crowhurst & Sons, Inc., and A. L. Malain, as the Employees' Representative, Sept. 2, 1936. *Archives of the Furriers Joint Council of New York:* Minutes of the Joint Council Jan. 8, 1937. *AFL Archives:* W. E. Bryan to William Green, May 13, 1937.

BOOKS AND PAMPHLETS. Leo Cyril Brown, S. J., *Union Policies in the Leather Industry,* Cambridge, Mass., 1947, pp. 137-56.

NEWSPAPERS AND MAGAZINES. *Peabody Times,* Apr. 7, 14, 28, May 5, 12, Nov. 21, 1933, May 11, 1934; *Norwood Messenger,* Dec. 8, 26, 1933; *Daily Worker,* Aug. 25, Nov. 8, 21, 25, 1933; *The Needle Worker,* Dec. 1933-Jan. 1934, p. 32, Feb.-Mar. 1944, p. 16; *Woburn Daily Times,* Dec. 9, 1937.

CHAPTER 47

MANUSCRIPTS. *IFLWU Archives:* "Proceedings 6th Annual Convention, National Leather Workers Association, 1939," pp. 9-10; "Proceedings of the Fifth Annual Convention, National Leather Workers Association . . . . 1938"; Proceedings Annual Convention Leather Division, International Fur and Leather Workers Union . . . . , Boston, Massachusetts, April 27-28, 1940, pp. 130-31, 194, 206.

BOOKS AND PAMPHLETS. *Proceedings Thirteenth Biennial Convention, International Fur and Leather Workers Union . . . . 1939,* pp. 8-10, 183-85, 297-323, 457-59.

NEWSPAPERS AND MAGAZINES: *The Fur Worker,* Feb.-Mar. 1938, Jan., May, July, 1939, Jan. 1940.

CHAPTER 48

MANUSCRIPTS. *IFLWU Archives:* "Proceedings Annual Convention Leather Division, International Fur and Leather Workers Union . . . . 1940," pp. 27-28, 31-33, 41-42, 60, 139-41, 147-48, 151-53, 157-58.

BOOKS AND PAMPHLETS. *Proceedings Ninth Annual Convention Leather Division, International Fur and Leather Workers Union . . . April 24-26, 1942, Detroit, Michigan,* pp. 128-29, 130-31; *Convention Proceedings, Fourteenth Biennial Convention, Fur Division, International Fur & Leather Workers Union . . . . , May 12-14, 1942, Chicago, Illinois,* p. 290; *Proceedings 15th Biennial Convention, International Fur and Leather Workers Union . . . May 14-20, 1944, Atlantic City, N. J., p. 200.*

NEWSPAPERS AND MAGAZINES. *Fur & Leather Worker,* Oct. 1939, Jan., Feb., Aug. 1940.

CHAPTER 49

BOOKS AND PAMPHLETS. *Convention Proceedings, Fourteenth Biennial Convention, Fur Division, International Fur and Leather Workers Union . . . . 1942,* pp. 77-79, 81-82.

NEWSPAPERS AND MAGAZINES. *New York Times,* Jan. 17, Nov. 5, 1940; *Furriers' Bulletin,* Jan. 15, 1937; *Fur Age Weekly,* July 13, 1942; *New York Sun,* June 27, 1941; *New York Herald-Tribune,* Sept. 4, 1942; *Daily Worker,* Jan. 17, 1936; *Fur & Leather Worker,* Jan.-Dec. 1940; Jan. Feb., Apr., May, 1941.

CHAPTER 50

MANUSCRIPTS. *District I, IFLWU Archives:* Preliminary Report on Investigation of March, 1940, Election of Peabody Local 21; Report of the National Executive Board Committee which investigated the March 29, 1940, Annual Election of officers held by Local 21 of Peabody, Mass.; Commonwealth of Massachusetts, Supreme Judicial Court for the Commonwealth, Imberiol Moroni *et al vs.* James Brawders *et al,* March sitting, 1944; Vote re International Constitution, Leather Division, May 17-20, 19-43; Local 21 to the Leather Workers of the Peabody and Salem are, 1943; National Leather Workers Association to Leather Manufacturers of the District, Aug. 24, 1943. *District III, IFLWU Archives:* Minutes of District III, June 28, 1942.

BOOKS AND PAMPHLETS. *Proceedings Annual Convention, Leather Division, International Fur and Leather Workers Union, . . . 1941,* pp. 18-19, 21-22, 164-66; *Proceedings Annual Convention, Leather Division, International Fur and Leather Workers Union . . . . 1942,* pp. 34, 38, 89-90; *Proceedings 15th Biennial Convention, International Fur and Leather Workers Union . . . . 1944,* pp. 96-102, 115, 190, 199-200, 264-65; *Proceedings 16th Biennial Convention, International Fur and Leather Workers Union . . . Atlantic City, N. J., May 19th to 25th, 1946,* pp. 85, 174, 215; Horace B. Davis, *op. cit.,* pp. 56 *ff.,* 86, 147-52, 179, 184.

NEWSPAPERS AND MAGAZINES. *Peabody Sunday Express,* Nov. 28, 1943, Oct. 29, 1944; *Fur & Leather Worker,* Jan., Feb., Apr., May, July, Aug.-Oct., Dec. 1940, Nov. 1941 Aug., Sept., Dec. 1942, Jan.-Mar., June, Sept., Oct. 1943, Jan. Mar., May, July-Sept. 1944.

CHAPTER 51

MANUSCRIPTS. *Archives of the Furriers Joint Council of New York:* Dr. Joseph Tennenbaum to Furriers Joint Council, Nov. 11, 1937.

BOOKS AND PAMPHLETS. *Report of the Officers Local 211, International Fur and Leather Workers Union, Williamsport, Pa., submitted to the members, Jan. 28, 1944; Convention Proceedings, Fourteenth Biennial Convention, Fur Division, International Fur and Leather Workers Union . . . . 1942,* pp. 119, 319; *Proceedings 15th Biennial Convention, International Fur and Leather Workers Union . . . . 1944,* pp. 56, 61, 49-50, 214-15; *Proceedings 16th Biennial Con-*

vention, *International Fur and Leather Workers Union . . . . 1946,* pp. 98-100.

NEWSPAPERS AND MAGAZINES. *Fur & Leather Worker,* Nov. 1939, Aug., Sept., Nov., Dec. 1941, Aug. 1942, Jan. 1943, May-Aug., Oct. 1, 15, Nov. 1944.

CHAPTER 52

BOOKS AND PAMPHLETS. *Proceedings 15th Biennial Convention, International Fur and Leather Workers Union . . . . 1944,* pp. 91-95; *Proceedings 16th Biennial Convention, International Fur and Leather Work-*

ers Union . . . . *1946,* pp. 4246, 62-65, 86-88, 89-90, 165.

NEWSPAPERS AND MAGAZINES. *The Fur Worker,* Oct. 1937; *Fur & Leather Worker,* Aug. 11, 1942, Jan., May, Oct., Dec. 1943, Jan.-Mar., Apr., July-Aug., Nov.-Dec. 1944, Jan.-Feb., June, Sept. 1945; *Women's Wear,* Apr. 29, 1944, Dec. 12, 1945.

CHAPTERS 53 and 54

Files of the *Fur & Leather Worker,* August 1945—March 1950. Files of other newspapers for the same period.

INDEX

Abelson, Paul, 181, 183, 184, 239, 241, 339, 425, 629-30
Algus, Harris J., 88-89, 92, 98, 99-100, 104, 108, 112, 114
Amalgamated Clothing Workers, 102, 115, 125, 196, 683
Amalgamated Leather Workers Union of America, 35-36
American Civil Liberties Union, 154, 191-92, 266-67, 286-87, 324, 425, 427
American Federation of Labor (AFL), early history of, 11; backward policies of, 24; policies of criticized by leather workers, 28-29; trade union policies of leadership, 62, 84, 122-23, 179; leaders conspire with police, 203-04, 348-51; role in 1926 strike, 197, 203-04, 208-14, 237; investigates 1926 strike, 249 ff.; leaders attack mass picketing, 280-81; admits "reorganization" conspiracy fails, 309-10, 362-65; policy during depression, 341-42, 358, 535; revolt of rank and file in, 447-48; leaders oppose unity of fur workers, 470-73, 491; leaders support corrupt elements in Toronto, 510-11; strike-breaking role of, 511-12, 579, 581-82, 625, 639, 669; aids union-wreckers in Peabody, 605
Angel, Morris, 412
Anti-Trust trials, 412-13, 576 ff.
Apostol, John, 491, 492
Apostolides, Nick, 492
Ash, Max, 106

Baraz, Benjamin, 259, 476, 478
Bearak, Joseph, 164, 224, 290, 331-32, 336-38
Beckerman, Abraham, 196, 397, 409, 412
Begoon, Harry, 147, 150, 275, 302, 316-17, 323, 330, 380, 403, 458, 466, 485, 491, 494, 505, 510, 522
Black, Walter, 590
Bobrowicz, Edmund V., 581, 590-91, 639
Boerum, Mark, 412, 519
Bolero, Natale, 393-94
Borochovich, Joseph, 320
Boyle, Daniel J., 542, 556
Bramen, Lina, 110, 130
Bridges, Harry, 680
Brissenden, Paul, 629-30
Bronsnick, Max, 488, 490

Brown, Philip, 373, 476
Brownstein, Abraham, 100, 104, 107, 113, 119, 139-40, 143-44, 147, 150
Brownstone, Frank, 259, 437-38, 515-16, 519, 563-64, 565 ff., 585, 592-93, 595
Bryan, William E., 34-35, 529-30, 532-33, 536, 546
Bunting, Howard, 505, 558-59
Burns, Benson, 589
Burt, Sam, 193, 222, 294, 317-18, 402, 411, 412, 413-14, 483, 504, 509, 576, 581

Cahan, Abraham, 125, 310, 332
Canada, organization of, 621-22
Carman, Harry J., 628-29
Carey, James B., 678, 682-83
Carlson, C. E., 22, 24
Carnegie Hall, meeting in, 208-14
Carr, Clarence, 544, 668
Chalkin, Abe, 41
Chalkin, Izzy, 41
Chase, Stuart, 152
Chenery, James J., 585, 600
Churka, John, 590-91
Citizens Committee to Investigate Conditions in the Fur Industry, 420-22
Cohen, Isidore, 41, 43, 63-69, 70, 423
Cohen, Leviche, 374, 475
Cohen, Maurice H., 74, 99, 104, 119, 190, 259, 296, 380, 412, 476, 576
Cohen, Max, 41
Cohen, Sam, 90, 96, 99, 102, 106, 115, 116, 132, 138, 147, 398
Collins, William, 309, 324, 362, 364-65, 371-72, 403, 471, 493, 582
Committee for Preservation of the Trade Unions, 256-57, 309-10
Committee of Fifty, 315
Committee of One Hundred, 266-67
Communist Party, 173-74, 342-43, 391
Company unionism, 537, 547-48
Compulsory arbitration, 31-32, 36
Congress of Industrial Organizations (CIO), birth of, 496-98; red-baiting attacks on, 496-500; expelled by AFL, 496-98; fur workers join, 499-503; supports 1938 furriers' strike, 517, 522; approves merger of fur and leather workers, 557; demands release of imprisoned furriers' leaders, 582;

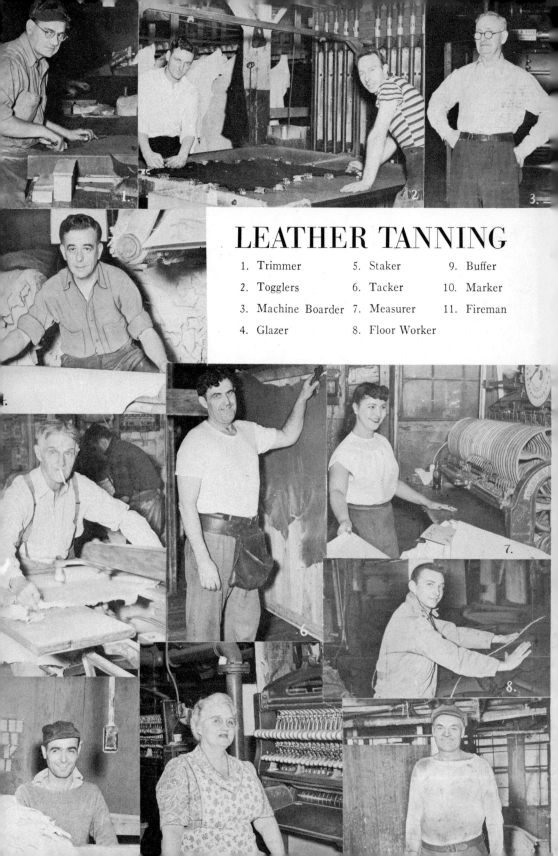

LEATHER TANNING

1. Trimmer   5. Staker   9. Buffer

2. Togglers   6. Tacker   10. Marker

3. Machine Boarder   7. Measurer   11. Fireman

4. Glazer   8. Floor Worker